THE OXFORD HANDBOOK OF

ASIAN AMERICAN HISTORY

THE OXFORD HANDBOOK OF

ASIAN

AMERICAN

HISTORY

Edited by

DAVID K. YOO

and

EIICHIRO AZUMA

OXFORD

UNIVERSITY PRESS

OXFORD
UNIVERSITY PRESS

Oxford University Press is a department of the University of Oxford. It furthers
the University's objective of excellence in research, scholarship, and education
by publishing worldwide. Oxford is a registered trade mark of Oxford University
Press in the UK and certain other countries.

Published in the United States of America by Oxford University Press
198 Madison Avenue, New York, NY 10016, United States of America.

© Oxford University Press 2016

First issued as an Oxford University Press paperback, 2020

Library of Congress Cataloging-in-Publication Data
The Oxford handbook of Asian American history / edited by David K. Yoo and Eiichiro Azuma.
pages cm
Includes index.
ISBN 978–0–19–986046–3 (cloth : alk. paper) | ISBN 978–0–19–754791–5 (paper : alk. paper)
1. Asian Americans—History.   I. Yoo, David, editor.   II. Azuma, Eiichiro, editor.
E184.A75O94 2016
973'.0495—dc23
2015032147

Contents

ACKNOWLEDGMENTS

THE completion of this book project represents the end of a lengthy process, and we especially are grateful for the patience and goodwill extended to us by the contributors whose work is featured in these pages and that constitutes a very high level of scholarship. While all published writings are a reflection of a certain time and place, we are confident that these essays will be an important touchstone for those of us who focus on Asian American history and others who have an interest in this area.

Thanks to Nancy Toff and the various editorial assistants at Oxford University Press. We would especially like to thank Phi Hong Su of the University of California, Los Angeles (UCLA), for her able and attentive research assistance.

Eiichiro would like to express his deep gratitude to colleagues, staff, and students at the University of Pennsylvania's History Department and Asian American Studies Program. Hiromi deserves a special mention for her unending emotional support.

From David, many thanks to colleagues, staff, and students at the UCLA Asian American Studies Center and the Department and the Institute of American Cultures. The bridging of research with our community partners in the greater Los Angeles area has been an especially meaningful dimension of being at UCLA. He also is thankful to his coauthors, Helen Jin Kim and Timothy Tseng, for the collaboration on their essay for this volume. As always, it is a joy to share life with Ruth, Jonathan, and Joshua.

Finally, we would like to dedicate this volume to the late Yuji Ichioka, our mentor and *sensei*. He taught us and many others about reclaiming the buried pasts of Asian Americans.

—David K. Yoo and Eiichiro Azuma

Contributors

Eiichiro Azuma is Alan Charles Kors Term Chair Associate Professor of History and Director of Asian American Studies at the University of Pennsylvania.

Keith L. Camacho is Associate Professor of Pacific Islander Studies in the Asian American Studies Department and a Faculty-in-Residence at the Office of Residential Life at the University of California, Los Angeles. He is also the senior editor of the *Amerasia Journal*; the author of *Cultures of Commemoration: The Politics of War, Memory, and History in the Mariana Islands*; and the coeditor of *Militarized Currents: Toward a Decolonized Future in Asia and the Pacific*.

Sucheng Chan is Professor Emerita of Asian American Studies and Global Studies at the University of California, Santa Barbara. She is the recipient of numerous awards for her scholarship, teaching, and service to students, the campus, and the Asian American community.

Gordon H. Chang is Professor in the Department of History at Stanford University and is the Olive H. Palmer Professor in Humanities. He has written extensively about Asian American history and America–East Asia relations. His more recent works include *Asian Americans and Politics: Perspectives, Experiences, Prospects*; *Asian American Art: A History, 1850–1970*; and *Fateful Ties: A History of America's Preoccupation with China*. He is the codirector of the Chinese Railroad Workers in North America Project at Stanford, a multidisciplinary and international effort to recover and interpret the history of Chinese workers who helped construct the first transcontinental and other rail lines throughout the country.

Jason Oliver Chang is Assistant Professor of History and Asian American Studies at the University of Connecticut (Storrs). He is the author of a book manuscript entitled *Chino: Racial Transformation of the Chinese in Mexico, 1880–1940*. He is also a coeditor of *Asian America: A Primary Source Reader* with K. Scott Wong and Cathy Schlund-Vials (forthcoming).

Kornel S. Chang is Associate Professor of History at Rutgers-Newark, State University of New Jersey. He is the author of *Pacific Connections: The Making of the U.S.-Canadian Borderlands*, winner of the 2014 Association for Asian American Studies History Book Award and a runner-up finalist for the 2013 John Hope Franklin Book Prize. He is currently working on a book about the U.S. occupation of Korea.

Catherine Ceniza Choy is Professor of Ethnic Studies at the University of California, Berkeley. She is the author of *Global Families: A History of Asian International Adoption in America* and *Empire of Care: Nursing and Migration in Filipino American History*.

Augusto Espiritu is Associate Professor of History and Asian American Studies (AAS) at the University of Illinois at Urbana-Champaign. He recently published the articles "Inter-Imperial Relations, the Pacific, and Asian American History" and "Planting Roots: Asian American Studies in the Midwest." He was the former head of the AAS Department, and he serves as a series editor for Southeast Asian Diasporas in the Americas (Brill) and as a member of the editorial board for *Amerasia Journal*.

Madeline Y. Hsu is Associate Professor of History at the University of Texas, Austin, and the former Director of the Center for Asian American Studies. Her first book, *Dreaming of Gold, Dreaming of Home: Transnationalism and Migration between the United States and South China, 1882–1943*, won the 2002 Association for Asian American Studies History Book Award. She coedited *Chinese Americans and the Politics of Race and Culture* with Sucheng Chan, and she edited Him Mark Lai's *Chinese American Transnational Politics*. Her second book, *The Good Immigrants: How the Yellow Peril Became the Model Minority*, was published in 2015.

Moon-Ho Jung is Associate Professor of History at the University of Washington. He is the author of *Coolies and Cane: Race, Labor, and Sugar in the Age of Emancipation* and the editor of *The Rising Tide of Color: Race, State Violence, and Radical Movements across the Pacific*.

Helen Jin Kim is a doctoral candidate in religion at Harvard University. She holds a B.A. in comparative studies in race and ethnicity and English literature from Stanford. Since 2006, she has been a member of the Asian Pacific American Religion and Research Initiative.

Lon Kurashige teaches at the University of Southern California, where he is Associate Professor and Director of Undergraduate Studies in the Department of History. He is the author of *Japanese American Celebration and Conflict: A History of Ethnic Identity and Festival, 1934–1990*, the winner of the History Book Award from the Association for Asian American Studies in 2004. He has written essays for many scholarly publications, including the *Journal of American History* and *Pacific Historical Review*, and he is a coeditor of the reader *Major Problems in Asian American History*. He is currently completing two book projects. "Perfect Storm of Exclusion: Asian Americans, Political Debate, and the Making of a Pacific Nation" (forthcoming) is a reinterpretation of the history of Asian immigration exclusion. He is also a founding coauthor of a forthcoming college-level U.S. history textbook.

Scott Kurashige is Professor in the School of Interdisciplinary Arts and Sciences at the University of Washington at Bothell. He is the author of *The Shifting Grounds of Race: Black and Japanese Americans in the Making of Multiethnic Los Angeles* and a coauthor with Grace Lee Boggs of *The Next American Revolution: Sustainable Activism for the Twenty-First Century*.

Erika Lee is the Rudolph J. Vecoli Chair in Immigration History and Director of the Immigration History Research Center at the University of Minnesota. She is the author of the award-winning books *At America's Gates: Chinese Immigration during the Exclusion Era, 1882–1943* and *Angel Island: Immigrant Gateway to America* (coauthored with Judy Yung), as well as *The Making of Asian America: A History*.

Daryl Joji Maeda is the author of *Rethinking the Asian American Movement* and *Chains of Babylon: The Rise of Asian America*. He is Chair and Associate Professor of Ethnic Studies at the University of Colorado at Boulder.

Sunaina Maira is Professor of Asian American Studies at the University of California, Davis. She is the author of *Desis in the House: Indian American Youth Culture in New York City* and *Missing: Youth, Citizenship, and Empire after 9/11*. Her coedited books include *Contours of the Heart: South Asians Map North America*, which won the American Book Award in 1997, and *The Imperial University: Academic Repression and Scholarly Dissent*.

Simeon Man teaches in the History Department at the University of California, San Diego. He is currently at work on his first book, *Soldiering through Empire: Race and the Making of the Decolonizing Pacific* (forthcoming).

Franklin S. Odo is currently the John Jay McCloy Visiting Professor of American Institutions and Foreign Diplomacy at Amherst College. He led the National Park Service Theme Study on Asian Americans and Pacific Islanders.

Greg Robinson, a native of New York City, is Professor of U.S. History at l'Université du Québec à Montréal. His books include *By Order of the President; A Tragedy of Democracy*; and *After Camp*. He has also published widely in law journals and legal media.

John P. Rosa is Assistant Professor of History at the University of Hawai'i at Mānoa. He has published *Local Story: The Massie-Kahahawai Case and the Culture of History*, as well as articles in *Amerasia Journal*, the *Journal of Asian American Studies*, and *AAPI Nexus Journal: Policy, Practice, and Community*.

Amy Sueyoshi is the Associate Dean of the College of Ethnic Studies at San Francisco State University and the author of *Queer Compulsions*. Her second book titled *Sex Acts* is forthcoming. She is also a founding cocurator of the GLBT History Museum in San Francisco, the first free-standing museum on queer history in the nation.

Eileen H. Tamura is Professor of History of Education and Chair of the Department of Educational Foundations, College of Education, at the University of Hawai'i. Her publications include *In Defense of Justice: Joseph Kurihara and the Japanese American Struggle for Equality; The History of Discrimination in U.S. Education: Marginality, Agency, and Power* (edited); *Asian and Pacific Islander American Education: Social, Cultural, and Historical Contexts* (edited); and *Americanization, Acculturation, and Ethnic Identity:*

The Nisei Generation in Hawaii. Tamura was a president of the History of Education Society.

Timothy Tseng is the Pastor of English Ministries at the Canaan Taiwanese Christian Church in San Jose, California, and was the founder and executive director of the Institute for the Study of Asian American Christianity. He has served as faculty at Denver Seminary, Colgate Rochester Crozer Divinity School, and as Associate Professor of American Religious History and Director of the Asian American Center at the American Baptist Seminary of the West/Graduate Theological Union.

Chia Youyee Vang is an Associate Professor of History at the University of Wisconsin–Milwaukee. Her research focuses on American involvement in Southeast Asia in the post–World War II era and on the large flow of refugees to the United States that resulted from the aftermath of the U.S. war in Vietnam. She is author of *Hmong America: Reconstructing Community in Diaspora.*

Adrienne Ann Winans is an Assistant Professor of History at Utah Valley University. Her current research project interrogates the intersection of gender, race, and space through the everyday experiences of Chinese American women and families. It re-maps exclusion-era Chinese America from the margins through the review of INS Chinese Exclusion Act files of women, transnational students, and mixed-race families.

K. Scott Wong is the James Phinney Baxter III Professor of History and Public Affairs at Williams College where he teaches a variety of courses in Asian American history, comparative immigration history, history and memory, and the history of race and ethnicity in American culture. In addition to numerous articles in journals and anthologies, he is the coeditor, with Sucheng Chan, of *Claiming America: Constructing Chinese American Identities during the Exclusion Era* and the author of *"Americans First": Chinese Americans and the Second World War.* He is also a series editor for the Asian American History and Culture series, which is published by Temple University Press.

Judy Tzu-Chun Wu is a Professor of Asian American Studies at the University of California, Irvine. She is the author of *Dr. Mom Chung of the Fair-Haired Bastards: The Life of a Wartime Celebrity* and *Radicals on the Road: Internationalism, Orientalism, and Feminism during the Vietnam Era.* She coedited *Frontiers: A Journal of Women's Studies, Women's America: Refocusing the Past* (8th edition), and a book series with Brill on "Gendering the Trans-Pacific World: Diaspora, Empire, and Race." She is working with Gwendolyn Mink on a political biography of Patsy Takemoto Mink, the first woman of color to serve as a U.S. congressional representative and as the cosponsor of Title IX.

David K. Yoo is Professor of Asian American Studies and Director of the Asian American Studies Center at the University of California, Los Angeles. He is the author or editor of seven books, including *Contentious Spirits: Religion in Korean American History, 1903–1945.*

Henry Yu received his B.A. from the University of British Columbia and a Ph.D. in history from Princeton University. After teaching at the University of California, Los Angeles for a decade, Yu returned to the University of British Columbia as a professor to build new on-campus and community-engaged programs to recover the histories of trans-Pacific migrants to Canada. The history of the Pacific region and the Americas as an engagement between transpacific migrants, transatlantic migrants, and indigenous peoples has been the focus of his scholarly research, student teaching, and university/community collaborations.

Xiaojian Zhao is Professor of Asian American Studies at the University of California, Santa Barbara. She is the author of *Remaking Chinese America: Immigration, Family, and Community, 1940–1965* (the winner of the History Book Award from the Association of Asian American Studies) and *The New Chinese America: Class, Economy, and Social Hierarchy*.

INTRODUCTION

DAVID K. YOO AND EIICHIRO AZUMA

EARLY traces of Asian American and Pacific Islander experiences have deep connections to water and land, from the traversing of great distances to inhabit islands in the Pacific Ocean to imperial routes that would reach to the Americas and the Caribbean over the course of at least five centuries. Glimpses into these experiences are offered in this collection of essays within a larger conversation about the development and future trajectories of the study of Asian American history. This academic field emerged from social movements during the 1960s and 1970s that, through struggle and protest, eventually gave rise to ethnic studies and Asian American studies programs based in universities and colleges—a period and a process now approaching fifty years.[1] While this volume primarily addresses the concerns of a particular area of study, it is critical to mark Asian American history as more than seeking inclusion. Instead, the roots of this field are linked to a deeper effort to transform the academy and to be involved with a production of knowledge engaged with local and global communities as part of a larger project aimed toward liberation, justice, and equity.

Indeed, the study of Asian American history is indebted to community-based, independent scholars, activists, writers, journalists, and artists as well as collectives and organizations for laying a foundation upon which academics have built. The lines between campus and community were blurred through collaborations that produced seminal anthologies like *Counterpoint*, edited by Emma Gee and her colleagues and published in 1976. Almost six hundred pages and truly expansive in scope, *Counterpoint* proved invaluable for instructors teaching the first Asian American history/studies courses.[2] Moving from Yale to the University of California, Los Angeles (UCLA) in 1971, the *Amerasia Journal* provided a critical space for Asian American studies scholarship when such spaces were virtually nonexistent in university settings.[3] Furthermore, the student-led and Los Angeles–based newspaper *Gidra* served as a national repository not only for news of the Asian American movement, but also for creative and artistic expression and for chronicling voices and perspectives of that period and the Asian American past.[4]

The ferment of the 1960s and 1970s in the United States contributed to the emergence of social history and the call to document and analyze history of everyday peoples. Individuals such as Yuji Ichioka and Him Mark Lai as well as organizations like the Filipino American National Historical Society painstakingly gathered important primary sources. In particular, Ichioka and Lai helped to reclaim the buried pasts of Asian Americans through the use of Asian-language sources.[5] Those working on various projects sought to foreground Asian Americans as subjects of historical narratives, breaking with the prevalent trends of either ignoring Asian Americans altogether or focusing upon what had happened to them. There was an engagement with immigration history and a push back against the assimilation framework of Oscar Handlin and the social science legacy of those like Robert E. Park of the Chicago School of Sociology.[6] Many of the early works were about the five Asian groups—Chinese, Japanese, Filipino, Korean, and Asian Indians—who had been in the United States in the pre–World War II era both in Hawai'i and on the mainland. The result was a richer and more nuanced understanding of how Asian immigration had shaped the contours of United States history.

Anticipating themes and issues of later works, pioneering studies by Roger Daniels and Alexander Saxton focused on the anti-Japanese and anti-Chinese movements in California.[7] These two studies were able to situate the efforts against the Chinese and Japanese within larger, structural issues of labor and politics. Lucie Cheng and Edna Bonacich coedited an important volume in 1984 that focused on labor and immigration in the pre–World War II era that addressed issues such as global capital and war and empire through transnational, diasporic, and world systems analyses. In terms of breadth and scope and theoretical concerns, their project, while not strictly historical in nature, provided richly suggestive frameworks for the future.[8]

The publication of Ronald Takaki's *Strangers from a Different Shore: A History of Asian Americans* (1989) and Sucheng Chan's *Asian Americans: An Interpretive History* (1991) signaled a coming of age for the field in which these narratives of the Asian American past synthesized the literature that had been produced to date.[9] Takaki's strengths in storytelling in a group-by-group approach helped to humanize Asian American history and to bring greater attention to Asian Americans as part of America's immigrant past. Although *Strangers from a Different Shore* had hints of the theoretical underpinnings of Takaki's earlier and more forceful work evidenced in *Iron Cages*, the book largely adopted the language and perspective that celebrated an American exceptionalism and multiculturalism of the times.[10] Chan's topical approach created a tighter frame of comparative work across Asian American groups through themes such as social organization, resistance, and women/families/second generation. Her densely packed prose situated Asian American history more fully within an international context for both the older groups as well as those who had come in the post-1965 period as immigrants and refugees.

The development of Asian American and ethnic studies programs on college campuses throughout the United States had led, among other things, to students entering graduate school to specialize in Asian American history. Many of these students received their degrees in the 1990s and 2000s. While certain subjects like the Japanese American incarceration during World War II have cast a long shadow, the body of scholarship produced over the past two decades or so has deepened and broadened the scope of knowledge. Numerous monographs and anthologies have included a greater number of racial-ethnic groups and issues. The influences of cultural studies, transnationalism, regional diversity, and interdisciplinary and comparative frameworks (to name only a few) have added to the richness of the theoretical and methodological approaches to the study of Asian American history. Established in 1979, the Association for Asian American Studies offered an important venue for the sharing of new perspectives and themes across the disciplines—the process is facilitated also by the publication of its quarterly, *Journal of Asian American Studies*.

Recent Trends and Developments in Asian American History

Toward the mid-1990s, there emerged notable changes—paradigm shifts of a sort—in Asian American history. Interlinked with what was going on in a larger scholarly discourse and production of academic knowledge in the U.S. academia, those changes included the following: the "transnational" and "cultural" turns in interpretive frameworks and research methodologies, a deeper conversation with and integration into many established fields of historical studies, and a rise of intersectional analyses beyond the earlier focus on race, class, and labor. Certain new themes have also captivated Asian American historians, who have become inclined to structure their queries around the problems of empire and war and international adoption, for example. At the same time, a number of historians have also extended their research beyond the World War II era to look into Asian American experience in the contexts of the Cold War and the antiwar/civil rights movement. As readers will see, these multifaceted developments in the field provide a background for the organization of this volume.

The so-called transnational turn has produced one of the most conspicuous paradigm shifts in the historical scholarship on Asian Americans. The publication of Madeline Hsu's *Dreaming of Gold, Dreaming of Home* (2000) signaled the rise of historical research that would attempt to demystify the salience of the nation-state and the spatial containment of the people's experience within the physical boundaries of the United States.[11] Nonetheless, transnationalism was not entirely new to Asian American history, though no such term—or associated theoretical formulation—was consciously deployed until the late 1990s. Coming out of the anti–Vietnam War movement, the first generation of Asian American historians was intellectually and politically under the heavy influence of radical leftist internationalism, which tended to focus a scholarly gaze on the capitalist nexus between the United States and Asia and the spread of and violent manifestations of U.S. militarism throughout the Pacific Basin. With an emphasis on race, labor, and nationalist politics, thus, the historians Yuji Ichioka and Him Mark Lai pioneered transnational bilingual research on Japanese and Chinese immigrants, respectively, in a transpacific context as early as the 1970s. Yet this initial form of transnationalism became less pronounced during the ensuing decades, partially because many scholars gravitated toward interpreting and narrating why and how Asian American experience was integral in U.S. national history—a primary intellectual challenge with which the first generation of Asian Americanists had to grapple due to the pervasiveness of Eurocentrism and Orientalism in academia and society, as well as the "Culture Wars" of the 1990s over U.S. multiculturalism. It was only at the turn of the twenty-first century when newer generations of Asian American historians, armed with the sophisticated theoretical language of transnationalism, rekindled the forgotten tradition in the field.

It is important to note that transnationalism has not arisen in Asian American history alone. In fact, it flourished with a synchronic intellectual trend in other fields of historical studies and disciplines, like African American studies and literary studies. Within the interdisciplinary field of Asian American studies, historians benefited from the simultaneous developments in other subfields, especially in their endeavor to de-center "nation" in their interpretive/analytical frames. For example, studies of certain themes, like Orientalism and diaspora, in literary studies had an enormous influence on the early phase of the transnational turn in Asian American history. This has also constituted a site of interaction between theory and history.

The transnational turn involves the redefinition of the United States as an empire—an active participant in the imperialist scramble for Asia and the Pacific between the mid-nineteenth century and World War II, and the most hegemonic power in Cold War geopolitics after the mid-1940s. Asian American historians embraced this emergent paradigm for various reasons. First, the empire framework allows for the envisioning of "America" as something larger than the physical bounds of its national sovereignty when they delve into Asian Americans' experiences of migration, family and community building, economic activities, cultural and intellectual production, political organization and struggle, and racial formation. Second, historians are able to examine how the articulations of U.S. imperialism were intertwined and integrated in domestic and international spheres when Asian America and Asia were concurrently being otherized, dominated, and co-opted. While commenting on the critical nexus between U.S. domestic race politics and its foreign policy mandate (including military violence), most chapters in this volume credit the salient role of such new analytical categories as empire, colonialism, and war. It is important to consider how the theoretical engagement with other disciplines—especially postcolonial scholarship—forms an indispensable background for this paradigm shift in Asian American history.

If one looks at the chronological trajectory of the transnational turn, Asian American history has somewhat lagged behind other disciplines. In other words, historians tend to be beneficiaries of new theoretical formulations and framing from other disciplines. Likely, the relative lateness of the transnational turn in Asian American history is related to the particular challenge with which the practitioners are often faced when they conduct research: the need for labor-intensive archival work and the problem of language. These methodological hurdles have made it more difficult and time-consuming for historians to take up a research project that would deal with the immigrant generation or their relationship to the "homeland." Whereas some fields may not require extensive archival research involving the reading of vernacular source material in exchange for a heavier emphasis on theoretical formulation, historians are generally compelled to harmonize these separate demands, thereby tending to take longer to produce a substantive, "transnational" scholarship.

In the context of the transnational turn, Asian American historians are often compelled to establish a meaningful relationship to non-U.S. area studies, especially various branches of Asian studies, Latin American/Caribbean studies, Pacific Islander studies, and Canadian studies.[12] The examination of transnational linkages, emergent networks, and practices and identities that transcend national borders requires serious engagement with the histories and historiographies of Asia (East, Southeast, and South), Pacific Islands, and the entire Western Hemisphere. In this vein, chapters in the section titled "Migration Flows" underscore either an ongoing intellectual dialogue or a need for a closer conversation with respective area studies.

What can be termed the "cultural" turn is another salient shift in the research and writing of Asian American history—a shift that dovetails with the rise of intersectional framing beyond the traditional thematic and paradigmatic focus on labor and class, and their relations to race (especially anti-Asian racism). Aided by literary and social science theories, a cultural studies approach has colored a poignant aspect of the new trajectories in the field. As the literary scholar Elaine Kim put it symbolically in 1996, the de-centering of the conventional Marxist gaze has expanded the scope of historical inquiries and analyses "beyond railroads and internment."[13] Indeed, in various subfields of Asian American history, the intersectional approach now renders gender, sexuality, culture, religion, and other axes of identity as important as the conventional categories of race/ethnicity, class, and labor.

Under the influence of the cultural turn, the recent intersectional scholarship encompasses a greater range of research agendas and chronological breadth—and hence a wider variety of historical agents than single male workers before World War II or loyal male citizens/soldiers during the wartime incarceration. Thus, on the one hand, historical research on religion, family, women, and post-1970s refugees—to name a few topics—have become not only legitimate but also more vigorous and widespread. On the other, the paradigmatic shift has brought forth multifaceted studies of Cold War cultural diplomacy, Asian American movement, international adoption, and postwar immigration of middle-class and professional Asians. In the meantime, Asian exclusion and Japanese American internment still form popular areas of historical research, but many scholars tackle the subjects with more theoretical sophistication and attention to issues beyond just race.

Simultaneously, intersectionality has revitalized the study of race relations in Asian American history. The growing interest in the interconnectedness of various analytical categories helps problematize the presumed integrity and discreteness of the racial category—always a focal point of Asian American history. In the past, like their counterparts in other ethnic studies fields, Asian Americanists generally privileged the centrality of Asianness to which they owed their primary "allegiance," juxtaposing it against whiteness in their studies of racial oppression and resistance. The institutionalization of four major ethnic studies branches (Asian American, African American, Chicano/a/Latino/a, Native American/Native Hawaiian) perhaps reinforced this binarism in the study of race relations. In 1994, the historian Gary Okihiro made a conscious move to destabilize that pervasive interpretive frame by asking "is yellow black or white?"[14] Not only did this simple but profound question anticipate the sophisticated theorization of racial triangulation of Asians vis-à-vis whites and blacks in social science disciplines, but it also paved the way to empirical historical studies of Asians' complex relations with other racialized minorities. A number of this volume's chapters look into this aspect of the recent historiographical and paradigmatic changes in Asian American history.

The new multiracial paradigm has helped disrupt a simplistic notion of Asian Americans as the oppressed. Compared and juxtaposed with the experiences of other racialized minorities, recent historical scholarship has shed light on the more ambiguous positionality of Asian Americans in U.S. race relations. After the mid-1990s, there has been an increasing number of scholarly works that critically examine the transformation of Asian Americans from the yellow peril to the model minority in the U.S. public discourse during the Cold War. This new racial stereotyping presented the group as an antithesis of the black racial threat while hailing them as honorary whites. Post-1990s scholarship on the Asian model minority has unveiled their frequent complicity with, if not embrace of, this discursive formation, and hence white supremacy, after World War II. Likewise, the multiracial paradigm has enabled scholars of Hawai'i's Asian Americans to complicate a one-dimensional narrative of the exploited plantation worker as well as the minoritized racial subject to the islands' *haole* elite. According to recent works on Hawai'i, Asian immigrants and their descendants have actually formed a linchpin of settler colonialism and local white supremacy, which continue, to this day, to alienate Native Hawaiians from their own land, tradition, and self-determination.

The post-1990s years mark a greater integration of Asian American history into the established subfields of historical studies and vice versa. Part IV of this volume illuminates the progress that historians of Asian America have made, albeit to varied degrees, in carving out a place and reputation in the mainstream historiographies. Some subfields of U.S. history, like immigration history, legal history, and urban history, have greatly benefited from and recognized the importance of Asian American perspectives. Mae Ngai's *Impossible Subjects* (2004), for example, is now treated as a canonical work in U.S. legal and immigration history and is on the reading list of practically every graduate student in American studies fields.[15] Other subfields, like political history, intellectual history, religious history, and education history, have been comparatively slower to embrace the contributions of Asian American scholarly production as the respective chapters speak to the situation. In non–U.S. history fields, too, the influence of Asian American history is evidenced, albeit more ploddingly. Takashi Fujitani's *Race for Empire* (2011) and Erika Lee's recent book on Asians in the Americas exemplify the signs of the breakthrough that the historical scholarship on Asian America, as well as its paradigms and perspectives, have made and will make outside U.S. history.[16] Despite variations, the trend seems to be there to stay and grow in the coming years: that Asian American history is deemed more and more relevant to scholars of "mainstream" U.S. history and various area studies fields.

THE *HANDBOOK*

Given the development of the field of Asian American history over the past four decades or so, the essays in the *Oxford Handbook of Asian American History* collectively provide a commentary on the state of the field at this moment in time. Although the chapters are historiographically informed, the emphasis is not on exhaustive overviews. Instead the authors have space to explore and to speculate on what kinds of questions and issues remain, how recent developments in related fields affect the historical treatment of Asian America, and what theoretical and methodological concerns have emerged. The time is ripe for a volume that simultaneously assesses where the scholarship has been and what the future holds.

One issue that several of the contributors have raised and that is not far below the surface in terms of the future is the contingent and ambiguous nature of the terms that have been used to designate groups such as "South Asian" or "Southeast Asian." Filipino Americans, for instance, have been included in essays in this volume as part of Southeast Asian Americans as well as Pacific Islanders. Moreover, the decision not to have entries for individual Asian ethnic groups was a conscious one in order to signal a focus on more collective forces like war and empire that have affected all groups, albeit in different ways at different times. The fact that this volume is about Asian American history suggests that there continues to be salience for the term. Nevertheless, tensions exist. For instance, there has been and continues to be an uncertain relationship between Asian American studies and Pacific Islander studies, even as both of these composite terms contain their own quandaries. Even more foundational is the term "Asian American" itself, a term credited to the historian Yuji Ichioka that emerged in the 1960s and 1970s in an effort to build coalitions across various Asian groups in the United States. The question remains as to what extent these categories obscure as much as they reveal, but the essays presented here raise important questions and issues, including about the shape of the field itself.

In exploring Asian American history, the *Handbook* follows up on several existing reference works on Asian American history such as Lon Kurashige and Alice Yang Murray, *Major Problems in Asian American History*; Franklin Odo, *The Columbia Documentary History of the Asian American Experience*; and Gary Y. Okihiro, *The Columbia Guide to Asian American History*. These helpful collections consist of selected primary and secondary sources and reprints of complete or partial essays as well as timelines and bibliographies.[17] These works include some essays that provide an overview and assessment of Asian American history, but much more work has been published since these works came out in the early 2000s. Shelley Sang-Hee Lee, Erika Lee, and Gary Okihiro have recently written general overviews of Asian American history that pick up from where Takaki and Chan left off. Their texts, albeit framed differently, are a welcome addition, especially for classroom usage and general readers.[18]

While no single volume could comprehensively cover the field of Asian American history, what is distinctive about the *Handbook* is that no existing book project draws together so many specialists in one place to engage and to critically assess key themes in the field. In that regard, the scope and the depth of the knowledge represented in these essays are its major contribution. Taking stock of any historical field, of course, speaks as much to present concerns as it does about the past. Asian American history and the movement that helped spawn it emerged during a time of great social unrest driven in part by visions of a nation and world marked by liberation, justice, and equity, especially for those who were considered Third World peoples in the United States and in other parts of the world. While it is easy to romanticize the 1960s and 1970s, the mass politics, creative expressions, and the imagination of that period are still as relevant for our times today as they were then, even recognizing the difference between that era and now. Certainly, the contributors to this volume attest to the ongoing importance of Asian American history to the understanding of self, society, and the world.

NOTES

1. For a sampling of related texts, see Daryl J. Maeda, *Chains of Babylon: The Rise of Asian America* (Minneapolis: University of Minnesota Press, 2009); Laura Pulido, *Black, Brown, Yellow and Left: Radical Activism in Los Angeles* (Berkeley: University of California Press, 2006); Sucheng Chan, *In Defense of Asian American Studies: The Politics of Teaching and Program Building* (Urbana: University of Illinois Press, 2005); Steve Louie and Glenn Omatsu, eds., *Asian Americans: The Movement and the Moment* (Los Angeles: UCLA Asian American Studies Center Press, 2001).
2. Emma Gee, ed., *Counterpoint: Perspectives on Asian America* (Los Angeles: UCLA Asian American Studies Center, 1976).
3. The journal has been published continuously since 1971 by the UCLA Asian American Studies Center. In 2003, the center launched a second journal, *AAPI Nexus Journal: Policy, Practice, and Community.*
4. Louie and Omatsu, *Asian Americans*, contains many excerpts from *Gidra*.
5. The late Yuji Ichioka, a longtime research associate and faculty member at the UCLA Asian American Studies Center, is credited with coining the terms "buried past" and "Asian American." Ichioka published many important works, especially *Issei: The World of First Generation Japanese Immigrants, 1885–1924* (New York: Free Press, 1988). The late Him Mark Lai was an independent scholar and is often seen as the dean of Chinese American history. See Him Mark Lai, *Him Mark Lai: Autobiography of a Chinese American Historian*, ed. Judy Yung, Ruthanne Lum McCunn, and Russell C. Leong (Los Angeles and San Francisco: UCLA Asian American Studies Center Press and the Chinese Historical Society of America, 2011); and Him Mark Lai, *Chinese American Transnational Politics*, ed. Madeline Y. Hsu (Urbana: University of Illinois Press, 2010). The Filipino American National Historical Society (FAHNS) was part of larger efforts dating to the 1950s around Filipino American community issues. See the FAHNS website at http://fanhs-national. org/filam/.
6. Oscar Handlin, *The Uprooted: The Epic Story of the Great Migrations That Made the American People* (Boston: Little, Brown, 1951); Robert E. Park and Fred Matthews, *The Quest for American Sociology: Robert E. Park and the Chicago School* (Montreal: McGill-Queens

University Press, 1977); Henry Yu, *Thinking Orientals: Migration, Contact, and Exoticism in Modern America* (New York: Oxford University Press, 2002).

7. Roger Daniels, *The Politics of Prejudice: The Anti-Japanese Movement in California and the Struggle for Japanese Exclusion* (Berkeley: University of California Press, 1962); Alexander Saxton, *The Indispensible Enemy: Labor and the Anti-Chinese Movement in California* (Berkeley: University of California Press, 1971).

8. Lucie Cheng and Edna Bonacich, eds., *Labor Immigration under Capitalism: Asian Workers in the United States before World War II* (Berkeley: University of California Press, 1984).

9. Ronald Takaki, *Strangers from a Different Shore: A History of Asian Americans* (Boston: Little, Brown, 1989); Sucheng Chan, *Asian Americans: An Interpretive History* (Boston: Twayne, 1991). There are two other publications, Roger Daniels, *Asian America: Chinese and Japanese in the United States since 1850* (Seattle: University of Washington Press, 1990); and H. Brett Melendy, *Asians in America: Filipinos, Koreans, and East Indians* (Boston: Twayne, 1978), but the works by Takaki and Chan were arguably the most influential in shaping courses and serving as a frame of reference for Asian American historical scholarship.

10. Ronald Takaki, *Iron Cages: Race and Culture in 19th Century America* (New York: Knopf, 1979). Takaki would continue the trend with the publication of *A Different Mirror: A History of Multicultural America* (Boston: Little, Brown, 1993).

11. Madeline Y. Hsu, *Dreaming of Gold, Dreaming of Home: Transnationalism and Migration between the United States and South China, 1882–1943* (Stanford, CA: Stanford University Press, 2000).

12. On the complicated relations between Asian American studies and Asian studies, see Shirley Hune, "Asian American Studies and Asian Studies: Boundaries and Borderlands of Ethnic Studies and Area Studies," in *Color-Line to Borderlands: The Matrix of American Ethnic Studies*, ed. Johnnella E. Butler (Seattle: University of Washington Press, 2001), 227–239; and Sucheta Mazumdar, "Asian American Studies and Asian Studies: Rethinking Roots," in *Asian Americans: Comparative and Global Perspectives*, ed. Shirley Hune et al. (Pullman: Washington State University Press, 1991), 29–44.

13. Elaine Kim, "Beyond Railroads and Internment: Comments on the Past, Present, and Future of Asian American Studies," in *Privileging Positions: The Sites of Asian American Studies*, ed. Gary Y. Okihiro et al. (Pullman: Washington State University, 1995), 1–9.

14. Gary Okihiro, *Margins and Mainstreams: Asians in American History and Culture* (Seattle: University of Washington Press, 1994), 31–63.

15. Mae Ngai, *Impossible Subjects: Illegal Aliens and the Making of Modern America* (Princeton, NJ: Princeton University Press, 2004).

16. Takashi Fujitani, *Race for Empire: Koreans as Japanese and Japanese as Americans during World War II* (Berkeley: University of California Press, 2011); and Erika Lee, *The Making of Asian America: A History* (New York: Simon and Schuster, 2015).

17. Lon Kurashige and Alice Yang Murray, eds., *Major Problems in Asian American History* (Boston: Houghton Mifflin, 2003); Franklin Odo, ed., *The Columbia Documentary History of the Asian American Experience* (New York: Columbia University Press, 2002); and Gary Y. Okihiro, *The Columbia Guide to Asian American History* (New York: Columbia University Press, 2001).

18. Shelley Sang-Hee Lee, *A New History of Asian America* (New York: Routledge, 2014); Erika Lee, *The Making of Asian America: A History* (New York: Simon and Schuster, 2015); Gary Y. Okihiro, *American History Unbound: Asians and Pacific Islanders* (Berkeley: University of California Press, 2015).

FURTHER READING

Chan, Sucheng. *Asian Americans: An Interpretive History*. Boston: Twayne, 1991.

Cheng, Lucie, and Edna Bonacich, eds. *Labor Immigration under Capitalism: Asian Workers in the United States before World War II*. Berkeley: University of California Press, 1984.

Daniels, Roger. *Asian America: Chinese and Japanese in the United States since 1850*. Seattle: University of Washington Press, 1990.

Ichioka, Yuji. *Issei: The World of First Generation Japanese Immigrants, 1885–1924*. New York: Free Press, 1988.

Lee, Erika. *The Making of Asian America: A History*. New York: Simon and Schuster, 2015.

Lee, Shelley Sang-Hee. *A New History of Asian America*. New York: Routledge, 2014.

Okihiro, Gary Y. *American History Unbound: Asians and Pacific Islanders*. Berkeley: University of California Press, 2015.

———. *Margins and Mainstreams: Asians in American History and Culture*. Seattle: University of Washington Press, 1994.

Saxton, Alexander. *The Indispensible Enemy: Labor and the Anti-Chinese Movement in California*. Berkeley: University of California Press, 1971.

Takaki, Ronald. *Iron Cages: Race and Culture in 19th Century America*. New York: Knopf, 1979.

———. *Strangers from a Different Shore: A History of Asian Americans*. Boston: Little, Brown, 1989.

Zia, Helen. *Asian American Dreams*. New York: Farrar, Strauss, and Giroux, 2001.

PART I

MIGRATION FLOWS

CHAPTER 1

....

FILIPINOS, PACIFIC ISLANDERS, AND THE AMERICAN EMPIRE

....

KEITH L. CAMACHO

THERE is a central, though rarely addressed, question in the historical study of Filipinos, Pacific Islanders, and the American empire:[1] if Filipinos and Pacific Islanders are linked by virtue of their historical relations with the United States, then why do their respective historiographies convey disconnected, even severed, records of these peoples? Granted, Filipinos and Pacific Islanders are not naturalized terms, let alone widely accepted categories of cultural, legal, and political recognition. Their historical relations with the United States are often tenuous, usually situational, and, in some cases, celebratory. It is true, as well, that no comparative history exists on the Carolines, Hawai'i, the Marianas, the Marshalls, the Philippines, and Sāmoa, areas variously and sometimes simultaneously colonized by the United States since the late nineteenth century. An absence of intellectual debates thus persists across these atolls and archipelagoes, even though historical studies of these areas have produced an imperial grammar akin to what the critic Allan Punzalan Isaac calls the "American tropics." As Isaac argues, American tropics make up "a set of regulatory tropes and narratives that reveal a particularly U.S. American imperial grammar that create ethnic, racial, and colonial subjects."[2] To varying degrees, these subjects have long informed historical discussions by and about Filipinos and Pacific Islanders, yet most conversations among these scholars have been temporary and peripheral. With few grassroots, organizational, and institutional opportunities to advance and connect their respective analyses of class, gender, race, religion, and sexuality, the historiographies on Filipinos and Pacific Islanders have become specialized and insular rather than intersectional and comparative in scope. Ultimately, area studies, disciplinary frameworks, nationalist agendas, modernization theories, and security paradigms account for the making of Filipinos and Pacific Islanders as recognizable, yet separate and unrelated peoples of study.

How might we address, then, the lacunae in the historiography? More important, how might we acknowledge and advance historical studies on Filipinos, Pacific Islanders, and the American empire? What kinds of methodologies and epistemologies might we consider, and for what intellectual and political purposes? As the ethnic studies scholar Joanne L. Rondilla reminds us, "The ties between Filipinos and Pacific Islanders run far and deep . . . we have a similar colonial history, and the ways in which we have had to deal with the effects of colonization are closely related."[3] By focusing on historical monographs and anthologies, this chapter addresses these questions by exploring the "ties between" Filipinos, Pacific Islanders, and the American empire. The goal is to survey the ways in which colonial and postcolonial bodies of knowledge have produced Filipinos and Pacific Islanders as subjects of study and as agents of history, illustrating the gaps and fissures in the historiography as much as reflecting on its links and ties. An inherently uneven process, the selection of these studies does not entail an exhaustive record of why and how scholars study Filipinos, Pacific Islanders, and the American empire. And although the publications examined in this chapter all address matters of historical importance, they do not necessarily employ historical analyses of continuity and change. Only studies of labor and migration, militarism and nuclearism, and empire and indigeneity are covered here, especially texts published from the mid-twentieth century to the present. Therefore, some sources of historical value, such as articles, novels, or plays, do not appear in this essay nor does every work under consideration receive fair treatment. With a few exceptions, oral histories—that is, chants, dreams, gossip, humor, and songs, to name a few examples—are not analyzed even though they largely account for the knowledge produced by Filipinos and Pacific Islanders.

LABOR AND MIGRATION

By the mid-twentieth century, historians concerned with the study of Filipinos or Pacific Islanders had begun to mark as separate and real the divisions that came with the study of these diverse societies. Take, for instance, *International Rivalry in the Pacific Islands, 1800–1875*, authored by Jean Ingram Brookes in 1941. In this study, Brookes traced the rise of American, English, and French colonial, missionary, and trade interests in the Pacific. As he understood the term, the "Pacific" encompassed the islands east of the Philippines, then described as the "Asiatic side" of the region.[4] For this reason, he chose not to study the Philippines, focusing instead on Fiji, Hawai'i, the Marquesas, New Zealand, and Sāmoa. On the other hand, A. Grenfell Price's *The Western Invasions of the Pacific and Its Continents: A study of Moving Frontiers and Changing Landscapes, 1513–1958* offered an encompassing notion of the Pacific, which included the aforementioned islands, as well as Australia, East and Southeast Asia, Latin America, North America, and Siberia. But for all its efforts of inclusion, this 1963 publication exemplified the Orientalist trends of that period wherein Pacific Islanders were considered inauthentic subjects by virtue of their exchanges with western diseases, governments, and technologies.

Notwithstanding analyses of Pacific Islander "chiefs" and "royalty," very seldom did historians consider other Pacific Islanders as agents of their narratives. Matters concerning European beachcombers, diplomats, explorers, and missionaries were more important. The American empire, if at all discussed alone or alongside these colonial histories, was usually described, to use A. Grenfell Price's words, as an "accident."[5] Reflective of a historiography influenced by what Brij V. Lal and Doug Munro describe as the "old guard of traditionalists," with whom the study of Europeans in the Pacific proved significant, no foundational works of Pacific Islanders and the American empire had yet to appear.[6] In fact, the usage of the term "Pacific Islander," as with that of "American empire," was virtually nonexistent.

Unlike the aforementioned historiography of the Pacific, whose intellectual and geographical purview excluded Filipinos and the American empire, the historiography on Filipinos at that time was already engaged in debates about Filipino laborers and migrants. Bruno Lasker's *Filipino Immigration to the Continental United States and to Hawaii* (1931) represented one such monograph. In this historical sociology of the "ethnic character of the Filipino people," Lasker interviewed nearly two hundred persons in the continental United States, Hawai'i and the Philippines for the purpose of examining American economic, legal, and political relations with Filipinos.[7] His focus on bachelor communities, exclusionary laws, fish canneries, plantation economies, and race relations, among other issues, foreshadowed the paradigmatic contours of later historical studies on Filipinos in the United States. The landmark publication of Jesse Quinsaat's edited pictorial history, *Letters in Exile: An Introductory Reader on the History of Pilipinos in America* (1976), nicely illustrated the making of these histories. The anthology featured the essay and photo contributions of labor organizers, student activists, teachers and others. In creating this oral history, Quinsaat called for the making of "Pilipino studies," a new field of study that would shed insights on Filipinos as "Asian" immigrants in the United States. In contrast to the Anglo-centric historiography of the Pacific, which had yet to face criticisms about its imperial dimensions, *Letters in Exile* demonstrated its commitment to a Pilipino studies premised on Filipino cultural nationalism, political solidarity, and anti-imperialism. As Quinsaat declared, the "construction of a Pilipino history in America should not be guided by a valueless pursuit of sheer knowledge for knowledge's sake. Pilipino studies must not become another market place for scholarly imperialism seeking to dump worthless intellectual goods."[8]

Other historical works published in the 1970s called for the decolonization of Filipino historiography, such as Renato Constantino and Letizia R. Constantino's *The Philippines: A Past Revisited* (1975) and *The Philippines: The Continuing Past* (1978). Although they primarily documented events in the Philippines, Constantino and Constantino nevertheless charted an intellectual trajectory that implicitly linked their methods with the burgeoning field of Filipino American studies in the United States. As they argued, "The task is to advance the writing of a truly Filipino history, the history of the Filipino people. This means that the principal focus must be on the anonymous masses of individuals and on the social forces generated by their collective lives and struggles."[9] With the Filipino as an accepted category of analysis, and with immigration and labor as the major "struggles" of this and later periods, an increasing number of studies emerged. Several methods proved appealing, with some scholars discussing these topics in comparative terms, some employing local lenses, and others taking transnational approaches. Collectively, they variously examined Ilocano, Pangasinan, Tagalog, and Visayan labor and migration circuits in and across Alaska, California, Hawai'i, the Philippines, and Washington, DC.

The monographs that explored Filipinos in comparative terms included H. Brett Melendy's *Asians in America: Filipinos, Koreans, and East Indians* (1977); Ronald Takaki's *Strangers from a Different Shore: A History of Asian Americans* (1989); Sucheng Chan's *Asian Americans: An Interpretative History* (1991); Chris Friday's *Organizing Asian American Labor: The Pacific Coast Canned-Salmon Industry, 1870–1942* (1994); and Mae N. Ngai's *Impossible Subjects: Illegal Aliens and the Making of Modern America* (2004). Often framed within the triangulation of migration, labor, and citizenship, these studies examined Filipinos in relation to the immigrant experiences of Chinese, Japanese, Koreans, and South Asian Indians. Equally significant were the localized studies of Filipino communities in Los Angeles and Seattle, many of which focused on citizenship movements, community newspapers, labor unions, and taxi halls, among other topics. They were especially critical of white racism and exclusionary laws and practices. As Sucheng Chan elaborates, these studies "adopted oppositional or revisionist paradigms that focused on the structural or institutional factors oppressing people of Asian ancestry, just as they did other peoples of color, women, workers and the poor."[10] These works included Fred Cordova's *Filipinos, Forgotten Asian Americans: A Pictorial Essay, 1763–circa 1963* (1983); Rick Bonus's *Locating Filipino Americans: Ethnicity and the Cultural Politics of Space* (2000); and Melinda Triakerkvliet's *Unbending Cane: Pablo Manlapit, a Filipino Labor Leader in Hawaii* (2002). Adding to this corpus was the emergence of transnational methodologies in the twenty-first century, a process described by the historian August Espiritu as producing more books "on Filipino American history than in the last three decades combined."[11]

Partly created in response to the assimilationist paradigm, a framework that informed previous studies of Filipinos, these historical monographs were no longer restricted by the binary study of Filipinos as successful or threatening immigrants. Nor were these studies limited to one national frame of reference. Transnational analysis offered, then, new ways of thinking about Filipinos across multiple national contexts. As the ethnic studies scholar Yen Le Espiritu explains, "The concept of transnationalism, used as a heuristic device, highlights instead the range and depth of migrants' lived experience in multinational social fields."[12] Some of these studies included Catherine Ceniza Choy's *Empire of Care: Nursing and Migration in Filipino American History* (2003); Yen Le Espiritu's *Home Bound: Filipino American Lives across Cultures, Communities, and Countries* (2003); Dorothy B. Fujita-Rony's *American Workers, Colonial Power: Philippine Seattle and the Transpacific West, 1919–1941* (2003); Martin F. Manalansan IV's *Global Divas: Filipino Gay Men in the Diaspora* (2003); Rhacel Salazar Parreñas's *The Force of Domesticity: Filipina Migrants and Globalization* (2008); and Rick Baldoz's *The Third Asiatic Invasion: Empire and Migration in Filipino America, 1898–1946* (2011).

With transnationalism as their analytic, these scholars opened up innovative ways of studying Filipinos across various geographic and national spaces. Manalansan's and Parreñas's contributions especially transformed the historiography to account for multiple gender and sexual orientations and ideologies in the United States and elsewhere. Issues of masculinity and femininity have thus become central to the study of Filipino labor and migration, as evidenced in recent works like Linda España-Maram's *Creating Masculinity in Los Angeles's Little Manila: Working-Class Filipinos and Popular Culture, 1920s–1950s* (2006).

Yet notwithstanding the few exceptions where indigenous peoples are discussed, as in the case of multiethnic fishing canneries in Washington, none of these studies fully addressed Filipino perceptions of and relations with indigenous peoples. For example, histories of Filipino experiences in California and Hawai'i are often devoid of indigenous presences and histories. These and other sites merely serve as entry and exit points for Filipino migration flows, if not as contested areas of white institutional racism and xenophobia. While new works like Roderick N. Labrador's *Building Filipino Hawai'i* (2015) further complicate this historiography, the overall strengths of these studies rest on their rigorous examination of class inequity, class mobility, and class solidarity. Elsewhere, these matters of class remain relatively absent in the historiography of Pacific Islanders and the American empire. Other than Donald Denoon's edited volume, *The Cambridge History of Pacific Islanders* (1997), no historical study exists on Pacific Islanders, labor, and migration, a lacuna that can be attributed to the bias in the historiography that privileges the study of indigenous cultures over indigenous economies. This partly explains why historians of Pacific Islanders and the American empire have rarely brought the Philippines into their frameworks of labor, migration, and, most especially, transnationalism. With respect to the U.S. context, the closest approximations of these themes appear in *Pacific Voices Talk Story: Conversations of American Experience* (2001), oral histories compiled and edited by the Samoan publisher Margo King-Lenson. With four volumes under the same title, King-Lenson's oral histories boast the most extensive collection of Pacific Islander views on labor, migration, and settlement in the continental United States. Chamorros, Chuukese, Cook Islanders, Hawaiians (or Kānaka Maoli), Maori, Marshallese, Samoans, Tahitians, and Tongans, among Pacific Islanders, are featured in these volumes. They come from various class backgrounds, and a few individuals even identify their mixed-race heritages, demonstrating the complexity of Pacific Islander identities.

The anthology *Pacific Diaspora: Island Peoples in the United States and across the Pacific* (2002) also examined Pacific Islanders as an identifiable people of study. Edited by Paul Spickard, Joanne L. Rondilla and Debbie Hippolite Wright, this volume analyzed the multidirectional mobility of Pacific Islanders in the United States and elsewhere in the Pacific. For the most part, then, very seldom have scholars examined Filipinos and Pacific Islanders in the contexts of labor and migration in the United States. While we know much about the histories of Filipinos in the agriculture, care, and service industries, we have yet to understand the impact and implications of Pacific Islanders in these and other economies. Herbert R. Barringer, Robert W. Gardner, and

Michael J. Levin's monograph *Asians and Pacific Islanders in the United States* (1993) addressed some of these issues in its sociological analysis of Filipinos, Pacific Islanders, and Asian Americans, offering directions for new research in the future. Still, much work remains unexamined with respect to Pacific Islanders, labor, and migration, let alone comparative treatments of these issues with Filipinos and others in the American empire and elsewhere.

MILITARISM AND NUCLEARISM

The historiography on Filipinos, Pacific Islanders, and the American empire pertains to the topics of militarism and nuclearism as well. Considered marginal fields when compared to labor and migration studies, the historiography on militarism and nuclearism examined here mainly applies to the western Pacific, a region also designated as Micronesia. Encompassing Chuuk, Guam, Kosrae, the Northern Mariana Islands, the Marshalls, Palau, Pohnpei, and Yap, Micronesia signifies these "American" islands, but excludes the independent countries and neighboring atolls of Kiribati and Nauru. Hawai'i, Hawaiians, and Kānaka Maoli also figure in this historiography of militarism and nuclearism, as do the Philippines and Filipinos to a lesser degree. Like the study of colonial wars in the Philippines that distinguish Southeast Asia as distinct from Micronesia, as in Leon Wolff's *Little Brown Brother: How the United States Purchased and Pacified the Philippine Islands at the Century's Turn* (1961) and Stuart Creighton Miller's *"Benevolent Assimilation": The American Conquest of the Philippines, 1899–1903* (1982), so, too, have studies on militarism and nuclearism in Micronesia treated Filipinos and Pacific Islanders as separate peoples of study. Historical analyses of World War II are particularly noteworthy for making these distinctions real but relevant, as in the landmark publications of Lin Poyer, Suzanne Falgout, and Laurence Marshall Carucci's *The Typhoon of War: Micronesian Experiences of the Pacific War* (2001) and Suzanne Falgout, Lin Poyer, and Laurence Marshall Carucci's *Memories of War: Micronesians in the Pacific War* (2008). As one of the few studies of Pacific Islander views of the war, these books significantly advanced some of the earlier works on global conflicts, indigenous peoples, and state formations, such as Geoffrey M. White's anthology *Remembering the Pacific War* (1991) and Geoffrey M. White and Lamont Lindstrom's volume *The Pacific Theater: Island Representations of World War II* (1989). They are welcome additions to the dearth of research on colonial wars in Micronesia.

Roger W. Gale's *The Americanization of Micronesia: A Study of the Consolidation of U.S. Rule in the Pacific* (1979) was another instrumental publication in this regard. As a study of the Trust Territory of the Pacific Islands in Micronesia, a United Nations "trust" created under the administration of the United States, Gale demonstrated how the United States developed Micronesia into a political identity premised on the deterrence of communism in East and Southeast Asia. He, among others, charted the "militarily strategic" importance of Micronesia to the United States. Later studies like

Grant K. Goodman and Felix Moos's edited volume *The United States and Japan in the Western Pacific: Micronesia and Papua New Guinea* (1981) and David Hanlon's *Remaking Micronesia: Discourses over Development in a Pacific Territory, 1944–1982* (1998) likewise explored the Cold War politics, economic dependencies, and security regimes, which underscored the making of American hegemony in Micronesia. As Goodman and Moos affirmed, the United States "retained political control of Micronesia for the purposes of strategic denial."[13] As in these and related studies, Micronesia became a bounded unit of study, as well as an ideological apparatus of and saltwater region for the Cold War brands of American militarism.

Subsequent historical research on Micronesia revealed the pervasiveness of American militarism, with its influencing of island constitutions in "free association" with the United States. Carl Heine's *Micronesia at the Crossroads: A Reappraisal of the Micronesian Political Dilemma* (1974), Norman Meller's *Constitutionalism in Micronesia* (1985), Bob Aldridge and Ched Myers's *Resisting the Serpent: Palau's Struggle for Self-Determination* (1990), Arnold H. Leibowitz's *Embattled Island: Palau's Struggle for Independence* (1996), and Howard P. Willens and Deanne C. Siemer's *An Honorable Accord: The Covenant between the Northern Mariana Islands and the United States* (2002) all variously examined the force of American militarism in the making of customary rights, territorial doctrines, indigenous constitutions, and bilateral treaties in Micronesia. Other studies like Robert F. Rogers's *Destiny's Landfall: A History of Guam* (1995) and Brian McAllister Linn's *Guardians of Empire: The U.S. Army and the Pacific, 1902–1940* (1997) celebrated American militarism as benign and beneficial to indigenous societies. While many of these histories linked the atomic diplomacy of the United States with the rise of indigenous nation-states in Micronesia, studies on nuclearism more explicitly conveyed the environmental, human, and political consequences of American militarism. Although most of these works have focused on the U.S. nuclear testing program in the Marshall Islands (1946–1958), many of which are ethnographic in form, these studies have historical value, given the relatively little research on or historical amnesia about American nuclearism in Micronesia.

Beginning with the anthropologist Robert C. Kiste's *The Bikinians: A Study in Forced Migration* (1974), several studies emerged thereafter with their analyses of antinuclear movements, displaced indigenous communities, nuclear-free zones, radioactive contamination, and uranium mining, among other topics. Jonathan M. Weisgall's *Operation Crossroads: The Atomic Tests at Bikini Atoll* (1994); Jane Dibblin's *Day of Two Suns: U.S. Nuclear Testing and the Pacific Islanders* (1990); Jack Niedenthal's *For the Good of Mankind: A History of the People of Bikini and Their Islands* (2002); Holly M. Barker's *Bravo for the Marshallese: Regaining Control in a Post-Nuclear, Post-Colonial World* (2004); and Barbara Rose Johnston and Holly M. Barker's *Consequential Damages of Nuclear War: The Rongelap Report* (2008) represent a sampling of the studies on the U.S. nuclear testing program and its effects on the atoll communities of Bikini, Enewetak, Rongelap, and Rongerik, among other sites. Given the regional and global reach of these issues, other studies engaged U.S. nuclearism in comparative terms, as evidenced in Peter Hayes, Lyuba Zarsky, and Walden Bello's *American Lake: Nuclear Peril in the Pacific* (1986); Stewart Firth's *Nuclear Playground* (1987); and Yoko S. Ogashiwa's *Microstates and Nuclear Issues: Regional Cooperation in the Pacific* (1991). With their emphasis on French, Soviet, and U.S. atomic diplomacy in Micronesia and elsewhere, these studies forewarned the possibility of nuclear conflicts, fallout, and apocalypse. But rather than merely create narrative histories of U.S. nuclearism, many of these studies strongly advocated interethnic solidarity among and social justice for indigenous peoples across the Pacific. Zohl dé Ishtar's *Daughters of the Pacific* (1994), an oral history of indigenous women organizers for a "nuclear-free" Pacific, crucially exemplified these activist sensibilities.

Another notable publication, the first of its kind created by Marshallese authors, is *Life in the Republic of the Marshall Islands/Mour ilo Republic eo an Majol* (2004). Edited by Anono Lieom Loeak, Veronica C. Kiluwe, and Linda Crowl, this volume features a broad array of topics, from environmental knowledge to indigenous medicine, and from family histories to navigational technologies. Marshallese experiences of the U.S. nuclear testing program are also discussed in ways that intersect with the different worldviews and needs of their generations, thereby demonstrating that nuclearism represents one of many historical events in their lives. Rounding out this historiography is Barbara Rose Johnston's anthology *Half-Lives and Half-Truths: Confronting the Radioactive Legacies of the Cold War* (2007). Drawing from the contributions of cultural, medical, and scientific anthropologists, her volume examines nuclearism through the lens of "radiogenic communities," or peoples who have been variously affected by nuclearism. As Johnston exclaims, "For the majority of the atmospheric tests conducted by the United States, the Soviet Union, China, France, and Great Britain, ground zero was the ancestral homeland for indigenous peoples, tribal groups, and other ethnic minorities."[14] Some of these radiogenic communities include the Australian Aboriginals, the Dene of Canada, the Marshallese, and the Navajo Diné, among others.

Despite the significant interventions of these studies on militarism and nuclearism, however, there have been few efforts to engage these works in the historiography on Filipinos and the American empire. Partly because of the marginal positions of Pacific Islanders in Asian American studies, very few historians have acknowledged the historiography on militarism and nuclearism in Micronesia and the Pacific as sources for teaching and research. The main exception concerns the study of American militarism in Hawai'i, with Haunani-Kay Trask's *From a Native Daughter: Colonialism and Sovereignty in Hawai'i* (1993) as its signature and widely circulated monograph. The peculiarity of Hawai'i can be attributed to its role as a nexus for transnational migration and global sugar production, first under the Kingdom of Hawai'i in the nineteenth century and then under the American empire in the twentieth century. With scholarship and nostalgia informing studies of Filipinos and other Asian Americans in Hawai'i, the land of Kānaka Maoli has thus become the signifier of American empire in the Pacific Islands, even though California, Micronesia, and the Philippines equally figure into these issues. Primarily concerned with the decolonization of Hawai'i, a goal honed by her indigenous and feminist methodologies, these locales fell beyond the purview of Trask's analysis of American empire. Instead, she analyzed the links among American colonialism, militarism, and tourism in Hawai'i, and she highlighted the structural challenges and possibilities of decolonization.

For these and other reasons, *From a Native Daughter* inspired the making of other studies on militarism in Hawai'i, such as Kathy E. Ferguson and Phyllis Turnbull's *Oh, Say, Can You See? The Semiotics of the Military in Hawai'i* (1999) and Brian Ireland's *The U.S. Military in Hawai'i: Colonialism, Memory, and Resistance* (2011). Edited anthologies on militarism are also indebted to Haunani-Kay Trask's contributions. These volumes, moreover, have begun to bridge the intellectual and political divisions in the study of Filipinos and Pacific Islanders. As the product of exchanges between anthropologists, ethnic studies scholars, and social historians, these volumes signal increasing efforts to analyze militarism and, to a lesser degree, nuclearism in ways not previously enabled by Cold War disciplines and area studies paradigms. T. Fujitani, Geoffrey M. White, and Lisa Yoneyama's *Perilous Memories: The Asia-Pacific War(s)* (2001), Catherine Lutz's *The Bases of Empire: The Global Struggle against U.S. Military Posts* (2009), and Setsu Shigematsu and Keith L. Camacho's *Militarized Currents: Toward a Decolonized Future in Asia and the Pacific* (2010) represent these efforts to analyze antibase movements, collective memory, environmental pollution, government propaganda, indigenous soldiering, multiethnic solidarity, sexual slavery, and war reparations, among other topics.

EMPIRE AND INDIGENEITY

Whereas historical studies on labor and migration in the 1970s had signaled the making of Pilipino studies, especially privileging Filipino perspectives in national and transnational terms, some histories of the American empire in the Philippines had yet to address these critical sensibilities. From examining the appointment of colonial governors like William Howard Taft to analyzing the political implications of the Tydings-McDuffie Act of 1934, much of the initial historiography focused on American actors, ideas, and events. In *Social Engineering in the Philippines: The Aims, Execution, and Impact of American Colonial Policy, 1900–1913* (1980), the historian Glenn Anthony May succinctly stated that a "study of American colonial policy is by its very nature U.S.-centered. Americans, after all, made the policy. Unfortunately, the Filipino component of the problem—that is, how Filipinos reacted to U.S. policies—is far more difficult to ascertain."[15] On the one hand, the historiography examined the U.S. conquest and administration of the Philippines, with a strong, if not nationalist, focus on studies of American commissions, governors, and laws. Viewed in this light, May is correct about his observations. On the other hand, the historiography featured studies of Filipino-American migrant and laborer experiences in Hawai'i and the continental United States, reflecting another place-based and often transnational method in how scholars understand Filipino historical agencies.

This is not to say, though, that Philippine-centered studies were less critical of the American empire, as works like William J. Pomeroy's *American Neo-Colonialism: Its*

Emergence in the Philippines and Asia (1970) and *The Philippines: Colonialism, Collaboration, and Resistance!* (1992) appropriated Marxist lens to analyze the economic dynamics of Philippine-U.S. relations. Some histories even demonstrate the co-constitutive elements of colonial pacification, police authoritarianism, and state formation in the Philippines, as in Alfred W. McCoy's *Policing America's Empire: The United States, the Philippines, and the Rise of the Surveillance State* (2009). One of the most comprehensive of these studies, combining both primary sources and historical analyses, is Daniel B. Schirmer and Stephen Rosskamm Shalom's volume *The Philippines Reader: A History of Colonialism, Neocolonialism, Dictatorship, and Resistance* (1987). They analyzed the Hukbalahap rebellion of World War II, martial law under Ferdinand Marcos, the development of Clark Air Base and Subic Naval Base, the Moros National Liberation Front, the Nacionalista and Liberal political parties, and the Philippine independence movement. These and other studies historicized the "special relationship" between the Philippines and the United States from the late nineteenth century to the late twentieth century.

The historiography on Filipinos and the Philippines is clearly robust in its Marxist histories of geopolitics, political collaboration, and revolutionary struggle. Several global conflicts—notably, the Philippine American War, the Spanish American War, World War II, and the Cold War—anchor the themes that comprise these studies. Following the publication of Edward Said's *Orientalism* (1978), the historiography on Filipinos and the Philippines became increasingly informed by postcolonial studies and its critique of discourse, knowledge, and power. Coupled with its materialist tradition, this new historiography welcomed new, compelling, and, as Vicente L. Rafael once put it, "episodic rather than epic" treatments of elitism, empire, gender, governance, language, medicine, nationalism, print media, religion, and race, to name a few examples.[16] Michael Salman's *The Embarrassment of Slavery: Controversies over Bondage and Nationalism in the American Colonial Philippines* (2001); Augusto Fauni Espiritu's *Five Faces of Exile: The Nation and Filipino American Intellectuals* (2005); Warrick Anderson's *Colonial Pathologies: American Tropical Medicine, Race, and Hygiene in the Philippines* (2006); and Paul A. Kramer's *The Blood of Government: Race, Empire, the United States and the Philippines* (2006) signaled the methodological turn to postcolonial studies. By focusing on the United States as an empire, these histories collectively refuted the benign, colonial, and paternalistic portrayals of American governance in the Philippines.

Pushing the historiography even further were analyses of the American empire that employed anthropological and literary approaches—interdisciplinary methods that were central to the making of postcolonial studies. These approaches enabled scholars to analyze art, literature, music, photography, textiles, theater, and other media as sources of historical value, thereby challenging the notion that only archives constitute the sole repositories of historical knowledge. Many of these scholars also questioned the supposed national cohesion that comes with studying "Filipino" and "Filipino American" subjects, even calling for critical reassessments of the historiography on diaspora, identity, labor, nationalism, and resistance. Commenting on Filipinos and

Asian Americans, for example, Antonio T. Tiongson, Jr., explained that "Filipinos may indeed share some affinities with Asian American groups, but because of their status as colonized subjects, it makes more sense to group them with Chicanos, Puerto Ricans, Native Americans, and Pacific Islanders."[17] He continued, "Conflating 'Filipino American' and ' / Asian American,' therefore, forecloses the potential of generating alternative ways of narrating Filipino history and subjectivities informed by the histories and situated knowledges of other colonized groups that speak to the violence of conquest and empire building and the realities of globalization and that, ultimately, better illuminate the particularities of Filipinos."[18] Favoring paradigms that center the experiences of Filipinos and other colonized peoples, these studies represent another recent transformation in the historiography. Such works include Vicente L. Rafael's *White Love and Other Essays in Filipino History* (2000), E. San Juan, Jr.'s *After Postcolonialism: Remapping Philippine–United States Confrontations* (2001), Angel Velasco Shaw and Luis H. Francia's volume *Vestiges of War: The Philippine-American War and the Aftermath of an Imperial Dream* (2003), Victor Bascara's *Model-Minority Imperialism* (2006), Allan Punzalan Isaac's *American Tropics: Articulating Filipino America* (2006), and Lucy Mae San Pablo Burns's *Puro Arte: Filipinos on the Stages of Empire* (2013).

In many ways, these and other studies can be credited for advancing conversations on a theme-by-theme basis, rather than on the assumed coherence of ethnic, national, or racial categories. Expanding the comparative study of patron-client ties, for instance, takes place in Julian Go's *American Empire and the Politics of Meaning: Elite Political Cultures in the Philippines and Puerto Rico during U.S. Colonialism* (2008). The implications of Filipinos and other nonindigenous groups participating in the discourse of "settler colonialism" are also explored in anthologies like Antonio T. Tiongson, Jr., Edgardo V. Gutierrez, and Ricardo V. Gutierrez's *Positively No Filipinos Allowed: Building Communities and Discourse* (2006) and Candace Fujikane and Jonathan Y. Okamura's *Asian Settler Colonialism: From Local Governance to the Habits of Everyday Life in Hawai'i* (2008). The analytic of genocide, another emergent lens, finds resonance in Dylan Rodríguez's *Suspended Apocalypse: White Supremacy, Genocide, and the Filipino Condition* (2010), demonstrating the interdisciplinary rigor of these works. And unlike the historiography of Pacific Islanders, which boasts a poor record of both class and comparative analyses, the historiography of Filipinos and the American empire has demonstrated otherwise. Julian Go and Anne L. Foster's anthology *The American Colonial State in the Philippines: Global Perspectives* (2003), Alfred W. McCoy and Francisco A. Scarano's volume *Colonial Crucible: Empire in the Making of the Modern American State* (2009), Vernadette Vicuña Gonzalez's *Securing Paradise: Tourism and Militarism in Hawai'i and the Philippines* (2013), and JoAnna Poblete's *Islanders in the Empire: Filipino and Puerto Rican Laborers in Hawai'i* (2014) variously examine the ascendancy, maintenance, or decline of empires in British Malaya, Cuba, Hawai'i, Panama, the Philippines, Puerto Rico, and Taiwan.

With respect to studies of Pacific Islanders and the American empire, some of the early histories on these subjects either ignored the topics altogether or drew primarily from colonial archives to narrate stories of American expansionism, commerce, and war in the Pacific. Arrell Morgan Gibson's *Yankees in Paradise: The Pacific Basin Frontier* (1993), for example, examined the agrarian, military, mining, and missionary "frontiers" of America in the Pacific. Gibson's focus on "frontiers" reflected his training as an historian of the "American West," a period and genre that would later inform Bruce Cumming's *Dominion from Sea to Sea: Pacific Ascendancy and American Power* (2009). But for all their efforts, these studies failed to analyze indigenous primary sources so as to nuance their understandings of the United States and the Pacific Islands. Countering this brand of the historiography, some of the first studies to incorporate both colonial and indigenous sources included K. R. Howe, Robert C. Kiste, and Brij V. Lal's volume *Tides of History: The Pacific Islands in the Twentieth Century* (1994) and Francis X. Hezel's *Strangers in Their Own Land: A Century of Colonial Rule in the Caroline and Marshall Islands* (1995). And comparable to the turn to postcolonial studies in the historiography of Filipinos and the American empire, cultural anthropologists, literary critics, and social historians are likewise responsible for advancing theoretical concepts and frameworks in their respective critiques of American representations of the Pacific. Sally Engle Merry's *Colonizing Hawai'i: The Cultural Power of Law* (2000), Rob Wilson's *Reimagining the American Pacific: From South Pacific to Bamboo Ridge and Beyond* (2000), Paul Lyons's *American Pacificism: Oceania and the U.S. Imagination* (2006), and Elizabeth M. DeLoughrey's *Routes and Roots: Navigating Caribbean and Pacific Island Literatures* (2007) represent these efforts to deconstruct the discursive continuities and indigenous appropriations of American law and literature in the Pacific.

The rise of Pacific Islander scholarship especially honed the methodological significance of postcolonial studies, whereby indigenous critics attempted to balance critiques of colonial state formations with (ironic) calls for indigenous national formations. As Frantz Fanon and other critics have already demonstrated, the replacement of one colonial apparatus often leads to its reproduction in the form of a native, bourgeois apparatus. Notwithstanding this political predicament, Pacific Islander critics like Vicente M. Diaz, Vilsoni Hereniko, Epeli Hau'ofa, Teresia K. Teaiwa, and Konai Thaman, among others, nevertheless pushed for the inclusion of indigenous concepts and theories in their respective works. The late Tongan writer Epeli Hau'ofa is especially credited for advancing an inclusive, decolonized Oceania, as illustrated in his book, *We Are the Ocean: Selected Works* (2008). Indeed, postcolonial studies and its antecedents in Marxism (in the eastern Pacific) and feminism partly enabled these discussions, as did the foment of various indigenous social movements since the 1950s. Anthologies like Vilsoni Hereniko and Rob Wilson's *Inside Out: Literature, Cultural Politics and Identity in the New Pacific* (1999), Robert Borofsky's *Remembrance of Pacific Pasts: An Invitation to Remake History* (2000), and David Hanlon and Geoffrey M. White's *Voyaging through the Contemporary Pacific* (2000) reflect the results of these individual and collective endeavors.

Unfortunately, however, the reach of these methodologies has been largely restricted to the study of Hawai'i and Guam whenever the question of the American empire arises. As the two main Pacific colonies of the United States, it is no surprise that historians and others tend to focus on these sites to the detriment of understanding the broader western Pacific and American Sāmoa. With this caveat in mind, Jonathan Kay Kamakawiwoʻole Osorio's *Dismembering Lāhui: A History of the Hawaiian Nation to 1887* (2002) and David E. Stannard's *Honor Killing: Race, Rape, and Clarence Darrow's Spectacular Last Case* (2005) are instructive for their respective analyses of Hawaiian Kingdom law and American colonial law in Oʻahu. Noenoe K. Silva's *Aloha Betrayed: Native Hawaiian Resistance to American Colonialism* (2004) was particularly pathbreaking for its usage of Hawaiian-language sources and for refuting the historiography that cast Hawaiians as an indigenous people without a history of resistance toward the American empire. As Silva asserted, "One of my goals in this work is to denaturalize these [historiographical] notions and practices, because it is still possible to obtain a doctorate in history specializing in Hawaiʻi and not be required to learn the Hawaiian language or use Hawaiian-language sources."[19] J. Kēhaulani Kauanui's *Hawaiian Blood: Colonialism and the Politics of Sovereignty and Indigeneity* (2008), Gary Y. Okihiro's *Island World: A History of Hawaiʻi and the United States* (2008), and Ty P. Kāwika Tengan's *Native Men Remade: Gender and Nation in Contemporary Hawaiʻi* (2008) likewise placed Hawaiian understandings of custom, genealogy, and place at the center of debates on the American empire in Hawaiʻi.

Chamorro scholars and others in Guam were also at the forefront of developing new studies on indigenous political survival and sovereignty. Laura M. T. Souder and Robert A. Underwood's *Chamorro Self-Determination* (1987) was a landmark collection in this regard. Several texts of equal significance were later produced by the Government of Guam's Political Status Education Coordinating Commission and distributed for use by the island's K–12 and college systems. They included *Hinasso': Tinige' Put Chamorro/ Insights: The Chamorro Identity* (1993) and *Kinalamten Pulitikåt: Siñenten I Chamorro/ Issues in Guam's Political Development: The Chamorro Perspective* (1996). Penelope Bordallo-Hofschneider's *A Campaign for Political Rights on the Island of Guam, 1899–1950* (2001), printed by the Northern Mariana Islands Humanities Council, also addressed Guam's struggle for political sovereignty. As local publications, these works targeted audiences in Guam and, to a lesser extent, the Northern Mariana Islands and greater Micronesia. Other university publications, though, had wider audiences, as in Ronald Stade's *Pacific Passages: World Culture and Local Politics in Guam* (1998), Anne Perez Hattori's *Colonial Dis-Ease: U.S. Navy Health Policies and the Chamorros of Guam, 1898–1941* (2004), Vicente M. Diaz's *Repositioning the Missionary: Rewriting the Histories of Colonialism, Native Catholicism, and Indigeneity in Guam* (2010), and Keith L. Camacho's *Cultures of Commemoration: The Politics of War, Memory, and History in the Mariana Islands* (2011). These studies variously examined Chamorro negotiations of American colonialism and militarism in ways that illuminated the power of both indigenous agency and colonial governance, with Julian Aguon's *The Fire This Time: Essays on Life under U.S. Occupation* (2006) as the most trenchant critique of the American empire in Guam.

Toward a Shared Historiography

As this chapter has demonstrated, the imperial grammar of U.S. governance in Asia and the Pacific Islands created the study of two, imagined subjects: "Filipinos" and "Pacific Islanders." In their respective historiographies, historians and other scholars have variously examined these societies in the contexts of labor and migration, militarism and nuclearism, and empire and indigeneity. Despite the historical processes that emanate from and converge across these peoples, however, the combined English-language historiography of Filipinos and Pacific Islanders tells a story of amnesia, fracture, and incoherence. That is to say, canonical treatments of the American empire in the Pacific Islands, the Philippines, and their respective diasporas have discouraged, if not altogether suppressed, histories about Filipino and Pacific Islanders in local, comparative, and transnational terms. But, as this chapter has shown, the histories of these and other colonized subjects increasingly meet at the intersections of colonial racialization, economic exploitation, indigenous survival, militarist violence, nationalist aspiration, and political emancipation. Richard Drinnon's *Facing West: The Metaphysics of Indian-Hating and Empire-Building* (1980) was a remarkable early monograph in this regard.

With his focus on "civilization," "racism," and "repression," Drinnon traced the discursive and material links between what he called the metaphysics of "Indian-hating" and "empire-building" in Native America, the Pacific Islands, the Philippines, and Southeast Asia. His treatment of the interrelated processes of Indian-hating and empire-building in and across these locales—a compelling but unlikely comparison for its time—demonstrated the potential for an intersectional historiography on empire, race, and nation. As Drinnon put it, "All along, the obverse of Indian-hating had been the metaphysics of empire-building—the backwoods of 'captain in the vanguard of conquering civilization' merely became the overseas outrider of the same empire. Far out on the boundless watery prairies of the Pacific, the twin metaphysics became nation-building and native-hating."[20] Several decades later, there has been an increased reckoning of these historical issues and processes, whether metaphysical, postcolonial, or otherwise. Take, for instance, Joanne Barker's edited volume *Sovereignty Matters: Locations of Contestation and Possibility in Indigenous Struggles for Self-Determination* (2005), which demonstrates the strong degree to which these conversations have begun to influence American Indian, Pacific Islander, and indigenous studies more broadly. With its emphasis on Cuba, Guam, Hawai'i, and the Philippines, Lanny Thompson's *Imperial Archipelago: Representation and Rule in the Insular Territories under U.S. Dominion after 1898* (2010) likewise illustrates the possibilities for an expansive and inclusive historiography across the Atlantic and Pacific worlds. As Vicente M. Diaz, Antonio T. Tiongson, Jr., Joanne L. Rondilla, and others have demonstrated, perhaps the time has come to fully advance these and other studies on Filipinos, Pacific Islanders, and the American empire. This process can continue by rethinking how colonial and postcolonial bodies of knowledge constitute Filipinos and Pacific Islanders as subjects of study and as agents of history. A shared historiography can accomplish this and more, if not generate further questions and debates about the links and fissures between Asian American studies and Pacific Islander studies more broadly.

NOTES

1. Vicente M. Diaz, a Carolinian Filipino critic, has long produced works that transcend the bifurcated study of Filipinos, Pacific Islanders, and the American empire. See his foundational essays, "Bye Bye Ms. American Pie: The Historical Relations between Chamorros and Filipinos and the American Dream," *ISLA: A Journal of Micronesian Studies* 3, no. 1 (1995): 147–160; and "To P or Not to P: Marking the Territory between Asian American and Pacific Islander Studies," *Journal of Asian American Studies* 7, no. 3 (2004): 183–208.
2. Allan Punzalan Isaac, *American Tropics: Articulating Filipino America* (Minneapolis: University of Minnesota Press, 2006), xxv.
3. Joanne L. Rondilla, "The Filipino Question in Asia and the Pacific: Rethinking Regional Origins in Diaspora," in *Pacific Diaspora: Island Peoples in the United States and across the Pacific*, ed. Paul Spickard, Joanne L. Rondilla, and Debbie Hippolite Wright (Honolulu: University of Hawai'i Press, 2002), 62.
4. Jean Ingram Brookes, *International Rivalry in the Pacific Islands, 1800–1875* (Berkeley: University of California Press, 1941), ix.
5. A. Grenfell Price, *The Western Invasions of the Pacific and Its Continents: A Study of Moving Frontiers and Changing Landscapes, 1513–1958* (Oxford: Clarendon, 1963), 122.
6. Brij V. Lal and Doug Munro, "The Text in Its Context: An Introduction," in *Texts and Contexts: Reflections in Pacific Islands Historiography*, ed. Doug Munro and Brij V. Lal (Honolulu: University of Hawai'i Press, 2006), 4.
7. Bruno Lasker, *Filipino Immigration to the Continental United States and to Hawaii* (Chicago: University of Chicago Press, 1931), x.
8. Jesse Quinsaat, ed., *Letters in Exile: An Introductory Reader on the History of Pilipinos in America* (Los Angeles: UCLA Asian American Studies Center, 1976), v.
9. Renato Constantino, with Letizia R. Constantino, *The Philippines: A Past Revisited* (Manila: Renato Constantino, 2002), 5.
10. Sucheng Chan, "The Changing Contours of Asian-American Historiography," *Rethinking History* 11, no. 1 (2007): 128.
11. Augusto Espiritu, "Transnationalism and Filipino American Historiography," *Journal of Asian American Studies* 11, no. 2 (2008): 172.
12. Yen Le Espiritu, *Home Bound: Filipino American Lives across Cultures, Communities, and Countries* (Berkeley: University of California Press, 2003), 4.
13. Grant K. Goodman and Felix Moos, eds., *The United States and Japan in the Western Pacific: Micronesia and Papua New Guinea* (Boulder, CO: Westview, 1981), 4.
14. Barbara Rose Johnston, "Half-Lives, Half-Truths, and Other Radioactive Legacies of the Cold War," in *Half-Lives and Half-Truths: Confronting the Radioactive Legacies of the Cold War*, ed. Barbara Rose Johnston (Santa Fe, NM: School for Advanced Research, 2007), 6.
15. Glenn Anthony May, *Social Engineering in the Philippines: The Aims, Execution, and Impact of American Colonial Policy, 1900–1913* (Westport, CT: Greenwood, 1980), xv.

16. Vicente L. Rafael, *White Love and Other Events in Filipino History* (Durham, NC: Duke University Press, 2000), 4.

17. Antonio T. Tiongson, Jr., "Introduction: Critical Considerations," in *Positively No Filipinos Allowed: Building Communities and Discourse*, ed. Antonio T. Tiongson, Jr., Edgardo V. Gutierrez, and Ricardo V. Gutierrez (Philadelphia: Temple University Press, 2006), 6.

18. Ibid.

19. Noenoe K. Silva, *Aloha Betrayed: Native Hawaiian Resistance to American Colonialism* (Durham, NC: Duke University Press, 2004), 3.

20. Richard Drinnon, *Facing West: The Metaphysics of Indian-Hating and Empire-Building* (Minneapolis: University of Minnesota Press, 1980), 464.

FURTHER READING

Brookes, Jean Ingram. *International Rivalry in the Pacific Islands, 1800–1875*. Berkeley: University of California Press, 1941.

Chan, Sucheng. "The Changing Contours of Asian-American Historiography." *Rethinking History* 11, no. 1 (2007): 125–147.

Constantino, Renato, with Letizia R. Constantino. *The Philippines: A Past Revisited*. Manila: Renato Constantino, 2002.

Diaz, Vicente M. "Bye Bye Ms. American Pie: The Historical Relations between Chamorros and Filipinos and the American Dream." *ISLA: A Journal of Micronesian Studies* 3, no. 1 (1995): 147–160.

———. "To P or Not to P: Marking the Territory between Asian American and Pacific Islander Studies." *Journal of Asian American Studies* 7, no. 3 (2004): 183–208.

Drinnon, Richard. *Facing West: The Metaphysics of Indian-Hating and Empire-Building*. Minneapolis: University of Minnesota Press, 1980.

Espiritu, Augusto. "Transnationalism and Filipino American Historiography." *Journal of Asian American Studies* 11, no. 2 (2008): 171–184.

Espiritu, Yen Le. *Home Bound: Filipino American Lives across Cultures, Communities, and Countries*. Berkeley: University of California Press, 2003.

Goodman, Grant K., and Felix Moos, eds. *The United States and Japan in the Western Pacific: Micronesia and Papua New Guinea*. Boulder, CO: Westview, 1981.

Isaac, Allan Punzalan. *American Tropics: Articulating Filipino America*. Minneapolis: University of Minnesota Press, 2006.

Johnston, Barbara Rose. "Half-Lives, Half-Truths, and Other Radioactive Legacies of the Cold War." In *Half-Lives and Half-Truths: Confronting the Radioactive Legacies of the Cold War*, edited by Barbara Rose Johnston, 1–24. Santa Fe, NM: School for Advanced Research, 2007.

Lal, Brij V., and Doug Munro. "The Text in Its Context: An Introduction." In *Texts and Contexts: Reflections in Pacific Islands Historiography*, edited by Doug Munro and Brij V. Lal, 1–16. Honolulu: University of Hawai'i Press, 2006.

Lasker, Bruno. *Filipino Immigration to the Continental United States and to Hawaii*. Chicago: University of Chicago Press, 1931.

May, Glenn Anthony. *Social Engineering in the Philippines: The Aims, Execution, and Impact of American Colonial Policy, 1900–1913*. Westport, CT: Greenwood, 1980.

Price, A. Grenfell. *The Western Invasions of the Pacific and Its Continents: A Study of Moving Frontiers and Changing Landscapes, 1513–1958*. Oxford: Clarendon, 1963.

Quinsaat, Jesse, ed. *Letters in Exile: An Introductory Reader on the History of Pilipinos in America*. Los Angeles: UCLA Asian American Studies Center, 1976.

Rafael, Vicente L. *White Love and Other Events in Filipino History*. Durham, NC: Duke University Press, 2000.

Rondilla, Joanne L. "The Filipino Question in Asia and the Pacific: Rethinking Regional Origins in Diaspora." In *Pacific Diaspora: Island Peoples in the United States and across the Pacific*, edited by Paul Spickard, Joanne L. Rondilla, and Debbie Hippolite Wright, 40–55. Honolulu: University of Hawai'i Press, 2002.

Silva, Noenoe K. *Aloha Betrayed: Native Hawaiian Resistance to American Colonialism*. Durham, NC: Duke University Press, 2004.

Tiongson, Antonio T., Jr. "Introduction: Critical Considerations." In *Positively No Filipinos Allowed: Building Communities and Discourse*, edited by Antonio T. Tiongson, Jr., Edgardo V. Gutierrez, and Ricardo V. Gutierrez, 1–16. Philadelphia: Temple University Press, 2006.

CHAPTER 2

···

TOWARD A HEMISPHERIC ASIAN AMERICAN HISTORY

···

JASON OLIVER CHANG

THE history of Asians in Latin America is a rapidly growing area of Asian American history. This subject of inquiry has been "hidden in plain view" but systematically overlooked for too long.[1] Records of Asians in Latin America predate the existence of the United States by several centuries, yet only recently has serious attention been given to this subject. For those with little knowledge of the presence of Asians in Latin America, they are sometimes referred to as Latin Asian Americans. The term refers to the ethnically diverse peoples from Asia, and their descendants, who traveled to the Western Hemisphere to reside in Latin America and the Caribbean (see figure 2.1). Such terminology does not represent a pan-ethnicity of Spanish- or Portuguese-speaking Asians as one might make reference to Asian American political identity. The scope and depth of the history of Latin Asian Americans is only now being assessed as Asians and their past were silenced from many of the national ideologies to emerge during struggles for national independence and revolutions over the last two hundred years. In an effort to confront their historical erasure and investigate the history of Asians in Latin America, the term Latin Asian American must resist the tendency to flatten the ethnic differences of those Asian populations or their regional and national location within Latin America and the Caribbean. Their history spans the entire modern period beginning in the sixteenth century and involves a multitude of Asian ethnicities and differentiated migration streams. The production of historical knowledge about Asians in Latin America is quite varied and spans numerous academic fields from history and area studies to anthropology and literary studies. The scholarly investigation of Latin Asian Americans was not established by Asian Americanist scholars, although Asian American studies has become a prominent and fertile intellectual community for its contemporary resurgence. Indeed, following the theoretical advances of diaspora and transnational studies, the subject of Latin Asian Americans has generated interest in a "hemispheric" reconceptualization of the concerns of Asian American studies. To paraphrase David Palumbo-Liu, we might approach the history of Latin Asian Americans as an important "proving ground" for the field of Asian American studies.[2]

The history of Asian migration to the Americas is inseparable from the larger history of colonialism and imperial capitalism. The social structures generated by these projects of human domination were promulgated by both the Euro-American West as well as by Asian regimes. These geopolitical struggles authored push-and-pull forces that inaugurated and sustained transpacific migration over the last four and a half centuries.

Asian Americanists have both much to learn from Latin America, as well as much to offer. What seems to be a unique contribution for Asian Americanists is the rich historical knowledge of Asian diasporas and a theoretical foundation in interpreting transnationalism as well as racialized and intersectional subjectivity. Because multiple generations of Latin Americanist historians have failed to acknowledge or consider the significance of the Asian presence in Latin America, distinctive trends among hemispheric approaches by Asian Americanists have been reconstructing diasporic spaces, tracing transnational social histories, and documenting the mechanisms of racialization. When Latin Americanists do consider the Asians in their midst, it is frequently done within the boundaries of a national state. The Latin American destinations of Asian migrants were also of little significance to Asian studies before there was a turn to the study of overseas Asian populations. However, scholarship on Latin Asian Americans remains fragmented and divided by disciplines and their respective publishing channels. Nevertheless, the scholarship produced by Latin Americanist historians is an indispensable intellectual launching point—their historiographies serve as both a guide and a mark of erasure. Asian American studies has become an appropriate site for the study of Asians in Latin America because it has always sought to correct the same Euro-Atlantic focus in U.S. history that has plagued the study of migration in Latin America. Furthermore, the recovery of their histories has spurred a resurgence of inquiry into Latin American racial states and their national histories that had become accustomed to pasts devoid of Asians. Still there are serious questions about how one might proceed.

Despite the resurgence of interest in this topic and the temptation to map the hemispheric dimensions of greater Asian America too quickly, historians of Asians in Latin America have proceeded with caution. Translating an Asian Americanist critique, if we may say such a thing exists, to the in situ domestic Latin American regimes of power and contested postcolonial states demands attention to at least two pressing concerns.[3] First is an accounting of Latin Asian American subjectivities with alternative chronologies and geographies from received notions of time and space defined by U.S. empire. This is an important first step because some histories of Asians in Latin America predate the existence of the United States, and many immigrants have never set foot in U.S. territory after 1776. Mapping the presence of Asians in Latin America is also a crucial exercise in contextualizing the environments in which Asians became a part of. This means accounting for a different and diverse set of actors with different genealogies of race, gender, and sexuality. To embark on this path, it would be foolish to discard the insights from U.S. contexts in the contested gendered and racial citizenship in immigration exclusion acts, the infamy of Japanese incarceration during World War II, and Cold War militarized refuge. Yet it would be equally foolish to project them everywhere we might find co-ethnic Asians elsewhere in the hemisphere. Likewise, it is important to resist using the U.S. experience as a measuring stick to evaluate the cultural and political meaning of Latin American discourses of Asian racial difference. We must write new and comparative histories, and many are doing so with tremendous force.

The interdisciplinary field of Asian American studies has generated important insights for the pursuit of Latin Asian American history. Historians, like Evelyn Hu-DeHart and Erika Lee, were among the first to articulate a hemispheric vision for Asian American history. However, literary scholars, like Lisa Lowe and Kandice Chuh, have pioneered an interpretive paradigm to fundamentally unhinge the nationalist trappings of a U.S.-centered Asian American studies. The provocation to go "beyond" the United States might reignite concerns raised by Sau Ling Wong more than twenty years ago in her cautionary "Denationalization Reconsidered." However, the basis of the hemispheric revisionist paradigm is not the "deterritorialization" of Asian American political subjectivity but the *re*-territorialization of subjecthood in the heterotopic space of the Western Hemisphere.

The second concern is related to this assertion. In order to write new histories of Asians in Latin America it is necessary to seriously deal with the complexity of what Charles Hale has described as the cultural politics of *mestizaje*, or race mixing. Traditionally, these cultural politics have been defined by the process of acculturation, integration, and transformation of the indigenous people, white settlers, and enslaved African populations that made up Latin American colonial societies—for the most part, Asians have been relegated to the footnotes of discussions of mestizaje in Latin American studies if mentioned at all. Throughout the hemisphere, centuries of European colonization and racial discipline through a mixed-race caste system produced ideologies of mixedness, or of the mestizo, that became central to reworking the terms of rule and consent in almost every Latin American national state in the nineteenth and twentieth centuries. Hale astutely points out that the term "mestizo" is multifarious, contextual, and disputed. He writes, "Far from a homogeneous category, discourses that invoke mestizaje, hybridity and difference have a great diversity of political motivations, contents and consequences. It then becomes crucial to examine the varying material contexts of these new political interventions, and relate them systematically to the varying consequences that follow."[4] The term "mestizo" is derived from the colonial label for the progeny of the union of a European man and an indigenous woman; however, the term is sometimes used to describe indigenous populations that have undergone some degree of acculturation and integration with settler groups.

There are at least two sides to the cultural politics of mestizaje for Latin Asian Americans: their explicit exclusion from nationalist renderings of ideal mestizo composites (a condition also shared with some Afro-Latin populations in their various national contexts like Afro-Mexicans, for example) and how mixed Asian subjects are recognized, valued, and signified. The first side of explicit exclusion reflects more state ideologies of *blanqueamiento*, or whiting, a pervasive notion across Latin America that the immigration of white Europeans to Latin America, especially to those countries with large indigenous and enslaved African populations, would eventually lead to a whitening of the overall population and thus to capitalist modernity.[5] Asians became a part of Latin American modernity, but frequently not as invited settlers but as disposable workers. In the twentieth century, several Latin American nations with large indigenous populations explicitly excluded Asians as a method to redefine national identity with a mestizo figure. Another side of the cultural politics of mestizaje is the mixed Asian subject. One example of how mixed Asian subjects were valued comes from colonial Peruvian *criollos'* (Europeans born in the colonies) use of the term "injerto," or corruption, to describe the result of Chinese/indigenous unions.[6] Another insightful rendering of mixed Asian subjectivity can be found in Lisa Yun's *Coolie Speaks*, in which she recovers a 1927 communal biography of Antonio Chuffat Latour, an Afro-Chinese Cuban, who recounts the collapse of the Cuban practice of Chinese indenture as an entangled Chinese and African struggle for life after bondage.[7] Alternatively, we might consider the ways that the Chinese Mexican artist Eduardo Auyón describes his Chinese heritage in the 1990s as an indigenous credential, reasoning that Native Americans were prehistoric Asian migrants, to thus gain backdoor access to a respectable Mexican identity—at least in his own mind.[8] These examples all illustrate a more general problematic of introducing the forgotten Asian subjects in ongoing discussions of the cultural politics of mestizaje.

This call to ground any instance of mestizaje in a cultural context and historical evolution is reminiscent of Lisa Lowe's call for the deconstruction of the Asian American subject to account for the multiplicity, heterogeneity, and hybridity found in the U.S. context. However, her point is more closely related to the first question of alternative and disaggregated Latin Asian American chronotropes. Instead, the difference that Hale underscores is the way that mestizaje operates in different instances as an imagined community, a racial state, a subaltern caste, a nationalist ideology, or a strategy of indigenous negotiation. These differences might exist synchronically across different regions of the same national state or they might identify a process of political transformation for one population, or the transnational development of racial governance. Therefore, the mestizo, and its relationship of Asian racial difference, is never just an insider "mestizo" population and an outsider "Asian" population, but a set of evolving power relations between sovereign state authority and the ruled population. A crucial role for Latin Asian American history is to use the restoration of Asian subjects in Latin American history to rethink the political function that Asianness plays in various forms of governmentality. It is the context and historical unfolding of the idiomatic expression of mestizaje, or the mestizo, that should be attended to in writing Latin Asian American histories. For this reason the history of Latin Asian Americans must go beyond a social history to account for the historical production of the Latin American ideologies of racial Asianness and the discursive figures they conjure. This point is made not to merely identify anti-Asian politics in other places, but to investigate what cultural and political meanings such projects of racial difference were attached to. For instance, Jeffrey Lesser's *Negotiating National Identity* illustrates that Brazilian notions of Japanese racial superiority were appropriated to reflect Brazilian national modernity and should resist an easy alignment with a more familiar U.S. model minority discourse. The historical recuperation of Latin Asian American pasts provides an opportunity to reexamine mestizo cultural politics from the perspective of Asians and thus begin to investigate the various functions of Asian racialization and historical erasure in Latin America.

Asian migrants came to the Americas under a variety of conditions, ranging from slavery, voluntary sojourn, or indenture (sometimes coerced, frequently through deception) to state-sponsored colonists. The Latin American destinations of Asian migrants were composed of indigenous republics, colonies, settler societies, and national states. Asians were also part of the complex and violent period of independence, revolution, and transformation in Latin America either as actual actors or as racialized figures in Latin American public spheres. The history of Asians in Latin America is fundamentally a transnational story of diaspora, yet one that insists on the importance of place, locality, and the specificity of connection to Asia, the hemisphere, and the globe. As most Latin Americanists can attest to, the specificity of local conditions is an analytical starting point for the study of race and ethnicity in Latin America because national identity and state power are usually situated within regional and local negotiations of sovereignty, frequently positioned against or within indigeneity. This means that the cultural meaning of racial codes must be figured within an appropriate national rubric of local/regional politics. For instance, constitutional independence in Latin America frequently abolished official racial designations, making racial meaning and identity a complex, coded, and contingent process that softened the state's responsibility but strengthened the reliance on racist local and regional customary laws to exercise sovereign authority. It bears noting that even based on these general outlines of the subject one may already get the sense that the historical record of Latin Asian Americans is scattered around the world's archives of numerous colonial administrations and national repositories, recorded in more than a dozen languages.

While the subject of Asians in Latin America is becoming popular, its significance is difficult to surmise. It is particularly so because this subject has emerged at the intersection of several fields of study. For this reason there is little agreement on periodization, prevailing theory, and terminology. One outcome of this condition is that the history of Asians in Latin America frequently creates more problems of inquiry than it seeks to resolve debates in historiography—more as a set of problems and questions than a clearly delimited subject of inquiry. This outcome occurs because this research is largely a project of recovery and restoration, butting up against historiographies and narratives that have marginalized, overlooked, or erased the Asian presence and contribution in the historical record. The analysis of many historical origins, consequences, fractures, convergences, and contingencies of Latin Asian American history allows us to represent some of the ferment that this subject brings. By bringing together some of the disparate threads and wagering their bearing for the field of Asian American history, it is possible to illuminate the ways that Asians in Latin America present a challenge to rethink the core concerns of Asian American history.

THE EARLY COLONIAL PERIOD

The early colonial period begins in the sixteenth century with the European colonization of the Americas and ultimately taking up the original European fantasy of a sea
route to Asia. In this period Filipinos were among the first Asian arrivants, as sailors
aboard Spanish galleons. For instance, in 1587 Filipino crew members of the Spanish
galleon *Nuestra Señora Esperanza* anchored in Morro Bay of New Spain's California
coast and established a small settlement at this site along the galleon's return from
Manila. The galleon trade between Acapulco in Spanish Mexico and Lima farther
south in the Peruvian viceroyalty and Manila in the Philippines marked the initiation
of a transpacific passage that would eventually bring hundreds of thousands of ethnically different Asians to the European colonies and indigenous lands of the Americas.
While Slavic Russians had imperial operations across the Pacific's northern Bering Sea
to Alaska and down the coast to present-day California, it did not lead to the systematic migration of people racialized as Asian. For example, the Spanish Filipinos, also
called *indios chinos*, who landed in Mexico, established settlements along the Pacific
coast of present-day Mexico and integrated with autonomous Indian republics. Floro
Mercene's *Manila Men in the New World* provides details that help reconstruct early
Filipino life in the Americas and the terrible conditions of the three-month Manila
passage.[9] Whereas the economic structure of the Hispanic Pacific has dominated
the study of this region, with tallies of silver bullion going west and silk and porce-
lains going east, new works focus on the subjectivities and lives of these early Asian
migrants. While such histories sought to correct an overemphasis on Atlantic commerce in world economic history, the Asian crews, passengers, and slaves held as
cargo were frequently ignored or noted with a nod of recognition. Edward Slack, Jr.'s
article "The Chinos in New Spain" clarifies the importance and scale of the human
dimension of the Pacific passage, although much less is known about chinos in Peru
over the same period.

Despite the humanistic oversight by economic historians, many specialists of the
early modern Pacific have identified important capitalist structures of exchange and
ideologies of rule that have shaped how Asians crossed the Hispanic Pacific and entered
the Americas. Examples are André Gunder Frank's seminal *ReOrient: Global Economy
in the Asian Age*, which identifies the capitalist logic of Pacific mercantilism, and Rainer
Buschmann, Edward Slack, Jr., and James Tueller's *Navigating the Spanish Lake: The
Pacific in the Iberian World, 1521–1898*, which describes how Guam and the Philippines
became key to power in the Hispanic Pacific.[10] Revealing the maritime world of the
early modern Pacific has been a generative area of research to document how empires
have made and remade the Pacific to their interests, thus altering the sources, paths,
and means of Asian migration to the Americas. David Igler's recent *The Great Ocean*
illustrates how Spanish, British, and later U.S. imperial regimes "assembled" their own
Pacific projects.[11]

This seventeenth-century maritime route became an occupation for recruited Asian seamen and a conduit for the trafficking of Asian slaves, the migration of Asian merchants, and the passage for Filipino indios chinos as vassals of the Spanish Crown. Some of the galleon's sailors were volunteers but others were coerced or enslaved to fulfill menial occupations during the transpacific voyage. In this early period, Spanish and Portuguese traders engaged in a brutal traffic in Asian slaves. Tatiana Seijas's *Asian Slaves in Colonial Mexico: From Chinos to Indians* (2014) is the first to conduct a systematic study of the subject, documenting the acquisition of male and female slaves from Japan, China, the Philippines, Mogul India, and Southeast Asian kingdoms.[12] The purchase and sale of Asian slaves created the racial category *chino* to denote all enslaved Asians. This differed from the category of indios chinos, who were subjects of Spain's Philippine colony and thus exempt from slavery. While women were trafficked for prostitution, males were enlisted in numerous types of oceanic and terrestrial labor—in particular textile occupations and domestic servant positions thought to correspond with particular racialized Asian qualities. The most famous chino to enter colonial Mexico was a Mogul princess, Mirrha, or, as she would later become known, Catarina de San Juan. Her figure would become a pivotal cultural icon in the central Mexican state of Puebla to signify beauty, devotion, healing, and benevolent care. Roshni Rustomji-Kerns has published numerous works to explore a history that represents one of the many ways in which enslaved Asians used the cultural traditions of colonial Mexico to work toward their emancipation.[13] Hopefully these pioneering historians' works will inspire more research into these hidden subjectivities and subaltern agencies.

The production and management of Asian racial difference within the Spanish empire presents new questions for the history of mixed-race identity formation in Latin America. The administrative reckoning of Asian subjects in New Spain facilitated an ethnic integration with the indigenous population and also an extremely vulnerable social category—yet we know little about the lives of chinos in the Indian republics of Mexico and Peru of the sixteenth and seventeenth centuries. Nevertheless, the research on Spanish Mexico informs us that chinos lived in multiethnic and multiracial communities across the Spanish colony and surrounding indigenous republics. Despite the vulnerability of chinos, we learn that enterprising chinos and indios chinos also conducted business in Mexico City and presented some unsettling competition for Spanish criollos. The Spanish Crown eventually barred Asian migration to New Spain in 1635 in order to protect the interests of Spanish colonists. By 1690 the chino slave trade was ended by pleas of Atlantic slavers to the Crown eager to cut out the Pacific competition. Yet small Filipino and Chinese enclaves did persist until the period of independence in the early nineteenth century. This area remains a rich and wide-open field of research.

One question in particular that remains quite unanswered is the role that the 1763 Treaty of Paris played within imperial succession in the Pacific. The eighteenth-century accord ended the Seven Years' War, or the French and Indian Wars as it is known in North America, marking the victory of England and Portugal over Spain and France in gaining control over the colonies of the Western Hemisphere and in encouraging the imminent independence of the British American colonies. Much of the historiography focuses on contested lands in North America; however, more research is needed to understand how the shifting tides of power altered the Pacific passage. A significant consequence of British/Spanish rivalry during this period was the Anglo production of Black Legend discourses of Spanish degeneracy, despotism, and decadence. U.S. historians have productively traced origins of negative U.S. stereotypes of Mexicans and Spaniards in British Black Legend discourse—contributing to an influential jingoist ideology that fueled two wars of expansion (in 1846 and 1898).[14] We do not know the extent of Black Legend discourse in shaping European and U.S. perceptions of Asians in Asia or in the Americas, but further research could offer an insightful genealogical rendering of ruling Pacific ideologies.

In the eighteenth century, England began to assemble a Pacific that would link commodities like opium and tea in India and China with the trade of agricultural commodities in the Americas and thus it inaugurated new forces for migration and demands for labor—giving rise to the next period of Latin Asian American history. The early colonial period gradually ends through the dawn of the nineteenth century with the confluence of four trends: the national independence of Spain's American colonies, U.S. conquest in North America, declines in the African slave trade and movements for emancipation, and the British imperial ascendancy.

The Coolie System

This next period of Latin Asian American history has had the strongest and most sustained attention by historians; however, there remain fascinating new directions for research. Mainstream Asian American history begins with mid-nineteenth-century Chinese sojourners to the California Gold Rush in 1849, but in Latin America there were a variety of indentured Asian workers delivered to plantations, mines, and construction sites. To understand this period, we must begin with the wave of independence struggles across the Spanish empire. The Crown's efforts to control their Latin American colonies led to successive wars for independence and the creation of more than a dozen postcolonial national states in the Western Hemisphere. This change ultimately led to an unraveling of the Spanish transpacific galleon trade and with it the most reliable link between Asia and the Americas. As the imperial tides of the Pacific shifted to the naval and commercial power of England, the Spanish galleon trade did not so much disintegrate as it expanded through its fragmentation, as others picked up the pieces. The decline of Spanish power made room for other imperial competitors, namely the British but also burgeoning American merchant mariners, within the lucrative Pacific trades. Furthermore, British expansion into the Pacific region created new avenues for a greater diversity of Asian migration to the Americas. The diversity of Asian migrants coming to the Americas in the early nineteenth century reflects the dependence on Asian labor for the expansion of industrial capitalism and the global reconciliation of liberal rationales for colonial rule and the dependence on chattel slavery. Indian lascar sailors as well as

Chinese and Indian coolie laborers boarded ships bound for the Western Hemisphere in an effort to respond to the violent disruption by European incursion, seek greater returns for family members back home, and seek adventure. The dreams that indentured Asians brought with them to Latin America were usually replaced with nightmares.

By the start of the nineteenth century, tens of thousands of Indian lascars worked aboard European vessels—a practice that had slowly expanded since the seventeenth century. After the last Spanish galleon anchored in Manila in 1815, lascars aboard transpacific European vessels, particularly English vessels, became the next ethnic group of Asians to arrive. When those vessels reached the Americas, some absconded from their ships to escape the hard and poorly paid labor. As early as 1788 we know that Indian lascars jumped ship in places like British Jamaica, although very little research has been done on the extent of this practice in Latin America or of their lives once ashore.[15] What is clear is that British colonial administrators and Parliament were upset with the tendency for lascars not to stay on the ships they were hired to work and heavy penalties were laid upon them. Vivek Bald's recent *Bengali Harlem* has described lascar history as "lost in migration."[16] His work centers on the twentieth-century lives of Bengali lascars who circulated through the Americas to settle in African American communities in the New York area. The Pacific's oceanic labor constitutes an enormous field of maritime history left almost completely untouched by Asian American historians. If Indian lascars helped expand the English naval and merchant marine in the Pacific as with the East Indian Company, then coolies, or contracted laborers, had filled the demand for agricultural work, mining, and railroad construction.

While the Spanish Crown ended the chino slave trade and banned free immigration of chinos in the seventeenth century in order to preserve Spanish monopolies in both the Pacific and Atlantic, the English did the opposite. In the nineteenth century British officials gradually constructed a global bureaucratic system of recruiting, exporting, and regulating contracted Indian and Chinese workers, or coolies. This system of acquiring, distributing, and controlling labor began in the 1830s as plantation owners across Latin America began to face two new limitations: independent postcolonial states and the contradiction of slavery and liberalism. Both of these limitations severely constrained the use and trade of enslaved Africans. Eventually the emancipation of Latin America's enslaved Africans came in the form of national independence or by colonial decree. Yet neither of these political forms brought an end to the economic structure of industrial capitalism. Coolies became an important source of labor in this period of transformation. A clear example of the link between Asian coolies and African slaves is the transition of Atlantic slave ships to Pacific coolie ships. In certain places coolies were substitutes for enslaved Africans and in other places they merely augmented the supply of coerced labor. Coolie histories have become the most prominent subject for Latin Asian American history. Through the coolie system, the Chinese became the largest population of Asians in the Americas by the second half of the nineteenth century. During that same period migrants from India and Japan also came in increasing numbers. Hundreds of thousands of Chinese and Indian migrants were brought to the Americas as indentured workers; among the first was a group of two hundred migrants delivered to Trinidad in 1807. In 1838

Indian coolie families from Calcutta were first introduced to British Guiana in an effort to augment the South American colony's agricultural labor in the wake of emancipated African slaves. The journalist Gaiutra Bahadur has recently published *Coolie Woman: The Odyssey of Indenture* to document the lives of female Indian coolies in that English colony.[17] This pathbreaking work documents their voyage, living conditions, and callous treatment at the hands of South American plantation managers. By mid-nineteenth century Indian coolies were still being brought to Trinidad in the Caribbean. Aisha Kahn documents how these coolies acculturated to a distinctive Indo-Caribbean polycultural norm that generated unique traditions and rituals.[18] A practice that reflected the multiple and global origins of the peoples brought to labor in the island's plantations.

From 1847 to 1874 more than 220,000 contracted Chinese male workers were brought to newly independent Peru and the Spanish colony of Cuba. They worked on sugar plantations, in guano fields, in mines, and on railroads. They were contracted laborers who toiled under the dubious conditions of the legal agreement, a labor practice that continued slavery in another name. Were it not for the publication of government investigations of abuses in the coolie system, the dreadful practice might have continued longer than it had. The 1871 book *The Coolie: His Rights and Wrongs* by the Englishman Edward Jenks documented the abuses of South Asian coolies in British Guiana and the 1874 publication of the Chinese Commission investigated the brutality imposed on Chinese coolies in Cuba. Both reports provide important details about the lives of South Asian and Chinese coolies and offer striking examples of the insights possible in comparative coolie studies in Latin America. These reports helped shed light on the inhumane conditions of the coolie trade and led to its dismantling later in the decade. Since the early work of Watt Stewart's *Chinese Bondage in Peru* (1951), James Tigner's *The Okinawans in Latin America* (1956), Arnold Meagher's *The Coolie Trade* (1974), and Evelyn Hu-DeHart's comparative examinations of Chinese in Mexico, Cuba, and Peru since the 1980s, another generation of historians has begun to rewrite coolie history.[19]

Some notable examples of the Cuban case include Kathleen López's *Chinese Cubans* and Lisa Yun's *Coolie Speaks*.[20] Both texts recover the coolie as a historical subject and individuals as historical actors. Yun's approach from literary studies reads the modes of communication found in Cuban records of and by Chinese coolies in order to reconstruct their worldviews and politics of mixed African slave and Chinese coolie community formation. López's work traces the transnational history of Chinese coolies as they transitioned from indenture to freedom and negotiated an identity that was both Chinese and Cuban. Cuban Chinese coolies are important as an illustration of the significance of Latin Asian Americans for Asian American studies. They are important not because some eventually migrated to the United States after indenture but because Cuban coolie practices informed influential discourses of Chinese racial difference in the United States. Moon-Ho Jung's *Coolies and Cane* illustrates this particular revelation as an alternative genealogy of U.S. racialization. According to him, racial discourses surrounding the use of Asian coolie labor in the Caribbean were vital sources of inspiration for the articulation of U.S. ideologies of race, free labor, and liberal citizenship.

Such revisions to Asian American theories of racialization illustrate the impact that broadening the geographic scope of the field can have. Such studies of coolie discourse underscore the importance of attention to the hemispheric and global circuitry in which racialized Asian figures become appropriated and localized in ideological state formations.

There are far fewer studies of Chinese coolies in Peru. Peru's coolies were divided between the guano industry on the coast and the sugar plantations inland. The more than twenty-five guano islands, encrusted with centuries of bird dung, became the site of horrific working conditions with an incredible death rate. Some of the islands that took coolie lives still bear names of their origins, like Asia Island and China Point. Inland, coolies worked at a number of plantations and mining operations. By the turn of the twentieth century, Japanese *dekasegis*, or migrant laborers, began to enter Peru as agriculture expanded and Amazonian settlements flourished. Peru's ex-coolies and dekasegis gradually remigrated to other locations in South America. Diego Lin Chou's *Chile y China* traces the remigration of ex-coolies to Chile while Iyo Kunimoto's *La inmigracion Japonesa en Bolivia* illustrates how Peru was an important gateway for Japanese to enter the Bolivian and Brazilian Amazon basin.[21]

The web of coolie routes and numerous remigrations have inspired comparative coolie studies to reflect on national differences as well as the transnational, or more precisely, the hemispheric scope of Latin Asian American migration in the late nineteenth and early twentieth centuries. Importantly, Elliot Young's book *Alien Nation* traces the inter-American routes of the Chinese diaspora from the mid-nineteenth century to World War II. His approach to Chinese diaspora history links the coolie system, various national immigration restriction laws, and the racial nationalisms of twentieth-century Latin American revolutions as pivotal structural features that gave shape to Chinese migration throughout the hemisphere but also conditioned their experiences as racialized Chinese aliens. As Young makes clear, the historical restoration of Latin Asian American cultural and migratory space was deeply fragmented by multiple and contested sovereignties. It should come as no surprise that this book about the Chinese diaspora should be written by a seasoned scholar of the U.S.-Mexico border who is familiar with theories of border space, crossing, and the circulation of racialized bodies through the jurisdictions of competing national states. These same themes have certainly been taken up by others writing transpacific Asian American histories with Asian-sending locations in which the migratory subjects were the proper subjects/citizens of those states, the difference being these migrants circulated through the Americas as racialized aliens. In other words, borders feel different when neither side is home. While the field of U.S.-Mexico border studies had suffered from the same Asian amnesia as within Mexican history, the recent study of Chinese in *la frontera* has become a crucial site to articulate the grounds of comparativity with the United States.

In this paradigm, Asians, coolie or not, were characterized as disinterested, cheap, obedient laborers, instruments of industrialization, not as potential citizens. Chinese migrants were a diverse group that included coolies, but independent voluntary peasants and wealthy merchants also journeyed across the Pacific.[22] However, South Asians were overwhelmingly contracted coolies. The clear majority of Asian migrants to the United States during this period were voluntary Chinese sojourners, or temporary migrants, along the Pacific Coast of North America. While there were large populations of coolies elsewhere in the Americas (the largest being in Cuba with 125,000), the largest concentration of voluntary Chinese migrants in the Americas was at the epicenter of the 1849 Gold Rush in central California, numbering more than 138,941 by 1880.[23] Because of these trends, central California and Havana, Cuba, became the most important hubs in the Americas for Chinese migration.

Throughout the Americas the reputation of Chinese as dependable, cheap industrial labor led to their employment building railroads across the hemisphere. Following the labor demands from railroad capitalists, Chinese workers laid tracks throughout the Americas. They worked on the most dangerous and difficult sections of the Southern Pacific's U.S. transcontinental line (completed in 1869), Peru's Chimbote-Huallanca line (1876), and the Canadian Pacific Rail (1885) as well as nearly every main line in Mexico, including the Tehuantepec railway (1894).[24] All of these rail lines connected remote manufacturing zones or sites of resource extraction to Pacific ports for access to global markets. These routes of transshipment highlight the importance of the U.S. project to construct the Panama Canal, a massive industrial endeavor that consumed the lives of hundreds of Chinese workers hired through the decaying contracted-worker recruitment system. The completion of railroads coincided with the formal end of the British coolie system (1879) and a wave of expired coolie contracts at the end of the nineteenth century. While the bureaucratic British system was dismantled, the practice of recruiting contracted laborers from China remained in effect well into the twentieth century. These factors led to the dispersal, circulation, and formation of a plaited web of migration throughout the Americas at a time when they were becoming unwelcomed.[25]

A big question that hemispheric Asian American history has wrestled with is to what extent did the treatment of Chinese in the United States became a model for the hemisphere. U.S. courts and legislatures crafted a racial jurisprudence of citizenship—one that rationalized immigration restriction and selective naturalization, enforced segregation, prohibited intermarriage, regulated the circulation of migrants, and invented bureaucratic procedures to document, verify, and police the Chinese within and beyond their borders and were seemingly appropriated and instated elsewhere.[26] U.S. court decisions and federal statutes illustrate the piecemeal approach by which Chinese legal activism pushed the U.S. judicial system to define the boundaries of their exclusion; this precedence helped establish a juridical logic of Asian exclusion. The most important U.S. law was the passage of the Chinese Exclusion Act in 1882, the first to lay out the legal and bureaucratic parameters for defining and enforcing an immigration restriction based on ideas of racial threat.[27] Nevertheless, the cultural politics of mestizaje and the divergent ideological architectures of Latin American nationalisms suggest a cautious, if not skeptical, evaluation of the influence of U.S. ideology in shaping Latin American discourses of Asian racial difference. My own work in Mexico argues that U.S. and Mexican ideologies of Chinese racial difference were overlapping but early twentieth-century Mexican antichinismo was not derivative of U.S. anti-Chinese politics. Instead, Mexican antichinismo evolved out of the crisis of reconstructing the governmental state after the 1910 revolution. Mexican appropriation of discourses of Asian racial difference included sources from the United States but they were selective, partial, and had contributed to the creation of a state-disciplined mestizo racial project. To attribute U.S. racism to Mexican actors disconnects them from the material, social, and cultural conditions in which Chinese racial difference had consequence for them and the Chinese Mexicans framed by it. Discourses of Asian racial difference in the Americas need not exhibit a direct lineage with U.S. empire to fulfill the interests of hemispheric Asian American history. Put another way, the hemispheric project ought to include the documentation and analysis of the variety of ways that Asianness became instrumental to different projects of racial domination in the Americas and the identities fashioned by Asians in this context.

By the economic recession of the 1870s, the image of a Chinese man as a constructive laborer quickly shifted to him as being a public enemy. Across many countries the usefulness of Chinese labor dwindled as the intensification of industrial capitalism forced many national states to revise the class structure of criollos, the working classes, and indigenous peasants. In these transitions anti-Asian attitudes became pragmatic and instrumental to new forms of consent.[28] It is in this period that many Latin American nations begin to pass anti-Asian immigration laws. These immigration restrictions reduced mobility and shaped the contours of Latin Asian American political belonging. However, the effect on the greater Chinese diaspora was a splintering and rerouting of migration routes to circumvent U.S. enforcement. For example, after 1882 Chinese migration to Canada and Mexico increased as migrants sought clandestine routes to the U.S. interior.[29] After decades of highly regimented use of imported coolie labor and recruitment of voluntary workers on mega-infrastructure projects across the Americas, the sudden restriction on Chinese immigration in the United States coincided with a widespread untethering of Chinese workers from their projects of industrialization and a winding down of the coolie system. As Chinese and South Asian workers began to reconfigure their lives, they connected with other Asians in the Americas and wove together complex multisited migration routes. These routes facilitated clandestine entry to the United States but they also provided the means to construct pan-American political and cultural identities as well as transnational commercial franchises.[30] Nevertheless, U.S. restriction hindered all but the diaspora's wealthiest merchants who continued to circulate throughout the Americas.

In each country Asians became the target of hatred as more privileged groups of workers negotiated marginal benefits from an increasingly powerful class of industrial capitalists such as those in the United States, like the Forbes, Pearson, Rockefeller, Morgan, and Carnegie families.[31] Other countries borrowed the U.S. brand of anti-Chinese laws because it was perceived as an innovation of constitutional power to articulate racial limitations of liberal modern citizenship for the Chinese and thus a useful tool to shape a variety of other articulations of state power in Latin America.[32] We can go beyond identifying whether Latin American countries adopted anti-Asian laws to ask why and to what effect. While other countries steadily adopted anti-Chinese laws similar to those of the United States they did so partially, selectively, and for divergent utopias.[33] These measures of institutionalization, as described by Arjun Appadurai as the global Orientalist ideosphere, or by Erika Lee's notion of hemispheric Orientalism, reflected the usefulness of anti-Asian politics for domestic power struggles as well as a forceful U.S. paradigm of immigration control and racial citizenship.

Erika Lee's *At America's Gate* is a significant monograph because it established the importance of Mexico and the Caribbean for Chinese migrants as they sought to evade the enforcement of U.S. exclusion laws at Pacific ports.[34] Since then, other important works have highlighted the historical intimacy of Chinese Mexican and Chinese American populations, particularly along the U.S.-Mexico border. Books like Julia Schiavone-Camacho's *Transpacific Journey* and Grace Delgado's *Making the Chinese Mexican* demonstrate how Mexican treatment of the Chinese differed from the United States but nevertheless produced similar exclusionary practices and forced removals after the 1910 nationalist revolution.[35] These works assert that the hemisphere is the appropriate geographic frame for Asian American studies because it reflects the diasporic scope of Asian American populations in the United States. Others, like Adam McKeown's *Melancholy Order*, assert that even broader cartographies are appropriate because they must account for the global scope of modern governmentality and the ways that regulating Chinese immigration taught governments how to govern.[36]

EMPIRES AND *COLONOS*

By the third quarter of the nineteenth century, British power in the Pacific was giving way to the United States and its Asian rival, Japan. This rivalry began with the expedition of U.S. Navy Commodore Matthew Calbraith Perry to Japan in 1853 and 1854 to the self-isolated Tokugawa Shogunate of Japan. Having successfully blockaded the Caribbean coast of Mexico during the Mexican-American War (1846–1848) five years earlier, the Japanese were mindful of the result of Perry's previous victory in Mexico. While the United States was the first to open trade with Japan in the nineteenth century, Americans were latecomers to the booming commerce of coastal China and Southeast Asia, where Europeans had had trade colonies since the seventeenth century. Perry's visit to Japan was a catalyst for dramatic internal change in Japan. The demonstration of U.S. military prowess proved the inability of the Shogunate to protect Japan from the outside world. This led to the emergence of technocratic samurai leaders who instituted a regime of rapid transformation to restore Japan to greatness. Their revolution in 1867 was called *Meiji*, or the renewal. The program of national unification promulgated by the ascending Meiji samurai class transformed feudal life through pacification, industrialization, and reworking the caste system, in addition to intense xenophilia. These changes fueled emigration and created regular streams of dekasegis—a majority of which went to Hawai'i, although others ventured into South America's Amazon basin in search of tapping into the lucrative trade in rubber.[37] Japanese state-sponsored colonization enterprises gathered and distributed Japanese settlers throughout Latin America. Nevertheless, the Meiji formulation of a vigorous nationalism and swift industrial reorganization became the envy of other postcolonial countries, particularly in Latin America. Several state-led programs investigated conditions in Latin America conducive to the settlement of Japanese colonists. Paradoxically, when Chinese workers were beginning to be rejected, the leaders of Latin American countries also began to look toward Japan as a model of postcolonial modernization.[38] The Japanese Meiji government began to introduce state-sponsored colonists throughout Latin America, with particularly robust settlements in Brazil. Before Japanese colonization of Korea after the turn of the twentieth century, Korean families and workers also entered the stream of labor migration to Latin America.

The emigration of Japanese to Latin America reinforces the importance of work in transnational Japanese American studies. The importance of the Japanese state in shaping emigration, sponsoring settlement, and bolstering the racial credentials of its citizens abroad is no less significant in the many cases of Latin America. Toake Endoh's *Exporting Japan* is an important illustration of the critical role that emigration played in Japanese industrialization as well as the strategic nature of where and when Japanese settlers were sent to locations in Latin America.[39] The state-sponsored nature of Japanese immigration positioned them as unique and troubled subjects. Whereas Chinese were frequently cast as racial degenerates in Latin American ideologies of mestizaje, the Japanese were frequently touted as adequate substitutes for Europeans. The field of Japanese immigration to Latin America and its particular influence on shaping the cultural politics of mestizaje can be generalized from a few significant works such as Jeffrey Lesser's *Negotiating National Identity* on Brazilian Japanese, Jerry Garcia's *Looking Like the Enemy* on Mexican Japanese during World War II, Seiichi Higashide's *Adios to Tears* on Peruvian Japanese incarcerated in the United States, and Greg Robinson's *Tragedy of Democracy* on the World War II incarcerations of Japanese across North America.[40] These most excellent works also illustrate that the majority of attention has focused on the World War II era. An important exception is Taku Suzuki's *Embodying Belonging* about Okinawan settlers sent to Bolivia as a part of postwar U.S. occupation of Japan.[41] Nevertheless, the absence of more postwar Latin Asian American histories is striking since in the 1980s a Chinese-inspired rebellion, the Shining Path, broke out in central Peru, and then in 1990 Peru elected the first national president with Asian ancestry in all the Americas, Alberto Fujimori. Yet no comprehensive history of Asian Peru exists.

These seemingly anecdotal examples taken from five hundred years of Asian contact and interaction with the Americas are the basis for new directions in Asian American history. These examples highlight areas in which the subject of Asians in Latin America presents challenges and opportunities for the further development of hemispheric Asian American history.

Concluding Remarks

There are a number of signs that the Asian presence in Latin America is no longer an obscure topic. China's ongoing economic expansion in Latin America has become a routine reminder of the centuries of contact between Asia and the Western Hemisphere. Furthermore, the phenomenal growth of scholarly interest can be seen in the annual Asians in the Americas symposium.[42] The study of Asians in Latin America has emerged out of the blind spots of three fields: Asian American studies, Asian studies, and Latin American studies. Historians of Latin America have produced excellent research on Asian immigration and identity formation in colonial and national periods but their relationship to Asian American history remained referential, if at all. In short, early Asian American histories put political premiums on U.S. populations, and Latin American histories of Asians asserted the uniqueness of local conditions and renounced any U.S. intellectual influence. In addition to the historical divisions between these fields of scholarship, Latin American historiographies have developed interpretive norms whose coherence relies on the erasure of the Asian presence or the assertion that Latin America is in some way postracial because of its mestizo, or mixed-race, character. This will continue to be a point of tension so long as the field of Latin American studies clings to nationalist mythologies and academic careers are built upon scholarship that continues the historical erasure of Asians.

One aspiration for Latin Asian American history might be to use the investigation of occluded Asian pasts as the entry point to engage with Latin America's other Others. We might agree that an opportunity would be missed if, in restoring the place of Asian subjects in Latin America history, we also neglected its links to other regimes of silence, forgetting, and domination. This issue is particularly pressing in the current moment when Asian capital investment in Latin America has reached an unprecedented magnitude. Latin Asian American history has become politically viable in ways it wasn't before. Nevertheless, transpacific Asia/Latin American economic cooperation has only intensified the domination and disavowal of Latin America's indigenous and racialized Others. It would seem that visibility does not come without a price, although Latin Asian American histories can reject this transaction by remaining committed to Asian American critiques of relational racial formations and identifying the ways in which this interracial nexus preserves the means of reproducing the state.

The production of historical knowledge regarding Asians in Latin America has engaged three broad themes of consequence: alternative chronologies and cartographies of the hemisphere that predate and decenter the United States; the comparative study of imperial regimes and colonial settler-states; and the documentation of the nested scale of synchronic multifarious racial projects in empires and across Latin America's heterogeneous regions and nations. This subject helps to reorient the temporal and spatial coordinates of the field to reflect the globalized nature of the early modern world when Asian diasporas began to cross the Pacific and become a part of the Americas as well as the hemispheric dimensions of actual diasporas and the various national silences in which Latin Asian Americans have endured. Through comparative study, we can discover the breadth of variation in Asian racialization and political formations of Latin Asian Americans. The hemispheric paradigm might suggest that to be inclusive of a broader cartography is not to use historical interpretation to appropriate a Latin Asian American past to cater to a U.S. ethnic studies intellectual project but to think, imagine, and narrate the past from alternative Asian subjectivities with agendas unrelated to U.S.-based Asian American politics. These themes illustrate why the study of Asians in Latin America goes beyond merely rendering more focused accounts of Asians in unexpected places. They challenge historical narratives bounded by nationalism, develop a transnational discourse of human rights and an articulation of diasporic citizenship, and lastly document the diverse and divergent ways that various racial ideologies have shaped the reception, integration, and subjectivity of Asians in Latin America.

NOTES

1. Rudy P. Guevarra, Jr., "Introduction to the Special Issue," *Journal of Asian American Studies* 14, no. 3 (2011): 323–329.
2. David Palumbo-Liu, "Asian Diasporas, and Yet . . . , " in *Asian Diasporas: New Formations, New Conceptions*, ed. Rhacel Salazar Parreñas and Lok C. D. Siu (Stanford, CA: Stanford University Press, 2007), 279–284.
3. Lisa Lowe, *Immigrant Acts: On Asian American Cultural Politics* (Durham, NC: Duke University Press, 1996).
4. Charles R. Hale, "Mestizaje, Hybridity, and the Cultural Politics of Difference in Post-Revolutionary Central America," *Journal of Latin American Anthropology* 2, no. 1 (1996): 34–61.
5. Tanya Katerí Hernández, *Racial Subordination in Latin America: The Role of the State, Customary Law, and the New Civil Rights Response* (Cambridge: Cambridge University Press, 2013).
6. Isabelle Lausent-Herrera, "Tusans (*Tusheng*) and the Changing Chinese Community in Peru," *Journal of Chinese Overseas* 5 (2009): 115–152.
7. Lisa Yun, *The Coolie Speaks: Chinese Indentured Laborers and African Slaves in Cuba* (Philadelphia: Temple University Press, 2008).
8. Eduardo Auyón Gerardo, *El dragón en el desierto: Los pioneros Chinos en Mexicali* (Mexicali: Instituto de Cultura de Baja California, 1991).
9. Floro L. Mercene, *Manila Men in the New World: Filipino Migration to Mexico and the Americas from the Sixteenth Century* (Quezon City: University of the Philippines Press, 2007).
10. André Gunder Frank, *ReOrient: Global Economy in the Asian Age* (Berkeley: University of California Press, 1989); Rainer Buschmann, Edward Slack, Jr., and James Tueller, *Navigating the Spanish Lake: The Pacific in the Iberian World, 1521–1898* (Honolulu: University of Hawai'i Press, 2014).
11. David Igler, *The Great Ocean: Pacific Worlds from Captain Cook to the Gold Rush* (Oxford: Oxford University Press, 2013).

12. Tatiana Seijas, *Asian Slaves in Colonial Mexico: From Chinos to Indians* (Cambridge: Cambridge University Press, 2014).

13. Roshni Rustomji-Kerns, "Mirrha-Catarina de San Juan: From India to New Spain," *Amerasia Journal* 28, no. 2 (2002): 28–37.

14. Philip Wayne Powell, *Tree of Hate: Propaganda and Prejudices Affecting United States Relations with the Hispanic World* (Albuquerque: University of New Mexico Press, 2008).

15. History of the Proceedings and Debates of the House of Commons, 1st Session of the 14th Parliament of Great Britain, vol. XXIV (1788): 373; Jordana Rosenberg and Chi-ming Yang, "Introduction: The Dispossessed Eighteenth Century," *Eighteenth Century* 55, no. 2 (2014): 137–152.

16. Vivek Bald, *Bengali Harlem and the Lost Histories of South Asian America* (Cambridge, MA: Harvard University Press, 2013).

17. Gaiutra Bahadur, *Coolie Woman: The Odyssey of Indenture* (Chicago: University of Chicago Press, 2013).

18. Aisha Kahn, *Callaloo Nation: Metaphors of Race and Religious Identity among South Asians in Trinidad* (Durham, NC: Duke University Press, 2004).

19. Watt Stewart, *Chinese Bondage in Peru* (Durham, NC: Duke University Press, 1951); James Tigner, "The Okinawans in Latin America" (PhD diss., Stanford University, 1956); Arnold J. Meagher, *The Coolie Trade: The Traffic in Chinese Laborers to Latin America 1847–1874* (Bloomington, IN: Xlibris, 1974); Evelyn Hu-DeHart, "Immigrants to a Developing Society: The Chinese in Northern Mexico, 1875–1932," *Journal of Arizona History* 21 (1980): 275–312.

20. Kathleen López, *Chinese Cubans: A Transnational History* (Chapel Hill: University of North Carolina Press, 2013); Yun, *Coolie Speaks*.

21. Diego Lin Chou, *Chile y China: Inmigración y relaciones bilaterales (1845–1970)* (Santiago: Pontificia Universidad Catolica de Chile Inst, 2004); Iyo Kunimoto, *Los Japoneses en Bolivia: 110 años de historia de la inmigracion Japonesa en Bolivia* (La Paz: Asociación Nippon-Bolivia, 2013).

22. Philip A. Kuhn, *Chinese among Others: Emigration in Modern Times* (Plymouth: Rowman and Littlefield, 2008).

23. Evelyn Hu-DeHart, "Chinese Coolie Labor in Cuba in the Nineteenth Century: Free Labour or Neo-Slavery?" *Slavery and Abolition* 14 (1993): 67–86; Erika Lee, *At America's Gate: Chinese Immigration during the Exclusion Era, 1882–1943* (Chapel Hill: University of North Carolina Press, 2003).

24. Richard White, *Railroaded: The Transcontinentals and the Making of Modern America* (New York: W. W. Norton, 2011); Eugenio Chang-Rodriguez, "The Chinese in Peru: Historic and Cultural Links," *Review: Literature and Arts of the Americas* 39, no. 1 (2006): 131–145; Timothy J. Stanley, "'Chinamen, Wherever We Go': Chinese Nationalism and Guangdong Merchants in British Columbia, 1871–1911," *Canadian Historical Review* 77, no. 4 (2008): 475–503; Teresa Van Hoy, *A Social History of Mexico's Railroads: Peons, Prisoners and Priests* (Plymouth, UK: Rowman and Littlefield, 2008), 61–63.

25. Elliot Young, *Alien Nation: Chinese Migration in the Americas from the Coolie Era through World War II* (Chapel Hill: University of North Carolina Press, 2014).

26. Adam M. McKeown, *Melancholy Order: Asian Migration and the Globalization of Borders* (New York: Columbia University Press, 2013).

27. Lowe, *Immigrant Acts*.

28. Erika Lee, "Orientalisms in the Americas: A Hemispheric Approach to Asian American History," *Journal of Asian American Studies* 8, no. 3 (2005): 235–256.

29. Lee, *At America's Gate*; Grace Delgado, *Making the Chinese Mexican: Global Migration, Localism, and Exclusion in the U.S.-Mexico Borderlands* (Stanford, CA: Stanford University Press, 2012).

30. Lok C. D. Siu, *Memories of a Future Home: Diasporic Citizenship of Chinese in Panama* (Stanford, CA: Stanford University Press, 2005); Robert Chao Romero, *The Chinese in Mexico, 1882–1940* (Tucson: University of Arizona Press, 2012).

31. Alexander Saxton, *The Indispensable Enemy: Labor and the Anti-Chinese Movement in California* (Berkeley: University of California Press, 1975).

32. Bill Ong Hing, *Defining America: Through Immigration Policy* (Philadelphia: Temple University Press, 2012).

33. David Scott FitzGerald and David A. Cook-Martín, *Culling the Masses: The Democratic Origins of Racist Immigration Policy in the Americas* (Cambridge, MA: Harvard University Press, 2014).

34. Lee, *At America's Gates*, 2003.

35. Julia Maria Schiavone Camacho, *Chinese Mexicans: Transpacific Migration and the Search for a Homeland, 1910–1960* (Chapel Hill: University of North Carolina Press, 2012); Delgado, *Making the Chinese Mexican*.

36. McKeown, *Melancholy Order*.

37. Eiichiro Azuma, *Between Two Empires: Race, History, and Transnationalism in Japanese America* (New York: Oxford University Press, 2005); Andrea Geiger, *Subverting Exclusion: Transpacific Encounters with Race, Caste, and Borders, 1885–1928* (New Haven, CT: Yale University Press, 2011).

38. Jeffrey Lesser, *Negotiating National Identity: Immigrants, Minorities and the Struggle for Ethnicity in Brazil* (Durham, NC: Duke University Press, 1999).

39. Toake Endoh, *Exporting Japan: Politics of Emigration to Latin America* (Champaign: University of Illinois Press, 2009).

40. Lesser, *Negotiating National Identity*; Jerry Garcia, *Looking Like the Enemy: Japanese Mexicans, the Mexican State, and U.S. Hegemony, 1897–1945* (Tucson: University of Arizona Press, 2014); Seiichi Higashide, *Adios to Tears: The Memoirs of a Japanese-Peruvian Internee in U.S. Concentration Camps* (Seattle: University of Washington Press, 2012); Greg Robinson, *A Tragedy of Democracy: Japanese Confinement in North America* (New York: Columbia University Press, 2009).

41. Taku Suzuki, *Embodying Belonging: Racializing Okinawan Diaspora in Bolivia and Japan* (Honolulu: University of Hawai'i Press, 2010).

42. "Asians in the Americas 2014," Rutgers School of Arts and Sciences, accessed March 7, 2015, https://sites.google.com/site/asiansintheamericas2014/home.

FURTHER READING

Azuma, Eiichiro. *Between Two Empires: Race, History, and Transnationalism in Japanese America*. New York: Oxford University Press, 2005.

Hing, Bill Ong. *Defining America: Through Immigration Policy*. Philadelphia: Temple University Press, 2012.

Lee, Erika. *At America's Gate: Chinese Immigration during the Exclusion Era, 1882–1943*. Chapel Hill: University of North Carolina Press, 2003.

Lesser, Jeffrey. *Negotiating National Identity: Immigrants, Minorities and the Struggle for Ethnicity in Brazil*. Durham, NC: Duke University Press, 1999.

Lowe, Lisa. *Immigrant Acts: On Asian American Cultural Politics*. Durham, NC: Duke University Press, 1996.

McKeown, Adam M. *Melancholy Order: Asian Migration and the Globalization of Borders*. New York: Columbia University Press, 2013.

Saxton, Alexander. *The Indispensable Enemy: Labor and the Anti-Chinese Movement in California*. Berkeley: University of California Press, 1975.

Siu, Lok C. D. *Memories of a Future Home: Diasporic Citizenship of Chinese in Panama*. Stanford, CA: Stanford University Press, 2005.

Stewart, Watt. *Chinese Bondage in Peru*. Durham, NC: Duke University Press, 1951.

Yun, Lisa. *The Coolie Speaks: Chinese Indentured Laborers and African Slaves in Cuba*. Philadelphia: Temple University Press, 2008.

CHAPTER 3

....

SOUTH ASIAN AMERICA

Histories, Cultures, Politics

....

SUNAINA MAIRA

THE literature on South Asians in the United States has grown rapidly in the last ten to fifteen years, including historical research on South Asian America. This is partly due to the expansion of the South Asian community in the United States and the entry of a new generation of scholars into Asian American studies and American studies who have developed the subfield of South Asian American studies. The historical experiences of South Asians in the United States (generally hailing from India, Pakistan, Bangladesh, Nepal, Sri Lanka, and Afghanistan) have called for a theoretical and political critique that has produced not just an empiricist account of South Asian American history and investigation of new archives, but a reframing of several areas of research key to Asian American studies. Over the last twenty years, and particularly in the last decade, it is apparent that burgeoning work on South Asians in the United States, including historiographically informed research, has shifted in approach from a largely empirical focus on documenting South Asian American histories and experiences to a theoretical and political critique that has, in some cases, opened up or reframed core debates in Asian American studies. These theoretical and political interventions have foregrounded debates about the relationship of race to Orientalism; the links between citizenship, rights, and imperialism; the politics of immigrant-led social movements; the articulations of gender and sexuality with the multicultural security state; and the ways in which regimes of surveillance, detention, and deportation in the War on Terror are reshaping political subjectivity and racial categories.

Scholars have used new and existing archives to insert and interrogate the concepts of race, Orientalism, citizenship, rights, labor, sexuality, and the state. In fact, some of these authors have reconceptualized the archive itself, discovering or producing knowledge of migration and colonialism in protest movements as archives, archives of racialized sexuality in police records or asylum cases, and bodily archives in news reports about and performances of Indian dance in the United States. Two works in particular speak to the important historiographical interventions made from the vantage point of South

Asian American studies and that illustrate the arc, in a sense, of the particular set of critiques that I am going to discuss: Vijay Prashad's *The Karma of Brown Folk* and Junaid Rana's *Terrifying Muslims*.[1] Prashad's first booklength work about South Asian America, published in 2000, is arguably the most important book in South Asian American studies in the last two decades, given that it draws on key moments in South Asian American history to offer an incisive critique of the politics of South Asian America in the pre- and post-1965 period and of the racialization of Asian Americans writ large. It has become a seminal work not only because it was the first monograph in South Asian American studies with such a sweeping historical scope, but also because it critiques the production of a South Asian American subject as a model minority subject pitted against other minoritized subjects, particularly against African Americans, since the 1970s. The book spoke to the growing interest at the time in comparative ethnic studies and the turn to African American/Asian American studies, which it was in many ways responsible for crystallizing, and it also shed light on political interventions and coalitions being forged on the ground by South Asians in the United States in the post-1965 period. Prashad drew on historical archives to demonstrate that while the South Asian American subject was constructed in U.S. racial formations as a docile or model minority subject, in fact, the South Asian American was also a radical political subject; or to put it another way, as argued by Prashad and Maia Ramnath, *radicalism* is also the subject of South Asian America.[2] In the post-9/11 moment, the notion of radicalism has been ideologically rewritten in mainstream discourse to strip it of its progressive possibilities and to conflate it with a specific counterterrorism doctrine focused on the "radicalization" of Muslim Americans.[3]

This shift, from the model minority and "good" citizens subject before 9/11 to the potentially "radical" (especially if Muslim) national security threat after 9/11, has generated new alliances between South Asian Americans and Middle Eastern and Arab Americans, as well as solidarity with Japanese Americans who suffered incarceration during World War II, Latino(a)s resisting deportation and the War on Immigration, and African American and other communities challenging criminalization, profiling, and white supremacy. The question of the limitations and possibilities of South Asian America as a terrain from, and in, which to carve out cross-racial alliances and build movements for emancipation is a theme that runs through several of the most important works in the field that I discuss here as well as those that I have not been able to address.[4] Arguably, it is the fragility of the pan-ethnic/national project that is South Asian America that is also its radical potential, as in the case of the pan–Asian American project.

Terrifying Muslims, published in 2011, focuses on Pakistani American subjects, particularly transnational Pakistani labor migrants, and the racialization of South Asians in the United States after the attacks of September 11, 2001. The book marks the shift away from the earlier focus on Indian American experiences, which has dominated much of this field, partly due to the much larger presence of Indian Americans and hence also of Indian American scholars. Rana tracks the consolidation of the Muslim/non-Muslim divide after 9/11 as the salient racial boundary in the War on Terror, overlapping with the black/white and black/nonblack color lines. He incisively argues that the ambiguous racialization of "the Muslim," and specifically of the Pakistani migrant, must be situated in the imperial geography of the warfare state and also in an older colonial archive of racial thinking that links Muslims to immigrants, indigenous peoples and blacks. One of the crucial insights posited in the book is that the post-9/11 racialization of the Muslim as the terrorist, the antithesis to Western liberal democracy and secular modernity, emerges from a global racial system and from longer histories of colonialism and displacement. The events of 9/11 and the intensified Islamophobia they generated, as well as the U.S. invasion and occupation of Afghanistan and drone attacks in Pakistan, led to intense state scrutiny of Pakistani, Bangladeshi, Afghan, and Indian Muslim communities who were targeted by policies of surveillance, detention, and deportation. In fact, Pakistanis in the United States have been disproportionately targeted by the post-9/11 regime of incarceration and deportation, as Rana points out, for they constituted a significant pool of low-wage and undocumented immigrant workers in the United States. Thus they were deeply affected by the Special Registration program and other policies of detention and deportation, which propelled an out-migration of Pakistanis from the United States and a shift in Pakistani migration circuits since 9/11.

This book is important because it is also one of the few studies of Muslim Americans after 9/11 that offers a theory of Muslim racial formation in the context of international and regional migration systems, examining the historical development of the Pakistani labor diaspora in the United States and the Gulf. Technologies of policing, containment, and disappearance of Pakistani migrants and Muslim bodies are sites of racial boundary making, according to Rana, in which the "war on immigrants" overlaps with the "War on Terror" and the "yellow peril" of Asian aliens blurs into the "green peril" of alien Muslims. Echoing the critique in Prashad's *Uncle Swami* and in *Missing: Youth, Citizenship, and Empire*,[5] Rana argues that the racialization of South Asians and Muslims through the paradigm of "security" and "terror" is rooted in the imperial logic of the War on Terror and so linked to U.S. foreign policy in West and South Asia, particularly U.S. support for colonial and repressive regimes such as Israel and Saudi Arabia and historical backing of dictatorships in Pakistan and Egypt. As the United States has increasingly shifted the front of the War on Terror to Southwest Asia (the invented border territory of "Af-Pak"), those who migrate from or resist imperial violence in this region are racialized through well-established archives that cast the Muslim, the Arab, or the Iranian as the archetypal other of Western modernity and civilization. In *Karma*, Prashad argues that South Asians, particularly those who are upwardly mobile and politically moderate, have been framed since the late 1960s as a "solution" to the "problem" of black America, and were used as a weapon against struggles for civil rights and social and economic justice. But after 2001, the problem was Muslim Americans, particularly South and West Asian Americans (including Indian Muslims and also Arab Christians), as racial formations shifted and racial profiling targeted ambiguous categories of "Muslim-looking" people. The (re)racialization of these groups as the "terrorist" enemy became the primary site of struggle for civil rights and against the ravages of the neoliberal, warfare state.

The constitution of "South Asian America" as a pan-ethnic rubric, on the ground and in fields of scholarship, offers an important epistemological critique of the shifting historical production of racial and ethnic categories that are ambiguous and contingent. Both Prashad's and Rana's works are fundamentally addressing the deeper question (explicitly, in the case of *Karma of Brown Folk*) of whether this pan-ethnic coalitional category—of South Asian or "desi"—can be the site of resistance to neoliberal capitalism and imperial nationalism. While Nayan Shah considers South Asia to be a cartographic formation produced by Cold War mappings of the world in social science and area studies, it is also evident that the national boundaries of the subcontinent are themselves colonial constructions of a region whose borders looked quite different before colonial powers partitioned and created nation-states such as India, Pakistan, Bangladesh, Sri Lanka, and Afghanistan.[6] In the diasporic context, migrants from this region have attempted to challenge nationalist divisions on the subcontinent and to mobilize around the unifying category of "South Asian" or desi (a more colloquial term but also one with a different social and political resonance), while there has been a concurrent move to participate in, and challenge the political and epistemic borders of, the category of "Asian American."[7]

Prashad and Rana are also responding, as do other authors whose works I discuss here, to ethnic identity politics in the moment of multicultural nationalism emerging since the 1980s, when white supremacy continues to secure its privilege and neoliberal capitalism is consolidated through, not against, racial and cultural difference. This has necessitated a crucial shift in South Asian American studies, as in Asian American studies. For example, Sharmila Rudrappa points out that the neoliberal turn has shaped the cultural sphere through "difference talk," where the politics of containment operates through the co-optation and commodification of difference; she observes that South Asian community organizations can no longer be considered a priori to be sites of resistance in an era of state funding for Asian American nongovernmental organizations (NGOs).[8] Similarly, Chandan Reddy argues that ethnic studies has been vulnerable to the institutional pressures of the neoliberal university and runs the risk of collusion with the imperial state's violence, at home and overseas, if it is complacent in its deployment of difference, belonging, and representation on the terms provided by the liberal, multicultural state and political modernity.[9]

ORIENTALISM, IMPERIALISM, AND THE MODEL MINORITY

The battles over multiculturalism, as well as ethnic studies, have complicated an easy drawing of political lines based on racial categories with the emergence of right-wing Asian and Indian American commentators since the 1980s. Prashad, in particular, responds to conservative political ideologues of the culture wars of the 1990s, such as

Dinesh D'Souza, and he critiques brownness as an alibi for the autonomous, self-reliant individual who succeeds under neoliberal capitalism. The cultural superiority of the hard-working, "pliant" Indian American (vis-à-vis the militant or disruptive African American), Prashad argues, is embedded in an Orientalist archive that extols the spirituality and docility of the mystical, Indian East.[10] Prashad draws on a range of sources to show how proponents of nineteenth-century U.S. Orientalism viewed India as the repository of a transcendental but impractical wisdom, as "poor and unfree" but able to provide redemption for the materialist West.[11] He points out that this ahistorical view of India was embedded in materialist relations of trade, missionary travel, and imperial relations linking the United States and South Asia. Yankee clippers had been bringing Indian goods to New England ports since the eighteenth century, and the earliest records of an Indian presence are from towns such as Salem, Massachusetts, where Indians arrived with Yankee traders and where some apparently married African American women.[12] Vivek Bald's new research has shifted our understanding of this period by exploring the migration of Muslim men from East Bengal (now Bangladesh) in 1880–1950, who came as maritime workers to port cities such as New Orleans and New York and who married, lived, and had children with African American and Puerto Rican women.[13]

Just as Edward Said argued in the case of British and French Orientalisms, Prashad demonstrates that U.S. Orientalism historically obscured imperial, racial, and capitalist relations and has continued to do so effectively at various moments through the figure of the Indian or South Asian. He is thus able to deploy genealogies of Orientalism as a key analytic through which the construction of the South Asian and Indian American as a pliant, rather than dissident, subject is continually shored up in a broad range of cultural and political arenas. Tracing the evolving Orientalization of India in the U.S. public sphere, from the visit of Swami Vivekananda in 1893 to the World Parliament of Religions and the late nineteenth- and early twentieth-century interest in Hindu gurus and "yogic science" to the fascination with Hinduism and Eastern religions in the counterculture of the 1960s, Prashad argues that this Orientalist turn to India coexisted with a different relationship to many African Americans (and progressive Americans) whose affiliations with India were rooted in anticolonial struggle and antiracist solidarity.[14] While Prashad acknowledges that India simultaneously provided a complex cultural symbol that was not without its own fantasies of redemption for African Americans, his valuable insight here is that the Orientalism of the late 1960s and 1970s occurred in the context of cultural, economic, and political shifts in the wake of the civil rights and antiwar movements.[15] The fetishization of Indian spirituality and pacifism associated with Asian religions must be situated in relation to the dismantling of the welfare state as well as the growing backlash against the militant struggles and alliances of Asian and African Americans and Latinos and Native Americans. Indians and South Asians could once again be admired as god-men and mystics, that is, as apolitical and uncritical figures, along with the emergence of Asian Americans as the model minority since 1965.

In the late twentieth century, Orientalism was intertwined with neoliberal multiculturalism via the figure of the South Asian; for example, Prashad shows how Dr. Deepak

Chopra embodies the neoliberal paradigm of the self-reliant individual, who can live on meditation and without secure employment, healthcare, or education. The emergence of various manifestations of Orientalism must be historicized and deconstructed to understand the material and political relations between the United States and South Asia that they generally obscure. I have similarly argued that the commodification of India as "trendy" in U.S. popular culture at the turn of the millennium, and the emergence of Indo-chic and a fascination with yoga and henna, must be understood in relation to global capital flows and the economic liberalization of India since the early 1990s, the increasing visibility of working-class Indian migrants, and incidents of anti–South Asian violence.[16] Indo-chic allowed for a domestication of certain aspects of South Asian culture through consumption while South Asian bodies continued to be marked as racially different and targeted in racist violence, most dramatically in the case of the Dotbuster attacks against South Asian small business owners in New Jersey in the late 1980s. The cultural appropriation of Indian or South Asian practices and symbols in various U.S. youth subcultures, whether in the form of henna artists or New Age ravers, is thus related to different streams of South Asian and labor migration and economic and national insecurities.

Research on South Asian America has thus made significant contributions to cultural studies, American studies, and ethnic studies in exploring the shifts in U.S. Orientalism and their implications for analyses of racial formation and global capitalism, given the historical preoccupation with South Asia as a repository of ancient wisdom and redemption for the West. This, of course, broke open to some extent after 2001 as South Asia splintered in the American cultural imaginary, with an imagined, militant, anti-Western Muslim zone of terrorism pitted against a non-Muslim/Hindu/secular zone friendly to neoliberal capitalism and Western liberal democracy. This is the moment addressed in *Uncle Swami*, Prashad's update to *Karma*, and in *Missing*, both of which examine the line drawn through South Asian communities after 9/11 so that Pakistanis, Bangladeshis, Afghans, and Indian Muslims found themselves in the bull's-eye of the security state's surveillance and policing apparatus, while those on the other side of the line positioned themselves as good, patriotic, minority/Asian subjects.

Orientalism, in South Asian American studies, is thus tied to various moments of empire, late U.S. empire, and also the collusion between the United States and the British empire. Keya Ganguly's literary ethnography of Indian immigrant professionals in New Jersey in the late 1980s and early 1990s astutely theorizes the investments of Indian immigrants in multiculturalism and ethnic authenticity as a postcolonial predicament, one that arises at the conjuncture of the legacy of British colonialism and the exceptionalism of U.S. imperialism.[17] While Orientalist imaginaries in the early twentieth century created the figure of the docile, mystical Indian or South Asian (often called "Hindoo," regardless of religion), work by Prashad and also Ramnath shatters this cultural mythology by examining the history of radicalism among South Asian farmworkers, students, and anticolonial revolutionaries in the first three decades of the twentieth century. Ramnath's book, *Haj to Utopia*, is a brilliant exploration of Ghadar (mutiny), a transnational movement opposing British colonialism that linked radical South Asians from

San Francisco, Vancouver, and New York to those in Calcutta, Berlin, Paris, Tokyo, and Moscow. This leftist, anti-imperial network involved alliances with Irish, Chinese, and Egyptian nationalist revolutionaries and the pan-Islamic Khilafat movement as well as with American leftists and the Communist International. In Ramnath's analysis, Ghadar provides the "missing link" between anarchist, syndicalist, and communist movements in which they were involved globally; in fact, in her view the movement overlapped to some extent with nearly "every radical tendency of its time."[18] Ghadar also provided another crucial political link between North American racism and labor exploitation and British colonial domination and plunder of South Asia. Ramnath observes, as have other historians, that the Ghadar movement was able to "articulate American class and race relations to the economics and geopolitics of empire, by linking the grievances of discrimination against a low-wage immigrant force to the colonized status of their home country."[19] This research is significant for Asian American history and American studies, as well as for political and labor history, for it shows the sophisticated, transnational framework of this early twentieth-century movement that was founded in California and spread around the globe.

Indeed, one of the most fascinating aspects of Ghadar, and the network of radicals that it generated, who traveled from China and Japan to Canada and Germany, was its cosmopolitanism. Radicals got weapons training in France, went undercover in Afghanistan, studied in Russia, and revolted and, in some cases, were killed or hanged by the colonial regime in South Asia. The exploration of this transnational movement for national liberation has been built on the pioneering work of Joan Jensen, whose book *Passage from India: Asian Indian Immigrants in North America* was the first monograph on Ghadar.[20] It is her archival research that brought to light for many contemporary readers the famed protest poetry written by Ghadarites, verses such as:

> The whole world calls us black thieves,
> the whole world calls us "coolie.
> Some push us around, some curse us.
> Where is your splendor and prestige today?
> Why doesn't our flag fly anywhere?
> We are all inhabitants of India,
> Offspring of one-Mother.[21]

Ghadar was a leftist, militant, anticolonial movement, and it was also secular and opposed to communal, ethnic, and regional divisions. It included Hindus, Sikhs, Muslims, Zoroastrians, Christians, and atheists and while it was largely male, scholars such as Prashad point out that Ghadarites were attempting not just to liberate their nation from the noose of British imperialism, but also to envision a different social order. For example, Prashad cites an exchange between a Ghadarite communist, Sohan Singh Bhakna, and a U.S. immigration officer about the practice of polygamy and polyandry in his home region of Punjab. Sohan Singh responded pointedly, "Everyone has the right to reject a particular tradition or custom which he does not like."[22]

The ideological underpinnings of Ghadar's vision of radical egalitarianism and freedom, however, is a point of some dispute among scholars such as Ramnath and Prashad. Ramnath, who has also published *Decolonizing Anarchism*, a companion book to *Haj to Utopia*—written for a general audience but drawing on the same archival material—argues that Ghadar's politics is "legible through a logic of anarchism."[23] She demonstrates, quite convincingly, that many Ghadarites combined their commitments to anticolonialism and socialism with an increasingly systematic critique of state power developed in conversations with anarchist thinkers. However, while Ramnath is right to read Ghadar's politics as "eclectic" rather than incoherent, it is also apparent that this eclecticism included strands of communism and Pan-Islamic socialism as well as anarchistic thought and tactics, sometimes in combination and shifting over time and space.[24] While Ramnath argues, quite eloquently, that a strand of Ghadar became increasingly critical of the state as the endpoint of the national liberation struggle, and was influenced by the global anarchist movement, Prashad highlights in *Uncle Swami* the involvement of Ghadarites in international communist movements. As Ramnath points out, the movement "forked" after World War I and many radical Ghadarites, what she calls "the Bolshevik mujahireen," returned to India after studying Marxism-Leninism in Russia or mobilizing in China.[25]

Ultimately, what is striking is that South Asian migrants in the first part of the twentieth century were very much a part of radical, anti-imperial, transnational movements, and of the debates these movements raised, of secular versus pan-Islamic frameworks for resistance, of autonomous or state-based Marxism, of symbolic direct action or mass-based organizing, and of the various positions that combine or synthesize these ideologies and strategies that still resonate deeply today and infuse post-9/11 politics in South Asian communities in the United States. An important contribution of Ramnath's work, like Prashad's, is that it reframes South Asian immigrant politics by situating it squarely within internationalist movements and political debates raging at that historical moment, demonstrating through careful archival research how deeply Ghadar was imbricated with a range of nationalist and socialist movements of the era and shaped by alliances with progressive-left Americans, Europeans, Arabs, Latin Americans, and other Asians.

This transnational, cross-ethnic approach does justice to the cosmopolitan lives and worldviews of migrant subjects, such as the Ghadarites, and it also inserts South Asian America into a political and intellectual conversation that goes beyond questions of immigration, assimilation, ethnicity, and cultural representation to foregrounding imperialism, colonialism, and capitalism. Bakirathi Mani observes that "the impact of South Asian anticolonial nationalism on Asian American politics is rarely discussed, even though these same movements against British imperialism shaped the broader context of the civil rights movement."[26] These works go a long way toward inserting the colonial question into Asian American politics and Asian American studies, but they also go further in acknowledging that there were also *other* anticolonial movements, in Asia and around the world, that informed and inspired diasporic South Asian nationalists and that these cross-currents have often remained hidden from view in a narrowly defined South Asian diasporic studies.

SEXUALITY AND THE STRANGER

Nayan Shah's *Stranger Intimacy*, likewise, reframes work on South Asian America by shifting focus to the notion of transiency, rather than arrival or settlement, and examining the complex, often secret, and sometimes illicit relationships and intimate ties produced by South Asians, generally men, in the "transient migrant world" of the early twentieth century.[27] Examining the experiences of South Asian farmworkers, manual laborers, business owners, and landlords on the West Coast, spanning the United States and Canada, Shah argues that these transient male migrants formed "subaltern counterpublics" with others, of diverse ethnic and racial backgrounds, in opposition to "bourgeois social expectations and state regulation." This produced, in Shah's view, a form of "stranger intimacy" expressed in "experiments in social relations" and a "desire for visceral solidarity."[28]

While this social experiment proffered a more nuanced form of solidarity, whose politics were complex and often ambiguous, given that it involved property owners as well as transient workers and did not always lead to organized politics in the spheres Shah examines, it did unsettle prevailing heteronormative, nationalist conceptions of citizenship, family, and belonging and challenge attempts to stabilize racial hierarchies and gender inequality. At a time of vigorous anti-immigrant campaigns and racially exclusionary laws, such as the Alien Land Laws (1913), the Barred Zone Immigration Act (1917), and the disbarring of Indians from naturalization (1923), Shah's research suggests that homosocial spaces involving South Asians, white Americans, African Americans, Latinos, and Native Americans contested the hardening of racial and gender boundaries. Using police records, vice committee reports, court records of sodomy and indecency, and other archival materials, Shah explores how sites of stranger intimacy were subjected to "state surveillance, intrusion, and exclusion" as well as to "press and reformer surveillance."[29] The state targeted and constructed the "ordinary Hindu" as unfit for immigration and naturalization and antithetical to white civilization and its privileges of property and citizenship.[30] While immigration policies restricted the entry of South Asian women during this period and thus contributed to the creation of new forms of kinship and (homo)sociality, the state managed intimacy through the regulation of racialized bodies and legislation that defined the boundaries of morality and degeneracy based on age, sexual behavior, and, in some cases, religion.

Shah's work examines the same migrant worlds that produced the radical activity of the Ghadar movement explored by Ramnath, Prashad, and Jensen, but he uses different archives and approaches archives that have already been researched with new questions, uncovering the gender and sexual politics that were not really discussed in other works. His work speaks to debates about kinship and offers a different, complementary window into the cross-racial and interethnic affiliations that Prashad and Ramnath have charted. There are multiple, subaltern counterpublics that emerge from this body of new work about South Asian America and that complicate earlier, pioneering but largely descriptive works such as Karen Leonard's study of Punjabi agricultural workers and Punjabi-Mexican marriages in California.[31] For example, Bald's pioneering research has uncovered the history of a racially mixed, working-class South Asian Muslim community during the first half of the twentieth century on the East Coast, shifting away from the focus in the existing Asian American studies literature on Punjabi labor migrants on the West Coast and South Asian–Mexican encounters in California as the archetypal experiences of early twentieth-century South Asian migration. Furthermore, this new body of work has increasingly challenged nation-based frameworks for studying South Asians in the United States, using a far more expansive, transnational, and critical approach that situates South Asians in the United States in relation to imperialism, global capital, radicalism, and social worlds that do not fit neatly into dominant or prescribed categories. In this regard, Shah's work in social history is groundbreaking because it inserts the question of gender, and in particular sexuality, into studies of labor and immigration in North America, as well as the analytic of race into work on queer kinships and intimacies. South Asian American studies has, in fact, been central to the development of queer-of-color critique and queer theory in Asian American studies, through the important work of scholars such as Gayatri Gopinath, Jasbir Puar, and Chandan Reddy.[32]

CITIZENSHIP, RIGHTS, AND NEOLIBERAL DEMOCRACY

One of the key questions in *Stranger Intimacy* and in other works such as *Missing*, Sharmila Rudrappa's *Ethnic Routes to Citizenship*, and Monisha Das Gupta's *Unruly Immigrants: Rights, Activism, and Transnational South Asian Politics in the United States* is that of citizenship and its related question, that of democracy.[33] What are the boundaries of citizenship, and what are its potential and pitfalls as a site for contesting the state—particularly at a moment when the multicultural, liberal, democratic state works through disciplinary inclusion? Can democracy be the horizon of progressive politics if it is the linchpin of the U.S.-led War on Terror and a rationale for military invasion and occupation? *Stranger Intimacy* traces the gendered and racial logics of the relationship of South Asians to U.S. citizenship and attempts to offer an alternative notion of democratic community. Shah explores, on the one hand, the ways in which South Asian migrant lives, at least in the world of transience and mobility, challenged the "importance and value of the married, heterosexual household to national citizenship."[34] On the other hand, he meticulously examines the state's attempt to fix the boundary of "white" and "Asiatic" in federal court cases that adjudicated the ambiguous racial classification

of migrants from South, West, and Central Asia. Contradictory rulings on the eligibility for naturalization of immigrants from the Arab world, Afghanistan, Palestine, Syria,
and India indicated the "unsettled state of jurisprudence," or "legal borderlands," that
emerged in the state's citizenship policies.[35] Shah highlights the famous case of *United
States v. Bhagat Singh Thind* in 1923, in which an Indian immigrant appealed for naturalization on the grounds that he was technically Caucasian and in which the court ruled
that he was ineligible for U.S. citizenship because he would not be considered white in
the understanding of the "common man."

Priya Srinivasan, however, argues that because most scholarship in South Asian
American, and Asian American studies on the racialized politics of citizenship has
focused on the Thind case, there has been a lack of attention to racial exclusion and
anti-Asian discrimination against (South) Asians *before* 1923 and, in particular, to the
experiences of South Asian *female* migrants.[36] Srinavasan's fascinating research focuses
on Indian women dancers as transnational labor migrants who came to the United
States beginning in the late nineteenth century and whose bodily labor in the formal
and informal economy was a site in which gendered understandings of citizenship,
whiteness, Americanness, and Asianness were constructed. Uncovering the presence
of "nautch" dancers from India in dance performances, circuses, and dime shows as
early as 1880—before the arrival of Indian contract workers who came after the Chinese
Exclusion Act of 1882—Srinivasan deftly challenges the focus on immigrant males in
much South Asian American historiography before 1965. Using archival research, performance studies, and dance ethnography, her work breaks new ground in South Asian
and Asian American studies by focusing on the "bodily archive," drawing on "signs and
traces of the laboring dancing body" of racially ambiguous Indian women to offer a new
reading of Orientalism, citizenship, and racial formation.[37]

Given the ways that South Asians have often been perceived to occupy a liminal position on white/nonwhite borders, work on South Asians in the United States has revealed
the contradictions of the "legal borderlands" of racialized citizenship.[38] After the
Immigration Act of 1965, South Asian migrants who were generally technically skilled
workers or professionals were quickly absorbed into the category of the model minority
and thus positioned as "almost white."[39] Their aspirations to whiteness were increasingly
channeled through the form of multicultural citizenship beginning in the 1980s, as the
U.S. state recuperated the dissent of oppositional and minority movements in the context
of right-wing assaults on affirmative action and civil rights. This was a contested cultural
turn in American politics, for as Rudrappa astutely argues, the backlash against growing
immigration from Latin America, Asia, and the Caribbean and fears of an "alien nation"
coexisted with the notion that the "ethnic values" of some of these immigrants facilitated their assimilation into U.S. capitalism and the neoliberal state.[40] In other words,
the shift to a racism predicated on culture, not on biology, operated both ends of the
switch through nativism *and* multiculturalism. South Asians were the exemplar of the
model minority/migrant, but this myth was destabilized and complicated by the arrival
of working- and lower-middle-class South Asians, often through family reunification,
who did not assimilate so easily into neoliberal multiculturalism—whatever their own

desires for assimilation may be. Reddy astutely points out that, since the 1980s, the state has increasingly recruited immigrant workers for low-wage, low-skill jobs through family reunification, so that as the welfare state was dismantled, a pool of flexible labor was imported whose welfare was the responsibility of immigrant communities themselves.[41]

The increasing class stratification of South Asian immigrant communities also produced sharp class schisms, which were not easily resolved on the terrain of multiculturalism but sometimes spilled over into tensions framed through contestations over culture and ethnic authenticity. For example, Rudrappa's study of two South Asian community organizations founded in the late 1980s in Chicago thoughtfully explores the ways in which they mobilized the notion of culture and difference along fault lines of class, nationality, and religion. This ethnographic study offers a nuanced analysis of the ways in which neoliberal multiculturalism has meant that on the one hand, state funding for nonprofit organizations serving ethnic or immigrant communities has privatized social services, and on the other hand, the language of diversity is used to contain dissent and commodify difference. The main thrust of Rudrappa's analysis is that South Asian community organizations have in some cases participated in this project of assimilation into neoliberal (multi)cultural citizenship themselves, even as they struggled with its contradictions in the context of the multicultural logic of citizenship in the late 1980s and early 1990s. So Apna Ghar, an anti–domestic violence organization and women's shelter, attempted to initiate South Asian women into late modern, American consumer culture while blaming Pakistani and working-class cultures for the existence of domestic violence. The Indo American Center was a space in which South Asian immigrant professionals wielded the notion of a superior ethnic Indian culture, echoing Prashad's critique of model minority Orientalism, as part of a program of schooling working-class Indian immigrants in U.S. cultural citizenship.

Missing: Youth, Citizenship, and Empire after 9/11 is an ethnographic study that examines the politics of cultural citizenship at a different moment, after the attacks of September 11, 2001. It explores the ways in which working- and lower-middle-class South Asian Muslim immigrant youth coming of age during the War on Terror understood national belonging in their everyday lives. The notion of model minorityhood cracked open even wider after 9/11 and with the intensification of the regime of surveillance, detentions, and deportations targeting Arab, South Asian, and Muslim Americans. Young people who were Muslim, immigrant, and part-time, low-wage workers in the service economy were vulnerable to exclusion and policing on multiple fronts. In the context of this precarity, I found that the logic of cultural rights as a framework for resistance to the imperial state was even more fraught than it had been, perhaps, before 9/11, for those seen as inherently anti-American and also militant, fundamentalist, antimodern, and antidemocratic in the "clash of civilizations." These South Asian immigrants belonged to transnational social networks that attempted to enact a form of flexible citizenship, but they faced much greater challenges in stretching their lives beyond the nation-state than upwardly mobile migrants, especially in the post-9/11 context.[42] Cosmopolitanism and transnational social, economic, and political ties—as in the era of the Ghadar movement—came under heightened state scrutiny and surveillance as a breeding ground for "radicalism" (now a dirty word) and terrorism.

Muslim immigrant youth, I argued in this book, attempted to find in the cracks and crevices of cultural citizenship, and to some extent in the language of rights, room for a different notion of belonging and for solidarity with other communities considered threatening or disposable by the imperial state. This research explored the ways in which immigrant high school youth reframed multicultural citizenship, resting on a liberal notion of cultural difference, as polycultural citizenship. Drawing on the work of Vijay Prashad and Robin Kelley, the concept of polyculturalism suggests forms of affiliation based not on difference, but on shared political struggles that produce cultures of solidarity. Some youth were also drawn into rights talk, using the notion of civil rights and human rights to engage in expressions of a dissenting citizenship that contains within it the paradox of reformist strands of mobilization that petition the state, often through the law, while simultaneously opposing it. So one of the key critiques in *Missing* is that post-9/11 exclusion from cultural citizenship for South Asian or Muslim American communities must be understood not as a failure of civil rights or U.S. democracy but in relation to the politics of U.S. empire, for various racialized groups have been targets of these policies of exclusion, expulsion, incarceration, and annihilation at different historical moments. Framing the exclusion of and violence against South Asian, Middle Eastern, and Muslim Americans simply as a problem of "racial profiling" or Islamophobia is to miss the ways in which these processes are actually constitutive of the imperial state, and create a state of permanent war and permanent surveillance, an argument also made by Prashad in *Uncle Swami*.

Work in South Asian American studies has thus attempted to link questions of citizenship, rights, and multiculturalist democracy to empire and imperialism in the context of shifting migration patterns, the intensified policing of the post-9/11 state, and the landscape of labor and political organizing. Recent work using a historicized ethnographic approach has examined how South Asian progressive movements have reconceptualized notions of rights and citizenship since the 1980s. It is not surprising that much of this work on post-1965 South Asian American politics has been focused on communities or movements in urban areas, particularly in cities such as New York, Boston, and Chicago, given the concentration of South Asian migrants and the emergence of new social movements in these metropolises. These large South Asian enclaves are also sites of collision and interaction between the professional-managerial class and service and low-wage workers. Inevitably, this has generated significant accounts of labor history, even if not by traditional historians, with a notable example being Biju Mathew's *Taxi!*[43] This is a historicized, ethnographically informed analysis of the ways in which South Asian taxi drivers in New York City, working with other immigrants, organized a new labor movement that staged a series of historic strikes in 1998 and challenged the antiworker and anti-immigrant policies of the taxi industry and the city's service economy. Mathew uses the mobilization by the New York Taxi Workers' Alliance (NYTWA) to illustrate the new labor paradigms that were created with the neoliberal restructuring of the taxi industry since the 1970s and the shift to a predominantly Third

World workforce beginning in the mid-1980s. The NYTWA is an important example of the immigrant worker movement that has grown since the 1980s and of the pan–South Asian and cross-ethnic coalitions that have emerged in labor movements and new social movements, as also discussed by Das Gupta, Prashad, and others.

Das Gupta's ethnographic study examines South Asian American labor movements, women's organizations, and queer organizations on the East Coast as examples of "transnational social change organizations."[44] She suggests that, from the mid-1980s through the 1990s, new political groups emerged in the South Asian community that participated in larger movements responding to the vicissitudes of immigration policies and the contradictions of neoliberal multiculturalism by arguing for a "transnational complex of rights" and disarticulating rights from citizenship.[45] These organizations claimed the rubric of "South Asian," rather than specific ethnic or national labels, a shift that Prashad notes began in the mid-1980s with feminist and women's groups.[46] South Asian queer groups, Das Gupta observes, emerged from a transnational network of queer organizations linking various nodes of the South Asian diaspora from North America and South Asia to the Caribbean and East Africa.[47] Groups such as the South Asian Lesbian and Gay Association (SALGA), formed in New York, were able to link histories of colonialism with experiences of racism and displacement and offer a different model of queer politics from that of the mainstream LGBT movement in the United States.

Challenging the neoliberal model of the "citizen-consumer" that shaped a liberal politics of sexual citizenship based on a politics of recognition and inclusion, Das Gupta argues that South Asian queer groups such as SALGA rejected the model of the ideal LGBT subject based on white, urban affluent gay and lesbian lifestyles and on consumerism and representation. Instead, they attempted to create alternative structures of kinship and community, echoing Shah's argument, unsettling both the notion of model South Asian minority subjects invested in cultural and social reproduction and also a fixed LGBT identity based on "coming out" and individual emancipation.[48] Alliances emerged between queer activists in New York and feminist groups, movements resisting Hindu nationalism and communal violence, and labor organizers opposing surveillance and criminalization by the city and state.

Reddy takes the queer-of-color critique offered by Das Gupta even further, arguing that the "contemporary antiradical liberalization of U.S. gay and lesbian politics through the movement for marriage rights and the repeal of 'don't ask, don't tell'" since the 1990s, resting on the notion of individual "sexual freedom" and sexual rights, shores up "sexuality's institutional role as the promissory that will settle the past" by erasing U.S. empire and racial violence.[49] He uses the example of the Mathew Shepard and James Byrd, Jr. Hate Crimes Prevention Act that amended the National Defense Authorization Act of 2010, allocating the highest defense budget in U.S. history, in the wake of the renewed war in Afghanistan and drone attacks on Pakistan; this hate crime bill was hailed as a major victory for sexual and national freedom. For Reddy, the celebration of this legislation by liberal-progressive groups and national LGBT organizations underscores the collusion of gay rights and civil rights with national security, and also with the exceptionalism of the liberal modern state that couples "freedom with violence."[50]

Reddy uses this instance of what Puar has described as a politics of "homonational-ism" to trace the neoliberal restructuring of the modern, liberal state committed to the principles of universal racial equality and the violence this entails, here and elsewhere.[51] Analyzing the figure of the gay Pakistani immigrant and cases of sexual asylum in the mid-1990s, Reddy argues that the appearance of this figure in "immigration proceed-ings, court cases, and legal journals" illustrates how the state has refashioned itself as the site of sexual freedom and liberation for migrants, including South Asian and espe-cially Muslim queers.[52] Sexual and gender freedom has been a cornerstone in the War on Terror to liberate Muslim/brown women or queers from Muslim/brown men and cultures, as Puar has brilliantly argued in her critique of the sexual exceptionalisms of the United States as gay-friendly, and thus modern, in opposition to Iraq, Afghanistan, Pakistan, or Palestine.[53]

Like Shah, Reddy argues that the "legal sphere" is an archive of "racialized sexual-ity" that "organizes social and historical differences."[54] Immigration or asylum law is not a neutral apparatus but promotes the citizen as an agent of universality; the law is "an active archive, or technique of self-making and the making of selves."[55] Reddy thus explicitly theorizes the notion of the legal archive, suggesting that it not only inscribes the past but also imagines the future. Reading the figure of the gay Pakistani immigrant "against the grain of the archive," Reddy links legal history to new archives of sexual his-tory and to a meta-critique of queer studies and ethnic studies. He argues eloquently that the project of these interdisciplinary intellectual formations should be to interro-gate what lives are "socially knowable and validated."[56]

Linking Reddy's powerful notion of politics as marking the boundary between "life that is known," and hence "politically meaningful," and "life that has no consequence for meaning," to the question of what it means to think about racial formation and radical-ism from the site of South Asian America, I want to return to the works that I have high-lighted in this essay.[57] Prashad's and Rana's works explore the ways in which the figure of the South Asian has been used to mark the boundary between the model and mili-tant minority and thus between acceptable and illicit politics. In Ramnath's and Shah's archival research, we see the traces of transient South Asian migrants trying to carve out alternative lives, through radical internationalist networks and homosocial encounters. Work on South Asian community organizing from the 1980s through the 2000s probes new politics movements based on gender, sexuality, and class in national and transna-tional contexts.

Bookending this discussion with Prashad's newest work, *Uncle Swami*, allows us to see how the criminalization of South Asian Muslims has fractured the model minor-ity subject associated with South Asian America and has generated new, cross-ethnic affiliations. These shifts in racial formations linked to national and global politics after 9/11 have led to new, or in some cases deeper, fissures and alliances among South Asian communities in the United States. One notable phenomenon is that progres-sive South Asian American groups have built civil rights and antiwar coalitions with Arab, Middle Eastern, and Muslim Americans and also created new pan-ethnic catego-ries such as AMSA (Arab/Muslim/South Asian). At the same time, in response to the consolidation of the "Islamic terrorist" as the enemy in the War on Terror, Indian supporters of Hindutva (Hindu nationalist) politics have forged or strengthened alliances with right-wing supporters of Israel and the Israel lobby (AIPAC) in the United States, even as India has forged closer military and economic ties with both Israel and the United States. Right-wing Indian Americans have aligned themselves with anti-Arab/anti-Muslim political constituencies through a discourse of shared cultural values and model minorityhood.[58] This right-wing Indian-Zionist alliance has positioned itself as the "vanguard of the new, antiterrorist battleship America" in the global war for democracy by the proxies of Western civilization in South and West Asia.[59] The point is that the fulcrum of these racialized alliances forged since 9/11, on the right as well as the left, is that of imperialism and colonialism. South Asian radicals at various historical moments may have embarked on a "haj to utopia," in envisioning alternative futures and rethinking pasts, but one cannot offer a utopian reading of the highly contradictory political aspirations and exit strategies of South Asians in the United States without simplifying the diverse and complex world of South Asian Americans.

METHODOLOGIES AND PUBLICS

The works discussed here are clearly political interventions concerned with reframing dominant discourses about South Asian America, critiquing neoliberal citizenship and model minorityhood, and reconceiving subaltern counterpublics and the very notion of the public itself. Most of this recent work in South Asian American studies is deeply interdisciplinary, and so it draws on history as well as anthropology, sociology, cultural studies, feminist studies, queer theory, and performance studies. It is also worth noting that Mathew, Prashad, and also the literary/cultural studies scholar Amitava Kumar are part of a group of Marxist South Asian/South Asian studies scholars who have produced a body of work on the politics of the South Asian diaspora in the United States that is intentionally written as public scholarship and political intervention.[60] Their books are written for a general public and offer a historical and political economic analysis that is both critical and engaging.

In a moment in which the notion of "engaged scholarship" is increasingly used by the neoliberal university as a marketing tool to promote the relevance of the university, defining and often restricting what public intellectuals can and should critique, it is significant that South Asian American studies has produced rigorously critical public scholarship against the grain of the figure of a safely commodifiable public intellectual. One of the methodological strategies used by this truly critical public scholarship is self-reflexivity, for Mathew, Prashad, Rudrappa, Srinivasan, and Das Gupta all situate themselves in their historical and ethnographic writing, disrupting both the positivist conservativism of the "neutral" scholar and also the solipsism of the navel-gazing anthropologist. As in *Missing*, which is written in a self-reflexive register and draws on my own accounts of involvement in political organizing after 9/11, this methodology is driven by an ethical imperative to reveal what is at stake: our own investments, collusions, failures, and hopes. Putting these new and not so new works about South Asian America into conversation with one another allows us to trace the shift in U.S. racial formations, when viewed through the palimpsest of "enemy alien" onto "model minority," and also to introduce a debate about what South Asian America can tell us about epistemologies of race, nation, empire, the state, and the politics of labor, gender, sexuality, and popular culture.

NOTES

1. Vijay Prashad, *The Karma of Brown Folk* (Minneapolis: University of Minnesota Press, 2000); Junaid Rana, *Terrifying Muslims: Race and Labor in the South Asian Diaspora* (Durham, NC: Duke University Press, 2011).
2. Maia Ramnath, *Haj to Utopia: How the Ghadar Movement Charted Global Radicalism and Attempted to Overthrow the British Empire* (Berkeley: University of California Press, 2011).
3. Sunaina Maira, "Deporting Radicals, Deporting La Migra: The Hayat Case in Lodi," *Cultural Dynamics* 19, no. 1 (2007): 39–66.
4. Jasbir K. Puar and Amit S. Rai, "Monster, Terrorist, Fag: The War on Terrorism and the Production of Docile Patriots," *Social Text*, 20, no. 3 (2002): 117–148; Jasbir K. Puar and Amit S. Rai, "The Remaking of a Model Minority: Perverse Projectiles under the Specter of (Counter)Terrorism," *Social Text*, 22, no. 3 (2004): 76–104; Sandhya Shukla, *India Abroad: Diasporic Cultures of Postwar America and England* (Princeton, NJ: Princeton University Press, 2003).
5. Vijay Prashad, *Uncle Swami: South Asians in America Today* (New York: New Press, 2012); Sunaina Maira, *Missing: Youth, Citizenship, and Empire after 9/11* (Durham, NC: Duke University Press, 2009).
6. Nayan Shah, *Stranger Intimacy: Race, Sexuality, and the Law in the North American West* (Berkeley: University of California Press, 2012), 14.
7. Shilpa Dave, Pawan Dhingra, Sunaina Maira, Partha Mazumda, Lavina Dhingra Shankar, Jaideep Singh, and Rajini Srikanth, "De-privileging Positions: Indian Americans, South Asian Americans, and the Politics of Asian American Studies," *Journal of Asian American Studies* 3, no. 1 (2000): 67–100; Lavina D. Shankar and Rajini Srikanth, eds., *A Part Yet Apart: South Asians in Asian America* (Philadelphia: Temple University Press, 1998).
8. Sharmila Rudrappa, *Ethnic Routes to Becoming American: Indian Immigrants and the Cultures of Citizenship* (New Brunswick, NJ: Rutgers University Press, 2004), 6–7, 14–15.
9. Chandan Reddy, *Freedom with Violence: Race, Sexuality, and the U.S. State* (Durham, NC: Duke University Press, 2011), 41; Maia Ramnath, *Decolonizing Anarchism* (Oakland, CA: AK Press and the Institute for Anarchist Studies, 2011).
10. Prashad, *Karma of Brown Folk*, 3–4.
11. Ibid., 12.
12. Shah, *Stranger Intimacy*, 19.
13. Vivek Bald, "Overlapping Diasporas, Multiracial Lives: South Asian Muslims in U.S. Communities of Color, 1880–1950," *Souls* 8, no. 4 (2006): 3–18.
14. Prashad, *Karma of Brown Folk*, 32, 36.
15. Ibid., 50.

16. Sunaina Maira, "Henna and Hip Hop: The Politics of Cultural Production and the Work of Cultural Studies," *Journal of Asian American Studies* 3, no. 3 (2000): 329–369.
17. Keya Ganguly, *States of Exception: Everyday Life and Postcolonial Identity* (Minneapolis: University of Minnesota Press, 2001).
18. Ramnath, *Haj to Utopia*, 3.
19. Ibid., 3.
20. Joan Jensen, *Passage from India: Asian Indian Immigrants in North America* (New Haven, CT: Yale University Press, 1988) .
21. Ibid., 42, 57, 121, 139, 270.
22. Prashad, *Karma of Brown Folk*, 127.
23. Ramnath, *Haj to Utopia*, 6.
24. Ibid., 3.
25. Ibid., 123.
26. Bakirathi Mani, *Aspiring to Home: South Asians in America* (Stanford, CA: Stanford University Press, 2012), 10.
27. Shah, *Stranger Intimacy*, 40.
28. Ibid., 55.
29. Ibid., 88, 54.
30. Ibid., 199.
31. Karen Leonard, *Making Ethnic Choices: California's Punjabi Mexican Americans* (Philadelphia: Temple University Press, 1992).
32. Gayatri Gopinath, *Impossible Desires: Queer Diasporas and South Asian Public Cultures* (Durham, NC: Duke University Press, 2005); Jasbir Puar, *Terrorist Assemblages: Homonationalism in Queer Times* (Durham, NC: Duke University Press, 2007).
33. Rudrappa, *Ethnic Routes*; Monisha Das Gupta, *Unruly Immigrants: Rights, Activism, and Transnational South Asian Politics in the United States* (Durham, NC: Duke University Press, 2006); Maira, *Missing*.
34. Shah, *Stranger Intimacy*, 233.
35. Ibid., 130–131.
36. Priya Srinivasan, *Sweating Saris: Indian Dance as Transnational Labor* (Philadelphia: Temple University Press, 2012), 45.
37. Ibid., 17, 16.
38. Shah, *Stranger Intimacy*.
39. Gary Okihiro, *Margins and Mainstreams: Asians in American History and Culture* (Seattle: University of Washington Press, 1994), 31–63.
40. Rudrappa, *Ethnic Routes*, 15.
41. Reddy, *Freedom with Violence*, 158–159.
42. Aihwa Ong, *Flexible Citizenship: The Cultural Logics of Transnationality* (Durham, NC: Duke University Press, 1999).
43. Biju Mathew, *Taxi! Cabs and Capitalism in New York City* (New York: New Press, 2005).
44. Das Gupta, *Unruly Immigrants*, 4.
45. Ibid., 9, 16.
46. Prashad, *Uncle Swami*, 18.
47. Das Gupta, *Unruly Immigrants*, 160.
48. Ibid., 171, 186.
49. Reddy, *Freedom with Violence*, 35, 18.

50. Ibid., 5, 13.
51. Puar, *Terrorist Assemblages*.
52. Reddy, *Freedom with Violence*, 150.
53. Puar, *Terrorist Assemblages*, 2–9.
54. Ibid., 165.
55. Ibid., 166.
56. Ibid., 170.
57. Ibid.
58. Ibid., 48–49, 68–69.
59. Prashad, *Uncle Swami*, 64.
60. For example, Amitava Kumar, *A Foreigner Carrying in the Crook of His Arm a Tiny Bomb* (Durham, NC: Duke University Press, 2010); Amitava Kumar, *Passport Photos* (Berkeley: University of California Press, 2000).

FURTHER READING

Bald, Vivek. "Overlapping Diasporas, Multiracial Lives: South Asian Muslims in U.S. Communities of Color, 1880–1950." *Souls* 8, no. 4 (2006): 3–18.
Das Gupta, Monisha. *Unruly Immigrants: Rights, Activism, and Transnational South Asian Politics in the United States*. Durham, NC: Duke University Press, 2006.
Dave, Shilpa, Pawan Dhingra, Sunaina Maira, Partha Mazumda, Lavina Dhingra Shankar, Jaideep Singh, and Rajini Srikanth. "De-privileging Positions: Indian Americans, South Asian Americans, and the Politics of Asian American Studies." *Journal of Asian American Studies* 3, no. 1 (2000): 67–100.
Ganguly, Keya. *States of Exception: Everyday Life and Postcolonial Identity*. Minneapolis: University of Minnesota Press, 2001.
Gopinath, Gayatri. *Impossible Desires: Queer Diasporas and South Asian Public Cultures*. Durham, NC: Duke University Press, 2005.
Jensen, Joan. *Passage from India: Asian Indian Immigrants in North America*. New Haven, CT: Yale University Press, 1988.
Kumar, Amitava. *A Foreigner Carrying in the Crook of His Arm a Tiny Bomb*. Durham, NC: Duke University Press, 2010.
Leonard, Karen. *Making Ethnic Choices: California's Punjabi Mexican Americans*. Philadelphia: Temple University Press, 1992.
Maira, Sunaina. "Deporting Radicals, Deporting La Migra: The Hayat Case in Lodi." *Cultural Dynamics* 19, no. 1 (2007): 39–66.
———. "Henna and Hip Hop: The Politics of Cultural Production and the Work of Cultural Studies." *Journal of Asian American Studies* 3, no. 3 (2000): 329–369.
———. *Missing: Youth, Citizenship, and Empire after 9/11*. Durham, NC: Duke University Press, 2009.
Mani, Bakirathi. *Aspiring to Home: South Asians in America*. Stanford, CA: Stanford University Press, 2012.
Mathew, Biju. *Taxi! Cabs and Capitalism in New York City*. New York: New Press, 2005.
Okihiro, Gary. *Margins and Mainstreams: Asians in American History and Culture*. Seattle: University of Washington Press, 1994.

Ong, Aihwa. *Flexible Citizenship: The Cultural Logics of Transnationality.* Durham, NC: Duke University Press, 1999.

Prashad, Vijay. *The Karma of Brown Folk.* Minneapolis: University of Minnesota Press, 2000.

———. *Uncle Swami: South Asians in America Today.* New York: New Press, 2012.

Puar, Jasbir. *Terrorist Assemblages: Homonationalism in Queer Times.* Durham, NC: Duke University Press, 2007.

Puar, Jasbir K., and Amit S. Rai. "Monster, Terrorist, Fag: The War on Terrorism and the Production of Docile Patriots." *Social Text* 20, no. 3 (2002): 117–148.

———. "The Remaking of a Model Minority: Perverse Projectiles under the Specter of (Counter)Terrorism," *Social Text,* 22, no. 3 (2004): 76–104.

Ramnath, Maia. *Decolonizing Anarchism.* Oakland, CA: AK Press and the Institute for Anarchist Studies, 2011.

———. *Haj to Utopia: How the Ghadar Movement Charted Global Radicalism and Attempted to Overthrow the British Empire.* Berkeley: University of California Press, 2011.

Rana, Junaid. *Terrifying Muslims: Race and Labor in the South Asian Diaspora.* Durham, NC: Duke University Press, 2011.

Reddy, Chandan. *Freedom with Violence: Race, Sexuality, and the U.S. State.* Durham, NC: Duke University Press, 2011.

Rudrappa, Sharmila. *Ethnic Routes to Becoming American: Indian Immigrants and the Cultures of Citizenship.* New Brunswick, NJ: Rutgers University Press, 2004.

Shah, Nayan. *Stranger Intimacy: Race, Sexuality, and the Law in the North American West.* Berkeley: University of California Press, 2012.

Shankar, Lavina D., and Rajini Srikanth, eds. *A Part Yet Apart: South Asians in Asian America.* Philadelphia: Temple University Press, 1998.

Shukla, Sandhya. *India Abroad: Diasporic Cultures of Postwar America and England.* Princeton, NJ: Princeton University Press, 2003.

Srinivasan, Priya. *Sweating Saris: Indian Dance as Transnational Labor.* Philadelphia: Temple University Press, 2012.

CHAPTER 4

....

ASIANS, NATIVE HAWAIIANS, AND PACIFIC ISLANDERS IN HAWAI'I

Place, People, Culture

....

JOHN P. ROSA

THERE is a Hawaiian saying: "'A'ohe pau ka 'ike i ka hālau ho'okahi [All knowledge is not taught in the same school]."[1] Let me tell you a story, a *mo'olelo*, about the many ways that people are learning the histories of Asians, Native Hawaiians, and Pacific Islanders in Hawai'i. It weaves seemingly disparate things together in order to create a larger picture. Historians in Hawai'i in the broadest sense—be they scholars, teachers, cultural practitioners, or community members—are turning to a variety of methods and sources in thinking about and researching the past. They work in archives and go beyond them in order to make meaning for themselves and multiple publics. These historians from within and beyond the academy often fashion more organic, holistic views of the past rather than versions that are solely analytical. They also use new ways to carry out and present their views of the past by using contemporary technologies like digital media and the Internet with its global reach.

In thinking about the history of Asians in Hawai'i one used to turn first to works by Ronald Takaki, a "local boy" from Palolo Valley on the island of O'ahu, who earned history degrees and taught ethnic studies in the University of California system. He wrote *Pau Hana: Plantation Life and Labor in Hawaii, 1835–1920* (1983) upon the urging of his uncle who had asked why there were no stories about people like him, an immigrant sugar-plantation worker. Takaki used a variety of plantation records, and, being the social historian that he was, he wove in accounts of everyday life that used Hawai'i Creole or pidgin in "talk story" fashion. Research on Hawai'i has developed so much since the publication of Takaki's works in the 1980s, and much of it now includes Hawaiian-language materials that shed light on the complex politics and social interactions of the multiethnic kingdom, territorial, and early statehood periods. The field is more interdisciplinary and examines a wider range of cultural forms in different ways. Interestingly enough, Hawai'i-born scholars have been rather central to the general field of Asian American history. For example, Lowell Chun-Hoon from Honolulu was a founding editor of the landmark *Amerasia Journal* while an undergraduate at Yale, and the scholarship and professional leadership of historians like Franklin Odo, Gary Okihiro, Gail Nomura, the literature scholar Stephen Sumida, and the anthropologist Franklin Ng, all from Hawai'i, have shaped how we think about the institutionalization and professionalization of Asian American studies.

Work by Native Hawaiian and other Hawai'i scholars has come of age in the last two decades. Historians trained at the University of Hawai'i at Mānoa like Davianna Pōmaika'i McGregor, Lilikalā Kame'eleihiwa, Jonathan Kamakawiwo'ole Osorio, and Kanalu Young were some of the first historians (as opposed to anthropologists) to take a look at Native Hawaiian experiences more closely. Scholars from other disciplines like Haunani-Kay Trask (political science), Jonathan Okamura (anthropology), and Amy Ku'uleialoha Stillman (ethnomusicology) have also added new conceptualizations when thinking about Hawai'i. Terminology and starting points, for example, have changed. The term "Asian American" is rarely used in Hawai'i and, in some ways, it emphasizes a relationship of immigrant groups in the islands rather narrowly to the United States alone. These days, new research and teaching often focuses first on the place of Hawai'i and its indigenous people, the Native Hawaiians (or *Kānaka Maoli*).

Not everyone in Hawai'i is Native Hawaiian, but the descendants of immigrants—mainly from Asia—have the common experience of living in Hawai'i's Island environment for many generations. Native Hawaiian understandings of the past can often provide some of the core frameworks for thinking about Hawai'i's history, even as the islands have become increasingly multicultural and multiethnic.

In contemporary Hawai'i, researching, learning, and sharing activities take place both indoors and outdoors—in libraries, archives, and classrooms; and in *lo'i* (agricultural fields), on the ocean, and in various *hālau* (schools) for traditional arts like hula, *mele* (song), and *'oli* (chant). As one of my students once told me, one cannot merely learn about Hawai'i from books alone: one must also take part in the world and be active within it.

PLACE

Before talking about the people of this mo'olelo, we need to talk about the setting: the time and place of Hawai'i and its relationship to other places. Hawai'i is one of the most geographically isolated places on earth, but as we shall see in another part of this essay, it has historical relationships to other places in the Pacific and along the Pacific Rim. Hawai'i is not exceptional in its island geography and physical isolation: it shares many similar characteristics with other Pacific Island places, but drawing attention to the place as a set of islands makes the experience different from larger, continental-based places.

Before we even think of the categories of "Asian" or "Pacific Islander," let us look at the place and how its location and geography have affected the islands' multiple histories. We can also talk about creation itself—or, at the very least, the ways in which people in Hawai'i think about their origins and their past.

Thinking about the Kumulipo, a Native Hawaiian origins chant, can help us to see Hawai'i through a different worldview. The nineteenth-century Native Hawaiian historian David Malo identified the Kumulipo as just one of a list of creation chants that also include the Paliku, Lolo, and other chants.[2] He mentions it early in his text *Ka Mo'olelo Hawai'i* when putting forth some general remarks on the history of Hawai'i.

Malo also sought to reconcile his native view of the origin of the islands with a new one put forth by Western scientists who speculated that the Hawaiian Islands "rose up out of the ocean as a result of volcanic action."[3] In considering the history of Hawai'i, we can be more expansive in our imaginations and do away with the boundary between natural history and human history. People, the land, and the ocean are intertwined. In the Kumulipo, literally, the "source of deep darkness," the first creature to be born is the coral polyp, followed by other creatures of the sea. First there is life in the water and then the land. Later in the creation chant, the genealogy of the gods associated with the water, sky, and earth is traced down to the creation of the first humans: Wākea (Sky Father) meets Papa (Earth Mother), who eventually gives birth to Hāloa and the Native Hawaiian people.

The Kumulipo was an important oral chant that was recited on special occasions only. King David Kalākaua had it transcribed into written Hawaiian and printed during his reign, and after his death, his sister, Queen Lili'uokalani, translated it into English while she was imprisoned at 'Iolani Palace. Its publication was just one way that these two *mo'i* (monarchs) were able to remind people of their *mana* (spiritual power) and their inherited ability to rule. The last section of the chant shows that the Kalākaua dynasty traces its genealogy all the way back to Wākea and Papa and thus to the beginnings of the world. In Lili'uokalani's translation, the Kumulipo opens this way:

> At the time that turned the heat of the earth,
> At the time when the heavens turned and changed,
> At the time when the light of the sun was subdued
> To cause light to break forth,
> At the time of the night of Makali'i [winter]
> Then began the slime which established the earth,
> The source of deepest darkness.[4]

It is important to look at Hawai'i in its relationships not only to the United States, but also to the greater Pacific—an area sometimes called Oceania by Pacific Islander scholars. Epeli Hau'ofa, a Tongan anthropologist who spent a lot of time in Hawai'i, commented in his well-known "Our Sea of Islands" essay that "continental" thinking since the eighteenth century had made colonial boundaries that confined ocean peoples. Hau'ofa argues that for the people of Oceania "their universe comprised not only land surfaces, but the surrounding ocean as far as they could traverse and exploit it."[5]

We are reminded of the great distances that people traveled in order to come to the islands. Voyaging without modern instruments—now called wayfinding—is an art that has been revived in Hawai'i and other parts of Polynesia, thanks to the assistance of Micronesian expertise through individuals like Mau Piailug. The revival of voyaging began with the work of the Polynesian Voyaging Society (PVS) in the 1970s under the leadership of Ben Finney, a University of Hawai'i anthropologist, and assisted by the expertise of skilled watermen like Nainoa Thompson and the legendary Eddie Aikau. People wishing to know more about wayfinding can now look to the community colleges of the University of Hawai'i like Honolulu Community College, which is home to the *Hōkūle'a* itself, moored at the Marine Education Training Center (METC) in Honolulu Harbor. In these community college settings, students learn both traditional culture and modern skills. Those unable to travel to Hawai'i can also explore the archives of the PVS online.[6]

Examinations of Hawai'i's history often have been limited to just a few islands—namely O'ahu, Hawai'i, Maui, and Kaua'i—instead of including more thorough studies of the smaller, major islands like Moloka'i, Lana'i, Ni'ihau, and Kaho'olawe. More work also needs to be done on the population shifts among islands that took place increasingly after World War II made O'ahu even more of a center of commerce, education, and social mobility. Davianna McGregor's *Nā Kua 'āina: Living Hawaiian Culture* (2007) looks at more than one island at a time, examining what she calls cultural *kīpuka*, or oases of traditional Native Hawaiian communities found in places like contemporary Moloka'i and Hawai'i Island. McGregor's book is also the first to chronicle the more recent revitalization of Kaho'olawe, an island seized by the U.S. Navy during World War II for bombing practice and only returned to the people of Hawai'i in the late twentieth century after protests in the 1970s.

Geographically speaking, the Hawaiian Island chain stretches over 1,500 miles from Hawai'i Island to Kure Atoll. Native Hawaiians long knew the extent of their islands and *ali'i* (chiefs) mention Nihoa and Kaula, smaller islands near Kaua'i, for example, in their writings. Smaller islands near the shores of major islands were also integrated into the worldview of Native Hawaiians because they were integral to fishing, sailing, and other activities. Sometimes known by English-language names today, their Hawaiian-language names tell us how they are linked to other places. The Hawaiian name for Chinaman's Hat on the windward side of O'ahu is Mokoli'i, telling of the *moko* (mythical lizard; *li'i* meaning little) that was part of the Pele story associated with the larger area of Kualoa. Photographic work by Kapulani Landgraf, accompanied by Hawaiian- and English-language text by Kalani Meinecke, helps current generations to rethink the past. As Cristina Bacchilega has noted, the photographs are not "landscapes" in a Western tradition; instead, Landgraf's photographs prompt us to see the land and sea differently. The work of Landgraf and other photographers like Jan Becket enable us to rethink how earlier Native Hawaiians saw their natural environment and its *wahi pana* (sacred sites).[7]

In looking at the islands further to the northwest of the main Hawaiian Islands, we have islands and atolls that are part of the Papahānaumokuākea Marine National

Monument, now designated as a World Heritage Site. These Northwestern Hawaiian Islands "are considered a sacred place, a region of primordial darkness from which life springs and spirits return after death."[8] The protected region is named after Papahānaumoku (literally the "one who gives birth to islands") who paired with Wākea to give birth to the Kānaka Maoli. The monument is the largest marine-protected area on the planet and is a research site, even for historians. It has, for example, archaeological sites showing human habitation on some islands, maritime history in the evidence of shipwrecks, and World War II history with the Battle of Midway. Even if a scholar does not specialize in the areas of whaling and military history, the ocean inspires us also to think beyond human activities on the land alone.

Upon encountering the Hawaiian Islands in the eighteenth and nineteenth centuries, Westerners assessed the islands for a variety of resources, whether they could be deep harbors, provide places for defensible forts, or generate possible trade goods like sandalwood. The British explorers James Cook and George Vancouver are the best-known visitors to the islands, but more work needs to be done on the impact of maritime trade that subsequently developed throughout the nineteenth century—seafaring that often included the use of Asian and Pacific Islander sailors.

An exceptionally detailed travel narrative, focused especially on the natural environment of Hawai'i, is that of Charles Wilkes who led an official United States exploring expedition that traveled from 1840 to 1841, mapping parts of the Pacific for the U.S. shipping industry. While on Hawai'i Island, he took scientists to the summit of Mauna Loa. The scientific information gathered was valuable, and for our historical purposes, we can examine how Wilkes enlisted the help of more than three hundred Native Hawaiians on this five-day journey from the volcanic Kilauea Crater to the top of Mauna Loa.[9]

Work in the ecological sciences can also help us in our historical understanding of how Native Hawaiians lived in and altered their natural environment. The current interest in sustainable, "place-based" management borrows from studies of the Hawaiian *ahupua'a* system where a *konohiki* (land manager) managed the natural resources that ran from the mountains to the sea. The ahupua'a system, in conjunction with a *kapu* system that restricted the use of some resources, resulted in a management system that protected the environment. Contemporary geologists like Charles Fletcher, who studies sea-level and coastal changes, and historical geographers like Carlos Andrade urge us to look beyond land use alone in thinking about the past and planning more wisely for the future.[10]

Historians can also learn from more accessible works on shorelines and beaches that were originally geared toward the general public. John R. K. Clark's series of books on Hawai'i's beaches, for example, helps us to take notice more of the importance and fragility of beaches as liminal places between ocean and land. Clark, a former president of the Hawaiian Historical Society and a retired lifeguard and deputy fire chief, has a deep knowledge of the ocean. His most recent book, *Hawaiian Surfing: Traditions from the Past* (2011), makes extensive use of Hawaiian-language newspapers of the nineteenth century as translated by Keao NeSmith. A related book, Isaiah Helekunihi Walker's *Waves of Resistance: Surfing and History in Twentieth-Century Hawai'i* (2011), looks at the modern surf scene, showing how highly coveted surf breaks like the North Shore of O'ahu can tell us about the competition between local and Native Hawaiian surfers and newly arrived surfers from Australia and California. In writing about the experiences and media coverage of Da Hui, a group of surfers on the North Shore, Walker is one of the first scholars to write about Native Hawaiian masculinity, thus joining ranks with the anthropologist Ty Kāwika Tengan, the author of *Native Men Remade: Gender and Nation in Contemporary Hawai'i* (2008). Both of these books complement works on gendered depictions of Native Hawaiian women as analyzed, for example, in Haunani-Kay Trask's often-cited essay "Lovely Hula Hands" or in Adria Imada's *Aloha America: Hula Circuits through the U.S. Empire* (2012).[11]

Geography was part of Hawaiian life since very early on. David Malo and other seminary students at Lahainaluna School on the island of Maui created some of the first school texts while under the instruction of missionaries like William Richards. Looking at these early primers gives us insight into the early nineteenth-century interactions between Native Hawaiian scholars and missionaries as they worked out a new orthography for the Hawaiian language.[12]

Work by twenty-first-century Native Hawaiian geographers like Kamana Beamer shows that even during the drastic social and political changes of nineteenth-century Hawai'i, Native Hawaiians adapted Western mapping techniques strategically in order to assist the development of the Hawaiian Kingdom and preserve its lands. Though Western mapping can often be used to dispossess native peoples, all was not lost in nineteenth-century Hawai'i. Hawaiians themselves did the surveying and mapping, consulted with native informants, and often used traditional *palena* (land boundaries).[13]

The Māhele of 1848 was the introduction of a Western land-tenure system—the establishment of fee-simple private property that eventually led to the dispossession of Hawaiians from their land. The geographer Donavan Preza has reexamined how the Māhele unfolded, emphasizing that the Māhele was a long process and that it was more of a Hawaiian process than a Western one. Hawaiians were active agents in seeking to secure land and in petitioning the government for fee-simple titles to land that they could live on and cultivate. Contrary to older views of the Māhele, Hawaiians were not dispossessed of their land quickly in the mid-nineteenth century. Preza argues that drastic political change—like the overthrow of the Kingdom of Hawai'i in 1893—was *the* sufficient condition for dispossession. Dispossession took place unevenly, depending upon location, and it would unfold over the course of two to three generations (fifty to seventy-five years).[14]

PEOPLE

When exactly the first humans arrived in the islands is likely to always be an ongoing mystery. Only a few decades ago, anthropologists thought that the islands were settled as early as somewhere around 0–300 CE, but now some anthropologists are estimating more conservative arrival dates of 1200 to 1277 CE, based on a more selective group of radiocarbon dating samples.[15] Questions about whether or not Captain James Cook's visit in 1778 was the first Western one to the islands are also likely to come up occasionally, with popular media periodically speculating that Spanish or Portuguese navigators had visited in the 1500s. Nearly all scholars in Hawai'i have gone beyond this fascination with Cook studies. Lilikalā Kame'eleihiwa, for example, believes that the heated debate in the 1990s between Gananath Obeyesekere and Marshall Sahlins about the supposed apotheosis or deification of Cook by Native Hawaiians is really more about the peculiarity of Western anthropological studies and how they treat native peoples than anything else. Furthermore, the political scientist Noenoe Silva argues that if one studies Hawaiian oral traditions that were later printed in Hawaiian-language newspapers, there are other Western visitors with "light eyes" that visited the islands, thus showing that Cook was not the first and was not all that distinctive.[16]

The historian David Stannard argued in 1988 that there were as many as 800,000 to 1,000,000 Hawaiians at the time of Cook's arrival in 1778—a population estimate that has come to be used quite commonly in the islands, even in public history accounts like the timeline of Hawaiian Hall displays at the Bishop Museum. Historical demographers and other social scientists can now study the first several decades of Western contact more closely. O. A. Bushnell initiated studies into how biological interactions decimated the Native Hawaiian population in his *Gifts of Civilization* (1993), and now others can explore how the Native Hawaiian society was not stable enough to handle the sheer number of deaths.[17] Numbers of Native Hawaiian men also left the islands in order to take part in whaling and maritime trade throughout the Pacific and many would eventually settle in the Pacific Northwest and American West. Asians and other Pacific Islander sailors were part of this early trade period that, as of yet, is still understudied.[18] We see evidence of this diaspora not only in Native Hawaiian newspapers, but also in U.S. newspapers that can be more readily researched through the Chronicling America database.[19]

In the early trade period, the term *haole* initially meant any foreigner who came to the islands, but by the late nineteenth century, the term was used almost exclusively for those with a white European or American background. Whites intermarried with Hawaiians, even ali'i. In the late nineteenth and early twentieth centuries, working-class whites—notably the Portuguese who, at the time, were not always considered "white"— also intermarried with Hawaiians and Asian immigrants. From the mid-nineteenth century onward, interethnic marriages—and, thus, interethnic communities—were common. By the 1930s, the University of Hawai'i sociologists Romanzo Adams and Andrew Lind were studying these intermarriages and examining the rapidly changing demographics of the islands.[20] The anthropologist Jonathan Okamura is one of the first in decades to thoroughly examine the multiethnic character of Hawai'i. His book *Ethnicity and Inequality in Hawai'i* (2008) reminds us to look more at *ethnicity* and not race when examining the relative power differences among groups. More work needs to be done in examining the histories of Hawai'i's ethnic groups in conjunction with one another instead of solely on a group-by-group basis.

Of course, it was the sugar industry that drew the majority of immigrants, mainly from East Asia, to Hawai'i in the first place. The main groups and the years of their first arrival in large numbers are the Chinese (1852), Japanese (1885), Koreans (1903), and Filipinos (1906). We must keep in mind, however, that these groups also interacted significantly with non-Asian laborers, namely Portuguese (1878) and Puerto Ricans (1900). Native Hawaiians worked on the first sugar plantation in Kōloa, Kaua'i, starting in 1835, and their experiences on sugar plantations as a native people with centuries of knowledge of the land are a subject for more thorough examination. The population specialist Eleanor Nordyke details the smaller numbers of other European and Pacific Islander groups that sugar planters experimented with in her *Peopling of Hawai'i* (1989).[21]

We also need to study how exactly movement off the sugar plantations and into other industries took place. Some workers continued with agricultural work, for example, by entering the pineapple industry, but by the last quarter of the twentieth century, the role of agriculture in the islands' economic life shrank drastically. Work in the tourism industry and the military and government sectors has made up much of the economy for over five decades—and scholars need to study these economic activities.[22]

Detailed descriptions of each ethnic group's history are no longer the only or preferred route to follow when researching Hawai'i's social history. Recently published works tell us that the trajectory of scholarship and publishing includes political histories, labor histories, and contemporary studies that provide only brief histories of migration. The journalist and filmmaker Tom Coffman, for example, has two recent books that examine the prominent role of Japanese Americans in Hawai'i's politics—his *Island Edge of America: A Political History of Hawai'i* (2003) and *I Respectfully Dissent: A Biography of Edward H. Nakamura* (2012). The latter is a study of a 442nd Regiment veteran who was later involved in labor organizing for the International Longshore and Warehouse Union and who then became a Hawai'i State Supreme Court Justice.

Masayo Duus's *Japanese Conspiracy: The Oahu Sugar Strike of 1920* (1999) is one of the first labor histories of Hawai'i to be published in decades. Drawing on Japanese- and English-language sources, Duus describes the labor leaders who organized the strike and the actions of the Hawaiian Sugar Planters' Association against them. Ronald Takaki depicted the 1920 strike in his *Pau Hana: Planation Life and Labor in Hawaii, 1835–1920* (1983) as being a working-class alliance between Japanese and Filipino laborers. In Takaki's labor-history narrative, the strike was in stark contrast to the 1909 strike where Japanese workers organized on the basis of "blood unionism." Duus's work suggests that there was some communication between Japanese and Filipino labor leaders in the 1920 strike, but it was not necessarily as fully a coordinated effort as Takaki had suggested. A strong class-based alliance among workers from different ethnic groups would not come together until shortly after World War II, says Moon-Kie Jung in his *Reworking Race: The Making of Hawaii's Interracial Labor Movement* (2006). In his conceptualization of Hawai'i's labor movement in the mid-twentieth century, Jung argues that class did not just replace ethnicity and race—the labor movement redefined the meanings of "race" and "class" by developing an ideology of class in Hawai'i that incorporated and reworked racial meanings and practices among laborers and their organizers.

Journals, memoirs, and oral histories published in the last two decades also help to complement many of the older, standard historical accounts about well-known events or people. Angeles Monrayo's diary from 1924 is readily accessible in *Tomorrow's Memories: A Diary, 1924–1928* (2003), edited by Rizaline Raymundo. The entries by this young Filipina chronicle the experiences of her family as they moved from a plantation in Waipahu on the island of O'ahu to the strike camp of the labor leader Pablo Manlapit in Honolulu. This social and cultural account provides a more personal, day-to-day account of living through the strike than the standard labor history detailed in John Reinecke's *The Filipino Piecemeal Sugar Strike of 1924–1925* (1996).

Diaries and oral histories give us insight into everyday details that are not always mentioned with the same emotion that scholarly syntheses do. Other kinds of firsthand accounts are particularly insightful in exploring lesser-known experiences—for example, like that of the internment experience in Hawai'i. The professional journalist and poet Yasutaro Soga was skilled in describing his own arrest on December 7, 1941, followed by his internment on Sand Island on the island of O'ahu and, later, in two camps in New Mexico. This *issei* account in Japanese has only recently been translated into English and published in 2008 for a wider audience. The Honouliuli camp that opened as the Sand Island internment site closed has been the subject of research by faculty and students from the University of Hawai'i—West O'ahu and by staff and volunteers from the Japanese Cultural Center of Hawai'i and Japanese American Citizens League Honolulu Chapter. Since 2012, there is an ongoing special resource study that is assessing the possibility of Honouliuli becoming a National Park Service site.[23] These projects show how internment experiences in Hawai'i were often quite different from those on the continental United States.

Hawai'i's history as a constitutional monarchy that was then overthrown has also created unique historical questions. Conditions for U.S. citizenship, for example, were different for Chinese in Hawai'i because those who were naturalized citizens of the Kingdom of Hawai'i automatically became U.S. citizens after the Organic Act of 1900. Another federal law in 1900 required all Chinese in Hawai'i to register and obtain a certificate of residence in order to distinguish them from Chinese living in the continental United States.[24] These certificates can be found at branches of the National Archives and Records Administration.

It is also helpful to see Asian migration to Hawai'i as part of a much larger picture. Adam McKeown shows migration to the islands as being part of a larger diaspora in his book *Chinese Migrant Networks and Cultural Change: Peru, Chicago, Hawaii, 1900–1936* (2001).[25] McKeown takes a transnational perspective, examining how migrant Chinese formed an extensive network of family connections, merchant relations, and shared institutions that linked communities thousands of miles apart. A more contemporary example of transnationalism can be seen in the sociologist Mary Yu Danico's book *The 1.5 Generation: Becoming Korean American in Hawaii* (2004), which touches on Korean experiences in the islands since the early twentieth century. Comparable works on more recent groups, notably Southeast Asians, Pacific Islanders, and other post-1965 immigrants, have yet to emerge. One possible research site is the ever-changing nature of Honolulu's Chinatown and its surrounding neighborhoods, which have Vietnamese, Thai, Asian Indian, and Micronesian grocery stores, restaurants, and other businesses. Language training to carry out such research can be found at the University of Hawai'i's federally funded National Foreign Language Resource Center, which includes the less commonly taught languages of Southeast Asia and the Pacific.

When we look at immigration history, we also need to consider the larger, international political and legal landscape. Work coming out of the University of Hawai'i's Political Science Department, for example, examines how the Kingdom of Hawai'i often granted Asian and other non-Hawaiian residents rights as naturalized subjects in its constitutional monarchy. The political scientist David Keanu Sai has ushered in a new way of looking at Hawai'i's political status: since the islands were never annexed by an internationally recognized treaty, Hawai'i can be said to be illegally occupied by the United States. This line of reasoning has already been acknowledged in international circles and is the basis of current legal challenges in U.S. federal courts and at the United Nations.[26] Recognizing the continued sovereignty of the Kingdom of Hawai'i is a more positive way of looking at its historical and contemporary political status in the community of nations. Scholars, students, and community members no longer need to use a colonial model to view Hawai'i as a weak, colonized place, doomed to be dependent on or subservient to the United States.

Records from the U.S. Census Bureau or the Kingdom of Hawai'i can help ground us when we evaluate the size of different population groups and their changing social and economic characteristics over the decades. Data for labor, economic, and citizenship status in the nineteenth and twentieth centuries can be found in Robert Schmitt's *Historical Statistics of Hawaii* (1977). For more recent decades, the statistics compiled by the State of Hawai'i's Department of Economic Development and Tourism are an excellent source for examining economic trends and the increasing numbers of visitors that come to the islands from all parts of the world.[27]

For convenience, we often look at histories, group by group. But there has been a long history of interracial or, more precisely, interethnic mixing in Hawai'i. According to the 2010 U.S. Census, more than 80 percent of people in Hawai'i identify themselves as having Native Hawaiian, Pacific Islander, or Asian ancestry. No ethnic group constitutes a majority, but when whites of various ethnic backgrounds are lumped together, people who are white or part white make up more than 40 percent of the islands' population. Many people who self-designate as part white are also Asian and/or Native Hawaiian, and more than 20 percent of people identified themselves as being of two or more racial groups. Multiethnic individuals have been a significant portion of Hawai'i's population for decades, as seen in studies by sociologists like Romanzo Adams and Andrew Lind that go back to the 1930s. Since then, however, there has not been extensive research on people of mixed ancestry.[28]

CULTURE

In a new place, people grow new cultures and cultural forms. The new histories that are emerging in Hawai'i are cultural histories, building on older social histories and adding to older, traditional economic and political histories. Perhaps the biggest innovation in the writing of Hawai'i's histories is the revitalization of the Hawaiian language. The number of *mānaleo*, or native language speakers, had dwindled throughout the mid- to late twentieth century, but since the Hawaiian cultural renaissance of the 1970s, curricular materials for the study of the Hawaiian language have matured. By the early 1990s, courses in 'Ōlelo Hawai'i were becoming increasingly popular at the high school and college levels; at the turn of this century, contemporary television, radio, and print media had also begun to incorporate the Hawaiian language in their broadcasts and publications.

When print culture was adopted by the Hawaiian kingdom in the middle of the nineteenth century, Hawaiians became one of the most literate populations in the world. Oral traditions like the Kumulipo were transcribed into Hawaiian and English by the end of the nineteenth century. The move from orality to literacy and its multiple effects is deftly described in Elizabeth Buck's *Paradise Remade: The Politics of Culture and History in Hawai'i* (1993). The most widespread form of literacy can be seen in newspapers, Hawaiian and otherwise, that proliferated since the early nineteenth century. Helen Chapin tells us in her complete reference guide to Hawai'i's newspapers that, between 1834 and 2000, there were approximately 1,250 different newspapers in at least twelve languages.[29] Other than English, some of the main languages for these newspapers are Hawaiian, Chinese, Japanese, and Portuguese. One good example of utilizing newspapers in different languages for scholarship is work by James Mohr, who used the skills of Hawaiian, Chinese, and Japanese translators in writing *Plague and Fire: Fighting the Plague and the Chinatown Fire of 1900* (2005). Portuguese-language newspapers give us insight into the politics of the times and the actions of haole, Hawaiian, Chinese, and, to a lesser extent, Japanese populations during the late nineteenth century. These fragile newspapers, held at the Hawaiian Historical Society, are being digitized thanks to funding from the Ferreira-Mendes Portuguese-American Archives at the University of Massachusetts Dartmouth and a local preservation fund drive in Honolulu.[30]

Several projects aim to reconstruct an archive of Hawaiian-language materials from the nineteenth century and early twentieth century. Ho'olaupa'i, a collaborative project of the Bishop Museum, Hale Kuamo'o, and Alu Like, is digitizing dozens of Hawaiian-language newspapers—a collection that amounts to approximately 125,000 pages and the largest collection of native language writings in the Pacific. Its website is nested within a larger online resource, Ulukau, the Hawaiian Electronic Library, which features Hawaiian-language dictionaries, reference materials, and portals to other databases.[31]

Hawaiian-language materials from the nineteenth century have been reprinted for wider distribution. One example is the *Buke Mele Lahui* (2003), which is part of the

Hawaiian Historical Society's Ke Kupu Hou series. It is a collection mainly of political and patriotic songs that were originally published in Honolulu during the turbulent 1890s. M. Puakea Nogelmeier and Amy Ku'uleialoha Stillman provide an introduction in both Hawaiian and English. Stillman, an ethnomusicologist, places these mele within a larger sociopolitical context with other cultural forms, like hula. Her *Sacred Hula: The Hula 'Āla'apapa in Historical Perspective* (1998) is another excellent work essential to the study of the history of hula.

Nogelmeier, a professor of Hawaiian language, has noted that older, well-known translations of works by Native Hawaiian historians like David Malo and Samuel Kamakau have been used so often that they have become a limited canon for scholars unable to read Hawaiian-language materials written by other native scholars. Nogelmeier and others are going beyond this "discourse of (in)sufficiency" by training a new generation of Hawaiian-language translators who are familiar with the idioms of nineteenth-century Hawaiian publications. Smaller contemporary presses like Nogelmeier's Awaiaulu Press have also been able to broaden the kinds of materials published dually in Hawaiian and English—as in the case of the 2006 publication of *Ka Mo'olelo O Hi'iakaikapoliopele* (a Hawaiian volume), or *The Epic Tale of Hi'iakaikapoliopele* (its English volume), which tells the epic of the goddess Pele and her sisters. The revitalization of Hawaiian print culture is also done with community members, as seen in *'Ike Kū'oko'a*—an innovative project headed by Nogelmeier in 2012 where thousands of volunteers logged in to a website in order to transcribe Hawaiian newspaper pages that were not able to be read by current optical character recognition technology.[32]

The archives, libraries, and museums have a culture of their own. The main archives for historical research are nearly all located in Honolulu. The Hawai'i State Archives, next to 'Iolani Palace and the Capitol building, houses records from the kingdom, territorial, and state government eras. Aside from these public records, there are private papers and photograph collections often used by professional historians and documentary filmmakers. Genealogists use the archives to look at the passenger records of ships that brought immigrants to the islands. Also downtown are the collections of the Hawaiian Historical Society and the Hawaiian Children's Mission, which share a vault in the Mission Houses Museum complex next to Kawaiaha'o Church, less than a block from 'Iolani Palace. The Hawaiian Historical Society is especially strong on missionary materials dating from the 1820s onward; it holds, for example, the most extensive collection of Hawaiian-language bibles in the world. David Forbes's four-volume annotated bibliography of Hawaiian-language materials is just one aid in previewing publications that might be found in these three archives downtown. His bibliography also helps in identifying rare materials held in the British Public Records Office and other European archives.[33] For those looking into territorial or military records, trips to the National Archives and Records Administration (notably its San Bruno, California, branch) might also be necessary.

The Hawaiian-Pacific Collection at the University of Hawai'i's Hamilton Library has an easily accessible set of reference materials to use while paging for primary and secondary source materials from its stacks. The Hawaiian Collection is strongest in its collection of published books and other bound materials about Hawai'i that are not always kept by archives. The collection now holds the Hawaiian Sugar Planters' Association Plantation archives and the Dole Corporation archives. Among the library's major but underutilized collections are ones on World War II domestic experiences when Hawai'i was under martial law. Even the records regarding Japanese experiences in Hawai'i during the war have not been used extensively when looking at the larger history of Japanese in the United States.

The Bishop Museum Archives hold many private manuscripts and papers, mainly from Native Hawaiian ali'i and other elites who donated them to the museum in the late nineteenth century. The museum's archives are also an excellent source of popular materials like magazines and film and television clips from throughout the twentieth century. One should also visit the museum's Hawaiian Hall, reopened in 2008 after it was restored by Mason Architects, a local firm that specializes in historic preservation and is headed by a former Hawaiian Historical Society president Glenn E. Mason. Much of the reenvisioning of the hall's layout was provided by Native Hawaiian academic historians like Davianna McGregor and Jonathan Osorio and museum specialists like Noelle Kahanu.[34]

EDUCATIONAL INSTITUTIONS AND THEIR RESOURCES

Institutions have a strong influence on what is researched and written. In 2007 the University of Hawai'i at Mānoa established an entire college devoted to the study of Native Hawaiian knowledge, named Hawai'inuiākea. It is composed of two academic units (one focusing on Hawaiian studies, and another on Hawaiian language) and it tends to one traditional cultural garden (a lo'i, or taro, patch). The college serves its own majors as well as thousands of university students who pass through its popular Hawaiian Studies 107 course, which familiarizes undergraduates with Hawaiian culture while also serving as a graduation requirement.

The Hawaiian Studies unit has a partnership with the Edith Kanaka'ole Foundation on an ancestral knowledge and land project called Kamakakūoka'āina. This project is training young Hawaiians in ancestral understandings of the land and in traditional land-management practices. Students work with archival records and maps from the Kingdom of Hawai'i and learn how to use modern computer technology to organize data and eventually make it available online. The project will result in a database of more than 12,000 digitized archival land records and maps, mainly for the island of O'ahu.[35]

The University of Hawai'i at Mānoa's Ethnic Studies Department has served many students since its founding as a program in 1970. It has a small collection of papers that are important to the study of community organizing on the island of O'ahu since the 1970s. Of particular note are ephemera like student and community newspapers, pamphlets, and fliers that were not always kept by the University of Hawai'i libraries. The University of Hawai'i at Mānoa's Center for Pacific Islands Studies focuses mostly on those residents who live in their islands of origin. Through its outreach efforts, however, the center's faculty and students have begun to educate the larger public about the steady increase of migration from Micronesia to Hawai'i in the last few decades.

Another university-based resource of use to the public is the Center for Oral History, established in 1976 with funding by the State of Hawai'i's legislature. Projects are organized mainly by geographical location, historical events, or ethnic group; all of the projects have extensive indexes and glossaries for non-English-language terms. The center's anthology, *Talking Hawai'i's Story: Oral Histories of an Island People* (2010), gives readers a better feel for the everyday life experiences of Hawai'i residents from different ethnicities and islands. Though researchers might not use these oral histories directly, they provide a valuable context when examining larger events like World War II or the development of the tourism industry. One of the newest and most unique projects is *Hui Panala'au: Hawaiian Colonists in the Pacific, 1935–1942*, which interviews Native Hawaiian men who were sent as colonists to the uninhabited equatorial Line Islands of Baker, Howland, and Jarvis. Barely out of high school at Kamehameha Schools, these young men were part of a secret enterprise to assert the United States' claim to these islands in anticipation of war with Japan.[36]

CONCLUSION

For centuries, histories in Hawai'i were oral in form; only recently have they been written down and put into print. In contemporary times, nothing limits us from going back to oral forms and sharing our histories. Talking story about the past, whether in the classroom or beyond it, is a way to build bonds of community. Storytelling is important because it shows how people and places are interrelated in an island society. Drawing on oral histories in order to teach or do research helps us to uncover the feelings and emotions associated with carrying out the process of discovery in the first place.

History is alive and well in Hawai'i. The Kumulipo is still studied by academic scholars, but cultural practitioners are also working to come up with new understandings of the text. For example, the Papakū Makawalu research team of the Edith Kanaka'ole Foundation, most often known for its acclaimed *hālau hula*, has produced three publications in order to give community members an in-depth look at the *wā'akahi* (first section) of the Kumulipo. People in Hawai'i see how they are connected to other people throughout the Pacific. Native Hawaiians can see themselves connected by their ancestor Hāloa across all the Hawaiian Islands. One stated goal of the University of Hawai'i's School of Hawaiian Knowledge, for example, is to help "strengthen genealogical ties to Papahānaumoku, our earth mother, and Hawai'i as our ancestral homeland."[37]

We can improve upon our older historical narratives of Asians in Hawai'i by not solely focusing on immigrants in search of better financial times or leaving undesirable situations in their countries of origin. Academic research needs to be shared with the multiple communities that universities and scholars are deeply indebted to. Research in Hawai'i cannot be carried out responsibly without honest interactions and commitments to places and people. Knowledge is nothing without respect for people and place. Native Hawaiian or not, we all have a *kuleana*, or responsibility, for preserving histories by preserving our archives and libraries. And at a most basic level, we have a responsibility to the ocean and the land that came before us—and that provides for us. Communal histories in Hawai'i, woven from various sources and approaches, have much to teach us about the way that our natural, social, and cultural worlds come together.

Notes

1. Mary Kawena Pukui, *'Ōlelo No'eau: Hawaiian Proverbs and Poetical Sayings, Collected, Translated, and Annotated by Mary Kawena Pukui* (Honolulu: Bishop Museum Press, 1983), 24, proverb #203.
2. David Malo, *Hawaiian Antiquities: Moolelo Hawaii* (Honolulu: Bishop Museum Press, 1951), 2.
3. Ibid., 3.
4. Lili'uokalani, *The Kumulipo: An Hawaiian Creation Myth* (Kentfield, CA: Pueo, 1978), 1–2.
5. Epeli Hau'ofa, *We Are the Ocean: Selected Works* (Honolulu: University of Hawai'i Press, 2008), 32.
6. The Honolulu Community College website for the Polynesian Voyaging Society is http://hokulea.org/. Funding for these digital resources was provided by the U.S. Department of Education's Title III Native Hawaiian Serving Institutions Program. See also the older companion site maintained at Kapi'olani Community College: http://pvs.kcc.hawaii.edu/.
7. Anne Kapulani Landgraf, *Nā Wahi Pana O Ko'olau Poko: Legendary Places of Ko'olau Poko* (Honolulu: University of Hawai'i Press, 1994); Jan Becket and Joseph Singer, *Pana O'ahu: Sacred Stones, Sacred Land* (Honolulu: University of Hawai'i Press, 1999); Cristina Bacchilega, *Legendary Hawai'i and the Politics of Place: Tradition, Translation, and Tourism* (Philadelphia: University of Pennsylvania Press, 2006).
8. "Papahānaumokuākea Marine National Monument," www.papahanaumokuakea.gov/heritage/welcome.html/.
9. "United States Exploring Expedition, 1838–1842," www.sil.si.edu/digitalcollections/usexex/follow.htm.
10. Charles Fletcher, Robynne Boyd, William J. Neal, and Virginia Tice, *Living on the Shores of Hawai'i: Natural Hazards, the Environment, and Our Communities* (Honolulu: University of Hawai'i Press, 2010); Carlos Andrade, *Hā'ena: Through the Eyes of the Ancestors* (Honolulu: University of Hawai'i Press, 2008).
11. Haunani-Kay Trask, *From a Native Daughter: Colonialism and Sovereignty in Hawai'i* (Monroe, ME: Common Courage, 1993), 179–197; Adria L. Imada, *Aloha America: Hula Circuits through the U.S. Empire* (Durham, NC: Duke University Press, 2012).
12. David W. Forbes, *Engraved at Lahainaluna: A History of Printmaking by Hawaiians at the Lahainaluna Seminary, 1834–1844* (Honolulu: Hawaiian Mission Children's Society, 2012).

13. B. Kamanamaikalani Beamer and T. Kaeo Duarte, "I palapala no ia aina—Documenting the Hawaiian Kingdom: A Colonial Venture?" *Journal of Historical Geography* 35, no. 1 (2009): 66–86.

14. Donovan C. Preza, "The Empirical Writes Back: Re-examining Hawaiian Dispossession Resulting from the Mahele of 1848" (M.A. thesis, University of Hawai'i at Mānoa, 2010).

15. For recent work by the University of Hawai'i anthropologist Terry Hunt, see T. M. Rieth, T. L. Hunt, C. Lipo, and J. M. Wilmshurst, "The 13th Century Polynesian Colonization of Hawai'i Island," *Journal of Archaeological Science* 38 (2011): 2740–2749. See also J. Wilmshurst, T. Hunt, C. Lipo, and A. Anderson, "High-Precision Radiocarbon Dating Shows Recent and Rapid Initial Human Colonization of East Polynesia," *Proceedings of the National Academy of Science* 108 (2011): 1815–1820.

16. Noenoe K. Silva, *Aloha Betrayed: Native Hawaiian Resistance to American Colonialism* (Durham, NC: Duke University Press, 2004), 16–23.

17. David E. Stannard, *Before the Horror: The Population of Hawai'i on the Eve of Western Contact* (Honolulu: University of Hawai'i Press, 1988); O. A. Bushnell, *Gifts of Civilization: Germs and Genocide in Hawai'i* (Honolulu: University of Hawai'i Press, 1993).

18. David A. Chappell, *Double Ghosts: Oceanian Voyagers on Euroamerican Ships* (Armonk, NY: M. E. Sharpe, 1997).

19. The Chronicling America webpage is available at http://chroniclingamerica.loc.gov/.

20. Romanzo Adams, *Interracial Marriage in Hawaii: A Study of the Mutually Conditioned Processes of Acculturation and Amalgamation* (New York: Macmillan, 1937); Andrew W. Lind, *Hawaii's People* (Honolulu: University of Hawai'i Press, 1980).

21. Eleanor C. Nordyke, *The Peopling of Hawai'i* (Honolulu: University of Hawai'i Press, 1989), 43–50, 94–96.

22. Historical statistics compiled by the State of Hawai'i's Department of Business Economic Development and Tourism are an excellent source for examining these economic trends. See http://hawaii.gov/dbedt.

23. Yasutaro Soga, *Life behind Barbed Wire: The World War II Internment Memoirs of a Hawai'i Issei* (Honolulu: University of Hawai'i Press, 2008); Japanese Cultural Center of Hawai'i, "The Untold Story: Internment of Japanese Americans in Hawai'i," http://www.hawaiiinternment.org. This web source is part of a larger Education through Cultural and Historical Organizations project—a collaborative education partnership of museums and cultural institutions in Hawai'i, Alaska, Massachusetts, and Mississippi with support provided by the U.S. Department of Education. See www.echospace.org. See also Alan Rosenfeld, "Honouliuli (detention facility)," *Densho Encyclopedia*, http://encyclopedia.densho.org/Honouliuli (detention facility)/.

24. "Chinese Immigration and the Chinese in the United States," http://www.archives.gov/research/chinese-americans/guide.html.

25. Adam McKeown, *Chinese Migrant Networks and Cultural Change: Peru, Chicago, Hawaii, 1900–1936* (Chicago: University of Chicago Press, 2001).

26. David Keanu Sai, *Ua Mau Ke Ea—Sovereignty Endures: An Overview of the Political and Legal History of the Hawaiian Islands* (Honolulu: Pū'ā Foundation, 2011). See also "Hawaiian Kingdom Government," http://www.hawaiiankingdom.org/.

27. See http://dbedt.hawaii.gov/.

28. For a brief discussion of Hawai'i's contemporary racial and ethnic characteristics, see John P. Rosa, "Race/Ethnicity," in *The Value of Hawai'i: Knowing the Past, Shaping the Future*, ed. Craig Howes and Jonathan Kamakawiwo'ole Osorio (Honolulu: University of

Hawai'i Press, 2010), 53–59. For "mixed" individuals, see John Chock Rosa, "'The Coming of the Neo-Hawaiian American Race': Nationalism and Metaphors of the Melting Pot in Popular Accounts of Mixed-Race Individuals," in *The Sum of Our Parts: Mixed Heritage Asian Americans*, ed. Teresa Kay Williams-Léon and Cynthia Nakashima (Philadelphia: Temple University Press, 2001), 49–56.

29. Helen G. Chapin, *Guide to Newspapers of Hawai'i, 1834–2000* (Honolulu: Hawaiian Historical Society, 2000). See also Helen Chapin, *Shaping History: The Role of Newspapers in Hawai'i* (Honolulu: University of Hawai'i Press, 1996).

30. "A New Portuguese Language Newspaper Initiative," https://www.hawaiianhistory. org/a-new-portuguese-language-newspaper-initiative/.

31. Ho'olaupa'i can be found at www.nupepa.org. The Hawaiian Electronic Library can be found at www.ulukau.org.

32. M. Puakea Nogelmeier, *Mai Pa'a i Ka Leo: Historical Voice in Hawaiian Primary Materials: Looking Forward and Listening Back* (Honolulu, Hawai'i: Bishop Museum Press, 2010).

33. David W. Forbes, ed., *Hawaiian National Bibliography, Volumes 1–4* (Honolulu: University of Hawai'i Press, 1998–2003).

34. *Restoring Bishop Museum's Hawaiian Hall: Ho'i Hou Ka Wena I Kaiwi'ula* (Honolulu: Bishop Museum Press, 2009). (This work has contributions by Samuel M. 'Ohukani'ōhi'a Gon III et al.)

35. The principal investigator for this project is the historian Lilikalā Kame'eleihiwa. Kame'eleihiwa's larger project is at http://www.avakonohiki.org/ava-team.html.

36. "University of Hawai'i Center for Oral History: Hui Panala'au," http://www.oralhistory. hawaii.edu/pages/historical/panalaau.html.

37. "Kamakakūokalani Center for Hawaiian Studies," http://manoa.hawaii.edu/hshk/ kamakakuokalani/.

FURTHER READING

Howe, K. R., ed. *Waka Moana: Voyages of the Ancestors: The Discovery and Settlement of the Pacific*. Honolulu: University of Hawai'i Press, 2007.

Howes, Craig, and Jonathan Kay Kamakawiwo'ole Osorio. *The Value of Hawai'i: Knowing the Past, Shaping the Future*. Honolulu: University of Hawai'i Press, 2010.

Kame'eleihiwa, Lilikalā. *Native Land and Foreign Desires: Pehea Lā E Pono Ai? How Shall We Live in Harmony?* Honolulu: Bishop Museum Press, 1992.

McGregor, Davianna Pōmaika'i. *Nā Kua 'āina: Living Hawaiian Culture*. Honolulu: University of Hawai'i Press, 2007.

Nogelmeier, M. Puakea. *Mai Pa'a i Ka Leo: Historical Voice in Hawaiian Primary Materials: Looking Forward and Listening Back*. Honolulu: Bishop Museum Press, 2010.

Okihiro, Gary. *Island World: A History of Hawai'i and the United States*. Berkeley: University of California Press, 2008.

Osorio, Jonathan Kay Kamakawiwo'ole. *Dismembering Lāhui: A History of the Hawaiian Nation to 1887*. Honolulu: University of Hawai'i Press, 2002.

Sai, David Keanu. *Ua Mau Ke Ea, Sovereignty Endures: An Overview of the Political and Legal History of the Hawaiian Islands*. Honolulu: Pū'ā Foundation, 2011.

Schmitt, Robert C. *Historical Statistics of Hawaii*. Honolulu: University of Hawai'i Press, 1977.

Silva, Noenoe K. *Aloha Betrayed: Native Hawaiian Resistance to American Colonialism.* Durham, NC: Duke University Press, 2004.

Spickard, Paul, Joanne L. Rondilla, and Debbie Hippolite Wright, eds. *Pacific Diaspora: Island Peoples in the United States and across the Pacific.* Honolulu: University of Hawai'i Press, 2002.

Stillman, Amy Ku'uleialoha. *Sacred Hula: The Hula 'Ala'apapa in Historical Perspective.* Honolulu: Bishop Museum Press, 1998.

Tengan, Ty P. Kāwika. *Native Men Remade: Gender and Nation in Contemporary Hawai'i.* Durham, NC: Duke University Press, 2008.

CHAPTER 5

SOUTHEAST ASIAN
AMERICANS

CHIA YOUYEE VANG

To understand Southeast Asian American history requires an examination of the complex histories of colonialism, imperialism, and war from the late nineteenth century through the end of the twentieth century. While some of the migration experiences of this varied community reflect the search for a better economic life elsewhere, others are entangled in homeland political transformations that have generated diverse movements across multiple national borders before their ultimate settlement in the United States. What Americans of Southeast Asian descent have in common is that their immigration history resulted from U.S. political and military activities aimed at building the United States as a global power. From Filipinos during the Spanish-American War in 1898 to Vietnamese from the U.S. Vietnam War, military interventions created opportunities for migration to the United States. This chapter examines the global intersections that resulted in the diverse migration experiences of Americans with origins in Southeast Asia, and it excavates the trends in knowledge production about people from this region.

DEFINING SOUTHEAST ASIAN AMERICANS

As the historian Sucheng Chan has noted, no satisfactory term exists to collectively refer to people living in America who are from Southeast Asia.[1] Thus, it is imperative to clarify what constitutes Southeast Asia and the ensuing category of Southeast Asian Americans. In geopolitical terms, the Asian subregion of Southeast Asia consists of ten countries that are organized under the Association of Southeast Asian Nations. Current member nations include Brunei, Cambodia, Indonesia, Lao People's Democratic Republic (Laos), Malaysia, Myanmar (Burma), the Philippines, Singapore, Thailand, and Vietnam. Of the 17.3 million Asian Americans, 37 percent have Southeast Asia origins. According to the U.S. Census Bureau data for 2010, more than half are Filipinos, and Vietnamese are the second largest group.[2] Because the Hmong living in the United States are those from Laos, when this population is added to the Laotian group those with origins in Laos constitute nearly half a million.[3]

MIGRATION AND WAR

The number of Americans with origins from Southeast Asian nations reflects the level of American involvement in particular locations as well as the liberalization of U.S. immigration policies during the mid-1960s. Any attempt to understand their histories requires an examination of the lasting effects of militaristic understandings and of these migrants' motivation to move. For groups like Filipinos, migration has occurred over the course of one hundred years while refugees from the Vietnam War era have arrived in significant numbers only in the last few decades. Although the initial goal of American involvement in specific countries was not to promote migration of the native population to the United States, unintended consequences have emerged in most cases. Once the migration process began, it became difficult to completely put an end to it, due to multiple factors, including the sponsorship of family members through regular U.S. immigration channels. It is evident that war instigated migration, but the underlying reasons for movement differed across the heterogeneous Southeast Asian groups. Thus, it is necessary to identify the different ways in which Americans of Southeast Asian descent have come to the United States.

Filipinos

The U.S. occupation of the Philippines following the Spanish-American War in 1901 marked the American entry into world affairs and set in motion U.S. interests in Southeast Asia. Under American rule, Filipino development mirrored many aspects of American society, including education and politics. Thousands of Filipino students attended American schools and universities. Many more would come to California and Hawai'i as agricultural workers during the 1920s. Their status was altered by the 1934 Tydings-McDuffie Act (Philippine Independence Act), which put the Philippines en route to self-rule and changed Filipinos to aliens instead of U.S. nationals. Providing the Philippines with an annual quota of only fifty individuals reduced Filipino migration, and thus their overall U.S. population, by 1940. Like other countries torn by the politics of World War II, Filipinos were also divided. Japanese invasion and occupation of the Philippines following the attack on Pearl Harbor generated tremendous tension between those who viewed the Japanese as liberators and those who joined forces with Americans against the Japanese. While the United States recognized Philippine independence in 1946, it maintained substantial military bases there. Consequently, Filipino women married to American servicemen accounted for a significant portion of migration in the ensuing decades. Additionally, the Education Exchange Act of 1946 facilitated the migration of nurses from the Philippines to the United States. Upon completion of their training, many nurses remained in the United States rather than returning to the Philippines.

In addition to this act, Americanized hospital training systems set in place during the colonial period contributed to the large influx of nurses.[4] Though small in comparison to European nations, the 1946 Luce-Celler Act doubled the annual Filipino quota. The spike in Filipino migration, however, came following the passage of the 1965 Immigration and Nationality Act (Hart-Celler Act). Changes in immigration policies enabled Filipino Americans to bring family members who were outside of the quota system. The need for medical workers in the United States allowed nurses, physicians, and medical technicians who were already trained with U.S. standards to emigrate in sizable numbers. Furthermore, the Health Professions Assistance Act of 1976 allowed American hospitals to recruit nurses directly from the Philippines. The phenomenon of military brides continued with the increase of U.S. military personnel based in the Philippines during the Vietnam War. In addition to military brides, many American men received "mail-order brides," where they arranged marriages by mail between men in the United States and women in the Philippines. All of these post-1965 policies and practices contributed to the dramatic increase in the Filipino American population.

Vietnam War Refugees

The areas known today as Cambodia, Laos, and Vietnam had endured foreign occupation and domination, so contact with intrusive foreigners was not new to the inhabitants. Cultural and political influences absorbed by the native populations from outsiders have been integral in their developments. The region was influenced by traditions and religion from China and India in immeasurable ways. While they are multiethnic countries with groups embracing a variety of religious beliefs, Buddhism is the dominant religion. Centuries of Chinese influence meant that the ethnic Chinese presence in these countries was common, most significantly in Vietnam. Although other European powers were present earlier, the French conquest of Cambodia, Laos, and Vietnam began in the mid- to late 1800s, resulting in the establishment of the concept of Indochina. Though varied in terms of investment, colonial rule influenced these societies in multiple ways. During French colonial rule, educated and ambitious Vietnamese were encouraged to settle in Cambodia and Laos where they dominated government posts and commerce. World War II changed France's great power status in Europe and contributed to its inability to maintain its colonies amid a tremendous decolonization fervor throughout much of the colonized world. Under the leadership of communists, Vietnamese nationalists rallied people throughout Indochina to rise up against the French. The Franco-Vietnam War (also known as the First Indochina War) would last for eight years (1946–1954).

The U.S. decision to support the French in 1950 marked direct American interests in Indochina. The French defeat by Vietnamese nationalists in 1954 ended France's colonial rule. When the French departed, the United States moved in to support anticommunist groups throughout Indochina. As the Cold War gained momentum, the presence of American military advisers during the mid-1950s resulted in a twenty-five-year commitment. Full-scale warfare compounded by internal political and military divide within the three countries led to tragic outcomes for all involved. Although U.S. military and political commitments were focused on Vietnam, the conflict spread to neighboring Cambodia and Laos. The nature of the American war in Vietnam coincided with domestic turmoil in the United States and, in Cambodia, Laos, and Vietnam, it led to the displacement of huge numbers of people and strained the fabric of Cambodian (Khmer), Laotian, and Vietnamese society. The 1973 cease-fire agreement let the United States disengage from the region, but it set in motion the biggest exodus to date of people in these countries toward the West. American military engagement in their nations would facilitate for the first time ever a large-scale arrival of people who had not previously migrated to the United States. For those who witnessed the end of the American war in Vietnam, images of people clinging to ships and narratives of near-death escapes are common. The exponential increase in the number of displaced persons from the region makes it difficult to erase these images. Although the war was responsible for the displacement of the native population, their response in its aftermath depended on the extent to which they were involved with American military and humanitarian efforts throughout the war.

While during the war many in neighboring Laos and Cambodia were pulled into the debacle due to their proximity, other Southeast Asian nations such as Hong Kong, Indonesia, Thailand, Indonesia, the Philippines, Malaysia, and Singapore were heavily affected by the arrival of thousands of refugees in the aftermath. As first asylum nations, refugee camps were set up to receive those fleeing war-torn Cambodia, Laos, and Vietnam. Because the duration of the camps and volume of arrivals varied, each first asylum host country responded differently. From the mid-1970s through early 2010, refugees from the American war represented nearly half of the 2.9 million people who entered the United States as refugees, of which the Vietnamese were the vast majority. Postwar political and economic conditions also played an important role in influencing people's decisions to emigrate. Although there are similarities across the former French colonies in terms of the retribution imposed by the new regime on those who collaborated with Americans during the war, significant differences existed within each nation that either promoted or prevented local populations from leaving their homes to seek refuge elsewhere.

Vietnam

The first phase of Vietnamese emigration in the days leading to the collapse of the South Vietnamese government on April 30, 1975, consisted primarily of people who possessed marketable skills for survival in America. Many were educated and spoke some English due to their previous work either with the South Vietnamese government or directly with Americans in Vietnam. During the couple of weeks following the air evacuation, thousands left on their own in small boats, ships, and aircraft. U.S. Navy and cargo ships operating near the coast of Vietnam rescued some at sea. The first group of Vietnamese refugees who left in April 1975 did not experience living in refugee camps in Southeast Asia. In fact, accommodation for this group was established at four military bases in the United States, including Camp Pendleton in California, Fort Chaffee in Arkansas, Eglin Air Force Base in Florida, and Indiantown Gap in Pennsylvania.[5] Some basic needs support was provided to the refugees as they waited to be sponsored out of the camps.

The second phase of Vietnamese emigration began in 1978 when many fled political repression and social and economic reforms. Some of the "boat people" who left Vietnam in the late 1970s were ethnic Chinese who feared persecution due to their ethnicity. Many perished at sea due to sea pirates and the lack of well-built boats. Because this second group of refugees came from poor backgrounds and many were not educated, they experienced greater adjustment challenges than those who fled in 1975. Those in the second phase would linger in refugee camps in the various first asylum countries, hoping for opportunities to settle in other countries. Several U.S. congressional actions would help to facilitate Vietnamese immigration. In 1980 Congress established the Orderly Departure and the Humanitarian Operation programs, which enabled those who had arrived earlier to sponsor family members. The programs enabled several categories of people to immigrate: those with family members living in the United States, former U.S. government or firm or organization employees, and reeducation center detainees. The 1988 Amerasian Homecoming Act was passed to allow children born in Vietnam of American fathers to immigrate. By 2009, more than 25,000 Amerasians and 60,000 to 70,000 of their relatives had immigrated through this act. Since 1975, about one million Vietnamese have immigrated to the United States.

Cambodia

Cambodian neutrality was stipulated in 1954 by the Geneva Accords, but the hot war across the border in Vietnam could not allow Cambodia to be uninvolved. Even though both the U.S. and Vietnamese communist forces used Cambodian territory, it was the 1970 invasion that made U.S. expansion of the war beyond Vietnam visible to Americans. Besides the bombing of Cambodian territory, American-backed forces were trained and provided with resources to battle the communist Khmer Rouge. As the situation in Vietnam deteriorated following the cease-fire agreement, internal struggles intensified. Consequently, American personnel were evacuated from Cambodia on April 12, 1975. Khmer Rouge forces took over the country soon thereafter and, in their attempts to create an agrarian utopia, murdered more than one million Cambodians during the next few years. In 1978, Vietnam invaded Cambodia, instigating the flight of many Cambodians to refugee camps in Thailand. More than 100,000 Cambodian refugees have immigrated to the United States. Following Vietnam's troop withdrawal from Cambodia in the late 1980s, the United Nations supervised the repatriation of more than 350,000 Cambodian refugees who had been living in Thai camps.

Laos

Like Cambodia, Laos's proximity forced it to be dragged into the conflict. Its own internal political struggles indeed mirror more closely what occurred in Vietnam. American military and humanitarian aid to the country commenced in the mid-1950s. The difference, however, is that U.S. combat troops were not sent to Laos. Instead, counterinsurgency efforts were used over the course of the Vietnam War. The U.S. Central Intelligence Agency (CIA) recruited local people, trained and supplied them with weapons, and paid them to be America's foot soldiers in Laos. These covert operations subsumed a great number of Laotians, and their involvement with American Special Forces had tragic consequences.

The most well known were Hmong ethnic minorities who lived in the northeastern part of the country bordering Vietnam, but other ethnic minorities such as Khammu and Mien fought alongside the Hmong. Because of the contentious political split within the ruling Lao elite, the majority ethnic Lao population also became American allies. In addition to CIA activities, the U.S. Agency for International Development provided humanitarian aid to the local population, which was an integral part of the military efforts because it responded to the needs of thousands of people internally displaced due to the fighting on Lao territory. In mid-May of 1975, a CIA evacuation of Hmong military leaders from their base in northeastern Laos airlifted about 2,500 people to Thailand. The exodus of people from Laos officially came to a halt in the mid-1990s as United Nations–sponsored camps closed. Of the more than 200,000 refugees from Laos who resettled in the United States, half are Hmong. In addition, 10,000 Mien and 4,000 Khammu fled the country following the communist takeover in 1975. Today, more than 260,000 people of Hmong ethnicity, 230,000 Lao, 60,000 Mien, and 8,000 Khammu, live in the United States.

Other Southeast Migrants and Refugees

The presence of Thai and Burmese Americans reflects the historical migration trajectory of Filipinos and refugees from Cambodia, Laos, and Vietnam, but at the same time, they depart slightly from the processes that occurred in these nations. The difference was Thailand's position in the region and Burma's contentious past resulting from British rule.

Thailand

As the only Southeast Asian nation not colonized by European powers, Thailand, which was known as Siam until 1938, established firm rapprochement with Western powers from the late 1800s to the early 1900s. The first Thais set foot in the United States in 1829. They settled in North Carolina and were officially naturalized in 1839. However, prior to the late 1960s, very few Thai migrated; less than 5,000 people of Thai ancestry lived in the United States.[6] Although some Thai sought employment in America following changes in U.S. immigration policies in the mid-1960s, like some Filipinos had, Thai migration occurred largely through spousal migration. In 1967, a treaty signed by the Thai government and the U.S. military allowed American soldiers to come to Bangkok for rest and recreation (R&R), which led to the explosion in Thailand's sex industry. Thousands of bars, nightclubs, and massage parlors were established to provide sex services to American servicemen. Not only did R&R help to fuel the Thai economy, but the American military presence in Thailand during the Vietnam War also resulted in many marriages between Thai women and American men who served in Vietnam. Consequently, more foreign-born Thai Americans living in the United States are women than men. In recent years the number of Thai who arrive in the United States as professionals or students has contributed to the diversity of Thai Americans. Their largest concentration is in the Los Angeles area. Thai American community leaders were successful in leading a campaign to designate a section of East Hollywood as "Thai Town."[7]

Burma/Myanmar

Refugees from Burma (known as Myanmar since the 1990s) are the newest Southeast group to settle in the United States in large numbers, but the migration of people from Burma began in the mid-1960s. Modern-day Burma was conquered by the British in 1824, and, like French Indochina, Burma consisted of many ethnic groups. The Burmans are the majority but ethnic groups such as the Karen make up a significant portion of the population. British colonial rule brought about some educational and economic changes for ethnic minorities who had previously been repressed by the majority. Missionaries were successful in converting many Karen to Christianity, and these converts eventually became separatist nationalists. Like other colonized people, World War II opened up new opportunities for Burmese nationalists who desired independence from Great Britain. Through political and military struggles, Burma gained independence from Great Britain in 1948, and until 1962 the country operated under democratic rule; however, a coup in 1962 placed the country under military rule. The one-party system led to further repression of ethnic minorities who desired separation. The antagonistic political situation resulted in decades-long military struggles between the military government and its ethnic minorities.[8]

Burmese nationalists' xenophobia led to the implementation of prejudicial policies. Those of Chinese descent who were primarily Buddhists became victims of socioeconomic oppression and race-based educational discrimination.[9] Such internal political instabilities and the promise of opportunities in the West encouraged the first wave of Burmese immigrants to the United States during the mid-1960s. Many Burmese of Chinese descent left following the 1967 anti-Chinese riot in Burma. Unlike ethnic Chinese, other ethnic minorities did not have the same means to leave. Ethnic armed groups have fought with the central government since then. A major offensive against the Karen National Union in 1984 caused the flight of about 10,000 refugees to Thailand. During the August 8, 1988, "Democracy Uprising," spearheaded by students and monks and known as "8 8 88," hundreds of thousands of people took part in protests throughout the country demanding democracy. Since 1984, an estimated 140,000 refugees have lived in nine refugee camps on the Thai-Burmese border. The conflicts have also generated the internal displacement of more than one million people in addition to the hundreds of thousands who have sought refuge in other neighboring countries, including Bangladesh, India, and Malaysia. Since the early 1990s, the United States has settled about 100,000 refugees from Burma, the majority of whom arrived between 2007 and 2010.[10]

The majority of Burmese Americans also settled in California, but there are sizable populations in Indiana, New York, Texas, Arizona, and Minnesota. Although it is too early to tell how the political climate in Burma will evolve, there are signs of change. Former U.S. Secretary of State Hillary Clinton's visit to Burma in December 2011 was the first visit to the country by an American diplomat in fifty years. Some Americans believe that this marks the beginning of efforts to improve relations between the two countries, which they hope will lead to greater social and political change in Burma, though this optimism is met with defiance by some in the exiled communities and antigovernment groups inside Burma. Aspiration for self-determination of ethnic minority groups such as the Karen continues to be full of uncompromising rhetoric, in particular from those living outside of Burma. This challenge to the government and the misery generated by sustained low-level conflict continue to get in the way of a peaceful solution.

The Politics of Forced Migration

The displacement of such an intense volume of people brings into question the responses by actors such as the United States, whose intervention often contributed to their plight in the first place. The extent to which states offer temporary and permanent refuge depends on a number of critical factors. The anthropologist Liisa Malkki argues that the factors influencing human displacement are not only complex, but also encompass many levels. She writes, "Nationalism and racism, xenophobia and immigration policies, state practices of violence and war, censorship and silencing, human rights and challenges to state sovereignty, 'development' discourse and humanitarian interventions, citizenship and cultural or religious identities, travel and diaspora, and memory and historicity are just some of the issues and practices that generate the inescapably relevant context of human displacement today."[11] Upon displacement, the refugee becomes a problem to be solved by state actors. Freedom of movement varied across refugee camps and first asylum countries. Regardless of where they first sought refuge, however, the camp experience of most Southeast Asian refugees was one of isolation because refugee camps were usually located in areas away from the local population.

The controversial and unpopular Vietnam War generated social, economic, and political devastation; thus, most Americans were pleased to see it come to an end in the early 1970s. Instead of cutting all ties to the region, the United States was confronted with an increasing flow of people who sought refuge as a result of both their entanglement with American efforts during the war and the ensuing economic and political repressions implemented by the victorious regime. Instabilities on all fronts within American society meant that the refugees confronted a dichotomous response from U.S. citizens. Because many Americans also faced issues of joblessness and diminishing resources during the late 1970s and 1980s, they were openly antagonistic toward the refugees. This hostility was indeed a reflection of the legacy of discrimination against newcomers outside of Western Europe. Interestingly, however, the racial and economic-based resentment was accompanied by unprecedented humanitarian aid provided by thousands of individuals and groups. American voluntary organizations throughout the country identified sponsors for refugee families, allowing them to leave the uncertain refugee-camp life. Dispersal policies implemented at the federal level resulted in refugees being distributed across the country. With the exception of some 15,000 Vietnamese foreign exchange students on temporary visas or wives of U.S. soldiers who had served in Vietnam, the refugees had no established community in the United States. This lack of a community to receive them has not prevented the refugees from establishing thriving communities during the last few decades.

Southeast Asian Americans' integration into U.S. society has indeed varied, depending largely on their personal backgrounds before arriving in America. Some came with professional experiences that were transferable or they had education skills to obtain necessary training to enter the U.S. job market; however, the majority of refugees arrived with little or no formal education. Many either took low-paying jobs to make ends meet or relied on public resources for survival. Due to social and political climate changes in the United States by the time Southeast Asian refugees arrived, those who wanted to better their socioeconomic conditions to enter a variety of spaces that were not previously available to people of color were able to do so.

The majority of these former refugees and their American-born children reside in states such as California, New York, and Texas that have large immigrant and/or Asian American populations. Refugee resettlement policies and practices of dispersing refugees throughout the country resulted in Southeast Asian Americans building new ethnic communities in areas that have not traditionally had large numbers of people of Asian descent. In states with large Asian American populations, they have not stood out, but in states with very small numbers, they have changed the demographic landscapes of those locations. For example, in Minnesota and Wisconsin, both of whom have about 12 percent people of color, Hmong Americans are the largest Asian groups. Furthermore, by 2010 Vietnamese Americans became the fourth largest Asian community in the United States.[12]

Southeast Asian refugees have built permanent communities in numerous locations, such as the Vietnamese in Westminster, California; Houston, Texas; and New Orleans, Louisiana. Also there were the Cambodians in Long Beach, California, and Lowell, Massachusetts; the Hmong in Fresno, California, and St. Paul/Minneapolis, Minnesota; and the Laotians in San Francisco, California. They start small businesses that often cater to their respective ethnic communities. Self-help community-based organizations are established to facilitate the transition to U.S. society. Southeast Asian American–elected officials include the Hmong American Choua Lee, who was elected to the Saint Paul Public Schools in 1991; the Vietnamese American Tony Lam, elected to

Westminster City Council in 1992; the Hmong American Mee Moua, who won a special election to the Minnesota Senate in 2001; and the Vietnamese American Anh "Joseph" Cao, who was elected to the U.S. House of Representatives in 2008. Their contributions to American society during the short time that they have been in the country are notable in the areas of education, business, and civic engagement. Consequently, the types of scholarship about these groups have begun to shift to better reflect their dynamic communities.

Contrary to many success stories of individuals beating the odds to succeed in education and in various sectors, Southeast Asian refugees continue to face challenges with youth and adults who have little or no formal education to enter the labor force. This segment of the population often lives under dire conditions. As a group, Hmong Americans remain the most impoverished Asian Americans. Youth from all of the Southeast Asian American groups who engage in crime-related activities have received much attention by law enforcement. Vietnamese organized crimes and Hmong, Lao, and Cambodian gangsters and delinquents are the subjects of many scholarly studies. Rather than embracing white middle-class American values, they have fallen prey to stereotypes of problem minorities who experienced downward assimilation into the underclass.[13]

State of the Field

Despite the diversity of ethnic groups from Southeast Asian countries, since the mid- to late 1970s the category "Southeast Asians" has primarily referred to post–Vietnam War refugees from Cambodia, Laos, and Vietnam. In fact, the term became synonymous with "Southeast Asian refugees," "Vietnam War refugees," or "Indochinese refugees." Lumping these diverse ethnic groups into undifferentiated categories neglects the diversity previously discussed. Consequently, the burden has remained with individuals and groups to distinguish their distinct cultures and histories to others in the United States who cannot tell them apart. Furthermore, many scholarly studies have focused on certain ethnic groups while very little is known about others.

The vast majority of scholarly studies about Southeast Asian Americans centers on refugee resettlement and issues of acculturation and adaptation. More research has been conducted on Vietnamese and Hmong refugees than the other groups. The lowland Lao have received the least attention. More recently, refugees from Burma have become subjects of great interest to scholars. Interestingly, however, they are often referred to as Burmese refugees or Karen refugees and not automatically funneled into the Southeast Asian refugee category.

Early research conducted by outsiders with support from bilingual ethnic community leaders highlighted the difficulties of adjusting to life in America. Such studies focus primarily on those who are known to community leaders in ethnic organizations and who are most in need. Studies funded by the federal Office of Refugee Resettlement primarily measured the extent to which the refugees were able to obtain suitable employment that would lead to self-sufficiency. Those refugees who relied on community-based orga-nizations for support tended to consist of the most vulnerable. Issues most commonly examined in scholarly and community-based studies include mental health, educa-tion, crime-related incidents, culture, and poverty. The adjustment experiences of those who do not become clients of such social service agencies were rarely documented. Consequently, early studies on Southeast Asian refugees did not fully capture the broad spectrum of integration into American society.

The trend in scholarship about Vietnamese Americans outlined by Yen Le Espiritu somewhat reflects studies about other Southeast Asian refugees. Initial studies charac-terized them as helpless and demoralized refugees who were victims of the Vietnam War in need of care to be provided by Americans. Researchers often portrayed Vietnamese refugees as passive objects to be rescued, focusing on a moral responsibility of the West to lend a helping hand. After arrival, studies of adaptation focused on the Vietnamese as problems to be solved at the same time that they began to highlight the successful eco-nomic adaptation of some.[14] The bulk of the early research studies are based on either sample surveys or ethnographic investigations, where the former constitute biased sam-ples and the latter case studies.[15] These studies are generally conducted with one of two purposes: a "disinterested stance" of "objective" academicians to produce knowledge for its own sake, or an advocacy stance of community spokespersons to demand actions. The latter is aimed at program implementation and set ideological or moral principles for public policy, which includes policy research and progress reports to funding orga-nizations.[16] Again, the challenge with these biased studies is that they focus on vulner-able populations that are known to institutions; thus the voices and experiences of those not known to the agencies are left out, resulting in the inability to generalize findings. As Malkki has argued, "Although many refugees have survived violence and loss that are literally beyond the imagination of most people, we mustn't assume that refugee status in and of itself constitutes a recognizable, generalizable psychological condition."[17]

Ethnic-specific social science studies clearly dominate the field, with some trying to compare the groups. Although some researchers use the term "Southeast Asian," they do not include all groups; thus, it is not always possible to tell who exactly is the subject of some studies. The shared experiences of war and displacement have enabled schol-ars to analyze their sense of community and livelihood within particular U.S. locations. Elders whose lives were often turned upside-down as a result of migration encounter isolation and loss of social status, regardless of ethnicity.[18] Furthermore, changes in fam-ily relationships require new approaches for women to negotiate their roles as mothers and wives amid challenging and sometimes dysfunctional situations.[19]

A number of personal narratives by former refugees have emerged to reveal wounds during and after the Vietnam War. A few that have frequently become required reading in literature and Asian American studies courses include Le Ly Hayslip's 1990 memoir, *When Heaven and Earth Changed Places: A Vietnamese Woman's Journey from War to Peace*, and Andrew X. Pham's *Catfish and Mandala: A Two-Wheeled Voyage through the Landscape and Memory of Vietnam* (1999).[20] While Hayslip provided an account of severe personal experiences that made survival difficult to imagine, Pham offers a compelling narrative of identity crisis and immigrant success. Published after U.S.-Vietnam relations had improved, Pham's biography of life during and after the war, growing up in the United States, and returning to his country of origin explores the tension that refugees from war-torn nations often encounter. Kao Kalia Yang's *The Latehomecomer: A Hmong Family Memoir* (2008) traces her family's escape from Laos and their experiences growing up in the Midwest while trying to hold on to Hmong culture and its traditions.[21]

NEW TRAJECTORIES

While social science research on adjustment and adaptation continues to be conducted, new works of scholarship during the last decade on Southeast Asian Americans have begun to explore the diversity within the groups. In particular, they critique Southeast Asians' transformations from refugees to citizens. Though refugees do find themselves in situations where they become victims to be rescued by states and the international humanitarian regime, the refugee status enabled them to exercise agency.[22] This agency has transferred from the immigrant generation to their children, who are transforming themselves into new Asian Americans.[23] They are reproducing ethnic culture and recreating new identities in diasporic locations.

Southeast Asian American scholars have actively contributed to the production of knowledge about their communities. Two *Amerasia Journal* volumes in 2003 and 2005 on Vietnamese Americans changed the landscape of refugee studies in general and Vietnamese American studies in particular.[24] The articles moved beyond describing Vietnamese identity and cultural production to critical analyses of the various dimensions of Vietnamese American life. While publication of research in mainstream scholarly journals is more common, several peer-reviewed, interdisciplinary academic journals have been established to focus on specific ethnic issues. They include the *Journal of Vietnamese Studies, Hmong Studies Journal*, and *Journal of Lao Studies*. Interestingly, however, the *Journal of Southeast Asian American Education and Advancement* was established to provide a publishing venue for Southeast Asian American studies scholars. As a peer-reviewed journal, it is open to all scholars; however, the journal does emphasize the importance and need for more research conducted by native Southeast Asian American researchers. Since 2006, when its first volume appeared, both Southeast Asian American and non–Southeast Asian American scholars have contributed to the journal.

Recent works on diaspora, identity, and citizenship have emerged to capture the dynamic communities that the former refugees have created. These works are placed within the Asian American context and they not only critique the factors in local contexts that either maintain continuity or facilitate changes, but also examine the transnational practices that influence Southeast Asian Americans. Changing relations with their homelands in Southeast Asia as well as their interactions with other co-ethnics in various places in the West have resulted in new frameworks to examine the flow of people and ideas across national borders.[25]

CHALLENGES AND OPPORTUNITIES

The American conquest and occupation of the Philippines set in motion the migration of people from Southeast Asia to the United States more than one hundred years ago. Military activities during the Cold War in addition to the liberalization of U.S. immigration policies during the mid-1960s enabled the entry of many different groups from the region. The American war in Vietnam generated the most diverse flow of people from Southeast Asia. In addition to the more than one million refugees from Cambodia, Laos, and Vietnam, the American military personnel presence in the Philippines and Thailand made possible the migration of thousands of women married to U.S. servicemen who had been stationed in those two countries. The emigration of children born to Vietnamese women by American servicemen and of refugees propagated by sustained internal political and military struggles in Burma continues to broaden what constitutes Southeast Asian American history.

While those who became refugees before settling in the United States often experienced loss and trauma, their life experiences reveal that, like immigrants, they do eventually transition to create meaningful communities. The refugees may begin their lives working in janitorial services or as factory workers, but their children often adapt well and enter professions such as engineering and medicine. Those who arrive as professionals and/or spouses of American citizens may not encounter the same problems as refugees, but they often face similar difficulties as racial minorities. The challenge for scholars and other researchers interested in studying Southeast Asian Americans is to continue to explain the experiences of diverse groups that have been subsumed under an ambiguous category. Furthermore, the migration experiences of Southeast Asians have been products of war, both directly and indirectly. With the exception of Filipino Americans, the histories of more recent arrivals have shaped their place in Asian America. Researchers who study these groups often find themselves not able to engage in conversations about such issues as race because their communities arrived in significant numbers in the post–civil rights era. At the beginning of the twenty-first century, Asian American scholars can embrace the diverse histories of those from Southeast Asia as an integral part of the Asian American experience rather than place them on the margins. Southeast Asian Americans should also actively engage in larger conversations about Asian America in addition to strengthening knowledge production about individual ethnic groups. Such incorporation of Southeast American history will enhance the larger body of knowledge about Americans of Asian origin.

NOTES

1. Sucheng Chan, *Survivors: Cambodian Refugees in the United States* (Urbana: University of Illinois Press, 2004), xxiii.

2. Asian American Center for Advancing Justice, *A Community of Contrasts: Asian Americans in the United States, 2011,* www.aajc.advancingjustice.org. Note that Cambodians (276,000) are the third largest single ethnic group and Malaysians (26,000) are the smallest.

3. Groups such as Iu Mien, Tai Dam, and Cham are not distinguished by the Census due to their small numbers.

4. Catherine Ceniza Choy, *Empire of Care: Nursing and Migration in Filipino American History* (Durham, NC: Duke University Press, 2003).

5. Gail Paradise Kelly, *From Vietnam to America: A Chronicle of Vietnamese Immigration to the United States* (Boulder, CO: Westview, 1977).

6. Todd LeRoy Perreira, "The Gender of Practice: Some Findings among Thai Buddhist Women in Northern California," in *Emerging Voices: Experiences of Underrepresented Asian Americans,* ed. Huping Ling (New Brunswick, NJ: Rutgers University Press, 2008), 160–182.

7. Chanchanit Martorell and Beatrice "Tippe" Morlan, *Thais in Los Angeles* (Charleston, SC: Arcadia, 2011).

8. Ashley South, "Karen Nationalist Communities: The 'Problem' of Diversity," *Contemporary Southeast Asia* 29, no. 1 (2007): 55–76.

9. Joseph Cheah, "The Function of Ethnicity in the Adaptation of Burmese Religious Practices," in *Emerging Voices: Experiences of Underrepresented Asian Americans,* ed. Huping Ling (New Brunswick, NJ: Rutgers University Press, 2008), 199–217.

10. Office of Refugee Resettlement, U.S. Department of Health and Human Services, http://www.acf.hhs.gov/programs/orr/data/refugee_arrival_data.htm.

11. Liisa H. Malkki, "Refugees and Exile: From 'Refugee Studies' to the National Order of Things," *Annual Review of Anthropology* 24 (1995): 495–523.

12. Asian American Center for Advancing Justice, *Community of Contrasts,* 9.

13. See Stacey Lee, "More Than 'Model Minority' or 'Delinquents': A Look at Hmong American High School Students," *Harvard Educational Review* 71, no. 3 (2001): 505–528; Ruben G. Rumbaut and Kenji Ima, *The Adaptation of Southeast Asian Refugee Youth: A Comparative Study. Final Report to the Office of Resettlement* (San Diego: San Diego State University, 1988); Mary Bulcholtz, "Styles and Stereotypes: The Linguistic Negotiation of Identity among Laotian American Youth," *Pragmatics* 14, no. 2/3 (2004): 127–148.

14. Ye Le Espiritu, "'We Don't Sleep around Like White Girls Do': Family, Culture, and Gender in Filipina American Lives," *Signs* 26, no. 2 (2001): 415–440.

15. Elena S. H. Yu and William T. Liu, "Methodological Problems and Policy Implications in Vietnamese Refugee Research," *International Migration Review* 20, no. 2 (1986): 483–501.

16. Ibid., 496–497.

17. Malkki, "Refugees and Exile," 510.

18. See Dan F. Detzner, *Elder Voices: Southeast Asian Families in the United States* (Walnut Creek, CA: AltaMira, 2004); Jeremy Hein, *Ethnic Origins: The Adaptation of Cambodian and Hmong Refugees in Four American Cities* (New York: Russell Sage Foundation, 2006).

19. Tuyet-Lan Pho and Anne Mulvey, "Southeast Asian Women in Lowell: Family Relations, Gender Roles, and Community Concerns," in *Contemporary Asian America: A Multidisciplinary Reader,* ed. Min Zhou and J. V. Gatewood (New York: New York University Press, 2007), 181–205.

20. Le Ly Hayslip, *When Heaven and Earth Changed Places: A Vietnamese Woman's Journey from War to Peace* (New York: Plume, 1990); Andrew X. Pham, *Catfish and Mandala: A Two-Wheeled Voyage through the Landscape and Memory of Vietnam* (New York: Farrar, Straus, and Giroux, 1999).

21. Kao Kalia Yang, *The Latehomecomer: A Hmong Family Memoir* (Minneapolis, MN: Coffee House, 2008).

22. Aihwa Ong, *Buddha Is Hiding: Refugees, Citizenship, the New America* (Berkeley: University of California Press, 2003).

23. Wanni W. Anderson, "Between Necessity and Choice: Rhode Island Lao American Women," in *Displacements and Diaspora: Asians in the Americas*, ed. Wanni W. Anderson and Robert G. Lee (New Brunswick, NJ: Rutgers University Press, 2005), 194–226.

24. Linda Trinh Vo, "Vietnamese Americans: Diaspora and Dimensions," *Amerasia Journal* 29, no. 1 (2003): ix–xviii; Yen Le Espiritu and Thu-Huong Nguyen-Vo, eds., "30 Years AfterWARD: Vietnamese Americans and U.S. Empire," *Amerasia Journal* 31, no. 2 (2005).

25. See Karin Aguilar-San Juan, *Little Saigons: Staying Vietnamese in America* (Minneapolis: University of Minnesota Press, 2009); Chia Youyee Vang, *Hmong America: Reconstructing Community in Diaspora* (Urbana: University of Illinois Press, 2010).

FURTHER READING

Aguilar-San Juan, Karin. *Little Saigons: Staying Vietnamese in America*. Minneapolis: University of Minnesota Press, 2009.

Anderson, Wanni W. "Between Necessity and Choice: Rhode Island Lao American Women." In *Displacements and Diaspora: Asians in the Americas*, edited by Wanni W. Anderson and Robert G. Lee, 194–226. New Brunswick, NJ: Rutgers University Press, 2005.

Chan, Sucheng. *Survivors: Cambodian Refugees in the United States*. Urbana: University of Illinois Press, 2004.

Cheah, Joseph. "The Function of Ethnicity in the Adaptation of Burmese Religious Practices." In *Emerging Voices: Experiences of Underrepresented Asian Americans*, edited by Huping Ling, 199–217. New Brunswick, NJ: Rutgers University Press, 2008.

Choy, Catherine Ceniza. *Empire of Care: Nursing and Migration in Filipino American History*. Durham, NC: Duke University Press, 2003.

Detzner, Dan F. *Elder Voices: Southeast Asian Families in the United States*. Walnut Creek, CA: AltaMira, 2004.

Hayslip, Le Ly. *When Heaven and Earth Changed Places: A Vietnamese Woman's Journey from War to Peace*. New York: Plume, 1990.

Hein, Jeremy. *Ethnic Origins: The Adaptation of Cambodian and Hmong Refugees in Four American Cities*. New York: Russell Sage Foundation, 2006.

Kelly, Gail Paradise. *From Vietnam to America: A Chronicle of Vietnamese Immigration to the United States*. Boulder, CO: Westview, 1977.

Lee, Stacey. "More Than 'Model Minority' or 'Delinquents': A Look at Hmong American High School Students." *Harvard Educational Review* 71, no. 3 (2001): 505–528.

Malkki, Liisa H. "Refugees and Exile: From 'Refugee Studies' to the National Order of Things." *Annual Review of Anthropology* 24 (1995): 495–523.

Martorell, Chanchanit, and Beatrice "Tippe" Morlan. *Thais in Los Angeles*. Charleston, SC: Arcadia, 2011.

Ong, Aihwa. *Buddha Is Hiding: Refugees, Citizenship, the New America.* Berkeley: University of California Press, 2003.

Perreira, Todd LeRoy. "The Gender of Practice: Some Findings among Thai Buddhist Women in Northern California." In *Emerging Voices: Experiences of Underrepresented Asian Americans,* edited by Huping Ling, 160–182. New Brunswick, NJ: Rutgers University Press, 2008.

Pham, Andrew X. *Catfish and Mandala: A Two-Wheeled Voyage through the Landscape and Memory of Vietnam.* New York: Farrar, Straus, and Giroux, 1999.

Pho, Tuyet-Lan, and Anne Mulvey. "Southeast Asian Women in Lowell: Family Relations, Gender Roles, and Community Concerns." In *Contemporary Asian America: A Multidisciplinary Reader,* edited by Min Zhou and J. V. Gatewood, 181–205. New York: New York University Press, 2007.

Rumbaut, Ruben G., and Kenji Ima. *The Adaptation of Southeast Asian Refugee Youth: A Comparative Study. Final Report to the Office of Resettlement.* San Diego: San Diego State University, 1988.

South, Ashley. "Karen Nationalist Communities: The 'Problem' of Diversity." *Contemporary Southeast Asia* 29, no. 1 (2007): 55–76.

Vang, Chia Youyee. *Hmong America: Reconstructing Community in Diaspora.* Urbana: University of Illinois Press, 2010.

Yang, Kao Kalia. *The Latehomecomer: A Hmong Family Memoir.* Minneapolis, MN: Coffee House, 2008.

Yu, Elena S. H., and William T. Liu. "Methodological Problems and Policy Implications in Vietnamese Refugee Research." *International Migration Review* 20, no. 2 (1986): 483–501.

CHAPTER 6

··

EAST ASIAN IMMIGRANTS

··

K. SCOTT WONG

EAST ASIAN immigrants will be considered those who came, and continue to come, to the United States from China, Japan, and Korea. For the most part, the immigrant streams from these three countries have been treated separately, but it is useful as well to view them together—not as a singular unit, but as three countries that have been in a close relationship with each other. Emigration trends from each country have been influenced by the events and policies of the others. The reasons that motivated the emigration of Chinese, Japanese, and Koreans to the United States from the mid- to late nineteenth century to the present reflect the international and transnational causes of emigration and immigration. This perspective goes beyond the traditional "push-pull" paradigm of immigration history to consider the reasons and impact of the movement of peoples across borders, cultures, and nation-states in ways that may offer us new ways to consider the presence of East Asian immigrants in the Americas. As immigration historians look to more nuanced and complex reasons for emigration from one country to another, they have employed transnational studies, the intersections of race and empire, and the impact of imperialism to provide a more comprehensive understanding of the immigration process. Having said this, however, I think it is important to note that these new approaches to immigration history do not necessarily imply a complete rejection of the traditional "push-pull" model, but simply demand that more factors be simultaneously taken into account so that we can better understand that aspiring immigrants were frequently "pushed and pulled" in a number of directions and for a wider confluence of reasons than we have previously taken into account.

As in other areas of immigration studies, we know that Asian emigrants left their homelands for a variety of reasons, but the overwhelming factor was an economic one. The sources of economic disruption in nineteenth-century China, Japan, and Korea may have differed, but the search for jobs and possible economic security was certainly the overriding cause for so many Asians to leave their homes and venture to the United States and its territories. In fact, well before Hawai'i became an official American territory, it became a site where race, empire, labor, and global capitalism came together to change the trajectory of Asian labor migration as well as America's relationship to East

Asia and the Pacific Islands. In addition, Hawai'i was a site in which Asian and Pacific cultures would be transformed through American imperialism and Christian missionaries, a process that would be repeated in various Asian countries and Asian American communities in the United States. Although American ships had long plied the Pacific trade routes, the gradual usurpation of power in Hawai'i from the 1840s through the overthrow of the Hawaiian monarchy by American sugarcane plantation owners, with the support of political and military powers in 1893, marked the beginning of American imperialism in that area, which set the conditions for America's emergence as a world power (formal annexation would take place in 1898). Hawai'i was "caught in the cross-currents of global mercantile trade involving Europe, the United States, and China and at the center of the burgeoning Pacific whale fishery" and it would be these competing economic, legal, and ideological forces that would eventually lead to the American domination of Hawai'i, including the use of the U.S. legal system to transform the socioeconomic, political, and religious cultures of the islands. As Sally Engle Merry points out, "It was Massachusetts prototypes that formed the basis of Hawaiian criminal law, for example, because these law books happened to be in Honolulu. But it was global trade networks that brought the ships that carried the books from New England to Hawai'i."[1]

The most obvious transformation that took place in Hawai'i, however, was the creation of a plantation economy based on sugarcane production and, later, on the growing and export of pineapples. And it was in the microcosm of the plantations that one could see the politics of Western imperialism, global capitalism, internal Asian politics, and labor migration play out. As a number of historians have documented, once American sugarcane and missionary interests increasingly took control of Hawaiian lands and sovereignty, they began recruiting labor from a variety of places, but most prominently from Asia, including China, Japan, and Korea. Because the Chinese had had a presence in Hawai'i well before American sugar concerns established themselves on the islands, and because the Chinese were already experienced in sugar production, they were the first to be recruited for plantation work. In a pattern that would be repeated later in other locations, once the Chinese became a sizable portion of the workforce, some groups found fault with them and they were considered a threat to labor stability. This then led the planters to turn to the Japanese as labor recruits to offset the power of the Chinese. As the Chinese population began to decline due to their leaving the sugar industry or because of the restrictions of the Chinese Exclusion Act, more Japanese emigrants began to arrive in Hawai'i. One important difference between Chinese and Japanese immigration to Hawai'i was the emigrants' relationship to the governments of their homelands.

The Chinese government had long considered emigrants to be on their own once they left China. Believing that China was the center of the civilized world, the Chinese government offered emigrants little help in foreign countries. This attitude often left the Chinese with little protection while abroad, falling victim to corruption on the part of their own less scrupulous countrymen, anti-Chinese violence, and ever-increasing anti-Chinese legislation. Thus, they had little recourse when they encountered such obstacles abroad. In many ways, their weakness abroad was reflective of how the Chinese responded to the Western presence in China. The Chinese imperial court and the scholar-official class that dominated the ruling elite on all levels of the Chinese bureaucracy were steeped in a Sinocentric worldview that saw little need to deal with the West on a basis of equality. Their sense of moral and cultural superiority, coupled with a corrupt and weak central government, the Chinese paid little attention to their countrymen who ventured abroad. In 1842, when China lost to the British in the first Opium War, one of the most important concessions the Chinese had to make was the opening of more ports to Western trade, including with the United States. The increasing presence of American ships in Chinese harbors cannot be underestimated in the importance of later Chinese emigration to the Americas. The Japanese, on the other hand, responded to the presence of the West in Japan in a very different manner. When Matthew Perry sailed into Edo Bay in 1853 and 1854, the Japanese, although initially dismissive of the foreign presence, eventually embarked on a program of modernizing reforms culminating in the Meiji Restoration in 1868. When the Japanese observed the Western "carving of the melon" in China, they vowed that they would not be put in the same position. Along with various reforms and modernizing efforts, the Japanese instituted ways in which to protect their overseas emigrants or to at least curtail some of the problems that the Chinese encountered. While the Chinese were pretty much left to their own devices to survive abuses abroad, the Japanese government tried to regulate the conditions under which Japanese emigrants traveled abroad, especially to Hawai'i, where the labor recruiters worked closely with the Japanese authorities.

Once China and Japan were "opened" by the West, the United States began making inroads in Korea, also recruiting laborers to Hawai'i to work on the sugarcane plantations with the additional enticement of advertising Hawai'i as a place where Koreans could freely practice Christianity. This is an essential point in understanding Korean immigration to the United States. Christianity played a role in Korean emigration in ways that were not relevant to Chinese or Japanese immigrants. As David Yoo points out in his *Contentious Spirits*, "Protestant Christianity provides the primary lens to examine the broader sweep of Korean America during this era. . . . Religion provides the most important entry point to Korean American history because it attended to the full range of human experience marked by complexity and contention. Churches provided an institutional structure for community and everyday life, while the sensibilities of Christianity touched upon the moral and the sacred."[2] Thus the American push into Asia and the Pacific in search of global markets and labor, and, for some, the desire to convert Asians to Christianity, had a direct impact on the emigration patterns of Chinese, Japanese, and Korean laborers, and, later, merchants and those with other occupations. However, Japanese imperialism in Korea, which led to the outright annexation of Korea by Japan, led to a quick decline of Korean emigration to Hawai'i and the American mainland as the Japanese sought to keep Korean laborers in Korea for two primary reasons: to ensure a full workforce in Korea and to lessen any competition with Japanese laborers abroad. Therefore, the policies and practices of imperialism and expansionism can be seen as active determinants in the flow of Asian labor to America and American territories by both governments on both sides of the Pacific Ocean.

While Hawai'i was the first site of large-scale Asian labor recruitment and emigration, the mainland of the United States was where one of the next important eras of Asian American history took place: the growth of the anti-Asian movement and the eventual exclusion of Asian immigrants. While there were cultural reasons for the anti-Asian movement, a brand of racism rooted in Orientalism and white supremacy, much of the antipathy that whites held toward Asian immigrants was focused on anxieties about the nature of Asian labor and the threat it posed to American culture and civilization. Here, too, these three groups can be seen in relation to each other as well as their shared exclusion from the United States. The historical development of the anti-Asian movement and the steady addition of exclusion legislation is well documented, so there is no need to retrace those histories in great detail here, but it is significant to remember that the manner in which these laws were passed and how they were framed reflected how the United States viewed China, Japan, and Korea. While most attention has been given to the Chinese Exclusion Act of 1882, the Page Law of 1875 set an important precedent that would have an important impact on aspects of future exclusion legislation. The Page Law targeted two distinct groups: Asian contract laborers and Chinese women who were thought to be or who might become prostitutes. This law set the stage for excluding Chinese (and later all aspiring Asian immigrants) based on their class, gender, and supposed sexual predilections. The subsequent Chinese Exclusion Act prohibited the immigration of Chinese laborers and their wives for a period of ten years and it codified that Chinese could not become American citizens. The act, however, did not exclude all Chinese. It allowed for the immigration of merchants and their families, students, diplomats, clergy, and tourists. However, these so-called exempt classes were often subjected to very harsh and humiliating interrogations and treatment while attempting to enter the country. Much of this was done without fear of Chinese reprisal because of the weakness of the Chinese government. The Japanese, on the other hand, had won the respect of the American government when Japan defeated Russia in the Russo-Japanese War in 1905. Although Japanese immigrants had inherited the anti-Asian sentiments directed toward the Chinese, the American authorities chose not to ban Japanese labor immigration outright as they had the Chinese but instead worked with the Japanese government to craft the Gentlemen's Agreement in 1907 in which the Japanese would agree to stop issuing passports to laborers wanting to go to the United States. The Americans did, however, allow Japanese women to join their husbands in the United States, a right that was denied to Chinese women until after World War II.

There was less of a need to develop an anti-Korean strategy because Japanese colonialism had limited Korean emigration, and whatever American laws were used to exclude the Japanese applied to Koreans as well since the United States had recognized Japanese sovereignty over Korea. This angered Koreans in America perhaps more than any hostile treatment they might have received at the hands of Americans. A prime example of this took place in Hemet, California, in 1913. A small number of Korean farmworkers were driven out of the town, and the Southern California branch of the Japanese Association reported it to the Japanese consulate in San Francisco, which forwarded the news to the Japanese embassy in Washington, DC. The Japanese ambassador soon filed a protest with the U.S. State Department. The Koreans in America, however, were angered by the actions of the Japanese. The president of the Korean National Association, Reverend David Lee, sent a letter to Secretary of State William Jennings Bryan, stating, "We, the Koreans in America, are not Japanese subjects, . . . we will never submit to her as long as the sun remains in the heavens. The intervention of the Japanese Consulate-General in Korean matters is illegal, so I have the honor of requesting you to discontinue the discussion of this case with the Japanese government representatives. . . . We will settle it without Japanese interference." Bryan reported to the press that the investigation was discontinued and that the United States would, in the future, deal directly with the Korean National Association in relation to all manners involving Koreans in the United States.[3] As a result of Japanese colonialism in Korea, Hawai'i and the American mainland became important sites for the development of Korean nationalism. Thus the development of Korean nationalism operated "within a triangulated web of geopolitical relations involving the interests of a colonized Korea, imperialist Japan, and exclusionist United States."[4] And by the 1930s, when Japanese aggression in China took the lives of hundreds of thousands of Chinese, and Japanese troops occupied Chinese territory, activities in both Hawai'i and the mainland would also foster Chinese nationalism.

If there was any "favorable" treatment afforded to Japanese immigrants, compared to that of Chinese and Koreans in America, that came to an end in 1922 with the U.S. Supreme Court decision in *Ozawa v. U.S.* In this landmark case, a Japanese national was denied the right of becoming a naturalized American citizen because he was a member of the "yellow race." Previously, only Chinese had been explicitly denied citizenship on the federal level, but this case now placed Japanese in the same racial category as Chinese. In the following year South Asians would also be declared ineligible for citizenship, and the Immigration Act of 1924 prohibited the immigration of all people who were ineligible for citizenship, thus effectively shutting down the immigration of all Asians to the United States.

The major turning point in Asian American history was World War II. The international conflict brought all of the tensions between these three Asian groups to the surface in traumatic developments, especially for Japanese and Chinese Americans. Because of the smaller Korean American population, that community would not be affected as significantly as the other Asian immigrant groups, but the war would certainly have important implications for Koreans in America as well. Obviously, the most traumatic and best-documented impact of World War II on East Asian immigrants and their offspring was the incarceration of more than 110,000 Japanese nationals and Japanese Americans, of whom 70 percent were American citizens. The impact of internment was not merely the temporary loss of civil rights and liberties, but the long-term effects were deeply felt throughout Japanese American communities. For many more, the American national consciousness had to confront serious questions concerning race, rights, and legal actions during wartime, as the moral compass of the nation was thrown off course.

The incarceration of most of the Japanese American population on the mainland United States in a sprawling network of internment camps and prisons disrupted lives and livelihoods for those in their working years, and the effects were felt by at least three generations. The immigrant generation, the *Issei*, who by law were ineligible for citizenship, lost most of their businesses, property, and any hope of belonging in their adopted home. Their *Nisei* children, American citizens by birth, also lost their jobs if they were of working age, while others lost out on college educations, their childhoods, and, for many, their sense of being Americans. Most of the *Sansei*, or third-generation Japanese Americans who were alive during the war, were very young and have little memory of the experience. This lack of historical memory was exacerbated by the fact that many Japanese American families chose not to talk about their internment experiences but preferred to maintain a silence about those painful years, a practice that denied the Sansei the knowledge of a vital part of their family's and community's history. But, for some, that history would come back to haunt them during the Vietnam War. While the military heroism of Nisei combat soldiers during World War II is well known, military service of Japanese Americans after World War II has not been covered in depth. However, one can point to a link between the socioeconomic effects of internment to the Vietnam-era generation of Japanese Americans. A number of Japanese Americans who were agriculturalists before the war lost their farms due to internment. After the war, they were unable to regain their land and consequently many used their agricultural skills to become gardeners, especially in Southern California. This downward social mobility often prevented their sons from attending college, which made them vulnerable to the draft during the war in Vietnam. And some of these Japanese American veterans have spoken to the issues of having to go to combat against other Asians in Vietnam and the prevalence of anti-Asian racism among the ranks of the American military during the war.

World War II, however, brought different fortunes to Chinese Americans. One could say that their experience was nearly the opposite of that of Japanese Americans. Because China and the United States were allies during the war against the Axis Powers, the image of China and the Chinese (including Chinese Americans) became more positive in the eyes of many Americans. The wartime economy called for more workers and Chinese Americans were eager to fill that void. For many, they found work outside of the Chinatown economy, which allowed them to work and associate with non–Chinese Americans for the first time. This increased exposure to mainstream American society hastened their assimilation into the American social landscape as they gradually became more accepted by other Americans. Chinese Americans took all kinds of jobs during the war, including in the defense industries and the military, as well as taking over some of the farms that Japanese Americans lost because of being interned.

One of the most important results of the improved status of Chinese Americans and China's relationship to the United States was the repeal of the Chinese Exclusion Acts in 1943. After sixty-one years of exclusionary legislation, regulations against Chinese immigration to the United States began to loosen up and Chinese immigrants could apply for American citizenship. In addition, in 1945, the War Brides Act was passed, which allowed Chinese women to enter the country as either new brides of Chinese Americans or, more important, as wives who had been separated from their husbands for decades and were finally able to join the latter in the United States. This enabled thousands of Chinese American families to be established and to flourish and grow as other American families did during this "baby boom" period.

The presence of the American military in East Asia has had a profound impact on both East Asia and the development of the Asian population in the United States as well. This has been especially so in the case of "military brides" and for the adoption of children who are the offspring of Asian and American unions. In addition, Chinese women came to America as new brides of Chinese American military personnel who returned to China to marry once the War Brides Act was passed (Ben Loy's wife, Mei Oi, in Louis Chu's *Eat a Bowl of Tea* is an example of such a "war bride") and also long-married wives came to the United States once the exclusion laws were lifted. The American occupation of Japan led to tens of thousands of marriages between Japanese women and American military personnel, most of whom were white or African American. (Velina Hasu Houston's play "Tea" is about Japanese military brides living at Fort Riley in Kansas.) Often overlooked in Asian American studies, these biracial families were in many ways pioneers in the realm of "mixed-race" marriages that produced bicultural/biracial children in an era when miscegenation was still illegal in many states of the union; the lives of these individuals have begun to be examined in depth only in recent years.

Korea is another site in East Asia where the American military has had a long history of influence. Since the beginning of the Korean War, the American military has maintained a high-profile presence in South Korea. There have been many ways in which Korean women and American soldiers and civilians have interacted: as workers on American military installations, as coworkers in transnational businesses, as bar girls and prostitutes, and in many other occupations. Since 1950, more than 100,000 Korean women have immigrated to the United States as wives of American military personnel alone. These marriages, like those of the Japanese American marriages mentioned above, are usually mixed-race unions. However, one important role that these Korean women played, especially those who came before the passage of the Immigration Act of 1965 (which went into effect in 1968) was that once they became legal residents or citizens of the United States, they could act as sponsors for family members to immigrate to the United States in accordance with the family reunification provisions of the immigration bill. Thus, they served as anchors for future Korean immigration, although that was not their intention when they initially married and migrated to America.

Another result of the American presence in Korea has been the adoption of Korean children into American families. Due to World War II and the subsequent Korean War, thousands of Korean children were orphaned by the ravages of war or had been the children of Korean women and occupying soldiers. A great many of these children ended up in orphanages. Eventually, Americans often with religious affiliations became involved with these orphanages and set up adoption agencies in the United States, which served to facilitate the adoption of Korean children by American families. Until recent decades, the majority of Asian children adopted by Americans have been Korean, numbering well over 100,000. In the past two decades, there has been a dramatic increase in the number of children adopted from China, reaching perhaps 60,000, but exact numbers are difficult to obtain. While the adoption of Korean children can be somewhat linked to the American presence in Korea (many of the children are mixed-race offspring of American service personnel), the reasons for the adoption of Chinese children are more due to internal factors in China (poverty, the One Child Policy) and the global reach of American economic power. Similar to transnational or international marriages, most of these Asian children were adopted by white families, rather than Asian American families. Hence, while these adoptees may be phenotypically Asian American, they may not identify as such at all. Thus, the presence of immigrant Asian wives and children in America speaks to issues of race, identity, nationality, and culture. Does a country of origin assume an embracing of that culture? In America, an Asian American's physical appearance may or may not send cultural signals about the degree of their "Americanness," but that same Asian American while in China will often meet with different reactions. When in China, my adopted Chinese daughter is often asked by strangers, "Do you speak Chinese? Can you use chopsticks?" For Chinese, these two "abilities," not her physical appearance, seem to be the cultural markers of being Chinese. In the United States, she is clearly seen as Asian American, but she is rarely asked these two questions.

In the past decade, a number of Asian American historians who study Chinese, Japanese, and Korean Americans have moved beyond World War II into the Cold War era. There have been two primary areas of this time period that have caught the attention of these historians: Asian Americans in the international reach of U.S. Cold War foreign relations and the domestic politics of the era, especially in terms of residential patterns and interracial relations. As of this writing, the exciting work on Asian Americans in international relations during the Cold War have not yet reached publication, but one can look at three important works that focus on shifts in Asian American residential choices and circumstances in postwar America. Scott Kurashige's *The Shifting Grounds of Race* examines how Japanese Americans and African Americans competed for space and resources in the aftermath of World War II and how their struggles were both in opposition to each other as well as how both groups found common ground in their resistance to white supremacy. Allison Varzally's *Making a Non-White America* increases the scope of these residential issues by exploring the complex relationships among Asian Americans, African Americans, Mexican Americans, Native Americans, and white ethnics who shared neighborhoods in Los Angeles and the developing suburbs. And, most recently, Charlotte Brooks's *Alien Neighbors, Foreign Friends* expanded the scope of such studies to focus on how Asian Americans, African Americans, and Latinos responded to the segregated housing market in postwar Los Angeles and San Francisco. Most important, all three of these studies not only address Asian American history, but also place Asian American history in dialogue with African American and Latino history, as well as the history of the American West in general. Furthermore, the authors are all aware that events taking place or socioeconomic and political trends elsewhere in the country or in Asia can affect how Asian Americans are perceived and treated during the time and locations their studies analyze.

There is no doubt that the study of East Asian immigrants and their descendants has grown enormously over the past few decades. There is, however, more fertile ground to till as we continue to unearth our "buried pasts" as well as new models we might consider as we explore new directions and methodologies in our research. Given my own early training as a historian of China, I have always advocated that Asian American historians acknowledge the importance of Asia in Asian American studies. When considering the immigration of East Asians to the United States, it is important to keep in mind that East Asia, especially China and, later, Japan, has long been a part of American history and the American imaginary of Asia. (Although it is beyond the scope of this essay, India was also an early influence on the trade patterns of British North America and the early republic.) Whether one examines immigration trends through the older "push-pull" model or the more recent focus of globalization and transnationalism, the nation-states and cultures of Asia should still play a vital role in our analysis. In addition to acknowledging the centrality of Asia in Asian American studies, it is also important to use Asian-language sources when possible. The pioneers of this approach to Asian American history were Yuji Ichioka and Him Mark Lai. In the past decade, a new generation of historians has been influenced by the works of Ichioka and Lai to produce a number of important works. Two recent studies in Japanese American history have demonstrated how the use of Japanese-language sources can open up new perspectives on Japanese immigration to the United States. Eiichiro Azuma's *Between Two Empires* shows that Japanese immigrants maintained a close relationship with their homeland, though often at odds with Japan's foreign policies, while Andrea Geiger's *Subverting Exclusion* has revealed a tension among Japanese immigrants, between the *burakumin* (outcastes) and those who resented their presence among the Japanese immigrant community.

The use of Chinese-language sources has had a profound impact on our understanding of the Chinese experience in America. Historians such as Xiaolan Bao, Shehong Chen, Yong Chen, Madeline Hsu, Huping Ling, Haiming Liu, Renqiu Yu, and Xiaojian Zhao have enriched our knowledge of Chinese immigration and settlement in the United States, which only Chinese-language sources, either in print or through oral histories, could reveal. It is also important to note that a number of these historians are among the 50,000 Chinese nationals who received permanent residency status after the 1989 Tiananmen incident.

Increased use of Asian-language sources could also open up new research on these post-Tiananmen Chinese immigrants and their families, the long-lasting impact of the Los Angeles riots of 1992, the history of Asian religions and their transformation in the United States, and the shadowy world of undocumented Asians living and working in America. While these are certainly sensitive areas of research, we all know that Asian Americans are part of the "illegal immigrant" population of this country, but we have remained fairly silent on the issue, allowing Latinos to take the brunt of the backlash against the undocumented.

Great strides have been made in the study of women, gender, and sexuality among East Asian immigrants. Earlier studies by Sucheng Chan, Lucie Cheng, Evelyn Nakano Glenn, and Judy Yung paved the way for more recent books by Wendy Rouse Jorae, Erika Lee, Karen Leong, Mary Ting Yi Lui, Valerie Matsumoto, Judy Tzu-Chun Wu, and

Ji-Yeon Yu, as well as the pan-Asian anthology *Asian/Pacific Islander American Women*, edited by Shirley Hune and Gail M. Nomura.

The last direction in recent Asian American history that I would like to draw attention to is the growing interest in linking Asian American history and environmental studies. Inspired by environmental history and studies of race and place, two recent publications point us in new directions to where Asian American history can be found and among whom it can be found. Connie Chiang's *Shaping the Shoreline* is a study of Chinese laborers in the fishing industry on the Monterey Coast, their interactions with Japanese and Italian immigrants within the same industry, and that business's role in shaping the changing nature and personality of Monterey Bay, as it transformed from a seaside resort to a working-class fishing town and finally to a tourist attraction. *Haunted by Waters* by Robert T. Hayashi takes the reader inland to Idaho, where he contrasts and analyzes the overlapping histories of Chinese Americans, Japanese Americans, African Americans, Mormons, and Native Americans and their relationships to that particular landscape, while weaving his own experiences there as an "Eastern traveler, explorer, researcher, angler, and third-generation Japanese American."[5]

By no means exhaustive, this essay has attempted to outline some of the major themes and developments in the study of East Asian (Chinese, Japanese, Korean) immigrants in the United States. It is obvious that there has been more historical work done on Chinese and Japanese Americans, mainly because of the length of time they have been in the country and because of their larger populations. Despite the enormous amount of material on the anti-Chinese movement and the incarceration of Japanese Americans during World War II, there are still areas of Chinese and Japanese American history that call for more detailed study from a fresh perspective. In recent decades, Korean immigrants have far outnumbered Japanese immigrants, and their story has been documented by sociologists and their own voices have been expressed by a growing number of novelists and poets. In time, more historians can fit their stories into the broader picture of Asia America. At the same time, it is not simply a matter that we should produce more studies on each group, but we should also continue the comparative work that has been introduced in recent years; make more attempts to link Asian American history to environmental studies, labor history, gender and sexuality studies, transnational and global studies, and Asian studies; and, perhaps most important, ensure that Asian American history is seen as a vital part of American history.

Notes

1. Sally Engle Merry, *Colonizing Hawai'i: The Cultural Power of Law* (Princeton, NJ: Princeton University Press, 2000), 4–6.
2. David Yoo, *Contentious Spirits: Religion in Korean American History, 1903–1945* (Stanford, CA: Stanford University Press, 2010), 3–4.
3. Mary Paik Lee, *Quiet Odyssey: A Pioneer Korean Woman in America* (Seattle: University of Washington Press, 1990), xlix–l.

4. Richard S. Kim, *The Quest for Statehood: Korean Immigrant Nationalism and U.S. Sovereignty, 1905–1945* (New York: Oxford University Press, 2011), 7.

5. Robert T. Hayashi, *Haunted by Waters: A Journey through Race and Place in the American West* (Iowa City: University of Iowa Press, 2007), 5; and Connie Y. Chiang, *Shaping the Shoreline: Fisheries and Tourism on the Monterey Coast* (Seattle: University of Washington Press, 2008).

FURTHER READING

Azuma, Eiichiro. *Between Two Empires: Race, History, and Transnationalism in Japanese America*. New York: Oxford University Press, 2005.

Brooks, Charlotte. *Alien Neighbors, Foreign Friends: Asian Americans, Housing, and the Transformation of Urban California*. Chicago: University of Chicago Press, 2009.

Chiang, Connie Y. *Shaping the Shoreline: Fisheries and Tourism on the Monterey Coast*. Seattle: University of Washington Press, 2008.

Chu, Louis. *Eat a Bowl of Tea*. New York: Lyle Stuart, 2002 [1961].

Dorow, Sara K. *Transnational Adoption: A Cultural Economy of Race, Gender, and Kinship*. New York: New York University Press, 2006.

Geiger, Andrea. *Subverting Exclusion: Transpacific Encounters with Race, Caste, and Borders, 1885–1928*. New Haven, CT: Yale University Press, 2011.

Hayashi, Robert T. *Haunted by Waters: A Journey through Race and Place in the American West*. Iowa City: University of Iowa Press, 2007.

Houston, Velina Hasu. "Tea." In *Unbroken Thread: An Anthology of Plays by Asian American Women*, edited by Roberta Uno, 155–200. Amherst: University of Massachusetts Press, 1993.

Hsu, Madeline Y. *Dreaming of Gold, Dreaming of Home: Transnationalism and Migration between the United States and South China, 1882–1943*. Stanford, CA: Stanford University Press, 2000.

Hune, Shirley, and Gail M. Nomura, eds. *Asian/Pacific Islander American Women: A Historical Anthology*. New York: New York University Press, 2003.

Ichioka, Yuji. *Before Internment: Essays in Prewar Japanese American History*. Stanford, CA: Stanford University Press, 2006.

Kim, Richard S. *The Quest for Statehood: Korean Immigrant Nationalism and U.S. Sovereignty, 1905–1945*. New York: Oxford University Press, 2011.

Kurashige, Scott. *The Shifting Grounds of Race: Black and Japanese Americans in the Making of Multiethnic Los Angeles*. Princeton, NJ: Princeton University Press, 2008.

Lai, Him Mark. *Chinese American Transnational Politics*. Urbana: University of Illinois Press, 2010.

Lee, Erika. *At America's Gates: Chinese Immigration during the Exclusion Era, 1882–1943*. Chapel Hill: University of North Carolina Press, 2003.

Lee, Mary Paik. *Quiet Odyssey: A Pioneer Woman in America*. Seattle: University of Washington Press, 1990.

Lui, Mary Ting Yi. *The Chinatown Trunk Mystery: Murder, Miscegenation, and Other Dangerous Encounters in Turn-of-the-Century New York City*. Princeton, NJ: Princeton University Press, 2005.

Merry, Sally Engle. *Colonizing Hawai'i: The Cultural Power of Law*. Princeton, NJ: Princeton University Press, 2000.

Varzally, Allison. *Making a Non-White America: Californians Coloring Outside Ethnic Lines, 1925–1955*. Berkeley: University of California Press, 2008.

Wong, K. Scott. *Americans First: Chinese Americans and the Second World War*. Cambridge, MA: Harvard University Press, 2005.

Wu, Judy Tzu-Chun. *Doctor Mom Chung of the Fair-Haired Bastards: The Life of a Wartime Celebrity*. Berkeley: University of California Press, 2005.

Yoo, David K. *Contentious Spirits: Religion in Korean American History, 1903–1945*. Stanford, CA: Stanford University Press, 2010.

Yuh, Ji-Yeon. *Beyond the Shadow of Camptown: Korean Military Brides in America*. New York: New York University Press, 2002.

Zhao. Xiaojian. *Remaking Chinese America: Immigration, Family, and Community, 1940–1965*. New Brunswick, NJ: Rutgers University Press, 2002.

CHAPTER 7

....

ASIAN CANADIAN HISTORY

....

HENRY YU

THE term "Asian Canadian" enjoys virtually no popular usage in Canada. Unlike the term "Asian American," which began in the United States, to be used in the 1970s as a replacement for those historically racialized as "Orientals," no parallel adoption occurred in Canada. Even recently, as Asian Canadian has gained more usage in Canadian academia (in particular with the increasing use of the category of "Asian Canadian literature" as a subject of analysis, the development of national networks of scholars, and the launch of Asian Canadian studies programs at the University of Toronto and the University of British Columbia), Asian Canadian has itself remained limited in popular use. This difference in usage reflects fundamental historical differences in how anti-Asian political movements developed in Canada and the United States, in how antiracist coalitions formed in response, and in how the Canadian national state has dealt with racial categories in its census and policy. The relative utility of the term (in comparison to the term "Asian American" in the United States) either as an analytical category for scholars or as a term for politically organizing pan-ethnic coalitions in Canada mirrors, in consequence, these historical differences, and it should be understood within such contexts.

The history of anti-Asian political movements in Canada might usefully be refracted through three main lenses: the use of anti-Asian rhetoric and the politics of white supremacy by labor organizers, the expansion of anti-Chinese politics to encompass other transpacific migrants, and the development of the means to evade, circumvent, and subvert anti-Asian legislation and practices by those targeted. Of these three, the first two in Canada would appear to be in parallel to the history of anti-Asian movements in the United States. First, the use of anti-Asian exclusion in the late nineteenth and early twentieth centuries by labor unions and white supremacist organizers was similar (and shared) up and down the Pacific coast. Indeed, political organizers across locations on the West Coast shared intelligence and adopted best practices in the use of anti-Chinese rhetoric in order to create political coalitions built around white supremacy in the late nineteenth century. The shift to broader anti-"Asian" (or "Asiatic" or "Oriental") rhetoric targeting migrants from Japan in addition to those from China at the turn of the nineteenth and early twentieth centuries similarly reflected an adoption of organizing tools for white supremacy that spanned national borders.[1] Both in Canada and the United States, transpacific migrants were lumped together as unwelcome competition as a way to organize new migrants arriving from Atlantic migration networks.

However, it has been in the continual process by which targeted migrants worked to undermine and outwit anti-Asian legislation and discrimination that the most significant variations in the patterns and practices north and south of the forty-ninth parallel have developed. Working within colonial and newly incorporated territories increasingly responsive to democratic polities that used white supremacy to organize and expand, targeted migrants seized upon openings and weaknesses in the legalized regimes of surveillance and control developed by these states. In an ongoing struggle as openings were closed and newly passed discriminatory laws necessitated new means of circumventing exclusionary practices, local variations developed as time passed, even as the sharing of information and techniques by white supremacist legislators and political organizers continued.[2]

The dominance of Chinese migrants in the flows of early labor migration around the Pacific, from Sydney through San Francisco and Victoria, was the direct consequence of the creation of the British treaty port of Hong Kong. When the Gold Rushes of the 1850s began bringing nonindigenous peoples to the Pacific coast of North America, one of the most efficient existing transportation routes was by boat across the Pacific from Hong Kong. A triumvirate of newly energized ports—Hong Kong, San Francisco, and Victoria—developed directly out of these Gold Rushes and created the basic infrastructure for transpacific migration. Because British imperial shipping through Hong Kong was such a formative factor, several hundred rural villages in only eight small counties in Guangdong province supplied most of the manual labor for the expansion of resource extraction and agricultural industries around the Pacific in the late nineteenth century. Speaking various rural dialects of Cantonese, these migrants created long-distance trade networks that expanded on existing connections across Southeast Asia (the "Nanyang" or "South Sea"). Labor was only one of the commodities moved by Cantonese merchants across and within the Pacific, but it was a formative catalyst for industrial agriculture, mining, logging, fishing, and manufacturing in virtually every new territory acquired and developed by European or American colonial expansion.

One of the crucial uses of Cantonese labor in the North American context was toward the building of the Pacific sections of each of the transcontinental rail networks that were completed in the late nineteenth century, beginning with the route terminating in San Francisco in 1865. Without tens of thousands of Cantonese laborers easily transported to the West Coast by transpacific shipping, these large-scale capital projects would have been prohibitively expensive and taken much longer to complete. The completion of these transcontinental rail systems made it possible to transport European laborers and other migrants from the Atlantic coast at a similar cost-basis as Cantonese labor from Hong Kong, creating for the first time large-enough numbers of such laborers to facilitate mass white supremacy as an organizing tool. It is no coincidence that anti-Chinese political movements occurred at the terminus of transcontinental rail systems. The historical irony lies in the rhetoric used by anti-Chinese organizers that Chinese threatened to take the jobs of "white" workers, when in practice the actual effect of white supremacy and union organizing in the late nineteenth century up and down the Pacific coast was the opposite. Late arriving white workers coming off the railroad often replaced Cantonese workers in industry after industry—not the other way around. By the 1920s, there had been almost half a century of struggles to remove Chinese, Japanese, South Asian, and aboriginal workers from workplaces as part of the organizing of unions built around white supremacy.

The completion of the transcontinental rail system terminating in Vancouver in 1885 exemplified how the rise of mass anti-Chinese politics coincided with the arrival of large numbers of laborers from the Atlantic region riding the very railroad that the Cantonese helped build. The Chinese Head Tax was passed by the federal government of Canada in 1885, charging individual Chinese migrants to Vancouver $50 upon their arrival, and signaling the increasing importance of anti-Chinese agitation for the organizing of democratic politics in British Columbia. Because the Dominion of Canada was forged in 1867 out of a string of British imperial colonies, including the recently established colony of British Columbia on the West Coast (1858), the founding of Canada as a nation was coincident with the rise of anti-Asian, white supremacist politics.[3] Although the presence of nonindigenous peoples in general on the Pacific coast was relatively small and recent in contrast to the indigenous First Nations who greeted them, the creation of the transcontinental railroad became a mythic act of nation building. The general pattern of migrants arriving along both transatlantic and transpacific migration networks was at first similar, dominated by young men aspiring to social mobility through geographic mobility. But the use of white supremacy to determine political inclusion in the new nation quickly distinguished European and British-descent migrants as "settlers" with privileged access to land and resources. British Columbia, as a settler state similar to others developing around the Pacific, used a democratic process restricted to "whites" to displace and remove indigenous peoples and to exclude and remove Asian migrants.[4]

In Canada, the imposition of a "capitation" or "head" tax paralleled similar "poll" taxes in New Zealand, generating revenue for the state by creating one-time payments by individual Chinese upon arrival. This "penalty" for being Chinese, although financially punitive, allowed a legal opening for further migrants, especially in comparison to the Chinese exclusion passed by the United States in 1882, and Cantonese migrants continued to arrive in Canada despite being forced to begin in considerable debt. Between 1885 and 1923 (when Canada cut off further migration by passing legislation that mirrored the U.S. exclusion act of 1882), more than 97,000 Cantonese migrants entered Canada. They overwhelmingly began their stay as laborers, but those who were enterprising and saved enough earnings could enter into profitable small businesses with cafés, laundries, and stores that spread all across Canada, travelling along the railroad their forebears helped build, in the opposite direction of European migrants. The Canadian head tax was also profitable for the provincial government of British Columbia, which split the over $23 million in revenue (equivalent to more than $1.5 billion in contemporary currency) with the Canadian federal government. Indeed, the Canadian Pacific Railway also depended heavily for its profits upon the continuing flow of Chinese migrants who rode restricted below decks in bulk third class on the ocean liners that it operated between Hong Kong and Vancouver.

Despite anti-Chinese movements and the opportunity cost of migration imposed by exclusionary legislation and taxes, the Cantonese built a complex and persistent network of trade and migration that sustained for multiple generations, connecting small rural villages in Guangdong province with an array of ports, urban centers, and small towns all across Southeast Asia, Australasia, Hawai'i, the Americas, and the Caribbean. The network that populated Canada was exactly the same network that populated the United States, with a demographic and gendered mix of migrants dominated by the same villages from the same eight counties. The term they used for their destinations in the Americas and Australia was "Gum San" (金山)—gold mountain—naming a geographic imaginary stretching beyond nations that captured their aspirations for wealth and upward social mobility rather than political units or nations. They had names for Canada, Australia, and the United States as well, but in referring within their own narratives of mobility to the destinations of journeys, Gum San was the name they used. They created a world that lasted well until the late twentieth century, interrupted by the Great Depression, the World War II, and the Cold War, but enduring precisely because of their alacrity and ability to circumvent and subvert the strictures placed upon them. Despite the suffering and cost imposed by white supremacy, one of the remarkable achievements of the "lo wah kiu" (老華僑)—the "old timer Overseas Chinese" who dominated the Cantonese Pacific networks for over a century—was to create the basic structures of labor migration, small business accumulation, split and dispersed families, and long-distance trade and capital remittance that endured for almost a century.

For the migrants from post–Meiji Restoration (1867) Japan who crossed the Pacific to Canada beginning in the 1890s, they were distinctly unlike their Cantonese counterparts in that they were not an extension and expansion upon preexisting long-distance migration networks.[5] And yet they similarly brought the social organization and kinship networks of small rural villages into new uses when adapting to transpacific migrations. As discriminatory laws and practices were extended, adapted, and newly formulated to apply to Japanese migrants in the early twentieth century, they responded with a vigorous resistance that reflected the strengthening power of post–Meiji Japan, as well as their place within a broader set of rapidly growing migrations out of Japan to the Americas and the northeast and southeast of Asia. Japanese Canadian communities self-consciously weighed options and decided how to fight back against anti-Asian practices with an array of strategies, ranging from local legal challenges and diplomatic appeals to the increasingly powerful Japanese imperial government, to organized long-term self-adaptation to local social norms, and—in the case of the 1907 anti-Asian riots in Vancouver—to arming themselves and fighting violence with violence.[6]

At first glance, the history of the Japanese in Canada seems parallel to that of the United States, with for instance the passage of the Hayashi-Lemieux "Gentleman's Agreement" between Canada and Japan in 1908 at the same moment and in concert with the Gentlemen's Agreement between the United States and Japan for formal limits on Japanese emigration. However, there were distinct and major differences in how anti-Japanese discrimination was implemented, with much of that difference the result of the very different possibilities for resisting or avoiding the consequences of racism in Canada. For example, when Canada forcibly removed over 23,000 Japanese Canadians from the Pacific coast in 1942, the process seemed parallel to what occurred in the United States to over 110,000 Japanese Americans on the West Coast. However, partially because of the ability of Japanese Americans to use birthright citizenship and other legal means to protect the private property of American-born members of their families, the loss of personal property did not occur on the same scale as in Canada. There was no legal enshrinement of birthright citizenship in Canada until after World War II (in the Canada Citizenship Act of 1947, delayed in application to Japanese Canadians until 1949), and there were no constitutional amendments for equal protection under the law or for other civil rights to which Japanese Americans could appeal legally (Canada had constitutional acts that brought it into being as a nation, but a Charter of Rights similar to the U.S. constitutional amendments was not enacted until 1982). Few Japanese Canadians held civic privileges such as voting, with only a small number of Japanese Canadian veterans of the World War I who had fought for Canada receiving the franchise.[7] The forcible removal of Japanese Canadians from the West Coast of Canada was in many ways much harsher than the internment process in the United States. Private property of Japanese Canadians was seized and sold to pay for the process in Canada, and Japanese Canadians were not allowed back to coastal British Columbia until after 1949, well after the end of the war. The long-term ethnic cleansing of Japanese Canadians from British Columbia was effective and sustained, with the dispersal of Japanese Canadians to other parts of Canada and the destruction of communities in British Columbia a permanent legacy.

This distinction in the treatment of Japanese Canadians is sometimes misapprehended as a difference between Canada and the United States merely in terms of government structure or the nature of anti-Japanese politics in each nation. However, the differences are best understood as the cumulative result of the long-term historical processes by which the targets of similar anti-Asian movements both north and south of the border found ways to respond to, combat, and circumvent anti-Asian legislation. Birthright citizenship, for instance, was universal in the United States not because the United States had constitutional rights and Canada did not: birthright citizenship was the result of legal challenges by Chinese Americans and others that resulted in the Supreme Court decision of 1898 in *United States v. Wong Kim Ark* that forced the government to grant citizenship to "native-born" Asian Americans, despite the desire of anti-Asian organizers. In other words, by the time that both the Canadian and American removal of Japanese communities occurred in 1942, an accumulation of differences had built up iteratively over eight decades of struggles by those targeted by anti-Asian legislation and practices.

South of the border, legal challenges using constitutional appeals were effective for much of the late nineteenth century.[8] Although the continual effort to remake anti-Asian legislation in the face of constitutional challenges meant that an array of discriminatory legislation littered American law at almost every level from municipal to federal statutes, there were also considerable gains made by Asian Americans in terms of legal protection. In Canada, the avenue of legal challenge to legal discrimination, although pursued, was in comparison neither as effective nor as available as a strategy as in the United States. And yet Chinese Canadians and Japanese Canadians in the late nineteenth century retained the best lawyers just as their counterparts did south of the border, and the accumulative changes they could effect were what over time created a different legal landscape of racialization than in the United States.[9] When municipal authorities in Victoria in the early twentieth century attempted to segregate Chinese Canadian schoolchildren, part of the spectrum of responses was to take legal action in addition to organized protests and strikes.[10] The organizers shared information and strategies with those in San Francisco fighting school segregation at the same time. But as with so many of the historical moments when anti-Asian practices were similarly organized and enacted north and south of the border, the localized processes by which struggles played out created ever greater differences in opportunities for response, and the institutional and legal arrangements that shaped these possibilities were left as a legacy.

During World War II, both Chinese Canadians and Japanese Canadians placed great emphasis on joining the war effort, even as the Canadian government consciously resisted including them in the military. The Canadian federal government made this explicit decision after having seen how Japanese Canadian veterans of World War I were able to demand the franchise and other rights reserved for whites. Ironically, the eventual success of efforts of young men initially denied the possibility of serving in the military was due to the decision by the British intelligence services to force Canada to allow them to recruit men of Chinese and Japanese heritage. They needed Chinese Canadians because they believed they could blend into the local populace easier than white soldiers if they were dropped behind Japanese lines as commandos. Young Japanese Canadians were needed by the intelligence services as Japanese-language translators to aid in interrogating prisoners and monitoring enemy communications, just as they were in the United States, but in comparison the number of young Chinese Canadians and Japanese Canadians who were able to join the military was much smaller.

Locally, one of the most common strategies in response to anti-Asian discrimination was to adapt symbolically meaning changes in practices and behaviors. As in the United States, for instance, Japanese communities in Canada often worked hard to conform schoolchildren to local practices and customs—learning and primarily speaking English, adopting local clothing styles, even altering food consumption practices—as a way to lessen anti-Japanese hostility. Although such changes were officially demanded in the United States as part of formal assimilation campaigns, they were actually much less explicit in terms of government mandate in Canada. Public school education was less segregated in general than in the United States, and young Chinese Canadians and Japanese Canadians alike actively used the selective adaptation of practices, especially the use of English, in order to gain leverage in a social order marked by racial hierarchy. Even so, Chinese- and Japanese-language schools operated as community initiatives throughout the twentieth century, designed to maximize the possibilities for social mobility and ethnic solidarity for younger generations. After the forced removal of Japanese Canadians left them dispersed across Canada, the adaptation of local practices as a means to survive and at times thrive created a stark feature of Japanese Canadian history, an almost indefatigable overcoming of what seem in retrospect insurmountable obstacles by individuals and families coercively spread across Canada.

One of the great distinctions in the history of transpacific migration to Canada in contrast to the United States is a consequence of differing imperial contexts. The mobility of large numbers of Filipino migrants to the United States in the early twentieth century, for instance, was directly related to the imperial expansion of the United States into the Philippines in 1899 and the creation of networks that facilitated migration to Hawai'i and the U.S. mainland. Some of these Filipino migrants traveled through the networks of seasonal labor migration that ran from Alaska through British Columbia down to California. The entry points and the nodes of this migration, however, were related to the expanding colonial territories of the United States, whereas a contrasting example of South Asian migrants from India in this same period, for instance, was tied to the very different processes of the British empire.

The confederation of Canada in 1867 united British colonies acquired as part of an expansive empire. Each of the colonies had its own unique history, but Canada shared with other nations formed from British settler colonies (such as Australia) the use of democratic politics to enforce and expand white supremacy. This created tensions between the mass politics of these new white settler nations and the imperial interests of the British empire, with no clearer example than in the history of South Asian migrants to Canada from the British colony of India. Beginning in the last decades of the nineteenth century, Punjabi Sikh soldiers in British Indian Army regiments had caught glimpses of British Columbia as they were being transported in their duties across the empire. After mustering out of the British military, some of them returned to Canada to look for better opportunities than at home in the Punjab. Following much the same pathway that Cantonese migrants took through Hong Kong (where Punjabi Sikhs were also deployed in large numbers as colonial police), an expanding migration network connected rural villages in the Punjab region of northern India with Vancouver, Hong Kong, Singapore, and Shanghai. By the turn of the century, Punjabi Sikh migrants were entering Vancouver in increasing numbers to work in lumber, fishing, mining, and agriculture, with many continuing across the border into the United States all the way down to California as migratory labor. In the early fall of 1907, an anti-Punjabi Sikh riot in Bellingham, Washington, was organized by the Asiatic Exclusion League, driving nearly two hundred Punjabi workers out of town, ostensibly back to Canada. Almost immediately afterward, A.E. Fowler, the leader of the Asiatic Exclusion League (which had originally been named the Japanese-Korean Exclusion League), worked with the Vancouver District Trades Council to organize a mob to attack Chinese Canadian and Japanese Canadian businesses in Vancouver.

The long-term legacy of the vigilante violence and destruction of the anti-Asian riots in Bellingham and Vancouver was a shift in the balance between the local politics of white supremacy in British Columbia and the broader global politics of the British empire. Anti-Chinese legislation such as the 1885 Head Tax had balanced imperial interests against those of local political demands. Avoiding the outright exclusion of Chinese migrants, the Head Tax continued to provide Chinese passengers for imperial shipping companies and Chinese labor for imperial investors keen on exploiting British Columbia's rich resources. Furthermore, although discriminatory, a tax applied to Chinese migrants only did not overly damage trade and diplomatic relations, because it took the form of a tariff borne by individual migrants. However, in the wake of the 1907 riots, the federal government of Canada acquired for the first time from British authorities the right to negotiate its own diplomatic treaty, the 1908 Hayashi-Lemieux Agreement—the so-called Gentlemen's Agreement that was negotiated in parallel with the American treaty of the same name.

Another statute, the so-called Continuous Journey Act, was passed in order to curb the flow of migrants from India. Couched in language that never named the targets of the act directly (a tactic much more commonly used in the United States, where the success of Asian American legal appeals to federal judiciary review had triggered the necessity of seemingly nondiscriminatory language in anti-Asian laws), the 1908 law was designed to disable migrants from landing in Canada unless they had "come from the country of their birth or citizenship by a continuous journey." In practice, the law was aimed at Indian migrants, who would have found no way to accomplish such a direct passage after the sole direct shipping route between India and Canada—run by Canadian Pacific between Calcutta and Vancouver—was discontinued under pressure from the government of Canada. Unlike in the United States, the pretense of neutral, nondiscriminatory language was not the result of legal considerations, but because of the need to balance Canadian calls for Asian exclusion against imperial political considerations in the governance of colonial India. Explicit anti-Indian laws passed anywhere in the British dominion—including Canada—threatened to trigger Indian nationalism. The balance, however, was now tipping to the side of local calls for exclusion in settler colonial nations such as Australia and Canada. Indian migration would be stopped, but without naming India directly.

Although not the main consideration for the compromise, avoiding the naming of Indians as the target paid lip service to the privileges that Punjabi Sikhs had earned as honored British subjects through their loyal military service to the empire. Not fooled by the empty respect displayed in the Continuous Journey Act, many Punjabi Sikhs responded by immediately beginning to challenge the prohibition and by actively organizing across their global migration networks. In 1913, a group of mostly Punjabi Sikh migrants founded the Ghadar Party in Astoria, Oregon, with the explicit goal of the overthrow of British colonial rule in India. The next year, Gurdit Singh, a Sikh merchant who had spent much of his life in British Singapore and Malaya, chartered the *Komagata Maru*, a Japanese coal ship docked in Hong Kong, with the deliberate aim of challenging the Continuous Passage Act. The 376 Indian passengers were mostly Punjabi Sikhs, but there was a deliberate mixture of Hindus and Muslims to represent the challenge as one on behalf of all Indians denied passage to Canada. Arriving in Vancouver Harbour in May 1914, Canadian authorities denied their landing, leading to a three-month incident that had ramifications across the world (for instance, in South Africa, the young law-yer Mohandas Gandhi closely followed the news of what was happening in Vancouver). In July, the *Komagata Maru* was forced to leave Vancouver Harbour, with all but twenty-four of its passengers prohibited from disembarking. The incident became one of the rallying points for Indian nationalism, and it reflects how anti-Asian politics in Canada were embedded within the larger structures of white supremacy across the British empire.[11]

Although for the next half a century, virtually no Indian migrants were allowed into Canada, the initial migration network between the Punjab and British Columbia cre-ated by the early Sikh migrants allowed a rapid resurgence of Punjabi Sikh mobility to Canada after 1967, when Asian exclusion in immigration policy was finally removed. A similar phenomenon occurred with the resumption of Cantonese migration from Hong Kong in large numbers in the 1970s—as with Punjabi Sikhs, new migrants tended to already have relatives and family connections in Canada. The Immigration Act of 1967, like the immigration reforms passed in the United States in 1965, created a new sys-tem that ended nearly a century of anti-Asian immigration policy, and like its American counterpart, it opened the way for family reunification as well as the preferential migra-tion of those who were educated and in needed professions.

By the beginning of the twenty-first century, a sea change had occurred in Canada, shifting immigration from the dominant transatlantic flows mandated by white suprem-acy for the first century of Canada to transpacific flows. The top three sending countries to Canada in its 2006 census were all Asian nations—the People's Republic of China, India, and the Philippines. These new migrants tended overwhelmingly to migrate to urban centers, transforming the three major cities of Canada—Toronto, Vancouver, and to a lesser extent, Montreal. Immigration policies in the 1980s and 1990s that encour-aged business investors had also created favored openings for migrants with wealth, and Canada became in the words of one observer the "Switzerland of the Pacific," idealized by the elite of Asia as a safe place to send children for education and to safely stow away wealth made in the rapidly expanding economies of Asia.

Hong Kong Chinese, looking for a safe refuge in anticipation of the reversion of Hong Kong from British to Chinese political rule in 1997, made a particularly powerful impact on Canada, specifically on Vancouver, long an epicenter of anti-Asian politics. Well acquainted with how to operate within the British colonial society of Hong Kong, these migrants often refused to quietly accept or evade the restrictions of long-standing structures of white supremacy. They wrought changes simply by using money to outbid privileges long reserved for whites, in particular in terms of residential segregation in real estate and de facto segregation in private schooling. Able to buy their way straight into neighborhoods long considered segregated bastions of white supremacy, or able to circumvent the power of an existing financial elite by bringing their own often greater sources of capital, the Hong Kong Chinese tended to use financial leverage to effect change, just as they had in Hong Kong, where formal political structures ignored the Chinese in ways similar in outcome to Canada's long history of disenfranchisement of nonwhites.

The initial response in the 1990s to these changes reflected a century of anti-Asian politics—Vancouver was dubbed "Hongcouver" in the popular media and "Asian" homeowners were accused of building "monster houses." As a way of naming the unwanted changes wrought by these newer migrants, the public rhetoric was revealing of the rapidity by which the new migrants were able to confront and sometimes obliterate the subtle racial boundaries of the older social order. The surprise, in many ways, was that this rhetorical echo of earlier periods of anti-Asian politics was so short-lived and ineffectual. By the end of the 1990s, despite global attention to the tensions within an older racial order laid bare by the new ethnic Chinese migrations, Vancouver had been transformed.[12]

Less noticed, but just as important, was the diversity of origin of new transpacific migrations. Ethnic Chinese came from all around the decolonized societies of Southeast Asia—Malaysia, Vietnam, Indonesia—often fleeing policies enacted by postcolonial national governments that were aimed at eroding the status of ethnic Chinese within reimagined states. Koreans, Taiwanese, and Mainland Chinese—traveling along the same networks of educational mobility as those going to the United States—filled high schools, colleges, and universities in every city. From the Philippines, a particularly bifurcated migration pattern emerged, with large numbers of nannies and low-wage service industry workers recruited from the Philippines employed in every urban center, growing in numbers in parallel with the migration of highly educated Tsinoys (Chinese Filipinos) from the strata of ethnic Chinese who had long enjoyed economic power in the Philippines. As in the United States, the new diversity of origins mapped onto earlier migration networks—in particular with those of Cantonese and Punjabi Sikh origin—but there were also brand-new migrations from all around south and west of continental Asia, from Pakistan through Iran.

No definition of "Asian" except the most superficial and empty could encompass the range of these new migrations, and there has been little attempt in Canada to do so. Older anti-Asian definitions of "Asiatics" and "Orientals" that lumped together Chinese, Japanese, Koreans, and "East Indians" (a term commonly used until the 1980s) were no longer salient, and in a crucial contrast to the United States, the Canadian census did not enshrine such a broad racial classification into the practical operations of the Canadian government. Perhaps no other difference is more telling than this longstanding difference in aggregate census categories. Although the country of origin was a category of the Canadian census from its beginnings in 1871, no umbrella category that lumped together all "Asians" as a race was ever created, mirroring the same lack of broad policies at the governmental level organized around a pan-Asian racial category. Anti-Asian measures were concerted and part of a broad framework of white supremacy that disenfranchised and disempowered nonwhites, but the organization of discriminatory legislation by an articulated category of "Asians" as a single race was mostly absent in Canada. Anti-Asian discrimination, in other words, was disarticulated into ethnic-specific measures.

The reason for this disarticulation has much to do with the ways in which those targeted responded to discrimination. They organized around preexisting family and community networks that had aided in their migration and adjustments to new locations, just as they had in the United States. They also built coalitions across ethnic communities, but these tended to cohere and fade in utility with the demands of the particular moment. Antiracist coalitions forming in the last half of the twentieth century, for example, brought together an array of political partners—faith-based charities, feminist organizations, progressive and humanitarian activists arguing for immigrant and refugee rights, labor organizations, radical political activists, First Nations and aboriginal sovereignty activists, local community action groups—but almost wholly missing were coalitions justified solely around pan-Asian issues. In some ways, the sophistication of political organization in the Canadian context has been more effective in creating rapid political and social change in Canadian society, so that the quiet and peaceful transition away from white supremacy has been quicker and more thorough than in the United States. In other ways, the relative lack of political organizing around "race" in comparison to the United States has meant that enduring legacies of white supremacy that had been highlighted and transformed in the United States by the civil rights movement remain as seemingly archaic vestiges when American observers notice them in Canada.

Perhaps one of the most interesting parallels between Canada and the United States in terms of transpacific migration has to do with the enduring practices of geographically dispersed family networks. A century ago, when Cantonese networks stretched around the Pacific, the gendered pattern by which families were split by location was stark. Young men traveled afar, migrating almost continuously in search of better opportunities. Young women in home villages aspired to marry into such "Gold Mountain guest" (金山客) families or, like most of the men, were already a part of such families even as children. A self-perpetuating system spanned the Pacific persistently because it functioned so well to exploit the economics of relative location in moving labor and other commodities from places where they were plentiful to where they were scarce. The relative buying power of money by location even determined the direction by which financial remittances flowed. A century ago, children were left in villages to be raised and educated because money earned overseas went farther in home villages. A century later, as educational mobility became one of the primary rationales for geographically split families among Chinese migrants to North America, women and children migrate while men stay in China or other parts of Asia to make money. The "astronaut" family and "parachute kids," marked by highly mobile men and women traveling by commercial airliner, or children and mothers dropped temporarily into wide-flung locations for schooling, have largely reversed the gender dynamics of migration. A process that initially was common among Hong Kong Chinese at the end of the twentieth century, it is now commonplace among many transpacific migrants to Canada, including those from China, Taiwan, and Korea.

In comparison, working-class Filipina migrants to Canada—like their counterparts leaving the Philippines for contract labor around the globe as domestics, as service industry workers, and as nurses and medical service providers—have adopted a parallel gendered pattern of leaving husbands at home with children to be educated in the Philippines by using money earned by them overseas. Their ability to strategize and use the economies of relative location across the Pacific is exemplified by the sacrifices made in geographically dispersing their families, a set of decisions reminiscent of those made by Cantonese men a century before. Canada was for decades seen as one of the most favored destinations by Filipina migrants; however, opportunities that existed in the last three decades of the twentieth century to reunite families in Canada have increasingly been curtailed as Canadian immigration policy expands temporary foreign worker programs (where the worker is forced to leave Canada at the end of the contract) and closes off opportunities for Filipina workers to become Canadian permanent residents and citizens.[13]

Although educational aspirations for children often play a role in the migration of Filipina workers, educational mobility as a primary means of strategizing life-cycle migrations has also marked the development of economically privileged, urban transpacific migrant communities in Canada. Focusing in particular on the migration of schoolchildren into Canada with an eye toward university education in North America, Canada has become a crucial stepping-stone for many aspiring migrants with hopes for English-language higher education for their children. Although Canada is not alone in this regard, with cities in Australia and the United States also envisaged by transpacific migrants as strategic locations for educational mobility, the ways in which Australia and Canada have aimed immigration policy since the 1990s toward the capturing of educated migrants have created persistent and recurring migrations for the last three decades. A hallmark of educational mobility has been the indeterminate endpoint of strategic migration. The aspirations revolve around English-language acquisition and the status of North American or other English-language university degrees, and national border crossings are challenges to be overcome through the process of choosing the best location among an array of global possibilities. Multiple migrations after each stage of education is achieved are common, and the transnational movement is often the by-product of the comparative consideration of educational institutions more than national or local considerations.

A particularly interesting development within the study of Chinese migrations to Canada as well as to Australia, New Zealand, and other locations such as Southeast Asia, Latin America, and the Caribbean has been the great propensity for young Chinese male migrants to marry into indigenous families and to use strategic marriage alliances to gain a foothold and status within aboriginal communities. There has been a long history of intimate contact and engagement that has only recently been recovered by scholars. In Canada, the forgetting of this rich history has been the result of the genocidal effects of Canadian policy toward First Nations and aboriginal peoples. The reserve system, residential schooling, and myriad other practices designed to remove and erase the presence of First Nations and aboriginal peoples are still being overcome only in small steps. One of the consequences of the devastating effects of residential schooling on family life in general among aboriginal communities has been the erasure of the memory of many mixed Chinese-aboriginal families. Perhaps one of the most suggestive parallels would be the history of Cantonese marriages into Native Hawaiian families in the nineteenth and twentieth centuries. As in the Australasian colonies and much of the Malay Peninsula, young Chinese men aspiring to engage with indigenous communities often used marriage as a strategy, opening small stores or restaurants amid new relations who anchored their place in local networks. That these marriages were often one of multiple marriages (commonly in addition to a village wife in China) has created a sense of shame and revelation in contemporary discourses about these unions that was generally not an issue historically. More studies, and in particular comparative studies across the broader Cantonese migration networks, will reveal that in Canada, as in other locations around the Pacific, the interactions among transpacific migrants, transatlantic migrants, and indigenous peoples both at the local level and across long distances were much more complex and interesting than has been imagined. Indeed, if we take into account the seafaring of the indigenous peoples of the Pacific and the arrivals of *kanakas* (Native Hawaiians) on the northwest coasts of the Americas along with the earliest coming of Cantonese and British in the late eighteenth century, the transoceanic migrations of people from the continents of Asia and Europe are inextricably entwined with that of the indigenous peoples in the Pacific in ways that involve the long-distance mobility of indigenous peoples themselves.

Even as differences among the historical experiences of Asian Canadian, Asian American, and Asian migrant communities around and within the Pacific are considered, the number of heuristic parallels remains large. Perhaps most important of all is that the migrants targeted by anti-Asian discrimination played a crucial role both within white settler colonies and postcolonial nations in shaping the development of racialized practices, as well as in their dismantling and transformation. As in the United States, those targeted by anti-Asian practices in Canada organized and developed strategies on how to respond to racism, often sharing strategies and working in concert by publicizing what was happening and being done in other places. Because they were often part of the same migration networks, and shared family links and connections to the same counties or prefectures in home countries as well as other network nodes around the globe, their ability to organize both locally and across long distances was remarkable.

It should not be surprising—given the relative lack of use of the category of "Asian Canadian" as an analytical framework—that there is no parallel in Canada to the historiography that has developed around "Asian American history" in the decades since that term was first used. But this is not the same as saying that there has been a dearth of excellent scholarship on the complementary processes of migration, anti-Asian discrimination, exclusion, and white supremacist nation building that took place in Canada, nor has there been a lack of literary and cultural production that from a U.S. perspective might even be labeled as Asian American (e.g., Japanese Canadian novels such as Joy Kogawa's *Obasan* (1981) were quickly adopted into the Asian American literature canon). Political activism in Canada produced strong literary and artistic communities that in turn received attention from scholars; however, these movements often reflected the local and regional engagements and antiracist coalitions that Asian Canadians made with other peoples of color or within class-based, feminist, and queer struggles. The career of Roy Miki, as a political activist, artist, and scholar, perhaps exemplifies how broad-based connections between scholarly production and community-based politics existed from the 1970s onward.

Scholars in Canada could analyze the decades of literary production of writers such as Miki both within the framework of "Asian Canadian" as well as "Asian North American" literature, using each as framing devices for interpreting what in Canada was similar and dissimilar to the United States, as well as what was connected and unconnected. However, scholarly analyses also accurately portrayed the specific local and regional character of political activism, community organizing, and cultural production, as well as its global contexts.[14] South Asian Canadian artists and writers, for example, were often placed within diasporic or postcolonial frames of analysis, emphasizing the importance of global migration and the legacies of colonialism and decolonization.

In terms of historical scholarship, key works that described anti-Asian politics as tools of Canadian nation building, as well as studies of Japanese Canadian removal and the history of anti-Chinese and anti-South Asian movements, were produced in the 1970s and 1980s. Indeed, a strong argument can be made that the connections between imperial migration, anti-Asian politics, white settler colonial politics, and nation building that took place in the Australasian and North American white settler colonies were more clearly seen by historians working outside the contexts of Asian American historiography. Scholars in Canada like Hugh Johnston saw the important place of anti-Asian policies in British Columbia within the framework of British imperial politics rather than just the Canadian nation-state, and Edgar Wickberg was able to understand Chinese communities in Canada within the perspective of larger transpacific Cantonese migration networks. As Asian American historiography over the last two decades has increasingly emphasized the global context of Asian American history, the long continuity of approaches that connect local and global processes has been a crucial feature of what may be seen in hindsight as a well-developed historiography of Asian Canadian history, perhaps because of the lack of the use of the term "Asian Canadian" rather than in spite of its absence.

Perhaps the most useful point to be made in thinking about the comparisons, connections, and parallels among Asian American and Asian Canadian history (if such a conception is to be intellectually useful rather than an empty parallel), is that the political border that marks the forty-ninth parallel has been as conceptually destructive to understanding historical processes as it has been generative of distinct national narratives and mythologies. For instance, for most of the nineteenth century and into the early twentieth century, it was a trivial matter to cross from Canada into the United States and vice versa. Letters written in Cantonese in the 1900s—when strict policing of the land border was seemingly in place—talk casually about going from Victoria to destinations in Washington and Oregon as if there were no impediment. The reason was that until recent decades, the main way to travel up and down the Pacific coast was by waterways, and landing in a small vessel almost anywhere was straightforward and avoided any contact with border guards. The vast majority of Cantonese migrants who came from or through Canada who were exposed as illegal entrants to the United States before the 1960s were caught long after they had been living and working there—crossing the border was itself trivial. It should be hoped that at some point the conceptual borders created by focusing on national boundaries will become just as trivial. Any consideration of connections and comparisons among transpacific migrations to locations in the United States and Canada, and the anti-Asian politics that arose there and were shaped by the local responses of the targeted migrants, will most usefully be considered in the multiple contexts of local and global connections first, with national generalizations a useful heuristic device only afterward.

This focus on the local and global contexts of history, simultaneously emphasizing the importance of these two registers as the generative founts of historical processes that create narrative meanings for time and space, has been a long-term trend. The placing of categories such as national, racial, ethnic, and other forms of identity (including "Asian Canadian") as the products of history rather than as pre-existing categories for analysis is perhaps the clearest legacy of the historiographic trends of the last several decades, as well as the most productive factor for developing Asian Canadian studies in the future. At the University of British Columbia, for instance, studying "Asian migrations" in global and local contexts, with a particular focus on colonialism, was emphasized as (or more) strongly as understanding the national context of "Asian Canadian" studies. Students and researchers alike have been more likely to be personally engaged with these approaches both because of the dynamic demographic profile of Canadian cities and universities in the late twentieth and early twenty-first centuries (with an almost universal experiential connection to migration, colonialism, and decolonization as processes) and the relative weakness of Canadian nationalism as an affective force. Colonial processes of dominance and exploitation around the Pacific region, in particular connections to local indigenous histories, are a powerful generative framework that has both been harder to ignore and easier to conceptualize outside of the United States. As programs develop institutionally at universities in Canada, scholarly connections that have already existed between researchers north and south of the forty-ninth parallel will continue to develop most generatively not in modes that emphasize national comparisons, but through approaches that explore the interlinked historical processes that enmesh local and regional histories in the Americas and within and across the Pacific.

NOTES

1. Kornel Chang, *Pacific Connections: The Making of the U.S.-Canadian Borderlands* (Berkeley: University of California Press, 2012); Elliot Young, *Alien Nation: Asian Migration from the Coolie Era through World War II* (Chapel Hill: University of North Carolina Press, 2014).

2. Lisa Mar, *Brokering Belonging: Chinese in Canada's Exclusion Era, 1885–1945* (New York: Oxford University Press, 2010).

3. Peter Ward, *White Canada Forever: Popular Attitudes and Public Policy towards Orientals in British Columbia* (Montreal: McGill-Queens University Press, 2002); Patricia Roy, *The Oriental Question: Consolidating a White Man's Province, 1914–1941* (Vancouver: University of British Columbia Press, 2003).

4. Marilyn Lake and Henry Reynolds, *Drawing the Global Colour Line: White Men's Countries and the International Challenge of Racial Equality* (Cambridge: Cambridge University Press, 2008); Young, *Alien Nation*.

5. Michiko Ayukawa, *Hiroshima Immigrants in Canada, 1891–1941* (Vancouver: University of British Columbia Press, 2007).

6. Andrea Geiger, *Subverting Exclusion: Transpacific Encounters with Race, Caste, and Borders, 1885–1928* (New Haven, CT: Yale University Press, 2011); John Price, *Orienting Canada: Race, Empire, and the Transpacific* (Vancouver: University of British Columbia Press, 2011).

7. Ken Adachi, *The Enemy That Never Was: A History of Japanese Canadians* (Toronto: McClelland and Stewart, 1976).

8. Lucy Salyer, *Laws as Harsh as Tigers: Chinese Immigrants and the Shaping of American Immigration Law* (Chapel Hill: University of North Carolina Press, 1995); Charles McClain, *In Search of Equality: The Chinese Struggle against Discrimination in Nineteenth-Century America* (Berkeley: University of California Press, 1996).

9. Mar, *Brokering Belonging*.

10. Timothy Stanley, *Contesting White Supremacy: School Segregation, Anti-Racism, and the Making of Chinese Canadians* (Vancouver: University of British Columbia Press, 2011).

11. Hugh Johnston, *The Voyage of the "Komagata Maru": The Sikh Challenge to Canada's Colour Bar* (Vancouver: University of British Columbia Press, 1995); Ali Kazimi, *Undesirables: White Canada and the Komagata Maru* (Toronto: Douglas and Mcintyre, 2012).

12. David Ley, *Millionaire Migrants: Trans-Pacific Lifelines* (Oxford: Wiley-Blackwell, 2010).

13. Roland Sintos Coloma, Bonnie McElhinny, Ethel Tungohan, John Paul C. Catungal, and Lisa M. Davidson, *Filipinos in Canada: Disturbing Invisibility* (Toronto: University of Toronto Press, 2012).

14. Donald Goellnicht and Eleanor Ty, eds., *Asian North American Identities: Beyond the Hyphen* (Bloomington: Indiana University Press, 2004).

FURTHER READING

Adachi, Ken. *The Enemy That Never Was: A History of Japanese Canadians.* Toronto: McClelland and Stewart, 1976.

Ayukawa, Michiko. *Hiroshima Immigrants in Canada, 1891–1941.* Vancouver: University of British Columbia Press, 2007.

Chang, Kornel. *Pacific Connections: The Making of the U.S.-Canadian Borderlands.* Berkeley and Los Angeles: University of California Press, 2012.

Coloma, Roland Sintos, Bonnie McElhinny, Ethel Tungohan, John Paul C. Catungal, and Lisa M. Davidson. *Filipinos in Canada: Disturbing Invisibility.* Toronto: University of Toronto Press, 2012.

Con, Ronald, Harold Con, and Edgar Wickberg. *From China to Canada: A History of the Chinese Communities in Canada.* Toronto: McClelland and Stewart, 1982.

Geiger, Andrea. *Subverting Exclusion: Transpacific Encounters with Race, Caste, and Borders, 1885–1928.* New Haven: Yale University Press, 2011.

Goellnicht, Donald, and Eleanor Ty, eds. *Asian North American Identities: Beyond the Hyphen.* Bloomington: Indiana University Press, 2004.

Johnston, Hugh. *The Voyage of the Komagata Maru: The Sikh Challenge to Canada's Colour Bar.* Vancouver: University of British Columbia Press, 1989.

Joseph, Maia, Christine Kim, and Christopher Lee, eds. *Tracing the Lines: Reflections on Contemporary Poetics and Cultural Politics in Honour of Roy Miki*. Vancouver: Talon, 2013.

Kazimi, Ali. *Undesirables: White Canada and the Komagata Maru*. Toronto: Douglas and Mcintyre, 2012.

Lake, Marilyn, and Henry Reynolds. *Drawing the Global Colour Line: White Men's Countries and the International Challenge of Racial Equality*. Cambridge: Cambridge University Press, 2008.

Lee, Josephine, Imogene Lim, and Yuko Matsukawa. *Re/collecting Early Asian America: Essays in Cultural History*. Philadelphia: Temple University Press, 2002.

Ley, David. *Millionaire Migrants: Trans-Pacific Lifelines*. Oxford: Wiley-Blackwell, 2010.

Li, Xiaoping. *Voices Rising: Asian Canadian Cultural Activism*. Vancouver: University of British Columbia Press, 2007.

McClain, Charles. *In Search of Equality: The Chinese Struggle against Discrimination in Nineteenth-century America*. Berkeley and Los Angeles: University of California Press, 1996.

Mar, Lisa. *Brokering Belonging: Chinese in Canada's Exclusion Era, 1885–1945*. New York: Oxford University Press, 2010.

Price, John. *Orienting Canada: Race, Empire, and the Transpacific*. Vancouver: University of British Columbia Press, 2011.

Roy, Patricia. *The Oriental Question: Consolidating a White Man's Province, 1914–1941*. Vancouver: University of British Columbia Press, 2003.

Salyer, Lucy. *Laws Harsh as Tigers: Chinese Immigrants and the Shaping of American Immigration Law*. Chapel Hill: University of North Carolina Press, 1995.

Stanley, Timothy. *Contesting White Supremacy: School Segregation, Anti-Racism, and the Making of Chinese Canadians*. Vancouver: University of British Columbia Press, 2011.

Ward, Peter. *White Canada Forever: Popular Attitudes and Public Policy towards Orientals in British Columbia*. Montreal: McGill-Queens University Press, 2002.

Young, Elliot. *Alien Nation: Asian Migration from the Coolie Era through World War II*. Chapel Hill: University of North Carolina Press, 2014.

Yu, Henry and Guy Beauregard, eds. "Pacific Canada: Beyond the 49th Parallel." *Amerasia Journal* 33, no. 2 (2007): xi–xxviii, 1–148.

PART II

TIME PASSAGES

CHAPTER 8

....

INTERNMENT AND WORLD WAR II HISTORY

....

EIICHIRO AZUMA

WORLD War II is often characterized as one of the most important watershed events in Asian American history. The interconnected themes of race, loyalty, and citizenship have formed major underpinnings of scholarly production relating to the period. Not only did it catalyze a notable shift in domestic race relations under the political pressure for national mobilization, but the war also created a decisive rupture in the intraracial formation processes of Asian Americans. Much of the World War II scholarship is split into the literature on Japanese Americans and that on other Asian ethnics. It is important to note that the genre spills over the chronological confines of the Pacific War to include various political, social, and cultural formations in postwar Japanese/Asian America.

The academic research on the internment of Japanese Americans (and Canadians) began even before the war's end, intersecting with the general historiographies of U.S. political, legal, military, and race history. Tangential to the voluminous academic study on Japanese internment is a cottage industry of popular history that has cranked out hundreds of publications, including personal memoirs and semifictional accounts. The "internment studies"—or the historical scholarship that revolves around the legacies and consequences of Japanese American mass incarceration—also extend to the postwar periods. On the other hand, the scholarship on the wartime experience of non-Japanese Asians is much more limited in number and scope, and it is only within the last two decades that we have witnessed a real growth in serious archival-based research—mainly on Chinese and Korean Americans during the Pacific War.

INTERNMENT HISTORY I: THE PROBLEM OF RESPONSIBILITY AND THE CONSTITUTIONAL QUESTION

The forced removal and incarceration of 120,000 Japanese Americans from the West Coast have, without question, constituted the most pivotal aspect of wartime Asian American history. The internment history initially started as a self-reflective liberal response to what was deemed "our worst wartime mistake" from a racial and legal stand-point. Perhaps it was Carey McWilliams who, as early as 1944, most succinctly captured the thinking of white racial integrationists that problematized the racist nature of the internment saga. Though having earlier supported the removal of Japanese residents from the West Coast, McWilliams eventually recanted his position and advocated the primacy of individual behavior over racial affiliation in the evaluation of one's national loyalty.[1] His antiracist argument against the 1942 military policy to intern all West Coast Japanese corresponded to the subsequent official stance that Americanism was "a mat-ter of the mind and heart" rather than that of "race or ancestry" as President Franklin D. Roosevelt stated in early 1943. Buoyed by the rise of a new national discourse of color-blind democracy, McWilliams's 1944 publication set the basic tone of the ensuing scholarly research that called into question the official "military necessity" argument for the mass internment. Simply put, the initial phase of the internment study aspired to understand why such an anomalous racist incident had taken place in a nation that had been supposedly fighting for universal democracy and human equality.

Concurrently, some legal experts grappled with a fundamental constitutional prob-lem that had smoldered since the beginning of the forced removal and incarceration of Japanese Americans. In September 1945, Eugene Rostow articulated the legalist approach to the internment study for the first time. Following McWilliams's conten-tion that "racial prejudice" had shaped the "military necessity" justification, the Yale University law professor criticized the violation of Nisei citizenship rights at the level of political decision making and judicial ruling. First, in rounding up all Japanese resi-dents on grounds of their "undiluted racial strains," the Roosevelt administration and the U.S. Army denied them their due process rights and hence broke the fundamen-tal American legal principle of equal justice under law. Then, as Rostow argued, the Supreme Court added insult to injury by failing to apply a proper judicial review—the rule of strict scrutiny—to the constitutional issues presented in *Korematsu v. U.S.* Rostow showed his profound concern about the elevated war powers of the military vis-à-vis the constitutional demands for civil liberties in the absence of the martial law regime. As he saw it, the complacent high court ruling resulted in the judicial con-struction of "second-class citizens" who stood on a different legal footing before the courts. This was, according to Rostow, "the worst blow our civil liberties have sustained in many years."[2]

McWilliams's criticism of "racial prejudice" and Rostow's legalist rendition of the government's "mistake" set the basic terms upon which the historiography of the internment studies would evolve in the years to come. Many liberal white scholars of the 1950s and 1960s endeavored to locate causation in shameful wartime racism—whether harbored by military leaders, government brass, or West Coast residents. In the immediate postwar period, the Japanese Evacuation and Relocation Study (JERS), a major research project spearheaded by Dorothy Swaine Thomas, a sociologist from the University of California at Berkeley, made it possible to address these central themes in a scholarly manner. During the Pacific War, Thomas organized troops of graduate students and young scholars, who engaged in field research in three of the ten War Relocation Authority (WRA) camps, as well as in resettlement communities in the Midwest and the East. Along with many articles, four major monographs came out of this project.[3]

Americans Betrayed (1949) by Morton Grodzins and *Prejudice, War, and the Constitution* (1954) by Jacobus tenBroek and colleagues carried the contentions of McWilliams and Rostow into the realm of full-fledged scholarly research. In terms of the legal question, the latter expanded on the set of issues introduced by Rostow, offering an extensive analysis of Ex Parte *Milligan* (1866), the legal precedence against the elevated emergency powers of the federal government when the civilian court was fully functional without the declaration of the martial law. Just like Rostow, tenBroek and colleagues described the Supreme Court ruling as the "blow . . . at the liberties of us all."[4]

As for the problem of racial prejudice, a locus of scholarly debate lay in whom to blame the most regarding the formulation of the internment policy. Grodzins's study offered a detailed analysis of the bigoted rhetoric that the "interest groups" and "politicians" of California had employed against Japanese Americans for selfish gains in 1941–1942. In turn, tenBroek and colleagues refuted Grodzins's indictment of Californians, particularly key state officials, as the chief culprits with ulterior motives. Their monograph emphasized a racist "state of mind" of Americans across the board, tracing its origin to the prewar "anti-Japanese heritage" in the nation. The authors' strongest criticism focused on Lt. General John DeWitt, simply because he was the military commander in California who issued various orders leading to the removal of Japanese Americans from the coast.[5]

Following these conflicting interpretations, the continuous scholarly interest in causation and responsibility paved the way for further research on the thinking and practice of major players in the government decision-making process. Generally, political and military historians played a central role in pushing the historiographical development forward, especially before the establishment of Asian American history as an academic field in the early 1970s. The discussion of responsibility was often mired in contemporary political concerns, interests, and agendas. For example, tenBroek's attack on Grodzins's argument mirrored an effort to rehabilitate the name of the former California State Attorney General Earl Warren during the time when he was enjoying a reputation as a trailblazer of minority civil rights.[6] Only twelve years after his anti-Japanese scaremongering, Warren was responsible for dismantling the separate but equal doctrine as the Chief Justice of the U.S. Supreme Court. Because McWilliams and Rostow had already set up the basic premise that the "racist" policy of Japanese American internment was of an "un-American" nature, the postwar academic inquiry into responsibility frequently entailed a battle over the images of political and military leaders as outstanding Americans according to America's disavowal of Nazi-style, blood-will-tell racism—the very pattern of thinking that had rationalized the 1942 U.S. government policy toward the West Coast Japanese.

Before the 1970s, the politics of interpretation in the internment studies betrayed the limitation of postwar racial liberalism. While reducing the causality of the unconstitutional policy to episodic racial prejudice—individual or societal—most authors avoided serious deliberation on the institutionalized dimensions of anti-Asian racism, whose origin goes back to the era of Chinese exclusion in the late nineteenth century. Liberal scholars of U.S. political and legal history also tended to treat the Japanese American internment as an aberration in a teleological history of the United States as the defender of liberty and equality. As Rostow so succinctly put, it was a "mistake," but not a logical consequence of systemic racial exclusion or inherent structural flaws. Insofar as postwar U.S. democracy could disown this "anomalous incident" of the past, the critical examination of wartime racial prejudice, and the search for guilty parties still implicitly suggested—if not outright celebrated—the progress of postwar America as a true democracy in the context of the Cold War. The internment studies, in this fundamental sense, formed a nationalist intellectual project—yet another manifestation of scholarly American exceptionalism.

In 1971, Roger Daniels published the first booklength studies of the Japanese American internment from what can be termed an "ethnic studies" perspective. Unlike racial liberalists of the earlier decades, this pioneering Asian American historian takes the question of institutionalized racism more seriously. Rather than describing individual behavior in terms of racial prejudice, Daniels offers a more sophisticated analysis of the complex decision-making process at the heart of the U.S. government that gave birth to the political machination of the race-based incarceration. According to the author, Provost Marshal General Allen Gullion and his right-hand man, Colonel Karl Bendetsen, managed to convince the indecisive DeWitt to support the idea of Nisei citizens as the most dangerous from the vantage point of national security. Formulated by these uniformed military men, the racist policy, disguised as military necessity, was subsequently embraced by the leadership of the War Department, as well as by President Roosevelt. To elucidate the oppressive nature of the mass incarceration, Daniels also takes issue with the euphemisms associated with the government policy, including "evacuation," "relocation," and so on. Indeed, he purposefully refers to the "relocation centers" as "concentration camps," prompting a wholesale epistemological shift in the internment studies.[7]

Peter Irons and Greg Robinson have further complicated the understanding of the wartime internment by presenting it as yet one more manifestation of a general U.S. institutionalized racism, and subsequent systemic government failure, if only in a more extreme shape. Setting up the dual contexts of institutional politics and racial politics, Irons's *Justice at War* (1983) looks at how the rivalry and complicity between the War Department and the Justice Department helped seal the fate of Japanese Americans under the pervasive influence of anti-Japanese ideology. As a crucial link between General DeWitt and War Department brass, Bendetsen played a decisive role

in manipulating the vacillating mind of the army commander in California. In conjunction, Assistant Secretary of War John J. McCloy reinforced the idea that Nisei citizenship
posed a greater and immediate threat to the defense of the West Coast within the executive branch of the government. In the end, antiracist officials in the Justice Department,
like Edward Ennis and James Rowe, yielded to the War Department's attempt to tip
the balance between the military powers versus civil liberties in favor of the former,
when Attorney General Francis Biddle caved in to DeWitt's demand for the wholesale
Japanese "evacuation."[8]

Greg Robinson's *By Order of the President* (2001) tackles the hitherto-neglected subject of President Roosevelt's role in the policy formulation and ensuing developments
in internment history. Robinson's meticulous research on government papers provides
a glimpse into the thinking of the president, whose beliefs in social Darwinism, lack of
empathy for Japanese Americans, and pragmatic political calculations allowed "misin-
formation" and "bad counsel" from the likes of McCloy and Bendetsen to prevail over
the minority voice that criticized the wholesale removal of U.S. citizens without regards
to due process.[9] Having been integral to the racist political structure, Roosevelt could
pose no check on the process of the systemic failure in wartime democracy.

Exemplified in the works of Daniels, Irons, and Robinson, the ethnic studies mode of
historical interpretation mirrors a notable change in research methodology. Until the
1970s, the military origin of the internment policy rendered much of the government
source material classified and hence inaccessible to researchers. It is for this reason that the
earlier studies failed to illuminate the entanglements of key government officials beyond
the analysis of their public statements. Because the press most frequently quoted General
DeWitt as the military commander in charge of the "Japanese problem" on the West
Coast, he naturally received disproportionately greater attention than mid-level government insiders, like Bendetsen and Ennis. It was difficult, if not impossible, to discern the
nuances and complexities behind the public utterances of DeWitt and other officials. The
dearth of government source material allowed the pre-1970s scholarship to only scratch
the surface of the decision-making process regarding Japanese American internment.

Starting in 1972, historians enjoyed better access to internal government documents.
The U.S. National Archives formalized the declassification of confidential government papers, thereby facilitating the public release of War Department source material
up to the 1970s. Roger Daniels used this previously unobtainable material to write his
groundbreaking monographs. In the early 1980s, Irons gained initial access to declas-
sified Justice Department papers, which enabled him to discuss the crucial role of government lawyers. Moreover, since ethnic studies scholars tend to look at the wartime
Japanese American experience in terms of its linkage to the long-standing tradition of
anti-Asian public policies and ideologies, they generally cast a much wider net over the
source material that ranges from government papers to newspapers, and from personal
papers to various publications at the local and national levels. Consequently, they are
able to construct more comprehensive and substantive narratives.

In 1982, the United States Commission on the Wartime Relocation and Internment
of Civilians (CWRIC) built on the accumulated scholarship to address the questions of

causation and responsibility in a semi-official capacity. Established by an act of Congress, the CWRIC sponsored extensive archival research while conducting nationwide hearings from both surviving policy makers and former internees. Combining conventional archival sources with oral testimonies, *Personal Justice Denied* (1982) presents a formal report, in which the CWRIC singles out "race prejudice, war hysteria, and a failure of political leadership" as the "broad historical causes" for the promulgation of Executive Order 9066, the basis for the internment policy. Because the order violated the constitutional rights of Japanese American citizens without probable cause, the CWRIC declared that it "was not justified by military necessity."[10] This view not only enlivened the ensuing political process toward the passage of a redress bill in Congress, but also gave something akin to a government's seal of approval for the race-based interpretation of causation and responsibility.

Yet such progress does not mean the disappearance of contrary interpretations, which bolster the "military necessity" justification for the mass internment. Because the study of this historical subject is inseparable from the fundamental question of America's national identity—and that of the government role in defending the nation at the time of crisis—certain key moments in postwar U.S. history have sparked an intense struggle over the meaning of the internment in public and scholarly discourse. At the fifty-year anniversary of the end of the Pacific War, for example, the renowned historian Page Smith published a monograph, in which he defended—indeed extolled—the virtue of military necessity, attempting to dress wartime American democracy and the military policy of the "greatest generation" in positive clothes.[11] Some six years later, the tragedies of September 11, 2001, revived public and academic interest in internment history. Proponents of racial/religious profiling and Islamophobic pundits presented a skewed rendition of the wartime Japanese American experience as acceptable precedence for elevated government powers in the name of national security.[12] Both instances involve the use of selective evidence, misquotes, and arbitrary interpretations, especially in relation to the intertwining notions of a Nisei/Muslim being inherently dangerous due to ancestry, and military necessity. The history and historiography of Japanese American internment still create discursive contestation and political polemics over the questions of race, minority citizenship rights, and national security—as well as America's national image as the defender of democracy and freedom.

INTERNMENT HISTORY II: LOYALTY/ DISLOYALTY, COOPERATION/RESISTANCE, AND THE QUESTION OF HISTORICAL AGENCY

In the internment body of literature, "loyalty" and "disloyalty" have also formed a set of fundamental analytical categories. In the immediate postwar period, some of the JERS publications compounded a notable mode of historical interpretation based on these categories. Compiled chiefly by Dorothy Swaine Thomas, *The Spoilage* (1946) concentrated on the Nisei and Issei who failed the WRA's loyalty registration and hence were segregated within the Tule Lake Segregation Center. *The Salvage* (1952) examined the experiences of the Japanese Americans who were allowed to resettle in the Midwest and the East after passing the loyalty test. Although these studies delved into the subjectivity of the internees, they did not scrutinize the biases and presumptions that sustained the official categories of "loyalty" and "disloyalty" against which the various forms of internee protest and dissent took shape.

Before the 1970s, virtually no academic studies, let alone popular histories, questioned the validity of relying on these analytical and political constructs. The long-standing master narrative of the U.S. government, which arbitrarily sifts the Japanese American internees according to the binary criteria, dovetails with the Japanese American Citizens League (JACL)'s interpretation of their members' wartime experiences. Both state and ethnic orthodoxy celebrate a portrait of undiluted Americanism of loyal Nisei, especially JACL members and servicemen, while ostracizing the disloyal from the narrative history of assimilated "Americans with the Japanese face," to borrow a description of Bill Hosokawa's *Nisei* (1969).[13] Whether penned by WRA administrators, JERS researchers, or JACL leaders, the characterizations of ordinary Japanese Americans have suffered extremely skewed renditions and narrations. Their practice and thinking are almost always represented in terms of either their alleged embrace of American democracy or of Japanese militarism. There is little consideration for a non-politico-ideological form of internee behavior or concern in the master narrative.

With attention to its nuances and complexities, many Asian American historians are ready to grapple with the question of internee historical agency outside the confines of the bounded categories of loyalty and disloyalty. With an eye to understanding Japanese American thinking and practice from their vantage point, Arthur Hansen (with David A. Hacker) and Gary Okihiro published groundbreaking studies in 1973. Hansen argues that the conventional perspectives are too inappropriate to elucidate the mindset of most Nisei and Issei internees, who continued to live by the traditional Japanese group norms. Hansen's "ethnic perspective" attempts to delve into the internal logic of internee practices during the Manzanar "rebellion" from the perspective of their culturally prescribed notions of right and wrong. The destruction of Issei leadership by the WRA, as well as its favoritism toward Nisei JACL members, defied the commonly shared "cultural" common sense of proper social order, defined by status and age hierarchy. Instead of national loyalty/disloyalty, the internees' anger at the imperious violation of ethnic community rule caused a large number of them to rebel against the WRA and JACL in the Manzanar camp. Instead of depicting them as anti-American "troublemakers" or as mindless masses under the yoke of "pro-Fascist agitators," Hansen proposes that their actions be put in proper perspective, in line with their cultural heritage and sensitivities.[14]

Drawing from postcolonial African studies scholarship, Okihiro considers the internee action as an expression of resistance against forced Americanization. Throughout the 1970s and the 1980s, he published a series of articles in terms of a resistance paradigm. The resurgence of Buddhism in the camp, Okihiro explains, exemplified a popular disavowal of the government attempt to Americanize them in accordance with its Eurocentric standards. The uprising of disloyal internees in the segregation center was emblematic of their struggle for ethnic preservation and dignity under the dehumanizing condition of militarized detention.[15] With these new interpretive frames, both Okihiro and Hansen have contributed to the rise of a historical literature that narrates the experiences of Nisei and Issei internees in a more sophisticated and sensible manner than the WRA/JACL orthodoxy.

While underscoring the failure of loyalty and disloyalty as analytical categories, the serious reevaluation of internee agency induced a shift in research methodology. Official government papers, mainstream press reports, and JACL documents, including the *Pacific Citizen* newspaper, generally constituted the chief source materials for the conventional scholarship. Not only have ethnic studies scholars carefully reread such documents, but they have also devised innovative ways to salvage the neglected voices of ordinary internees, including those of the disloyal. The types of new source material that they often turn to include life histories and oral interviews, personal diaries and letters, court records, and literary works and cultural artifacts.

After the early 1970s, the topics of new research on Japanese American resistance range from the reevaluation of internee struggle against military orders to organized draft objection, and from Tule Lake camp rebellions to mass renunciation. Michi Weglyn's *Years of Infamy* (1976) and Eric Muller's *Free to Die for Their Country* (2001) are poignant examples that draw on the alternative interpretive frames and new research methodology. In particular, Muller's work brings back to the forefront the question of Japanese American constitutional rights. He combines a legalist discussion with a bottom-up analysis of Nisei draft resisters in the Heart Mountain camp. Donald Collins's *Native American Aliens* (1985) also applies a legalist analysis to the wartime and postwar struggle of Nisei renunciants, who lost their birthright citizenship due to their disloyal standing.[16]

Along the same line, Nisei litigants in historic Supreme Court cases emerged as an important research subject within the resistance paradigm. Having disobeyed the military's curfew order and/or evacuation order in the spring of 1942, Min Yasui, Gordon Hirabayashi, and Fred Korematsu became representatives of the test cases that challenged the constitutionality of the internment policy. The government convicted them as criminals, and the JACL lambasted them as "self-styled martyrs," who allegedly tarnished the good name of patriotic Japanese Americans. Without losing sight of national priority during a time of total war, ethnic leadership reasoned, most other Nisei had quietly demonstrated their loyalty through self-sacrifice and cooperation with the government—a view that the JACL orthodoxy continued to hold up in the postwar years. In their studies, however, Peter Irons and other scholars illuminate the alternative definition of loyalty that the three men propounded, just as draft resisters did. The test case litigants felt that every self-respecting "loyal" American had the responsibility to protest an unlawful government policy and to seek redress—even when it was carried out in the name of military necessity and national security.[17] The new paradigm allows historians to complicate the notion of loyalty because the resisters were, in their thinking and practice, every bit as patriotic as JACL leaders claimed to be.

Aided by innovative research methodology, the new scholarship on Japanese American agency also unveils how all strata of social relations in Japanese America transformed during the torturous wartime processes of forced migration, incarceration, and resettlement/segregation. Under an overbearing pressure to prove allegiance to the government that had incarcerated them, the preexisting community's spirit and bonds gave way to mutual suspicions and resentments. Not only did the WRA strip the immigrant men of all authority and status in favor of JACL leaders, but internees found their family ties fraying, the generations becoming more distant and acrimonious to one another, and gender relations mutated in a fundamental way. The consequences of these changes were still felt strongly in postwar Japanese America—even in the era of the third generation, Sansei. Tackling these issues, the literature on social and psychological effects on Nisei and Sansei occupies an important place in contemporary internment studies.

Other works also examine the paradox of "democratic" education in captivity, the role of spirituality and religious institutions in everyday camp life, the practice of internee cultural citizenship, and the grassroots proliferation of artistic production under incarceration. Thomas James (1987) shows how white camp administrators and teachers executed a progressive curriculum—including the "Problems of Democracy" courses—for Nisei pupils, resulting in an ironic effect of highlighting the state of their own political repression in captivity. Yet, as Yoon Pak (2001) reveals, such contradictions simultaneously enabled Japanese American youth to develop a more nuanced understanding of democracy and freedom vis-à-vis the reality of racism—one that Eurocentric racial liberalism of the time could not capture. As Okihiro suggests, the involvement of internees in Buddhist activities likewise calls into question the meaning of the assimilationist ideal propagated by the WRA and JACL. Furthermore, starting with Karin Higa's work (1992), studies of camp art have brought to light the creative activities of ordinary Issei and Nisei that ranged from painting to sculpture and from photography to poetry.[18] Having been deprived of the opportunity to express their complex emotions and heterodox viewpoints, new studies reveal, Japanese Americans relied on informal cultural production to resist the imposed virtues of loyalty and Americanism.

Finally, it is necessary to situate another set of literature in the trajectory of the recent scholarly endeavors rooted in the resistance paradigm. Research on the movement for Japanese American redress and reparations deals with the 1970s and the 1980s; however, the central theme revolves around the question of how Japanese Americans—Nisei and Sansei—have come to terms with the painful memory of wartime racial persecution through new renditions of government responsibility and internee behavior. This literature offers an intriguing look at the ramifications of internment history beyond the chronological confines of World War II. Moreover, it also unravels the entanglements of historical revisionism with the political activism that the ethnic studies scholarship has generated since the 1970s. While Yasuko I. Takezawa (1995) uncovers a simultaneous development of political mobilization and ethnic identity formation in Seattle, Mitchell

Maki and colleagues (1999) and Leslie Hatamiya (1993) detail the tumultuous process through which the Japanese American community managed to push the redress legislation forward in the national politics. These studies suggest, in various ways, that the remaking of post-1970s Japanese America—its group identities and collective historical memories and consciousness—is deeply intertwined with the alternative understandings of the internment past. Alice Yang Murray (2008) expounds explicitly on these themes in her major monograph.[19]

OUTSIDE THE WRA CAMPS

Because they see the Japanese American internment as a culmination of institutionalized racism, some Asian American scholars are interested in understanding how Nisei and Issei coped with different, if somewhat milder, expressions of white racism outside the West Coast during the war. With a larger Japanese population than the West Coast, Hawai'i is a logical point of comparison. Following Japan's attack on Pearl Harbor, the islands were placed under martial law. Even though the same kind of legal constraints did not exist in Hawai'i's martial law regime as in the continental United States, no mass removal or incarceration, paradoxically, took place there. The U.S. Army nonetheless did issue a variety of military orders to restrict the activities and movements of Hawai'i's Japanese residents. Gary Okihiro (1992), Tom Coffman (2003), and Franklin Odo (2003) narrate aspects of these developments, as well as local Nisei and Issei responses to such trying situations. Similar to the research on the West Coast internee agency, their studies entail a sensible analysis of nuanced popular resistance, maneuvering, and adaptation to the martial law regime. This scholarship poses a powerful challenge to the oversimplified account of Hawai'i Nisei's allegiance to American democracy that was put forth earlier by Andrew Lind (1946).[20] Furthermore, the army's treatment of Hawai'i Japanese, who were allowed to remain in the islands, also raises a critical question regarding the government's justification for the West Coast incarceration as a matter of military necessity.

The experience of former internees outside the camps constitutes another popular theme of recent historical research. Adopting a less chronologically bound vision of internment history, some historians find it necessary to look at the repeated processes of forced migration and resettlement during and after the war. The mobility of "loyal" Japanese Americans from captivity into the Midwest, the East, and later back to the West Coast mirrored a significant shift in dominant racial discourse. In dialogue with the study of Cold War Asian American history, the scholarship on postinternment resettlement often looks at how Nisei men and women negotiated what Okihiro calls the "antiracism" of postwar white America, where "Americanism" was measured according to one's embrace of democratic values, not one's skin color. This new national practice renounced biological racism in order to facilitate minority integration on the basis of their professed allegiance to color-blind democracy (and, implicitly, their opposition to communism and other forms of "radicalism"). Situating the research subject in that context, Okihiro (1999), Allan W. Austin (2005), Greg Robinson (2012), and Ellen D. Wu (2014) have published solid monographs on wartime and postwar Nisei resettlement and experiences. A powerful corrective to the superficial treatment of Nisei agency in the earlier JERS publications, the emergent literature explores the complex meanings of their loyalty, the difficulties of social assimilation, and the challenge of balancing their American identity with their ethnic/cultural heritage under a postwar racial liberalism that was still Anglo-centric in nature.[21]

Outside the U.S. national context, the scholarship on Japanese Canadian internment reveals a divergent trajectory of historiographical development relative to its U.S. counterpart. Canada's invocation of the War Measures Act removed legal deterrents against the mass detention of civilians, forced labor, confiscation of private properties, and denaturalization and deportation to which Japanese Canadians were subjected. Of the 22,000 internees, three-quarters were native-born Canadian citizens yet they were treated as "enemy aliens" under the law. Men were separated from women and children; the former were placed in labor camps and the latter in interior internment camps. After the war, the internees were faced with the choice of moving to eastern Canada or losing citizenship and being deported to Japan. Western Canada was closed to them until 1949.

The overwhelming emergency powers of which the Canadian government could freely avail itself provided for no constitutional question equivalent to the U.S. internment. Thus, Canadian scholars have not been fixated on legalist concerns. Nor did they start to examine the subject closely until the problem of race emerged as the major issue in the historical research and political consciousness in Canadian academia. Except for a 1948 study by Forrest La Violette—who was a former WRA staff researcher in the United States—the Canadian internment literature took shape primarily after the mid-1970s in conjunction with state-sponsored multiculturalism and the community-led redress movement, the converging political forces that propelled Canada to come to terms with its racist actions against Japanese residents. Ken Adachi's *The Enemy That Never Was* (1976) set off the publication of one historical monograph and another that presented a common narrative of egregious racist persecution and the Japanese struggle against it.[22] Despite similarity in the narrative schema, however, the Canadian studies are rarely in dialogue with their U.S. counterparts, and vice versa, for both sides tend to restrict their respective internment histories to the domains of domestic race relations and/or ethnic formations. Whether being narrated from the standpoint of citizenship rights or multiculturalism, or from that of minority assimilation or resistance, Japanese internment is almost always rendered as part of a national history.

MILITARY SERVICE AND PATRIOTISM

Material to internment history, a study of Japanese American military service reveals an even more nation-bound orientation. The story of Nisei military service is well documented in both popular and scholarly publications. Loyalty remains a central paradigm in this major subfield of World War II history. Combined with the 100th Battalion from Hawai'i, the famed 442nd Regimental Combat Team (RCT) consisted almost exclusively of "loyal" Nisei volunteers and, later, of draftees from within and without the internment camps. Because the War Department, WRA, and JACL made concerted efforts to publicize their patriotic accomplishments on the European warfront in the official propaganda, Nisei soldiers became something of a national icon that supposedly epitomized the antiracist national identity of a new America.

Since before the end of the war, the intertwining stories of Nisei's martial Americanism and of America's embrace of nonwhite citizen patriots have shored up a liberal exceptionalist narrative of national progress. In 1946, Orville Shirley compiled a volume, entitled *Americans*, to detail how valorously Nisei had fought against Nazism and Fascism in Europe due to their unshaken commitment to color-blind democracy, despite the temporary setback for their civil liberties. A subsequent, more scholarly work by John Rademaker, a former WRA researcher, also presented a pointed account of Hawai'i Nisei's military heroism in terms of the integrationist paradigm that his book title— *These Are Americans* (1951)—crystallized.[23] Just as President Harry S. Truman did, these works valorized the idea that Nisei patriots embodied America's double victory over racial bigotry at home and totalitarianism abroad, with the goal of portraying the nation as a true defender of freedom and equality. It was a triumphant narrative of America's progress as much as it was a poignant tale of Nisei's patriotism.

The ensuing decades have witnessed the publication of similar books—both popular and academic—that follow the basic narrative scheme set by the aforementioned. In the post-1970s era, Masayo Umezawa Duus (1987) and Robert Asahina (2006) have arguably produced some of the most representative studies on the 442nd RCT. Some authors have also applied the same celebratory storyline to the exploits of Nisei members of the Military Intelligence Service in the Pacific theater. Joseph Harrington's *Yankee Samurai* (1979) and James McNaughton's *Nisei Linguists* (2007) are good examples.[24] To compound a personalized feel in the narrative, these works commonly feature Nisei veterans themselves as the main storytellers, whose life histories, personal correspondences, and diaries are combined with the analysis of recently released government source material.

Many Asian American historians are critical of the ideological ramifications for the dominant interpretive and narrative scheme, however. Rather than contending that democracy corrected itself through Nisei patriotism and the goodwill of enlightened white Americans, they elucidate the irony of fighting for a nation that denied them and their parents a legitimate place within it. With an eye on historical continuities, Franklin Odo connects the wartime experience of Nisei volunteer soldiers in Hawai'i to the prewar tradition of racial discrimination in the islands and their postwar struggle with a more subtle, and yet stubborn, undercurrent of racism embedded in Cold War liberalism. Takashi Fujitani is perhaps among the first scholars who brings the perspective of empire to the center of historical analysis in a booklength study. Most other studies of World War II are deficient of an empire paradigm. In his *Race for Empire* (2011), Fujitani sheds light on the imperialist nature of minority military service by comparing Nisei soldiers in the U.S. armed forces with Korean soldiers in the Japanese imperial army.[25] These works compel readers to better understand not only the deeper meaning of Japanese American patriotism but also the role of the conventional master narrative in sustaining and reinforcing U.S. exceptionalist nationalism in the era of diversity and multiculturalism.

Some Chinese American and Korean American scholars have examined the wartime experiences of the respective groups through the lenses of military service and national allegiance. According to K. Scott Wong's *Americans First* (2005), the political exigencies of the Pacific War facilitated the breakdown of racial barriers for non-Japanese residents, splitting the monolithic category of "Asian" into the good and the evil. Through new opportunities in war industries and the armed forces, Chinese American men and women negotiated the turbulent processes of social integration and economic mobility. Their growing identification with, and loyalty to, color-blind Americanism was accompanied by their conscious self-representation as a model minority—at the cost of creating a rupture with Nisei, the symbol of "evil Asians" in the wartime American imagination. The Chinese American pursuit of equal treatment and inclusion involved a racial formation of a different sort, because wartime racial liberalism only managed to realign the asymmetry of racial differences and boundaries rather than eliminating them. Indeed, America's general acceptance of Chinese Americans was far from automatic or unconditional. It was still contingent on their public display of undiluted patriotism—one usually juxtaposed against the supposedly treacherous nature of Japanese Americans.[26]

Similar dilemmas constituted the wartime social reality for Korean Americans, especially immigrants. Lili M. Kim's research unveils how they struggled to establish an identity as patriotic ethnic Americans while consciously and loudly emphasizing their unambiguous difference from the Japanese—both here and in Asia. Yet even though they wholeheartedly supported U.S. war efforts to defeat Japanese imperialism and liberate Korea, their legal status as colonized subjects of the enemy empire added more complications to the wartime story of intra-Asian disidentification. Not only were Korean Americans compelled to distance themselves from everything Japanese, but they were also faced with the equally difficult task of convincing the U.S. government that they were on the American side in the war against Japan—despite, or because of, colonial Korea's enemy standing.[27] Some activists and scholars have also documented the valor of Filipino American soldiers who fought alongside American soldiers against imperial Japan. As in the Korean American case, that history also exposes the paradox of their military service due to their unique colonial position; on the grounds that they were colonized U.S. nationals, not full-fledged citizens, Filipino American servicemen were denied veterans' benefits until 2009. These ironic stories of Asian American military heroism accentuate the nuanced meanings and equivocal consequences of loyalty and Americanism.

NEW DEVELOPMENTS AND FUTURE OUTLOOK

Despite many notable changes during the past several decades, academic research on internment history has generally maintained one consistent feature. Scholars have kept their inquiry within the national bounds of the United States (or Canada). The domestic orientation of internment studies is wedded to the pivotal theme of civil liberties (or multiculturalism in the case of Canada). Because the main argument has revolved around the violation of Nisei citizenship rights via a racist policy, the resultant narratives have restricted the geographic scope of research and interpretation within the reach of U.S. constitutional rule. The preoccupation with citizenship rights has also generated an asymmetric scholarly gaze at native-born Nisei and foreign-born Issei. The prevailing focus on the second generation in the existing literature is entangled with an excessive emphasis on civil rights concerns. Combined, these twin biases have perpetuated a nation/citizen-based frame of research and analysis in the internment studies.

To counter these biases, transnational and comparative perspectives have emerged in the last decade. These approaches signal new directions in the field. Brian Hayashi (2004) not only contests accepted interpretations about causation and responsibility, but also expands the contours of historical knowledge on the Japanese American internment by looking at "international linkages" and the geopolitical "landscape."[28] On the question of causation, Hayashi's monograph takes race and military concerns seriously, rather than putting an overbearing emphasis on one or the other. Considering "foreign factors" in a "wider, global context" of the Pacific War, Hayashi argues that government leaders had to evaluate the domestic Japanese problem in terms of pressing geopolitical concerns, including military situations in the Philippines and diplomatic pressures from Mexico, Canada, and Peru. The decision to intern Japanese Americans was inseparable from such developments outside the United States.

Decentering constitutional concerns within internment studies allows noncitizen internees to occupy a more prominent place in a historical narrative. Conventionally, Issei have been subjected to historical oblivion in a scholarship that concentrates on Nisei citizenship rights. Though his use of vernacular immigrant source material is limited and hence problematic from a methodological standpoint, Hayashi still gives life to those forgotten historical agents—especially the ambiguities and ambivalence of their allegiances and actions—who were stuck between two countries of varied importance to them. Similarly, through the lens of human rights rather than of civil rights in the internment saga, John Howard (2008) manages to discuss questions relating to gender and sexuality in an unprecedented manner.[29] These approaches move readers away from the polarized, essentialized categories of "loyal" versus "disloyal," "American" versus "Japanese," and "good" versus "evil"—the binaries that past scholarship hardly complicated. Even the resistance paradigm largely fails to disrupt the dichotomy between "American" and "Japanese," as it tends to fit noncitizen internees into the mold of "loyal" victims insofar as it was the U.S. racial regime that had denied their rights/chance for naturalization and hence national inclusion.

Comparative studies of "enemy" internment cases also signal the burgeoning of a new transnational approach. Following his work titled *Concentration Camps North America: Japanese in the United States and Canada during World War II* (1993), Roger Daniels, with an Australian scholar, put together *Alien Justice* (2000), an anthology that juxtaposes the varied experiences of peoples of Axis ancestry in the United

States, Canada, and Australia. Though not closely meshed, the chapters form a comparative frame to reveal the differences and similarities of concurrent historical developments, which revolved around the problems of race/ethnicity, citizenship, and national security in the three Allied countries. Greg Robinson tries to coalesce the disparate national histories of Japanese internment into a cohesive narrative in *A Tragedy of Democracy* (2009). Dismantling the fixed spatial boundaries, the author adopts a hemispheric approach. He is interested in unveiling how the mass incarceration of U.S. resident Japanese influenced the historical unfolding of other areas in the Western Hemisphere—notably Hawai'i, Canada, and Latin American nations (Mexico, Panama, and Peru)—where no legal deterrent against mass removal or civilian detention was present.[30]

The works of Hayashi, Daniels, and Robinson reveal new possibilities in internment history. In terms of the interpretive frames, their studies prove that the transnational and comparative paradigms can shift a scholarly gaze to the neglected aspects of the human experience—aspects not contained within the bounds of national(ized) narratives. The field should anticipate more historical studies with these new approaches if it wishes to remain intellectually viable and relevant to the general transnational turn in Asian American history, U.S. history, and historical scholarship in general. Of course, seen from the standpoint of countering politicized attempts to exploit the internment past for contemporary nationalist/racialist politics, it is understandable that many ethnic studies scholars insist on the importance of the civil rights perspective. Nevertheless, it is also high time that scholars give serious thought to an intellectual demand for the vigorous critiquing of a national exceptionalist narrative that exclusively favors the analytical categories of loyalty and citizenship rights.

Aside from the subject of Japanese American incarceration, general studies of World War II history may also benefit from revamping and enlarging the scope of research and analysis. The conventional themes of military service, national inclusion, and ethnic identity formation have presented an important glimpse into wartime Asian American experiences, yet they have created particular biases and oversights in the scholarship. For example, the emphasis on the military experience inevitably results in an ignorance of women's agency as much as the denial of noncitizens' places in history. Moreover, in comparison with other subfields of Asian American history, World War II history has seldom probed how Asian Americans negotiated changing relations with other racial minorities once they found an increasing opportunity for integration—and, hence, growing frequency of intergroup contact—in daily life. A serious inquiry into the wartime experience of Asian Americans in the context of multiracial relations would be a welcome development.

Furthermore, World War II history needs to extend beyond the "war" itself as a primary focus of analysis. While Asian Americans were certainly concerned with and swayed by the Pacific War, they also went on with everyday routines as men, women, and children; eked out livings as workers, store owners, and farmers; and engaged in recreational and communal activities unrelated to national defense and/or ancestral lands. Just as historians have explored these aspects of Asian American history in the prewar context, they may well look at the war years from the similar vantage point of historical mundanity—one that is fundamental to social and cultural history. The war is an extraordinary event in history that allows historians to grapple head-on with many intriguing questions, like national identity, loyalty, and the complex meaning of citizenship. But World War II history also entails many commonplace affairs and issues that define the wholeness of human experience beyond (albeit not free from) the mandates and imperatives of the warring states. For the next generation of Asian American historians, these areas of research remain wide open and hence form unexplored opportunities.

NOTES

1. Carey McWilliams, *Prejudice, Japanese Americans: A Symbol of Racial Intolerance* (Boston: Little, Brown, 1944).
2. Eugene Rostow, "Our Worst Wartime Mistake," *Harper's Magazine* 191 (1945): 193–201, esp. 194.
3. They are Dorothy Swaine Thomas and Richard S. Nishimoto, *The Spoilage* (Berkeley: University of California Press, 1946); Morton Grodzins, *Americans Betrayed: Politics and the Japanese Evacuation* (Chicago: University of Chicago Press, 1949); Dorothy Swaine Thomas (with assistance of Charles Kikuchi and James Sakoda), *The Salvage* (Berkeley: University of California Press, 1952); and Jacobus tenBroek et al., *Prejudice, War and the Constitution* (Berkeley: University of California Press, 1954);
4. TenBroek et al., *Prejudice, War and the Constitution*, 334.
5. Grodzins, *Americans Betrayed*, 92–128; tenBroek et al., *Prejudice, War and the Constitution*, 185–208.
6. See Peter T. Suzuki, "For the Sake of Inter-University Comity: The Attempted Suppression by the University of California of Morton Grodzins' *Americans Betrayed*," in *Views from Within: The Japanese American Evacuation and Resettlement Study*, ed. Yuji Ichioka (Los Angeles: UCLA Asian American Studies Center, 1989), 95–123.
7. Roger Daniels, *Concentration Camps USA: Japanese Americans and World War II* (New York: Holt, Rinehart and Winston, 1971), 42–73.
8. Peter H. Irons, *Justice at War: The Story of Japanese-American Internment Cases* (New York: Oxford University Press, 1983), 3–74.
9. Greg Robinson, *By Order of the President: FDR and the Internment of Japanese Americans* (Cambridge, MA: Harvard University Press, 2001), 109–124.
10. United States Commission on Wartime Relocation and Internment of Civilians, *Personal Justice Denied: Report of the Commission on Wartime Relocation and Internment of Civilians* (1982; repr., Seattle: University of Washington Press, 1997), 1–23, esp. 18.
11. Page Smith, *Democracy on Trial: The Japanese American Evacuation and Relocation during World War II* (New York: Simon and Schuster, 1995). Note the use of euphemisms, like "evacuation" and "relocation," that underscore Smith's argument for the nonracist nature of the internment policy.
12. See Michelle Malkin, *In Defense of Internment: The Case for "Racial Profiling" in World War II and the War on Terror* (Washington, DC: Regnery, 2004).
13. Bill Hosokawa, *The Nisei: The Quiet Americans* (New York: William Morrow, 1969), 494.

14. Arthur A. Hansen and David A. Hacker, "The Manzanar Riot: An Ethnic Perspective," *Amerasia Journal* 2, no. 2 (1973): 112–157.

15. Gary Y. Okihiro, "Religion and Resistance in America's Concentration Camps," *Phylon* 45, no. 3 (1984): 220–233. The following essay marked the beginning of his writings on Japanese American resistance. Gary Okihiro, "Japanese Resistance to America's Concentration Camps: A Re-evaluation," *Amerasia Journal* 2, no. 1 (1973): 20–34.

16. Michi Weglyn, *Years of Infamy: The Untold Story of America's Concentration Camps* (New York: Quill, 1976); Eric L. Muller, *Free to Die for Their Country: The Story of Japanese American Draft Resisters in World War II* (Chicago: University of Chicago Press, 2001); Donald Collins, *Native American Aliens: Disloyalty and the Renunciation of Citizenship by Japanese Americans during World War II* (Westport, CT: Greenwood, 1985).

17. Irons, *Justice at War.*

18. See Thomas James, *Exile Within: The Schooling of Japanese Americans, 1942–1945* (Cambridge, MA: Harvard University Press, 1987); Yoon Pak, *Wherever I Go, I Will Always Be a Loyal American: Seattle's Japanese American Schoolchildren during World War II* (New York: Routledge, 2001); and Karin M. Higa, *The View from Within: Japanese American Art from the Internment Camps, 1942–1945* (Los Angeles: UCLA Asian American Studies Center, 1992).

19. Yasuko I. Takezawa, *Breaking the Silence: Redress and Japanese American Ethnicity* (Ithaca, NY: Cornell University Press, 1995); Mitchell Maki, Harry H. L. Kitano, and S. Megan Berthold, *Achieving the Impossible Dream: How Japanese Americans Obtained Redress* (Urbana: University of Illinois Press, 1999); Leslie T. Hatamiya, *Righting a Wrong: Japanese Americans and the Passage of the Civil Liberties Act of 1988* (Stanford, CA: Stanford University Press, 1993); Alice Yang Murray, *Historical Memories of the Japanese American Internment and the Struggle for Redress* (Stanford, CA: Stanford University Press, 2008).

20. Gary Y. Okihiro, *Cane Fires: The Anti-Japanese Movement in Hawaii, 1865–1945* (Philadelphia: Temple University Press, 1992); Tom Coffman, *The Island Edge of America: A Political History of Hawai'i* (Honolulu: University of Hawai'i Press, 2003); Franklin Odo, *No Sword to Bury: Japanese Americans in Hawai'i during World War II* (Philadelphia: Temple University Press, 2003); Andrew Lind, *Hawaii's Japanese, An Experiment in Democracy* (Princeton, NJ: Princeton University Press, 1946).

21. Gary Y. Okihiro, *Storied Lives: Japanese American Students and World War II* (Seattle: University of Washington Press, 1999); Allan W. Austin, *From Concentration Camp to Campus: Japanese American Students and World War II* (Urbana: University of Illinois Press, 2005); Greg Robinson, *After Camp: Portraits in Midcentury Japanese American Life and Politics* (Berkeley: University of California Press, 2012); Ellen D. Wu, *The Color of Success: Asian Americans and the Origins of the Model Minority* (Princeton, NJ: Princeton University Press, 2014); Matthew M. Briones, *Jim and Jap Crow: A Cultural History of 1940s Interracial America* (Princeton, NJ: Princeton University Press, 2012), 162–191.

22. Ken Adachi, *The Enemy That Never Was: A History of the Japanese Canadians* (Toronto: McClelland and Stewart, 1976).

23. Orville C. Shirley, *Americans: The Story of the 442nd Combat Team* (Washington, DC: Infantry Journal Press, 1946); John A. Rademaker, *These Are Americans: The Japanese Americans in Hawaii in World War II* (Palo Alto, CA: Pacific Books, 1951).

24. Masayo Umezawa Duus, *Unlikely Liberators: The Men of the 100th and 442nd*, translated by Peter Duus (Honolulu: University of Hawai'i Press, 1987); Robert Asahina, *Just Americans: How Japanese Americans Won a War at Home and Abroad* (New York: Gotham, 2006); Joseph D. Harrington, *Yankee Samurai: The Secret Role of Nisei in America's Pacific*

Victory (Detroit, MI: Pettigrew, 1979); James C. McNaughton, *Nisei Linguists: Japanese Americans in the Military Intelligence Service during World War II* (Washington, DC: U.S. Army Center of Military History, 2007).

25. Odo, *No Sword to Bury*; T. Fujitani, *Race for Empire: Koreans as Japanese and Japanese as Americans during World War II* (Berkeley: University of California Press, 2011). See also Wu, *The Color of Success*, 72–110.

26. K. Scott Wong, *Americans First: Chinese Americans and the Second World War* (Cambridge, MA: Harvard University Press, 2005). See also Wu, *The Color of Success*, 43–71.

27. Lili M. Kim, *Resisting the Orientalization of the Enemy: Korean Americans, World War II, and the Transnational Struggle for Justice on the Homefront* (Stanford, CA: Stanford University Press, forthcoming).

28. Brian M. Hayashi, *Democratizing the Enemy: The Japanese American Internment* (Princeton, NJ: Princeton University Press, 2004), esp. 2–12.

29. John Howard, *Concentration Camps on the Home Front: Japanese Americans in the House of Jim Crow* (Chicago: University of Chicago Press, 2008).

30. Roger Daniels, *Concentration Camps North America: Japanese in the United States and Canada during World War II* (Malabar: Krieger, 1993); Kay Saunders and Roger Daniels, eds., *Alien Justice: Wartime Internment in Australia and North America* (St. Lucia: University of Queensland Press, 2000); Greg Robinson, *A Tragedy of Democracy: Japanese Confinement in North America* (New York: Columbia University Press, 2009).

FURTHER READING

Adachi, Ken. *The Enemy That Never Was: A History of Japanese Canadians*. Toronto: McClelland and Stewart, 1976.

Austin, Allan W. *From Concentration Camp to Campus: Japanese American Students and World War II*. Urbana: University of Illinois Press, 2005.

Daniels, Roger. *Concentration Camps USA: Japanese Americans and World War II*. New York: Holt, Rinehart and Winston, 1971.

Fujitani, Takashi. *Race for Empire: Koreans as Japanese and Japanese as Americans during World War II*. Berkeley: University of California Press, 2011.

Grodzins, Morton. *Americans Betrayed: Politics and the Japanese Evacuation*. Chicago: University of Chicago Press, 1949.

Hayashi, Brian M. *Democratizing the Enemy: The Japanese American Internment*. Princeton, NJ: Princeton University Press, 2004.

Ichioka, Yuji, ed. *Views from Within: The Japanese American Evacuation and Resettlement Study*. Los Angeles: UCLA Asian American Studies Center, 1989.

Irons, Peter. *Justice at War: The Story of Japanese-American Internment Cases*. New York: Oxford University Press, 1983.

McWilliams, Carey. *Prejudice, Japanese Americans: A Symbol of Racial Intolerance*. Boston: Little, Brown, 1944.

Muller, Eric L. *Free to Die for Their Country: The Story of Japanese American Draft Resisters in World War II*. Chicago: University of Chicago Press, 2003.

Murray, Alice Yang. *Historical Memories of the Japanese American Internment and the Struggle for Redress*. Stanford, CA: Stanford University Press, 2008.

Odo, Franklin. *No Sword to Bury: Japanese Americans in Hawai'i during World War II.* Philadelphia: Temple University Press, 2003.

Okihiro, Gary Y. *Storied Lives: Japanese American Students and World War II.* Seattle: University of Washington Press, 1999.

Robinson, Greg. *By Order of the President: FDR and the Internment of Japanese Americans.* Cambridge, MA: Harvard University Press, 2001.

———. *A Tragedy of Democracy: Japanese Confinement in North America.* New York: Columbia University Press, 2009.

TenBroek, Jacobus, Edward H. Barnhart, and Floyd W. Matson. *Prejudice, War and the Constitution.* Berkeley: University of California Press, 1954.

Thomas, Dorothy Swaine, and Richard S. Nishimoto. *The Spoilage.* Berkeley: University of California Press, 1946.

Thomas, Dorothy Swaine, with assistance of Charles Kikuchi and James Sakoda. *The Salvage.* Berkeley: University of California Press, 1952.

United States Commission on Wartime Relocation and Internment of Civilians. *Personal Justice Denied: Report of the Commission on Wartime Relocation and Internment of Civilians.* Edited by Tetsuden Kashima. 1982. Reprint, Seattle: University of Washington Press, 1997.

Weglyn, Michi. *Years of Infamy: The Untold Story of America's Concentration Camps.* New York: Quill, 1976.

Wong, K. Scott. *Americans First: Chinese Americans and the Second World War.* Cambridge, MA: Harvard University Press, 2005.

CHAPTER 9

....

RECONSIDERING ASIAN
EXCLUSION IN THE
UNITED STATES

....

KORNEL S. CHANG

On October 6, 2011, the United States Senate, in a resolution with unanimous bipartisan support, apologized for the Chinese Exclusion Act of 1882 and the subsequent laws that restricted the movements of Chinese immigrants and denied them citizenship. The chief sponsor of the bill, Dianne Feinstein, a Democratic senator from California, issued this statement following its passage in the upper chamber: "The enactment of Chinese exclusionary laws is a shameful part of our history that must not be forgotten. I hope this resolution will serve to enlighten those who may not be aware of this regrettable chapter in our history, and bring closure to the families whose loved ones lived through this difficult time." But if this was a moment to shine light on a past injustice, it also served as an occasion to recuperate the liberal narrative of immigration and assimilation. "Despite these hardships," Feinstein added, "Chinese immigrants persevered, and they continue to make invaluable contributions to the development and success of our country." In this rendering of an immigrant America, the unjustly treated foreigner serves, as the Bonnie Honig has pointed out, as "an agent of national reenchantment that might rescue the regime from corruption and return it to its first principles."[1] In this process, the once-excluded Chinese is transformed into the iconic good immigrant who, in overcoming racial exclusion, redeems the promise of an exceptional America.

In recent years, scholars of Asian American history have produced a rich body of work that has complicated, and in some cases, overturned, the traditional liberal narratives of assimilation and inclusion. Inspired variously by the transnational and cultural turn in the social sciences and the humanities, and a growing interest in writing imperial histories of migration, a new generation of scholars has reshaped and transformed our understanding of Asian exclusion so that it is no longer simply a tale of exclusion and the inevitable triumph of liberal citizenship. Instead, by embedding Asian exclusion within broader histories and wider fields of power, these scholars have revealed how the exclusion of Asian immigrants—the concerted effort to bar them from the country, and to deny those within its boundaries the full rights of citizenship—was constitutive of U.S. nation building, emerging as a preeminent site for developing the state's triad strategies of "discipline, normalization, and regulation," and deployed as part of America's repertoire of imperial power in the late nineteenth and early twentieth centuries.[2] This chapter provides a brief overview of the literature, tracing how historical interpretations of Asian exclusion have changed and been recast over time, and it then turns its focus to the methodological innovations and the temporal and spatial reorientations that have attended the recent reappraisal of Asian exclusion in the United States.

EXCLUSION WITHIN A NATION OF IMMIGRANTS

The earliest writings on Asian exclusion in the United States were typically lumped in with discussions of immigration restriction. Joining Southern and Eastern Europeans, Asian immigrants were viewed as a social problem that threatened the racial integrity of the nation, which was imagined as being Anglo-Saxon in character. Yet, even as they fit into a more general pattern of American history, immigrants from Asia were also conceptually and intellectually set apart, given the distinct designation of the "Oriental problem" by social scientists in the early twentieth century. This splitting had profound consequences for the academic study of immigration in the mid-twentieth century, when it emerged as an important subfield of American history. Consider John Higham's classic account of nativism, *Strangers in the Land*, first published in 1955, which methodically traced antiforeign sentiment in the United States from the late nineteenth century to the early twentieth century, showing how it culminated with the passage of the National Origins Act in 1924. Conspicuously absent from Higham's genealogy of American nativism, however, was the Chinese Exclusion Act, the nation's first attempt to ban immigrants on the basis of race, as well as the subsequent laws restricting Asian immigration to the United States. In the tradition of the Chicago School of Sociology, Higham thought that the experiences of the Chinese and Japanese represented "somewhat separate phenomena, historically tangential to the main currents of American nativism."[3]

But if this absent presence was a legacy of interwar social science theories, its influence loomed large even when Asian immigrants were treated as subjects of historical inquiry. Gunther Barth, a student of Oscar Handlin, published one of the first academic studies of Chinese immigration and exclusion. Writing from the dominant perspectives of the social sciences, in *Bitter Strength* (1964), Barth replaced the European immigrant of Handlin's *Uprooted* with the Chinese "sojourner" in the assimilation cycle. For Barth, the process was far more vexing and protracted for the Chinese because they migrated to the United States under coercion as "coolie" laborers, and, thus, unlike Europeans, they were not truly free immigrants. This led a white public to conflate Chinese labor with servitude and African American slavery. This condition of unfreedom reinforced a sojourning mentality among the Chinese, nativists argued, that stubbornly resisted assimilation. As sojourners, the Chinese in America became associated with subservience, filth, vagrancy, and immorality. Opposition to these real and imagined characteristics of the Chinese (and their places of settlement) galvanized a social movement to exclude them from the body politic. Thus, Barth held Chinese "sojourners" responsible, at least in part, for their own marginalization.[4] Other studies written around the same time were more categorical in its denunciation of Asian exclusion, declaring it a blot on America's liberal democratic traditions, but their arguments for inclusion continued to rest on an appeal to the social worthiness of the Asian immigrant.[5]

The publication of Alexander Saxton's *Indispensable Enemy* in 1971 signaled a shift away from the Asian immigrant and a focus on the white exclusionists themselves. The Chinese exclusion movement was, according to Saxton, animated by a Jacksonian producer ethic and grew out of the seemingly irresistible westering thrust of Manifest Destiny. Transplanted white Europeans, coming to California as part of westward expansion, carried with them notions of "free labor" that profoundly shaped their commitment to exclude the Chinese, both from working-class membership and the body politic.[6] Anticipating critical whiteness studies by several decades, Saxton argued that organized labor opposition to the Chinese facilitated the development of a white working-class identity in which "free labor" became coterminous with white labor. Integrating psychoanalysis into a materialist framework, Saxton showed how the struggle for Chinese exclusion enabled a diverse array of Euro-American workers to constitute themselves into self-conscious white working-class subjects on the western frontiers.

Like Saxton, Stuart Creighton Miller traced the roots of Chinese exclusion to America's expansionist agenda and fantasies of imperial dominance. However, by identifying the building blocks of exclusion in an earlier effort to open the mythical China markets, Miller relocated the origins of Chinese exclusion to an earlier period and to far-flung places outside of California. Decades before San Francisco sandlot orators were chanting the "Chinese must go," Americans in China were drawing negative images of the Chinese that ultimately circulated back to the United States. Frustrated with the lack of progress in converting pagan souls to Christianity and making inroads into the China markets, U.S. traders, missionaries, and diplomats fixed on the lack of morality, industriousness, and intelligence among the Chinese in order to account for their failures. These earlier images of an irredeemable people and a civilization in irreversible decline would serve as usable material later on for white nativists to push their exclusionist agenda.[7]

ORIENTALISM AND STATE FORMATION

The core theses of these pioneering studies stood as the standard interpretations of Chinese exclusion for decades, and, in many respects, they continue to constitute the conventional wisdom on the subject. But beginning in the 1990s and 2000s, a new wave of scholarship, which accompanied the institutionalization of Asian American studies and ethnic studies more broadly, reconsidered Asian exclusion by moving beyond the questions of why and how the Chinese Exclusion Act was passed. Instead, scholars, inspired by Edward W. Said's seminal text *Orientalism*, began to ask what "work"— politically, culturally, and socially—Asian exclusion performed in service to the nation and empire. Bringing to bear the methods and approaches of cultural, critical race, and postcolonial studies, a new generation of scholarship showed how Asian exclusion was generative of white national identity and belonging in the United States.

John Kuo Wei Tchen's *New York before Chinatown*, published in 1999, was an exemplar of this new scholarship. Writing Orientalism into the postcolonial history of the United States, Tchen showed how white American revolutionaries' encounters with and consumption of Chinese goods and culture helped a people without a history forge a postcolonial identity.[8] This fascination with all things Chinese continued through the early nineteenth century in the form of a "commercial orientalism," which shaped the diverse plebian cultures of the antebellum urban North. Identifying both "positive" and "negative" representations of the Chinese, Tchen complicated Miller's earlier account of American perceptions of China, but only so slightly. The qualities that had invoked fascination in an earlier period would give rise to racial hate by the mid-nineteenth century, transforming the Chinese from objects of fascination to despised peoples. As it were, desire and contempt constituted flip sides of the same coin. This third and final form of Orientalism, which Tchen identified as "political orientalism," "recast desire-imbued and ambiguous representations into an exclusionary and segregationist discourse."[9]

Nayan Shah and Mary Ting Yi Lui followed up with case studies of San Francisco's and New York City's Chinatown, respectively, that examined the ways Asian exclusion mapped unto urban spaces. Drawing imaginatively from queer and feminist theory, Shah's *Contagious Divide* (2001) explored biomedical discourses of disease, health, and the body at the turn of the century showing how they created the image of San Francisco's Chinatown as a "perverse space," a place of "prostitute cribs, concubine apartments, bachelor bunkhouses, and opium dens" that "fostered perverse intimate relationships and bred contagion."[10] The failure of its residents to comport to bodily norms and adhere to standards of respectable domesticity (constituting a "queer domesticity," in Shah's words) justified violence, harassment, surveillance, and denying them access to a liberal welfare state. The technocratic construction of the normal/queer binary formed a crucial pivot around which an emerging public health bureaucracy and its cadre of self-confident experts enacted new rituals of inclusion and exclusion.[11]

Similarly, Mary Ting Yi Lui described anxieties and fascinations surrounding Chinese male sexuality and how they, in turn, galvanized a concerted political campaign to contain the menace of interracial sex and mixing in turn-of-the-century New York City. Concerns about interracial liaisons between Chinese immigrant men and white (mostly, working-class) women sparked new efforts to police racial and gender boundaries in lower Manhattan, resulting in the demarcation of Chinatown—a space of racial quarantine, where deviant Chinese men and the threat they posed to white racial purity could be safely tucked away.[12] But if it constituted an actual physical space, Chinatown was also a product of white imagination that "reproduced Euro-American notions of racial and cultural superiority against an immoral and vice-ridden Chinese immigrant community."[13] As both Shah and Lui suggest, Asian exclusion was not only a matter of immigration restriction but also a form of social control to regulate gender roles and interracial intimacies in the state's articulation of normative citizenship.

In addition to cultural analysis, Asian American and U.S. historians revisited Asian exclusion by way of political and legal history. Scholars interested in questions of state power and sovereignty began to look more closely into the assemblage of laws, statutes, precedents, and enforcement mechanisms that made up the legal regime of Asian exclusion in the late nineteenth and early twentieth centuries. Building on the earlier works of Sucheng Chan, Him Mark Lai, and Charles J. McClain, Lucy Salyer's book, *Laws Harsh as Tigers* (1995), started this trend by looking closely at the legal challenges brought forth by Chinese immigrants to the Chinese Exclusion Act of 1882 and subsequent related legislation. As Salyer's study showed, excluded Chinese with the help of their white lawyers were incredibly adept at using the American court system to gain redress. Appealing to the foundational principles of due process legal rights—habeas corpus, for example—Chinese litigants mounted successful challenges to provisions contained in the Chinese Exclusion Act.[14] However, resorting to the court system to overturn the administrative decisions of the Immigration Service only served to stiffen the nativist opposition in Congress and led to initiatives to insulate immigration law from judicial oversight. For years, constitutional experts and legal scholars had puzzled over how it became that U.S. immigration law was "so radically insulated and divergent from those fundamental norms of constitutional right, administrative procedure, and judicial role that animate the rest of our legal system."[15] Salyer's meticulous study traced the origins of Congress's plenary power over immigration back to the government's attempts at honing and perfecting Chinese exclusion in the late nineteenth century.

Erika Lee, similarly, insisted on the centrality of Chinese exclusion in the centralization and bureaucratization of the U.S. Federal Government at the turn of the twentieth century. Like Salyer, Lee showed that the enactment of the Chinese Exclusion Act did not of itself make exclusion a reality. *At America's Gates* (2003) documented the numerous ways in which Chinese immigrants evaded the law after its passage, ranging from the "paper son" scheme to surreptitious border crossings across the U.S.-Mexican and U.S.-Canadian borders.[16] Extending Salyer's argument, Lee contended that the struggle over the enforcement of Chinese exclusion not only established the doctrine of plenary power over immigration but also lay the very foundations for a national system of immigration and border controls. "State mechanism used to regulate immigration, enforce national borders, and distinguish U.S. citizens, legal immigrants, and illegal immigrants, such as the U.S. Immigration and Naturalization Service, U.S. passports, 'green cards,' and illegal immigration and deportation policies, can all be traced back to the Chinese exclusion era."[17] By tracking the formative regulatory powers that were accrued to the federal government in the course of its campaign to exclude the Chinese, Lee placed immigration restriction and the racial-based forms of segregation it generated at the heart of American state-building.

Writing a comparative history of "illegal" immigration in the United States, Mae M. Ngai's *Impossible Subjects* (2004) considered Asian exclusion relationally, in connection with other forms of immigration restriction.[18] In doing so, Ngai showed how Asian exclusion calibrated, and was calibrated against, the inclusions and exclusions of other racialized groups. In a rereading of the National Origins Act (1924), *Impossible Subjects* showed that while the quota system erected a hierarchy of racial desirability among European immigrants, with those from Southern and Eastern Europe finding themselves on the bottom rungs, it also paradoxically "redrew the color line around Europe instead of through it," which would facilitate the assimilation of Europeans, regardless of national origins, into white Americans. But whereas the National Origins Act (also known as the Johnson-Reed Act) uncoupled the racial and ethnic identities of European immigrants, it subsumed race and ethnicity for Asian and Latino immigrants. "The legal racialization of these ethnic groups' national origin," Ngai argued, "cast them as permanently foreign and unassimilable to the nation."[19] Just as profoundly, Ngai linked the racial construction of Asians and Latinos as "illegal aliens," "alien citizens," "U.S. nationals," and perpetual guest workers in the twentieth century to U.S. wars of conquest in the Southwest and U.S. colonial interventions in Asia and the South Pacific in the mid- to late nineteenth century.

Historians writing in transnational frameworks added additional layers to this reassessment of Asian exclusion. Based on archival research on both sides of the Pacific and in Asian-language sources, their findings questioned some of the core assumptions of an assimilationist narrative that portrayed immigration as a one-way journey from the Old World to the New World (which was also sometimes presumptively framed as a movement from tradition to modernity). Collectively, their research unearthed previously obscured connections, processes, and crisscrossing passages that linked a global Chinese diaspora to their homeland, and, in doing so, revealed the multiple and complex ways their transnational lives and movements were enmeshed in intricate global networks of kinship, trade, and movement.[20] Bridging the divide between Asian history and Asian American history yielded more nuanced accounts of Chinese immigration to the United States, showing that while their lives and communities may have bore the mark of exclusion, they were not entirely defined by it either.

Viewing Japanese immigrant experiences through a transnational lens, Eiichiro Azuma and Andrea Geiger analyzed the ideas that Japanese immigrants brought with them to the North American West, and they looked at how they shaped their responses to Asian exclusion and white supremacy.[21] Japanese immigrants, according to Azuma, were transnational subjects who found themselves caught between two empires, having to negotiate the imperial aspirations of both the United States and Japan. But this tightrope, which included appeals to Americanism and assertions of racial superiority over other nonwhite groups, did not result in equal rights for Japanese immigrants and did not shield them from the stigma of racial exclusion. Taking a slightly different tack, Geiger's book, *Subverting Exclusion* (2011), looked at how Tokugawa-era ideas about caste informed Japanese immigrants' negotiation, adaptation, and resistance to race-based exclusion laws in Canada and the United States. Their immigrant acts of subverting exclusion, which Japanese immigrants considered to be entirely legitimate in the face of racist legal barriers, ran up against Japan's aspirations to be recognized as an advanced, modern nation worthy of recognition on the world stage. These national insecurities, Geiger argues, led Meiji officials into accepting and, ultimately, reinforcing the racist logic of Asian exclusion in Canada and the United States. "The Meiji government's policy of accommodating and even anticipating the demands of the U.S. and Canadian governments contributed, in turn, to creating the conditions that allowed both Western nations to mark Japanese subjects as excludable in some of the very ways Japan tried to avoid."[22]

IMPERIAL ROOTS

The transnational turn in Asian American and U.S. immigration history also included efforts to write empire into the histories of Asian migration and exclusion. The calls to do so came as early as the mid-1990s when Oscar V. Campomanes critiqued Asian American studies for its insufficient attention to empire. "The major problem," as Campomanes saw it, was "the tendency of Asian American studies to 'domesticate' the questions of U.S. nationality and nation building, leaving untouched their imperialist mooring." His critical assessment of the field, along with those of Lisa Lowe and Sucheta Mazumdar, was to remind its practitioners of the radical origins of Asian American studies and ethnic studies.[23] More recently, scholars in Asian American studies have called for imperial histories of migration as a corrective to a transnational scholarship that too often imputes cross-national mobility, interactions, and connections with emancipatory meaning and significance, which have the effect of "removing those stories from struggles against a world governed by white supremacy and uneven flows of capital and labor."[24]

Tracing the imperial pathways that brought Chinese laborers, real and imagined, to the U.S. South and the Caribbean, Moon-Ho Jung offered an important reinterpretation of Chinese exclusion that relocated the origins of U.S. immigration restriction both temporally and spatially. Jung's *Coolies and Cane* (2006) eschewed the conventional starting point of Asian American history—the railroads and mines of California, that is—and began instead with southern white planters' importation of overseas Chinese laborers as a possible solution to the problem of labor scarcity in the mid-nineteenth century.[25] The recruitment of so-called coolie labor provoked intense debates about the nature of free-dom and slavery from which a national consensus emerged that the coolie trade should be suppressed, and that the Chinese—who were imagined as its living embodiment—should be excluded by extension. As such, the coolie, Jung argued, made "possible the passage of the nation's first restrictions on immigration under the banner of 'freedom' and 'immigra-tion.'"[26] The campaign to outlaw the coolie also served to remake a slaveholding nation into an "empire of liberty," as spreading freedom became the justifying rationale for deep-ening U.S. interventions in China and the Asia-Pacific.

Drawing our attention to what Ann Laura Stoler has identified as the moving car-tographies of U.S. imperial rule, scholars of U.S. colonialism in the Philippines and of Filipino migration have revealed that Asian exclusion was not about erecting impen-etrable borders but calibrating their permeability in such a manner to maximize the exploitation of overseas labor and markets without compromising the nation's racial integrity. This was a case, then, of a gatekeeping nation finding it in its interest to carve out "privileged exemptions" and "ad hoc exceptions" to Asian exclusion. This began with exemptions in the Chinese Exclusion Act for merchants, diplomats, and students. These exempt classes were thought to be crucial intermediaries for realizing U.S. ambi-tions for an "open door" empire in Asia. Several decades later, with U.S. expansion into Asia and the South Pacific proceeding apace, the United States elaborated new exemp-tions and legislated a sliding scale of rights to integrate Filipinos (as well as Puerto Ricans, American Samoans, and other Pacific Islanders) into an intra-imperial cir-cuitry of labor. By assigning its colonial subjects the ambiguous noncitizen status of the "U.S. national," these legal carve-outs created a politically vulnerable, yet highly mobile, population, which could be mobilized and distributed to sites of labor demand in the North American West and across the Pacific.[27] Catherine Ceniza Choy identified vestiges of this colonial strategy of shifting and redefining legal criteria of member-ship in the postwar recruitment of Filipino nurses, in which the material exploitation of a former colony continued.[28] Seen from this perspective, the Immigration Reform Act of 1965, which enabled this "brain drain," rather than representing a major point of departure from the recent past, was old policies and colonial mentalities reworked to protect and extend America's privileged position in the world in the making of an "American century."

The imperial project to calibrate the nation's borders so that they were porous to some things while remaining barriers to others was, of course, not without its tensions. Indeed, the contradictions between the inclusive racism of empire building and its impulse to incorporate differences hierarchically for the benefit of the metropole and the exclusive racism of white nationalism that imagined a racially homogeneous national commu-nity was a recurrent source of conflict, pitting imperial anti-exclusionists against nativ-ist protectionists in the late nineteenth and early twentieth centuries. These tensions between imperial expansion and national protection first flared up with Chinese exclu-sion, manifesting itself most vividly in the 1905 Chinese boycott of U.S. goods, which was organized by Chinese merchants and students in response to Congress's decision to make the exclusion acts permanent. In the case of the Philippines, the efforts to manage and reconcile these tensions and contradictions resulted in that peculiar, adjoined outcome of Filipino exclusion and independence in 1934.

The growing migration of Filipinos to the West Coast of the United States during the 1920s and early 1930s sparked fears of another "Asiatic invasion." The white working-class response to this new pattern of Asian migration was, predictably, to fasten the old rhetoric of cheap labor to the Filipinos. But what really drew the ire of white nativists, prompting a wave of anti-Filipino violence in the region, was the ease with which Filipino men interacted and consorted with white women. Deemed a threat to both white manhood and womanhood—and thus imperiling the racial purity of the nation—nativists targeted Filipinos for exclusion. But in order to enact Filipino exclusion, they had to figure out a way to denationalize the Filipinos—strip them of their status as U.S. nationals, that is—which had guaranteed their rights to migration and mobility. The road to Filipino exclusion would therefore have to go through decolonization. But exclusionists faced strong opposition from U.S. imperialists who continued to imagine the Philippines as a gateway to the fabled China markets and to a boundless maritime empire in the Pacific. As Mae Ngai and Paul Kramer showed, this struggle brought together strange bedfellows, as restrictionists allied themselves with Filipino nationalists in a struggle for Philippine independence, culminating with the passage of the Tydings-McDuffie Act in 1934, which set a timetable for independence while turning Filipinos into "aliens" overnight.[29]

But although tensions between nation and empire flared out into the open on occasion, more often than not, national protection and imperial expansion were quite compatible, operating in tandem to shore up Anglo-American empires along the Pacific Rim. The U.S. and British imperial drive into the Pacific had established circuits of power and culture that integrated people, goods, and markets beyond the nation's reach into a hierarchically ordered polity. But anticolonial revolutionaries, militant labor activists, and radical nationalists found ways to reconfigure these imperial transits to mount cross-cutting challenges to global capitalism and Euro-American imperial domination in the late nineteenth and early twentieth centuries. The rising tide of radicalism was deemed an existential threat to "white men's countries" across the Pacific Rim and was therefore met with state repression and violence.[30]

Scholars focusing on the organizing of South Asian revolutionaries in the western U.S.-Canadian borderlands, for instance, reveal how Canada, Britain, and the United States, often in collaboration, reworked the mechanisms of Asian exclusion into counterinsurgency measures to infiltrate their worldwide movement. Indeed, the surveillance techniques devised to keep out "illegal" Asian aliens were now being arrayed against foreign insurrectionists and seditionists. This in turn enforced and concretized the western U.S. Canadian border in the early twentieth century. By showing how the boundary line was drawn and delimited against the "Hindu menace," these recent works reinterpret border enforcement from strictly being about national protection, of keeping out undesirable foreigners, to consider how it was a foundational strategy of U.S. and British imperial rule.[31] Still others like Alfred McCoy have traced the origins of the modern surveillance state to America's brutal campaign to pacify the Philippines at the turn of the twentieth century. Sheltered from observing constitutional protections and norms, the U.S. military government in the Philippines experimented with "clandestine penetration, psychological warfare, disinformation, media manipulation, assassination, and torture."[32] But these highly objectionable tactics would not be contained to the periphery; they would eventually find their way to the metropole, to be deployed against new "foreign" enemies at home. The U.S. national security state was thus forged in the crucible of empire and built on the foundations of Asian exclusion.

Other scholars have taken a broad imperial view of Asian migration and exclusion by resituating the United States into a global history of white settler colonialism. Building on the seminal insights of the Aristide Zolberg, this new body of scholarship analyzes the rise of white settler sovereignty, arguing that it emerged out of a struggle to restrict and regulate Asian movement in the Pacific world. They explore how the legal and institutional precedents that were established during the course of this contest went on to form the backbone of an international regulatory system of migration control in which technologies of surveillance—border patrol and checkpoints, immigrant detention and deportation, and travel and identification documents—became standard expressions of state territorial sovereignty. These studies further argue that the effort to control Asian migration legitimized white settlers' claims to self-government, which in turn facilitated their passage from colony to nation-state.[33]

Writing in this vein, Marilyn Lake and Henry Reynolds tracked the white elite exchange of ideas, knowledge, and experiences across the Pacific, showing how they bound empire builders, figures like President Theodore Roosevelt and Charles Pearson, together into inter-imperial communities of solidarity. But while "this imagined community of white men" may have been "transnational in its reach," it was, as Lake and Reynolds astutely point out, "nationalist in its outcome, bolstering regimes of border protection and national sovereignty."[34] This transnational comity of whiteness, which was nurtured out of a shared commitment to Asian exclusion and Indian removal, would then, ironically, nationalize "white men's countries," birthing distinct, self-governing territories within the British imperium in the late nineteenth and early twentieth centuries.

Taking a similar approach, my work similarly describes the intercolonial exchanges and movements that generated a white settler pattern of anti-Asian agitation and politics in the Pacific world, demonstrating how it coalesced around points of dense white working-class migration and contact. Extending Saxton's seminal analysis of white working-class racism beyond the boundaries of the nation, I argue that the mass politics of anti-Asian agitation in the American West energized, and was energized by, similar movements in Australia, Canada, New Zealand, and South Africa, as white laborers circulated the empire and carried their accumulated racial knowledge of "coolie" labor and the "yellow peril" with them.[35] As these works clearly indicate, intensifying cross-border mobility and contact, so often captured under the celebratory rubric of globalization, constituted the moving parts of Asian exclusion and helped to solidify white supremacy in the Pacific.

CONCLUSION

Since 2000, the scholarship on Asian American history has grown substantially and it has been recognized for making important contributions to U.S. history, in particular to the subfields of immigration, labor, Western, and urban studies, as well as to the emerging field of Pacific history. As part of this trend, historians have revisited Asian exclusion, by asking new questions and adopting new perspectives in the process. Inspired by different intellectual trends and methodological models, this reappraisal was broad in its scope and impressively diverse in its approach. Interest in the cultural dimensions of state power and forms of domination, for example, had scholars looking for Asian exclusion in places formerly unseen—amusement parks, medical wards, and street corners—and, in doing so, they brought previously hidden nodes of state power into view. Then there were legal histories—inspired by critical race theory—that studied the ways in which restrictive immigration law emerged as a preeminent site for the production of racial knowledge upon which citizenship and nation was elaborated and constructed in the United States. More recently, scholars, by writing the United States into a history of the white settler world, have illustrated how Asian exclusion was part of a global pattern, a product of intercolonial exchanges that crossed and collapsed national spaces. This wide-ranging reassessment of Asian exclusion has suggested new places to look for the origins of immigration restriction; teased out the multiple and varied work that Asian exclusion performed in constructing race, gender, sexuality, and nation in the United States; and identified in Asian exclusion an important technology of U.S. imperial rule.

NOTES

1. Bonnie Honig, *Democracy and the Foreigner* (Princeton, NJ: Princeton University Press, 2001), 74. Honig's book is a brilliant meditation on the multiple and contradictory "work" that the figure of the "immigrant" performs in service to the nation.
2. On how the policing of immigrants emerged as a preeminent site for developing the state's triad strategies of "discipline, normalization, and regulation," see Ali Behdad, "Nationalism and Immigration in the United States," *Diaspora: A Journal of Transnational Studies* 6, no. 2 (1997): 155–179.
3. John Higham, *Strangers in the Land: Patterns of American Nativism, 1860–1925* (New Brunswick, NJ: Rutgers University Press, 1955), along with Oscar Handlin's *The Uprooted: The Epic Story of the Great Migrations that Made the American People* (Boston: Little, Brown, 1951) established, according to Mae M. Ngai, "the intellectual framework for immigration reform in the post–World War II period." But if it did so, this founding historiography also established "a normative theory of American immigration" that made the immigrant coterminous with European in the popular imagination. See Ngai's essay, "Immigration and Ethnic History," in *American History Now*, ed. Eric Foner and Lisa McGirr (Philadelphia: Temple University Press, 2011), 358–375. On the social science

construction of the "Oriental problem," see Henry Yu, *Thinking Orientals: Migration, Contact, and Exoticism in Modern America* (Oxford: Oxford University Press, 2001).

4. Gunther Barth, *Bitter Strength: A History of the Chinese in the United States, 1850–1870* (Cambridge, MA: Harvard University Press, 1964).

5. See Roger Daniels, *The Politics of Prejudice: The Anti-Japanese Movement in California and the Struggle for Japanese Exclusion* (Berkeley: University of California Press, 1962); Roger Daniels and Harry H. Kitano, *American Racism: Explorations of the Nature of Prejudice* (Englewood Cliffs, NJ: Prentice-Hall, 1970); and William Peterson, *Japanese Americans: Oppression and Success* (New York: Random House, 1971).

6. Alexander Saxton, *The Indispensable Enemy: Labor and the Anti-Chinese Movement in California* (Berkeley: University of California Press, 1971). In locating the working-class origins of Chinese exclusion, Saxton was building on the early works of Mary Roberts Coolidge, *Chinese Immigration* (New York: Holt and Company, 1909); and Elmer Clarence Sandmeyer, *Anti-Chinese Movement in California* (Urbana: University of Illinois Press, 1939).

7. Stuart Creighton Miller, *The Unwelcome Immigrant: The American Image of the Chinese, 1785–1882* (Berkeley: University of California Press, 1969).

8. John Kuo Wei Tchen, *New York before Chinatown: Orientalism and the Shaping of American Culture, 1776–1882* (Baltimore, MD: Johns Hopkins University Press, 1999). On how the consumption of Chinese material goods helped a revolutionary elite to make the transition from colony to nation, see Kariann Akemi Yokota, *Unbecoming British: How Revolutionary America Became a Postcolonial Nation* (Oxford: Oxford University Press, 2011).

9. Tchen, *New York before Chinatown*, xxii.

10. Nayan Shah, *Contagious Divides: Epidemics and Race in San Francisco's Chinatown* (Berkeley: University of California Press, 2001), 13.

11. Ibid. On the state's management of same-sex relations in the polyglot North American West, and how it drew the boundaries of national membership around heteronormative standards and the white nuclear family, see Shah's more recent work, *Stranger Intimacy: Contesting Race, Sexuality, and the Law in the North American West* (Berkeley: University of California Press, 2011).

12. Mary Ting Yi Lui, *The Chinatown Trunk Mystery: Murder, Miscegenation, and Other Dangerous Encounters in Turn-of-the-Century New York City* (Princeton, NJ: Princeton University Press, 2005). On how "Chinatown" was as much the product of white imagination as it was an "objective" physical space, see Kay Anderson, *Vancouver's Chinatown: Racial Discourse in Canada, 1875–1980* (Montreal: McGill-Queens University Press, 1995).

13. Lui, *Chinatown Trunk Mystery*, 5.

14. Lucy E. Salyer, *Laws Harsh as Tigers: Chinese Immigrants and the Shaping of Immigration Law* (Chapel Hill: University of North Carolina Press, 1995). On the enforcement of the Chinese exclusion laws and how they justified the expansion of bureaucratic state power in the United States and China, see Adam M. McKeown, "Ritualization of Regulation: The Enforcement of Chinese Exclusion in the United States and China," *American Historical Review* 108, no. 2 (2003): 377–403.

15. Peter H. Schuck, "The Transformation of Immigration Law," *Columbia Law Review* 84, no. 1 (1984): 1–90.

16. Erika Lee, *At America's Gates: Chinese Immigration and American Exclusion, 1882–1943* (Chapel Hill: University of North Carolina Press, 2003).

17. Ibid., 10.

18. Mae M. Ngai, *Impossible Subjects: Illegal Aliens and the Making of Modern America* (Princeton, NJ: Princeton University Press, 2004).

19. Ibid., 17.

20. For examples, see Yong Chen, *Chinese San Francisco, 1850–1943: A Trans-Pacific Community* (Stanford, CA: Stanford University Press, 2000); Madeline Y. Hsu, *Dreaming of Gold, Dreaming of Home: Transnationalism and Migration between the United States and South China, 1882–1942* (Stanford, CA: Stanford University Press, 2000); Adam McKeown, *Chinese Migrant Networks and Cultural Change: Peru, Chicago, Hawaii, 1900–1936* (Chicago: University of Chicago Press, 2001).

21. Eiichiro Azuma, *Between Two Empires: Race, History, and Transnationalism in Japanese America* (Oxford: Oxford University Press, 2005); Andrea Geiger, *Subverting Exclusion: Transpacific Encounters with Race, Caste, and Borders, 1885–1928* (New Haven, CT: Yale University Press, 2011), 192.

22. Geiger, *Subverting Exclusion*, 192.

23. Oscar V. Campomanes, "New Formations of Asian American Studies and the Question of U.S. Imperialism," *Positions* 5, no. 2 (1997): 523–550; Lisa Lowe, *Immigrant Acts: On Asian American Cultural Politics* (Durham, NC: Duke University Press, 1996); Sucheta Mazumdar, "Asian American Studies and Asian Studies: Rethinking Roots," in *Asian Americans: Comparative and Global Perspectives*, ed. Shirley Hune et al. (Pullman: Washington State University Press, 1990), 29–44.

24. Moon-Ho Jung, "Beyond these Mythical Shores: Asian American History and the Study of Race," *History Compass* 6, no. 2 (2008): 633. Paul Kramer has leveled a similar critique, arguing that "transnational scholarship often unconsciously partakes in a language of post-sovereignty—of flows, exchanges, connections, and interactions—that closely resembles social-scientific, journalistic, and corporate narratives of capitalist globalization since the early 1990s." See his "Power and Connection: Imperial Histories of the United States in the World," *American Historical Review* 116, no. 5 (2011): 1348–1391.

25. Moon-Ho Jung, *Coolies and Cane: Race, Labor, and Sugar in the Age of Emancipation* (Baltimore, MD: Johns Hopkins University Press, 2006). On imagining the "coolie" and the political and cultural work it performed on behalf of liberal modernity, see Lisa Lowe, "The Intimacies of Four Continents," in *Haunted by Empire: Geographies of Intimacies in North American History*, ed. Ann Laura Stoler (Durham, NC: Duke University Press, 2006).

26. Jung, *Coolies and Cane*, 13.

27. Dorothy B. Fujita-Rony, *American Workers, Colonial Power: Philippine Seattle and the Transpacific West, 1919* (Berkeley: University of California Press, 2003); Rick Baldoz, *The Third Asiatic Invasion: Empire and Migration in Filipino America, 1898–1946* (New York: New York University Press, 2011); and JoAnna Poblete, *Islanders in the Empire: Filipino and Puerto Rican Laborers in Hawai'i* (Champaign: University of Illinois Press, 2014).

28. Catherine Ceniza Choy, *Empire of Care: Nursing and Migration in Filipino History* (Durham, NC: Duke University Press, 2003). For traces of U.S. colonialism in postindependence Filipino migration patterns, see Robyn Magalit Rodriguez, *Migrants for Export: How the Philippine State Brokers Labor to the World* (Minneapolis: University of Minnesota Press, 2010).

29. Ngai, *Impossible Subjects*, 96–126; Paul A. Kramer, *The Blood of Government: Race, Empire, the United States, and the Philippines* (Chapel Hill: University of North Carolina Press,

2006), 347–432. Examining its provisions closely, Kramer has argued against seeing the Tydings-McDuffie Act as an "early act of decolonization," and instead concluded that it was "yet another moment in the unfolding of calibrated colonialism." Kramer, *Blood of Government*, 424.

30. For some of these anti-imperial struggles and resistance taking place in the North American West and across the Pacific, see the essays in Moon-Ho Jung, ed., *The Rising Tide of Color: Race, Radicalism, and Repression on the West Coast and Beyond* (Seattle: University of Washington Press, 2013).

31. Kornel S. Chang, *Pacific Connections: The Making of the U.S.-Canadian Borderlands* (Berkeley: University of California Press, 2012); Seema Sohi, *Echoes of Mutiny: Race, Surveillance, and Indian Anticolonialism in North America* (Oxford: Oxford University Press, 2014). This recent scholarship is indebted to the earlier groundbreaking work of Joan Jensen, *Passage from India: Asian Indian Immigrants in North America* (New Haven, CT: Yale University Press, 1988).

32. Alfred McCoy, *Policing America's Empire: The United States, the Philippines, and the Rise of the Surveillance State* (Madison: University of Wisconsin Press, 2009), 5. Also see Joan M. Jensen, *Army Surveillance in America, 1775–1980* (New Haven, CT: Yale University Press, 1991), 88–108; and Moon-Ho Jung, "Seditious Subjects: Race, State Violence, and the U.S. Empire," *Journal of Asian American Studies* 14, no. 2 (2011): 221–247.

33. Aristide Zolberg, "The Great Wall against China: Responses to the First Immigration Crisis, 1885–1925," in *Migration, Migration History, History: Old Paradigms and New Perspectives*, ed. Jan Lucassen and Leo Lucassen (Bern: Peter Lang, 1997). See also Adam McKeown, *Melancholy Order: Asian Migration and the Globalization of Borders* (New York: Columbia University Press, 2008); and Marilyn Lake and Henry Reynolds, *Drawing the Global Colour Line: White Men's Countries and the International Challenge of Racial Equality* (Cambridge: Cambridge University Press, 2008). On the white Pacific, see Gerald Horne, *The White Pacific: U.S. Imperialism and Black Slavery in the South Seas after the Civil War* (Honolulu: University of Hawai'i Press, 2007); and John Fitzgerald, *Big White Lie: Chinese Australians in White Australia* (Sydney: University of New South Wales Press, 2007).

34. Lake and Reynolds, *Drawing the Global Colour Line*, 4.

35. Chang, *Pacific Connections*.

FURTHER READING

Anderson, Kay. *Vancouver's Chinatown: Racial Discourse in Canada, 1875–1980*. Montreal: McGill-Queens University Press, 1995.

Azuma, Eiichiro. *Between Two Empires: Race, History, and Transnationalism in Japanese America*. New York: Oxford University Press, 2005.

Baldoz, Rick, *The Third Asiatic Invasion: Empire and Migration in Filipino America, 1898–1946*. New York: New York University Press, 2011.

Barth, Gunther. *Bitter Strength: A History of the Chinese in the United States, 1850–1870*. Cambridge, MA: Harvard University Press, 1964.

Behdad, Ali. "Nationalism and Immigration in the United States." *Diaspora: A Journal of Transnational Studies* 6, no. 2 (1997): 155–179.

Campomanes, Oscar V. "New Formations of Asian American Studies and the Question of U.S. Imperialism." *Positions* 5, no. 2 (1997): 523–550.

Chang, Kornel S. *Pacific Connections: The Making of the U.S.-Canadian Borderlands*. Berkeley: University of California Press, 2012.

Chen, Yong. *Chinese San Francisco, 1850–1943: A Trans-Pacific Community*. Stanford, CA: Stanford University Press, 2000.

Choy, Catherine Ceniza. *Empire of Care: Nursing and Migration in Filipino History*. Durham, NC: Duke University Press, 2003.

Coolidge, Mary Roberts. *Chinese Immigration*. New York: Holt and Company, 1909.

Daniels, Roger. *The Politics of Prejudice: The Anti-Japanese Movement in California and the Struggle for Japanese Exclusion*. Berkeley: University of California Press, 1962.

Daniels, Roger, and Harry H. Kitano. *American Racism: Explorations of the Nature of Prejudice*. Englewood Cliffs, NJ: Prentice-Hall, 1970.

Fitzgerald, John. *Big White Lie: Chinese Australians in White Australia*. Sydney: University of New South Wales Press, 2007.

Fujita-Rony, Dorothy B. *American Workers, Colonial Power: Philippine Seattle and the Transpacific West, 1919*. Berkeley: University of California Press, 2003.

Geiger, Andrea. *Subverting Exclusion: Transpacific Encounters with Race, Caste, and Borders, 1885–1928*. New Haven, CT: Yale University Press, 2011.

Handlin, Oscar. *The Uprooted: The Epic Story of the Great Migrations That Made the American People*. Boston: Little, Brown, 1951.

Higham, John. *Strangers in the Land: Patterns of American Nativism, 1860–1925*. New Brunswick, NJ: Rutgers University Press, 1955.

Honig, Bonnie. *Democracy and the Foreigner*. Princeton, NJ: Princeton University Press, 2001.

Horne, Gerald. *The White Pacific: U.S. Imperialism and Black Slavery in the South Seas after the Civil War*. Honolulu: University of Hawai'i Press, 2007.

Hsu, Madeline Y. *Dreaming of Gold, Dreaming of Home: Transnationalism and Migration between the United States and South China, 1882–1942*. Stanford, CA: Stanford University Press, 2000.

Jensen, Joan M. *Army Surveillance in America, 1775–1980*. New Haven, CT: Yale University Press, 1991.

———. *Passage from India: Asian Indian Immigrants in North America*. New Haven, CT: Yale University Press, 1988.

Jung, Moon-Ho. "Beyond These Mythical Shores: Asian American History and the Study of Race." *History Compass* 6, no. 2 (2008): 627–638.

———. *Coolies and Cane: Race, Labor, and Sugar in the Age of Emancipation*. Baltimore, MD: Johns Hopkins University Press, 2006.

———. "Seditious Subjects: Race, State Violence, and the U.S. Empire." *Journal of Asian American Studies* 14, no. 2 (2011): 221–247.

———, ed. *The Rising Tide of Color: Race, Radicalism, and Repression on the West Coast and Beyond*. Seattle: University of Washington Press, 2013.

Kramer, Paul A. *The Blood of Government: Race, Empire, the United States, and the Philippines*. Chapel Hill: University of North Carolina Press, 2006.

———. "Power and Connection: Imperial Histories of the United States in the World." *American Historical Review* 116, no. 5 (2011): 1348–1391.

Lake, Marilyn, and Henry Reynolds. *Drawing the Global Colour Line: White Men's Countries and the International Challenge of Racial Equality*. Cambridge: Cambridge University Press, 2008.

Lee, Erika. *At America's Gates: Chinese Immigration and American Exclusion, 1882– 1943.* Chapel Hill: University of North Carolina Press, 2003.

Lowe, Lisa. *Immigrant Acts: On Asian American Cultural Politics.* Durham, NC: Duke University Press, 1996.

———. "The Intimacies of Four Continents." In *Haunted by Empire: Geographies of Intimacies in North American History,* edited by Ann Laura Stoler, 191–212. Durham, NC: Duke University Press, 2006.

Lui, Mary Ting Yi. *The Chinatown Trunk Mystery: Murder, Miscegenation, and Other Dangerous Encounters in Turn-of-the-Century New York City.* Princeton, NJ: Princeton University Press, 2005.

Mazumdar, Sucheta. "Asian American Studies and Asian Studies: Rethinking Roots." In *Asian Americans: Comparative and Global Perspectives,* edited by Shirley Hune et al., 29–44. Pullman: Washington State University Press, 1990.

McCoy, Alfred. *Policing America's Empire: The United States, the Philippines, and the Rise of the Surveillance State.* Madison: University of Wisconsin Press, 2009.

McKeown, Adam. *Chinese Migrant Networks and Cultural Change: Peru, Chicago, Hawaii, 1900–1936.* Chicago: University of Chicago Press, 2001.

———. *Melancholy Order: Asian Migration and the Globalization of Borders.* New York: Columbia University Press, 2008.

———. "Ritualization of Regulation: The Enforcement of Chinese Exclusion in the United States and China." *American Historical Review* 108, no. 2 (2003): 377–403.

Miller, Stuart Creighton. *The Unwelcome Immigrant: The American Image of the Chinese, 1785–1882.* Berkeley: University of California Press, 1969.

Ngai, Mae M. "Immigration and Ethnic History." In *American History Now,* edited by Eric Foner and Lisa McGirr, 358–375. Philadelphia: Temple University Press, 2011.

———. *Impossible Subjects: Illegal Aliens and the Making of Modern America.* Princeton, NJ: Princeton University Press, 2004.

Peterson, William. *Japanese Americans: Oppression and Success.* New York: Random House, 1971.

Poblete, JoAnna. *Islanders in the Empire: Filipino and Puerto Rican Laborers in Hawai'i.* Champaign: University of Illinois Press, 2014.

Rodriguez, Robyn Magalit. *Migrants for Export: How the Philippine State Brokers Labor to the World.* Minneapolis: University of Minnesota Press, 2010.

Salyer, Lucy E. *Laws Harsh as Tigers: Chinese Immigrants and the Shaping of Immigration Law.* Chapel Hill: University of North Carolina Press, 1995.

Sandmeyer, Elmer Clarence. *Anti-Chinese Movement in California.* Urbana: University of Illinois Press, 1939.

Saxton, Alexander. *The Indispensable Enemy: Labor and the Anti-Chinese Movement in California.* Berkeley: University of California Press, 1971.

Schuck, Peter H. "The Transformation of Immigration Law." *Columbia Law Review* 84, no. 1 (1984): 1–90.

Shah, Nayan. *Contagious Divides: Epidemics and Race in San Francisco's Chinatown.* Berkeley: University of California Press, 2001.

———. *Stranger Intimacy: Contesting Race, Sexuality, and the Law in the North American West.* Berkeley: University of California Press, 2011.

Sohi, Seema. *Echoes of Mutiny: Race, Surveillance, and Indian Anticolonialism in North America.* Oxford: Oxford University Press, 2014.

Tchen, John Kuo Wei. *New York before Chinatown: Orientalism and the Shaping of American Culture, 1776–1882*. Baltimore, MD: Johns Hopkins University Press, 1999.

Yokota, Kariann Akemi. *Unbecoming British: How Revolutionary America Became a Postcolonial Nation*. New York: Oxford University Press, 2011.

Yu, Henry. *Thinking Orientals: Migration, Contact, and Exoticism in Modern America*. New York: Oxford University Press, 2001.

Zolberg, Aristide. "The Great Wall against China: Responses to the First Immigration Crisis, 1885–1925." In *Migration, Migration History, History: Old Paradigms and New Perspectives*, edited by Jan Lucassen and Leo Lucassen, 291–315. Bern: Peter Lang, 1997.

CHAPTER 10

··

THE COLD WAR

··

MADELINE Y. HSU

AMERICA's post–World War II campaign for global leadership led it to intensify efforts to accumulate and extend its influence across the Pacific. The unanticipated "loss" of China to the communists provoked a maelstrom of recriminations and hard-line commitments to securing beachheads of American dependencies—styled as fellow democracies and capitalist partners—against the sinister, inexplicable, expanding threat of communism. To this end, the United States increased the scope and degree of its engagements in East and Southeast Asia in ways that in turn reshaped domestic ideologies and practices of immigration restriction, citizenship, and race relations with transformative consequences for the numbers, characteristics, and trajectories of Asians in the United States. The newly decolonized Philippines experienced many of the kinds of programs reflecting America's extending reach into Asia, such as the establishment of bases for military operations, patronage of politically dependent leaders, provision of economic guidance and resources, aid for refugees and other kinds of humanitarian needs, and technical, cultural, and educational exchanges. Other Asian allies such as Japan, "Free China" on Taiwan, South Korea, Thailand, Hong Kong, and South Vietnam similarly became targets of such American imperialist projects.

These efforts had unanticipated but wholly explicable outcomes in serving both to humanize and to domesticate Asian political allies, making them more welcome as visitors, political allies, immigrants, and potential U.S. citizens through the piecemeal breakdown of immigration restrictions that had previously conceptualized Asians as intrinsically foreign, inassimilable, and therefore necessary targets for exclusion. Extensive overseas military deployments during and after World War II offered greater opportunities for the forging of international, often interracial friendships, romances, and family relationships. However, the system of highly restrictive race and national origins–based immigration quotas imposed by the 1924 Johnson-Reed Immigration Act and its predecessors made it nearly impossible for the foreign partners in most such pairings to enter and reside with their spouses or fiancés in the United States. The valor and sacrifices of America's military personnel required that Congress pass the so-called War Brides Act in 1945 to honor their patriotism and family bonds.

This law, however, accommodated only some Asian spouses and fiancés. The 1924 act had prohibited altogether the immigration of "aliens ineligible for citizenship," a legal category referring to Asians based on long-standing prohibitions against their rights to citizenship by naturalization. Wartime alliances had gradually reduced such discriminations, with first Chinese gaining a repeal of the Chinese exclusion laws and naturalization rights in 1943, then Filipinos and Indians becoming eligible in 1946. As wartime enemies, Japanese were the last major Asian group to attain access as war brides. Although interned en masse during World War II as "enemy aliens," the Japanese American Citizens League (JACL) nevertheless pressed Congress to acknowledge the demonstrated heroism and loyalty of the 442nd Infantry Regiment of Nisei—second-generation Japanese American—soldiers and to uphold constitutional guarantees of equality to also admit Japanese spouses and fiancés. In passing the amendment to do so in 1947, Congress elevated constitutional ideals over previously legislated, and judicially upheld, race-based inequities in immigration laws while also tacitly acknowledging the legality of mixed-race marriages two decades before the Supreme Court abolished antimiscegenation laws in *Loving v. Virginia*. At first, the military establishment made it procedurally difficult for white and black Americans and their Japanese partners to qualify, but, in the decades since, military marriages of primarily Asian women to American men has been a major route of entry into America and has resulted in the highest levels of out-marriage in Japanese, Korean, Filipino, and Vietnamese populations that host American military bases.[1]

Military deployments fostered other forms of intimacy that produced new immigration flows, which placed Asians into mixed-race American families. War, occupation, and the long-term presence of military bases perhaps inevitably produced orphans, mixed-race children, and impoverished children who became ready subjects for American succor. Bedraggled children were the most alluring recipients of G.I. generosity, presented in the form of much-appreciated candy and gum. Such innocently friendly encounters masked the seamier reality that the significantly greater material comforts and wealth associated with American bases and personnel fostered extensive ancillary services in the form of nightlife, entertainment, and prostitution businesses among local populations. Through the series of American military ventures into Asia—World War II; the Korean War; the occupation of Japan; bases in Thailand, Taiwan, and Okinawa; and the Vietnam War—Americans encountered impoverished, orphaned, or cast-off biracial children demanding American sympathy. Celebrity advocates such as the author Pearl Buck and the evangelists Harry and Bertha Holt urged fellow Americans to undertake the benevolence of intercountry, transracial adoptions. Starting in 1948, refugee legislation provided for the entry of adopted children although initially these laws were framed with Europeans in mind. Adoption from Asia became popular with the Korean War under the leadership of the Holts, who launched a well-publicized, successful campaign for Congress to pass special legislation that would allow them to adopt eight Korean children and encouraged other American Christians to undertake salvation of Asian children in dire need. This powerful movement promoted the legal claims of American families and their would-be adoptees.

Until 1961, contingency refugee laws remained the chief way that transnational adoptees could enter America. Passage of the McCarran-Walter Act in 1952 had affirmed the congressional commitment to the discriminatory quota system of 1924 while providing for nonquota immigration by immediate family members such as spouses, minor children, and parents but not transnational adoptees. Opposed by immigration reformers but supported by the JACL, the McCarran-Walter Act granted Asians symbolically significant but tiny, token quotas (for example, China's was only 105) and eliminated the racial restriction on naturalized citizenship, but capped annual immigration from the Asia-Pacific Triangle at 2,000. Intercountry, transracial adoptions were feasible under piecemeal refugee legislation but continued advocacy by highly outspoken evangelical Christian groups transformed the public image of destitute Asian children from that of refugees to valued potential family members, thereby persuading Congress to permanently legislate adoptees as eligible for nonquota family admissions in an act on September 26, 1961.[2]

In parallel with the vision of shared humanity that impelled greater immigration rights for Asian war brides and adopted children, admissions of refugees, students, and trainees highlighted shared political causes and economic values against the backdrop of America's responsibility to provide humanitarian relief to its allies. For example, the 1948 Displaced Persons Act did not allocate any visas to Asians but allowed thousands who were already resident in the United States to adjust their status rather than be forced back to homelands that had fallen to communism. In perhaps the most striking demonstration of these reworked priorities, Congress took the unprecedented step of directing unused war-relief funds to aid Chinese scholarship students, trainees, and visitors cut off from nationalist government funding and their homeland by the anticipated victory of Mao Zedong and the Chinese Communist Party in late 1948. About 12,000 highly select Chinese, with powerful connections and many holding elite academic credentials, were thus able to remain in the United States, with many completing degrees to the level of Ph.D.s, and eventually obtain legal employment. This considerable break with past practices of prohibiting students from seeking employment and requiring their departure upon completion of academic programs made sense in light of heightened sympathy for Chinese lingering from World War II propaganda on one hand and, on the other, from practical considerations that highly educated and talented individuals should not be forced into communist hands. The most visible of these "stranded students" included Tsung-dao Lee (Li Zhongdao) and Chen-ning Yang (Yang Zhenning), who would share the 1957 Nobel Prize in Physics and provide potent evidence that America should liberalize its immigration laws to account for individual abilities, potential for contributing to the United States, and shared political goals, rather than race and national origins.

The politics of refugee admissions advanced the possibility of viewing Asians as compatriots and allies, rather than as fundamentally, racially incompatible. The 1953 Refugee Relief Act, passed in response to the limitations of the McCarran-Walter Act, allocated a total of 214,000 refugee visas with 2,000 designated for Chinese and 3,000 to other recipients in the Far East generally. Congress thereby conveyed its preoccupation with European affairs, but at the steadfast urging of Congressman Walter Judd of

Minnesota, who had also led the charge for repeal and quotas for Asian nations in the McCarran-Walter Act, gestured toward superficial forms of equity. Successive refugee acts of 1956 and 1957 redirected unused visas from the European quotas to Asians, particularly Chinese, who remained in need of new homes. The Office of Refugee and Migration Affairs within the State Department sought to use the programs to highlight American benevolence overseas and its functioning domestic democracy by ensuring smooth resettlement even as it attempted to reassure Americans that refugee admissions, often of peoples kept out by the existing quota system, presented no strain upon the American economy, social dynamics, or political security. Its publicity stressed the family values, educational attainments, work ethic, political conformity, and ready assimilability of those granted refugee visas. In the case of Chinese, these efforts were so successful that in 1962, when a resurgence of refugee arrivals into Hong Kong spurred global outbursts of alarm and sympathy, President John F. Kennedy was able to authorize with bipartisan support the parole of 15,111 into the United States, a decision also intended to underscore the inadequacy of existing immigration laws.[3]

During this time, tens of thousands of other Asians entered the United States without consideration for quota restraints as students, a status that provided no guarantees that they could legally remain although many found ways to do so in a flow of educated elites from Taiwan, India, and South Korea that became known by the mid-1960s as the world's most serious cases of "brain drain." After World War II, Congress and the State Department sought to promote American influence through educational and cultural exchanges, priorities embodied perhaps most visibly by the Fulbright program. Leadership and technical training programs targeted potential future leaders from developing allied nations for junkets to expose them to the democracy and advanced economic and scientific civilization of the United States. Programs coordinated through the State Department's Institute for International Education brought the numbers of international students to unprecedented levels at several thousand per year. In the case of Taiwan, through the 1970s, about 90 percent of such students remained in the United States. The Exchange Visitor Program (EVP) was another example of a "temporary" training program, first established in 1948, that resulted in permanent resettlement of skilled or professional workers. Under the EVP, about 11,000 Filipina nurses arrived to work in the United States between 1956 and 1968 with many finding ways of remaining in the country by marriage, reapplication, or migration to Canada, often with the facilitation of the hospitals in which they worked.[4]

Like their "stranded student" predecessors, many Asian students, particularly those trained in the sciences and engineering, readily found employment upon graduation and worked out means to legally remain in the United States. Some did so through the refugee laws, others through stays of deportation that privileged applicants for "first-preference" admission for those with skills needed in the United States, marriage to citizens, and private bills to Congress. The expanding American economy, and in particular the hotly contested nuclear arms and space races against the Soviet Union, rendered such individuals highly employable with consequences for reforms of immigration law. Public Law 87-885, passed in 1962, removed quota restrictions on thousands of first-preference applicants waiting in line for permanent residency, a privileging of economically useful immigrants that only increased with passage of the 1965 Hart-Celler Immigration Act and its employment and investment preference system. Once-excluded populations of Asians became the leading group of brain-drain immigrants to the United States as medical personnel, engineers, scientists, and other employees with useful skills. Cold War politics had laid the foundations for the dramatic transformations of Asian immigration usually credited to the 1965 immigration act.

Asian American populations became increasingly diverse along vectors of socio-cultural capital, class, gender, family status, generation, access to mainstream employment and suburban residence, and places of origin, with some new arrivals construed as outsiders to established communities. Although many Asians immigrated through the family reunification clauses of the McCarran-Walter Act or as refugees sponsored by relatives or friends, thousands of others entered without ties to Asian Americans largely mired in the working classes and small ethnic businesses. For example, 84,000 Japanese foreign spouses emigrated from 1945 until 1985, constituting over half of the total arrival of 154,000 Japanese. Apart from those who married Nisei, most were situated in the United States through the families and communities of white or black military spouses. Between 1965 and 1975, an almost entirely new immigration of about 8,000 Vietnamese war brides also emerged. Most Koreans entering from 1951 until 1964 did so without ties to the relatively small Korean American community, in the form of about 6,500 war brides, 6,300 adopted children, and 6,000 students. From 1959 until 1965, 70 percent of Koreans arriving as immigrants were women under the status of military spouses. Mixed in with these largely unskilled workers were 6 percent arriving as professionals and managers, indicating that even before 1965, Koreans had begun shifting toward arriving with greater education and skills. With college and advanced degrees, those arriving as students could then become brain-drain immigrants who nonetheless also experienced some discrimination in employment and residential selection. Through such influxes, the tiny population of about 7,500 Koreans in 1950 multiplied five-fold to about 45,000 in 1965.

Between 1952 and 1965, Japanese emigrated in greater numbers than any other Asian nationalities, primarily as war brides and other family reunification statuses. Japanese remained the largest Asian American population from 1910 until 1970, after which emigration by other Asian nationalities overtook them in numbers. Although most of these *shin issei* arrived without professional or technical backgrounds, the Japanese American community's overall educational and employment profiles improved. After 1924, growing numbers of Nisei and then Sansei had attended college, many through the GI Bill after 1945, and became a core of professional doctors, dentists, and lawyers.

From 1940 to 1960, the Chinese American population more than doubled from 106,334 to 237,292, in large part through a natural increase as women joined husbands and sons through family reunification categories. By 1965, about 55 percent of Chinese Americans were American-born. However, perhaps the most visible of Chinese Americans during these years were immigrants arriving with technical, scientific, and professional skills—such as the computer entrepreneur An Wang who founded Wang

Computers—who reached previously unattainable levels of success and integration. In conjunction with growing numbers of American-born citizens entering technical and professional fields, these new immigrants contributed to the segmented representation of Chinese Americans in the labor market characterizing the early twenty-first century.

Asian Indians started exhibiting this bifurcation as well. A small group before World War II, Asian Indians continued to migrate in low numbers before 1965 with the population increasing from only 2,405 in 1940 to about 72,500 in 1970. Much of this new immigration consisted of Western-educated intellectuals and the wealthy fleeing the leftward turn in India's government.

The shifts in immigration law brought a greater gender balance to the largely male Filipino American community. World War II brought those serving in the U.S. military service the opportunity for naturalization, which several thousand Filipinos undertook annually through the 1940s and 1950s, thereby gaining the ability to bring over wives and children. Through these processes, by 1965, the numbers of adult Filipino men and women had reached parity. For this reason, despite relatively modest immigration numbers, the community did grow through a natural increase from 122,707 in 1950 to 176,310 in 1960. Among low numbers of immigrants, increasing percentages arrived as professionals, growing from 9.2 percent in 1959 to 18.1 percent in 1963.[5]

Despite improving immigration access for Asians during the 1950s and early 1960s, the Cold War also imposed greater pressures for political conformity, presenting both crisis and opportunity for Asian Americans. Chinese, in particular, faced suspicions because their homeland had become communist. The highly politicized "loss of China" fueled the earliest of McCarthy's witch hunts and continued as a key security issue pressed by the China Lobby, which managed to delay the People's Republic of China (PRC)'s entry into the United Nations until 1971. Long-standing practices of immigration through fraudulent statuses—the so-called paper-son system—drew close scrutiny as a possible means of entry for communist spies. The Drumwright Report, authored by the consul general in Hong Kong, fueled such fears by documenting the extent of such practices. In response, the FBI and Immigration and Naturalization Service (INS) implemented the controversial Confession Program in 1956 in efforts to induce Chinese Americans to voluntarily reveal their paper-son lineages in exchange for regularized status and use of their real names. After decades of mistreatment by immigration authorities, only about a quarter of Chinese Americans participated, most unwillingly implicated in the confessions of others. Evidence of fraudulent entry gained in this way was used to deport those Chinese Americans suspected of leftist sympathies. For self-protection, many Chinese American individuals and organizations claimed allegiance to the Nationalist government on Taiwan, a key American ally in the fight against communist China. The mishandled case of the brilliant Cal Tech rocket scientist Qian Xuesen vividly illustrated how political paranoia entwined with immigration enforcement to try to identify "good" Chinese and deport the "bad." When he attempted to visit his parents in China in 1950, Qian was accused of past Communist Party membership despite his recent conversion to U.S. citizenship and marriage to the daughter of a prominent Nationalist official. Qian was placed under house arrest and refused access to research facilities. After five years of such treatment, Qian was eager to leave when his name appeared at the top of a 1955 PRC list of persons to be exchanged in return for American Korean War prisoners of war. Qian returned to found the PRC's rocket program, in what is often seen as a significant loss to the United States in a key example of how Cold War zealotry generated unnecessary and destructive divides.

Christina Klein has explained the imperatives demanding the inclusion of allied or sympathetic Asians and the exclusion of the politically hostile by juxtaposing "the global imaginary of integration" with "the global imaginary of containment." Even as the Cold War justified intensified surveillance and control of left-leaning or even neutral Asian subjects, it also provided "an opportunity to forge intellectual and emotional bonds with the people of Asia and Africa. Only by creating such bonds . . . could the economic, political, and military integration of the 'free world' be achieved and sustained."[6] Toward the goal of improved integration, Asian Americans could gain political ground by exhibiting their American patriotism through the embrace of democratic and capitalist values. The immigrant Dalip Singh Saund became a U.S. citizen by naturalization as soon as legally permitted and was the first South Asian and Asian American elected to Congress in 1956. With Japan's emergence as a key American ally in East Asia, Japanese Americans were able to parlay the heroism of the 442nd, which received a sympathetic Hollywood treatment in the 1951 movie *Go for Broke!* and their acquiescence to internment, to claim a fuller set of civil rights. After 1952, Issei rushed to claim the citizenship that had long been denied to Asians just a few years after being interned as enemy aliens. Internment had dismantled West Coast Japanese American communities, leading some to resettle in the Midwest, South, and East Coast states where they had been imprisoned or released. Such patterns were interpreted by some observers as positive indicators that Japanese Americans were finally integrating. Lack of employment opportunities, however, led most Japanese Americans to recongregate on the West Coast. The back of the ethnic enclave economy had been broken, however, and Japanese Americans found jobs in gardening and domestic service while growing numbers of American-born Nisei and Sansei with college educations were able to enter white-collar and professional fields. Military service with its ensuing veterans' benefits, the throwing out of discriminatory residential covenants, and mandates to integrate workplaces and schools provided access to middle-class residences and employments, which contributed to impressions that Japanese Americans were attaining upward social mobility. The apparent successes of Japanese Americans, after the discriminations of World War II, would provide fodder for one of America's most powerful claims to have attained equity as a functioning multiracial democracy.

The imperative of integration required that the territory of Hawai'i finally attain its almost forty-year quest for statehood in 1959. Before World War II, a coterie of southern conservatives had steadfastly opposed Hawai'i's admission to the union, fearing that the majority ethnic Asian population would elect an "Oriental" representative to Congress. The Cold War rendered such racial rationales insupportable, and the longest campaign for conversion from territory to state finally ended with Hawai'i gaining equal status. As anticipated, it sent the Japanese American Democrat Daniel Inouye and the Chinese

American Republican Hiram Fong to Congress where they became advocates on behalf of Asian American concerns such as redress for internment and immigration reform.

During the Cold War, popular cultural products celebrated ethnic cultures, depicted interracial friendships, and even advocated for acceptance of miscegenation. Mainstream publishing houses issued autobiographical writings by ethnic Asian writers such as Jade Snow Wong (*Fifth Chinese Daughter*; 1950) and Monica Sone (*Nisei Daughter*; 1953), which revealed for general audiences the struggles of American-born Asians to carve an identity and sense of home out of the often conflicting burdens of family and tradition and the racial exclusions of the United States. As do many other ethnic immigrant narratives, Wong's and Sone's accounts produced the happy endings of racialized American individuals finding their sense of belonging and purpose in the United States.[7]

In contrast to the blatantly stereotypical literary and film depictions of Asians that prevailed in the pre–World War II era, such as the series of novels and movies featuring Sax Rohmer's diabolical Fu Manchu and Earl Derr Biggers's obsequious Charlie Chan, Cold War cultural productions—on page, stage, and screen—celebrated ethnic communities and peoples while emphasizing American commitments to the inclusion of Asians in America and outreach to Asian peoples and cultures overseas. The Chinese immigrant author C. Y. Lee's 1957 novel, *Flower Drum Song*, became the basis for Rodgers and Hammerstein's highly successful Broadway musical in 1958, which in turn produced the popular screen adaptation in 1961, memorably featuring Nancy Kwan. *Flower Drum Song* was but one of three Broadway musicals and films generated by Rodgers and Hammerstein, alongside the Tony Award–winning *The King and I* (1946), based on the 1944 novel *Anna and the King of Siam* by Margaret Landon and also depicted in the Academy Award–winning film of 1956. Rodgers and Hammerstein also produced the Pulitzer Prize–winning musical *South Pacific* (1949), which was based on the Pulitzer Prize–winning book by James Michener, *Tales of the South Pacific* (1947), and resulted in a movie version in 1958. Some best-selling Michener-authored books featuring Americans in Asia and the Pacific Islands included *Hawaii* (1959), *The Bridges at Toko-ri* (1953), and *Sayonara* (1954), which served as the basis for the Marlon Brando film of 1957 that sympathetically portrayed romances and marriages between white military officers and Japanese women in occupied Japan. Brando had also starred in the 1956 screen adaptation of the Pulitzer Prize–winning play *Teahouse of the August Moon* (1953), written by John Patrick and adapted from the 1951 novel by Vern J. Sneider depicting comedic collusions between U.S. military officers and Japanese villagers on Okinawa. Patrick also wrote the screenplay for the 1960 movie *World of Suzie Wong*, based on the 1957 novel by Richard Mason and again starring Nancy Kwan as a prostitute redeemed through her love for a poor American painter.[8]

Asians gained acceptance as Americans but with the caveat that integration required them to remain identifiably ethnic. Multicultural American democracy now allowed Asians to participate as citizens, but their chief symbolic value relied not on their disappearing into the mainstream with other Americans, but on their remaining visibly ethnic in order to demonstrate the United States' capacity to incorporate difference.

During this era, celebrations of America's participation in a multiracial Asian Pacific became something of a cottage industry for several high-profile authors and other cultural producers who emphasized the benevolence of the United States' expanding influence in the region. As described by Naoka Shibusawa, however, the greater emphasis on women and children, portrayed as dependent and malleable subjects, naturalized American dominance and patriarchal leadership while masking the ongoing inequalities of power and privilege in the region. Perhaps most starkly, festive depictions of cheerfully mixed-race Pacific Islander communities contrasted with U.S. nuclear arms testing and population decimations in the region.[9]

The Cold War applied contradictory forces to Asian American lives. America's expanding imperialism in Asia produced wars, refugees, and exacerbations of global inequalities even as more Asian immigrants gained access to the United States, with some managing to attain celebrity status. The China-born architect I. M. Pei, for example, received the commission to design the Kennedy Library in Boston in 1964, while the Zen Buddhist master D. T. Suzuki became the toast of New York.[10] Artists such as Isamu Noguchi, Chang Dai-chien, Mine Okubo, and Dong Kingman garnered critical acclaim and lucrative sales. Despite the highly visible inroads made by a select few, and the professional, technical, scientific, and white-collar employment attained by another tier of well-educated immigrants and those American-born, many Asian Americans remained trapped in low-paying, low-skill labor sectors of the economy such as laundries, restaurants, textile manufacturing, agriculture, domestic service, and gardening. Although far greater numbers of ethnic Asians were able to gain university positions than in the past, many with doctoral degrees remained in ancillary roles as librarians or language lecturers rather than as fully fledged faculty. Starting in the tumultuous 1960s, college-educated Asian American activists tackled community problems enduring from the era of Asiatic exclusion, such as urban overcrowding, poor access to public housing and health services, high rates of school dropouts and juvenile crime, and underrepresentation on university campuses even as they protested America's war in Vietnam.

Despite these ongoing challenges and struggles, in 1966 articles in two popular magazines promoted a celebratory image of Asian Americans that has since become a dominant trope: one that elides the experiences of working-class and refugee Asian Americans still struggling to escape low-paying, unskilled employments and ethnic enclave housing. That year, the conservative sociologist William Petersen published "Success Story, Japanese American Style" in the *New York Times Magazine*, using statistical data to argue that despite being the ethnic group to have arguably faced the severest racial discrimination during their lifetime by having been interned, Japanese Americans had managed to attained educational and employment levels comparable to, and even bettering, that of native-born whites. According to the 1960 Census data, 56 percent of Japanese Americans worked in white-collar jobs compared with 42 percent for whites while 26 percent were professionals or technicians compared with 12.5 percent of whites. Petersen attributed Japanese American success not to protests or government programs, but to their commitment to education, which by 1960 reached a median of 12.2 years compared with 11.1 for Chinese, 11.0 for whites, and far above the 9.2 achieved by Filipinos and 8.6 for blacks.[11]

Later that year, *U.S. News and World Report* published a parallel article that made similar claims regarding the Chinese.[12] This "model minority" image coexists with the "yellow peril" stereotype that had once justified Asiatic exclusion, and it retains a pernicious influence well into the twenty-first century that situates Asian Americans, despite their tremendous diversity of ethnic, socioeconomic, religious, and migration characteristics, as a population of color whose attainments validate democratic processes in the United States even as the risk of persecution as invading foreigners remains. The Cold War provided the conditions for greater attainments and access by Asian Americans even as it retained the possibility of their threat to national security, producing conditions of political and social ambivalence whose lingering shadows have yet to be dispelled.

NOTES

1. Masako Nakamura, "Families Precede Nation and Race: Marriage, Migration, and Integration of Japanese War Brides after World War II" (Ph.D. diss., University of Minnesota, Twin Cities, 2010).

2. See Arissa H. Oh, "From War Waif to Ideal Immigrant: The Cold War Transformation of the Korean Orphan," *Journal of American Ethnic History* 31, no. 4 (2012): 34–55.

3. See Madeline Y. Hsu, "The Disappearance of America's Cold War Chinese Refugees, 1948–1966," *Journal of American Ethnic History* 31, no. 4 (2012): 12–33. This article and Oh's appear in a special issue titled "Ethnic History and the Cold War, Part II: Refashioning Asian Immigration during the Cold War."

4. Catherine Ceniza Choy, *Empire of Care: Nursing and Migration in Filipino American History* (Durham, NC: Duke University Press, 2003), 56–82.

5. Statistics regarding demographic changes in this and the previous three paragraphs are drawn from Bill Ong Hing, *Making and Remaking Asian America through Immigration Policy, 1850–1990* (Stanford, CA: Stanford University Press, 1993), chapter 2.

6. Christina Klein, *Cold War Orientalism: Asia in the Middlebrow Imagination, 1945–1961* (Berkeley: University of California Press, 2003), 23, 40.

7. Jade Snow Wong, *Fifth Chinese Daughter* (New York: HarperCollins, 1950); Monica Sone, *Nisei Daughter* (Seattle: University of Washington Press, 1953).

8. C. Y. Lee, *Flower Drum Song* (New York: Dell, 1961); Margaret Landon, *Anna and the King of Siam* (New York: Garden City, 1944); James Michener, *Tales of the South Pacific* (London: Macmillan, 1947); James Michener, *Hawaii* (New York: Random House, 1959); James Michener, *The Bridges at Toko-ri* (New York: Random House, 1953); James Michener, *Sayonara* (New York: Random House, 1954); Vern J. Sneider, *Teahouse of the August Moon* (New York: Penguin, 1951); Richard Mason, *World of Suzie Wong* (New York: Penguin, 1957).

9. See Naoko Shibusawa, *America's Geisha Ally: Reimagining the Japanese Enemy* (Cambridge, MA: Harvard University Press, 2006).

10. See Jane Iwamura, *Virtual Orientalism: Asian Religions and American Popular Culture* (New York: Oxford University Press, 2011).

11. William Petersen, "Success Story, Japanese American Style," *New York Times Magazine*, January 9, 1966, 20–21, 33, 36, 38, 40–41, 43.

12. "Success Story of One Minority Group in U.S.," *U.S. News and World Report*, December 26, 1966, 73–76.

Further Reading

Brooks, Charlotte. *Alien Neighbors, Foreign Friends: Asian Americans, Housing, and the Transformation of Urban California*. Chicago: University of Chicago Press, 2009.

Bu, Liping. *Making the World Like Us: Education, Cultural Expansion, and the American Century*. Westport, CT: Praeger, 2003.

Choy, Catherine Ceniza. *Empire of Care: Nursing and Migration in Filipino American History*. Durham, NC: Duke University Press, 2003.

Hing, Bill Ong. *Making and Remaking Asian America through Immigration Policy, 1950–1990*. Stanford, CA: Stanford University Press, 1994.

Hsu, Madeline Y. "The Disappearance of America's Cold War Chinese Refugees." *Journal of American Ethnic History* 31, no. 4 (2012): 12–33.

Iwamura, Jane. *Virtual Orientalism: Asian Religions and American Popular Culture*. New York: Oxford University Press, 2011.

Klein, Christina. *Cold War Orientalism: Asia in the Middlebrow Imagination, 1945–1961*. Berkeley: University of California Press, 2003.

Kung, S. W. *Chinese in American Life: Some Aspects of Their History, Status, Problems, and Contributions*. Seattle: University of Washington Press, 1962.

Kurashige, Lon. *Japanese American Celebration and Conflict: A History of Ethnic Identity and Festival, 1934–1990*. Berkeley: University of California Press, 2002.

Lai, Eric, and Dennis Arguelles, eds. *The New Face of Asian Pacific America: Numbers, Diversity, and Change in the 21st Century*. Los Angeles: *AsianWeek* and UCLA Asian American Studies Center Press, 2003.

Marchetti, Gina. *Romance and the "Yellow Peril": Race, Sex, and Discursive Strategies in Hollywood Fiction*. Berkeley: University of California Press, 1993.

Ngai, Mae. *Impossible Subjects: Illegal Aliens and the Making of Modern America*. Princeton, NJ: Princeton University Press, 2004.

Robinson, Greg. *After Camp: Portraits in Midcentury Japanese American Life*. Berkeley: University of California Press, 2012.

Shibusawa, Naoko. *America's Geisha Ally: Reimagining the Japanese Enemy*. Cambridge, MA: Harvard University Press, 2006.

CHAPTER 11

THE ASIAN AMERICAN MOVEMENT

DARYL JOJI MAEDA

ALTHOUGH the Asian American movement remains "one of the least-known" or even "most invisible" social movements of the 1960s and 1970s, a remarkable body of scholarship examining Asian American activism has emerged in the last two decades, especially since the year 2000.[1] Monographs, journal articles, book chapters, anthologies, and dissertations have examined the movement from new perspectives, mined new sources, and built new interpretations. Diane Fujino's outstanding historiographical essay (2008) partitions writing on the Asian American movement chronologically into four discrete periods: the movement era of the late 1960s and mid-1970s, the "vacuum" of scholarship from the late 1970s to the late 1980s, the "slow upsurge" of the late 1980s to late 1990s, and the "coming of age" of movement historiography in the twenty-first century.[2] Rather than retracing Fujino's steps, in this essay I concentrate on recent developments in what she describes as the fourth era by surveying definitional questions posed by the historiography, highlighting broad intellectual trends that have affected its study, and thematizing approaches to the movement. Doing so reveals contestations and alterations in the ways the Asian American movement has been defined and framed, along with the growing set of perspectives and sources that historians and other scholars have used in their quest to uncover its past.

The earliest writings on the history of the Asian American movement emerged from the movement itself, which was remarkably self-reflexive and theoretically engaged. It is often said that journalism writes the first rough draft of history, and, indeed, movement participants reflected in newspapers and periodicals on the beginnings of Asian American activism as a way to contemplate the way forward. For example, in 1973 the I Wor Kuen newspaper *Getting Together* published a history of the Red Guard Party (one of the most important early movement organizations), in which former Red Guards critiqued the party for sexism and ultra-militarism, while calling for greater community engagement ("mass work") and theoretical grounding in the ideas of Marx, Lenin, and Mao. Similarly, *Gidra*, the most significant and widely read movement publication, concluded its print run in April 1974 with a lengthy summation of the newspaper's history, in which Mike Murase chronicled the political evolution of the paper and its staffers and pondered the relationship of the paper to the larger movement.[3] The desire to understand the history and future of the Asian American movement—already evident in the movement's own earliest reflections—continued on in the explorations of scholars and former movement participants in subsequent decades.

PERIODIZATION: A SHORT OR LONG SIXTIES?

One of the most fundamental issues posed by the historiography on the Asian American movement concerns periodization: when did the movement begin and when did it end? Many recent studies of the 1960s in general have embraced a "long sixties" approach, proposed by Arthur Marwick and others, which stretches the periodization of the era backwards into the mid- to late 1950s and forward into the mid-1970s.[4] Peniel Joseph argues that the historiography on the Black Power movement is undergoing just such a chronological expansion, with new accounts examining the Black Power movement's pre-1960s roots and its post-1960s tendrils.[5] Going further, Jaqueline Dowd Hall traces the "long civil rights movement" from the New Deal to Reagan.[6] The historiography on the Asian American movement has only partially embraced the long sixties perspective, continuing to locate its commencement within the 1960s but finding that it ended well after 1970, if it ever ended at all.

Scholars agree that although various Asian ethnic groups in the United States mobilized politically in the nineteenth and early to mid-twentieth centuries, a new form of activism emerged in the late 1960s. The year 1968 is generally understood as the beginning of the Asian American movement. In May of that year, Yuji Ichioka—a graduate student at University of California, Berkeley, who would go on to become an eminent Asian American historian—coined the term "Asian American" when he cofounded the Asian American Political Alliance (AAPA).[7] AAPA and the social movement that it spawned was characterized by multiethnic solidarity forged within a racial framework that foregrounded how Chinese, Japanese, and Filipino Americans (the three dominant Asian ethnic groups in the United States at that time) suffered from similar economic exploitation, legal disfranchisement, and social discrimination.

In contrast to concurrence on its beginning, scholars differ on when the Asian American movement ended. On one hand, some scholars contend that it lasted at least until 1990. William Wei discusses mobilization around the Vincent Chin murder (1983), Don Nakanishi's tenure fight (1987), and Asian American immersion in electoral politics, including Jesse Jackson's presidential campaigns of 1984 and 1988—events that were nearly current during the publication of his book in the early 1990s.[8] In *The Snake Dance of Asian American Activism* (2008), Michael Liu, Kim Geron, and Tracy Lai label the period from 1976 to 1982 as "the Mature Movement," and though they acknowledge that changing international politics altered the movement, like Wei they include 1980s events—including the Chin case and Jackson campaigns, as well as the push for redress and reparations for Japanese Americans interned during World War II—within its purview. They mark the end of the movement around 1990 and acknowledge that Asian American activism after that point constitutes a resurgence or rearticulation of politics not coterminous with the earlier movement.[9]

On the other hand, a far greater number of activists and scholars pinpoint the movement's end in the late 1970s. Three documentary collections make that case through their selections and framing. *Asian Americans: The Movement and the Moment* (2001), edited by Steve Louie and Glenn Omatsu, includes recollections of activists and documents from a staggering array of activities, including "Serve the People" programs in Asian American ghettoes; the fights for ethnic studies at San Francisco State and Berkeley; the anti–Vietnam War movement; the movement against martial law in the Philippines; the campaign to save the International Hotel; Asian American women's organizing; solidarity work with African Americans, Latinos, and Native Americans; and many others. What unites these campaigns is that they occurred overwhelmingly within the 1970s. Although the recollections of twenty-eight activists stretch forward into the present, they tend to discuss the legacy of the movement that existed in the past. Louie writes that the movement "charged forward during the Seventies" but had institutionalized by the end of that decade, and, as a result, the movement's "ideas morphed" and it "began to fade."[10] Omatsu asks whether the "legacy" of the Asian American movement is still relevant thirty years later—a clear indication of his belief that the movement reached a high point during the 1970s.[11] Even the subtitle of the collection, *The Movement and the Moment*, suggests that the movement existed within a particular, bounded historical moment, rather than continuing on unabated into the present. While *Asian Americans* amasses a social history of the Asian American movement, *Legacy to Liberation: Politics and Culture of Revolutionary Asian America* (2000), edited by Fred Ho, Carolyn Antonio, Diane Fujino and Steve Yip, draws a combined social and cultural history of the movement through its greater inclusion and discussion of art, literature, and music. It also contains more extensive coverage of recent events and issues. However, *Legacy to Liberation* shares with *Asian Americans* a primary concentration on the 1960s and 1970s and the demarcation between the movement of that period and Asian American activism of the present. As Diane Fujino and Kye Leung state, "The Asian American Movement today is qualitatively different than in the 1960s and 70s."[12]

Both *Asian Americans* and *Legacy to Liberation* adopt a self-consciously catholic approach and endeavor to represent the wide array of radical organizations that composed the Asian American movement. In contrast, *Stand Up: An Archive Collection of the Bay Area Asian American Movement, 1968–1974* (2009), documents the progression of a cohort of activists who gravitated from the Berkeley AAPA to the Asian Community Center and Wei Min She. The depth of *Stand Up* provides a different type of utility than the breadth of its two predecessors, especially because it provides a level of detail on the range of activities engaged in by these activists—from the Third World Liberation Front strike at Berkeley to Serve the People programs to labor organizing. As the title suggests, the editors locate the Asian American movement in the period from 1968 to 1974, though they include limited material on the International Hotel campaign, which ended in 1977.[13]

A number of dissertations and monographs also periodize the Asian American movement within the late 1960s and 1970s. Three doctoral dissertations completed in the last decade agree on its general parameters, varying only slightly on its precise beginning and end points. The scholar-activist Harvey Dong (2002) carefully divides Asian American activism in the Bay Area into three periods: emergence on college campuses (1968–1972), transition into communities (1972–1977), and decline (1977–1980) due to the end of the Vietnam War, China's rightward turn after the death of Mao Zedong, and the institutionalization of Asian American studies and ethnic studies.[14] Though less explicit in explaining the reasons for their periodization, Jason Ferreira (2003) constrains his discussion of "Third World radicalism" (including Asian American radicalism) in San Francisco to the period from 1968 to 1974,[15] and May Fu (2005) limits her examination of community organizing in Los Angeles, Detroit, and San Francisco to the years from 1969 to 1977.[16] Despite the fact that all three periodize Asian American activism within specific geographical areas, their observations overlap and can safely be extended to a discussion of the national Asian American movement.

Monographs on the Asian American movement concur with the periodization presented by the documentary collections and dissertations. Although the International Hotel anti-eviction struggle in San Francisco cannot be understood to stand in for the entire Asian American movement, it does represent one of its most important and visible campaigns. *San Francisco's International Hotel*, Estella Habal's scholarly account of the struggle and her personal role in it, covers the period from 1968 to 1979, with a very brief epilogue of sorts discussing the transition from the Filipino/Filipino American organization Katipunan ng mga Demokratikong Pilipino (KDP) to the multiracial party Line of March.[17] Like Habal, I also identify the heart of the Asian American movement as occurring in the late 1960s and 1970s in both *Chains of Babylon: The Rise of Asian America* (2009) and *Rethinking the Asian American Movement* (2012). I contend that the movement reached an inflection point in the mid- to late 1970s due to three factors: first, the end of the antiwar movement and diminution of the Black Power movement, both of which had galvanized Asian American activism; second, the wave of consolidations in which Asian American organizations merged into multiracial parties; and third, a reconfiguration of global politics that took the luster off of China's status as a revolutionary model.[18] All of these authors concur that the Asian American movement existed from 1968 or 1969 to somewhere in the mid- to late 1970s. This is not to say that Asian American activism ceased at the end of the 1970s, but rather to acknowledge the shifts in priority and changes in forms of mobilization that occurred over the course of the decade.

Although the tendency of the literature on the Asian American movement to bound it within the 1960s and 1970s might be seen as a historiographical lag in comparison to the "long sixties" approach that characterizes the study of other movements, there are good reasons to believe that the Asian American movement represents a unique case, both in terms of its beginning and its end. The relatively late start of the Asian American movement derives from two factors. First, World War II and the Cold War dampened

Asian American radicalism in particularly racial ways. The labor organizer Karl Yoneda notes that Japanese American communists were unceremoniously ousted from the American Communist Party (CPUSA) after Pearl Harbor, due to the CPUSA's Popular Front stance, and Japanese American radicals, traumatized by the internment, may have drifted away from activism after the war.[19] During World War II, Filipino American radicals like Carlos Bulosan supported the United States in solidarity with its struggle against Japanese fascism, yet during the Cold War were harassed and threatened with deportation, a penalty not enforceable against white or black American citizens.[20] The strong Chinese American left that existed prior to World War II fell dormant in the 1950s due not only to McCarthyism, but also to the ethnically specific repression in Chinatowns from right-wing, Kuomintang-affiliated elites who were especially virulent after the communist Chinese revolution of 1949.[21] Furthermore, the hottest flare-ups of the Cold War were located in Asia (China, Korea and Vietnam), transforming Asian Americans—whose fate has long been tied via Orientalism to Asia—into racialized political threats, which provides a plausible reason for the Asian American left's shallower institutional roots in the 1950s. Second, and most important, the Asian American movement hailed into existence the very category of "Asian American" as a multiethnic formation. Pre-1968 activism by Asian ethnics in the United States proceeded in ethnic, national, or class forms that were therefore not recognizably Asian American in post-1968 terms.

The Asian American movement's endpoint in the 1970s may also be seen as the result of two unique factors. First, the composition of Asian America changed more drastically in the 1970s than that of any other racial group due to the immigration reforms of 1965 and the end of the Vietnam War. The post-1965 flow of immigrants transformed Asian America from primarily native-born to majority foreign-born, dramatically increased its ethnic and national diversity, and brought in many well-educated immigrants entering under professional quotas. In addition, the end of the Vietnam War in 1975 created a stream of Southeast Asian refugees, many of whom were anticommunist.[22] Second, as Laura Pulido argues, of all members of the multicolored left in Los Angeles, Asian American organizations were perhaps the most assiduously interethnic and interracial in their theory and practice, in part because the Asian American movement never hewed to Asian American nationalism.[23] It was therefore a natural progression for Asian American organizations to participate in the wave of multiracial consolidations that Max Elbaum describes occurring in the new communist movement in the mid- to late 1970s.[24] As the center of gravity among Asian American radicals shifted into multiracial parties, the Asian American movement ceased to exist as an identifiably Asian American formation. While participants in other movements also took part in these consolidations, blacks, Chicanos, and Puerto Ricans inherited a wider spectrum of nationalisms, which enabled their movements to retain more ethnically and racially specific characteristics. Given the historiography's general concurrence that the Asian American movement occurred from approximately 1968 to around 1980, it makes sense to consider the Asian American movement as a product of a "long Seventies" rather than the 1960s, a reframing that suggests its congruence with the Black Power, Chicano, Puerto Rican, American Indian, and women's liberation movements.

FRAMEWORKS: CIVIL RIGHTS VERSUS
THIRD WORLD SOLIDARITY

Despite wide-ranging agreement on when the Asian American movement started, explanations of why it began diverge. In the first monograph on the movement, *The Asian American Movement* (1993), the historian William Wei set the terms of the debate by arguing that the Asian American movement was "[i]nspired by" and "owes a debt of gratitude" to the civil rights movement "for exposing the gap between the country's image of itself and reality."[25] Wei has been widely criticized for what Fujino aptly terms his "misplaced civil rights etiology,"[26] which has led to a spurious framing of the movement. Wei partitions the movement into "reformers" (whom he lauds for their positive contributions to their communities) versus "revolutionaries" (whom he derides as "Maoist sects" and criticizes as divisive, sectarian, and obsessed with ideological correctness).[27] He finds the Asian American movement commendable to the extent that it mirrored the reformist civil rights movement—which critiqued racism but tended to seek equal entry into the American body politic—but ignoble when it called for radical changes to American political and economic systems as the revolutionary Black Power movement did. But the dichotomy between reformers and revolutionaries is a false one, for revolutionaries were often among the most ardent and committed community activists on issues such as healthcare and working and living conditions. The useful work performed by revolutionaries—in communities, on campuses, for gender equality, and against the Vietnam War—outweighed the sectarian squabbles that did occur.

Aside from Wei, the vast majority of the literature on the Asian American movement links it to the Black Power movement, rather than the civil rights movement. As early as 1969, Amy Uyematsu penned one of the movement's first self-conscious definitions, a widely read essay entitled "The Emergence of Yellow Power in America," in which she quoted the famed Black Power advocate Stokely Carmichael's rejection of integrationism and stated that "yellow power" was "derived from the black power ideology."[28] The historiography on the movement that has emerged after Wei's opening salvo bears out Uyematsu's early insistence that Black Power rather than civil rights galvanized the Asian American movement, as will become clear in the remainder of this essay.

TWENTY-FIRST-CENTURY APPROACHES
TO THE MOVEMENT

The sociologist Yen Le Espiritu proffered the highly influential theory of "Asian American panethnicity" in 1992. She argued that, in the United States, Asians of various ethnicities coalesced in a multiethnic coalition under the rubric of "Asian American" in order to exercise greater leverage on the state for social service funding, gaining electoral office, and protection from hate crimes.[29] Espiritu credited the Asian American movement with building the first instance of panethnicity, and while I agree that the movement created a multiethnic Asian American identity, I contend that a state-centric notion of panethnicity cannot fully explain the anti-imperialism of the Asian American movement.[30] The following year, William Wei published *The Asian American Movement*, a social history of ambitious scope that unfortunately decontextualized the movement in relationship to its contemporary power movements and undertheorized the meaning of the emergent category "Asian American." Since 2000, scholars have investigated the Asian American movement through an expanding range of historiographical, social scientific, and cultural studies frameworks that have challenged Espiritu's and Wei's interpretations.

Social Movement Theory

In *The Snake Dance of Asian American Activism*, Liu, Geron, and Lai attempt to systematize the study of the Asian American movement through the use of social movement theory. They examine how the movement emerged at a moment of what Sidney Tarrow terms "political opportunity," acknowledge that resource mobilization theory (which arose from studies of the civil rights movement) does not fully apply to the Asian American case, and engage briefly with the idea of framing, or how a social movement creates, sustains, and relies on a set of meanings.[31] In contrast to Wei's assertion that the Asian American movement was an outgrowth of the civil rights movement, these authors state unequivocally, "The new generation of Asian Americans became active in support of the emerging, Black, brown, and Red power movements in this country."[32] Indeed, the presence of those movements provided one form of political opportunity that enabled the Asian American movement to thrive, and the Asian American movement framed the plight of Asian ethnics in the United States as a problem of racism.

Cultural History

Cultural histories of the Asian American movement do not explicitly invoke framing theory but take as their central problematic the creation of a politicized Asian American identity in the realm of representation and performance. Gisele L. Fong's dissertation (2003) examines how cultural workers of the Asian American movement formed an oppositional Asian American identity through publications, posters, and music. According to Fong, the cultural work of the movement focused on the collective racialization of Asian ethnics into a panethnic formation, advocated for interracial and Third World solidarity, and addressed class and gender oppression.[33] In *Chains of Babylon* (2009), I contend that culture provided an arena in which an antiracist and anti-imperialist Asian American identity could be articulated. The political theater of protests and rallies performed Asian American militancy, and the music of A Grain of Sand expressed its commitment to interracial and international solidarity.[34] In *Rethinking the Asian American Movement* (2012), I extend my analysis to cultural institutions such as theatrical companies and community-based art workshops, arguing that these organizations brought together multiethnic Asian American artists and audiences in the practice of coalition building.[35] Fong and I concur on the antiracist, anti-imperialist, pro-solidarity nature of Asian American movement culture and agree that cultural work empowered Asian American communities to define their own identities, claim their spaces, and make the movement's politics accessible to wider audiences.

Biography and Institutional History

Methodologically, nearly all historians of the Asian American movement rely at least in part on oral histories gathered from participants. However, Diane Fujino stands apart in her extensive use of oral history to build biographies of critical movement figures. Her first book, *Heartbeat of Struggle: The Revolutionary Life of Yuri Kochiyama* (2005), portrays the legendary woman not only as an extraordinary activist, but also as a profoundly human figure. Drawn from "thirty-four hours of recorded interviews, in addition to hundreds of hours of informal conversations and interactions," Fujino's account traces Kochiyama's political journey from her beginnings as a Japanese American girl raised in a middle-class family in San Pedro before World War II, who retained her "optimistic naivete" and patriotism even during her incarceration in camps at Santa Anita and Jerome, through her political education in Harlem in the 1960s and encounters with Malcolm X, to her emergence as an influential Asian American radical. Throughout, Fujino captures Kochiyama's humanity and shows how her innate warmth and incessant networking enabled her organizing, but she also notes how Kochiyama's dedication to activism sometimes exacted personal tolls.[36] In many ways, Fujino's second biography, *Samurai among Panthers: Richard Aoki on Race, Resistance, and a Paradoxical Life* (2012), functions as a companion to the first. This methodologically rich study draws on an impressive array of archival sources; twenty-six interviews with friends, family members, and political associates; and more than a hundred hours of interviews with Aoki himself.[37] Written as a dialogue between Aoki's voice and Fujino's contextualizations, it portrays a boy raised in an unstable home, who came to value machismo as a way of negotiating the streets of Oakland during the Cold War, spent time in the military, dabbled with socialism, became a field marshal in the Black Panther Party, cofounded AAPA, and participated in the Third World Liberation Front (TWLF) strike at Berkeley. After Aoki's death, his critical role in the Asian American movement was remembered by veteran movement participants like Mo Nishida, who called him "Chairman Richard, our own Lenin, a theoretician and practical leader," and Harvey Dong, who called him the "toughest Oriental to come out of West Oakland"—both appellations referring to his machismo and visibility.[38] Aoki's complex, confrontational masculinity contrasts with Kochiyama's resolute yet embracing style, but both managed to become highly admired avatars of Asian American radicalism because they shared an unceasing commitment to social justice for all, regardless of race. Furthermore, the stories of Kochiyama and Aoki bear witness to the Black Power impact on the nascent Asian American movement.

The genre of biography provides an important way of expanding the temporal span of Asian American movement historiography in terms of individuals, given the paucity of institutional connections from the Asian American Old Left to the New Left. Fujino's work shows how individuals became politicized in the pre-movement period—Kochiyama in the political hotbed of Harlem, and Aoki through engagement with the Socialist Workers Party—before emerging into 1960s activism. The life story of Kazu Iijima, whom Karen Ishizuka memorializes as "one of the mothers of the Asian American movement" (2009), provides one example of a personal bridge from the Old Left to the Asian American movement. Iijima was a member of the Young Communist League before World War II, but she eschewed politics after the war while she raised her children, one of whom was Chris Iijima, the well-known movement musician and activist. Her political revival came about in the 1960s when she drew inspiration from Black Power advocates like H. Rap Brown and James Farmer, and she subsequently cofounded one of the most important movement organizations, Asian Americans for Action (AAA), in 1969.[39] If other backward linkages to the Old Left are to be discovered, they will be found by exploring the experiences of individuals like Iijima in the form of personal profiles. Biographical examinations can also illuminate how movement participants developed their racial awareness and sense of justice.[40]

If biography can stretch Asian American movement periodization backward, institutional history provides a way to extend it forward, for many of the institutions that the movement created have outlasted the movement itself. *At 40* (2009) reflects on four decades of the Asian American Studies Department at San Francisco State University, one of the primary institutions created by the movement. Documents and reminiscences of the TWLF strike and the groundbreaking implementations of an Asian American studies curriculum, along with essays on the evolution of the department, provide a sense of how it grew out of the movement and became institutionalized.[41] More institutional histories are needed to show how the movement's aims have been realized, evolved, and contested in long-standing educational, legal, nonprofit, and arts and cultural organizations.

Intersectional Explorations

Examinations of the intersections of gender with race and the crucial roles played by women in the Asian American movement form one of the most critical developments in movement historiography. Early on in movement studies, Susie Ling's "The Mountain Movers" (1989) argued that, for many Asian American women, a growing awareness of gender oppression formed a critical part of their dawning racial consciousness. Within spaces carved out inside the Asian American movement, women shared their frustrations with being restricted to subordinate roles such as typing and making coffee, and about their experiences of being silenced, sexually exploited, and even physically abused. Ling catalogs the array of Serve the People programs created by and for women in Los Angeles. Most critically, she highlights their "triple oppression" framework, which put opposition to sexism on an equal footing with struggles against racism and class exploitation.[42] Mary Kao calls the development of this tripartite consciousness a "three-step boogie," which enabled Asian American women to conceptualize U.S. imperialism as a totality "that used racism, sexism, and classism to maintain its rule." Because of this intersectional vision, female activists saw their male cohorts as "comrades and allies," even as they struggled against male chauvinism within the movement.[43]

In "'Serve the People and You Help Yourself'" (2008), May Fu provides a more detailed picture of the work of Asian Sisters, an antidrug organization that focused on barbiturate overdoses by young women. Asian Sisters linked substance abuse to racism, which damaged Asian American women's self-esteem by holding them up to a white standard of beauty, as well as sexism, which objectified their bodies. Fu notes that Asian Sisters eschewed the belligerent tactics of male antidrug programs in organizations like Yellow Brotherhood and Asian American Hardcore, opting instead to nurture supportive relationships with at-risk young women. Their politically engaged framework combined antiracism, antisexism, and community empowerment.[44] Fu also examines the Detroit Asian Political Alliance (APA), a study group composed of Asians and Asian Americans, including the veteran Marxist theorist Grace Lee Boggs, a figure more closely associated with black radicalism than the Asian American movement.[45] In contrast to the normative analysis that situates Boggs and the APA as marginal to the Asian American movement,[46] Fu notes APA's anti-imperialist opposition to the war in Vietnam, its rigorously internationalist politics, and Boggs's attendance at the early and important Asian American Reality conference at Pace University in 1970. This reinterpretation raises the definitional question of who and what counts as part of the Asian American movement.

Comparative Approaches

In my recent synthesis of the Asian American movement, I argue that interracialism and internationalism formed two of the most important characteristics of the movement.[47] Scholars using comparative frameworks have produced some of the best work on the Asian American movement of the past decade, and have revealed its interracialism in three different ways. The first strand of comparative work examines Asian Americans operating within multiracial coalitions. In their respective dissertations, Jason Ferreira (2003) and Angela Ryan (2010) argue that Asian Americans participating in the 1968–1969 TWLF strike at San Francisco State College shared a Third World vision with Black, Chicano, and American Indian comrades. This collectively held ideology linked racism, colonialism, and economic exploitation, and it called for self-determination for, and solidarity among, people of color in the United States and around the globe. Furthermore, this global vision informed local practices. Like other members of the TWLF at San Francisco State, the Asian American Political Alliance (AAPA), Intercollegiate Chinese for Social Action (ICSA), and Pilipino American Collegiate Endeavor (PACE) began outreach and tutoring programs in their communities prior to the strike and continued their community engagement after its conclusion.[48] Though they shared much in common with the rest of the multiracial coalitions, Asian Americans stood alone in confronting a fellow Asian, the San Francisco State president S. I. Hayakawa, as the most powerful opponent of the strike.[49] Ferreira notes that the strike constituted one instance among many of Third World radicalism in San Francisco, and Ryan compares the action at State with a similar strike at City College of New York, which gestured toward, but never truly achieved, inclusion of Asian Americans due to the demographics of the city and school. Harvey Dong's dissertation (2002) provides the best Asian American–centered picture of the TWLF strike at Berkeley. He reveals that the members of the original Berkeley AAPA chapter hailed from a variety of backgrounds. Some were the children of "garment workers, restaurant workers, and small farmers," while others had parents who had only recently ascended into the middle class; they came from Hawai'i, rural farming towns, cities, and suburbs, and some were international students from Hong Kong. A few had already been politicized in organizations such as the United Farm Workers, the Student Nonviolent Coordinating Committee, the Black Panther Party, and the Peace and Freedom Party, while others were drawn from culturally oriented student associations. This diverse grouping forged a politics of antiracism and anti-imperialism that plugged seamlessly into the ideologies of the TWLF and its push for ethnic studies.[50] My own synthesis of Asian American student activism draws extensively from these excellent dissertations, all of which certainly deserve wider circulation.[51]

The second strand of comparative work situates Asian American activism alongside activism by other people of color. Laura Pulido's *Black, Brown, Yellow, and Left* (2006) stands as the most important work of this type published to date. A finely wrought portrait of what Pulido terms the "Third World Left" in Los Angeles, it places the largely Japanese American radical collective East Wind in the context of groups like the Black Panther Party and the Chicano group El Centro de Acción Social y Autonomo (CASA). Pulido concludes that, in comparison to its cohorts, East Wind was less nationalistic, most thoroughly interracial and interethnic in its work, and least sexist, though its women members did experience sexism.[52] Although East Wind cannot represent the entirety of the Asian American movement, it did confront many of the same issues faced by other Asian American organizations around the nation and underwent similar changes over time. In contrast to Pulido's local focus, Max Elbaum narrates the historical transitions that Asian American radicals and other radicals of color across the nation underwent in the evolution from Third World Marxism to the new communist movement. *Revolution in the Air: Sixties Radicals Turn to Lenin, Mao, and Che* (2002) shows how intensifying efforts to achieve theoretical and political orthodoxy and increasing desires to build vanguard parties drove Asian American groups—including East Wind, I Wor Kuen, Wei Min She, KDP, and Workers Viewpoint Organization—into mergers with non–Asian American groups that formed a number of multiracial communist parties in the mid- to late 1970s, including the League of Revolutionary Struggle (Marxist-Leninist), Revolutionary Communist Party (RCP), Line of March, and Communist Workers Party (CWP).[53] Elbaum's overarching framework demonstrates that by 1980 the key Asian American radical organizations had faced similar challenges, undergone comparable transformations, and in many cases reached the same conclusion that a revolution would best be incited by multiracial parties.

The third strand of comparative work explores how understandings of race and empire provided conceptual and ideological bridges between Asian American radicals and other radicals of color, particularly African Americans. Robin D. G. Kelley and Betsy Esch's provocative essay "Black Like Mao" (1999) traces the influence of the Chairman's Third World Marxism on black radicals.[54] Vijay Prashad's *Everybody Was Kung Fu Fighting* (2001) narrates a "mongrel Afro-Asian history" that unfolded over centuries and across the globe. Prashad catalogs the racist and colonialist machinations that interpellated Africans and Asians into similar positions, as well as the resistances practiced by these subjugated others, and concludes with a chapter on the 1960s and 1970s that briefly discusses the Red Guard Party and I Wor Kuen.[55] I argue in "Black Panthers, Red Guards, and Chinamen" (2005) that Asian American movement participants like the Red Guards worked out their sense of racial and political identity in part by contemplating blackness in the form of Black Power, particularly the masculinity of the Black Panther Party.[56] The cultural studies scholar Rychetta Watkins continues the exploration of the black-Asian encounter in *Black Power, Yellow Power, and the Making of Revolutionary Identities* (2012). Watkins compares how African Americans and Asian Americans envisioned "power" as a method by which to achieve radical change in the 1960s and 1970s. Although her explorations of Yellow Power tread the familiar ground of *Gidra* and the literary anthology *AIIIEEEEE!!!*, Watkins's most useful contributions to our understanding of the Asian American movement include her careful tracing of the influence of Fanon's anticolonialism within movement writings and her elaboration on both the liberatory possibilities and constraints of representing the guerrilla as the ultimate agent of social change.[57] These authors collectively assert the necessity of understanding the Asian American movement's ideologies and political understandings within a comparative framework that acknowledges interracial and transnational cross-pollinations.

Transnational Perspectives

While interracialism anchored the Asian American movement's activism within the United States, the ideology of internationalism informed its global vision. Cutting-edge works of the past decade have revealed the Asian American movement's transnational dimensions, and this line of inquiry forms the most exciting avenue for future explorations. Jonathan Okamura (2003) persuasively argues that transnational consciousness undergirded much of the Asian American movement. Countering Sau-Ling Wong's widely read caution against adopting an uncritical "denationalization" of Asian American studies, Okamura suggests that the Asian American movement's community orientation should not be mistaken for a lack of international awareness; instead, he points out that the foundational movement-era anthologies, *Roots* (1971) and *Counterpoint* (1976), contain what today we would call a transnational framework for understanding the United States in Asia and Asians in America.[58] Recent work has begun to further excavate the Asian American movement's transnational crossings.

Asian American activists constructed transnational affiliations with Asians across the Pacific in many ways. Opposing U.S. aggression in Southeast Asia enabled Asian American radicals to express transnational sympathies with the Vietnamese people to whom they felt racially bound, and with whom they shared a common subjugation with U.S. imperialism. It also aided in building the Asian American movement as a multiethnic U.S. coalition, as Asians of many ethnicities marched together in antiwar protests under the banners of the leftist nations of Asia—China, North Vietnam, and North Korea.[59] Antiwar activism mobilized the multiethnic Asian American movement largely through symbolic and ideological means, but more material traces can be found that speak to the international roots of the movement.

Certain Asian diasporic radicals exercised considerable influence on American-born activists of the fledgling Asian American movement, but their stories have yet to be fully told. Though chiefly concerned with post-1980 Korean diasporic radicalism, Miriam Ching Yoon Louie (2004) points intriguingly to the influence of Harry Chang, a relatively unknown first-generation Korean mathematics professor who in the 1960s and 1970s introduced young Bay Area activists to the serious study of Marxism and sustained a historical materialist analysis of racism in the United States.[60] Like Chang, the Japanese activist Shin'ya Ono was born in Asia before migrating to the United States. Ono became involved in radical politics in the 1960s, served as editor of *Studies on the Left*, joined the Weathermen in 1969, and served jail time in Chicago for his participation in the Weathermen-sponsored Days of Rage. As Ryan Fukumori argues, Ono had a brief and contentious membership in I Wor Kuen, the radical organization based out of New York's Chinatown, but gained celebrity in Asian American radical circles on the basis of his high-profile actions and incarceration. After being released from jail, Ono relocated to Los Angeles, where he worked as a labor organizer until returning to Japan in 1982.[61] In contrast to the fragmentary evidence for the influence of Chang and Ono (both of whom deserve further examination), the case of Filipino radicals and their influence on the Asian American movement has been far better documented.

Catherine Ceniza Choy insists that the history of the Asian American movement must account for its connections to the Philippine left. In "Towards Trans-Pacific Social Justice" (2005), she recuperates the stories of women who began their activism in the

Philippines, fled political persecution, and helped to foster Filipino American radicalism in the 1970s.[62] Helen Toribio notes that the Filipino American movement in the United States combined American-born Filipinos politicized in the heady environment of 1960s Third World activism with Philippine radicals who were members or supporters of the Communist Party of the Philippines (CPP).[63] CPP cadres exiled to the United States helped to organize Filipino American leftist formations such as the Kalayaan collective and KDP. KDP proclaimed a dual focus on ending Ferdinand Marcos's repressive martial law regime in the Philippines and establishing socialism in the United States. Choy and Toribio deliver valuable, if fragmentary, reconstructions of the influence of the CPP on the Filipino American left and KDP's anti–martial law work; their accounts suggest that KDP provides arguably the strongest example of internationalist influences and practices within the Asian American movement.

Another way to transnationalize the study of the Asian American movement is to compare it to movements in other nations during the 1970s. The resurgence of Asian pride in North America is generally thought of as a U.S. phenomenon, but Masumi Izumi (2007) draws parallels between movements by Japanese Americans and Japanese Canadians, who, like their counterparts south of the border, rejected assimilationism, revitalized Japanese culture, recuperated the history of Japanese immigrants, and delivered social services to the elderly.[64] Opposition to the Vietnam War also occurred on both sides of the U.S.-Canadian border. In fact, one of the most important events for the Asian American antiwar movement occurred in Canada.

In April 1971, U.S. and Canadian women gathered together to meet with Southeast Asian women from Vietnam and Laos at the Indochinese Women's Conferences (IWC) held in Vancouver and Toronto. The historian Judy Tzu-Chun Wu's article "Rethinking Global Sisterhood" (2010) chronicles the tensions based on race, nationality, and sexuality that manifested at the IWC and argues that many of the IWC delegates suffered from "radical Orientalism," her term reworking Edward Said's notion of Orientalism by noting that the Southeast Asian women were romanticized and essentialized as the locus of revolutionary perseverance and power. White antiwar activists sought to gain soulful connections with the Vietnamese representatives, but in doing so they marginalized Asian American women.[65] Wu also studies journeys by multiracial delegations that included Asian Americans to Hanoi, South Vietnam, Cambodia, North Korea, and the People's Republic of China.[66] These leftist delegations drew revolutionary inspiration from radical Asia and also built Third World American antiwar coalitions. By studying the international travels of the antiwar movement, Wu simultaneously internationalizes the Asian American movement, which was mobilized by opposition to the war and prioritized ending it.[67]

CONCLUSION

Works on KDP and the Asian American antiwar movement point to the leading edge of Asian American movement historiography by combining attention to women and gender with a keen analysis of internationalism. Both cases demonstrate that internationalism formed a critical component of the Asian American movement and argue for expanding notions of what counts as part of the movement. These accounts suggest that the movement must be understood as the product of transnational flows of ideologies and activists and as the source of transnational border crossings and solidarities. Wu's work in particular examines the Asian American movement within a Third World, interracial framework; attends to the gendered nature of the movement and role that women played in it; and highlights its global crossings. Twenty-first-century historiography of the Asian American movement will move further in all of these directions. Many intriguing topics remain relatively unexplored and deserve greater scrutiny. Organizational histories of AAA, AAPA, IWK, Wei Min She, and KDP have yet to be written, as do biographies of any number of prominent activists and leaders. No monograph on the Asian American antiwar movement exists yet, nor do we have available a monograph on Asian American labor organizing during the movement era. Intriguingly, the field of Asian American studies has yet to produce a definitive monograph on its own history and development. And though the historiography has begun to address gender in the Asian American movement, sexuality remains relatively unexplored, in spite of the participation of gays and lesbians in the movement.[68] Studies of movement-era activism in the urban centers of Los Angeles, San Francisco, and New York have dominated the literature, despite the fact that the movement surfaced in college towns in the Midwest and East Coast, Chicago, Seattle, Philadelphia, Hawai'i (though in specific forms there), and elsewhere. As it continues to develop, the historiography on the Asian American movement will undoubtedly continue to illuminate the interlocking workings of race, class, gender, and nation within a radical movement that fought against inequality and exploitation along all of those axes simultaneously.

NOTES

1. Daryl Joji Maeda, *Rethinking the Asian American Movement* (New York: Routledge, 2012); Diane C. Fujino, "Race, Place, Space, and Political Development: Japanese-American Radicalism in the 'Pre-Movement' 1960s," *Social Justice* 35, no. 2 (2008): 58.
2. Diane C. Fujino, "Who Studies the Asian American Movement? A Historiographical Analysis," *Journal of Asian American Studies* 11, no. 2 (2008): 127–169.
3. "A History of the Red Guard Party," *IWK Journal: The Political Organ of I Wor Kuen* 2 (1975): 81–88; Mike Murase, "Towards Barefoot Journalism," *Gidra* (1974): 1, 34–46.
4. Arthur Marwick, *The Sixties: Cultural Revolution in Britain, France, Italy, and the United States, c.1968–c.1974* (New York: Oxford University Press, 1998).
5. Peniel E. Joseph, *Waiting 'Til the Midnight Hour: A Narrative History of Black Power in America* (New York: Holt, 2007); Peniel E. Joseph, ed., *The Black Power Movement: Rethinking the Civil Rights-Black Power Era* (New York: Routledge, 2006), 7–8.
6. Jacquelyn Dowd Hall, "The Long Civil Rights Movement and the Political Uses of the Past," *Journal of American History* 91, no. 4 (2005): 1233–1263.

7. Rick Baldoz pointed out the prehistory of the term "Asian American" in a Facebook exchange dated March 26, 2012, though he cautioned in an email follow-up dated March 28, 2012, that the pre-1960s usages differed dramatically in meaning from Ichioka's. As Baldoz notes, in the 1950s the sociologist Lawrence Fuchs used the term "Asian-American" in passing in "Some Political Aspects of Immigration," *Law and Contemporary Problems* 21, no. 2 (1956): 281.

8. William Wei, *The Asian American Movement* (Philadelphia: Temple University Press, 1993), 159, 193–194, 241–270.

9. Michael Liu, Kim Geron, and Tracy Lai, *The Snake Dance of Asian American Activism: Community, Vision, and Power* (Lanham, MD: Lexington, 2008), xv–xvi, 93–177.

10. Steve Louie, "When We Wanted It Done, We Did It Ourselves," in *Asian Americans: The Movement and the Moment*, ed. Steve Louie and Glenn Omatsu (Los Angeles: UCLA Asian American Studies Center Press, 2001), xxiv–xxv.

11. Glenn Omatsu, "Listening to the Small Voice Speaking the Truth: Grassroots Organizing and the Legacy of Our Movement," in Louie and Omatsu, *Asian Americans*, 315.

12. Diane C. Fujino and Kye Leung, "Radical Resistance in Conservative Times: New Asian American Organizations in the 1990s," in *Legacy to Liberation: Politics and Culture of Revolutionary Asian America*, ed. Fred Ho, Carolyn Antonio, Diane Fujino, and Steve Yip (San Francisco: AK Press, 2000), 141–158.

13. Asian Community Center Archive Group, *Stand Up: An Archive Collection of the Bay Area Asian American Movement, 1968–1974* (Berkeley, CA: Eastwind, 2009).

14. Harvey C. Dong, "The Origins and Trajectory of Asian American Political Activism in the San Francisco Bay Area, 1968–1978," Ph.D. diss., University of California, Berkeley (2002), 234–243. Dong also provides the reasoning for the periodization of *Stand Up* (217–219).

15. Jason Michael Ferreira, "All Power to the People: A Comparative History of Third World Radicalism in San Francisco, 1968–1974," Ph.D. diss., University of California, Berkeley (2003).

16. May Chuan Fu, "Keeping Close to the Ground: Politics and Coalition in Asian American Community Organizing, 1969–1977," Ph.D. diss., University of California, San Diego (2005).

17. Estella Habal, *San Francisco's International Hotel: Mobilizing the Filipino American Community in the Anti-Eviction Movement* (Philadelphia: Temple University Press, 2007).

18. Daryl J. Maeda, *Chains of Babylon: The Rise of Asian America* (Minneapolis: University of Minnesota Press, 2009), x–xi; Maeda, *Rethinking*, 136–146.

19. Karl Yoneda, *Ganbatte: Sixty-Year Struggle of a Kibei Worker* (Los Angeles: Asian American Studies Center Press, 1983).

20. Carlos Bulosan, *America Is in the Heart* (Seattle: University of Washington Press, 1973); Arlene de Vera, "Without Parallel: The Local 7 Deportation Cases," *Amerasia Journal* 20 (1994): 1–25.

21. Him Mark Lai, "A Historical Survey of the Chinese Left in American Society" in *Counterpoint: Perspectives on Asian America*, ed. Emma Gee (Los Angeles: UCLA Asian American Studies Center Press, 1976), 63–80; Dong, "Origins and Trajectory," 199–210, 214–219.

22. Bill Ong Hing, *Making and Remaking Asian America through Immigration Policy, 1850–1990* (Stanford, CA: Stanford University Press, 1993).

23. Laura Pulido, *Black, Brown, Yellow, and Left: Radical Activism in Los Angeles* (Berkeley: University of California Press, 2006), 106, 133–142, 154–160.

24. Max Elbaum, *Revolution in the Air: Sixties Radicals Turn to Lenin, Mao and Che* (London: Verso, 2002), 227–266; Maeda, *Rethinking*, 139–146.

25. Wei, *Asian American Movement*, 12–13.

26. Fujino, "Who Studies the Asian American Movement?," 138–141.

27. Wei, *Asian American Movement*, 169–240.

28. Amy Uyematsu, "The Emergence of Yellow Power in America," *Gidra* (October 1969); reprinted in *Roots: An Asian American Reader*, ed. Amy Tachiki, Eddie Wong, and Franklin Odo with Buck Wong (Los Angeles: UCLA Asian American Studies Center Press, 1971), 9–13.

29. Yen Le Espiritu, *Asian American Panethnicity: Bridging Institutions and Identities* (Philadelphia: Temple University Press, 1992). Espiritu offers the now-standard narrative of immigration and ethnic "disidentification" in the late nineteenth and early twentieth centuries, followed by the crucible of multiethnic activism in the 1960s.

30. Maeda, *Chains of Babylon*, 16.

31. Liu et al., *Snake Dance*, 6–11, 148–155.

32. Ibid., 1.

33. Gisele L. Fong, "The People United: Cultural Work and the Making of Asian America, 1968–1985," Ph.D. diss., University of California, Los Angeles (2003).

34. Maeda, *Chains of Babylon*, 127–153.

35. Maeda, *Rethinking*, 85–106.

36. Diane C. Fujino, *Heartbeat of Struggle: The Revolutionary Life of Yuri Kochiyama* (Minneapolis: University of Minnesota Press, 2005), xxx, 41.

37. Diane C. Fujino, *Samurai among Panthers: Richard Aoki on Race, Resistance, and a Paradoxical Life* (Minneapolis: University of Minnesota Press, 2012), xxv, xxvii.

38. Mo Nishida, "Komrad Richard," *Amerasia Journal* 35, no. 2 (2009): 233–239; Harvey Dong, "Richard Aoki (1938–2008): Toughest Oriental to Come Out of West Oakland," *Amerasia Journal* 35, no. 2 (2009): 223–232.

39. Karen L. Ishizuka, "Flying in the Face of Race, Gender, Class and Age: A Story about Kazu Iijima, One of the Mothers of the Asian American Movement on the First Year Anniversary of Her Death," *Amerasia Journal* 35, no. 2 (2009): 24–47. See Glenn Omatsu, "Always a Rebel: An Interview with Kazu Iijima," *Amerasia Journal* 13, no. 2 (1986–1987): 83–98.

40. A brief profile of Don Nakanishi, the longtime director of the UCLA Asian American Studies Center, hints that his identification with Mexican Americans, acquired from growing up in the multiracial neighborhood of Boyle Heights in Los Angeles, may have incubated his activism, which included his cofounding the pioneering scholarly periodical *Amerasia Journal*. See Karen L. Ishizuka, "A Portrait of the Scholar-Activist as a Young Man: Don Nakanishi," *Amerasia Journal* 35, no. 3 (2009): 211–232.

41. Asian American Studies Department, San Francisco State University, *At 40: Asian American Studies @ San Francisco State; Self-Determination, Community, Student Service* (San Francisco: Asian American Studies Department, San Francisco State University, 2009).

42. Susie Ling, "The Mountain Movers: Asian American Women's Movement in Los Angeles," *Amerasia Journal* 15, no. 1 (1989): 51–67.

43. Mary Uyematsu Kao, "Three-Step Boogie in 1970s Los Angeles: Sansei Women in the Asian American Movement," *Amerasia Journal* 35, no. 1 (2009): 112–138.

44. May Fu, "'Serve the People and You Help Yourself': Japanese-American Anti-Drug Organizing in Los Angeles, 1969 to 1972," *Social Justice* 35, no. 2 (2008): 80–99.

45. May C. Fu, "On Contradiction: Theory and Transformation in Detroit's Asian Political Alliance," *Amerasia Journal* 35, no. 2 (2009): 1–22. For more on Boggs, see Grace Lee Boggs with Scott Kurashige, *The Next American Revolution: Sustainable Activism for the Twenty-First Century* (Berkeley: University of California Press, 2011); and Grace Lee Boggs, *Living for Change: An Autobiography* (Minneapolis: University of Minnesota Press, 1998).

46. Jennifer Jung Hee Choi, "At the Margin of Asian American Political Experience: The Life of Grace Lee Boggs," *Amerasia Journal* 25, no. 2 (1999): 18–40.

47. Maeda, *Rethinking*.

48. Ferreira, "Dare to Struggle"; Angela Rose Ryan, "Education for the People: The Third World Student Movement at San Francisco State College and City College of New York," Ph.D. diss., Ohio State University (2010).

49. Maeda, *Chains of Babylon*, 40–72.

50. Dong, "Origins and Trajectory," 27–78.

51. Maeda, *Rethinking*, 27–51.

52. Pulido, *Black, Brown, Yellow, and Left*.

53. Elbaum, *Revolution in the Air*. Returning briefly to the subject of periodization, Elbaum marks 1992 as the end of the new communist movement (NCM), which could argue for extending the life span of the Asian American movement by over a decade. However, Asian American participation in the NCM differed so dramatically from the racially specific, community-oriented tenor of earlier formations that it makes more sense to treat the NCM as a distinct entity that followed after the Asian American movement.

54. Robin D. G. Kelley and Betsy Esch, "Black Like Mao: Red China and Black Revolution," *Souls* 1 (1999): 6–41.

55. Vijay Prashad, *Everybody Was Kung Fu Fighting: Afro-Asian Connections and the Myth of Cultural Purity* (Boston: Beacon, 2001), xii.

56. Daryl J. Maeda, "Black Panthers, Red Guards, and Chinamen: Constructing Asian American Identity through Performing Blackness, 1969–1972," *American Quarterly* 57, no. 4 (2005): 1079–1103.

57. Rychetta Watkins, *Black Power, Yellow Power, and the Making of Revolutionary Identities* (Jackson: University Press of Mississippi, 2012).

58. Jonathan Y. Okamura, "Asian American Studies in the Age of Transnationalism: Diaspora, Race, Community," *Amerasia Journal* 29, no. 2 (2003): 171–193; Saul-Ling C. Wong, "Denationalization Reconsidered: Asian American Cultural Criticism at a Theoretical Crossroads," *Amerasia Journal* 21, nos. 1–2 (1995): 1–27; Amy Tachiki, Eddie Wong, Franklin Odo, and B. Wong, eds., *Roots: An Asian American Reader* (Los Angeles: UCLA Asian American Studies Center, 1971); Emma Gee, ed., *Counterpoint: Perspectives on Asian America* (Los Angeles: UCLA Asian American Studies Center, 1976).

59. Maeda, *Chains of Babylon*, 97–126.

60. Miriam Ching Yoon Louie, "Doing *Durepae* Duty: Korean American Radical Movement after Kwangju," *Amerasia Journal* 30, no. 1 (2004): 88–106.

61. Ryan Fukumori, "'Our Asian Soul': The Nation as Problem and Promise in the Birth of 'Asian America,'" unpublished manuscript in author's possession. Fukumori presented a shorter version of this paper, "'Our Asian Soul': The Problem and Promise of Shin'ya Ono's Asian Nation," at the Association for Asian American Studies annual conference, Washington, DC, April 2012.

62. Catherine Ceniza Choy, "Towards Trans-Pacific Social Justice: Women and Protest in Filipino American History," *Journal of Asian American Studies* 8, no. 3 (2005): 293–307.

63. Helen C. Toribio, "We Are Revolution: A Reflective History of the Union of Democratic Filipinos (KDP)," *Amerasia Journal* 24, no. 2 (1998): 155–178; Helen C. Toribio, "Dare to Struggle: The KDP and Filipino American Politics," in Ho et al., *Legacy to Liberation*, 31–45.

64. Masumi Izumi, "The Japanese Canadian Movement: Migration and Activism before and after World War II," *Amerasia Journal* 33, no. 2 (2007): 49–66.

65. Judy Tzu-Chun Wu, "Rethinking Global Sisterhood: Peace Activism and Women's Orientalism," in *No Permanent Waves: Recasting Histories of U.S. Feminism*, ed. Nancy A. Hewitt (New Brunswick, NJ: Rutgers University Press, 2010), 193–220.

66. Judy Tzu-Chun Wu, "Journeys for Peace and Liberation: Third World Internationals and Radicalism during the U.S. War in Vietnam," *Pacific Historical Review* 76, no. 4 (2007): 575–584.

67. Judy Tzu-Chun Wu, *Radicals on the Road: Internationalism, Orientalism, and Feminism during the Vietnam Era* (Ithaca, NY: Cornell University Press, 2013).

68. Daniel C. Tsang, "Slicing Silence: Asian Progressives Come Out," in Louie and Omatsu, *Asian Americans*, 220–239; Gil Mangaoang, "From the 1970s to the 1990s: Perspective of a Gay Filipino American Activist," *Amerasia Journal* 20, no. 1 (1994): 33–44.

FURTHER READING

Boggs, Grace Lee. *Living for Change: An Autobiography.* Minneapolis: University of Minnesota Press, 1998.

Boggs, Grace Lee, and Scott Kurashige. *The Next American Revolution: Sustainable Activism for the Twenty-First Century.* Berkeley: University of California Press, 2011.

Bulosan, Carlos. *America Is in the Heart.* Seattle: University of Washington Press, 1973.

Choi, Jennifer Jung Hee. "At the Margin of Asian American Political Experience: The Life of Grace Lee Boggs." *Amerasia Journal* 25, no. 2 (1999): 18–40.

Choy, Catherine Ceniza. "Towards Trans-Pacific Social Justice: Women and Protest in Filipino American History." *Journal of Asian American Studies* 8, no. 3 (2005): 293–307.

de Vera, Arlene. "Without Parallel: The Local 7 Deportation Cases." *Amerasia Journal* 20 (1994): 1–25.

Dong, Harvey C. "Richard Aoki (1938–2008): Toughest Oriental to Come Out of West Oakland." *Amerasia Journal* 35, no. 2 (2009): 223–232.

———. "The Origins and Trajectory of Asian American Political Activism in the San Francisco Bay Area, 1968–1978." Ph.D. diss., University of California, Berkeley, 2002.

Elbaum, Max. *Revolution in the Air: Sixties Radicals Turn to Lenin, Mao and Che.* London: Verso, 2002.

Espiritu, Yen Le. *Asian American Panethnicity: Bridging Institutions and Identities.* Philadelphia: Temple University Press, 1992.

Ferreira, Jason Michael. "All Power to the People: A Comparative History of Third World Radicalism in San Francisco, 1968–1974." Ph.D. diss., University of California, Berkeley, 2003.

Fong, Gisele L. "The People United: Cultural Work and the Making of Asian America, 1968–1985." Ph.D. diss., University of California, Los Angeles, 2003.

Fu, May Chuan. "Keeping Close to the Ground: Politics and Coalition in Asian American Community Organizing, 1969–1977." Ph.D. diss., University of California, San Diego, 2005.

———. "On Contradiction: Theory and Transformation in Detroit's Asian Political Alliance." *Amerasia Journal* 35, no. 2 (2009): 1–22.

————. "'Serve the People and You Help Yourself': Japanese-American Anti-Drug Organizing in Los Angeles, 1969 to 1972," *Social Justice* 35, no. 2 (2008): 80–99.

Fujino, Diane C. *Heartbeat of Struggle: The Revolutionary Life of Yuri Kochiyama.* Minneapolis: University of Minnesota Press, 2005.

————. "Race, Place, Space, and Political Development: Japanese-American Radicalism in the 'Pre-Movement' 1960s." *Social Justice* 35, no. 2 (2008): 57–79.

————. *Samurai among Panthers: Richard Aoki on Race, Resistance, and a Paradoxical Life.* Minneapolis: University of Minnesota Press, 2012.

————. "Who Studies the Asian American Movement? A Historiographical Analysis." *Journal of Asian American Studies* 11, no. 2 (2008): 127–169.

Fujino, Diane C., and Kye Leung. "Radical Resistance in Conservative Times: New Asian American Organizations in the 1990s." In *Legacy to Liberation: Politics and Culture of Revolutionary Asian America*, edited by Fred Ho, Carolyn Antonio, Diane Fujino, and Steve Yip, 141–158. San Francisco: AK Press, 2000.

Gee, Emma, ed. *Counterpoint: Perspectives on Asian America.* Los Angeles: UCLA Asian American Studies Center, 1976.

Habal, Estella. *San Francisco's International Hotel: Mobilizing the Filipino American Community in the Anti-Eviction Movement.* Philadelphia: Temple University Press, 2007.

Him Mark Lai. "A Historical Survey of the Chinese Left in American Society." In *Counterpoint: Perspectives on Asian America*, edited by Emma Gee, 63–80. Los Angeles: UCLA Asian American Studies Center Press, 1976.

Hing, Bill Ong. *Making and Remaking Asian America through Immigration Policy, 1850–1990.* Stanford, CA: Stanford University Press, 1993.

Ishizuka, Karen L. "Flying in the Face of Race, Gender, Class and Age: A Story about Kazu Iijima, One of the Mothers of the Asian American Movement on the First Year Anniversary of Her Death." *Amerasia Journal* 35, no. 2 (2009): 24–47.

————. "A Portrait of the Scholar-Activist as a Young Man: Don Nakanishi." *Amerasia Journal* 35, no. 3 (2009): 211–232.

Izumi, Masumi. "The Japanese Canadian Movement: Migration and Activism before and after World War II." *Amerasia Journal* 33, no. 2 (2007): 49–66.

Joseph, Peniel E., ed. *The Black Power Movement: Rethinking the Civil Rights-Black Power Era.* New York: Routledge, 2006.

————. *Waiting 'Til the Midnight Hour: A Narrative History of Black Power in America.* New York: Holt, 2007.

Kao, Mary Uyematsu. "Three-Step Boogie in 1970s Los Angeles: Sansei Women in the Asian American Movement." *Amerasia Journal* 35, no. 1 (2009): 112–138.

Kelley, Robin D. G., and Betsy Esch, "Black Like Mao: Red China and Black Revolution." *Souls* 1 (1999): 6–41.

Ling, Susie. "The Mountain Movers: Asian American Women's Movement in Los Angeles." *Amerasia Journal* 15, no. 1 (1989): 51–67.

Liu, Michael, Kim Geron, and Tracy Lai. *The Snake Dance of Asian American Activism: Community, Vision, and Power.* Lanham, MD: Lexington, 2008.

Louie, Miriam Ching Yoon. "Doing *Durepae* Duty: Korean American Radical Movement after Kwangju." *Amerasia Journal* 30, no. 1 (2004): 88–106.

Maeda, Daryl J. "Black Panthers, Red Guards, and Chinamen: Constructing Asian American Identity through Performing Blackness, 1969–1972." *American Quarterly* 57, no. 4 (2005): 1079–1103.

———. *Chains of Babylon: The Rise of Asian America.* Minneapolis: University of Minnesota Press, 2009.

———. *Rethinking the Asian American Movement.* New York: Routledge, 2012.

Mangaoang, Gil. "From the 1970s to the 1990s: Perspective of a Gay Filipino American Activist." *Amerasia Journal* 20, no. 1 (1994): 33–44.

Marwick, Arthur. *The Sixties: Cultural Revolution in Britain, France, Italy, and the United States, c.1968–c.1974.* New York: Oxford University Press, 1998.

Nishida, Mo. "Komrad Richard." *Amerasia Journal* 35, no. 2 (2009): 233–239.

Okamura, Jonathan Y. "Asian American Studies in the Age of Transnationalism: Diaspora, Race, Community." *Amerasia Journal* 29, no. 2 (2003): 171–193.

Omatsu, Glenn. "Always a Rebel: An Interview with Kazu Iijima." *Amerasia Journal* 13, no. 2 (1986–1987): 83–98.

Prashad, Vijay. *Everybody Was Kung Fu Fighting: Afro-Asian Connections and the Myth of Cultural Purity.* Boston: Beacon, 2001.

Pulido, Laura. *Black, Brown, Yellow, and Left: Radical Activism in Los Angeles.* Berkeley: University of California Press, 2006.

Ryan, Angela Rose. "Education for the People: The Third World Student Movement at San Francisco State College and City College of New York." Ph.D. diss., Ohio State University, 2010.

Tachiki, Amy, Eddie Wong, Franklin Odo, and B. Wong, eds. *Roots: An Asian American Reader.* Los Angeles: UCLA Asian American Studies Center, 1971.

Toribio, Helen C. "Dare to Struggle: The KDP and Filipino American Politics." In *Legacy to Liberation: Politics and Culture of Revolutionary Asian America,* edited by Fred Ho, Carolyn Antonio, Diane Fujino, and Steve Yip, 31–45. San Francisco: AK Press, 2000.

———. "We Are Revolution: A Reflective History of the Union of Democratic Filipinos (KDP)." *Amerasia Journal* 24, no. 2 (1998): 155–178.

Tsang, Daniel C. "Slicing Silence: Asian Progressives Come Out." In *Asian Americans: The Movement and the Moment,* edited by Steve Louie and Glenn Omatsu, 220–239. Los Angeles: UCLA Asian American Studies Center Press, 2001.

Watkins, Rychetta. *Black Power, Yellow Power, and the Making of Revolutionary Identities.* Jackson: University Press of Mississippi, 2012.

Wei, William. *The Asian American Movement.* Philadelphia: Temple University Press, 1993.

Wong, Saul-Ling C. "Denationalization Reconsidered: Asian American Cultural Criticism at a Theoretical Crossroads." *Amerasia Journal* 21, nos. 1–2 (1995): 1–27.

Wu, Judy Tzu-Chun. "Journeys for Peace and Liberation: Third World Internationals and Radicalism during the U.S. War in Vietnam." *Pacific Historical Review* 76, no. 4 (2007): 575–584.

———. *Radicals on the Road: Internationalism, Orientalism, and Feminism during the Vietnam Era.* Ithaca, NY: Cornell University Press, 2013.

———. "Rethinking Global Sisterhood: Peace Activism and Women's Orientalism." In *No Permanent Waves: Recasting Histories of U.S. Feminism,* edited by Nancy A. Hewitt, 193–220. New Brunswick, NJ: Rutgers University Press, 2010.

Yoneda, Karl. *Ganbatte: Sixty-Year Struggle of a Kibei Worker.* Los Angeles: Asian American Studies Center Press, 1983.

PART III

VARIATIONS ON THEMES

CHAPTER 12

A HISTORY OF ASIAN INTERNATIONAL ADOPTION IN THE UNITED STATES

CATHERINE CENIZA CHOY

THE United States is the top recipient of internationally adopted children in the world. In the late twentieth century, adoption from Asia transformed the United States into an international adoption nation. According to the Evan B. Donaldson Adoption Institute, international adoptions in the United States have more than doubled between 1991 and 2001. While Russia, Guatemala, Romania, and Ukraine are top sending countries of adoptive children to the United States, Asian children have comprised the majority of children internationally adopted by U.S. citizens. Between 1971 and 2001, U.S. citizens adopted 265,677 children from other countries, and more than half (156,491) of those children were from Asian countries. Since the late 1990s, China has been a major sending nation of adoptive children to the United States. In 2000, China led the list of the top twenty primary sending countries, with 5,095 children from China adopted by U.S. citizens. South Korea, Vietnam, India, and Cambodia also placed in the top ten of primary sending nations.[1]

The phenomenon has become increasingly mainstream. As anthropologist Toby Alice Volkman observes:

> The mainstreaming of Chinese adoption has occurred in part through the incessant media attention that has been lavished on adopted Chinese girls over the past decade. This interest shows no signs of abating, with a steady stream of articles in disparate venues. On a page entitled boldly "How America Lives," the *Ladies' Home Journal* featured "Citizen Amy," an adoptive five-year-old Chinese girl in Kentucky, American flag in hand.[2]

The media attention given to celebrity adoptions of Asian children—such as Angelina Jolie and Brad Pitt's adoption of boys from Cambodia and Vietnam, and Katherine

Heigl's adoption of a Korean girl—further presents Asian international adoption as an acceptable and desirable way to make a family.

However, highly critical perspectives of international and transracial adoption of Asian children emerge alongside these celebratory narratives. The specter of American racism haunts the joyous imagery of these adoptive families. Since the late 1990s a growing body of memoirs, documentary films, and anthologies by primarily Korean American adoptees who have come of age underscore the theme of their numerous mundane encounters with American racism.

The seemingly positive stereotype of Asian Americans as "model minorities" in relation to negative stereotypes of African Americans adds another layer of complexity regarding how race informs the phenomenon of Asian international adoption. Sociologist Sara Dorow has argued that this stereotype creates a racial preference for Asian children over African American children. In her pioneering book of contemporary Chinese international adoption, *Transnational Adoption*, Dorow claims that these attitudes reflect ideologies of a "flexible Asian difference" that can be successfully integrated in American families and communities in contrast to a "less assimilable" African American difference. [3]

Furthermore, the decreasing supply of white babies in the United States in the late twentieth century—a result of the creation of the birth control pill, the legalization of abortion, and the increasing social legitimacy of single parenting—contributes to the commodification of Asian children for an international adoption market. Several scholars have strongly criticized international adoption by calling attention to the global market that transports babies from poorer to richer nations, likening it to a form of forced migration and human trafficking. For example, in his book *Comforting An Orphaned Nation* Korean studies scholar Tobias Hubinette writes that "contemporary international adoption, which has seen at least half a million children flown in to Western countries during a period of 50 years, has so many parallels to the transatlantic slave trade . . . and to present day's massive trafficking of non-Western women for international marriage and sexual exploitation."[4] Thus, Asian international adoption is simultaneously highly celebrated and deeply controversial.

ASIAN INTERNATIONAL ADOPTION IN ASIAN AMERICAN STUDIES

Despite the hypervisibility of Asian international adoption in the United States in the late twentieth and early twenty-first centuries, the history of Asian international adoption in the United States is not well known. The majority of previous scholarship on Asian international adoptees in the United States was rooted in psychological and social welfare studies, which focused on the adjustment of the adoptees.[5] They framed international adoption as a problem to be solved rather than as a historically rooted, dynamic phenomenon. In her ethnography of Korean adoptees, *Adopted Territory*, anthropologist Eleana Kim elaborates:

> These studies attempted to measure the mental health or 'adjustment' of children and adolescents adopted transracially and transnationally, and they are limited by their tendency to disembed the phenomenon of transnational adoption from its relevant historical, social, and political contexts. . . . The majority of these studies, for the most part based on samples of one hundred or fewer, determined that transnational adoptees are no different from and sometimes are better adjusted than domestic adoptees, as well as in comparison to nonadopted siblings. The power of these findings as 'expert knowledge' is often mobilized to support the so-called positive view of transracial adoption, despite problematic assumptions, methods, and measures.[6]

Book-length historical studies of U.S. domestic adoption by E. Wayne Carp, Barbara Melosh, and Ellen Herman produced more knowledge about the history of international adoption in the United States, which included adoption from Asia.[7] This scholarship located the origins of international adoption in post–World-War-II American prosperity and Cold War politics. Although most of the foreign-born adoptive children brought to the United States after 1945 came from war-torn Greece, Germany, and Japan, in subsequent decades, the aftermath of the Korean War would result in Korean children becoming the largest group of international adoptees in the United States. These studies also pointed to the advocacy of famed novelist Pearl S. Buck, who established the adoption agency Welcome House, as well as Harry Holt, the founder of the adoption program now known as Holt International, to explain the increasing popularity of international and transracial adoption from Asia.

In her history of adoption in the modern United States, Ellen Herman expounds upon these demographic changes and individual advocates by situating Asian (specifically Japanese, Korean, and later Vietnamese) international adoption in the broader historical context of humanitarian rescue efforts. According to Herman, these efforts recapitulated "the rhetoric of rescue and religious fervor that had animated many nineteenth-century domestic placements while echoing the sexualized racial anxiety that accompanied episodes of imperial intimacy, such as the case of children produced in the Dutch and French colonies of Southeast Asia during the first half of the twentieth century."[8] Herman frames the beginnings of international adoption in the United States as an organized movement that mobilized faith communities (Lutherans, Catholics, and Seventh-Day Adventists among others) and that inspired the creation of new organizations such as the American Joint Committee for Assisting Japanese-American Orphans. It was a movement fraught with conflict, especially between independent adoption advocates such as Buck and Holt and professional social workers over who should conduct international adoption placements.

In general, however, U.S. adoption history treated international adoption as an extension and radical expansion of domestic adoption, similar to transracial and special needs adoptions. Many questions went unanswered: How was a supply of Asian adoptive children created? What motivated American families to formally adopt Asian children? Why did international adoption from Korea and other specific Asian countries flourish? How did race as well as nation, gender and class play roles in this phenomenon? What is the relationship between Asian America and Asian adoptees?

Although Asian international adoption would seem like an obvious topic for Asian American Studies, in the late 1990s, little research had been conducted by and about Asian international adoption in the context of Asian American Studies. One notable exception was Mike Mullen's 1995 article, which suggested that young Korean adoptees could feel accepted by whites, but as they became older and their consciousness of physical differences grew, they began to raise questions about race. Mullen concluded that Korean children who had been adopted by white American families experienced a distinct identity development process that diverged from the more traditional minority identity development approach.[9] Recent psychological studies of Asian, American adoptees by Asian American Studies scholars continue to enrich the fields of psychology and Asian American studies. For example, a major question animating psychologist and Asian Americanist Rich Lee's work is: What can psychologists do to improve the lives of Asian American individuals and families? Lee is a member of the Minnesota International Adoption Team, which aims to develop a comprehensive picture of the successes and challenges of children who join their families through international adoption.[10]

Until recently, the history of Asian international adoption was a topic that was markedly absent in Asian American historiography. This blindspot can partly be attributed to the fact that during the Asian American Movement of the late 1960s to the 1980s, Asian international adoption was not the highly visible demographic and cultural phenomenon that it is today. Furthermore, the fact that the majority of the Asian adoptees were young children, whose dominant experience during this time period was their assimilation into predominantly white American families in rural, suburban, and urban areas throughout the United States went under the radar of Asian American Studies scholarship, which grew out of overtly confrontational social and political protests on college campuses.

In the past decade, however, a critical mass of historical scholarship on Asian international adoption has emerged. Most of these scholarly works are in the form of dissertations and new books. This important shift is the result of the increasing demographic significance of Asian international adoption, the coming of age of several generations of Asian American adoptees, and their growing presence in Asian American Studies classrooms. This recent scholarship calls for the need to study the history of Asian international adoption in the United States on its own terms.

A major strength of this historical research is its transnational focus on Korean international adoption. The significance of Korean international adoption is historical and demographic. Beginning in the mid-1950s, the phenomenon has spanned six decades and involved over 200,000 Korean children adopted by families in Western nations (primarily the United States, but also France and Sweden). Studies by Eleana Kim, Soojin Pate, Arissa Oh, Susie Woo, and Bongsoo Park use both Korean and English language sources to document and critically analyze the origins of Korean international adoption and its increasing popularity in the United States in the formative Cold War period of the 1950s and 1960s.[11] Some of their Korean archival sources include the Syngman Rhee Papers at Yonsei University and *Ko ah kuk-eh ip-yang* [Foreign Overseas Adoptions] and *Ko-a ku-oh* [Orphan Aid] records at the Ministry of Foreign Affairs. In the United States, archival records of the U.S. Children's Bureau, U.S. Army, and U.S. Department of Defense contain relevant primary source materials.

A treasure trove for the study of the history of Asian international adoption are the organizational records and adoption case records of the International Social Service-United States of America (ISS-USA) branch at the University of Minnesota's Social Welfare History Archives. The collection includes 56 linear feet of administrative records, and 500 linear feet of case records and case record indexes dating from 1929 to 1995.[12] Although the historical origins of the ISS-USA were rooted in family problems related to international migration more broadly, by the late 1950s, casework related to international adoption constituted the major activity of the ISS-USA. My book on the history of Asian international adoption in the United States utilizes these records to explore international adoption from Japan and Hong Kong as well as Korea in the 1950s and 1960s.[13]

Some points of consensus in this emergent scholarship include the following.

First, histories of race, gender, sexuality, and nation—especially regarding the emergence of a population of mixed-race children born to U.S. serviceman and Japanese, Korean, and Vietnamese women—informed early Asian international adoption history in ways that distinguished it from European international adoption. The actual numbers of mixed-race children in Japan and Korea were difficult to obtain, and fluctuated widely—from the thousands to tens of thousands to over one hundred thousand—depending upon who reported them. However, the attention given to the mixed-race population exceeded its numerical significance because of its symbolic importance for U.S.-Asian foreign relations and Asian and American national identities.

Media reports in both Asia and the United States publicized the plight of mixed-race Asian and American children in Japan, Korea, and later Vietnam. Their depiction of an inherent Asian prejudice toward mixed-race children resonated with American viewers in the 1950s. As the scholarship of Christina Klein and Naoko Shibusawa has shown, cultural productions—magazine and news articles, Hollywood movies, and Broadway musicals—during this time were not solely vehicles for entertainment.[14] Their narratives about U.S. moral responsibility in Asia (especially toward Asian women and children) made the U.S. occupation of Japan and U.S. Cold War involvement in Asia justifiable, palatable, and even desireable to the American general public.

Second, the recent scholarship is highly critical of the dominant narrative of Asian international adoption as the humanitarian rescue of mixed-race Asian and American children by white American adoptive families. Generalizations about Japan and Korea prejudices glossed over racism in the United States against Asian Americans, African Americans, and mixed-race people. In the history of anti-miscegenation laws in the United States, thirty-eight states banned black-white relationships and fourteen states prohibited Asian-white marriages. [15] They also did not acknowledge how an American military presence contributed to the hardships of these children. The U.S. military actively discouraged marriages between American servicemen and Japanese and Korean women. And American servicemen commonly deserted their children.[16]

By the 1950s, however, decolonization movements in Africa and Asia and the escalation of the Cold War posed fundamental challenges to American racism. The image of the United States at home and abroad became a cause for alarm.[17] Communist governments challenged U.S. claims of democracy and freedom by pointing to the social realities of racial segregation, violence, and protest in the United States. The role of Asian nations in the Cold War was a major concern of the U.S. government especially after the victory of the Chinese Communist Party in the Chinese Revolution of 1949. This international politics of race heightened debates about U.S. accountability for the population of mixed-race Asian and American children and informed the moral urgency to rescue them through formal adoption.

Third, this new body of scholarly work criticizes the overemphasis on the individual efforts of Americans, such Harry Holt and Pearl Buck, and instead emphasizes that multiple historical actors, including, but not limited to missionaries, soldiers, and social workers popularized and facilitated Asian international adoption in the United States. The participation of many different agencies and organizations illustrate that the history of Asian international adoption is rooted in a collective past, although competition between social service agencies and individuals dominated the discourses of how international adoption should work.

Finally, it calls for attention to the voices, experiences, and historical agency of Asian American adoptees. Adoptee voices are noticeably absent in the archival records. However, since the 1990s, the emergence of a sizable body of artistic work by and about Asian American adoptees has challenged the representation of Asian international adoption as a "quiet migration."[18] These cultural productions include, but are not limited to anthologies of poetry, essays, and creative nonfiction such as *Seeds from a Silent Tree*, *Voices from Another* Place, and *Outsiders Within*; documentary films such as *First Person Plural*, Wo *Ai Ni Mommy*, and *Operation Babylift*; and memoirs such as *A Single Square Picture* (2002), *The Language of Blood* (2003), and *Lucky Girl* (2009).[19] These works constitute an alternative and much-needed archive for the study of adoption.

THE UNITED STATES
OF INTERNATIONAL ADOPTION

Much has changed in international adoption since the 1970s. First, the phenomenon has become a truly global industry. The few thousand international adoptions that took place in the 1950s and 1960s pale in comparison to the tens of thousands in the late-twentieth and early-twenty-first centuries. As demographer Peter Selman notes in his study of the movement of children for international adoption between 1998 and 2004, "The number of intercountry adoptions has more than doubled in the last twenty years."[20] Between 1998 and 2004 the total number of children adopted in twenty receiving countries increased by 42 percent, from 31, 667 to 45, 016.

Second, the national origins of adoptive children in the United States have become much more diverse, involving different regions of the world. Specific Asian nations continue to supply adoptive children, but Eastern European, Latin American, and African countries have also become important sources. From 1993 to 2005, Russia was the largest or second largest sending country of adopted children to the United States. It led adoptions for the years 1997, 1998, and 1999. In 2006 and 2007, Guatemala was the second leading sending country of adopted children to the United States. International adoption from Ethiopia increased by 150 percent between 2002 and 2005. Ethiopia's popularity grew as a result of new restrictions—eligibility requirements, adoption agency regulations, domestic adoption initiatives—implemented in China, Russia, and South Korea.

Third, other countries have become important receiving nations of internationally adopted children. Peter Selman observes that, in 2004, the receiving states with the highest adoption ratios were Norway and Spain. In Spain, international adoptions doubled between 1998 and 2000 and nearly tripled by 2004, making Spain the second largest receiving country after the United States in terms of the actual number of international adoptions.[21] Other countries showing an above-average increase were Ireland, Italy, the Netherlands, and the United States.

Finally, new controversies have emerged such as the question of gay and lesbian adoption. Beginning in December 2000, international adoptive parents of Chinese children were required to sign a statement that they were not gay or lesbian. Chinese Center of Adoption Affairs regulations state that "foreign homosexuals are not allowed to adopt children in China."[22] In December 2001, China told U.S. adoption agencies that no more than 5 percent of their applicants could be unmarried. Sociologist Sara Dorow writes that "it is generally understood that the latter regulation is to further contain the placement of Chinese children with not just single but more specifically gay and lesbian parents."[23] In their 2009 anthology on international adoption, gender and women's studies scholar Laura Briggs and anthropologist Diana Marre observe, however, that "the ability of gay men and lesbians to adopt seems to be expanding within some countries—a third of the EU countries and South Africa now allow this practice—at the same time that it is contracting elsewhere, as conservative religious groups in the United States struggle to outlaw it."[24]

The devastating impacts of war and political instability create linkages between the contemporary landscape of international adoption and its historical origins in the post-World War II period. However, the new geographies of international adoption merit attention on their own terms. Thankfully, an emergent body of adoption studies scholarship has deepened our understanding of current practices.

While some of this pioneering work features specific Asian countries that send large numbers of adoptive children to the United States, such as Sara Dorow's *Transnational*

Adoption on China and Eleana Kim's *Adopted Territory* featuring South Korea, other works chart the rise of other international adoption nations. Barbara Yngvesson's 2010 book *Belonging in an Adopted World* focuses on Sweden, which in the late 1970s and early 1980s, was the country with the world's highest adoption rate.[25] In contrast to the United States and Sweden, the history of international adoption in Spain is quite recent. It is a phenomenon that became significant in the mid-1990s. Anthropologist Diana Marre points to the repeated broadcasting of a 1995 British television program, "The Rooms of Death," about orphanages in China, which inspired humanitarian impulses to adopt.

After the exponential growth of international adoption between 1998 and 2004, Peter Selman observed that a decrease in numbers in 2005 and 2006 affected many receiving countries, including Spain.[26] In the United States, this downturn made headlines. A 2008 *USA Today* story also highlighted that foreign adoptions by Americans dropped sharply: "The number of foreign children adopted by Americans fell 12 percent in the past year, reaching the lowest level since 1999 as some countries clamped down on the process and others battled with allegations of adoption fraud."[27] Given this decline, the premise that the United States is an international adoption nation might be more appropriately phrased as a question: "Is the United States *still* an international adoption nation?"

However, current demographic trends cannot undo the Cold War history and legacy of international adoption in the United States in the second half of the twentieth century and the first few years of the new millennium. The United States continues to be an international adoption nation through the presence of multiple social, educational, and entrepreneurial networks that serve global families, networks in which Asian international adoption has played a formative role.

Small groups founded by American parents of Korean adoptees in the late 1970s inspired the formation of one of the largest social networks, Families with Children from China (FCC). Anthropologist Toby Alice Volkmann characterizes the FCC as a major force in shaping and sustaining "a sense of kinship and community beyond the family."[28] In 1992, a few of the earliest adoptive parents of Chinese children met in New York's Chinatown to celebrate their new adoptions. Today FCC is a nondenominational organization comprised of more than one hundred separate organizations across the United States, Canada, and the United Kingdom. The organizations provide a network of support for families who have adopted from China as well as information to prospective parents.[29] Another organization with a similar mission is Families with Children from Viet Nam (FCV). Founded in 1997, FCV consists of local chapters from 31 states, the District of Columbia, and Toronto, Canada.[30]

Korean adult adoptees in Europe and the United States have also been a major force in creating a sense of community beyond the family. According to anthropologist Eleana Kim, they have been organizing regionally since 1986 when eighteen-year-old Mattias Tjeder founded *Adopterade Koreaners Forening* (Association of Adopted Koreans, AKF) in Stockholm, Sweden. When asked about the origins of AKF, Tieder explained that he had known only one other adoptee while growing up in the suburbs of Stockholm.

His desire to learn more about his background led to meetings with a handful of other adoptees. This small network blossomed into an organization *for* Korean adoptees *run by* Korean adoptees that has since served over nine hundred members.[31]

Minnesota Adopted Koreans (MAK), founded in 1991, would become the first official Korean adoptee organization in the United States.[32] Since then, Korean adult adoptees have organized in various parts of the country. Four Korean adoptees founded the Association of Korean Adoptees—San Francisco (AKASF) in 1997. It aims to serve as a support group for adult Korean adoptees living in the San Francisco Bay Area.[33] The inaugural meeting of Korean Adoptees of Hawai'i (KAHI) was held in 2006. KAHI offers resources and services for its members who wish to explore their Korean heritage while also striving to raise awareness about their unique identity. It provides opportunities for Korean adoptees in Hawai'i to connect with one another locally as well as with other adoptees on the mainland and internationally.[34]

Korean adult adoptees have also been at the forefront of creating organizations that serve the broader adoptee community and a pan-Asian adoptee community. For example, Also-Known-As began in May 1996 when a small group of Korean adoptees and friends in the New York metropolitan area planned a mentorship program for a new generation of international adoptees. Since then the outreach of the organization has expanded to recognize and celebrate "the community of people whose lives, through adoption, bridge nations, cultures and races."[35]

Based in Seattle, Asian Adult Adoptees of Washington (AAAW) provides mentoring and educational opportunities for Asian American and Pacific Islander adoptees. AAAW began when a group of adult adoptees met informally over dinner in December 1996. At that time, there were resources for adopted children as well as teens, but no existing networks for adult adoptees in Washington. Out of this void, AAAW formed to acknowledge the unique experiences of Asian adult adoptees as well as youth.[36]

Fueling the creation of international adoption networks is the Internet. Toby Alice Volkmann notes that the Internet and adoption from China began to grow at approximately the same time. The collusion of these phenomena has resulted in highly specialized virtual networks for Chinese international adoptive families that geographically and intellectually expand traditional notions of family and community. As Volkman writes:

> By 2002, the two largest China adoption lists had a combined membership of over thirteen thousand subscribers, and more than 350 other lists were devoted to more specialized interests, from *chinaboys* and *China Dads at Home* to born-again Christian lists. There are lists for those whose adoption dossier went to China in a particular month, and well over one hundred lists for families with children adopted from the same orphanage or region. Members of orphanage lists may come to think of all children in their child's orphanage as siblings.

The Internet has also played a central role in the development of Korean adoptee networks. Eleana Kim's ethnographic research revealed that Korean adoptees who were ambivalent about attending a face-to-face meeting with other adoptees used the

Internet to search for adoptee stories. Learning about these experiences and available resources for adoptees inspired and prepared them to attend networking meetings.[37] After Minnesota Adopted Koreans dissolved in the late 1990s, its successor organization AKConnection utilized the Internet to recruit fellow Korean adoptees.

The Internet also facilitated community building among Filipino adult adoptees. Co-founders Lorial Crowder and Sharon Cuartero of the Filipino Adoptees Network (FAN) thank the Internet for bringing them together and for inspiring the creation of a FAN website. The website aims to provide an online community that was unavailable to Filipino adoptees when Crowder and Cuartero were growing up. Launched in January 2005, FAN is the first web-based organization to provide support and resources for Filipino adoptees and their families.[38]

Listserves and blogs, however, have not supplanted the role of print media in creating and sustaining Asian international adoption communities. The non-profit quarterly newspaper *Korean Quarterly* features writing by and about the Korean American community of the Twin Cities and the upper Midwest. The staff, contributors, and advisory board define the Korean American community to include "first and second generation Korean Americans and their families (including non-Korean family members), adopted Koreans and their families, and bi-racial/bi-cultural Korean American people."[39] Its premiere issue, entitled "Who We Are," was published in fall 2007. The commemoration of "50 Years of Korean Adoption" was the focal point of the spring 2005 issue. However, every issue has included feature stories, reviews, and/or interviews with Korean adoptees, presenting them as central, as opposed to token, members of the Korean American community.

In 1993, Brian Boyd, the father of two Korean adopted children, founded Yeong & Yeong Book Company, which specializes in books on Asian international adoption. He felt that his Korean-born daughters needed a book about their lives in Korea before coming to their new family. The resulting book, *When You Were Born in Korea: A Memory Book for Children Adopted from Korea,* led to the creation of a similar title, *When You Were Born in China,* followed by *When You Were Born in Vietnam.* The books were published as fund-raisers, and a portion of their proceeds supports adoption agencies in Korea, China, and Vietnam. Since the early 1990s, Yeong & Yeong Press has published and/or distributed fifteen books related to Asian international adoption. Other books feature collected letters and stories by Korean birth mothers; prose, poetry, photography, and art by Asian adoptees; and essays by adoptive parents. These books also contribute royalties to adoption-related organizations such as Ae Ran Won (a home for birth mothers in Seoul, South Korea), Holt International, Children's Home Society of Minnesota, The Amity Foundation, The Catalyst Foundation, The Foundation for Chinese Orphanages, and Eastern Social Welfare Society among others.[40]

The rise of Chinese international adoption in the United States led to the publication of *Mei* Magazine, a quarterly magazine published in Florida since 1999 that features issues specific to Chinese adoptees between the ages of seven and fourteen. The magazine's website emphasizes the unique identities and broad kinship of Asian adoptees: "Mei girls need to see themselves and each other in print! They deserve a forum where they can share in their special sisterhood."[41]

As these personal, virtual, and print networks shape a broader sense of community and kinship, they create an audience and niche market for what sociologist Heather Jacobson has called "culture keeping." Jacobson defines culture keeping as the process through which adoptive parents attempt to ensure that their internationally adopted children have access to the culture of their national origins.[42] Culture keeping, Jacobson observes, is a standard practice in the adoption world. Both real and virtual encounters inspire, facilitate, and sustain culture-keeping industries. As Jacobson writes:

> International-adoptive parents are often told by the adoption community that their children *should* engage in their native cultures; some are told that they *must*. In adoption agency materials, on electronic mailing lists, and in memoirs, support groups, advice books, educational workshops, and conference presentations, culture keeping is framed as a mechanism for facilitating a solid ethnic identity and sense of self-worth in children who may experience difficulties because of their racial, ethnic, and adoptive statuses.[43]

Culture or heritage camps aimed at international adoptees and their families comprise one major culture-keeping industry. Given the longer history of Korean international adoption, camps for Korean adoptees and their adoptive families are the most numerous. The Korean American Adoptee Adoptive Family Network (KAAN) is an organization that aims to build strong connections among adoptees, birth and adoptive families, Koreans, and Korean Americans primarily through a national conference held annually in a different city in the United States. KAAN's website also attempts to facilitate these connections by featuring Korean programs such as culture camps. It lists 28 Korean culture camps in New York, Wisconsin, New Jersey, Indiana, North Carolina, Pennsylvania, Illinois, Washington, D.C., Maryland, Virginia, Michigan, Oregon, Nebraska, Iowa, Utah, Ohio, Oklahoma, Kentucky, and Massachusetts.[44] While some of these camps are open to other children of Korean heritage (such as second-generation Korean Americans), most of them are exclusively for Korean adopted children and their adoptive families.

The non-profit organization, Heritage Camps for Adoptive Families (HCAF), began in Colorado in 1991 with a summer heritage camp for 60 families with children adopted from Korea. It currently offers 11 different camps that reflect the diversity and growth of international adoption in the United States.[45] 10 camps are for families with internationally adopted children from the African Caribbean, Cambodia, China, the Philippines, India, Nepal, Latin America, Eastern Europe, and Vietnam.

Given the vibrancy of the communities formed through Asian international adoption, the field of Asian American Studies must include adoptee experiences in its teaching, research, and professional service. From its historical origins in the late 1960s, the scholarly field of Asian American Studies has focused on the histories, cultural expressions, and contemporary concerns of Asians in North America. Although seminal Asian American history texts to date have not included the history of Asian international adoption, an emergent critical mass of new scholarship is contesting this absence. Recent books and scholarly articles by Gregory Paul Choy, Sara Dorow, David Eng, Mark Jerng, Eleana Kim, Josephine Lee, Richard Lee, Andrea Louie, Jiannbin Lee Shiao, and Mia Tuan as well as myself aim to reach Asian American Studies as well as adoption studies audiences.[46]

In the 2011 anthology *Asian American Plays for a New Generation* edited by Josephine Lee, Don Eitel, and R. A. Shiomi, plays about Korean adoptees that have been produced by Theatre Mu in Minneapolis, Minnesota take center stage. As Josephine Lee writes in the introduction:

> The prevailing sensibility that Minnesota is 'white' is belied by the large concentrations of Hmong and Korean adoptees, both constituencies fairly new to claiming 'Asian American' identity. What is produced by way of theatre registers these distinctions. Mu's first production, *Mask Dance*, featured the stories of young Korean adoptees raised in Minnesota. This focus on adoptees, many of whom grew up as the only non-white individuals in their rural communities, departs radically from an understanding of Asian American stories as centered on immigrant families. These differences in the imagining of 'Asian America' cannot be dismissed as just a set of quaint regional distinctions. Titling a play *Walleye Kid* has relevance beyond associating transracial adoption with a notably Minnesota fish; it emphasizes the *prominence of the adoptee in refiguring what 'Asian American' is*. Racial isolation is an experience familiar to many in the Midwest, so much so that it should be thought of as paradigmatic rather than peripheral part of Asian American experience.[47]

In their 2011 book *Choosing Ethnicity, Negotiating Race: Korean Adoptees in America*, education studies scholar Mia Tuan and sociologist Jiannbin Lee Shiao compare the Korean adoptee experience to the experience of Asian Americans. They conclude:

> A part and yet apart, Korean adoptees are bound to other Asian Americans because of their race and, as a result, have overlapping experiences. However, their unique life and family circumstances make them a different type of Asian American: they harbor greater expectations for social acceptance from white people and experience greater disappointment when that acceptance is not forthcoming.[48]

The leadership of Korean adoptees artists and scholars has been pivotal in making Asian adoptee concerns integral to the field of Asian American Studies. Deann Borshay Liem's former position as Executive Director of NAATA (National Asian American Telecommunications Association, now named the Center for Asian American Media or CAAM) undoubtedly contributed to the organization's showcasing of films about international adoption, such as "Wo Ai Ni Mommy," "In the Matter of Cha Jung Hee," and "Passing Through," through development funding; screenings at its annual Asian American International Film Festival in San Francisco; and distribution to educational institutions as well as the general public. "Adoption" is a featured subject area of CAAM's catalog of video and DVD programs.

In sum, the crossover between Asian American Studies and adoption studies has begun, enriching Asian American Studies while insisting upon and maintaining the unique and autonomous identity of Asian adoptees. The national professional organization, Association for Asian American Studies (AAAS) features an Asian Adoptee section. Korean adoptee Kim Park Nelson, co-author of *Here: A Visual History of Adopted Koreans in Minnesota* and department chair of American Multicultural Studies at Minesota State University, Moorhead, founded the section in 2007. At the annual meetings of the AAAS, scholarly panels have featured recent research on Asian adoptee issues.

This scholarship should be used to expand as well as to complicate Asian American history's chronological and geographical scope and its major historical actors. Specifically, this book engages in that conversation by showcasing how the post–World War II and Cold War periods created the foundation for the multigenerational Asian adoptee community of the twenty-first century, and why it is important to view this history from the range of perspectives of its diverse participants—international social workers in the receiving and sending countries; independent adoption advocates; adoptive and birth parents; and the adoptees themselves.

Finally, this learning process must go both ways. Adoptive parents, policy makers, and social welfare workers need not solely turn to Asian heritages as resources for adopted children. They should also consider how Asian adoptees in the United States are part of the growing and increasingly diverse Asian American communities of the United States and a part of an Asian American history that is centuries old. As a result, their heritages are multiple. They are Asian adoptees, but they are also adopted Asian Americans.

NOTES

1. The Evan B. Donaldson Adoption Institute, "International Adoption Facts," available at http://www.adoptioninstitute.org/FactOverview/international.html, accessed October 6, 2009.
2. Toby Alice Volkman, "Embodying Chinese Culture: Transnational Adoption in North America," "Transnational Adoption" special issue ed. Toby Alice Volkman and Cindi Katz, *Social Text* 74 (2003): 30. Volkman's article was reprinted in Toby Alice Volkman, ed., *Cultures of Transnational Adoption* (Durham, NC: Duke University Press, 2005), 81–113. David Eng also writes about this phenomenon in a close reading of a John Hancock commercial aired on network television in 2000 that featured a white American lesbian couple at a U.S. airport with their newly arrived Chinese baby girl. See David L. Eng, *A Feeling of Kinship: Queer Liberalism and the Racialization of Intimacy* (Durham, NC: Duke University Press, 2010), 98–99.
3. Sara K. Dorow, *Transnational Adoption: A Cultural Economy of Race, Gender, and Kinship* (New York: New York University Press, 2006), 37–38.
4. Tobias Hubinette, *Comforting an Orphaned Nation: Representations of International Adoption and Adopted Koreans in Korean Popular Culture* (Jimoondang: Korean Studies Series, 2006), 17.
5. See for example, Nam Soon Huh and William J. Reid, "Intercountry, Transracial Adoption and Ethnic Identity: A Korean Example," *International Social Work* 43, no. 1 (2000): 75–87; Kevin L. Wickes and John R. Slate, "Transracial Adoption of Koreans: A Preliminary

Study of Adjustment," *International Journal for the Advancement of Counselling* 19 (1996): 187–195; Herma J. M. Versluis-den Bieman and Frank C. Verhulst, "Self-Reported and Parent Reported Problems in Adolescent International Adoptees," *Journal of Child Psychology and Psychiatry* 36, no. 8 (1995): 1411–1428; Wun Jung Kim, "International Adoption: A Case Review of Korean Children," *Child Psychiatry and Human Development* 25, no. 3 (1995): 141–154; and Nguyen My Lien, Knarig Katchadurian Meyer, and Myron Winick, "Early Malnutrition and 'Late' Adoption: A Study of Their Effects on the Development of Korean Orphans Adopted Into American Families," *American Journal of Clinical Nutrition* 30 (1977): 1734–1739.

6. Eleana Kim, *Adopted Territory: Transnational Korean Adoptees and the Politics of Belonging* (Durham, NC: Duke University Press, 2010), 9.

7. E. Wayne Carp, *Family Matters: Secrecy and Disclosure in the History of Adoption* (Cambridge, MA: Harvard University Press, 1998); Barbara Melosh, *Strangers and Kin: The American Way of Adoption* (Cambridge, MA: Harvard University Press, 2002); and Ellen Herman, *Kinship by Design: A History of Adoption in the Modern United States* (Chicago, IL: University of Chicago Press, 2008).

8. Ellen Herman, *Kinship by Design*, 217.

9. Mike Mullen, "Identity Development of Korean Adoptees," in *Reviewing Asian America: Locating Diversity*, ed. Wendy L. Ng, Soo-Young Chin, James S. Moy, and Gary Y. Okihiro (Pullman: Washington State University Press, 1995), 61–74.

10. University of Minnesota, "International Adoption Project, About," accessed June 13, 2012, available at http://www.cehd.umn.edu/icd/iap/About/default.html.

11. SooJin Pate, *From Orphan to Adoptee: U.S. Empire and Genealogies of Korean Adoption* (Minneapolis: University of Minnesota Press, 2014); Arissa Oh, *To Save the Children of Korea: The Cold War Origins of International Adoption* (Stanford, CA: Stanford University Press, 2015); Susie Woo, "A New American Comes 'Home': Race, Nation, and the Immigration of Korean War Adoptees, 'GI Babies,' and Brides" (PhD diss., Yale University, 2008); and Bongsoo Park, "Intimate Encounters, Racial Frontiers: Stateless GI Babies in South Korea and the United States, 1953-1965" (PhD diss., University of Minnesota, 2010).

12. The University of Minnesota Libraries' finding aid of the International Social Service United States of America Branch records written by Jon Davidann and revised by Linnea M. Anderson provides a collection summary and detailed descriptions of the records. It is available at http://special.lib.umn.edu/findaid/xml/sw0109.xml, accessed June 1, 2012.

13. Catherine Ceniza Choy, *Global Families: A History of Asian International Adoption in the United States* (New York: NYU Press, 2013).

14. Christina Klein, *Cold War Orientalism: Asia in the Middlebrow Imaginations, 1945–1961* (Berkeley: University of California Press, 2003); and Naoko Shibusawa, *America's Geisha Ally: Reimagining the Japanese Enemy* (Cambridge, MA: Harvard University Press, 2006).

15. Rachel F. Moran, *Interracial Intimacy: The Regulation of Race and Romance* (Chicago, IL: University of Chicago Press, 2001), 17.

16. American chaplains counseled against intermarriage and unit commanders separated American and Japanese couples through new assignments and transfers. U.S. military laws abrogated American servicemen's responsibility toward their mixed-race Asian and American children unless they admitted paternity and registered their children's births with the U.S. Consulate. As enemy aliens, Japanese mothers were prohibited from pursuing paternity or child-support suits. See Yukiko Koshiro, *Trans-Pacific Racisms and the U.S. Occupation of Japan* (New York: Columbia University Press, 1999), 162, 198, and Ellen

Herman, *Kinship by Design*, 216. For a detailed discussion of the attempt of the U.S. military to curtail marriages between American servicemen and Korean women, see Susie Woo, "A New American Comes 'Home,'" 75–87.

17. Mary Dudziak, *Cold War Civil Rights: Race and the Image of American Democracy* (Princeton, NJ: Princeton University Press, 2000), Thomas Borstelmann, *The Cold War and the Color Line: American Race Relations in the Global Arena* (Cambridge, MA: Harvard University Press, 2003), and Penny M. Von Eschen, *Satchmo Blows Up the World: Jazz Ambassadors Play the Cold War* (Cambridge, MA: Harvard University Press, 2006).

18. Richard H. Weil, "International Adoptions: The Quiet Migration," *International Migration Review* 18, no. 2 (1984): 276–293.

19. Tonya Bishoff and Jo Rankin, eds., *Seeds from a Silent Tree: An Anthology by Korean Adoptees* (San Diego, CA: Pandal Press, 1997); Susan Soon-Keum Cox, ed., *Voices from Another Place: A Collection of Works from a Generation Born in Korea and Adopted to Other Countries* (St. Paul, MN: Yeong & Yeong Book Company, 1999); and Jane Jeong Trenka, Julia Chinyere Oparah, and Sung Yung Shin, eds., *Outsiders Within: Writing on Transracial Adoption* (Boston, MA: South End Press, 2006). First *Person Plural*, directed by Deann Borshay Liem (San Francisco, CA: Center for Asian American Media, 2000), DVD, 59 minutes; *Wo Ai Ni* Mommy, directed by Stephanie Wang-Beal (New York: New Day Films, 2009), DVD, 75 minutes; and *Operation Babylift*, directed by Tammy Nguyen Lee (Dallas, TX: Against the Grain Productions, 2010), DVD, 72 minutes. Katy Robinson, *A Single Square Picture: A Korean Adoptee's Search for Her Roots* (New York: Berkley Books, 2002); Jane Jeong Trenka, *The Language of Blood: A Memoir* (St. Paul: Minnesota Historical Society, 2003); and Mei-Ling Hopgood, *Lucky Girl: A Memoir* (Chapel Hill, NC: Algonquin Books, 2009).

20. Peter Selman, "The Movement of Children for International Adoption: Developments and Trends in Receiving States and States of Origin, 1998-2004," in *International Adoption: Global Inequalities and the Circulation of Children*, ed. Diana Marre and Laura Briggs (New York: New York University Press, 2009), 33.

21. Peter Selman, "The Movement of Children for International Adoption," 32, 34.

22. Sara Dorow, *Transnational Adoption: A Cultural Economy of Race, Gender, and Kinship* (New York: New York University Press, 2006), 82 and fn 11 on 290–291.

23. Dorow, *Transnational Adoption*, 82.

24. Laura Briggs and Diana Marre, "Introduction: The Circulation of Children," in *International Adoption: Global Inequalities and the Circulation of Children*, ed. Diana Marre and Laura Briggs (New York: New York University Press, 2009), 19.

25. Barbara Yngvesson, *Belonging in an Adopted World: Race, Identity, and Transnational Adoption* (Chicago, IL: University of Chicago, 2010).

26. Peter Selman, "The Movement of Children for International Adoption," 34.

27. David Crary, "Foreign Adoptions by Americans Drop Sharply," *USA Today*, 17 November 2008, accessed on December 7, 2011, available at http://www.usatoday.com/news/nation/2008-11-17-3481490130_x.htm.

28. Toby Alice Volkman, "Embodying Chinese Culture: Transnational Adoption in North America," in *Cultures of Transnational Adoption*, ed. Toby Alice Volkman (Durham, NC: Duke University Press, 2005), 87.

29. "About Families with Children from China (FCC)," *Families with Children from China (FCC)*, September 20, 2009, accessed on December 5, 2011, available at http://fwcc.org/index.php?option=com_content&view=article&id=3&Itemid=10.

30. "Families with Children from Viet Nam," *Families with Children from Viet Nam*, accessed on December 5, 2011, available at http://www.fcvn.org/.

31. Eleana Kim, *Adopted Territory: Transnational Korean Adoptees and the Politics of Belonging* (Durham, NC: Duke University Press, 2012), 106–107.

32. Kim, *Adopted Territory*, 110.

33. "About Us," *Association of Korean Adoptees—San Francisco (AKASF)*, accessed on December 5, 2011, available at http://www.akasf.com/about-us.

34. "About KAHI," *KAHI (Korean Adoptees of Hawai'i)*, accessed December 5, 2011, available at http://www.kahawaii.org/about.html.

35. "History," *also-known-as*, accessed December 5, 2011, available at http://www.alsoknow-nas.org/organization/history.html.

36. "About AAAW," *Asian Adult Adoptees of Washington (AAAW)*, November 22, 2007, accessed December 5, 2011, available at http://aaawashington.org/wpress/about/.

37. Kim, *Adopted Territory*, 110–114.

38. "About FAN," *Filipino Adoptees Network*, 15 September 2009, accessed December 5, 2011, available at http://www.filipino-adoptees-network.org/?page_id=2.

39. "About Us," *Korean Quarterly*, accessed December 5, 2011, available at http://www.korean-quarterly.org/About.html.

40. "About Us," *Yeong & Yeong Book Company*, accessed December 5, 2011, available at http://www.yeongandyeong.com/about_us.php.

41. "Homepage," *Mei Magazine*, accessed December 5, 2011, available at http://www.meimag-azine.com/.

42. Jacobson, *Culture Keeping*, 1–2.

43. Jacobson, *Culture Keeping*, 2.

44. "KAAN: Korean Cultural Programs-Culture Camps," *Korean American Adoptee Adoptive Family Network (KAAN)*, accessed December 5, 2011, available at http://www.kaanet.com/korean_cultural_programs/camps.php.

45. "History," *Heritage Camps for Adoptive Families*, accessed December 5, 2011, available at http://heritagecamps.org/what-we-do/the-camps.html.

46. See Catherine Ceniza Choy and Gregory Paul Choy, "Transformative Terrains: Korean American Adoptees and the Social Constructions of an American Childhood," in *The American Child*, eds. Caroline Levander and Carol Singley (New Brunswick, NJ: Rutgers University Press, 2003), 262–279; Catherine Ceniza Choy, "Race at the Center: The History of American Cold War Asian Adoption," *Journal of American-East Asian Relations* 16, no. 3 (2009): 1–20; Dorow, *Transnational Adoption*; David Eng, *The Feeling of Kinship: Queer Liberalism and the Racialization of Intimacy* (Durham, NC: Duke University Press, 2010); Mark Jerng, *Claiming Others: Transracial Adoption and National Belonging* (Minneapolis: University of Minnesota Press, 2010); Kim, *Adopted Territory*; Josephine Lee, Don Eitel, and R. A. Shiomi, eds., *Asian American Plays for a New Generation* (Philadelphia: Temple University Press, 2011); Richard Lee, "The Transracial Adoption Paradox: History, Research, and Counseling Implications of Cultural Socialization," *Counseling Psychologist* 31, no. 3 (2003): 711–744; Andrea Louie, "'Pandas, Lions, and Dragons, Oh My!': How White Adoptive Parents Construct Chineseness," *Journal of Asian American Studies* 12, no. 3 (2009): 285–320; and Mia Tuan and Jiannbin Lee Shiao, *Choosing Ethnicity, Negotiating Race: Korean Adoptees in America* (New York: Russell Sage Foundation, 2011).

47. Josephine Lee, "Introduction," in *Asian American Plays for a New Generation*, 5 (emphasis mine).
48. Mia Tuan and Jiannbin Lee Shiao, *Choosing Ethnicity, Negotiating Race*, 145–146.

FURTHER READING

Bergquist, Kathleen Ja Sook, M. Elizabeth Vonk, Dong Soo Kim, and Marvin D. Feit, eds. *International Korean Adoption: A Fifty-Year History of Policy and Practice*. Binghamton: Haworth Press, 2007.

Choy, Catherine Ceniza. *Global Families: A History of Asian International Adoption in America*. New York: New York University Press, 2013.

Dorow, Sara K. *Transnational Adoption: A Cultural Economy of Race, Gender, and Kinship*. New York: New York University Press, 2006.

Eng, David L. *The Feeling of Kinship: Queer Liberalism and the Racialization of Intimacy*. Durham, NC: Duke University Press, 2010.

Herman, Ellen. *Kinship by Design: A History of Adoption in the Modern United States*. Chicago, IL: University of Chicago Press, 2008.

Hubinette, Tobias. *Comforting an Orphaned Nation: Representations of International Adoption and Adopted Koreans in Korean Popular Culture*. Seoul: Jimoondang, 2006.

Jerng, Mark. *Claiming Others: Transracial Adoption and National Belonging*. Minneapolis: University of Minnesota Press, 2010.

Kim, Eleana. *Adopted Territory: Transnational Korean Adoptees and the Politics of Belonging*. Durham, NC: Duke University Press, 2010.

Klein, Christina. *Cold War Orientalism: Asia in the Middlebrow Imaginations, 1945–1961*. Berkeley: University of California Press, 2003.

Lee, Richard. "The Transracial Adoption Paradox: History, Research, and Counseling Implications of Cultural Socialization." *Counseling Psychologist* 31, no. 3 (2003): 711–744.

Marre, Diana and Laura Briggs, eds. *International Adoption: Global Inequalities and the Circulation of Children*. New York: New York University Press, 2009.

Oh, Arissa. *To Save the Children of Korea: The Cold War Origins of International Adoption*. Stanford, CA: Stanford University Press, 2015.

Pate, SooJin. *From Orphan to Adoptee: U.S. Empire and Genealogies of Korean Adoption*. Minneapolis: University of Minnesota Press, 2014.

Trenka, Jane Jeong, Julia Chinyere Oparah, and Sung Yung Shin, eds. *Outsiders Within: Writing on Transracial Adoption*. Boston, MA: South End Press, 2006.

Volkman, Toby Alice, ed. *Cultures of Transnational Adoption*. Durham, NC: Duke University Press, 2005.

Weil, Richard H. "International Adoptions: The Quiet Migration." *International Migration Review* 18, no. 2 (1984): 276–293.

CHAPTER 13

CONFRONTING THE RACIAL STATE OF VIOLENCE

How Asian American History Can Reorient the Study of Race

MOON-HO JUNG

In his widely celebrated speech on race in March 2008, then presidential candidate Barack Obama seemed to portend a new kind of politician, a figure capable of speaking about race honestly and critically. Perhaps of greatest significance to Asian Americans (and Asian Americanists), he seemed particularly suited to speak to and about them. He has many family members with Asian backgrounds. Less than a minute into the speech, however, it became clear that there would be nothing revolutionary uttered that day. After an introductory paean to America's revolutionary Founding Fathers, Obama turned to "this nation's original sin of slavery." "Of course," he added quickly, "the answer to the slavery question was already embedded within our Constitution—a Constitution that had at i[t]s very core the ideal of equal citizenship under the law; a Constitution that promised its people liberty, and justice, and a union that could be and should be perfected over time." The person delivering the speech might have looked and sounded different, but his underlying message was the same. In racial matters, the United States was fundamentally about racial exclusion (the past) and national inclusion (the future), a promise supposedly inscribed in the Declaration of Independence and the Constitution.[1]

Obama did not ignore the Asian side of his family. His racial vision was indeed expansive, certainly more so than that of his peers, but his multiracial and multicontinental family came to stand for America's inclusive ethos and telos. "I have brothers, sisters, nieces, nephews, uncles and cousins, of every race and every hue, scattered across three continents," he said, "and for as long as I live, I will never forget that in no other country on Earth is my story even possible." Momentary nods to Asia and Asians—"Asian" appeared three times in the speech—had failed to disrupt racial narratives that have become commonplace every January (on Martin Luther King, Jr., Day). Condemning his former pastor's sermons, which had compelled him to deliver the speech in the first place, Obama called for a new beginning, a historical vision not bound to "a tragic past" but striving for "a more perfect union." Perhaps we cannot expect more from a mainstream presidential candidate, but we can and should expect more from the field of Asian American studies.

Over the past four decades, the field of Asian American studies has wrestled with two, if not more, epistemological and political tendencies and contexts. On the one hand, Asian American studies, as an intellectual and political project, emerged out of the struggles of student and community activists of the late 1960s. It was an unapologetically radical project, committed to democratizing higher education, to producing new forms of knowledge, and to critiquing the U.S. empire. "We seek . . . simply to function as human beings, to control our own lives," Filipino students at San Francisco State College stated. "So we have decided to fuse ourselves with the masses of Third World people, which are the majority of the world's peoples, to create, through struggle, a new humanity, a new humanism, a New World Consciousness, and within that context collectively control our own destinies."[2] On the other hand, our field has aspired to become historically visible and academically current and relevant. Absent for much too long in most U.S. history textbooks, Asian Americanists have struggled to insert Asian Americans into larger conversations on race and U.S. history. Although they need not represent opposing tendencies and contexts, the demand for intellectual and political transformation and the search for historical and academic recognition can and often do operate on different registers. As Obama's speech exemplified, the latter was not an easy task, but it has proven much easier than the first.

How might we then pursue and interpret Asian American history so that it transforms how we study race in U.S. history? The answer was already embedded within Obama's speech, within what he disavowed on behalf of the United States. Within the "profoundly distorted view of this country" articulated by his black pastor resided not a "divisive" cynicism, as Obama tried to dismiss Reverend Jeremiah Wright, but a larger sense of history that refused to be contained within the United States. It harkened back to a black radical tradition that had recognized the import and relevance of Asia and Asians long ago. In his searing critique of colonialism and white supremacy in the wake of World War I, for example, W. E. B. Du Bois exposed the historical forces ultimately responsible for multiracial and multicontinental families like Obama's. "The cause of war is preparation for war; and of all that Europe has done in a century there is nothing that has equaled in energy, thought, and time [than] her preparation for wholesale murder," he observed. "The only adequate cause of this preparation was conquest and conquest, not in Europe, but primarily among the darker peoples of Asia and Africa; conquest, not for assimilation and uplift, but for commerce and degradation." The United States was not exceptional, for, in standing "shoulder to shoulder with Europe in Europe's worst sin against civilization," Du Bois wrote, it "established a caste system, rushed into preparation for war, and conquered tropical colonies."[3]

Here was an intellectual vision and tradition capacious enough to recognize Asian American history and to demand radical transformations. In offering a "profoundly distorted view" of the United States, Du Bois recognized the need for historical and political visibility, not for visibility's sake but as a means to generate wider and deeper struggles. "Instead of standing as a great example of the success of democracy and the possibility of human brotherhood America has taken her place as an awful example of its pitfalls and failures, so far as black and brown and yellow peoples are concerned," he stated. "And this, too, in spite of the fact that there has been no actual failure; the Indian is not dying out, the Japanese and Chinese have not menaced the land, and the experiment of Negro suffrage has resulted in the uplift of twelve million people at a rate probably unparalleled in history." Casting his lot with what would later be called the Third World, Du Bois warned famously: "*The Dark World is going to submit to its present treatment just as long as it must and not one moment longer.*"[4] It is that kind of distorted view of U.S. and world history that some Asian Americanists have been producing over the past two decades and thereby challenging dominant narratives of race, in particular by placing state violence front and center. The end result has been not a story of national redemption but a history of ongoing struggles over race, empire, and social justice, struggles defiantly exceeding and challenging the temporal and spatial bounds of the United States.

SYNTHESES AND SIGNIFICANCE

Long before Asian American activists took to the streets in 1968, academics at some of the most prestigious U.S. universities studied Asian American history, to probe the deeper meanings of race and U.S. history. Not unlike the 1960s, Asian Americanists of the Progressive Era saw Asian American history in part as a means to articulate and advance their political agendas. Following the tradition of Protestant missionaries who had defended the Chinese in the nineteenth century, Mary Roberts Coolidge, Robert Ezra Park, and a legion of social scientists sought to explain anti-Asian racism on the Pacific coast, which came to represent a racial frontier with a new race problem, the "Oriental problem." Through detailed accounts of electoral politics or case studies on a universal race-relations cycle, the earliest generation of Asian Americanists located the origins of the exclusion movement in the minds and votes of white workers in the U.S. West. Hostility to Asian migrants, they believed, arose primarily from these workers' socioeconomic insecurities and foreign (especially Irish) and southern sensibilities. For these academics, the Chinese and the Japanese after them were misunderstood, misrepresented, and betrayed by the "nation of immigrants," whose central trait was its capacity for inclusion. It was their mission to correct a national mistake and to accelerate an irreversible path to assimilation.[5]

As much as Asian Americanists may wish to excise and exorcise the liberal genesis of our field, its intellectual foundation remains all too secure. The impulse to reclaim and proclaim our "American" roots has proven too seductive, too irresistible. When Ronald

Takaki set out to write a major synthesis of Asian American history in the 1980s, he seemed poised to break new ground. He was the author of *Iron Cages* (1979), a magisterial history of how the racialization of American Indians, African Americans, Mexicans, and Asians had enabled the birth of the United States as an independent republic and its development into an industrial and imperial power. When Takaki turned to Asian American history, however, first in *Pau Hana* (1983) and then in *Strangers from a Different Shore* (1989), the immigrant narrative took center stage. Highlighting personal stories, he presented Asian Americans as quintessential Americans—immigrants "overblown with hope" but struggling to overcome racial oppression and generational and cultural divides to join a wider community of national belonging. Perhaps overblown by his own hope for historical salvation, Takaki concluded: "The history of America is essentially the story of immigrants, and many of them, coming from a 'different shore' than their European brethren, had sailed east to this new world. . . . . Their dreams and hopes unfurled here before the wind, all of them—from the first Chinese miners sailing through the Golden Gate to the last Vietnamese boat people flying into Los Angeles International Airport—have been making history in America."[6]

Sucheng Chan, another pathbreaking historian in the field, worked on a major synthesis of her own around the same time. Stressing the global contexts to Asian migrations and struggles and integrating various ethnic groups into thematic chapters, *Asian Americans* (1991) appeared very different from Takaki's text in tone, approach, and content. Chan eschewed celebratory histories that drew attention to the "colorful cultural contributions" made by Asian Americans and others. Instead, she hoped to present Asian Americans as victims and agents of history, specifically "on how Asian immigrants themselves have fought against the discrimination they faced, as they tried to claim a rightful place for themselves in American society." Published in Twayne's Immigrant Heritage of America series, *Asian Americans* nonetheless subscribed to many of the same tenets as *Strangers from a Different Shore*. U.S. history was fundamentally about sanctioning immigration and overcoming racism. "The history of Asians in America can be fully understood only if we regard them as both immigrants and members of nonwhite minority groups," Chan concluded. "As immigrants, many of their struggles resemble those that European immigrants have faced, but as people of nonwhite origins bearing distinct physical features, they have been perceived as 'perpetual foreigners' who can never be completely absorbed into American society and its body politic." In the end, Chan suggested that national inclusion—to "become full participants in American life"—through "the curtailment of racial tensions" posed the ultimate challenge and objective for Asian Americans.[7]

Their invaluable efforts to make Asian American history coherent and visible notwithstanding, the pioneering syntheses by Takaki and Chan—notably their enduring and varied fixation on immigration and national inclusion—left little to no room to complicate the study of race more generally. Asian Americans ultimately represented a racial amalgam of sorts, a group encompassing and fusing aspects of whiteness (immigration) and blackness (racial exclusion) and implicitly standing somewhere in the middle of an assumed racial spectrum between white and black. That approach and perspective reflected and reproduced comparative studies of race published in the 1970s and 1980s that had tended to concentrate on explaining how Asian Americans were similar to or different from whites, blacks, or both. The sociologist James W. Loewen, for example, posed his study around how Asian Americans negotiated and navigated the Jim Crow world of Mississippi. Arriving as plantation laborers to replace and supplement black workers during Reconstruction, he argued, the Chinese looked inward culturally and socioeconomically to protect themselves from white supremacy and to open up small stores in black neighborhoods shunned by local whites. In their transition from "sojourners" to "immigrants," Loewen concluded, the Chinese began distancing themselves from African Americans, a tactic that purportedly enabled their rise to become "very nearly, and in some respects entirely, equal in status to Caucasians." In his estimation, Asian Americans had moved up racially, from almost black to almost white, but always between black and white.[8]

If the black-white dyad has loomed large in the study of race within and beyond Asian American studies, its broader meanings and logics received little theoretical and historical scrutiny. Gary Y. Okihiro stepped into the breach in 1994 by asking directly and explicitly in a chapter title, "Is Yellow Black or White?" Written amid the much-publicized Korean-black conflict culminating in four days of civil unrest in Los Angeles in 1992, the second chapter of *Margins and Mainstreams* provided a sweeping survey of global interactions and connections between Africans and Asians and pointed to a history and political possibility of African-Asian solidarity. "Yellow is emphatically neither white nor black," Okihiro wrote, "but insofar as Asians and Africans share a subordinate position to the master class, yellow is a shade of black, and black, a shade of yellow." But the hegemony of the black-white binary in U.S. racial discourse, he argued, generally reduced Asian Americans (and American Indians and Latinos) to representations of being like whites or like blacks, thereby eliding and disabling alliances among peoples of color. Seeing race in black and white, in short, according to Okihiro, constituted a central element in the logic of white supremacy in the United States, an "essential site of Asian American oppression" that Asian American studies had the capacity and the imperative to expose and deconstruct.[9]

Through that chapter and throughout *Margins and Mainstreams*, Okihiro sought to de-center the immigrant narrative in Asian American history, opening up new ways to frame and pursue the study of race. Building on his earlier studies on California and Hawai'i, Okihiro marked the origins of Asian American history not in the first Asians to immigrate to what would become the United States but in Europe's "expansion eastward and westward to Asia for conquest and trade." Within that colonial world, he argued, Asians traveled across the Pacific as migrant laborers, their journeys fundamentally shaped by and linked to the Atlantic slave trade and America's "manifest destiny" across North America. By calling for an expansive rendering of Asian American history, including a feminist periodization and spatialization, Okihiro argued for its broader significance. Asian Americans struggled "to transform, and not simply reform, American society and its structures," he argued, helping "to redefine the meaning of the American identity, to expand it beyond the narrower idea of only white and black, and to move it beyond the confines of the American state and the prescribed behaviors of loyalty and patriotism." If his efforts to reclaim "American democracy, equality, and liberty" on behalf of marginalized groups unwittingly sanctified the nation, Okihiro's critique challenged the field of Asian American studies to move beyond racial binaries and the nation-state in framing Asian American history in particular and U.S. history in general.[10]

RACIAL SOLIDARITIES AND DIVIDES

Asian Americanists responded to Okihiro's call, directly or indirectly, in multiple ways. Following his lead, scholars have probed a wider history of interactions between Africans and Asians. In a timely and forceful rebuke of "the diversity model of multiculturalism," wherein cultural and political identities become static and bounded entities, Vijay Prashad's *Everybody Was Kung Fu Fighting* (2001) demands that we see "polycultural" experiences and practices over the past five centuries, grounded in struggles against racism rather than in state responses to regulate difference. From the Hosay festival and Rastafarianism in the Caribbean to the formation of the Nation of Islam and the resonation of Bruce Lee and kung fu in urban communities, Prashad argues, history abounds with examples of Africans and Asians forging solidarities through intercommunal exchanges and innovations. "Polycultural solidarity is not the melancholic hope for unity that sometimes guides the imagination of the Left," he observes, "but it is a materialist recognition that people who share similar experiences create the platform for cultural interaction." And those countless cultural connections, Prashad argues, generated radical movements—Garveyism, Marxism, Third World coalitions, Black Power, Maoism—that exceeded and rejected the bounds of racial provincialism, even if many of their representatives have all too often fallen into the trap of staking claims to cultural authenticity.[11]

But, then, how are we to make sense of undeniable racial rifts, such as that between Korean shopkeepers and black residents in the 1980s and 1990s? Without denying their existence or intensity, Prashad suggests the need to enlarge our frames of reference and to put the spotlight on the U.S. state. The problem lay much deeper than in racial stereotypes or individual attitudes, he argues, for interracial shootings and lootings never took root in middle-class neighborhoods. It was, according to Prashad, fundamentally a matter of social relations under capitalism and empire. Koreans entered working-class black neighborhoods as small-scale merchants during a period of mass deindustrialization in U.S. cities and U.S. hegemony in East Asia. Those were interconnected developments, Prashad argues, as "the multiracist state" encouraged and guided Korean immigrants to such jobs as an "outlet" to stabilize the U.S. presence in Korea and simultaneously incarcerated black youth en masse and sustained credit regimes that disallowed the establishment of black businesses. The racial and imperial logic materially and ideologically positioned Koreans and African Americans against one another, absolving white elites of any responsibility in creating and profiting from systemic inequalities. "And the idea of the 'Korean,' forged in the smithy of U.S. imperial policies," Prashad concludes, "becomes the determinate contradiction to black liberation, while in fact it is that very conceit of imperialism that should be in the gunsights instead."[12]

Social scientists, in the meantime, produced a series of studies on the contemporary Korean-black conflict, mostly within what Claire Jean Kim calls the "racial scapegoating story" of black people lashing out irrationally against hardworking and vulnerable Korean merchants. Concentrating on the black boycott campaign against two Korean-owned stores in Brooklyn in 1990, Kim herself sought to study the Korean-black conflict as a way to expose the intricate and ongoing workings of "racial power" in the United States. Racial categories always emerge and operate relationally against one another, she argues, specifically around two axes of racial ordering in the U.S. context. The American racial order, according to Kim, is structured and reproduced around "superior/inferior" and "insider/foreigner" divides, wherein immigrants and other groups come to be positioned relative to whites (top) and blacks (bottom). As a result, Asian Americans, she posits, have historically been " 'triangulated' insofar as they have been racialized both as inferior to Whites and superior to Blacks (in between Black and White), and as permanently foreign and unassimilable (apart from Black and White)." The "racial triangulation" of Asian Americans, of Korean immigrants in particular, set the context to and set in motion the Korean-black conflict, Kim argues, enabling socioeconomic opportunities for Koreans systematically denied to African Americans and disabling Koreans' full inclusion into the U.S. body politic.[13]

Even as Kim's concept of racial triangulation moves the study of Korean-black relations beyond the realm of personal psychology and impersonal economic structure, especially through a careful analysis of the boycott's complex roots and dynamics, it ironically reifies a racial hierarchy she is attempting to resist. Kim stresses early on that she is not proposing "a single-scale hierarchy (A over B over C)," but it becomes nearly impossible to see how her triangulated model looks significantly different, apart from adding a second axis (insider/foreigner). Whites remain on top; blacks occupy the bottom; Asian Americans reside in the middle. Kim's theoretical construct rests on the premise that African Americans are "firmly at the bottom of the racial order," a position they have seemingly occupied across time and space since the days of slavery. Asian Americans, in turn, Kim suggests, have been racialized above blacks and below whites, again apparently across time and space. My point here is not to propose that African Americans have not occupied the bottom of the American racial order or that Asian Americans have suffered equally under white supremacy. But it is not clear what we gain theoretically and politically by proclaiming the reverse, as Kim does, that African Americans have indeed occupied the bottom and that Asian Americans have not suffered as much.[14]

Kim's triangulation model is not the problem per se. Her emphasis on the need to study racial formations mutually and relationally—in the case of Asian Americans, against whiteness and blackness—offers a critical and necessary intervention. She makes a strong case for the centrality of Asian Americans in structuring race more generally in U.S. history. Ever since the middle of the nineteenth century, Kim argues in a separate essay, racial triangulation has enhanced "White dominance over Asian Americans and Blacks alike." From alien workers without access to citizenship to a "model minority" enlisted to attack civil rights and affirmative action, she suggests, Asian Americans have been valorized relative to African Americans and ostracized from American cultural norms. The reproduction of white supremacy, in short, has rested on the racialization of Asian Americans vis-à-vis blacks and whites at particular historical moments. In her book, however, Kim curiously ends up claiming, in effect, that her triangulated model *describes* the American racial order. Turning to statistical data (e.g., poverty rates, income and education levels) usually invoked to construct the "black underclass" and the "model minority," two racial tropes she is challenging, Kim pursues racial triangulation as a theoretical explanation and an empirical truth. "As a triangulated group," she concludes matter-of-factly, "Koreans clearly enjoy greater freedom than do Blacks in choosing the spaces in which they reside, work, and travel."[15] That may very well be the case, but is the relative degree of racial oppression or marginalization something that can be measured empirically and definitively?

Kim is not alone. Studying race relationally beyond black and white has all too often translated into attempts to place racialized groups on a scale of racial oppression. In his historical study of California published in 1994, for example, the sociologist Tomás Almaguer argued that race had shaped and defined social relations on multiple "racial fault lines," not simply in bipolar terms. Cast as "uncivilized and heathen" in the extreme, he observed, the indigenous population suffered the brunt of white supremacy at the bottom of California's racial hierarchy. Whites ruled in California, as elsewhere, but, according to Almaguer, blacks fared relatively well. Having "assimilated important European cultural patterns," they were English-speaking Christians, "a fact that contributed directly to blacks not becoming the major target of racist initiatives in California that they were elsewhere in the country." And immediately below whites, and at times ambiguously racialized as white, were Mexicans, who likewise shared cultural values with Anglos and, in addition, wielded significant political and economic power. Deemed unambiguously nonwhite and culturally alien, Almaguer continued, Asian immigrants fared worse than Mexicans and blacks as they fell outside the "eurocentric cultural criteria" that whites used to racialize different peoples they encountered. Especially since his approach generally studied each group's "class-specific conflicts" with whites in relative isolation ("on their own terms"), Almaguer's insistence on such a distinct and tidy hierarchy—whites, Mexicans, blacks, Asians, and American Indians, in the order of power and status—appeared all the more gratuitous and oddly ahistorical (or transhistorical).[16]

In her comparative study of radical Third World organizations of the 1960s and 1970s, the geographer Laura Pulido likewise attempts to map a clear hierarchy of racialized groups in California. "A racial hierarchy is a specific configuration of power relations in a given place and time based on racial ideology," she argues. "Racial hierarchies are the mapping of power relations: Who is on top? Who is on the bottom? Who is in between? And how are racial groups related?" Through World War II in California, according to

Pulido, Asian Americans were "arguably the most despised racial/ethnic group in the state," as manifested in the mass incarceration of Japanese Americans. (Her study explicitly does not include American Indians.) By the late 1960s, however, African Americans had replaced Asian Americans on "the lowest rung in the racial hierarchy." How did the historical shift take place? After the war, Pulido states, Japanese Americans "responded by trying to blend in, becoming model citizens, and suppressing any criticism," a strategy that apparently moved them up the racial hierarchy. Whites, in turn, begrudgingly accorded Asian Americans respect and conferred them the title of "model minority." Although Pulido recognizes that the "model minority" was a myth and calls it as such, she simultaneously suggests that Asian Americans acted like "model citizens" and that "the 'model minority' myth also affected the racial hierarchy by enhancing the position of Asian Americans to the detriment of Blacks and Mexican Americans." A racial myth somehow became a racial reality.[17]

Pulido's reification of a racial hierarchy in general and the "model minority" myth in particular is especially striking, for it represents the foundation to her historical explanation of radical Third World organizations. Hers is a study of contrasts, seemingly reflective of the different positioning of blacks, Mexicans, and Asians on the racial hierarchy. Members of the Black Panther Party, she argues, focused their attention on armed self-defense and survival programs targeting the lumpen proletariat. El Centro de Acción Social y Autónomo (Center for Autonomous Social Action), on the other hand, according to Pulido, concentrated on immigrant workers' rights *sin fronteras*, since documented and undocumented Mexicans formed the backbone of the local labor force. Asian American activists in East Wind were also moved by revolutionary nationalism and socialism alongside other Third World radicals, but they alone had to grapple with "Asian Americans' ambiguous racial position." "While there was no doubt that Asian Americans were affected by white racism and imperialism," Pulido argues, "their partial acceptance by whites, which enabled both upward and spatial mobility, necessitated that activists clarify their position within the racial hierarchy." As self-conscious Third World radicals, she continues, Asian American activists contended with their "proximity to whiteness" by expending great energy trying to forge interracial alliances with other peoples of color, who did not respond in kind, and to distance themselves from whites.[18] Such was the price of placing second on the racial hierarchy.

All of these studies and many others laid the groundwork for investigating the mutual, relational, and divisive roots of racial formations, but those that presumed the empirical reality of a racial hierarchy obscured the complexity of race as much as it revealed. Relative racial valorization has been interpreted as having a positive impact on Asian American communities. As the "model minority," cast as being almost white, Asian Americans seemingly were viewed and treated as almost white, as if that provided real, enduring benefits to Asian Americans. To point out the obvious, to be represented as almost white—or almost beautiful, almost rich, almost powerful—is not the same as to be accepted as white. To the contrary, as Okihiro argued, race has historically ascribed apparently contradictory traits—"positive" and "negative" opposites—that were, at root, inherently related and gendered. Asian Americans may be lauded as "diligent" and "upwardly mobile" one moment and then demonized as "slavish" and "aggressive" the next. Not isolated to Asian Americans, contradictory racial representations run the gamut—"Uncle Tom" and "black beast rapist," for instance—that either justify the status quo or beckon a masculine response to maintain the status quo.[19] Who would ever suggest that "Uncle Tom" or "Mammy" materially benefited African Americans or moved them up the racial hierarchy? The intellectual question, or political project, should never be about trying to rank peoples of color on a racial hierarchy. It should be about deconstructing and dismantling white supremacy's pernicious logics and practices. Kim, Almaguer, and Pulido undeniably contribute to the latter but unfortunately engage in the former in the process.

THE RACIAL STATE OF VIOLENCE

In their seminal work originally published in 1986, Michael Omi and Howard Winant proposed that we approach race as "*an unstable and 'de-centered' complex of social meanings constantly being transformed by political struggle.*" Race was always in formation, they argued, both giving shape to and being shaped by social, economic, and political forces at particular historical moments. For most of U.S. history, they observed, racially subordinated groups had no choice but to engage in a "racial *war of maneuver,*" cultivating institutions, movements, and communities outside "the hegemonic racial state." Such maneuvers laid the groundwork for a racial "war of position," in the Gramscian sense, an open assault on the racial state for democratic change to transform the dominant racial ideology. Writing amid the so-called Reagan Revolution, Omi and Winant understood and underscored the dialectical relationship between the state, what they called the "racial state," and social movements in defining racial politics in the United States. The racial state did not embody and enact a linear, liberal progress toward equal rights and democracy—the inexorable march toward "a more perfect union." Rather, it has sought constantly to equilibrate (or stabilize) the racial order, according to Omi and Winant, through laws, policies, and "a repressive apparatus" in response to crises initiated by racially based social movements. State reform and state reaction proceeded apace, establishing "a new *unstable equilibrium*" in the racial order.[20]

The workings of the racial state, however, have remained largely indiscernible, as the U.S. state has been depicted and perceived generally as a neutral or benevolent force in matters of race. Beginning with Reconstruction—and perhaps even earlier with the Declaration of Independence and the Constitution, as Obama suggested in 2008—and culminating in the Civil Rights Act (1964) and the Voting Rights Act (1965), the U.S. state has seemingly stepped forward to advance and sanctify the nation's supposed commitment to racial equality and racial justice. The federal government finally mustered a national resolve to defeat racism once and for all, to enforce desegregation on a recalcitrant South, so the story goes. That historical depiction, in turn, has been essential to making the racial state appear nonracial and even antiracist, from the founding of the

United States. The state, in truth, has acted as a preeminent site of racial struggle, serving historically as the target of egalitarian movements and even more so as the chief agent of white supremacy. The state's adoption of civil rights reforms in the 1960s did not eclipse or sever that history, as Omi and Winant stressed, but exemplified the state's multiple and contradictory responses that produced a new racial order reflecting social demands for racial justice and "the heritage of deep-seated racism and inequality."[21] It is that history of the racial state that Asian American studies is acutely positioned to reveal, a history that can critique liberal narratives of national redemption.

My own work, for example, attempts to reframe entrenched understandings of emancipation and exclusion, specifically by explaining how thousands of Chinese migrants ended up working side by side with African Americans in Louisiana immediately after the Civil War. Reports from the Caribbean, where hundreds of thousands of South Asian and Chinese indentured recruits worked on sugar plantations beginning in the 1830s, proved deeply influential, as they indelibly racialized Asian workers as "coolies" in American culture. Deemed naturally docile and brutally enslaved, coolies emerged continually during Reconstruction as both the salvation of the reuniting nation and the scourge of American civilization, thereby justifying their recruitment and exclusion and reconstructing racial boundaries after emancipation. Coolies, for instance, confused and collapsed the seemingly indissoluble divide between slavery and freedom—they embodied slavery after emancipation—but campaigns to prohibit their migrations to the Caribbean and then to the United States remade America into a "free" nation and made "immigrants" white and European. Positioned between *and* beyond slavery and freedom as well as black and white, Asian workers posed a vexing anomaly, whose recruitment and exclusion facilitated and justified a series of critical transitions in U.S. history: from slave trade laws to racially coded immigration laws, from a slaveholding nation to a "nation of immigrants," and from a continental empire of "manifest destiny" to a liberating empire across the seas. The historical moment of slave emancipation and legal inclusion was also a moment of racial exclusion, a contradiction resolved and equilibrated by and through the racial state.[22]

Asian American history likewise has the potential to disrupt liberal narratives of race and civil rights in the twentieth century. Beginning with sprawling suburban developments that segregated Los Angeles through racial covenants and state subsidies in the decades before World War II, Scott Kurashige illustrates the historical origins of racial patterns and policies that would become the norm in postwar America. Like Kim, Kurashige probes the "triangular nature" of race, but, unlike Kim, he does so by highlighting their shifting ideological bases and material relations. In the 1920s and 1930s, for instance, African Americans and Japanese Americans waged multifaceted campaigns for housing and jobs that generated white hostility and black-Japanese interactions and alliances. That iteration of racial triangulation did not last, as Japanese Americans and African Americans came to occupy divergent paths in defining race and politics during World War II. Compelled to disprove their presumed "disloyalty," Japanese Americans found themselves on the defensive (and in concentration camps) against wartime U.S. nationalism and rabid anti-Japanese racism. African Americans, on the other hand, went on the offensive, claiming a "militant brand of patriotism" through a vibrant, progressive "Negro Victory" movement. With the rise of anticommunism and globalization, these contrasting views of the state—fears of state intervention versus demands for state intervention—would ironically recast Japanese Americans, and Asian Americans more generally, as "models" of success and assimilation and African Americans as "problems" responsible for urban blight.[23]

The prominence of the Korean-black conflict in the 1980s and 1990s no doubt directed historians to look for historical precedents and contexts, but reorienting the study of race through Asian American history need not hinge on triangulating or disrupting the black-white dyad. In a remarkable work published in 1987, Richard Drinnon studied the career of Dillon S. Myer "to bring together the vast bodies of evidence on the treatment of Native Americans and of Japanese Americans—materials too often studied separately—and trace these to their common matrix." As head of the War Relocation Authority and the Bureau of Indian Affairs, Myer oversaw the "relocation" of Japanese Americans and afterward the "termination" of American Indian lands and peoples that epitomized "the banality of evil, U.S. style." Myer was a typical New Deal bureaucrat, Drinnon emphasized, whose "so normal" worldview—including an utter incomprehension and disdain of American Indians and Japanese Americans and an unwavering faith in the administration of state power—resulted in the "twin calamities" of the twentieth century. *Keeper of Concentration Camps* encompassed much more than Myer's career, exploring in great detail the horrors experienced by those placed under his authority and the resistance they organized and expressed. Although Drinnon did not use the term, he provided an incisive critique of the U.S. racial state. "In Myer we have seen the disastrous consequences of coupling three centuries of racism to the positivistic scientism of the Progressives," Drinnon concluded.[24]

If the juxtaposition and integration of Asian American and American Indian histories compel us to center empire within the study of race, transpacific connections and perspectives can also illuminate the centrality of race and empire—rather than immigration and assimilation or racial exclusion and national inclusion—in shaping U.S. history. For decades, studies in Japanese American history generally have dismissed, ignored, or minimized the pro-Japan and racist ideas and practices of early Japanese migrants and their children. In the wake of their vilification and incarceration during World War II, historians and lay leaders understandably, if too stridently, stressed Japanese American "loyalty" to the United States. But, as Eiichiro Azuma argues, Japanese American history cannot be reduced to an American story, divorced from Japanese migrants' backgrounds and their ongoing engagement with the Japanese nation-state and empire. He calls instead for an "inter-National" approach that takes into account the enduring and uneven effects and affects that Japan and the United States had on Japanese American lives. In contrast to U.S. military and civilian leaders, Japanese Americans saw no contradiction in seeing themselves as modern Japanese citizen-subjects and assimilable Americans. Through largely Japanese-language sources, Azuma explains cogently how Japanese Americans responded to white supremacy in the United States by affirming and exploiting imperial Japan's racial and national declarations in a doomed effort to elevate themselves in a racialized society.[25]

Takashi Fujitani likewise challenges liberal framings of race, nation, and empire by traversing the Pacific. The total war regimes of Japan and the United States, he argues, marked a pivotal shift from "vulgar racism" to "polite racism" during World War II. Even as both states continued to practice widespread violence on racial grounds, according to Fujitani, they both commonly also began disavowing racism, a shift that hinged on the production of self-conscious liberal, national subjects. Building on Michel Foucault's concepts of "governmentality" and "biopower," Fujitani illustrates how Japanese and U.S. states projected onto Koreans and Japanese Americans the right to choose to serve the benevolent, inclusive nation (and empire). That putative choice to join the nation, however, came at a great price—the sacrifice of national subjects as coerced soldiers (e.g., 442nd Regimental Combat Unit), workers, and "comfort women" while those individuals evidently choosing not to become "loyal" subjects (e.g., "no-no boys") came to be renewed targets of state violence. Liberal governmentality shaped international relations as well. Rather than outright colonial subjugation, Fujitani suggests, imperial authority rested increasingly on creating nominally self-governing nation-states that allied to serve the interests of Japan and the United States, a logic heralded by Japan's call for the Greater East Asia Co-Prosperity Sphere. The United States and Japan, it turns out, fought an all-out war against each other and simultaneously converged around emergent notions of race and empire that would define the postwar order.[26]

CONCLUSION

From the nation's founding to the present day, state violence has lain at the heart of the U.S. empire, and race has lain at the heart of state violence. It is a history that is buried deep in the national consciousness. It is always there, hidden and distorted but inescapable. It is like the pervasive image of Martin Luther King, Jr., in American culture today, frozen in time, speaking before the Lincoln Memorial in 1963 of a dream "deeply rooted in the American dream that one day this nation will rise up and live out the true meaning of its creed." But King's critique ran much deeper, firmly rooted in a black radical tradition. On April 4, 1967, he broke his public silence on the Vietnam War and received an avalanche of personal attacks in response. Linking domestic and foreign policies and noting the irony of black and white soldiers dying together in Southeast Asia while disallowed from living and learning together in the United States, King said that he had to speak the truth. "I knew that I could never again raise my voice against the violence of the oppressed in the ghettos without having first spoken clearly to the greatest purveyor of violence in the world today—my own government," he said. Speaking as a "citizen of the world," King recalled a larger sense of history, "beyond the prophesying of smooth patriotism." "I speak for those whose land is being laid [to] waste, whose homes are being destroyed, whose culture is being subverted," he stated. "I speak for the poor of America who are paying the double price of smashed hopes at home and death and corruption in Vietnam."[27]

Uncovering layers of history, King's prophetic speech, in effect, marked African Americans and the Vietnamese as subjects of the U.S. racial state of violence. And both peoples, as Eric Tang argues, remember and use their varied and common histories everyday, in far-flung places like New Orleans. With mass white flight since the 1960s, racial dynamics in the Village de L'Est neighborhood could not be explained in familiar racial narratives. It was a neighborhood almost completely of Vietnamese and African Americans. In Hurricane Katrina's aftermath in 2005, both Vietnamese and black residents returned much earlier and in larger numbers than anticipated or desired by city, state, and federal officials. Almost immediately upon their return, they encountered a new threat nearby, in the form of a makeshift landfill ordered into existence by the mayor. With support from the Southern Christian Leadership Conference, King's venerable organization, the Southern Poverty Law Center, and other civil rights groups, local residents mobilized to shut it down. "The landfill struggle, everything we're fighting for out here—this is about the Vietnamese and the blacks together," a Vietnamese American organizer stated.[28] It is not that racial tensions and conflicts are absent in New Orleans East, but its history reminds us not to isolate the study of race to racial dyads, rigid hierarchies, or U.S. national borders. We must approach Asian American history critically, expansively, and imaginatively if we are to capture the complexities of race in our intellectual and political pursuit to create a more just world.

NOTES

1. "Race Speech," last modified March 18, 2008, http://www.constitutioncenter.org/amore-perfectunion/docs/Race_Speech_Transcript.pdf (accessed April 2, 2012). Subsequent quotes from the speech refer to this text.
2. Karen Umemoto, "'On Strike!' San Francisco State College Strike, 1968–69: The Role of Asian American Students," *Amerasia Journal* 15, no. 1 (1989): 15.
3. W. E. B. Du Bois, *Darkwater: Voices from within the Veil* (New York: Washington Square Press, 2004 [1920]), 33, 36.
4. Ibid., 35, 36. Emphasis in the original.
5. Some of the most influential studies were Mary Roberts Coolidge, *Chinese Immigration* (New York: Henry Holt, 1909); Elmer Clarence Sandmeyer, *The Anti-Chinese Movement in California* (Urbana: University of Illinois Press, 1991 [1939]); and Robert Ezra Park, *Race and Culture* (Glencoe, IL: Free Press, 1950). On Park and the Chicago School of Sociology, see Henry Yu, *Thinking Orientals: Migration, Contact, and Exoticism in Modern America* (New York: Oxford University Press, 2001).
6. Ronald Takaki, *Iron Cages: Race and Culture in Nineteenth-Century America* (New York: Knopf, 1979); Ronald Takaki, *Pau Hana: Plantation Life and Labor in Hawaii, 1835–1920* (Honolulu: University of Hawai'i Press, 1983); Ronald Takaki, *Strangers from a Different Shore: A History of Asian Americans* (Boston: Little, Brown, 1989).
7. Sucheng Chan, *Asian Americans: An Interpretive History* (Boston: Twayne, 1991), xiii–xiv, 187–188.
8. James W. Loewen, *The Mississippi Chinese: Between Black and White*, 2nd edition (Prospect Heights, IL: Waveland, 1988 [1971]), 2.

9. Gary Y. Okihiro, *Margins and Mainstreams: Asians in American History and Culture* (Seattle: University of Washington Press, 1994), 34, 62.

10. Ibid., 7, 155, 175.

11. Vijay Prashad, *Everybody Was Kung Fu Fighting: Afro-Asian Connections and the Myth of Cultural Purity* (Boston: Beacon, 2001), 148, 119. See also the special issue "The Afro-Asian Century," ed. Andrew F. Jones and Nikhil Pal Singh, *Positions: East Asia Cultures Critique* 11, no. 1 (2003); Bill V. Mullen, *Afro-Orientalism* (Minneapolis: University of Minnesota Press, 2004); Heike Raphael-Hernandez and Shannon Steen, eds., *AfroAsian Encounters: Culture, History, Politics* (New York: New York University Press, 2006); and Fred Ho and Bill V. Mullen, eds., *Afro Asia: Revolutionary Political and Cultural Connections between African Americans and Asian Americans* (Durham, NC: Duke University Press, 2008).

12. Prashad, *Everybody Was Kung Fu Fighting*, 103–104.

13. Claire Jean Kim, *Bitter Fruit: The Politics of Black-Korean Conflict in New York City* (New Haven, CT: Yale University Press, 2000), 2, 16.

14. Ibid., 10, 27.

15. Claire Jean Kim, "The Racial Triangulation of Asian Americans," *Politics and Society* 27, no. 1 (1999): 118; Kim, *Bitter Fruit*, 47.

16. Tomás Almaguer, *Racial Fault Lines: The Historical Origins of White Supremacy in California* (Berkeley: University of California Press, 1994), 8, 206.

17. Laura Pulido, *Black, Brown, Yellow, and Left: Radical Activism in Los Angeles* (Berkeley: University of California Press, 2006), 25–26, 41–44.

18. Ibid., 136, 161.

19. Okihiro, *Margins and Mainstreams*, 118–147.

20. Michael Omi and Howard Winant, *Racial Formation in the United States: From the 1960s to the 1980s* (New York: Routledge, 1986), 68, 74, 79, 82 (emphases in the original).

21. Nikhil Pal Singh, *Black Is a Country: Race and the Unfinished Struggle for Democracy* (Cambridge, MA: Harvard University Press, 2004), 4–5; Omi and Winant, *Racial Formation*, 75–76, 83.

22. Moon-Ho Jung, *Coolies and Cane: Race, Labor, and Sugar in the Age of Emancipation* (Baltimore, MD: Johns Hopkins University Press, 2006).

23. Scott Kurashige, *The Shifting Grounds of Race: Black and Japanese Americans in the Making of Multiethnic Los Angeles* (Princeton, NJ: Princeton University Press, 2008), 4, 133.

24. Richard Drinnon, *Keeper of Concentration Camps: Dillon S. Myer and American Racism* (Berkeley: University of California Press, 1987), xxvi–xxvii, xxviii, 25, 268.

25. Eiichiro Azuma, *Between Two Empires: Race, History, and Transnationalism in Japanese America* (New York: Oxford University Press, 2005).

26. Takashi Fujitani, *Race for Empire: Koreans as Japanese and Japanese as Americans during World War II* (Berkeley: University of California Press, 2011).

27. Singh, *Black Is a Country*, 1–6; James Melvin Washington, ed., *A Testament of Hope: The Essential Writings of Martin Luther King, Jr.* (San Francisco: HarperSanFrancisco, 1991), 219, 233, 231, 238.

28. Eric Tang, "A Gulf Unites Us: The Vietnamese Americans of New Orleans East," *American Quarterly* 63, no. 1 (2011): 128. In this vein, see also Daryl J. Maeda, *Chains of Babylon: The Rise of Asian America* (Minneapolis: University of Minnesota Press, 2009) and Diane C. Fujino, *Samurai among Panthers: Richard Aoki on Race, Resistance, and a Paradoxical Life* (Minneapolis: University of Minnesota Press, 2012).

FURTHER READING

Almaguer, Tomás. *Racial Fault Lines: The Historical Origins of White Supremacy in California.* Berkeley: University of California Press, 1994.

Azuma, Eiichiro. *Between Two Empires: Race, History, and Transnationalism in Japanese America.* New York: Oxford University Press, 2005.

Coolidge, Mary Roberts. *Chinese Immigration.* New York: Henry Holt, 1909.

Drinnon, Richard. *Keeper of Concentration Camps: Dillon S. Myer and American Racism.* Berkeley: University of California Press, 1987.

Fujitani, Takashi. *Race for Empire: Koreans as Japanese and Japanese as Americans during World War II.* Berkeley: University of California Press, 2011.

Jung, Moon-Ho. *Coolies and Cane: Race, Labor, and Sugar in the Age of Emancipation.* Baltimore, MD: Johns Hopkins University Press, 2006.

Kim, Claire Jean. *Bitter Fruit: The Politics of Black-Korean Conflict in New York City.* New Haven, CT: Yale University Press, 2000.

Kurashige, Scott. *The Shifting Grounds of Race: Black and Japanese Americans in the Making of Multiethnic Los Angeles.* Princeton, NJ: Princeton University Press, 2008.

Loewen, James W. *The Mississippi Chinese: Between Black and White*, 2nd edition. Prospect Heights, IL: Waveland, 1988.

Okihiro, Gary Y. *Margins and Mainstreams: Asians in American History and Culture.* Seattle: University of Washington Press, 1994.

Omi, Michael, and Howard Winant. *Racial Formation in the United States: From the 1960s to the 1980s.* New York: Routledge, 1986.

Park, Robert Ezra. *Race and Culture.* Glencoe, IL: Free Press, 1950.

Prashad, Vijay. *Everybody Was Kung Fu Fighting: Afro-Asian Connections and the Myth of Cultural Purity.* Boston: Beacon, 2001.

Pulido, Laura. *Black, Brown, Yellow, and Left: Radical Activism in Los Angeles.* Berkeley: University of California Press, 2006.

Takaki, Ronald. *Iron Cages: Race and Culture in Nineteenth-Century America.* New York: Knopf, 1979.

Tang, Eric. "A Gulf Unites Us: The Vietnamese Americans of New Orleans East." *American Quarterly* 63, no. 1 (2011): 117–149.

CHAPTER 14

....

THEORY AND HISTORY

....

LON KURASHIGE

HISTORIANS are often wary of theory. One reason for this is because they are more interested in particular national cases than generic, supra-national patterns of human behavior. Some historians dismiss theory as "scientized" speculation ungrounded in a broad and deep foundation of primary sources. They draw an ideological line that distinguishes history as an empirical discipline from more theoretically oriented fields in the humanities and social sciences. The result is a bunkerlike mentality preventing the free sharing of ideas and approaches across disciplinary divides.

The fact that students of the Asian American past have relied on theory to identify research topics, questions, and methods, as well as to guide their analysis, exposes the false dichotomy between history and theory. In nearly a century of studies, scholars of Asian American experiences have adopted different theoretical approaches, from the dawn of professional historical scholarship in the early twentieth century to the expansion of theoretical approaches in the latter part of the century, when Asian American history emerged as a legitimate field of study. Since the 1990s, the field moved from the margins to the center of American historical scholarship, generating an increasing diversity of approaches.

This analysis rests upon a Kuhnian notion of scientific revolutions as "paradigm shifts" in thinking associated with a foundational text and school of thought. Such an examination allows one to map broad patterns of scholarship rather than to provide "thick descriptions" of individual texts. This approach aims to *explain* the characteristics, context, and consequences of theoretical approaches rather than to *judge* their political value as tools for social change. The problem with existing reviews is they often privilege the theoretical orientation of ethnic studies as the standard for evaluating other approaches. While ethnic studies has had a great significance in research on Asian American history, there is not one but many insightful ways to study the past.

Theory during the Exclusion Era, 1907–1941

The study of Asian American history, like that of almost every historical subject studied today, grew out of the professionalization of scholarship in the late nineteenth and early twentieth centuries. An example of Progressive Era rationalization and respect for scientific authority, such scholarship rested upon a new class of university-trained and credentialed professionals who established standards of scholarship and policed them through organizations, journals, prizes, and other means to distinguish the "professional" from the self-trained, non-university-affiliated "amateur." The professionalization of scholarship coincided with the controversy surrounding Japanese and Chinese immigration. The contemporary nature of the "Oriental question" attracted social scientists, especially those in the new discipline of sociology, whose purpose was to explain the rise of urban problems associated with America's industrial revolution. One of these problems concerned the effect of immigration on native populations, institutions, and cultures. The first major study of what would later be called Asian American history examined the origins and process of Chinese immigration exclusion.[1] The author's sympathy for the excluded Chinese immigrants embodied the merging of social science analysis with social welfare activism during the Progressive Era. Such blending took root especially at the recently established University of Chicago, where forward-thinking missionaries and social workers built the school's sociology department into a national leader. It was not surprising that this department would have a major impact on the early study of Asian Americans.

No one did more to shape this research area than Robert Ezra Park. This Olympian figure in sociology came to Asian immigration issues through his interest in the promiscuous mixing of different types of persons in rapidly expanding cities like Chicago. Park's interest also stemmed from an earlier career where he worked closely with the leading African American spokesman and educator Booker T. Washington. Park had already come up with a theory about race relations before he applied it to the study of Asian immigrants. His famous "race-relations cycle" was influenced by larger historical circumstances of early twentieth-century globalization in which peoples foreign to each other came into increasingly close contact. Park's cycle has four successive and irreversible stages: contact, competition, accommodation, and assimilation. The process moves from the stage of the least amount of familiarity and trust (contact), to a crucible (competition) from which groups reach a level of understanding (accommodation) that eventually leads to a significant degree of familiarity and trust (assimilation). In the classic sense of a theory, Park saw the race-relations cycle as a universal law of human behavior not unique to Asian Americans per se.[2]

In addition to research, Park exerted a strong influence on the study of Asian Americans through his roles as teacher and data collector. As a teacher, he and his

University of Chicago colleagues trained scores of Ph.D. students who would provide the bulk of studies on Asian immigrants and their reception before World War II. The only school to rival University of Chicago in this regard was Stanford University. Thus it was not surprising that these two universities teamed up to produce the largest and most important Asian American research project of its day. The Survey of Race Relations, headed by Robert Park but originated and managed by social-gospel missionaries of Japan, collected a trove of materials documenting the Asian American experience. The study featured hundreds of interviews with Asian Americans and persons interested in their experiences. The missionaries who initiated and managed the survey sought to use objective research to defuse the lasting controversy about the alleged harms posed by Asian immigrants. Park, who treated all his subjects as if they were specimens in a petri dish, was more of a social scientist than social activist. But lending his name to the survey signaled his sympathy with the opposition to anti-Asian racism.

Thus research during the exclusion era had a forward-looking cast that opposed anti-Asian movements. Park's race-relations cycle offered a sense of hope that *over time* a society riven by sudden intergroup conflict would return to a level of homeostasis marked by the assimilation of Asian Americans. Researchers were particularly interested in the second generation because their cultural adaptation seemed to provide proof that Asian immigrant groups were progressing, as Park predicted, through the race-relations cycle. In this way scholars were in step with Asian immigrant leaders who looked hopefully to their children's birthright U.S. citizenship and cultural literacy to assuage yellow peril fears.

The noisy ruckus regarding the threats posed to American society by Asian immigrants died down considerably in the late 1920s after the nation had closed its immigration gates to all of Asia—and indeed most of the world. The 1930s witnessed Park's retirement and the subsequent and not unrelated decline of the Chicago School of Sociology from the discipline's cutting edge. Yet the Chicago sociologists continued to study Asian Americans, while the missionaries behind the Survey of Race Relations established a new resource for such studies in the internationalist "think tank" known as the Institute of Pacific Relations (IPR). Missionaries had long seen anti-Asian racism as a problem for international relations and America's standing in East Asia. As a result, the IPR, which focused primarily on the analysis of global affairs, also paid attention to Asian American experiences. Before his retirement, Robert Park, along with many of the survey missionaries, became one of the IPR's founding members.

THEORY DURING THE RISE AND TRIUMPH OF CIVIL RIGHTS, 1942–1988

The bombing of Pearl Harbor revived the hateful feelings of the exclusion movement and targeted these feelings toward a single group—Japanese Americans. Their subsequent evacuation and confinement to internment camps during World War II stemmed from the return of broad-based pessimism about the assimilation process. Again, it was largely missionaries and social scientists who sought to counter this pessimism with studies of the race-relations cycle. The best known of these endeavors was based at the University of California, Berkeley, and was headed by Dorothy Swaine Thomas, a demographer married to Robert Park's mentor and friend, W. I. Thomas. This project, the Japanese Evacuation and Resettlement Study (JERS), resembled the earlier Survey of Race Relations in that it collected a vast quantity of materials and interviews regarding historical and contemporary experience. Thomas's two books based on JERS research assured that, despite the internment and the disillusionment of some Japanese Americans, this immigrant group was proceeding along the path toward full assimilation. The internment, to Thomas and her research team, was a kind of painful crucible that Robert Park saw as necessary for improving intergroup relations.[3]

The wartime incarceration of Japanese Americans, however, was much worse than the earlier movements for immigration exclusion. While the racist rhetoric and justifications were similar, the forced relocation and confinement of the West Coast Japanese community was more coercive and did more immediate and sustained damage than any previous instance of anti-Asian discrimination in the United States. The personal suffering and the violation to the nation's constitutional heritage were simply too great for many scholars to dismiss as mere setbacks on the road to assimilation. The first critique of the internment came while it was happening from an IPR-sponsored study conducted by the activist historian Carey McWilliams. Others followed, especially after the end of the war removed concerns about publishing views that damaged American morale. After the war, legal scholars condemned the internment's constitutionality; a U.S. Army historian questioned its necessity; and scholars from the JERS project (from which Dorothy Thomas published two books underscoring Japanese American assimilability) produced a third book focusing squarely on the problem of white racial prejudice.[4]

Studies of the internment propelled the emergence of theoretical innovation in Asian American historiography. After World War II, Park's race-relations cycle no longer served as the default explanatory framework; instead it would become routinely criticized, or dismissed altogether, for playing down impediments to assimilation such as the internment. In postwar America signs of other state-sponsored oppression, including the Holocaust, Second Red Scare, and the Jim Crow South, were everywhere apparent. Scholars, like the public in general, grew more skeptical about government authority and the nature of democracy. A pathbreaking study during this time was *The Authoritarian Personality* (1950), in which a collection of scholars headed by Theodor Adorno offered a psychoanalytic theory to explain the prejudice behind fascism, totalitarianism, and the Holocaust. The theory, in brief, maintains that a certain "authoritarian" personality is prone toward projecting an individual's insecurities of himself (usually involving an inability to control sexual impulses) onto minority groups. These minority groups, in turn, are seen by that individual as dangers needing to be purged from society.[5]

Such a theory of oppression would be used to explain the aggressive behavior of not just individuals but whole societies. Scholars, thus, searched for the factors in a given historical situation that encouraged a kind of collective authoritarian person-ality geared toward the persecution of racial, religious, or ideological minorities. Roger Daniels's classic study of the exclusion of Japanese immigration exemplifies this new emphasis on state-sponsored oppression. First published in 1962, the *Politics of Prejudice* rejected the view that the anti-Japanese movement derived mainly from labor politics, political pressure groups, and war jingoism against Japan. Daniels, instead, argues that each of these factors grew out of a shared "frontier psychology" from which the vast majority of Americans developed "nonrational fears" about Japanese immi-gration.[6] In a series of subsequent books Daniels turned his attention to Japanese American internment, focusing on the significance of this nonrational racism for gov-ernment decision making and for the totalitarian nature of the internment camps. In the early 1980s the U.S. Congress, with strong encouragement from Daniels and other scholars, published its own oppression study of the internment. This research provided the intellectual backing for the passage of legislation in 1988 that redressed the wrong of internment.[7]

While oppression theory offered an oblique critique of Park's optimistic race-relations cycle, a new generation of sociologists provided a direct challenge to it. The leading influence was Milton M. Gordon, who developed a theory of ethnic group socializa-tion that underscored rigid barriers to their full inclusion in American life. Ethnic and racial minorities, he argued, adapted well to mainstream standards and expectations (a process Gordon called "behavioral assimilation"); however, because of institutional-ized prejudice, it was impossible for most of them to reach a level of "structural assimi-lation" in which their ethnic or racial difference would melt away. Consequently, their Americanism was filtered through the lens of their ethnic or racial group identity. Thus, unlike Robert Park, Gordon maintained that racism would remain a permanent feature of American society and not wither away inevitably through the crucible of group con-flict and competition. The lasting power of prejudice, to Gordon, led not to assimilation but to structurally conditioned pluralism.[8]

Gordon's theory of structural pluralism resonated with a cottage industry of stud-ies produced in the 1960s through the 1970s to explain the dramatic social mobility of Asian Americans after World War II. All of these works, most written by sociologists, identified the retention of ethnicity across the generations as the key ingredient to their social-economic success. While acknowledging the history of anti-Asian racism, they did not follow the doom and gloom of oppression theory, focusing instead on the con-structive aspects that came with retaining ethnicity. Some studies found that cultural practices from China and Japan gave immigrants from these countries advantages for social mobility overseas, while others claimed that such favorable advantages actually were an ironic consequence of discrimination. John Modell and Edna Bonacich, for example, contend that the segregation of Japanese Americans reinforced their ethnic group solidarity, which in turn made them more formidable economic competitors. By emphasizing the "economic basis of ethnic solidarity," their argument was in step with Bonacich's theories—"middleman minority" and "split labor market"—that saw eco-nomic structures behind both anti-Asian racism and Asian American ethnic retention and social mobility. Bonacich, with her fellow sociologist Lucie Cheng, would also play a role in developing theories to explain the waves of Asian migration before World War II as functions of global capitalism.[9]

Both oppression theory and structural pluralism moved the study of Asian American history beyond Park's race-relations cycle, but a third approach would exceed these two in uprooting Chicago School theories. This last approach emerged less from theoretical frameworks than radical social movements to empower minority groups. A major scholarly influence was E. P. Thompson's *The Making of the English Working Class*. Thompson, a British Marxist historian, shifted the study of the working classes away from unions and economic conflict toward everyday sites of culture and community where he argued class identity was really made. During the heyday of the New Left, Thompson's "bottom-up" approach appealed powerfully to a young generation of historians interested in approaches that meshed with the progressive social movement goal of "participatory democracy." The outcome was the concept of "historical agency," which viewed individuals and groups not as pawns of history but as active agents who had the power to negotiate although never to command social structures.[10]

The new social history would attract intellectual activists from the Asian American movement. While first drawn to oppression theory to raise awareness of Asian American victimization, these "amateur" historians embraced the new social history as a way to underscore the value of resisting and recasting oppression. Here was a way for history to not just raise awareness of social problems but also model progressive social action. Two of the most important historians in this regard were Him Mark Lai and Yuji Ichioka, each of whom used native language sources to document the agency of Chinese and Japanese immigrants, respectively. More than anyone else, these two pioneered an ethnic studies approach to Asian American history. Roger Daniels, the historian of oppression, would join them in calling for "bottom-up" studies—and he then wrote one of his own. Daniels's book *Asian America* was the first attempt to synthesize the new field of Asian American history.[11]

But more important was a younger generation of scholars who were drawn toward studying the history of people who looked like them and who faced some of the same social problems in the past as they did in the present. This form of identity politics drove the institutionalization of Asian American studies in journals like *Amerasia* (begun in 1969), ethnic studies programs, and a professional organization (begun in 1979). As a field of interdisciplinary ethnic studies, Asian American history embodied the social history orientation of the day; scholars produced bottom-up histories of ethnic groups and communities, internment camp life and resistance, work culture, migration patterns, women's oppression and agency, family roles, and other "buried" aspects of past Asian American experiences.

One study that stood out was Ronald Takaki's *Strangers from a Different Shore*, still today probably the most recognized and cited book on Asian American history. Takaki, like Daniels, came to the field from oppression studies to write a broad synthetic history. But Takaki's book became an instant classic, while Daniels's never received the attention that it deserved from historians of Asian America. One of the crucial differences

between the two books was that Takaki's better captured the Asian American movement's pan-ethnic identity by featuring Korean, Indian, Filipino, and other Southeast
Asian Americans along with the more intensely studied Chinese and Japanese
Americans. It also did not hurt that Takaki wrote as an Asian American "insider," a
claim that the white Daniels could not make. Indeed, the vast majority of new social
history studies were written by insiders like Takaki, Ichioka, Lai, and a host of others
including Sucheng Chan, Gary Okihiro, Judy Yung, Valerie Matsumoto, David Yoo,
Brian Hayashi, and Dorothy B. Fujita-Rony. For the first time, scholars of Asian descent
led the way in the professional study of Asian American history.[12]

But if Takaki's book benefited from the field's identity politics, *Strangers* fell victim to its ideological and ethical divisions. To some, Takaki's embrace of multicultural American nationalism and the aggressive marketing campaign for *Strangers*
went against the grain of the Asian American movement's self-consciously radical and
populist ethos. In this vein, one insider scholar criticized Takaki for co-opting Asian
American history to achieve mainstream status and commercial success. Others took
him to task less for violating the field's identity politics than for perpetuating its male
hegemony. And still more found fault with *Strangers* for ignoring transnational and
middle-class dimensions of the Asian American experience. While there is truth to each
of these claims, it is also true that Takaki's book was neither the first nor only study to
warrant such criticism. Whatever his motivations for publishing *Strangers,* Takaki probably did more than anyone else to expand the audience for Asian American history. It is
likely that countless numbers of scholars and university administrators came to recognize this history as a legitimate field of scholarship due in large part to the success of his
book. For better or worse, *Strangers* raised the field's national and international profile,
marking a key transition away from the utopian, community-based orientation of the
Asian American movement.

THEORY AND INCREASING DIVERSITY, 1989–2013

Since the publication of *Strangers*, the field has grown in legitimacy and theoretical
innovation. During this time the field has consisted of five interconnected, conceptual
orbits pertaining to (1) culture and discourse, (2) nationalism and the state, (3) diaspora
and transnationalism, (4) urbanism and interminority relations, and (5) biopolitics and
sexuality.

Perhaps the most profound theoretical shift during these years derived from the
growing popularity in the United States of Foucault, Derrida, and other linguistic and
cultural theorists who brought a new emphasis on the construction of knowledge. Their
"poststructural" theories suggested to social historians that, rather than seeking to reveal
action within predetermined structures, they should study the structures themselves as

historically contingent sites of construction. In this way, the "cultural turn" in scholarship politicized a wide range of actors, issues, and places that had been overlooked or understudied.

One of the first and most successful books to connect poststructural theory with ethnic studies was Michael Omi and Howard Winant's *Racial Formation in the United States* (1986). These scholars made a crucial distinction between racism and racial formation. In their eyes, racism, the subject of oppression theory and the fixed given for agency studies, is a set of social and cognitive structures that damage racial minorities. Racial formation, on the other hand, is a generative process through which these social and cognitive structures are themselves defined. The difference is between seeing racism as a predetermined act and seeing racial formation as an ongoing work in progress.[13]

Omi and Winant's conception of racial formation made it possible for scholars of Asian American history to study racism by paying attention to how anyone at anytime defined race. In this way, Lon Kurashige combined a racial formation framework with ethnographic theories regarding "invented traditions" to show how a seemingly unimportant ethnic festival embodied and enacted racial meanings that were instrumental to power relations affecting Japanese Americans. The politicization of popular culture and ethnic community practices is also the subject of histories written by Chiou-Ling Yeh, Linda España-Maram, and Shirley Jennifer Lim. Yeh follows in the mold set by Kurashige by exploring the politics among Chinese Americans through the study of a popular Chinatown festival. España-Maram and Lim showcase intersections of race and gender. España-Maram focuses on the creation of Filipino American masculinity through boxing, gambling, and taxi dance halls, while Lim addresses the bonds of Asian American sisterhood through sororities, consumption, Hollywood films, and beauty pageants.[14]

A related theoretical influence emerged in studies of Asian American history at the same time as racial formation theory. This was Edward Said's notion of Orientalism. Like Omi and Winant, Said explained how racism resulted not just from explicit structures of domination (e.g., racist laws, practices, and attitudes), but from unexamined, "poststructural" patterns of thought, perception, and representation that ostensibly have little to do with race. As a literary critic, Said placed literature at the center of analysis, and as a Palestinian exile, he focused attention on colonial European views of the near east "Orient." Thus it took time to adapt Orientalist theory to the North American context and to apply it to East, South, and Southeast Asians in the United States.[15]

Orientalist studies on Asian Americans reveal a clear indebtedness to Said's pioneering work. The titles of books by John Kuo Wei Tchen, Robert Lee, Henry Yu, Karen J. Leong, and Mari Yoshihara directly referenced Orientalism. Tchen acknowledged adapting Orientalist theory to explain the formation of white racial identity from the founding of the United States until the first Chinese Exclusion Act. Lee traced a pattern of Orientalist representation throughout the entire sweep of Asian American history, while Yu examined Chicago School sociologists, including a number of Asian Americans, as American Orientalists who carried on the forms of racial representation that Said argued served

European colonization so well. Leong took a different approach by studying how leading Chinese American women used Orientalism to resist anti-Chinese racism. Yoshihara also emphasized the gendered nature of Orientalism in shedding light on how white women infused Asian representations with American feminism.[16]

The combining of racial formation and Orientalist theories produced another major theoretical innovation that would guide the study of Asian American history. That this was achieved by an Asian American scholar of French Orientalism is not surprising. Lisa Lowe's *Immigrant Acts: On Asian American Cultural Politics* established a new conception of Asian American citizenship as not merely a legal fact, but as a struggle over racial discourse enacted through cultural and literary productions as well as more obvious policies and laws. In this way, Lowe contributed to a new wave of studies on citizenship that would turn increasingly from the politics of culture to politics proper. Omi and Winant contributed here as well; by theorizing the "racial state," they paved the way for discourse analysis of politics, policies, and state formation. Further explanations of the relationship between race and the nation-state came from legal scholars of "critical race theory" who used poststructuralist frameworks to expose and challenge Reagan-Bush era efforts to undo affirmative action and other antiracist policies. Also contributing to new understandings of the state was Benedict Anderson's theory of "imagined communities," which highlighted national identity itself as a cultural text inculcated through myriad often-overlooked state agencies and actions.[17]

The new theories of citizenship and the state influenced a quartet of highly acclaimed studies. The first is Nayan Shah's examination of racialized public health discourse regarding San Francisco's Chinatown. The next is Erika Lee's meticulous analysis of the influence of Chinese immigrants on U.S. immigration bureaucracy. Mae Ngai's expansive study of the construction of "illegal aliens," which includes Asian immigrants, is the third, while the fourth is Eiichiro Azuma's transnational and comparative examination of nationalist formation among Japanese immigrants.[18]

The recent boon in studies on the history of Asian diasporas cannot be traced to any specific theoretical innovation. In some ways it represents a fulfillment of calls made by ethnic studies historians to use Asian-language sources. Consequently, Madeline Hsu's and Yong Chen's different analyses of southern Chinese immigrants can be seen as following the path set by Him Mark Lai, while Eiichiro Azuma's and Brian Hayashi's different studies of Issei dual nationalism can been seen to have followed the path established by Yuji Ichioka. But Him Mark Lai and Yuji Ichioka used Asian-language sources to understand the experiences of Asian immigrants within the United States, whereas recent studies are equally interested in migrant homelands, return migration, and diasporic communities outside the United States. A better monographic precedent for today's studies is Gunther Barth's *Bitter Strength*, a study that views Chinese American communities as part of a larger pattern of overseas migration and settlement, which began centuries earlier in Southeast Asia. Barth was perhaps the first historian of Asian Americans to make extensive use of scholarship on Asian diasporas, and in this sense he anticipated the border crossings between the fields of U.S. history and Asian histories that define the recent studies.[19]

In the absence of a theoretical center, the analysis of Asian diaspora and transnationalism has gone in different directions. Historians of U.S. immigration, like Hayashi, use social history theory to uncover diasporic communities and identities in the United States, and they increasingly have turned their attention to Latin America, as evident in Julia Camacho's work. Those trained in East Asian history, like Hsu and Azuma, employ a comparative method that views Asian Americans as participants in two nations, while world historians such as Adam McKeown broaden the comparison to three or more nations. Historians of American empire, such as Augusto Espiritu, Paul Kramer, and Gary Okihiro, turn to the rich literature on modern colonialism to examine the diasporic consequences of U.S. colonization of the Philippines or, in Okihiro's case, the politics of transpacific commodity flows centering on Hawai'i. And, finally, those studying recent migration experiences, including Cathy Choy and Aihwa Ong, are in conversation with theories of globalization and global migration. A recent book by Kornel Chang combines theories of white settler colonialism with the study of U.S. borderlands to examine how Asian immigrants were instrumental to the historical construction of the U.S.-Canada border.[20]

The fourth cluster of studies developing since the 1980s derives from theories related to cities, geography, and urban planning that induced the "spatial turn" in historical scholarship. These studies mark the first meaningful convergence between Asian American history and urban history. While histories of Asian Americans often took place in urban settings, the cities themselves were merely the backdrop to the story. This began to change with the emergence of new insights about the role that housing segregation played in making the "urban crisis." The key works here are by Thomas Sugrue, Douglas S. Massey and Nancy A. Denton, and George Lipsitz.[21]

Another influence was the rise of the Los Angeles school of urbanism. "L.A. School" theories countered the traditional understanding of cities as organisms emanating out from an urban core, and instead it appreciated places like Los Angeles, with multiple cores, a broad matrix of suburbanization, and multiracial demographics. The urbanist Mike Davis's studies of Los Angeles racism, in particular, provided an entrée for Scott Kurashige and Charlotte Brooks to address processes of suburbanization, redevelopment, transportation, and globalization in urban California. Shelly Sang-Hee Lee's study of Seattle's racial cosmopolitanism moved in a different direction by recasting studies of Asian American communities to explore the process and consequences of the emerging "Pacific world." And on the East Coast, Mary Ting Yi Lui used Orientalist and racial formation theory to deconstruct fixed assumptions about the spatial and sexual boundaries of New York's Chinatown.[22]

Another impetus for the urban history subfield was the 1992 Los Angeles civil unrest and other expressions of black-Korean conflict occurring in the nation's increasingly multiracial cities. The political scientist Claire Jean Kim roots the tension between Asians and African Americans within a historical pattern of white domination. Kim argues that the tension between these groups is best explained by "triangulating" them with whites, the dominant group, who subordinate blacks by valorizing Asian Americans as "model minorities." At the same time, whites also maintain their racial

superiority by ostracizing Asian Americans as "perpetual foreigners." Kim's major contribution was to encourage historians to see the racialization of Asian Americans and
blacks (not to mention whites) as intertwined rather than parallel processes. One of
the most successful books to capitalize on this insight is Scott Kurashige's *The Shifting
Grounds of Race,* in which he traces how the racial representation of blacks and Japanese
Americans throughout twentieth-century Los Angeles were mutually constitutive and
how this intertwined racialization supported white dominance. Other scholars, such
as Vijay Prashad, Laura Pulido, Bill Mullen, and Claire Jean Kim have focused on the
resistance to racial triangulation by highlighting the lasting significance of Asian-black
alliance and coalition. Resistance studies, more recently, include biographies of Yuri
Kochiyama, Grace Lee Boggs, and other Asian American radicals whose lives and politics modeled interminority alliance. A final dimension of the interminority perspective is evident in research by Moon-Ho Jung and Najia Aarim-Heriot that examine the
triangulation of discourse about blacks, whites, and Chinese in the nineteenth-century
American South.[23]

The fifth and final set of recent theoretical influences focuses on the state's role in
creating and enforcing normative conceptions of the body and sexuality. One type of
study is Takashi Fujitani's groundbreaking U.S.-Japan comparative history of minority soldiers during World War II that fits with the previously addressed transnational
mode of Asian American history written by scholars of East Asia. But Fujitani's book
is also important for being the field's most fully realized engagement with Foucault's
notion of "biopolitics." Fujitani explains that a biopolitical regime relies on racism
to distinguish "between those who will foster the life and welfare of the [normative]
population and must be made to live, and those who hinder the life and welfare of
the population and must be made to die."[24] In this way, the author analyzes the racial
logic of military policies in Japan and the United States during World War II that
either ended up killing or increasing the risk of death for minorities (Koreans in
Japan, Japanese in the United States) so that the majority races could live. In addition, the biopolitics framework allows Fujitani to draw attention to the connection
between military policies (politics of killing) and social welfare policies (politics of
life) and how each of these types of politics discriminated against minorities within
each country.

Foucault's notion of biopolitics stems from his studies of human sexuality and in
this way is rooted as well in queer studies that historicize and disrupt heteronormative
understandings of sexuality and family. A notable connection between queer studies
and Asian American history is Nayan Shah's recent study of East Indian immigrants
during the first half of the twentieth century. In reconstructing the intimate and public
experiences of these immigrants, Shah deconstructs normative views of their permanent settlement, nuclear family households, and polarized sexuality as either and only
heterosexuals or homosexuals. Biographical accounts, too, have taken advantage of
queer theory to examine the blurred line between gay and straight sexuality as well as
masculine and feminine identities. These include Judy Tzu-chun Wu's study of Margaret
Chung, a well-respected American-born woman of Chinese descent who developed

erotic relationships with white and black women, and Amy Sueyoshi's analysis of the Japanese artist Yone Noguchi's male and female lovers.[25]

The five theoretical clusters discussed above—culture and discourse, nationalism and the state, diaspora and transnationalism, urbanism and interminority relations, and biopolitics and sexuality—exist like gravitational forces, drawing new research into their respective orbits. Of course, recent research escapes this gravitational pull to fall under the influence of two or more of the clusters. But what is striking, given the century of studies regarding Asian American history, is the diverse range of theories at work in the field. In the first half of the twentieth century, most scholarship on Asian American history, either directly or indirectly, addressed debates over the "Oriental question" and in doing so based their analysis on the assimilation process theorized in Robert Park's race-relations cycle. Indeed, until the 1950s the study of Asian American history was largely a branch of sociology conducted by scholars trained at or influenced by Park and his colleagues at the University of Chicago. Fresh theoretical options emerged after World War II in the form of theories of oppression and later theories of agency and resistance connected to the new social history. The emergence of Asian American studies as a field of scholarship combined oppression and agency theories in a new historical synthesis. Thus there were two major theoretical approaches to Asian American history by the late 1980s. The development of four more since that time reveals a pattern of an increasing range of theoretical options that has created an increasingly complex and specialized picture of the Asian American past. This trend will only continue as the field gains greater legitimacy, thus attracting more researchers and generating more competition for historical innovation.

NOTES

1. Mary Roberts Coolidge, *Chinese Immigration* (New York: Henry Holt, 1909).
2. Robert Ezra Park, *Race and Culture* (New York: Free Press, 1964).
3. Dorothy Swaine Thomas, *The Salvage: Japanese-American Evacuation and Resettlement* (Berkeley: University of California Press, 1952); Dorothy Swaine Thomas and Richard S. Nishimoto, *The Spoilage: Japanese-American Evacuation and Resettlement during World War II* (Berkeley: University of California Press, 1946).
4. Carey McWilliams, *Prejudice—Japanese-Americans: Symbol of Racial Intolerance* (New York: Little, Brown, 1944); Jacobus tenBroek, *Prejudice, War and the Constitution* (Berkeley: University of California Press, 1954).
5. Theodor W. Adorno, Else Frenkel-Brunswik, Daniel Levinson, and Nevitt Sanford, *The Authoritarian Personality Part One* (Hoboken: John Wiley and Sons, 1964 [1950]).
6. Roger Daniels, *The Politics of Prejudice: The Anti-Japanese Movement in California and the Struggle for Japanese Exclusion* (Berkeley: University of California Press, 1962), 105–107.
7. Roger Daniels, *Concentration Camps USA: Japanese Americans and World War II* (New York: Holt Rinehart and Winston, 1980); Tetsuden Kashima, *Personal Justice Denied: Report of the Commission on Wartime Relocation and Internment of Civilians* (Seattle: University of Washington Press, 1996).

8. Milton M. Gordon, *Assimilation in American Life: The Role of Race, Religion, and National Origins* (New York: Oxford University Press, 1964).

9. John Modell, *The Economics and Politics of Racial Accommodation: The Japanese of Los Angeles, 1900–1942* (Champaign: University of Illinois Press, 1977); Edna Bonacich and John Modell, *The Economic Basis of Ethnic Solidarity: Small Business in the Japanese American Community* (Berkeley: University of California Press, 1980); Lucie Cheng and Edna Bonacich, eds., *Labor Immigration under Capitalism: Asian Workers in the United States before World War II* (Berkeley: University of California Press, 1984); Ivan Light, *Ethnic Enterprise in America, Business and Welfare among Chinese, Japanese, and Blacks* (Berkeley: University of California Press, 1973); William Petersen, *Japanese Americans: Oppression and Success* (New York: Random House, 1971); Harry H. L. Kitano, *Japanese Americans; The Evolution of a Subculture* (Englewood Cliffs, NJ: Prentice-Hall, 1969).

10. E. P. Thompson, *The Making of the English Working Class* (New York: Vintage, 1966).

11. Yuji Ichioka, *The Issei: The World of the First Generation Japanese Immigrants, 1885–1924* (New York: Free Press, 1988); Him Mark Lai, *Chinese American Transnational Politics* (Champaign: University of Illinois Press, 2010); Roger Daniels, *Asian America: Chinese and Japanese in the United States since 1850* (Seattle: University of Washington Press, 1988).

12. Ronald Takaki, *Strangers from a Different Shore* (New York: Little, Brown, 1989); Sucheng Chan, *This Bittersweet Soil: The Chinese in California Agriculture, 1860–1910* (Berkeley: University of California Press, 1989); Gary Y. Okihiro, *Cane Fires: The Anti-Japanese Movement in Hawaii, 1865–1945* (Philadelphia: Temple University Press, 1992); Gary Y. Okihiro, *Margins and Mainstreams: Asians in American History and Culture* (Seattle: University of Washington Press, 1994); Judy Yung, *Unbound Feet: A Social History of Chinese Women in San Francisco* (Berkeley: University of California Press, 1995); Valerie J. Matsumoto, *Farming the Home Place: A Japanese Community in California, 1919–1982* (Ithaca, NY: Cornell University Press, 1993); David K. Yoo, *Growing Up Nisei: Race, Generation, and Culture among Japanese Americans of California, 1924–49* (Champaign: University of Illinois Press, 1999); Brian M. Hayashi, *For the Sake of Our Japanese Brethren: Assimilation, Nationalism, and Protestantism among the Japanese of Los Angeles, 1895–1942* (Stanford, CA: Stanford University Press, 1995); Dorothy B. Fujita-Rony, *American Workers, Colonial Power: Philippine Seattle and the Transpacific West, 1919–1941* (Berkeley: University of California Press, 2002).

13. Michael Omi and Howard Winant, *Racial Formation in the United States from the 1960s to the 1980s* (New York: Routledge, Chapman and Hall, 1986).

14. Lon Kurashige, *Japanese American Celebration and Conflict: A History of Ethnic Identity and Festival, 1934–1990* (Berkeley: University of California Press, 2002); Chiou-ling Yeh, *Making an American Festival: Chinese New Year in San Francisco's Chinatown* (Berkeley: University of California Press, 2008); Linda España-Maram, *Creating Masculinity in Los Angeles's Little Manila: Working-Class Filipinos and Popular Culture, 1920s–1950s* (New York: Columbia University Press, 2006); Shirley Jennifer Lim, *A Feeling of Belonging: Asian American Women's Public Culture, 1930–1960* (New York: New York University Press, 2005).

15. Edward W. Said, *Orientalism* (New York: Vintage, 1979).

16. John Kuo Wei Tchen, *New York before Chinatown: Orientalism and the Shaping of American Culture, 1776–1882* (Baltimore, MD: Johns Hopkins University Press, 2001); Robert G. Lee, *Orientals: Asian Americans in Popular Culture* (Philadelphia: Temple

University Press, 1999); Henry Yu, *Thinking Orientals: Migration, Contact, and Exoticism in Modern America* (New York: Oxford University Press, 2002); Karen J. Leong, *The China Mystique: Pearl S. Buck, Anna May Wong, Mayling Soong, and the Transformation of American Orientalism* (Berkeley: University of California Press, 2005); Mari Yoshihara, *Embracing the East: White Women and American Orientalism* (New York: Oxford University Press, 2002).

17. Lisa Lowe, *Immigrant Acts: On Asian American Cultural Politics* (Durham, NC: Duke University Press, 1996); Richard Delgado and Jean Stefancic, *Critical Race Theory: An Introduction, Second Edition* (New York: New York University Press, 2012); Kimberlé Crenshaw, Neil Gotanda, and Garry Peller, eds., *Critical Race Theory: The Key Writings That Formed the Movement* (New York: New Press, 1996); Benedict Anderson, *Imagined Communities: Reflections on the Origin and Spread of Nationalism* (New York: Verso, 1993).

18. Nayan Shah, *Contagious Divides: Epidemics and Race in San Francisco's Chinatown* (Berkeley: University of California Press, 2001); Shelley Sang-Hee Lee, *Claiming the Oriental Gateway: Prewar Seattle and Japanese America* (Philadelphia: Temple University Press, 2010); Mae M. Ngai, *Impossible Subjects: Illegal Aliens and the Making of Modern America* (Princeton, NJ: Princeton University Press, 2005); Eiichiro Azuma, *Between Two Empires: Race, History, and Transnationalism in Japanese America* (New York: Oxford University Press, 2005).

19. Madeline Hsu, *Dreaming of Gold, Dreaming of Home: Transnationalism and Migration between the United States and South China, 1882–1943* (Stanford, CA: Stanford University Press, 2000); Yong Chen, *Chinese San Francisco, 1850–1943: A Trans-Pacific Community* (Stanford, CA: Stanford University Press, 2002); Azuma, *Between Two Empires*; Brian Masaru Hayashi, *Democratizing the Enemy: The Japanese American Internment* (Princeton, NJ: Princeton University Press, 2008); Gunther Barth, *Bitter Strength* (Cambridge, MA: Harvard University Press, 1964).

20. Julia Maria Schiavone Camacho, *Chinese Mexicans: Transpacific Migration and the Search for a Homeland, 1910–1960* (Chapel Hill: University of North Carolina Press, 2012); Hsu, *Dreaming of Gold*; Azuma, *Between Two Empires*; Adam McKeown, *Chinese Migrant Networks and Cultural Change: Peru, Chicago, and Hawaii 1900–1936* (Chicago: University of Chicago Press, 2001); Adam M. McKeown, *Melancholy Order: Asian Migration and the Globalization of Borders* (New York: Columbia University Press, 2011); Augusto Espiritu, *Five Faces of Exile: The Nation and Filipino American Intellectuals* (Stanford, CA: Stanford University Press, 2005); Paul A. Kramer, *The Blood of Government: Race, Empire, the United States, and the Philippines* (Chapel Hill: University of North Carolina Press, 2006); Gary Y. Okihiro, *Pineapple Culture: A History of the Tropical and Temperate Zones* (Berkeley: University of California Press, 2010); Catherine Ceniza Choy, *Empire of Care: Nursing and Migration in Filipino American History* (Durham, NC: Duke University Press, 2003); Aihwa Ong, *Flexible Citizenship: The Cultural Logics of Transnationality* (Durham, NC: Duke University Press, 1999); Kornel Chang, *Pacific Connections: The Making of the U.S.-Canadian Borderlands* (Berkeley: University of California Press, 2012).

21. Thomas J. Sugrue, *The Origins of the Urban Crisis: Race and Inequality in Postwar Detroit* (Princeton, NJ: Princeton University Press, 2005); Douglas Massey and Nancy Denton, *American Apartheid: Segregation and the Making of the Underclass* (Cambridge, MA: Harvard University Press, 1993); George Lipsitz, *The Possessive Investment in Whiteness: How White People Profit from Identity Politics*, revised and expanded ed. (Philadelphia: Temple University Press, 2006).

22. Mike Davis, *City of Quartz* (New York: Pimlico, 1998); Scott Kurashige, *The Shifting Grounds of Race: Black and Japanese Americans in the Making of Multiethnic Los Angeles* (Princeton, NJ: Princeton University Press, 2010); Charlotte Brooks, *Alien Neighbors, Foreign Friends: Asian Americans, Housing, and the Transformation of Urban California* (Chicago: University of Chicago Press, 2009); Lee, *Claiming the Oriental Gateway*; Mary Ting Yi Lui, *The Chinatown Trunk Mystery: Murder, Miscegenation, and Other Dangerous Encounters in Turn-of-the-Century New York City* (Princeton, NJ: Princeton University Press, 2007).

23. Claire Jean Kim, "The Racial Triangulation of Asian Americans," *Politics and Society* 27, no. 1 (1999): 105–138; Kurashige, *Shifting Grounds of Race*; Vijay Prashad, *The Karma of Brown Folk* (Minneapolis: University of Minnesota Press, 2001); Vijay Prashad, *Everybody Was Kung Fu Fighting: Afro-Asian Connections and the Myth of Cultural Purity* (Boston: Beacon, 2002); Laura Pulido, *Black, Brown, Yellow, and Left: Radical Activism in Los Angeles* (Berkeley: University of California Press, 2006); Bill Mullen, *Afro-Orientalism* (Minneapolis: University of Minnesota Press, 2004); Diane C. Fujino, *Heartbeat of Struggle: The Revolutionary Life of Yuri Kochiyama* (Minneapolis: University of Minnesota Press, 2005); Diane C. Fujino, *Samurai among Panthers: Richard Aoki on Race, Resistance, and a Paradoxical Life* (Minneapolis: University of Minnesota Press, 2012); Moon-Ho Jung, *Coolies and Cane: Race, Labor, and Sugar in the Age of Emancipation* (Baltimore, MD: Johns Hopkins University Press, 2006); Najia Aarim-Heriot, *Chinese Immigrants, African Americans, and Racial Anxiety in the United States, 1848–82* (Urbana: University of Illinois Press, 2003).

24. Takashi Fujitani, *Race for Empire: Koreans as Japanese and Japanese as Americans during World War II* (Berkeley: University of California Press, 2011), 39.

25. Nayan Shah, *Stranger Intimacy: Contesting Race, Sexuality, and the Law in the North American West* (Berkeley: University of California Press, 2011); Judy Tzu-chun Wu, *Doctor Mom Chung of the Fair-Haired Bastards: The Life of a Wartime Celebrity* (Berkeley: University of California Press, 2005); Amy Sueyoshi, *Queer Compulsions: Race, Nation, and Sexuality in the Affairs of Yone Noguchi* (Honolulu: University of Hawai'i Press, 2012).

CHAPTER 15

···

EMPIRE AND WAR IN ASIAN
AMERICAN HISTORY

···

SIMEON MAN

IN 1971, as the U.S. war in Southeast Asia raged on unabated, Asian American students and community activists mounted protests across the country to demand its swift end. Galvanized by the antiwar slogan "Stop Killing Our Asian Brothers and Sisters!" they proclaimed an affinity with the Vietnamese that challenged conventional boundaries of race and nation. Their critique of U.S. state violence linked the freedom struggles of Asians in the United States with those of blacks, Chicanos, Puerto Ricans, and American Indians and with anticolonial revolutions across the globe, most notably the National Liberation Front in Vietnam. In recent years, Asian American studies scholars have reexamined these political movements to underscore the transnational and radical dimensions of Asian American activism. Asian American activists, they argue, became politicized not by identifying with U.S. nationalism, but by engaging in antiracist and anti-imperialist politics that challenged the core presumption of the United States as an arbiter of democracy. They saw themselves not as "Americans first," but as racialized subjects of the U.S. empire whose struggles for a more substantive democracy were deeply entwined with decolonization movements in the Third World. The Vietnam War, in short, emerged simultaneously as the object of their protest and the catalyst for their radical praxis.[1]

Invigorated by comparative and transnational methodologies, recent scholarship on the Asian American movement has offered a welcome critique of the liberal narrative of immigration and assimilation that has driven the field since its inception. According to this narrative, the history of Asians in the United States has been chiefly concerned about racial exclusion in the past and the steady progress toward national inclusion, with World War II marking the pivotal turning point when Asian Americans proved once and for all their capacity for citizenship by joining the military. At the heart of this redemptive story are the Japanese American soldiers of the 100th Infantry Battalion and 442nd Regimental Combat Team, who were called on to defend the nation when their families were confined in internment camps and who persevered by demonstrating their patriotism. This narrative has endured as one of the major thematic linchpins of the field, even as scholars have uncovered more nuanced accounts of Japanese American resistance during the war.[2] If World War II continues to be memorialized as the "good war," then the Vietnam War seems to tell a different story. Indeed, recent studies of Asian American activism in the 1960s and 1970s have reframed the centrality of "war" in Asian American history. Rather than reinforcing Asian Americans' abiding faith in U.S. nationalism, these studies focus on the Vietnam War to tell a history of race and radicalism that implicated and politicized Asian Americans alongside other racialized subjects in the United States and beyond.

These two approaches to the study of Asian Americans and war—one about military service in World War II, the other about activism during the Vietnam War era—recast the familiar tension of accommodation and resistance that has animated the field. The difference of their political critique is unmistakable. Yet to fixate on their difference risks eliding a fundamental similarity in their framing of war. In both cases, "war" functions as an essential ground for the enactment of Asian American politics. If World War II summoned Asian Americans to proclaim their national loyalty and belonging, then the Vietnam War compelled them to critique the nation-state and to articulate a politics of Third World solidarity. War, in both instances, is something that happens "over there," with implications for Asian Americans "back home." Instead of figuring war merely as an event, as something already known, what if we approached it as a site of contingency? That is, what if we approached war not as a backdrop of racial politics but as an active site of Asian American racial formation? More pointedly: how do we move beyond an episodic approach to Asian Americans and war and make "war" central to our under-standing of race?

These questions articulate a broader impasse in Asian American historiography, in which the study of war has remained largely separate from the study of empire. This problem is all the more remarkable given the tremendous growth in the scholarship on U.S. imperialism over the past three decades. Lucie Cheng and Edna Bonacich's edited collection of essays, *Labor Immigration under Capitalism* (1984), was the first to reinter-pret the history of Asian migrations to the United States by centering Euro-American imperialism and capitalist development as its pivotal driving force. Influenced by Immanuel Wallerstein's world systems theory, their framework of migrant labor recast the study of immigration beyond seemingly disconnected "push" and "pull" factors to account for the networks of capital and labor that linked the development of the core to the underdevelopment of the periphery in the world system. Edward Said's *Orientalism* (1979), a foundational text in postcolonial studies, pushed scholars to engage with the discursive regimes of knowledge that enabled and justified European colonial and imperial projects.[3] Together, these studies articulated new theoretical paradigms that expanded the geographical and temporal boundaries of Asian American history beyond the mythic narratives of Gold Rush California.[4] And yet even as these more critical works emerged over the past two decades, our field continued to witness a prolifera-tion of celebratory accounts of Asian Americans and their contributions to U.S. wars, a response in part to the multicultural impulse to claim and proclaim Asian Americans as rightful members of the "nation of immigrants."[5] In short, if empire has emerged as an important category of analysis, it has made glaring the degree to which the study of Asian Americans and war continues to elide the question of imperial formations to focus on a national history of patriotism and protest.

Bringing the study of war and empire into a single analytical frame has the potential to unsettle dominant discourses of Asian American citizenship by illumining the global processes of imperial state violence that are foundational to Asian American racial formation. Scholars of the U.S. colonial Philippines have been among the most persistent in taking on this task. As part of a wave of interdisciplinary historians and anthropologists seeking to interrogate the contradictions of European colonialisms in Southeast Asia and Africa—what Ann Laura Stoler and Frederick Cooper termed "tensions of empire"—as well as the broader inquiry into the "absence" of empire in American studies, Philippine scholars turned to colonial knowledge production as an object of analysis.[6] Vicente L. Rafael, for example, examined the census as a technique of U.S. colonial rule that targeted Filipinos as subjects of "benevolent assimilation" at the official end of the U.S. war in 1902. The work of enumerating the population became an ongoing function of pacification, he argued, such that violence and assimilation emerged as constitutive elements of the colonial project. Similarly examining the production of racialized difference in the U.S. colonial Philippines, Paul A. Kramer situates his study within a wider world of race and empire in the late nineteenth and early twentieth centuries. In his account, the "racial remaking of empire and the imperial remaking of race" worked in tandem to justify U.S. conquest and colonial state building as an endless project of transforming "savage" Filipinos into "civilized" subjects. The contradictions of benevolent assimilation, however, consistently confounded U.S. authorities. As the Tydings-McDuffie Act (1934) revealed, nativist demands to halt further Filipino migration to the United States would come at the cost of eventual Philippine independence, a compromise that signaled ultimately the incompatibility between exclusion and empire.[7]

If recent work on the U.S. colonial Philippines have brought postcolonial studies of empire to bear on transnational U.S. history, it also converged with the growth of Filipino American studies.[8] Over the past decade, a burgeoning body of scholarship on pre-1965 Filipina/o migration and gendered racial formation has worked to re-center empire in Asian American history. As Catherine Ceniza Choy demonstrates, for instance, the U.S. colonial drive to educate and "uplift" Filipina/os through a public health regime in the early twentieth century shaped the contours of Filipina nurse migration to the United States long after Philippine independence in 1946. Similarly, as Linda España-Maram, Rick Baldoz, and others have shown, Filipino labor migrants, first recruited to Hawai'i and then to the U.S. West, comprised a flexible labor force that fulfilled the demands of the region's agricultural industries. Their legal status as U.S. "nationals" delimited their claims to citizenship, and it worked to regulate their movements and social interactions that further entrenched their racialization as uncivilized subjects of the U.S. empire. Far from an anomaly, the U.S. empire has played a pivotal role in structuring the lives of Filipina/os in the Philippines and in the United States from the colonial era to the present.[9]

As colonized subjects whose legal and cultural inclusion in the U.S. nation-state could never be realized fully, Filipinos and their racialized liminality provide an opening into a broader critique of war and empire in Asian American history. To be sure, this critique has not been confined to Filipino American studies alone. A recent spate of scholarship on Asian Americans and the cold war has interrogated further the limits of liberal inclusion in the post–World War II era. Christina Klein's *Cold War Orientalism* examines the cultivation of a "global imaginary of integration" through middlebrow cultural productions such as *Reader's Digest* and Rodgers and Hammerstein's *The King and I* (1956), both of which translated U.S. foreign policy objectives into sites of sentimental ties between Americans and Asians. Focusing on U.S.-occupied Japan, Naoko Shibusawa similarly analyzes the discourses of American Orientalism rooted in ideologies of gender and maturity to explain the popular shift of Japan from a wartime enemy to postwar ally. As these works and others show, the integration of decolonizing nations into the U.S.-led capitalist free world was intimately bound up with the domestic integration of Asian and African Americans in the United States. The increasing tolerance toward, and celebration of, Asians as a "model minority" was a cold war imperative, but it nonetheless paved a path for Asian Americans to assert their claims to national belonging. As Ellen Wu and Cindy I-Fen Cheng demonstrate, Asian Americans indeed latched onto the rhetorical claims of U.S. democracy to wage meaningful struggles for civil rights reform in the 1950s and 1960s.[10]

These works on cold war civil rights and cultural diplomacy stand as a much-needed corrective to the triumphant and dominant narrative of post–World War II Asian American inclusion. The dismantling of legal and cultural barriers to Asian American citizenship after 1945 was not a story about the United States redeeming itself from a history of racial exclusion, they remind us, but was part of the project of deepening U.S. political, military, and economic power in the emerging global order. Moreover, the racialization of Asian Americans as "assimilating Others," to borrow Wu's term, was contingent upon generating "new modes of exclusion" targeting other racialized and indigenous subjects and political dissidents in the United States.[11] And yet at the same time that these studies on cold war civil rights have complicated our understanding of Asian American racial formation through a transnational and comparative framework, they also reproduced a domestic narrative of race and nation by emphasizing struggles for citizenship and national belonging as the ultimate goal. The question remains: in the age of global decolonization that has been forgotten as the "cold war," how did U.S. imperial violence in Asia—most notably in the "hot wars" in Korea and Vietnam—complicate the imperative of Asian American inclusion?

Transnational scholarship about Asian American racial formation at mid-century, in other words, must account for the production of U.S. state violence that has been obscured in part by the "cultural turn" in the study of U.S. foreign relations. If cultural representations of Asians as the "model minority" worked to suture U.S. claims to global power, then how did the mobilization of Asians in the service of the U.S. empire—in the work of occupation, pacification, prostitution, and other forms of militarized labor—complicate this narrative? Put differently, how might cultural histories of empire engage with the social dimensions of working, living, and dying within the U.S. empire? Feminist scholars have been at the forefront of addressing these questions. As Maria Höhn and Seungsook Moon argue in their edited anthology, *Over There*, to make visible the U.S. military empire after 1945 entails foregrounding the sexual and gender relations that have structured the presence of U.S. soldiers overseas. Camptown prostitution, for example, emerged as a vital institution for maintaining the U.S. military in South Korea while at the same time buttressing the militarized political economy of the South Korean state. The regulation of women's sexual labor in the service of U.S. soldiers, as Moon demonstrates, both normalized heterosexual desire and liaisons as a condition of the U.S. military presence and reinforced the class boundary that protected "respectable" Korean women from foreign soldiers at the expense of working-class women. And, as with the case of Filipino nationals in the early twentieth century, the experiences of laboring within the colonized space of camptowns indelibly shaped the lives of Korean "military brides" as they migrated and built their lives in the United States, as Ji-Yeon Yuh has documented.[12]

Eiichiro Azuma's study "Brokering Race, Culture, and Citizenship" likewise interrogates the racial politics of the U.S. military empire by focusing on the role of Nisei linguists in occupied Japan. His essay tackles one of the most glaring contradictions that has been obscured by conventional accounts of Japanese American military service: how did the wartime and postwar representations of Nisei soldiers as the "model minority" square with the reality of their complicity in bolstering the U.S. imperial project after World War II, specifically through the work of occupation? Taking aim at the popular narrative of Nisei servicemen as the conduit of democracy in postwar Japan, Azuma explains how some of these Nisei "cultural brokers," in an attempt to demonstrate themselves as full-fledged Americans in the wake of their wartime incarceration, actively distanced themselves from the Japanese that at times led to acts of violence against the local population. Capitalizing on their racial difference and status as U.S. citizens, the Nisei participated in a "unique form of racial maneuvering" that positioned themselves as a "colonial middleman" in relation to the conquered Japanese, thus reinforcing American hierarchies of race and power in post-1945 geopolitics. The struggle for Japanese American national inclusion after World War II, therefore, was waged not only through domestic reform or cultural diplomacy, but also through their engagements with the U.S. military empire that transformed them from the "oppressed to oppressor."[13]

As Azuma demonstrates, the military offers a rich site of investigation into the broader history of race and empire in the Pacific. Takashi Fujitani's *Race for Empire* takes this task head-on by turning to soldiering as an analytical lens to interrogate the shifting racial grounds of the U.S. and Japanese states during World War II. Writing against dominant interpretations that posit the U.S. and Japanese wartime regimes as incompatible projects of opposing means and ends—pushed to wage a "war without mercy," in John Dower's famous phrase—Fujitani examines the two regimes' similar treatments of ethnic minorities to demonstrate how racial liberalism emerged as a strategy of empire. Central to his story are Japanese Americans in the U.S. army and ethnic Koreans in the Japanese military, who both were mobilized in order to satisfy manpower shortages and the broader aim of disavowing racism in a war that was continually being cast as a "race war" by both sides. The inclusion of these racialized subjects into their respective regimes, Fujitani argues, signaled a broader shift from "vulgar racism" to "polite racism" in American and Japanese imperial cultures, a racial formation that would enable the United States to pursue its post-1945 imperial project in the name of racial equality. Far from being an uncomplicated narrative of liberal inclusion, however, the promise of national belonging for Japanese Americans and Korean colonial subjects was always articulated against their exploitation as soldiers and laborers—indeed, as subjects primed for death—a contradiction that reveals the heart of liberalism and its limitations.[14]

Approaching the Pacific as a site of sedimented colonial and imperial histories thus enables a reframing of Asian American soldiering beyond the rubrics of military service and citizenship. Specifically, it reveals how the incorporation of Asian ethnic minorities and colonial subjects into the nation through the military depended on their mobilization to police new boundaries of exclusion elsewhere in the decolonizing world. This conception of the Pacific as a region of overlapping imperial formations has come into sharper focus recently, in part through the efforts of Azuma, Fujitani, and others who have pushed the fields of Asian American studies and Asian studies in closer dialogue. Asian migrants, as soldiers, contract laborers, and itinerant workers who often traversed multiple nation-states and empires, tended to develop complex affiliations that did not align neatly with the imperatives of nation-states. Jun Uchida's *Brokers of Empire*, for example, delves into the history of Japanese settler colonialism in Korea to show how Japanese migrants became constituted as racialized subjects of the Japanese empire. In illustrating how Japanese settlers actively participated in the colonization of Korea, and thus helped mediate Japan's rise as a modern nation-state and empire in the early twentieth century, Uchida demonstrates both the complicity of Japanese settlers in the colonial enterprise and the fragility of the imperial project as settlers pursued their own commercial and political ambitions. Not framed as an American story, her study nonetheless compels American and Asian American studies scholars to interrogate the overlapping histories of race and empire that implicated Asian subjects on both sides of the Pacific.[15]

Emerging work on the mutual constitutions of the U.S. and Japanese empires has converged with—and indeed reinvigorated—scholarship in Pacific Islander studies. Long rendered marginal to both Asian American studies and studies of empire broadly, the Pacific Islands have played a crucial role in the expansion and consolidation of U.S. and Japanese imperialism throughout the twentieth century, bearing the deep social, political, and cultural costs of military interventions and imperial wars in Asia and the Pacific. Setsu Shigematsu and Keith Camacho's edited anthology, *Militarized Currents*, elucidates these historical relations by examining how the legacies of colonialism in places such as Guam, Okinawa, the Marshall Islands, the Philippines, and Korea have produced new forms of militarization and generated ongoing movements for decolonization in the present. In conceptualizing the Pacific, they simultaneously call for the need to critique Asian and American studies approaches that frame the Pacific as a site of crossings, conquest, and settlement, and to highlight the "decolonizing bodies of knowledge" produced by the peoples most directly affected by the processes of colonialism and militarization in the region. Further examining the colonial legacies that have shaped the histories of Guam and the Northern Marianas, Keith Camacho's *Cultures of Commemoration* examines how Chamorro have engaged in "indigenous cultural agency" and active forms of remembering that contest dominant and triumphant narratives of American "liberation" during World War II.[16]

Bringing Asian American studies in conversation with Pacific Islander studies has generated urgent discussions about the historical formations of Asian settler colonialism, most notably in Hawai'i. Candace Fujikane and Jonathan Y. Okamura's collection of essays, *Asian Settler Colonialism*, offers a formative critique. With the aim of unsettling the dominant nationalist narrative that Asian inclusion into the U.S. settler state signals a triumph of multiracial democracy, the anthology sought to make "visible the status of Asians as settlers," to highlight their complicity with the ongoing colonization of Native Hawaiians, and ultimately to strive for a kind of Asian American politics that accounts for Native struggles for decolonization.[17] Likewise interested in the convergent histories of Asian migration and settler colonialism, Renisa Mawani's *Colonial Proximities* turns our attention to the interracial encounters among Chinese, aboriginal, European, and mixed-race populations in British Columbia at the turn of the twentieth century. Examining these encounters as a point of departure to investigate the production of colonial knowledge and racial governance that were at the core of British imperial policy, Mawani builds on and ultimately goes beyond the critique of Asian settler colonialism by shifting the focus from personal and collective investments in the settler regime to how that regime was enacted and sustained through state practices of policing interracial intimacies.[18]

If the scholarship on settler colonial formations in Asia and the Pacific has shed light on Asians as agents of empire, it also has revealed new geographies and routes of radicalism and resistance forged across multiple imperial terrains. As Judy Tzu-Chun Wu demonstrates in *Radicals on the Road*, Asian American activists during the Vietnam War era not only formed multiracial coalitions at home but also traversed the Pacific in an effort to build a "global public sphere" against the war. Traveling abroad to Vietnam, North Korea, and China deepened these activists' commitment to anti-imperialism, Wu argues, which was premised on their conception of "radical orientalism" that both challenged and reproduced racialized gendered assumptions about the "Third World."[19] Shifting the focus to earlier histories of race, empire, and radicalism, Seema Sohi and Moon-Ho Jung illustrate how circuits of anticolonialism connecting Europe, Asia, and the U.S. West at the turn of the twentieth century threatened to undermine the U.S. and British empires. The emergence of the "Hindu menace" on the Pacific Coast and "seditious" subjects in the Philippines, they argue, respectively, were deeply entwined with the rise of a security state apparatus that proved crucial to the consolidation and maintenance of the two empires.[20]

As these studies make clear, wars in the age of empire have been defined less by temporal and geographical markers than by the constant legitimating functions of the state to police, criminalize, and expel undesirable subjects. This notion of war as state violence permeating everyday life unsettles dominant understandings of war as "the continuation of politics by other means," an exceptional state of violence that invariably gets resolved in the "postwar" period or war's "aftermath," often through the inclusion of peoples displaced by the war into the U.S. nation. The study of Southeast Asian refugees in the 1970s and 1980s traditionally have reinforced this narrative, as earlier scholars have tended to depict them as subjects deserving of sympathy and uplift as they transition to civilian life in the United States. Recent work in critical refugee studies has challenged this dominant discourse of rescue and liberation. Encapsulating this emerging interdisciplinary field, Yen Le Espiritu's *Body Counts* contends the need to approach "the refugee" not as an object of investigation but as a productive site of critique of the limits of U.S. national inclusion; the "refugee," in her framing, is both a "critical idea" *and* "a social actor" whose itinerant life illuminates the broad interconnections of war, colonialism, and empire.[21] Ma Vang, in a similar vein, argues that official state recognition of Hmong refugee soldiers through the Hmong Veterans' Naturalization Act of 1997 worked to obscure the U.S. "secret" war in Laos while restaging the violence of war through liberal inclusion. Extending this critique, Mimi Nguyen's *The Gift of Freedom* elaborates on "freedom" as a structuring force of U.S. imperial violence. Liberal peace and liberal war, she argues, operated in tandem to produce the Vietnamese refugee as a grateful subject of U.S. benevolence. Henceforth "indebted" to the U.S. empire, the refugee thus enables the United States to pursue ongoing wars in the name of freedom. Without losing sight of the social dimensions of refugees' experiences, Jana Lipman's accounts of Fort Chaffee and the refugee camp on Guam illustrate how Vietnamese challenged resettlement policy after 1975 and, in the process, revealed the connections among the legacies of war, empire, detention, and deportation.[22]

The circuitous routes traveled by Southeast Asian refugees across the Pacific and their liminal subjectivities as "stateless" persons capture the perilous and violent journeys that continued to shape their lives after the official end of war. Far from unique, their experiences indeed resonate in Asian American history broadly. Asian Americans are not "immigrants," Gary Y. Okihiro first reminded us; rather they are a kind of "post-imperial exile," whose histories of race and diaspora bear the traces of Euro-American imperial violence in Asia even if they have become incorporated in other ways into the imperial project.[23] Vernadette Vicuña Gonzalez offers a recent example of this critique. In *Securing Paradise*, she interrogates the enjoined processes of militarism and tourism in Hawai'i and the Philippines from the early twentieth century to the present, to illustrate the ways that the legacies of U.S. colonialism have continued to mobilize former colonial subjects through the neoliberal economies of desire and consumption.[24] In reflecting on the slippery ideologies of militarism and tourism that have structured U.S. neocolonialism in Asia and the Pacific, or, to use a different but related example, the recruitment of Filipino contract workers in Iraq, Afghanistan, and other parts of the Middle East for the "War on Terror," we would do well to remember that colonial wars do not simply end but get recalibrated in an age of permanent war through the ruses of freedom. Moving beyond the binaries of colonial and postcolonial, domestic and foreign, inclusion and exclusion—the rubrics that have organized narratives of American exceptionalism—Asian American history can reanimate a critique of war and empire. By foregrounding global histories of race and empire and by engaging critically with other interdisciplinary fields of study, including Pacific Islander studies and critical Asian studies, Asian American history can provide the means to reimagine and transform the politics of our present.

NOTES

1. Daryl J. Maeda, *Chains of Babylon: The Rise of Asian America* (Minneapolis: University of Minnesota Press, 2009); Diane Fujino, *Samurai among Panthers: Richard Aoki on Race, Resistance, and a Paradoxical Life* (Minneapolis: University of Minnesota Press, 2011); Judy Tzu-Chun Wu, *Radicals on the Road: Internationalism, Orientalism, and Feminism during the Vietnam Era* (Ithaca, NY: Cornell University Press, 2013).

2. Studies of Japanese Americans and World War II include Franklin S. Odo, *No Sword to Bury: Japanese Americans in Hawai'i during World War II* (Philadelphia: Temple University Press, 2004); and Masayo Duus, *Unlikely Liberators: The Men of the 100th and 442nd* (Honolulu: University of Hawai'i Press, 2007). For more critical approaches, see Eric L. Muller, *Free to Die for Their Country: The Story of the Japanese American Draft Resisters in World War II* (Chicago: University of Chicago Press, 2001); and Takashi Fujitani, *Race for Empire: Koreans as Japanese and Japanese as Americans during World War II* (Berkeley: University of California Press, 2011), especially chapter 4.

3. Lucie Cheng and Edna Bonacich, eds., *Labor Immigration under Capitalism: Asian Workers in the United States before World War II* (Berkeley: University of California Press, 1984); Edward Said, *Orientalism* (New York: Vintage, 1979).

4. See, for example, Gary Y. Okihiro, *Cane Fires: The Anti-Japanese Movement in Hawaii, 1865–1945* (Philadelphia: Temple University Press, 1991); John Wei Kuo Tchen, *New York before Chinatown: Orientalism and the Shaping of American Culture, 1776–1882* (Baltimore, MD: Johns Hopkins University Press, 1999); Mary Ting Yi Lui, *The Chinatown Trunk Mystery: Murder, Miscegenation, and Other Dangerous Encounters in Turn-of-the-Century New York City* (Princeton, NJ: Princeton University Press, 2005); Eiichiro Azuma, *Between Two Empires: Race, History, and Transnationalism in Japanese America* (New York: Oxford University Press, 2005); Moon-Ho Jung, *Coolies and Cane: Race, Labor, and Sugar in the Age of Emancipation* (Baltimore, MD: Johns Hopkins University Press, 2006); Kornel Chang, *Pacific Connections: The Making of the U.S.-Canadian Borderlands* (Berkeley: University of California Press, 2012).

5. Ronald Takaki, *Double Victory: A Multicultural History of America in World War II* (New York: Little, Brown, 2000); K. Scott Wong, *Americans First: Chinese Americans and the Second World War* (Cambridge, MA: Harvard University Press, 2005).

6. Frederick Cooper and Ann Laura Stoler, eds., *Tensions of Empire: Colonial Cultures in a Bourgeois World* (Berkeley: University of California Press, 1997); Amy Kaplan and Donald E. Pease, eds., *Cultures of United States Imperialism* (Durham, NC: Duke University Press, 1993).

7. Vicente L. Rafael, "White Love: Surveillance and Nationalist Resistance in the U.S. Colonization of the Philippines," in *Cultures of United States Imperialism*, ed. Amy Kaplan

and Donald E. Pease (Durham, NC: Duke University Press, 1993), 185–218; Paul A. Kramer, *The Blood of Government: Race, Empire, the United States, and the Philippines* (Chapel Hill: University of North Carolina Press, 2006), 3.

8. Warwick Anderson, *Colonial Pathologies: American Tropical Medicine, Race, and Hygiene in the Philippines* (Durham, NC: Duke University Press, 2006); Julian Go, *American Empire and the Politics of Meaning: Elite Political Cultures in the Philippines and Puerto Rico during U.S. Colonialism* (Durham, NC: Duke University Press, 2008).

9. Catherine Ceniza Choy, *Empire of Care: Nursing and Migration in Filipino American History* (Durham, NC: Duke University Press, 2003); Rick Baldoz, *The Third Asiatic Invasion: Empire and Migration in Filipino America, 1898–1946* (New York: New York University Press, 2011). See also Dorothy B. Fujita-Rony, *American Workers, Colonial Power: Philippine Seattle and the Transpacific West, 1919–1941* (Berkeley: University of California Press, 2003); Linda España-Maram, *Creating Masculinity in Los Angeles' Little Manila: Working-Class Filipinos and Popular Culture, 1920s–1950s* (New York: Columbia University Press, 2006); Dawn Bohulano Mabalon, *Little Manila Is in the Heart: The Making of the Filipina/o Community in Stockton, California* (Durham, NC: Duke University Press, 2013).

10. Mary Dudziak, *Cold War Civil Rights: The Image of American Democracy* (Princeton, NJ: Princeton University Press, 2000); Christina Klein, *Cold War Orientalism: Asia in the Middlebrow Imagination, 1945–1961* (Berkeley: University of California Press, 2003); Naoko Shibusawa, *America's Geisha Ally: Reimagining the Japanese Enemy* (Cambridge, MA: Harvard University Press, 2006); Cindy I-Fen Cheng, *Citizens of Asian America: Democracy and Race during the Cold War* (New York: New York University Press, 2013); Ellen D. Wu, *The Color of Success: Asian Americans and the Origins of the Model Minority* (Princeton, NJ: Princeton University Press, 2014).

11. Wu, *The Color of Success*, 8; Cheng, *Citizens of Asian America*.

12. Maria Höhn and Seungsook Moon, eds., *Over There: Living with the U.S. Military Empire from World War II to the Present* (Durham, NC: Duke University Press, 2010); Seungsook Moon, "Regulating Desire, Managing the Empire: U.S. Military Prostitution in South Korea, 1945–1970," in *Over There*, ed. Maria Höhn and Seungsook Moon (Durham, NC: Duke University Press, 2010), 39–77; Ji-Yeon Yuh, *Beyond the Shadow of Camptown: Korea Military Brides in America* (New York: New York University Press, 2004). See also Katherine H. S. Moon, *Sex among Allies: Military Prostitution in U.S.-Korea Relations* (New York: Columbia University Press, 1997); and Cynthia Enloe, *Globalization and Militarism: Feminists Make the Link* (New York: Rowman and Littlefield, 2007).

13. Eiichiro Azuma, "Brokering Race, Culture, and Citizenship: Japanese Americans in Occupied Japan and Postwar National Inclusion," *Journal of American-East Asian Relations* 16, no. 3 (2009): 186, 204.

14. Fujitani, *Race for Empire*.

15. Jun Uchida, *Brokers of Empire: Japanese Settler Colonialism in Korea, 1876–1945* (Cambridge, MA: Harvard University Press, 2011).

16. Setsu Shigematsu and Keith L. Camacho, eds., *Militarized Currents: Toward a Decolonized Future in Asia and the Pacific* (Minneapolis: University of Minnesota Press, 2010), xxx, xxxii; Keith L. Camacho, *Cultures of Commemoration: The Politics of War, Memory, and History in the Mariana Islands* (Honolulu: University of Hawai'i Press, 2011).

17. Candace Fujikane and Jonathan Y. Okamura, eds., *Asian Settler Colonialism: From Local Governance to Habits of Everyday Life in Hawai'i* (Honolulu: University of Hawai'i Press, 2008), 36, 13. See also Dean Saranillio, "Why Asian Settler Colonialism Matters: A Thought Piece on Critiques, Debates, and Indigenous Difference," *Settler Colonial Studies* 3, nos. 3/4 (2013): 280–294.

18. Renisa Mawani, *Colonial Proximities: Crossracial Encounters and Juridical Truths in British Columbia, 1871–1921* (Vancouver: University of British Columbia Press, 2009).

19. Wu, *Radicals on the Road*, 4.

20. Seema Sohi, *Echoes of Mutiny: Race, Surveillance, and Anticolonialism in North America* (New York: Oxford University Press, forthcoming); Moon-Ho Jung, "Seditious Subjects: Race, State Violence, and the U.S. Empire," *Journal of Asian American Studies* 14, no. 2 (2011): 221–247.

21. Yen Le Espiritu, *Body Counts: The Vietnam War and Militarized Refuge(es)* (Berkeley: University of California Press, 2014), 11.

22. Ma Vang, "The Refugee Soldier: A Critique of Recognition and Citizenship in the Hmong Veterans' Naturalization Act of 1997," *positions* 20, no. 3 (2012): 685–712; Mimi Thi Nguyen, *The Gift of Freedom: War, Debt, and Other Refugee Passages* (Durham, NC: Duke University Press, 2012); Jana K. Lipman, "'Give Us a Ship': The Vietnamese Repatriate Movement on Guam, 1975," *American Quarterly* 64, no. 1 (2012): 1–31; Jana K. Lipman, "A Refugee Camp in America: Fort Chaffee and Vietnamese and Cuban Refugees, 1975–1982," *Journal of American Ethnic History* 33, no. 2 (2014): 57–87.

23. Gary Y. Okihiro, *Margins and Mainstreams: Asians in American History and Culture* (Seattle: University of Washington Press, 1994), 28–29. On the term "postimperial exile," see Jodi Kim, *Ends of Empire: Asian American Critique and the Cold War* (Minneapolis: University of Minnesota Press, 2010), 6.

24. Vernadette Vicuña Gonzalez, *Securing Paradise: Tourism and Militarism in Hawai'i and the Philippines* (Durham, NC: Duke University Press, 2013).

FURTHER READING

Anderson, Warwick. *Colonial Pathologies: American Tropical Medicine, Race, and Hygiene in the Philippines.* Durham, NC: Duke University Press, 2006.

Azuma, Eiichiro. *Between Two Empires: Race, History, and Transnationalism in Japanese America.* New York: Oxford University Press, 2005.

———. "Brokering Race, Culture, and Citizenship: Japanese Americans in Occupied Japan and Postwar National Inclusion." *Journal of American-East Asian Relations* 16, no. 3 (2009): 183–211.

Baldoz, Rick. *The Third Asiatic Invasion: Empire and Migration in Filipino America, 1898–1946.* New York: New York University Press, 2011.

Bascara, Victor. *Model-Minority Imperialism.* Minneapolis: University of Minnesota Press, 2006.

Camacho, Keith L. *Cultures of Commemoration: The Politics of War, Memory, and History in the Mariana Islands.* Honolulu: University of Hawai'i Press, 2011.

Chang, Kornel. *Pacific Connections: The Making of the U.S.-Canadian Borderlands.* Berkeley: University of California Press, 2012.

Cheng, Cindy I-Fen. *Citizens of Asian America: Democracy and Race during the Cold War*. New York: New York University Press, 2013.

Cheng, Lucie, and Edna Bonacich, eds. *Labor Immigration under Capitalism: Asian Workers in the United States before World War II*. Berkeley: University of California Press, 1984.

Choy, Catherine Ceniza. *Empire of Care: Nursing and Migration in Filipino American History*. Durham, NC: Duke University Press, 2003.

Cooper, Frederick, and Ann Laura Stoler, eds. *Tensions of Empire: Colonial Cultures in a Bourgeois World*. Berkeley: University of California Press, 1997.

Dudziak, Mary. *Cold War Civil Rights: The Image of American Democracy*. Princeton, NJ: Princeton University Press, 2000.

Duus, Masayo. *Unlikely Liberators: The Men of the 100th and 442nd*. Honolulu: University of Hawai'i Press, 2007.

Enloe, Cynthia. *Globalization and Militarism: Feminists Make the Link*. New York: Rowman and Littlefield, 2007.

España-Maram, Linda. *Creating Masculinity in Los Angeles' Little Manila: Working-Class Filipinos and Popular Culture, 1920s–1950s*. New York: Columbia University Press, 2006.

Espiritu, Yen Le. *Body Counts: The Vietnam War and Militarized Refuge(es)*. Berkeley: University of California Press, 2014.

Feldman, Keith P. *A Shadow over Palestine: The Imperial Life of Race in America*. Minneapolis: University of Minnesota Press, 2015.

Fujikane, Candace, and Jonathan Y. Okamura, eds. *Asian Settler Colonialism: From Local Governance to Habits of Everyday Life in Hawai'i*. Honolulu: University of Hawai'i Press, 2008.

Fujino, Diane. *Samurai among Panthers: Richard Aoki on Race, Resistance, and a Paradoxical Life*. Minneapolis: University of Minnesota Press, 2011.

Fujita-Rony, Dorothy B. *American Workers: Colonial Power: Philippine Seattle and the Transpacific West, 1919–1941*. Berkeley: University of California Press, 2003.

Fujitani, Takashi. *Race for Empire: Koreans as Japanese and Japanese as Americans during World War II*. Berkeley: University of California Press, 2011.

Go, Julian. *American Empire and the Politics of Meaning: Elite Political Cultures in the Philippines and Puerto Rico during U.S. Colonialism*. Durham, NC: Duke University Press, 2008.

Gonzalez, Vernadette Vicuña. *Securing Paradise: Tourism and Militarism in Hawai'i and the Philippines*. Durham, NC: Duke University Press, 2013.

Höhn, Maria, and Seungsook Moon, eds. *Over There: Living with the U.S. Military Empire from World War II to the Present*. Durham, NC: Duke University Press, 2010.

Jung, Moon-Ho. *Coolies and Cane: Race, Labor, and Sugar in the Age of Emancipation*. Baltimore, MD: Johns Hopkins University Press, 2006.

———. "Seditious Subjects: Race, State Violence, and the U.S. Empire." *Journal of Asian American Studies* 14, no. 2 (2011): 221–247.

Kaplan, Amy, and Donald E. Pease, eds. *Cultures of United States Imperialism*. Durham, NC: Duke University Press, 1993.

Kim, Jodi. *Ends of Empire: Asian American Critique and the Cold War*. Minneapolis: University of Minnesota Press, 2010.

Klein, Christina. *Cold War Orientalism: Asia in the Middlebrow Imagination, 1945–1961*. Berkeley: University of California Press, 2003.

Kramer, Paul A. *Blood of Government: Race, Empire, the United States, and the Philippines*. Chapel Hill: University of North Carolina Press, 2006.

Lipman, Jana K. "'Give Us a Ship': The Vietnamese Repatriate Movement on Guam, 1975." *American Quarterly* 64, no. 1 (2012): 1–31.

———. "A Refugee Camp in America: Fort Chaffee and Vietnamese and Cuban Refugees, 1975–1982." *Journal of American Ethnic History* 33, no. 2 (2014): 57–87.

Mabalon, Dawn Bohulano. *Little Manila Is in the Heart: The Making of the Filipina/o Community in Stockton, California.* Durham, NC: Duke University Press, 2013.

Maeda, Daryl J. *Chains of Babylon: The Rise of Asian America.* Minneapolis: University of Minnesota Press, 2009.

Mawani, Renisa. *Colonial Proximities: Crossracial Encounters and Juridical Truths in British Columbia, 1871–1921.* Vancouver: University of British Columbia Press, 2009.

Moon, Katherine H. S. *Sex among Allies: Military Prostitution in U.S.-Korea Relations.* New York: Columbia University Press, 1997.

Moon, Seungsook. "Regulating Desire, Managing the Empire: U.S. Military Prostitution in South Korea, 1945–1970." In *Over There*, edited by Maria Höhn and Seungsook Moon, 39–77. Durham, NC: Duke University Press, 2010.

Muller, Eric L. *Free to Die for Their Country: The Story of the Japanese American Draft Resisters in World War II.* Chicago: University of Chicago Press, 2001.

Nguyen, Mimi Thi. *The Gift of Freedom: War, Debt, and Other Refugee Passages.* Durham, NC: Duke University Press, 2012.

Odo, Franklin. *No Sword to Bury: Japanese Americans in Hawai'i during World War II.* Philadelphia: Temple University Press, 2004.

Okihiro, Gary Y. *Cane Fires: The Anti-Japanese Movement in Hawaii, 1865–1945.* Philadelphia: Temple University Press, 1991.

———. *Margins and Mainstream: Asians in American History and Culture.* Seattle: University of Washington Press, 1994.

Rafael, Vicente L. "White Love: Surveillance and Nationalist Resistance in the U.S. Colonization of the Philippines." In *Cultures of United States Imperialism*, edited by Amy Kaplan and Donald E. Pease, 185–218. Durham, NC: Duke University Press, 1993.

Said, Edward. *Orientalism.* New York: Vintage, 1979.

Saranillio, Dean. "Why Asian Settler Colonialism Matters: A Thought Piece on Critiques, Debates, and Indigenous Difference." *Settler Colonial Studies* 3, nos. 3/4 (2013): 280–294.

Shibusawa, Naoko. *America's Geisha Ally: Reimagining the Japanese Enemy.* Cambridge, MA: Harvard University Press, 2006.

Shigematsu, Setsu, and Keith L. Camacho, eds. *Militarized Currents: Toward a Decolonized Future in Asia and the Pacific.* Minneapolis: University of Minnesota Press, 2010.

Sohi, Seema. *Echoes of Mutiny: Race, Surveillance, and Anticolonialism in North America.* New York: Oxford University Press, forthcoming.

Takaki, Ronald. *Double Victory: A Multicultural History of America in World War II.* New York: Little, Brown, 2000.

Tchen, John Wei Kuo. *New York before Chinatown: Orientalism and the Shaping of American Culture, 1776–1882.* Baltimore, MD: Johns Hopkins University Press, 1999.

Uchida, Jun. *Brokers of Empire: Japanese Settler Colonialism in Korea, 1876–1945.* Cambridge, MA: Harvard University Press, 2011.

Vang, Ma. "The Refugee Soldier: A Critique of Recognition and Citizenship in the Hmong Veterans' Naturalization Act of 1997." *positions* 20:3 (2012): 685–712.

Wong, K. Scott. *Americans First: Chinese Americans and the Second World War.* Cambridge, MA: Harvard University Press, 2005.

Wu, Ellen D. *The Color of Success: Asian Americans and the Origins of the Model Minority.* Princeton, NJ: Princeton University Press, 2014.

Wu, Judy Tzu-Chun. *Radicals on the Road: Internationalism, Orientalism, and Feminism during the Vietnam Era.* Ithaca, NY: Cornell University Press, 2013.

Yuh, Ji-Yeon. *Beyond the Shadow of Camptown: Korean Military Brides in America.* New York: New York University Press, 2004.

CHAPTER 16

QUEER ASIAN AMERICAN HISTORIOGRAPHY

AMY SUEYOSHI

QUEERNESS has only just become visible in Asian American studies. Before the mid-1990s few if any publications appeared on LGBT Asians in America. In the field of history itself, the dearth is even more pronounced. While queer texts in the past twenty years have multiplied significantly in literary criticism and cultural studies, they remain scant in number in Asian American history. So legitimated has queer studies become in some disciplines that those who do not identify as LGBT are taking up queer topics as a mark of edge and intellect. One faculty member in American Studies and Ethnicity at the University of Southern California went so far as to note that all scholars now must take into account queer theory and queer possibilities if they hoped their work to be seen as rigorous. Yet in Asian American studies, the LGBT experience remains marginal. In Asian American history in particular, the number of people specializing in queer studies might be counted on one hand. While five is better than zero and the Asian American queer experience is no longer in complete darkness, the field still remains in desperate need of robust growth even as the small numbers do tremendous intellectual work.

The dearth of queer historians can hardly be blamed on the individual Asian Americanist. A legacy of disincentives inhibits the historian from pursuing LGBT Asian America as a research area. In 2000, Susan Lee Johnson noted that despite the fact that scholarly inquiry into the history of sexuality has "exploded" in the past two decades, including the birth of the *Journal of History of Sexuality* in 1990, relative silence on sex and sexuality has reigned in the history of the North American West. Doubters assert that sexuality is "private," "individual," and without historical significance since it is a "trivial pursuit" motivated by "prurient" interests.[1] Within Asian American studies as well, founders of the field have severely restricted the proliferation of queer possibilities. Frank Chin, Jeffrey Paul Chan, and their yellow brethren no doubt dissuaded many from even touching queer topics with their homophobic diatribes of the 1970s.[2] Award-winning journalist and independent scholar Helen Zia remembers being subjected to a "lesbian trial" when fellow community organizers, both Asian and African American, invited her to a meeting to discuss her sexual orientation. If she were a lesbian she would "harm" their "organizing efforts." In that moment she remembers "stepping into the closet and slamming the door shut" to preserve her activist family.[3]

Writing about queer desires might additionally seem blasphemous in a field that has historically interpreted sexuality as a site of oppression. In the earliest publications on Asian American sexuality by historians such as Mary Roberts Coolidge, Yuji Ichioka, and Lucie Cheng Hirata, men languished painfully in bachelor societies and women endured forced sex work. These works laid the groundwork for later publications by Asian Americanists Robert Lee and George Anthony Peffer who highlighted sexually oppressed Asian men and women in America. Notably, in 2003 Madeline Hsu illuminated how Chinese men steeped in a tradition of homosocial interaction may not have been as deprived as more insistently heteronormative histories have declared.[4] Yet single-sex communities continue to appear as sites of deprivation in the popular imagination. As late as 2014, the award-winning journalist Nicholas Hune-Brown wrote of Chinese bachelor societies as "strange, often unhappy places"—"neighbourhoods of grown men living together, sleeping in bunk beds." Indeed, no amount of recent "gay streaming," the mainstreaming of gay characters on television, could eradicate the presumption that a bachelor society would be anything but oppressive.[5] Moreover as Asian Americanists criticize representations of emasculated Asian men as "faggots," embracing the "homo" within ourselves might be akin to subscribing to the stereotype.[6]

Being a queer historian seems to have financial consequences as well.[7] Even as America seems more accepting of gays and lesbians in recent years, in at least two faculty searches at research universities—one in Indiana and another in Texas—the dean refused to hire the search committee's top candidate who were each visibly queer historians specializing in LGBT history. While Nayan Shah described the "dramatic" development of the history of Asian American sexuality broadly since 1990, no wonder that works specifically on queer sexuality are still small in number.[8] Even if the historian-in-training decides to brave the barriers ahead of her in queer studies, she will likely find herself with compromised employment options, unable to convince the most powerful that a queer should be teaching LGBT history to America's young adults.

Among nonprofit organizations charged with bringing history to a broader public, we see the continued discounting of sexuality. One queer history museum took down its extremely popular sex toys exhibit that highlighted sexual pleasure as political power, due to fears that an exhibit case displaying a cityscape of dildos standing erect would dissuade politicians and banks from giving their support. More recently, when I was introduced as a possible resource for an Asian American historical society as a historian specializing in sexuality, the program director responded, "Ooh la la," with eyebrows raised followed by a chuckle. The response signaled the organization's devaluation of the history of sexuality as opposed to labor or politics, in its public programming and exhibits. For sure, queer history continues to face widespread public perception as illicit or recreational, but never as a serious intellectual endeavor.

Many attribute the Asian American community's reluctance to take on sexuality to the presumption that Asians are culturally conservative. Religious studies scholars attribute the Asian community's refusal to accept same-sex sexuality to Confucianism and Christianity. In 2005 Alain Dang and Mandy Hu, in their survey for the National Gay and Lesbian Taskforce, declared that homophobia and transphobia were "a problem" within Asian Pacific American communities.[9] Community denial fuels the continued erasure of queers in history. Though plainly visible evidence has pointed to people of prominence such as Margaret Chung and Yone Noguchi as likely queer, scholars of Asian descent have refused to address individual sexuality until recently.[10] Because heteronormativity compels people to presume that it must be better to be seen as "normal" than to carry the stigmatized label of queer, documenting a historical figure as queer requires definitive evidence of same-sex sexuality.[11]

As much as many of us have come to believe that Asian culture is at the root of Asian American homophobia, the political scientist Cathy Cohen's argument that a racially marginalized community such as African Americans striving for respectability within racist America would less likely embrace queerness may just as powerfully apply to an immigrant population.[12] Asians too struggle for acceptance in white America as they grapple also with the ignominy of shame within their own communities. Ironically, throughout numerous Asian countries, same-sex sexualities and queer genders existed acceptably before Western imperialism mandated strict moral codes that restricted native customs and people.[13]

While naysayers of queer history also cite a lack of sources for its documentation, the real trouble may lie in how materials deemed historically significant are collected and catalogued. If we imagined sex and love to be as crucial in understanding American politics as presidents, we would have more archives and libraries dedicated exclusively to sexuality and desire. Since the 1990s as well, technological developments in research tools such as LexisNexis have transformed the accessibility of source material on sexuality through instantaneous keyword searches using terms such as "crime against nature," "fellatio," and "buggery." Historians of sexuality no longer have to search court documents and newspapers page by page as if looking for a needle in haystack.

The most accessible records, however, can also be the most problematic. Because same-sex sexuality has a longer history of criminalization rather than acceptance, queers most readily appear in arrest records and court proceedings. Before World War II, men in their thirties having sex with young men in their late teens, and sometimes younger, appeared in criminal records all too often. In graduate school in the 1990s, a classmate also specializing in queer history confided in me, "What do we do with these sources?" Cases that suggested sexual abuse, rape, and violence upon male children seemed tricky to bring up in a field struggling for intellectual legitimacy, not to mention during a time when homophobes insisted homosexuality and pedophilia to be one and the same. Yet these very same cases, if we dare to engage them, hold untold stories of race, sexuality, power, and disability.

In 1912 Dong Pok Yip appeared before the California State Supreme Court in hopes of appealing his conviction of assault on nine-year-old Albert Hondeville. He had originally been charged with an attempt to commit sodomy but was convicted instead of the lesser offense of "simple assault." Dong Pok Yip contended that with the jury's acquittal of the higher offense, there remained no evidence that showed an intent to commit any other sort of assault. A Portuguese American bookkeeper by the last name of Rodrigues had spied the two sitting together on the Antioch Pier. Dong Pok Yip appeared to be teaching Hondeville how to fish. When Dong put his arm around Hondeville and whispered something in his ear, Rodrigues grew suspicious. Dong then helped Hondeville to his feet and the two walked hand-in-hand toward an oil tank near some brush about a foot in height. Rodrigues followed and found them stooping, Dong in the back of Hondeville and holding his waist. He noticed the "back of the boy's overalls hung down" and the "Chinaman's trousers unbuttoned in the front." When the two saw the peeping Rodrigues, they quickly stood up. Hondeville slipped on one of the suspenders of his overalls and Dong buttoned up his pants.[14]

In contrast to Rodrigues's account, the nine-year-old Hondeville testified that he was facing Dong the entire time. Dong had, in fact, made a "disgusting proposal" regarding his sister, promised to give him two dollars, and then exposed his penis. The court had decided to allow Hondeville's testimony after some deliberation about his questionable intelligence, which they characterized as "retarded mental development."[15]

While the Supreme Court upheld the decision of the lower court maintaining the simple assault conviction, Dong Pok Yip's case provokes a number of questions not easily answerable in a historical context uniformly understood as anti-Asian and homophobic. If Dong Pok Yip had just miraculously gotten away with the "intent to commit the felonious crime against nature," it seems absurdly bold for him to further attempt to reverse the decision of the lesser offense of simple assault. Dong Pok Yip's fishing lesson for Albert Hondeville and his acquaintance with his sister appear unusually friendly in a world in which whites appeared fearful and antagonistic toward Chinese. Moreover, how did Rodrigues suspect that Dong Pok Yip was "trying to use the boy as [a] female" had he not himself had some familiarity with anal sex? Finally, how is it that a "Chinaman" could be found not guilty of sodomy through the dissenting account of a child "not even of ordinary intelligence" as opposed to supposedly more reliable testimony from a white bookkeeper?

If we think sociologically, no occurrence, including what might appear to be anomalous, is random or simply an act of individual free will. Events and outcomes are embedded in a sociocultural context to make perfect sense in that given moment. Dong Pok Yip's case appeared as one of more than a handful in the early decades of the twentieth century in which an Asian man appeared to persuade a judge or jury that he was not morally degenerate even when caught literally with his pants down. As individual or private sex acts might appear, piecing them together to create a collective statement about race, gender, or desire remains the task of the historian of sexuality. The knot of Dong Pok Yip and his seeming contradictions if untied would likely reveal new complexities in the Asian American experience.

As early as 2003 Peter Boag had tackled a number of these court cases and placed them within a larger queer history of the Pacific Northwest. Two years later Nayan Shah gave more focused attention to these records, the majority involving Asian Indian men playing the active or insertive role in sex with white youth. Both argued that persecution of South Asian men as sodomizing white boys reflected a growing fear around the influx of immigrant men in the Pacific Northwest. Interestingly, these cases clearly defied established notions of the historically emasculated Asian men.[16]

Indeed, when the cultural critic Tina Takemoto closely analyzed the sparse records remaining on a confirmed gay Japanese immigrant, Jiro Onuma, incarcerated at the Topaz concentration camp during World War II, she brought new insight into sources typically read as American patriotism or perseverance in Japanese American history. By starting with the presumption that "gays in Topaz" in fact existed, she read dandyism, queer camp, alienation, and subversion in photographs historically viewed as evidence of Americanization among Japanese in the United States.[17]

Despite the significant potential of reframing history through the lens of marginalized desires, queer actors in Asian American history remain few and far between. Chris Friday in 1994 may have been the first historian to acknowledge the existence of queer desires among early Asians in America in his book on labor in the canned salmon industry. Just a few lines suggested same-sex intimacies taking place among Filipinos in the Pacific Northwest.[18] Not until 2002 would Eric Wat then publish what may have been the first booklength oral history on Asian American queer history. Wat deliberately chose to present his interviews as interviews rather than embed them in the conventional format of a linear narrative since history is "not linear or always progressive."[19] While Wat's book plays a foundational role in queer Asian American history, it hardly registers in the professional field of history, perhaps in part because of its format, the trade versus university press that published his book, or his position as an independent scholar with no academic affiliation. Three years later, Judy Wu declared in her book that Margaret Chung, considered to be the first Chinese American surgeon and the founder of the hospital of Western medicine in San Francisco Chinatown, may have been a lesbian.[20] While Wu's assertions about Chung's sexuality are more speculative than certain, her publication blasted open the possibility of queer Asians in American history before the 1960s when LGBT Asians became suddenly visible in social protest movements. In 2012, my own book on Yone Noguchi and his intimate affairs exposed the existence of same-sex desire and love among Japanese immigrants at the turn of the nineteenth century.[21] In the midst of these few published works, unpublished manuscripts on queer Asian and Pacific Islander history, such as dissertations by Trinity Ordona and Alice Hom, additionally fill an egregious void.[22]

Perhaps precisely because of the marginal status and resulting dearth of literature within queer Asian American history, the field borrows heavily from developments in the interdisciplinary field of queer studies. Queer Asian American historians incorporate theories from psychoanalysis, performance studies, literature, visual studies, and countless other disciplines to theorize and bring better context to private desires and sex acts in the past. These cross-disciplinary linkages enable the queer Asian Americanist to more successfully clarify and articulate the profound ideological significance of sexuality in history in the midst of intellectual opposition.

For example, the literary critic Andrew Leong proposed an "epistemology of the pocket" as opposed to the queer theorist Eve Sedgwick's "epistemology of the closet." Leong describes the pocket as a smaller space that "due to its proximity to the body, ought to be more 'private,' but because of its placement on the body, is subject to public view." It accommodates only partial concealment, since "you can hide a body in a closet but not in a pocket." Leong added, "For propertied, Anglo-American men with rooms of their own, the closet might be an appropriate figure for the possession of a hidden identity. The pocket might be more fitting for the countless others with more precarious relationships to individual property and identity: colonized peoples who have had their property taken from them; people who have been treated *as* property; aliens ineligible for citizenship; migrant workers."[23] For queer Asians who sought to keep their desires private particularly in early Asian American history, Leong's proposed pocket serves as a useful metaphor for their all-too-small shelter, which rendered them visible even as they hoped to be invisible. Historians of queer Asian America rely on these ill-fitting pockets, calling attention to parts protruding that persons more tasteful might respectfully ignore.

While unearthing queer people in history seems difficult, some have had more success "queering" familiar histories of Asian America steeped in unfaltering heterosexuality. In 2002 Melinda De Jesus "reclaimed queerness" by illuminating the homoerotic potential in Carlos Bulosan's *America Is in the Heart* and Bienvenido Santos's *Scent of Apples*, two classic texts in Filipino American history. Four years earlier, Daniel Y. Kim went so far as to queer even the aforementioned openly homophobic forefather of Asian American studies, Frank Chin, due to his obsession with men and their masculinity, both white and yellow. Andrew Leong, the previously cited theorist of the "pocket," also brought to light the queer and often unacknowledged "failures" of the Issei or the Japanese immigrant world in his translation of Shoson Nagahara's 1925 novel *Lament in the Night*. Many more who are queering the Asian American canon are, as De Jesus asserts, "speaking the unspeakable."[24]

As history drags its heels to the queer ball, others largely in English and cultural studies have enthusiastically taken up LGBT topics in a veritable explosion of works in the new millennium. David Eng, Martin Manalansan, Gayatri Gopinath, and Jasbir Puar all published groundbreaking books in queer Asian American studies. A younger generation of scholars such as Eng-Beng Lim and Nguyen Tan Hoang are upending standard tropes of oppression in their works by foregrounding queer Asian camp and pleasure even within postcolonial operations of power and desire.[25]

Scholarly publication on queer topics began most significantly in the 1990s outside the field of history, with *Amerasia Journal,* the first academic journal in Asian American studies. Its special issue titled "Dimensions in Desire," published in 1994, contained eighteen entries and inspired a second generation of queer Asian Americanists hoping to study sexuality in the field. A little over twenty years after the journal's first issue in 1971 and ostensibly the birth of Asian American studies as an academic field, the inclusion felt long overdue. Yet, if we consider the professionalization of the much older academic discipline of U.S. history in the 1890s and the rise of queer studies within the field in the 1980s, Asian American queer history seems to have arrived at warp speed. *Amerasia*'s editor Russell Leong would republish the "Dimensions in Desire" as a book retitled *Asian American Sexualities* with eight additional entries later in 1996. Two years later David Eng and Alice Hom produced a second edited collection on queer Asian America. Both anthologies, while interdisciplinary, had just one essay on queer Asian American history out of fifty entries total, though several more were historical in content in the form of an interview or memoir.[26]

Notably, before academia decided to open its doors to queer studies, Asian American activists joined with other queer people of color to self-publish their own experiences, in hopes of changing the heteronormative discourse around race, inequality, and gender. Radical women and feminists literally set up printing presses in their home to establish publishing houses such as Kitchen Table.[27] Lesbian and bisexual Asian women writers contributed to anthologies dedicated to women of color through poetry and prose. A number of writers such as Willyce Kim, Kitty Tsui, Merle Woo, and Chea Villanueva published their own single-authored books throughout the 1970s, 1980s, and 1990s.[28] Then, in 1994 Asian Pacific Islander lesbian and bisexual women produced an anthology of over one hundred entries under the editorship of Sharon Lim-Hing, titled *The Very Inside*. She began thinking about producing the book in the summer of 1990 as she walked home in defiant anticipation of the local teenagers calling her "chink" in Somerville, Massachusetts. After arriving home, in the heat of her apartment, and with the neighbor's dog barking incessantly, Lim-Hing in her discomfort decided that Asian and Pacific Islander lesbians should have a book of their own. At the time Asian women's writings appeared only as two or so contributions as part of women of color anthologies or as tokens toward diversity in white anthologies. There did exist an earlier anthology of Asian American lesbians titled *Between the Lines* with just six contributors from Santa Cruz. The publication, however, was out of print and hard to obtain. Lim-Hing sought to create something as large as Gloria Anzaldúa's and Cherrie Moraga's *This Bridge Called My Back* to speak to Asian Pacific bisexual and lesbian women's strength, beauty, creativity, and rage so that these women would be more than just "a blip on the graph at the intersection of 'race' and sexual preference, nor . . . the hub of triple oppressions."[29] Six years later, Quang Bao and Hanya Yanagihara published another anthology titled *Take Out* with the support of the Asian American Writer's Workshop in New York. More artistry and less activism motivated their publication, which the editors hoped would force readers "to reevaluate [their] conceptions of gay Asian America." The collection comprised articles mostly by men since the editors decided to not "worry too much about gender equity" since it was "far better to sacrifice quantity for quality."[30] Despite the editors' less-than-feminist impulse, writings in *Take Out*, along with the numerous creative works published earlier, fill out an otherwise undernourished field with a slew of primary sources that can be used in teaching and writing about Asian American queer history.

First-person queer and Asian American publications continue today, perhaps more robustly in the trade press rather than in the academic world. In 1997, *Honor Thy Children* detailed the loss of Al and Jane Nakatani's three sons. A decade later Thomas

Beatie, whose father was of Filipino and Korean descent, would also come out with his own memoir after storming the daytime television circuit as the "pregnant transman." Two years earlier the legal scholar Kenji Yoshino used his own sexuality as a springboard to discuss how coerced conformity stood as the final barrier to civil rights. In 2012 Marsha Aizumi authored *Two Spirits, One Heart* for her transgender son Aiden.[31] Countless blogs from queer Asians also fill the Internet to expound upon the importance of community engagement and queer empowerment through personal experiences.

No doubt queer Asian America has grown tremendously in the past two decades. In universities across the nation, queer and Asian student groups are cropping up. In the San Francisco Bay Area alone, four institutions—University of California at Berkeley, San Francisco State University, San Jose State University, and Stanford—all have student-run organizations that program and mount educational workshops centered around LGBT Asian issues. As more teenagers are arriving at college being already out, a growing queer field in Asian American studies will only engage and compel these youth craving to see themselves in the curriculum. For them, a reading assignment in queer Asian American studies can be earth-shattering. For others who do not identify as LGBT, learning about queer studies is life-changing in its transformative potential. Queer Asian American studies can eradicate sex negativity within the Asian American community and radicalize how people interact with one another. Theorists have pushed queer studies to be about revolution, building upon work from activists in the 1970s and 1980s who sought to up-end normative notions of desire, propriety, and success. In this version, women would shave just a part of their heads and wear combat boots. Men might dye their hair pink and purple and wear glitter lip gloss. Gay men and lesbian would have sex with each other, all the while still identifying as gay or lesbian. Most importantly, queers would band together to eradicate poverty, stamp out racism, and protest Western imperialism. All would not always work out perfectly, but these fairies, butches, and trannies would put their all into transforming the world into a queer nation.

As queer Asian American history forges ahead with a limited number of works in the field, the publications are nearly always informed by the most recent developments in both queer studies and Asian American studies. Notably postmodern, transnational, and postcolonial from its beginnings, queer Asian American history uncovers queers broadly without ascribing to more limited categories of "gay" and "lesbian" and elucidates queer ways of thinking, all the while insisting on the radical potential of a queer nation that is also Asian American.

Notes

1. Susan Lee Johnson, "'My Own Private Life': Toward a History of Desire in Gold Rush California," *California History* 79, no. 2 (2000): 317.
2. Frank Chin and Jeffrey Paul Chan, "Racist Love," in *Seeing Through Shuck*, ed. Richard Kostelanetz (New York: Ballantine, 1972), 65–79.

3. Helen Zia, *Asian American Dreams: The Emergence of an American People* (New York: Farrar, Straus and Giroux, 2000), 228–229.

4. Mary Roberts Coolidge, *Chinese Immigration* (New York: Henry Holt, 1909); Yuji Ichioka, "Ameyuki-san: Japanese Prostitutes in Nineteenth-Century America," *Amerasia Journal* 4, no. 1 (1977): 1–22; Lucie Cheng Hirata, "Free, Indentured, Enslaved: Chinese Prostitutes in Nineteenth Century America," *Signs* 5, no. 1 (1979): 3–29; George Anthony Peffer, *If They Don't Bring Their Women Here: Chinese Female Immigration before Exclusion* (Urbana: University of Illinois Press, 1999); Robert G. Lee, *Orientals: Asian Americans in Popular Culture* (Philadelphia: Temple University Press, 1999); Madeline Y. Hsu, "Unwrapping Orientalist Constraints: Restoring Homosocial Normativity to Chinese American History," *Amerasia Journal* 29, no. 2 (2003): 230–253.

5. Nicholas Hune-Brown, "The Return of Chinese Bachelor Societies," Hazlitt, last modified February 6, 2014, http://penguinrandomhouse.ca/hazlitt/blog/return-chinese-bachelor-societies; Eve Ng, "'A Post-Gay' Era? Media Gaystreaming, Homonormativity, and the Politics of LGBT Integration," *Communication, Culture, and Critique* 6 (2013): 258–283.

6. David Eng, *Racial Castration: Managing Masculinity in Asian America* (Durham, NC: Duke University Press, 2001); Celine Parreñas Shimizu, *Straitjacket Sexualities: Unbinding Asian American Masculinities in the Movies* (Stanford, CA: Stanford University Press, 2012).

7. Gayle Rubin, "Blood under the Bridge: Reflections on 'Thinking Sex,'" *GLQ: A Journal of Lesbian and Gay Studies* 17, no. 1 (2010): 15–48.

8. Nayan Shah, "Race-ing Sex," *Frontiers: A Journal of Women Studies* 35, no. 1 (2014): 26–36.

9. Sumie Okazaki, "Influences of Culture on Asian Americans' Sexuality," *Journal of Sex Research* 39, no. 1 (February 2002): 34–41; Yongliang Feng, Chaohua Lou, Ersheng Gao, Xiaowen Tu, Yan Cheng, Mark R. Emerson, and Laurie S. Zabin, "Adolescents' and Young Adults' Perception of Homosexuality and Related Factors in Three Asian Cities," *Journal of Adolescent Health* 50, no. 3 (2012): S52–S60; Boyung Lee, "Teaching Justice and Living Peace: Body, Sexuality, and Religious Education in Asian-American Communities," *Religious Education* 101, no. 3 (2006): 402–419; Alain Dang and Mandy Hu, *Asian Pacific American Lesbian, Gay, Bisexual and Transgender People: A Community Portrait. A Report from New York's Queer Asian Pacific Legacy Conference, 2004* (New York: National Gay and Lesbian Task Force Policy Institute, 2005).

10. Judy Tzu-Chun Wu, "Was Mom Chung 'A Sister Lesbian'? Asian American Gender Experimentation and Interracial Homoeroticism," *Journal of Women's History* 13, no. 1 (2001): 58–82; Amy Sueyoshi, "Intimate Inequalities: Interracial Affection and Same-sex Love in the 'Heterosexual' Life of Yone Noguchi, 1897–1909," *Journal of American Ethnic History* 29, no. 4 (2010): 22–44.

11. Amy Sueyoshi, "Finding Fellatio: Friendship, History, and Yone Noguchi" in *Embodying Asian/American Sexualities*, ed. Gina Masequesmay and Sean Metzger (New York: Rowman and Littlefield, 2009), 157–172.

12. Cathy Cohen, *Boundaries of Blackness: AIDS and the Breakdown of Black Politics* (Chicago: University of Chicago Press, 1999).

13. For the specific case of Japan, see Gary Leupp, *Male Colors: The Construction of Homosexuality in Tokugawa Japan* (Berkeley: University of California Press, 1995); Gregory M. Pflugfelder, *Cartographies of Desire: Male-male Sexuality in Japanese Discourse, 1600–1950* (Berkeley: University of California Press, 1999); Joseph Hawkins, "Japan's Journey into Homophobia," *Gay and Lesbian Review* 7, no. 1 (2000): 36–71.

14. *The People v. Dong Pok Yip*, 164 Cal. 143 (1912); Nayan Shah, *Stranger Intimacy: Contesting Race, Sexuality, and the Law in the North American West* (Berkeley: University of California Press, 2011).

15. *The People v. Dong Pok Yip*.

16. Peter Boag, *Same-sex Affairs: Constructing and Controlling Homosexuality in the Pacific Northwest* (Berkeley: University of California Press, 2003); Nayan Shah, "Between 'Oriental Depravity' and 'Natural Degenerates': Spatial Borderlands and the Making of Ordinary Americans," *American Quarterly* 57, no. 3 (2005): 703–725.

17. Tina Takemoto, "Looking for Jiro Onuma: A Queer Meditation on the Incarceration of Japanese Americans during World War II," *GLQ: A Journal of Gay and Lesbian Studies* 20, no. 3 (2013): 241–275.

18. Chris Friday, *Organizing Asian American Labor: The Pacific Coast Canned-Salmon Industry, 1870–1942* (Philadelphia: Temple University Press, 1994).

19. Eric C. Wat, *The Making of a Gay Asian Community: An Oral History of Pre-AIDS Los Angeles* (Boston: Rowman and Littlefield, 2002).

20. Judy Tzu-Chun Wu, *Doctor Mom Chung of the Fair-haired Bastards: The Life of a Wartime Celebrity* (Berkeley: University of California Press, 2005). John Howard similarly suggests the existence of gay men incarcerated at Rohwer and Jerome concentration camps through the eyes of the humanitarian Earl Finch, who would invite Japanese American men over for dinner at his home. See John Howard, *Concentration Camps on the Home Front: Japanese American in the House of Jim Crow* (Chicago: University of Chicago Press, 2008).

21. Amy Sueyoshi, *Queer Compulsions: Race, Nation, and Sexuality in the Affairs of Yone Noguchi* (Honolulu: University of Hawai'i Press, 2012).

22. Trinity Ann Ordona, "Coming Out Together: An Ethnohistory of the Asian and Pacific Islander Queer Women's and Transgendered People's Movement of San Francisco" (Ph.D. dissertation, University of California at Santa Cruz, 2000); Alice Hom, "Unifying Differences: Lesbian of Color Organizing in Los Angeles and New York" (Ph.D. dissertation, Claremont Graduate University, 2011).

23. Andrew Leong, "The Pocket and the Watch: A Collective Individualist Reading of Japanese American Literature," *Verge: Studies in Global Asias* 1.2 (2015): 76–114.

24. Melinda De Jesus, "Rereading History, Rewriting Desire: Reclaiming Queerness in Carlos Bulosan's 'America Is in the Heart' and Bienvenido Santos' 'Scent of Apples,' " *Journal of Asian American Studies* 5, no. 2 (2002): 91–111; Daniel Y. Kim, "The Strange Love of Frank Chin," in *Q&A: Queer in Asian America*, ed. David Eng and Alice Y. Hom (Philadelphia: Temple University Press, 1998), 270–303. See also Lee, *Orientals* and Shah, *Contagious Divides*.

25. Eng, *Racial Castration*; Martin Manalansan, *Global Divas: Filipino Gay Men in the Diaspora* (Durham, NC: Duke University Press, 2003); Gayatri Gopinath, *Impossible Desires: Queer Diasporas and South Asian Public Cultures* (Durham, NC: Duke University Press, 2005); Jasbir Puar, *Terrorist Assemblages: Homonationalism in Queer Times* (Durham, NC: Duke University Press, 2007); Eng-Beng Lim, *Brown Boys and Rice Queens: Spellbinding Performances in the Asias* (New York: New York University Press, 2014); Nguyen Tan Hoang, *A View from the Bottom: Asian American Masculinity and Sexual Representation* (Durham, NC: Duke University Press, 2014). See also Joon Oluchi Lee, "Joy of the Castrated Boy," *Social Text* 23, no. 3 (2004): 35–56.

26. *Amerasia Journal: Dimensions in Desire* 20, no. 1 (1994); Russell Leong, ed., *Asian American Sexualities: Dimensions of the Gay and Lesbian Experience* (New York: Routledge, 1996);

David L. Eng and Alice Y. Hom, *Q&A: Queer in Asian America* (Philadelphia: Temple University Press, 1998). Since 1994, *Amerasia* has published two additional special issues on same-sex sexuality. See *Amerasia Journal: Marriage Equality Debate* 32, no. 1 (2006), and *Amerasia Journal: Further Desire—Asian and Asian American Sexualities* 37, no. 2 (2011). For a more recently published interdisciplinary anthology after *Asian American Sexualities* and *Q&A,* see Metzger and Masequesmay, *Embodying Asian/American Sexualities.*

27. Jaime M. Grant, "Building Community-Based Coalitions from Academe: The Union Institute and the Kitchen Table: Women of Color Press Transition Coalition," *Signs* 21, no. 4 (1996): 1024–1033.

28. Cherrie Moraga and Gloria Anzaldúa, eds., *This Bridge Called My Back: Writings by Radical Women of Color* (Watertown, MA: Persephone, 1981); Willyce Kim, *Eating Artichokes* (Oakland, CA: Women's Press Collective, 1972); Willyce Kim, *Dancer Dawkins and the California Kid* (Boston: Alyson, 1985); Kitty Tsui, *The Words of a Woman Who Breathes Fire* (New York: Spinsters Ink, 1983); Kitty Tsui, *Breathless: Erotica* (Ithaca, NY: Firebrand, 1996); Merle Woo, *Yellow Woman Speaks: Selected Poems* (Seattle: Radical Women, 1986); Chea Villanueva, *Jessie's Song and Other Stories* (New York: Masquerade, 1995); Chea Villanueva, *Bulletproof Butches* (New York: Hard Candy, 1997).

29. Sharon Lim-Hing, *The Very Inside: An Anthology of Writing by Asian and Pacific Islander Lesbian and Bisexual Women* (Toronto: Sister Vision, 1994). For the earlier anthology from Santa Cruz, see C. Chung, A. Kim, and A. K. Lemeshewsky, *Between the Lines: An Anthology of Pacific/Asian Lesbians of Santa Cruz, California* (Santa Cruz, CA: Dancing Bird, 1987).

30. Quang Bao and Hanya Yanagihara, *Take Out: Queer Writing from Asian Pacific America* (New York: Asian American Writer's Workshop, 2000).

31. Molly Fumia, *Honor Thy Children: One Family's Journey to Wholeness* (Berkeley, CA: Conari, 1997); Thomas Beatie, *Labor of Love: The Story of One Man's Extraordinary Pregnancy* (Berkeley: Seal, 2008); Kenji Yoshino, *Covering: The Hidden Assault on Our Civil Rights* (New York: Random House, 2006); Marsha Aizumi, *Two Spirits, One Heart: A Mother, Her Transgender Son, and Their Journey to Love and Acceptance* (Bronx, NY: Magnus, 2012).

FURTHER READING

Aguilar-San Juan, Karin. "Landmarks in Literature by Asian American Lesbians." *Signs* 18.4 (1993): 936–943.

Ahmed, Sara. *The Promise of Happiness.* Durham, NC: Duke University Press, 2010.

Chin, John J. "Let's Not Ignore a Growing HIV Problem for Asians and Pacific Islanders in the U.S." *Journal of Urban Health* 84.5 (2007): 642–647.

Eng, David. *Feeling of Kinship: Queer Liberalism and the Racialization of Intimacy.* Durham, NC: Duke University Press, 2010.

Eng, David, Judith Halberstam, and José Esteban Múnoz, eds. *What's Queer About Queer Studies Now?* Durham, NC, Brooklyn, NY: Duke University Press; Ubiquity Distributors, 2005.

Hwang, David Henry. *M. Butterfly.* New York: American Library, 1989.

Luibheid, Eithne. *Entry Denied: Controlling Sexuality at the Border.* Minneapolis: University of Minnesota Press, 2002.

Manalansan IV, Martin F. "Queer Worldings: The Messy Art of Being Global in Manila and New York." *Antipode* 47.3 (2015): 566–579.

Masequesmay, Gina. "How Religious Communities Can Help LGBTIQQ Asian Americans Come Home." *Theology and Sexuality* 17.3 (2011): 319–335.

———. "Emergence of Queer Vietnamese America." *Amerasia Journal* 29.1 (2003): 117–134.

Massad, Joseph. "Re-Orienting Desire: The Gay International and the Arab World." *Public Culture* 14.2 (2002): 361–386.

Tongson, Karen. *Queer Suburban Imaginaries*. New York: New York University Press, 2011.

Uyehara, Denise. *Hello (sex) Kitty*. Alexandria, VA: Alexander Street, 2004.

Yew, Chay. *Porcelain, and A Language of Their Own: Two Plays*. New York: Grove Press, 1997.

CHAPTER 17

THE STUDY OF ASIAN AMERICAN FAMILIES

XIAOJIAN ZHAO

As the oldest human social institution, the family has received substantial attention and scrutiny since the 1960s. Academic interest in Asian American families started to grow in the 1980s, following a series of media reports that portrayed young Asian Americans as extraordinary achievers. The growth of the Asian American population and its improved public image have created a favorable climate for academic research. Given the diversity of the ethnic population, the fluidity of family patterns, and the complexity of social issues involved, discussions on the character of Asian American families are also open to dispute.

HISTORICAL FAMILIES

There are relatively few studies of historical Asian American families. Before World War II, having a family in the United States was considered a luxury for immigrants from Asia. Efforts to document early immigrant families are part of a scholarly maneuver to overturn negative stereotypical images of Asian Americans in "bachelor societies." Some studies show that, like their counterparts from other parts of the world, the majority of pioneering Asian immigrants first arrived without female companions. Once settled, they tried to send for their wives and children or to form families, but exclusion made it difficult. Based on systematic analysis of government documents—laws, congressional and court records, and immigration files—several studies argue that the imbalanced sex ratio of the Asian immigrant population before World War II was not due to the personal preferences of male immigrants, but a result of legal hurdles that prohibited Asian women from immigrating. Asian immigrant communities fought for decades to bring women to the United States; their collective efforts included filing grievances in court and lobbying Congress to amend exclusion laws. Meanwhile, individual immigrants developed tactics to circumvent legal restrictions.[1]

With slightly different angles, a few studies trace the myriad ways in which families were formed or functioned during the exclusion era. Based on census and local records, for example, one study tells the story of unions between male immigrants from India and women from Mexico, showing how the couples' race, religion, and cultural backgrounds shaped their family structure and childrearing. Shifting the focus from the United States to immigrants' native places and utilizing a variety of local documents in China, another study explores the ways that families were maintained and continued when husbands and wives lived an ocean apart. There are also books on family history that utilize letters, personal accounts, and immigration documents. One book examines the transnational natures of Chinese Americans, illuminating how complex historical circumstances in both the United States and China pushed the immigrants and their families back and forth across the Pacific. Another tells the story of a well-known Japanese American family from Hood River, Oregon. It illustrates the courage, determination, and aspirations of the immigrant generation to settle in the United States, the anti-Japanese sentiment that tore family members apart during World War II, and efforts of the third generation to preserve family legacy. The story of a Japanese family of farmworkers in California is told in two books, from the perspectives of an immigrant woman and then her husband. Another book documents four generations of an interracial Chinese American family in Los Angeles. The history of one pioneering Korean immigrant family was recorded in the voice of its daughter, who came to the United States at age five. Though books on early Asian American families are relatively few, marital patterns, gender relations, and generational conflicts inform the narratives of community formation, race and labor relations, and religious practices in many studies.[2]

The impact of World War II and postwar U.S. foreign relations on Asian American families has captured the attention of a number of scholars. Recent studies on family life, family formation, and gender relations during this time period offer fresh perspectives on not only the changing lives of the individuals involved, but also the communities that transformed around them. Combining documents, such as newspapers and letters, created in internment camps, one study shows how Japanese American men, women, and children experienced the forced internment differently. For example, immigrant women, the glue of their families, suffered traumatic strain during the war. Nevertheless, inside the camps they enjoyed ample leisure time that had not been available to them before the war. Immigration files, ethnic newspapers, and oral history interviews inform a study of Chinese American families that reveals tensions between Americanized husbands and their fresh-off-the-boat wives after the long-awaited family reunion finally took place. Families of American soldiers and their brides from Asia after World War II form the subject of two books, both of which make good use of oral history interviews. The first book illuminates how Japanese war brides followed in the footsteps of early immigrant women (and their daughters) and became domestic workers. The second situates the identity and family formation of Korean War brides in the context of U.S. colonialism in postwar Asia, providing the historical background for the post-1965 Korean American transnational community.[3]

Works published on early Asian immigrant families, regardless of their variations in methodology, approach, and use of source materials, tend to agree on a common theme: the severe racism of the late nineteenth and early twentieth centuries and the U.S.-imposed hardships on Asian American family life. Indeed, the contours of Asian immigrant families are largely defined by Asian exclusion and racial discrimination of the time.

Post-1965 Immigrant and Refugee Families

Immigration reform in 1965 opened the door for Asian immigration, opening a new chapter in Asian American history. The family-unification provision of the new law changed the demographic profile of Asian American communities. One notable difference was the sex ratio of new immigrants. While earlier immigrants had been predominantly male, women from Asia often outnumbered their male counterparts after 1965.

Of those arriving after 1965, Southeast Asian families received particular scholarly attention for two reasons. First, unlike East Asian immigrant families, they had no established ties in the United States to rely on. Second, in addition to the tragedy and trauma they had suffered during the Vietnam War and the journey to escape their homeland, few were financially, socially, and psychologically prepared for settlement in the United States. Two books document the ways that refugee families adjusted to life in the new land; both combine oral history interviews with participant observations. The first focuses on a community of ethnic Hmong families in Seattle in the early 1980s. Uprooted from their village homes in the mountains of Laos, these families encountered many difficulties in the urban surroundings of a completely foreign society. Utilizing government assistance as well as the support of their ethnic community, however, these families found ways to build a new life in America. The second investigates a group of Vietnamese families who settled in Philadelphia. Like the first one, this book shows the willingness of Southeast Asian refugees to invest in family life, which allowed them to survive under unusually difficult circumstances. A few other studies also examine social networks beyond the nuclear household that provide both material and emotional support.[4]

Gender and Generational Relations

Gender and generational relations are often studied in the framework of power structure. Based on the concept of the patriarchal Asian family structure, some studies examine the ways that family members are related to one another in a social hierarchy. Perpetuated by rural economies and kinship, the patriarchal family structure is believed to confine women's labor to the domestic sphere, and its cultural ideology requires women's subordination to men, giving men the authority to influence and control women's behaviors.

One important finding of the existing scholarship is that drastic social dislocation caused by war, revolution, and immigration often worked to undermine the foundation of the patriarchal structure by weakening those who possessed resources, power, and authority. Since women had relatively little to begin with, they had less to lose than their husbands in times of crisis or major social transformation. Access to the American job market, meanwhile, allowed immigrant women to gain economic independence and bargaining power within the family. Some studies also find a correlation between women's wage earning and their participation in family decision making. The general consensus is that immigration creates a basis for gender equality and helps improve gender relations, changes that could work to reverse the order of the patriarchal family.

A few studies, however, view power relations between married men and women in more complex ways. They find that although improvement in terms of women's resources is apparent, there are signs of resistance to change. Recognizing changing family dynamics, one study finds that the diminished resources of one family member or increased resources of another do not necessarily work to flip the family order. While many refugee women are able to find gainful employment in America, relatively few see their economic independence as an opportunity to compete against their husbands. Many Vietnamese women continue to situate their personal achievement in the context of the collective goals of their families.[5]

Studies exploring relations between parents and children also find the concept of the patriarchal Asian family structure useful. Because parents possess financial resources, some assume that they also have the power to make decisions and the authority to influence or control their children's behavior. Conflicts between parents and children in this context are often framed so that parents are the oppressors and children are the victims.

Instead of exploring a gap between individuals from different times, studies on Asian American generational relations often focus on a spatial dimension between immigrant parents and their American-educated children. Thanks to the large influx of new immigrants since 1965, Asian American generational relations have not failed to attract scholarly attention. Within the framework of patriarchal family structure, these studies tend to characterize Asian family culture as collectivistic and American culture as individualistic. The assumption is that in a culture of collectivism, the pride and shame of one individual are shared by the entire family. Accordingly, filial obligation is expected, requiring children to assume family responsibilities before entering adulthood. Conflict is then inevitable when the child is exposed to the dominant culture's idea of individualism. The dichotomy of collectivism versus individualism positions the family's goals in opposition to the children's desire to pursue their own dreams; it sees generational relations within the Asian American family as an inescapable struggle between Eastern and Western cultures. Advocating for children's freedom and rights, some studies express concerns about the unhappiness, stress, mental health problems, and incidents of suicide among Asian American children.[6]

Studies on Asian American generational relations are largely informed by autobiographies, personal accounts, and writings by members of the second generation. For example, Jade Snow Wong's *Fifth Chinese Daughter* and Monica Sone's *Nisei Daughter*, both about experiences of growing up female in early Asian immigrant families, have become classic texts. Studies focused on the first half of the twentieth century view the second generation as individuals living between two worlds: family and ethnic-exclusive communities on one side and American educational institutions on the other. This in-betweenness, they argue, is a characteristic that children of early Asian immigrants share, and it is critical to their identity formation.[7]

A few studies try to measure generational disagreements by using typical situations that reflect parent-child differences. Their research on several groups of Asian American adolescents and young adults shows that disagreements are more likely to occur in Asian immigrant families because immigrant parents tend to have high expectations for their children. They also attribute the generational distinctions to different paces of acculturation: Asian American families are more likely to have generational disagreements because immigrant parents move a step slower than their children in the acculturation process.[8]

Other studies, however, see strengths within the collectivistic ideology. They argue that, by instilling in children a sense of duty, the culture of collectivism tends to produce good students and responsible citizens. Some also discover that although cultural differences pose challenges to family harmony, many immigrant families are able to maintain healthy generational relations, especially in cases when supports from ethnic networks are utilized. Such observations are consistent with studies on other ethnic immigrant families. One comparative study finds that in contrast to their white peers, Asian and Latin American adolescents possess stronger values and higher expectations regarding their duty to assist, respect, and support their families. It argues that collectivistic traditions do not have a negative impact on the development of children.[9]

The benefits of collectivistic culture are revealed in a few studies on the care of the elderly, one of which examines the relationship between Chinese, Japanese, and Korean American adults and their aged parents. It finds that assistance to the elderly is not necessarily associated with individual financial resources. More than their compatriots who grew up in the United States, immigrant parents rely on their children for financial and emotional support. Regardless of their relatively limited income, adult children from immigrant families are more likely to reside close to the family elders, and they are more likely to provide their aged parents with financial and emotional support.[10]

The fact that a large number of post-1965 immigrants came to the United States at a young age makes it difficult to draw the generational line. These children spent some years in Asia before coming to the United States; they are native speakers of their ancestral languages, and some started formal education in Asia. More important than the native language are the values and norms that they carried with them to America. For these reasons, some studies argue that these children should not be lumped together with their U.S.-born siblings. The term "1.5 generation" is thus used to describe immigrants who came to the United States before entering adulthood. One book tells life stories of young Vietnamese refugees who fled with their family elders from Vietnam after the war. Through personal narratives, the book shows how wartime trauma and strenuous journeys to the United States gave young Vietnamese refugees courage and strength, which helped them build a new life in America. Unlike their U.S.-born siblings, the 1.5-generation Vietnamese Americans have complex views and observations on the values of the two societies in which they have lived. A second book examines young Korean immigrants in Hawai'i. It explores how the values and norms of two different cultures are instilled in these young immigrants through family life, schooling, and socialization. The book also illuminates how the cultural backgrounds of these children have turned into powerful forces in shaping their new identities.[11]

The study of generational relations is largely limited to children's personal narratives. Broadening the analysis to consider materials in the form of arts, music, sports, and consumer goods would help develop a better understanding of today's children. Further, while children's perceptions are crucial, it is also necessary to incorporate the views of their parents. The relatively few studies that examine the opinions of both adolescents and their parents offer more balanced insights into generational relations.[12] The uniqueness of growing up in Asian immigrant families is an important aspect of Asian American history, and a similar line of inquiry could be directed toward the parents. What are the challenges confronting immigrant parents in the United States? While Asian American children can express their thoughts and feelings freely in English, and these views are accessible in published autobiographies and other documents, immigrant parents' narratives are more difficult to find because many immigrants lack the English proficiency to voice their concerns in public. But they do share their stories with their peers in ethnic newspapers and online forums, and many would participate in oral history projects if approached. Through these sources, researchers could uncover a wide range of perspectives from parents. Without their input, the story of generational relations is incomplete. Understanding the aspirations, motivations, concerns, and frustrations of both children and parents would not only add depth and sophistication to our inquiries, but also help challenge stereotypical images of Asian Americans.

There are relatively few studies that look beyond the second generation. Cultural distance between immigrant parents and their U.S.-born children could lead to more generational disagreements, and cultural losses are probably inevitable. Thus, it would be worth exploring the extent to which cultural characteristics of Asian American families could survive through generations. This calls our attention to questions regarding immigrant agency in relation to culture. Recent studies have used "adaptation" or "acculturation" in place of "assimilation" to describe transitional adjustments to life in America. To survive in the United States and take advantage of what their adopted country has to offer, Asian immigrants are eager to familiarize themselves with American law, culture, and practices and adjust their behaviors and lifestyles accordingly. But this adjustment/adaptation process may or may not necessarily mean a complete divorce from one's past. As some studies have shown, Asian immigrants—men, women, and children—are agents in their own right. They have made conscious choices regarding what to take, what to discard, and what to keep. These studies do not view the process of cultural adjustment as a one-way street. Instead, they have used such processes to observe how one culture intersects with another.[13]

While power structure has been utilized as an important analytical framework for the study of gender and generational relations, relatively few studies view power as a relational or multidimensional concept. As a human institution, family is a basic economic unit, but financial benefit is not the only reason for bringing a family together. Family members—men, women, and children—can influence or be influenced by one another in myriad ways, regardless of one's contribution to the family wealth. While there have been efforts to document women's agency, little attention has been paid to that of children. Do they have the ability to act on their own right before they can bring money to their families? Studies on Southeast Asian immigrant families have revealed that some immigrant children possess a unique power because their parents, due to the lack of English proficiency, rely on them to translate financial documents or write checks, thereby allowing children and young adults to participate in decision-making processes before they can even make money on their own. These studies indicate a different way of understanding power; they also suggest different aspects of autonomy and agency among individual family members.

ASIAN AMERICAN CHILDREN

A considerable number of studies on Asian American families are devoted to assessing the status of the children, who constitute a large proportion of the Asian American population. They are an important part of the family structure, and their well-being provides clues of future families and society. How does immigration affect the life of Asian American children? What is it like growing up in Asian American families? How are Asian American children faring in American schools and making the transition to the larger world? How do Asian American children differ from children of other racial/ethnic backgrounds? What does the study of Asian American children have to offer to our understanding of American society? Assessing the well-being of Asian American children brings together issues concerning not only education and employment, but also race and class in American society, making controversy almost inevitable.

While studies on Asian American families during the exclusion highlight the hurdles that the children faced, studies on contemporary Asian American families acknowledge progress since the civil rights movement. Signs of progress were first exhibited in census statistics of the 1980s, which indicate the improved socioeconomic status of Asian and Pacific Islander Americans and their above-national-average college graduation rate. The perceived correlation between social mobility and educational achievements has encouraged more studies on children's performance. A number of studies find that compared to non-Asian groups, Asian Americans take less time to graduate from college, are admitted to prestigious colleges and universities at a higher rate, and receive higher high school grades and nationwide test scores. Such findings have been confirmed by the census and national surveys of the past few decades. The 2010 census shows that a higher proportion of Asian Americans earn college degrees than the general U.S. population. Of the 48,069 research doctorates granted at U.S. universities in 2010, U.S.-born and foreign-born Asian students account for 25 percent. Their share of Ph.D.s is especially high in engineering (45 percent), math and computer sciences (38 percent), physical sciences (33 percent), and life sciences (25 percent).[14]

Does the educational achievement gap suggest that children of different ethnic backgrounds inherit different levels of cognitive abilities? This question generates academic interest for both scientists and social scientists. A couple of studies claim that the average IQ of Japanese children exceeds that of American children, but subsequent research challenged their samples and methodologies, deeming such findings inconclusive.[15]

More studies emphasize the social upbringing of Asian American children. One book examines how family, community, and school helped post-1965 Chinese immigrant children adapt to a new life in New York City. Two books focusing on children of Southeast Asian refugees link family and community structure to children's school performance; their findings have been frequently cited. More research attributes common behaviors of Asian American children, such as respect for learning and willingness to make an effort to study, to cultural ideas developed in Asian traditions. They find that many students of immigrant parents perform well in school because their families are able to seize opportunities in the United States that were unavailable to them in Asia. These studies provide evidence that many immigrant families adhere to some of their traditional values and adapt to American life in selective ways. One interesting observation is the difference between children of immigrant families and those of long-settled Asian American families. Although immigrant children are expected to face greater difficulties in school, they often do better than their peers whose families have been in the United States longer. One study links the educational success of children of Sikh immigrants from southwestern India to some degree of resistance their families have to assimilation. Utilizing a large national database, another study argues that educational aspirations are a more important factor driving academic achievement than socioeconomic status and educational resources. Taking into consideration both their cultural values and their minority status in the society, one study proposes a theory of relative functionalism. It argues that education is functional as a means for Asians' mobility when other career choices are limited. Asian American students are more likely to work hard in school because of a belief that success in life depends on their performance in school; their desire to enter "safe" professions reflects the reality of ethnic minorities in American society.[16]

The success story of Asian American children, however, has generated heated debate; the central concern is its broad social and political implications. Does such a story promote the idea of the American dream and mask persistent inequalities in American society? Would the success story of one ethnic group lead to a battle over the appropriateness of another? If one minority group could achieve the American dream, why couldn't others, such as African Americans and Latinos? Should society be allowed to blame those who have failed? Similarly, if Asian Americans have an inherited merit of cultural strength, does it imply that some other minority groups suffer a lack of industry and values? There are also other concerns. Education advocates, for example, have worried that once Asian Americans were labeled a model minority they would no longer be considered an underprivileged group and therefore would be excluded from social assistance.[17]

Challenging the model minority theory, two recent books criticize the cultural interpretation of Asian American children. The first compares Chinese American students attending Columbia University with those enrolled in Hunter College in New York. It finds that race and class matter more than culture in determining whether a student attends an Ivy League university or a less prestigious public institution. The second examines Korean Americans in New York and compares students in a highly competitive magnet high school with dropouts from working-class neighborhood schools. Acknowledging functions of social networks, parental strategies, and school resources, it argues that children's school performance must be analyzed in the broader contexts of both class and race in American society.[18]

Many paper-length studies are designed to demonstrate, simply, that the model minority hypothesis is a myth. One argument is that the level of meritocracy in American society has been greatly exaggerated. Studies in this direction reveal the uneven achievements of Asian American children, showing that Asian America is a very diverse ethnic group. Originating from different parts of Asia, Asian Americans carry many different cultural, linguistic, regional, and religious distinctions. New immigrant families often have fewer resources than those who have been in the United States for generations, and resources in American schools of different urban and rural settings are not always equally distributed. A number of researchers have argued convincingly that while some Asian students have achieved success, others—children of Cambodian and Laotian refugees or Pacific Islander Americans, for example—are less fortunate and therefore do not fit into the model minority image.

A number of studies investigate problems involving Asian American children. Some studies find that Southeast Asian adolescents are often associated with school dropouts, gangsters, and welfare dependents. They show that Cambodian and Laotian American students who fall behind and are marginalized in school are more likely to be pushed into gang activities. These studies also show the negative effects their families have on their school performance.[19]

Scholars do not agree on the impact of family responsibility on a child's performance in school. Some studies argue that family obligations create tension between Southeast Asian adolescents and their parents because household chores take away free time for social life, making it difficult for immigrant children to make friends and adjust to school. One study, however, finds that although Filipino American children spend more time helping their family than their peers of other ethnic backgrounds do, they tend to have less conflict with parents and siblings. However, based on a comparative analysis of Chinese, Cambodians, Laotians or Mien, and Vietnamese American students, one study argues that parental attachment may not be a good predictor for academic achievement. It finds that peer affiliations directly affect school attitudes, which is a better predictor for academic achievement.[20]

There are also studies that examine the degree to which children are subject to domestic abuse. National data from the U.S. Department of Health and Human Services indicate that Pacific Islander American children, along with American Indian and African American children, had the highest rate of victimization: 21.4, 21.3, and 20.4 per 1,000 children in 2005. This rate is lower among white and Hispanic children (11.0 and 9.9 per 1,000) and the lowest among Asian American children (2.7 per 1,000). Some scholars, however, argue that the low rate of victimization may only reflect the fact that Asian American families are less likely to report incidents of child abuse. One study, for example, finds that Korean immigrant parents are more tolerant of using physical means to control children and tend to value physical punishment. Some studies also argue that due to high stress in immigrant families and parents' slow pace of acculturation, Asian American children are more likely to be physically abused. There are studies, however, that argue that physical abuse of children is not a product of cultural heritage. Based on data collected from several Asian American groups (Vietnamese, Filipino, Chinese, Korean, Japanese, Asian Indian, and others), one finds that children of more highly acculturated parents have a higher risk rate of physical abuse than those of less acculturated parents.[21]

ASIAN AMERICAN PARENTING

Most studies tend to agree that children's behaviors are closely related to their upbringing. Asian American parenting is therefore critically scrutinized. Research on Asian American parenting often uses existing typologies—authoritarian, authoritative, and permissive—conceptualized by the psychologist Diana Baumrind as an analytical tool. Based on European immigrant parenting patterns of early twentieth-century America, the term "authoritarian" is used to describe parents who are strict, harsh, and demanding. "Authoritative" parents also set rules and have high expectations for their children, but they balance firm discipline with love and affection. Parents who allow their children complete freedom are described as "permissive." Most studies characterize Asian American parents as "strict," "restrictive," and "controlling," terms commonly used to describe authoritarian parents.[22]

According to Baumrind, however, the authoritarian parenting style is a predictor for producing children with poor school performance, which does not apply to Asian American children. Seeking a different interpretation, studies on Korean American families find a difference between maternal and paternal parenting. They argue that Korean immigrant mothers have a higher level of acceptance than their husbands. Other studies argue that strictness may mean different things to people of different ethnic backgrounds. Based on observations of Chinese American parents, one study finds they have little hostility, aggression, mistrust, and dominance—characteristics of the authoritarian parenting style—toward their children. It argues that connotations of control and close supervision of Chinese immigrants reflect forms of parental concern, caring, or involvement, which work to produce positive school performance. In other words, Asian American parents are more "authoritative" than "authoritarian."[23]

A number of studies observe the cultural notion of training among Asian American parents. One examines the different parenting styles of Anglo, Mexican, and Chinese American mothers of different class backgrounds. It finds that Chinese mothers of young sons take their roles as teachers more seriously than Anglo and Mexican mothers. While all mothers are concerned about their children's education, middle-class mothers are more attuned to concepts of early education, environmental enrichment, and quality education. Another study reveals that although both immigrant Chinese mothers and their white counterparts view loving their children as their first priority, the effort of the former is collectivistic in nature while that of the latter is more individualistic. One study probes the perspectives of Asian parents in childrearing. It finds that Filipino immigrant mothers described their roles as facilitators, caregivers, and teachers, reflecting the ways that they interact with their young children.[24]

Several studies explore the effectiveness of Asian immigrant parents in helping their children adjust to American schools. They find that regardless of their lack of economic resources, English proficiency, and knowledge of the workings of American schools, these parents are more optimistic about their children's socioeconomic prospects and view education as a ladder to social mobility. Some studies discover that some Asian parents want their children to outperform their peers because they see the "glass ceiling" effect as an obstacle for their children. The negative impact of assimilation has also been investigated. One study argues that Asian American children score higher than their white peers on GPA and standardized tests because a significantly large proportion of them are children of immigrants. Most interestingly, the study shows that unlike their immigrant counterparts, third-generation Asian Americans do not perform better than their white counterparts. Another study finds that immigrant youth from Punjab in northwestern India adjust to school well partly because their parents discourage their interaction with peers from other ethnic backgrounds.[25]

One cross-cultural analysis provides important insights into the construction of Asian American parenting culture. Based on observations of Japanese nursery school and kindergarten activities, it finds that the cultures of home and school are defined differently in Japan and in the United States. Parents in Japan can depend on teachers for children's early academic socialization. When immigrants realize American teachers are too lenient and schools are less dependable, they search for other ways to compensate for the difference.[26]

Some studies find that effective parenting encourages mutual support among siblings. While sibling rivalry is an important theme in the study of family generally, analyses of Asian American families uncover the benefits of teamwork among siblings. One study on Southeast Asian families shows that although relatively few refugee parents have the time and knowledge to supervise their children's homework, their children learn to take care of themselves and each other from a young age. As this study demonstrated, supervision and instruction from elder siblings could be very effective in helping younger siblings achieve extraordinary educational success.[27]

A number of studies, however, express concerns about Asian American parenting. They deem Asian immigrant parents, regardless of their emphasis on education, as not closely bound to their children. They find that these parents are less likely to participate in school activities or stay in touch with teachers. Some studies also question the adequacy of Asian immigrants' parenting. One study, for example, concludes that immigrant mothers are less knowledgeable than average American mothers about child development and childrearing.[28]

One major concern regarding Asian American parenting is how parental pressure impacts their children's personality development, mental health, and suicide rates. A few studies view parents' high expectations as a major trigger of adolescent resentment. According to one study, some Lao youth do not care about school partly because they resent educational pressures from their family. Some studies find that compared to their white peers, Asian American students are more likely to have perfectionist tendencies, which make them more wary of making mistakes and more likely to have self-doubt. One study finds that Korean American adolescents reported more parental control and less parental care than their white peers did. Such control, it argues, has a negative correlation with self-esteem and a positive correlation with depression. A second study focuses on the parents' assimilation level. It finds fewer psychological distress symptoms among Korean immigrants when their parents adopted American parenting methods. A few studies claim that Asian American college students are at a higher risk for suicides than their peers, although reliable data are yet to be found. These studies identify a few unique risk factors for depression and suicidal behaviors among Asian American youth, including parent-child conflict, collectivistic family values, and poor school performance. A common concern found in most studies is that Asian Americans are less likely than their white peers to seek mental health treatment.[29]

CONCLUSION

Although scholars have different views on Asian American families, they are hardly divisive. To recognize the achievements of Asian Americans through education is to acknowledge progress in the past few decades, which reflects improvement in American society since the civil rights movement. However, recognizing diversity and exposing problems associated with underprivileged groups reveal that not everyone shares this success story; this serves as an important reminder that social injustice still exists. Together, these studies have identified several characteristics of Asian American families and tested established concepts, typologies, and frameworks. They have laid important groundwork for future research.

Although the importance of culture in understanding the workings of Asian American families, power relations, gender roles, generational gaps, and parenting style is recognized in existing scholarship, there is a great need to bring the study of culture to a higher level. First, there are relatively few studies that acknowledge the complexity of Asian cultures and societies, which have many influences. Chinese culture, for example, is more influential in East Asian and Southeast Asian nations than in South Asian and Pacific Islander nations. People who originated from one particular nation-state may also have their share of diverse ethnic, linguistic, and religious backgrounds. Fitting all Indian immigrants into one cultural pattern, for example, could be problematic. Pacific Islander Americans, for example, have inherited many distinctive cultures of their own and therefore deserve more scholarly attention. Second, Asian cultures are changing. Industrialization, urbanization, colonialism, war, revolution, and migration have challenged traditional patriarchal societies in profound ways, and advanced technological development in recent decades has made transnational cultural exchange frequent. Such changes obscure cultural boundaries, making it difficult to localize cultures. The East verses West dichotomy, therefore, has its limitations. Third, immigration provides a great opportunity to study how one culture intersects with another. Expanding academic inquiries to include migration families of the Asian diaspora, especially families that have settled in non-Western countries, would allow us to see how different cultures meet and intersect at various locations. Fourth, there is a great need for cross-cultural research. Studies that showcase broad social support for families and childrearing in Asia have shed light on our understanding of Asian American behaviors, which, after all, are socially constructed in the United States.[30]

Globalization poses a great challenge to the study of Asian American families. As the relatively few studies on transnational Asian American families show, geographical distance between husband and wife or between parents and children undermines family intimacy and disrupts perceived family order. Globalization also makes it possible for individuals to be exposed to different cultures while still living in one particular setting. Today, it is relatively easy to become a world traveler, physically and via television, video games, and the Internet. Asian languages and cultures, for example, are taught in American classrooms and through education abroad and other exchange programs. As the world gets smaller, people's thoughts and behaviors are increasingly influenced by what is happening globally, regardless of where they live. Taking into consideration the world outside the United States would help raise new questions regarding cultural differences across generations.[31]

Would the study of one ethnic group's achievements raise questions about the appropriateness of another ethnic minority group? It would if the research had been done out of historical and social context and if the emphasis were only on the accomplishments of Asian Americans. Studies on uneven development and the problems associated with Asian Americans are especially important in that they point out the limitations of cultural determinations. The question is not whether Asian Americans achieve more than other ethnic backgrounds, but that among Asian Americans there are both overachievers and underachievers. Good examples are found in two studies on adolescents in the

Philippines that investigate correlations between family structure/parents' behaviors and children's school performance. They conclude that parents play a valuable role in children's development and that marital problems and a negligent parenting style negatively affect children's educational achievement. There are good opportunities to engage in in-depth, cross-ethnic research. Are there family issues that black, Hispanic, and Asian American overachievers share in common? What do all underachievers share?[32]

Research exploring Asian American family variations is still limited. So much has changed in just a few decades, which means we need to think about Asian American families in different ways. Many now-common forms of Asian American families are understudied: single-parent families, gay or lesbian families, families with adopted children, families with disabled individuals, interracial families, and solo-living individuals, for example.

As a relatively new field, the study of Asian American families is still in progress. Asian Americans, along with their compatriots from other parts of the world, not only have contributed to the nation's economic development, but also have left deep imprints on American culture. More waves of Asian immigrant families from more diverse regions and cultures will arrive in the twenty-first century, which means there will be more opportunities for future research. The study of the Asian American family will have much more to offer to our understanding of family in a changing American society.

NOTES

1. Sucheng Chan, "The Exclusion of Chinese Women, 1870–1943," in *Entry Denied: Exclusion and the Chinese Community in America, 1882–1943*, ed. Sucheng Chan (Philadelphia: Temple University Press, 1991), 94–146; George Anthony Peffer, *If They Don't Bring Their Women Here: Chinese Female Immigration before Exclusion* (Urbana: University of Illinois Press, 1999); Xiaojian Zhao, *Remaking Chinese America: Immigration, Family, and Community, 1940–1965* (New Brunswick, NJ: Rutgers University Press, 2002).

2. Karen I. Leonard, *Making Ethnic Choices: California's Punjabi Mexican Americans* (Philadelphia: Temple University Press, 1992); Madeline Y. Hsu, *Dreaming of Gold, Dreaming of Home: Transnationalism and Migration between the United States and South China, 1882–1943* (Stanford, CA: Stanford University Press, 2000); Haiming Liu, *The Transnational History of a Chinese Family: Immigrant Letters, Family Business, and Reverse Migration* (New Brunswick, NJ: Rutgers University Press, 2005); Lauren Kessler, *Stubborn Twig: Three Generations in the Life of a Japanese American Family* (Portland: Oregon Historical Society, 2005); Akemi Kikumura, *Through Harsh Winters: The Life of a Japanese Immigrant Woman* (Novato, CA: Chandler and Sharp, 1981); Akemi Kikumura, *Promises Kept: The Life of an Issei Man* (Novato, CA: Chandler and Sharp, 1991); Lisa See, *On Gold Mountain: The 100-Year Odyssey of a Chinese-American Family* (New York: St. Martin's, 1995); Mary Paik Lee, *Quiet Odyssey: A Pioneer Korean Woman in America* (Seattle: University of Washington Press, 1990); Wayne Patterson, *The Ilse: First-Generation Korean Immigrants in Hawaii, 1903–1973* (Honolulu: University of Hawai'i Press, 2000).

3. Valerie Matsumoto, "Japanese American Women during World War II," *Frontiers* 8 (1984): 6–14; Zhao, *Remaking Chinese America*; Evelyn Nakano Glenn, *Issei, Nisei, War Bride: Three Generations of Japanese American Women in Domestic Service* (Philadelphia: Temple University Press, 1986); Ji-Yeon Yuh, *Beyond the Shadow of Camptown: Korean Military Brides in America* (New York: New York University Press, 2002).

4. Nancy D. Donnelly, *Changing Lives of Refugee Hmong Women* (Seattle: University of Washington Press, 1994); Nazli Kibria, *Family Tightrope: The Changing Lives of Vietnamese Americans* (Princeton, NJ: Princeton University Press, 1993); David Haines, Dorothy Rutherford, and Patrick Thomas, "Family and Community among Vietnamese Refugees," *International Migration Review* 15 (1981): 310–319.

5. Kibria, *Family Tightrope*.

6. See, for example, erin Khuê Ninh, *Ingratitude: The Debt-Bound Daughter in Asian American Literature* (New York: New York University Press, 2011).

7. Jade Snow Wong, *Fifth Chinese Daughter* (New York: HarperCollins, 1950); Monica Sone, *Nisei Daughter* (New York: Little, Brown, 1953); Zhao, *Remaking Chinese America*; K. Scott Wong, *Americans First: Chinese and the Second World War* (Cambridge, MA: Harvard University Press, 2005); Judy Yang, *Unbound Feet: A Social History of Chinese Women in San Francisco* (Berkeley: University of California Press, 1995); David Yoo, *Growing Up Nisei: Race, Generation, and Culture among Japanese Americans of California, 1924–49* (Urbana: University of Illinois Press, 2000); Matsumoto, "Japanese American Women during World War II."

8. Richard M. Lee, Jennifer Choe, Gina Kim, and Vicky Ngo, "Construction of the Asian American Family Conflict Scale," *Journal of Counseling Psychology* 47, no. 2 (2000): 211–222; Matthew J. Miller and Richard M. Lee, "Factorial Invariance of the Asian American Family Conflicts Scale across Ethnicity, Generational Status, Sex, and Nationality," *Measurement and Evaluation in Counseling and Development* 42 (2009): 179–196.

9. Andrew J. Fuligni, Vivian Tseng, and May Lam, "Attitudes toward Family Obligations among American Adolescents with Asian, Latin American, and European Backgrounds," *Child Development* 70 (1999): 1030–1044; Carola Suárez-Orozco and Marcelo M. Suárez-Orozco, *Children of Immigration* (Cambridge, MA: Harvard University Press, 2002).

10. Masako Ishii-Kuntz, "Intergenerational Relationships among Chinese, Japanese, and Korean Americans," *Family Relations* 46 (1997): 23–32.

11. Sucheng Chan, *The Vietnamese American 1.5 Generation: Stories of War, Revolution, Flight, and New Beginnings* (Philadelphia: Temple University Press, 2006); Mary Yu Danico, *The 1.5 Generation: Becoming Korean American in Hawaii* (Honolulu: University of Hawai'i Press, 2004).

12. Kyunghwa Kwak and John W. Berry, "Generational Differences in Acculturation among Asian Families in Canada: A Comparison of Vietnamese, Korean, and East-Indian Groups," *International Journal of Psychology* 36 (2001): 152–162.

13. Kibria, *Family Tightrope*.

14. Samuel S. Peng, "Attainment Status of Asian Americans in Higher Education" (paper presented at the Conference of the National Association for Asian Pacific American Education, Denver, Colorado, April 7–9, 1988); Jayjia Hsia, "Limits on Affirmative Action: Asian American Access to Higher Education," *Educational Policy* 2 (1988): 117–136; Pew Research Center, *The Rise of Asian Americans* (Pew Research Center: Social and Demographic Trends, 2012).

15. R. Lynn, "IQ in Japan and the United States Shows a Growing Disparity," *Nature* 297 (1982): 222–223; Harold W. Stevenson and H. Azuma, "IQ in Japan and the United States: Methodological Problems in Lynn's Analysis," *Nature* 306 (1983): 291–292; Harold W. Stevenson, James W. Stigler, Shin-ying Lee, G. William Lucker, Seiro Kitamura, and Chen-chin Hsu, "Cognitive Performance and Academic Achievement of Japanese, Chinese, and American Children," *Chinese Development* 56 (1985): 718–734.

16. Betty Lee Sung, *The Adjustment Experience of Chinese Immigrant Children in New York City* (New York: Center for Migration Studies, 1987); Nathan Caplan, Marcella H. Choy, and John K. Whitmore, *Children of the Boat People: A Study of Educational Success* (Ann Arbor: University of Michigan Press, 1991); Min Zhou and Carl L. Bankston III, *How Vietnamese Children Adapt to Life in the United States* (New York: Russell Sage Foundation, 1998); Margaret Gibson, *Accommodation without Assimilation: Sikh Immigrants in an American High School* (Ithaca, NY: Cornell University Press, 1988); Grace Kao and Marta Tienda, "Optimism and Achievement: The Educational Performance of Immigrant Youth," *Social Science Quarterly* 76 (1995): 1–19; Stanley Sue and Sumie Okazaki, "Asian American Educational Achievements: A Phenomenon in Search of an Explanation," *American Psychologist* 45 (1990): 913–920.

17. K. Osajima, "The Hidden Injuries of Race," in *Bearing Dreams, Sharing Visions*, ed. Linda A. Revilla, Shirley Hune, and Gail M. Nomura (Pullman: Washington State University Press, 1993), 81–91; Don Nakanishi, "A Quota on Excellence? The Asian American Admissions Debate," in *The Asian American Educational Experience*, ed. D. Nakanishi and T. Nishida (New York: Routledge, 1995), 273–284.

18. Vivian S. Louie, *Compelled to Excel: Immigration, Education, and Opportunity among Chinese Americans* (Stanford, CA: Stanford University Press, 2004); Jamie Lew, *Asian Americans in Class: Charting the Achievement Gap among Korean American Youth* (New York: Teachers College Press, 2006).

19. Patrick Du Phuoc Long, *The Dream Shattered: Vietnamese Gangs in America* (Boston: Northeastern University Press, 1996); Bic Ngo, "Learning from the Margins: Southeast and South Asian Education in Context," *Race, Ethnicity and Education* 9 (2006): 51–65; Bic Ngo, *Unresolved Identities* (Albany: State University of New York Press, 2010); Khatharya Um, *A Dream Denied: Educational Experiences of Southeast Asian American Youth* (Washington, DC: Southeast Asian Resource Action Center and Berkeley Southeast Asian Student Coalition, 2003); M. Baizerman and G. Hendricks, *A Study of Southeast Asian Youth in the Twin Cities of Minneapolis and St. Paul, Minnesota* (Washington, DC: U.S. Office of Refugee Resettlement, 1988).

20. Hendricks, *A Study of Southeast Asian Youth*; Danling Fu, *"My Trouble is My English": Asian Students and the American Dream* (Portsmouth, NH: Boynton/Cook, 1995); Andrew Fuligni and Carrie L. Masten, "Daily Family Interactions among Young Adults in the United States from Latin American, Filipino, East Asian, and European Backgrounds," *International Journal of Behavioral Development* 34, no. 6 (2010): 491–499; Janet Chang and Thao N. Le, "The Influence of Parents, Peer Delinquency, and School Attitudes on Academic Achievement in Chinese Cambodian, Laotian or Mien, and Vietnamese Youth," *Crime and Delinquency* 51 (2005): 238–264.

21. For a good summary, see Irene J. Kim, Anna S. Lau, and Doris F. Chang, "Family Violence among Asian Americans," in *Handbook of Asian American Psychology*, ed. Frederick L. Leong, Arpana Inman, Angela Ebreo, Lawrence Hsin Yang, Lisa Marie Kinoshita, and Michi Fu (New York: Sage, 2006), 363–378.

22. Diana Baumrind, "Current Patterns of Parental Authority," *Developmental Psychology Monographs* 4 (1971): 1–103.

23. Sanford M. Dornbusch, Philip L. Ritter, P. Herbert Leiderman, Donald F. Roberts, and Michael J. Fraleigh, "The Relation of Parenting Style to Adolescent School Performance," *Child Development* 56 (1987): 326–341; Ruth K. Chao, "Beyond Parental Control and Authoritarian Parenting Style: Understanding Chinese Parenting through the Cultural Notion of Training," *Child Development* 65 (1994): 1111–1119.

24. Margaret Steward and David Steward, "The Observation of Anglo-, Mexican-, and Chinese-American Mothers Teaching Their Young Sons," *Child Development* 44 (1973): 329–337; Ruth Chao, "Chinese and European American Mothers' Beliefs about the Role of Parenting in Children's School Success," *Journal of Cross-cultural Psychology* 27 (1996): 403–423; Rosa Milagros Santos, Laurie M. Jeans, Jeanette McCollum, Angel Fettig, and Amanda Quesenberry, "Perspectives of Roles during Parent-child Interactions of Filipino Immigrant Mothers," *Early Child Development and Care* 181 (2011): 809–826.

25. Grace Kao, "Asian Americans as Model Minorities? A Look at Their Academic Performance," *American Journal of Education* 103 (1995): 121–159; Grace Kao and L. T. Rutherford, "Does Social Capital Still Matter? Immigrant Minority Disadvantage in School-specific Social Capital and Its Effects on Academic Achievement," *Sociological Perspectives* 50 (2007): 27–52; Gibson, *Accommodation without Assimilation*.

26. Lois Peak, *Learning to Go to School in Japan: The Transition from Home to Preschool Life* (Berkeley: University of California Press, 1993).

27. Caplan et al., *Children of the Boat People.*

28. Marc H. Bornstein and Linda R. Cote, "'Who Is Sitting Across from Me?' Immigrant Mothers' Knowledge of Parenting and Children's Development," *Pediatrics* 114 (2004): 557–564.

29. Wansoo Park, "Parental Attachment among Korean-American Adolescents," *Child and Adolescent Social Work Journal* 26 (2009): 307–309; Eunjung Kim, Kevin Cain, and Marilyn Mccubbin, "Maternal and Paternal Parenting, Acculturation, and Young Adolescents' Psychological Adjustment in Korean American Families," *Journal of Child and Adolescent Psychiatric Nursing* 19 (2006): 112–129; Anna S. Lau, Nadine M. Jernewall, Nolan Zane, and Hector F. Myers, "Correlates of Suicide Behaviors among Asian American Outpatient Youths," *Cultural Diversity and Ethnic Minority Psychology* 8 (2002): 199–213; Rocco A. Cimmarusti, "Exploring Aspects of Filipino-American Families," *Journal of Marital and Family Therapy* 22 (1996): 205–217.

30. Robert Alan LeVine and Merry I. White, *Human Conditions: The Cultural Basis of Educational Development* (New York: Routledge and Kegan Paul, 1986).

31. Rhacel Parreñas, *Children of Global Migration: Transnational Families and Gendered Woes* (Stanford, CA: Stanford University Press, 2005); Mirca Madianou and Daniel Miller, "Mobile Phone Parenting: Reconfiguring Relationships between Filipina Migrant Mothers and Their Left-behind Children," *New Media and Society* 13 (2011): 457–470; Paula S. Fass, "Children in Global Migration," *Journal of Social History* 38 (2005): 937–953.

32. Michelle J. Hindin, "Family Dynamics, Gender Differences, and Educational Attainment in Filipino Adolescents," *Journal of Adolescence* 28 (2005): 299–316; Scott E. Harper, "Exploring the Role of Filipino Fathers: Paternal Behaviors and Child Outcomes," *Journal of Family Issues* 31 (2010): 66–89.

FURTHER READING

Chan, Sucheng. *The Vietnamese American 1.5 Generation: Stories of War, Revolution, Flight, and New Beginnings*. Philadelphia: Temple University Press, 2006.

Chao, Ruth K. "Beyond Parental Control and Authoritarian Parenting Style: Understanding Chinese Parenting through the Cultural Notion of Training." *Chinese Development* 65 (1994): 1111–1119.

Chee, Maria W. L. *Taiwanese American Transnational Families: Women and Kin Networks*. New York: Routledge, 2005.

Danico, Mary Yu. *The 1.5 Generation: Becoming Korean American in Hawaii*. Honolulu: University of Hawai'i Press, 2004.

Detzner, Daniel F. *Elder Voices: Southeast Asian Families in the United States*. Walnut Creek, CA: Altamira, 2004.

Donnelly, Nancy D. *Changing Lives of Refugee Hmong Women*. Seattle: University of Washington Press, 1994.

Kessler, Lauren. *Stubborn Twig: Three Generations in the Life of a Japanese American Family*. Corvallis: Oregon State University Press, 1984.

Kibria, Nazli. *Family Tightrope: The Changing Lives of Vietnamese Americans*. Princeton, NJ: Princeton University Press, 1993.

Leonard, Karen I. *Making Ethnic Choices: California's Punjab Mexican Americans*. Philadelphia: Temple University Press, 1992.

Haines, David, Dorothy Rutherford, and Patrick Thomas. "Family and Community among Vietnamese Refugees." *International Migration Review* 15 (1981): 310–319.

Hsia, Jayjia. "Limits on Affirmative Action: Asian American Access to Higher Education." *Educational Policy* 2 (1988): 117–136.

Liu, Haiming. *The Transnational History of a Chinese Family: Immigrant Letters, Family Business, and Reverse Migration*. New Brunswick, NJ: Rutgers University Press, 2005.

Patterson, Wayne. *The Ilse: First-Generation Korean Immigrants in Hawaii, 1903–1973*. Honolulu: University of Hawai'i Press, 2000.

Yoo, David. *Growing Up Nisei: Race, Generation, and Culture among Japanese Americans of California, 1924–1949*. Chicago: University of Illinois Press, 1999.

Yuh, Ji-Yeon. *Beyond the Shadow of Camptown: Korean Military Brides in America*. New York: New York University Press, 2002.

Zhao, Xiaojian. *Remaking Chinese America: Immigration, Family, and Community, 1940–1965*. New Brunswick, NJ: Rutgers University Press, 2002.

PART IV

ENGAGING
HISTORICAL FIELDS

CHAPTER 18

ASIAN AMERICAN ECONOMIC AND LABOR HISTORY

SUCHENG CHAN

LIKE immigrants from other areas of the world, Asians who have migrated to the United States—whether as temporary workers, immigrants who intend to settle permanently, cosmopolitan people who lead transnational lives pursuing activities in and forming linkages with two or more nation-states, or smuggled-in irregular entrants—have all come primarily in search of economic opportunities. Certainly, many had noneconomic motives as well, but financial calculations have been the paramount consideration that propelled Asians across the Pacific Ocean. Despite this central fact in Asian American history, the subfields of Asian American economic history and labor history have not received the scholarly attention they deserve. Due to the relatively sparse scholarship available, it is appropriate to discuss Asian American economic and labor histories together.

Studies of nineteenth-century Asian American economic and labor histories in the continental United States deal almost entirely with Chinese immigrants in California because the number of Japanese present before 1900 was small. Other Asian-origin groups did not arrive in significant numbers until the first decade of the twentieth century, and California was where a vast majority of the Chinese lived and worked. Two major conceptual issues related to this period remain unresolved to this day. First, were Chinese immigrant workers free, semifree (a term I coined that includes indentured, coerced, bound, and contract labor), or unfree (slave) labor? Second, regardless of their statutory status, were Chinese workers "cheap labor"? These questions fueled the vitriolic anti-Chinese movement and they remain salient in the twenty-first century, given the multitudes of contract and migrant workers from dozens of Asian countries now employed around the world.

The economic historians Patricia Cloud and David W. Galenson asked what the "contractual status" of Chinese immigrant workers "actually was." They claimed that the so-called Chinese Six Companies (the widely used informal name of the Chinese Consolidated Benevolent Association) used "extralegal means" to operate a "bound labor system" that circumvented a then-existing U.S. law prohibiting indentured or contract labor. According to them, the Chinese Six Companies imported tens of thousands of Chinese laborers but shrewdly did not give them *written* contracts because such papers were illegal in the United States. They concluded, however, that the Chinese Six Companies did in fact hold the workers in bondage by colluding with steamship companies that agreed not to sell tickets to individuals who wished to return to China unless each of them could produce a document issued by the Chinese Six Companies or one of its component district associations, indicating that the aspiring returnee had paid all his debts. In a critique of Cloud and Galenson's thesis, the legal historian Charles J. McClain, Jr., insisted that there was no credible evidence that the Chinese Six Companies imported laborers by the shipload or served as a large-scale labor contractor. As he saw it, Cloud and Galenson either misinterpreted their sources or ignored other evidence that did not support their conclusion. Cloud and Galenson retorted that it is McClain, and not they themselves, who used quotes selectively to buttress his own view.[1] The three scholars relied on the same set of evidence: testimonies given by individuals supposedly knowledgeable about Chinese immigration during government hearings in the late 1870s. And therein lies the problem: the people who testified did not have definitive, objective information that could have settled the disagreement satisfactorily. On both sides of the debate, the conclusions were *inferred* from anecdotal information that might or might not have been accurate but had nonetheless morphed into sweeping generalizations.

Two other perspectives have framed the issue of whether Chinese immigrants were unfree, bound, coerced, indentured, under contract, or free. The economic historians Ping Chiu and Sucheng Chan looked at the occupational structure of Chinese immigrants during the nineteenth century, while the cultural historian Moon-Ho Jung demonstrated compellingly how the image of the coolie was a malleable construct that could be manipulated by employers and politicians in accordance with their changing economic needs and shifting sociopolitical contexts.[2]

Chiu and Chan collected raw data pertaining to each Chinese individual from the manuscript censuses of the nineteenth century (each page of which was hand written and therefore not available as computer files). They tabulated the relative distribution of Chinese occupations by economic sectors and analyzed how those patterns changed over time. The picture that emerges shows clearly that Chinese who arrived during the California Gold Rush remained miners for several decades longer than any other ethnic group. In addition to raw census data, Chan systematically went through the official archives of California counties that contain thousands of original mining claims staked by Chinese as well as claims that Chinese gold miners purchased from European American miners, despite the fact that some gold-mining regions in California prohibited Chinese from staking or buying any claims at all. From the 1850s on, Chinese also grew vegetables, small fruit, potatoes, onions, wheat, barley, corn, and buckwheat. The first Chinese farmworkers helped harvest the huge crops of wheat produced in California from the 1850s to the 1880s. Later, they provided the harvest labor for many kinds of deciduous tree fruit and nuts as California's agriculture turned to the cultivation of specialty crops. The official archives of California counties are also full of leases, chattel mortgage, and deeds recorded at the request of Chinese tenant farmers and owner-operators who acquired land to grow a wide variety of crops.

Chinese construction workers built roads, tunnels, bridges, stone walls, and stone wine cellars. They helped build the western segments of five (and not just one, as commonly believed) transcontinental railroads—four across the United States (the Central Pacific, Northern Pacific, Great Northern, and Southern Pacific) and one across Canada (the Canadian Pacific)—as well as many shorter branch lines. As owners of small businesses, they operated laundries in towns and cities stretching from the Pacific Coast to the Atlantic Coast as they moved eastward across the continent; ran stores that sold both goods imported from China and products made in the United States; and catered to both Chinese and non-Chinese in restaurants that served Chinese, American, and "invented" Chinese American food such as chop suey and chow mein. They manufactured woolen textiles, sewed clothing, and made shoes, boots, cigars, and various household objects in small factories and workshops owned by European Americans as well as by Chinese. As service workers, they cleaned houses and worked as cooks in European American homes, hotels, farms, and work camps. They also earned a living as artisans plying myriad trades. Those who made the most money ran lucrative gambling joints, opium dens, and brothels; and some made good incomes as labor contractors.

In short, Chinese immigrant communities were internally stratified and economically complex. The Chinese immigrant population was not an amorphous, undifferentiated "horde" of "coolies" controlled by the Chinese Six Companies and their agents or foremen. Given their extremely diverse means of livelihood, even if the Chinese Six Companies did regulate their exit from the United States, that fact does not constitute proof that the organization controlled the geographic movements and job mobility of Chinese workers and entrepreneurs within the United States. Moreover, the wide range of entrepreneurial activities that the Chinese engaged in was *not* something that unfree laborers could carry out.

Asian American economic and labor historians can benefit by becoming conversant with a sizable literature on the historical evolution of the concept and reality of "free labor" and various forms of "unfree labor." Particularly useful is the work of the law professor Robert J. Steinfeld who argued that scholars should "give up the idea that so-called free and coerced labor inhabit completely separate universes" and think, instead, in terms of "a very broad continuum." He urged researchers to investigate what differences existed/exist in the *terms* of employment in each type of labor—that is, the degree of compulsion employers use, whether penalties are pecuniary (monetary fines and/or forfeitures of wages earned) or nonpecuniary (physical punishment and incarceration), whether workers can leave jobs without being charged with a crime, and what legal institutions are used to enforce contracts or adjudicate relationships between employers and employees.[3] The implication of Steinfeld's proposal for historians of Asian America is that instead of asserting simplistically that Chinese were or were not unfree labor, the more appropriate question to ask is where along the socially constructed continuum from "unfree" to "free" labor were various groups of nineteenth-century Chinese immigrant workers located? The wide-ranging occupational structure described above indicates that Chinese were located along many points, rather than a single one, of this continuum. Thus, no single labor category can describe their status adequately.

Moon-Ho Jung examined another facet of Chinese labor by analyzing how and why Chinese workers were brought to the American South and the discourse that emerged regarding their presence. The "coolie" image seeped into American consciousness via observations of events in Cuba and in the British-colonized Caribbean islands where sugar plantation owners were desperately trying to find new sources of labor after enslaved Africans were emancipated. In his view, "Coolies were never a people or a legal category. Rather, coolies were a conglomeration of racial imaginings that emerged worldwide in the era of slave emancipation." In the post–Civil War imaginary, "coolies came to epitomize enslaved labor, a foreign scourge." The term was a "vital instrument in the reproduction of racial, nationalist, and class provincialisms" that helped "justify racial exclusion in the aftermath of black inclusion." Once the 1863 Emancipation Proclamation had ended chattel slavery, admitting coolies into the United States would be "a reversion to slavery." To get around this semantic hurdle, sugar plantation owners in Louisiana, in need of workers to replace black freedmen, "recast" Chinese workers as "voluntary immigrants."

Whereas the idea of coolies was indeed useful symbolically, the fact that there *was* a materialist basis for coolies cannot be dismissed easily. The term's etymology goes back several centuries. It originated in India where, in the Hindi and Telugu languages, *kuli* refers to an unskilled laborer. When Europeans entered the Indian Ocean at the beginning of the sixteenth century and established trading stations along that ocean's littoral, an increasing number of laborers on the Indian subcontinent began working at docks loading cargo onto and unloading cargo off of ships plying the Asian trade routes. These porters and dockworkers were the first kuli that Europeans encountered. The Portuguese—the first Europeans to create a seaborne empire—introduced the term kuli to China. The word was transcribed in written Chinese with two characters: ku, meaning bitter, and li, meaning strength. The British spelled kuli as "coolie" and passed on that notion and spelling to Americans. There is a significant difference in how the term was understood in Asia and later on in North America, however. In Asian languages, kuli signifies the nature of the *work* a person does, whereas in North America, it references the innate attributes of a *person* occupying the negative pole of the binary, "free" versus "unfree" labor.

The second key issue, whether the Chinese were "cheap labor," can be assessed by examining how much railroad and agricultural employers, who hired the largest number of Chinese, paid them compared to what they paid white workers. Ping Chiu, Paul M. Ong, and William F. Chew have investigated the income that Chinese railroad builders earned vis-à-vis white workers.[4] Chiu found that when Chinese were initially hired by the Central Pacific Railroad Company, they received $26 a month without board. As the railroad expanded its employment of Chinese, it raised the pay several times until it reached $31 a month without board in order to lure the very large number of Chinese workers it desired. By 1867, the company was paying Chinese $35 a month without board.

European American workers (mostly Irish immigrants) started at $35 a month with board and made $45 a month plus board during the peak construction period. Food and beverages for white workers cost anywhere between 70 cents and $1 per capita per diem, which means that the total white wage varied from $56 to $65 a month during the early phase of construction and rose even higher when the pay of both Chinese and whites increased. Chiu calculated that white workers were paid anywhere from 64 percent to 90 percent more than the Chinese, who were aware of this discrepancy and apparently resented it. In late May 1867 they went on strike to demand initially $45 a month but soon lowered the amount asked to $40. They also wanted to be allowed to work only eight hours a day instead of the ten to twelve hours they had been putting in up to that point. "Eight hours a day good for white men, all the same good for Chinamen," they declared. The strike lasted only a week. It did not succeed because the railroad starved them out by refusing to bring in their provisions. They returned to work at a monthly wage of $35.

The economist Paul M. Ong used economic theory to estimate the income disparity between Chinese and white railway workers. Ong treated the railroad as a monopsonist (a single buyer facing many sellers, the opposite of a monopolist). In this case the commodity that the railroad bought and laborers sold was human strength. He argued that the railroad corporation had the market power to keep wages lower for its tens of thousands of Chinese employees than what it paid white workers who were far fewer in number and many of whom walked off the job after they discovered the extreme hardships involved. According to Ong, the wage discrimination suffered by Chinese workers was $13 a month per person, a 40 percent disparity. This is a smaller percentage than Ping Chiu's figure because Chiu took into account the value of board that was provided to white workers but not to Chinese while Ong did not.

William F. Chew, an engineer by vocation and a history buff by avocation, discovered that the California State Railroad Museum in Sacramento, California, holds a collection of the payrolls kept by the Central Pacific Railroad Company. Nineteen months of these payrolls have been preserved. The records contain the names of European American site foremen and Chinese "gang bosses" and labor contractors; the number of workers each gang boss or labor contractor supervised; each crew's length of employment; job classifications and their attendant pay scales; and the monthly total man-days of work each crew did. The railroad paid each man in charge of a crew a lump sum that he then divvied up, after deducting the expenses incurred by each worker. This treasure trove of numerical data allowed Chew to determine that the Central Pacific began hiring Chinese in January 1864—fifteen months *earlier* than scholars and popular writers had hitherto believed. It employed an estimated 23,000 Chinese, a far larger number than earlier estimates of 10,000 to 12,000 Chinese workers hired between January 1864 and May 1869 when the Central Pacific and Union Pacific railroads (the western and eastern segments, respectively, of the first transcontinental railroad) were connected at Promontory Summit, Utah. Chinese carried out sixteen different kinds of jobs and were paid less than European American workers performing the same tasks, regardless of what work was involved. Chinese did not all earn the same wage as some writers had thought.

Blacksmiths were the best paid. Chinese blacksmiths initially earned $1.34 a day, with their daily wage rising eventually to $1.53, while European American blacksmiths started at $2.50 a day and ultimately received $2.88 a day. Cooks and waiters had the lowest pay at less than $1 a day. Chinese who dug, chiseled, drilled, and blasted tunnels through solid granite got a monthly bonus of $1. Those who stood in chilly river water hour upon hour laying foundations for trestles and building bridges were rewarded with an extra $1.25 per month. Chinese labor contractors and headmen received $2.50 more a month than the amount paid to each member of their crews. However, the supervisory personnel's incomes could be considerably larger, depending on the size of their crews, as they collected a commission of $2 a month from each worker under their supervision. Everyone's income was in fact lower than the nominal wage because the railroad company did not provide tools free of charge. A Chinese worker had to pay $1.50 for a shovel and $2.50 for a pick. When removing the huge mountains of debris, Chinese gang bosses had to rent carts from the railroad for $5 per day or a horse and cart for $15 a day. Each Chinese worker gave his labor contractor or gang boss $6 a month for food, $1.50 for herbal medicine (that very likely included opium, an addictive drug that is an analgesic), and the monthly commission of $2 mentioned above. The district association to which each Chinese belonged also took a cut of $1 a month. If workers wanted to send letters home, letter writers were available, charging 50 cents a letter.

No comparable payroll records for Chinese farmworkers have been discovered. However, Ping Chiu, Richard Steven Street, and Sucheng Chan have ferreted out the wages of Chinese and European American farmhands from narrative sources.[5] Chiu and Chan both pointed out that subsistence family farms have never dominated California agriculture. The state's crops are grown on huge acreages—a form of farming called agribusiness. As Chiu noted, under such a system of production, farm prices and consequently the "upper limit of both profit and wages" are determined not by local supply and demand but by constantly fluctuating national or even world commodity prices. During the 1860s farm employers standardized the wages paid to farm laborers of various ethnic origins. Chiu's sources indicate that they paid Native Americans and Mexican Americans less than $1 a day, Chinese between $1 and $1.20 a day, and European Americans $30 to $40 a month. In those days, hired help worked twenty-six days a month. So the daily wage of white farmhands ranged from $1.15 to $1.50. In the 1870s, farm employers revised the standard wage rates, varying them according to season. During the slack winter season, they paid Chinese $22 a month and whites $30 a month. During the busy summer season, the monthly pay of Chinese was $30 and that of whites $40 to $50. Despite paying white farmworkers more, farm employers deplored their allegedly poor work ethic, calling them "lazy idlers" who quit as soon as they had earned a few dollars. In contrast, agricultural employers spoke approvingly of their Chinese employees who stayed on the job until all the work they had agreed to do was completed, who provided their own food, who were diligent and well organized, and who never became drunkenly rowdy during weekends as many white workers did.

Street, a professional photographer and historian, produced a nine-hundred-page exhaustively researched narrative history of California farmworkers, and he devoted several chapters each to Native Americans, Mexican Americans, Chinese Americans, Japanese Americans, and European American "bindlemen" or "bindlestiffs"—derogatory terms meaning tramps or hobos. Piecing together thousands and thousands of documents, Street painted detailed, three-dimensional portraits of farmworkers who have played such a crucial role in transforming California into the premier agricultural producer that it still is. Street's findings of wage rates are similar to Ping Chiu's with the exception of the amount paid Mexican Americans. Street's sources indicate that Chinese received $1 a day without board, Mexicans $1.25 a day, and whites $1.50 a day. Both Mexicans and whites received board, estimated at 60 cents per person per day. Street argued that even though "the Chinese certainly understood that they received smaller wages than whites, they did not see themselves as 'cheap laborers'" because when they converted their American earnings into Chinese currency, they were doing quite well. In the late 1870s and early 1880s, small groups of Chinese farm laborers went on strike in scattered locations to demand wages equal to those paid European Americans. To hang on to this indispensable farm labor force, agricultural employers had no recourse except to raise the Chinese daily wage from $1 to $1.25 and even $1.50. The wages that Chan found in the 1872 *Transactions of the California State Agricultural Society* were similar to the figures unearthed by Chiu and Street. She also discovered that when farm employers responded to critics who excoriated them for using cheap Chinese labor, they pointed out that Chinese farmhands in California made more than what white farm laborers did in some other parts of the United States. Thus, whether or not a particular group of workers was "cheap" depended in part on who they were compared to. California's high wages across the board were a legacy of Gold Rush days when there was a severe shortage of labor as men chose to dig for gold rather than settle for the pittance common laborers earned. After the 1882 Chinese Exclusion Law went into effect and their numbers dwindled, Chinese workers used their enhanced bargaining power to strike for higher wages and shorter working hours. The Bureau of Labor Statistics observed in 1900 that the Chinese were "becoming Americanized to the extent of enforcing such demands in some cases through the medium of labor organization." The changing behavior of Chinese farmworkers mandates that the question of Chinese "cheap labor" be rephrased: were Chinese cheap because they were a despicably "servile" people or because they lacked the leverage to demand higher wages until their declining numbers made them a less available, and thus more highly prized, source of labor? In both railroad construction and agriculture, the historical record can be summarized pithily: cheaper labor, yes; slavelike labor, no.

The economic and labor histories of Asians in the U.S. mainland during the first six decades of the twentieth century are at once more complicated and simpler than accounts of the nineteenth century—more complex because the number of Asian-origin groups had increased and they were spreading themselves all over the American West; simpler because the occupational structure of these groups was considerably narrower than that found among nineteenth-century Chinese. Fewer kinds of jobs were open to Asian immigrants who arrived during the early decades of the twentieth century because gold that could be mined profitably with the then-existing technology had been depleted, the transcontinental railroads had been completed, labor unions had consolidated themselves by strenuously keeping out nonwhite workers, white manufacturers had driven Chinese (and later-arriving Asian immigrants) out of light manufacturing by persuading the public to boycott Chinese-made goods, and large factories owned by corporations were rapidly displacing independent artisans and small proprietors.

Japanese immigrant workers did not build transcontinental railroads but thousands of them worked as "section hands" to maintain the tracks. Investigators for a congressional committee also found some (Asian) Indian and Korean section hands at work at scattered locations in the American West. Japanese worked for coal-mining companies but did not prospect for gold. Many Japanese earned a living as import-export merchants, storekeepers, shop assistants, sellers of fresh produce, and proprietors of boarding houses, hotels, pool halls, and restaurants, but few Korean, Indian, and Filipino immigrants did so. The number of Koreans and Indians was so small that opening their own businesses was not a viable option, given their potentially minuscule co-ethnic clientele, while Filipinos, who were familiar with small stores owned by Chinese in the Philippines, apparently felt no discomfort patronizing stores run by Chinese in the United States. Compared to the very large number of Chinese laundrymen, the number of Japanese laundrymen was smaller. Numerous Japanese immigrant youth became domestic servants but virtually no Koreans and Indians did. Filipinos found service jobs as hotel bellhops and railroad porters.

The one economic sector that all groups worked in was agriculture. Tens of thousands of Chinese, Japanese, and Filipino immigrants earned a living as farmworkers while a relatively smaller number of Chinese, Japanese, Koreans, and Indians (but not Filipinos) became tenant farmers. In the early twentieth century, Japanese immigrants dominated the cultivation of many crops despite the restrictions imposed upon them by the 1913 and 1920 Alien Land laws in California. Oregon, Washington, Idaho, Montana, Minnesota, Arizona, New Mexico, Texas, Louisiana, Missouri, Kansas, and Nebraska also passed alien land laws. Even in the face of such legal strictures, as the Nisei historian Masakazu Iwata has chronicled, Japanese immigrants farmed all over the American West and in Texas as they developed "a distinct agricultural system, encompassing production as well as wholesale and retail distribution." The largest concentration of Korean tenant farmers was in Dinuba and Reedley, two small towns in the San Joaquin Valley of central California where they cultivated deciduous tree fruit. Other Korean tenant farmers grew rice in the upper Sacramento Valley and row crops in the Sacramento–San Joaquin Delta. Asian Indians gathered mainly in the semi-arid Imperial and Coachella valleys in the southeastern corner of California to grow cotton, cantaloupes, and winter crops of lettuce on irrigated land.[6] Almost no Filipinos leased land to farm even though they were not "aliens ineligible to [sic] citizenship" (and thus were not barred from leasing or buying land under the alien land laws) but were, instead, American "nationals" who traveled with U.S. passports during the years when an American colonial administration governed the Philippines. No one has yet investigated the reason(s) for the absence of Filipino tenant farmers during the 1920s and 1930s. Filipinos finally gained access to farms in 1942 when the federal government removed approximately 120,000 Issei and Nisei from the Pacific Coast states and part of Arizona and incarcerated them. The Farm Security Administration was responsible for finding replacement tenants and it offered the farms that Issei families were forced to abandon to Filipino, Chinese, and European American tenants.

In Hawai'i, the major employers of Asian immigrants were sugar plantation owners. Native Hawaiians, the first plantation employees, could not meet the burgeoning demand for plantation labor because they were dying at an alarming rate due to their lack of immunity to Old World diseases and overwork. As contract labor was legal in the Hawaiian kingdom under the 1850 Master and Servants Act that remained in force until 1897, planters looked for potential workers beyond Hawai'i's shores. The first Chinese contract laborers arrived in 1852, and more trickled in during the next quarter century. After the United States and the then-independent Kingdom of Hawaii signed the 1876 Reciprocity Treaty, the tariff levied on Hawaiian raw sugar imported into the United States was lifted. Thereafter, sugar production expanded rapidly, which meant that more and more plantation workers were needed. The Board of Immigration's records indicate that between 1865 and 1899, 33,605 Chinese, 65,034 Japanese, 10,835 Portuguese (mostly from the Azores and Madeira islands where sugarcane had been cultivated for several centuries), 2,444 Pacific Islanders, and smaller numbers of Germans, Norwegians, and Spaniards came on contract to work in Hawai'i. Plantation owners did not start hiring Filipinos until the 1906–1907 season.

During the last three decades of the nineteenth century, contract laborers as a percentage of the total plantation workforce declined as the proportion of free laborers increased—a development that plantation owners did not welcome. In 1886, the year after Japanese mass immigration to Hawai'i began, my computation of available statistics[7] shows that (counting only male workers) the percentage of contract laborers out of the total number of plantation workers in each ethnic group ranged from a low of 15 percent for Chinese to a high of 99 percent for Japanese. Among Pacific Islanders (other than Native Hawaiians), the proportion was 86 percent, Portuguese and Germans were each at 75 percent, and Native Hawaiians, 62 percent. Ten years later, the percentage under contract stood at 69 percent for Chinese, 54 percent for Japanese, 26 percent for Native Hawaiians, and 20 percent for Portuguese. By then, there were very few non-Portuguese European and Pacific Islander plantation workers left. The large increase in the percentage of Chinese contract laborers in 1896 is a reflection of the fact that Hawai'i's legislature, pressured by plantation owners, passed a law in 1890 to allow the minister of foreign affairs to authorize Chinese contract laborers be admitted for five-year terms with the stipulation that they be confined to plantation work only. An 1892 revision limited the annual intake to 5,000 and allowed Chinese to work as domestic servants as well. Under another amendment approved in 1895, the recruits who had entered earlier under temporary permits could henceforth remain in Hawai'i permanently. By 1899, the year before contract labor was outlawed, 15 percent of Hawaiians, 8 percent of Portuguese, 46 percent of Chinese, and 75 percent of Japanese plantation workers were still working under contract.

At century's end, Japanese dominated the plantation labor force, comprising 71 percent of the total (counting both contract and free laborers), and it was they who participated in dozens of spontaneous, short-lived strikes in 1900 after the U.S. Congress passed the Organic Act to make Hawai'i's laws conform to U.S. laws—an important provision in the U.S. annexation of Hawai'i. Henceforth, contract labor would no longer be legal in the islands. Between 1907 and 1919, 24,113 Filipinos landed in Hawai'i; from 1920 to 1929, 47,481 did so. No longer bound by a labor system with punitive penalties, those Japanese and Filipino plantation workers who neither returned to their homelands nor sailed from Hawai'i to the U.S. mainland after their contracts ended carried out larger and longer strikes.

In response to this rising labor militancy, after the 1920 strike (described below) plantation owners formed the Hawaiian Emergency Labor Commission to lobby Washington, D.C., to seek permission to hire Chinese contract laborers even though that recruitment channel had been illegal for twenty years. As the historian and labor activist John E. Reinecke chronicled at length, this appeal was based on a "feigned necessity." What sugar planters really wanted was not simply more workers but "a return to the system of contract-bound labor."[8] However, after congressmen listened to testimony from anti-Chinese leaders from California, who conjured up the fearsome specter of Chinese coolies once again, they declined to grant the sugar planters their wish. The alleged labor shortage soon eased as an increasing number of Filipinos arrived.

Two pivotal issues emerge from the Asian American economic and labor historiography of the first half of the twentieth century. First, were Japanese in the U.S. mainland a sojourning middleman minority who planned to return to Japan after they had earned some money, or were they actually trying to colonize areas of the American West as they leased and bought agricultural land? Second, did Asian immigrant workers possess a working-class consciousness and, if so, in which setting and under what circumstances was that consciousness most clearly displayed?

The sociologist Edna Bonacich has applied middleman minority theory to Asian Americans. In a 1973 journal article and a 1980 book on Japanese Americans coauthored with the historian John Modell, she argued that the Chinese in Southeast Asia, Indians in East Africa, and Jews in Europe—the archetypical middleman minorities—were sojourners who maximized the liquidity of their assets so that they could pull up stakes and leave in a hurry should hostilities against them erupt. These groups evinced a very high level of ethnic solidarity and served as middlemen or buffers between the European colonial elite and the nonwhite masses, in the process bridging the "status gap" between these two groups while keeping largely to themselves socially and culturally. Analogously, Bonacich and Modell tried to prove that Japanese Americans were also a sojourning middleman minority because so many of them owned and ran small businesses or were tenant farmers during the pre–World War II decades. Even the Nisei had an occupational concentration in commerce, they averred, so Japanese Americans constituted an intergenerational middleman minority. As they saw it, being a sojourning middleman minority was supposedly a *culturally* determined trait that played a far more important role than *structural* factors—laws that barred Japanese Americans from many lines of work and severely limited the kind of occupations they could enter—in shaping the socioeconomic nature of Japanese American communities.[9]

V. S. McClatchy, a newspaper publisher and an actively outspoken anti-Japanese leader, framed the situation in the opposite way. He wrote and distributed widely a pamphlet entitled *Japanese Immigration and Colonization* to broadcast the alarmist idea that Japanese were invading the United States in order to colonize it. Indeed, Japanese immigrants did create several agricultural colonies—the Yamato colony near the town of Livingston; and the Cressey and Cortez colonies, located in Merced County, California. Abiko Kyutaro, the founder of the influential newspaper *Nichibei Shimbun*, who made money as a labor contractor and was a highly respected community leader, strongly urged Issei and their progeny to settle permanently in the United States and to abandon the practice of *dekasegi* (temporary labor migration). In 1906, he established the American Land and Produce Company and bought 3,200 acres, which he then divided into lots of forty acres each and sold to those who wished to become owner-operators of farms of their own. The first group of buyers moved onto their properties in 1907. The other two planned agricultural colonies came into being a decade or so later. The existence of these colonies, plus the increasingly visible Issei presence in other farming localities, intensified the paranoia felt by people who were vehemently anti-Japanese.

There was little clarity regarding whether the Japanese in the United States were sojourners or alleged invaders until the historian Eiichiro Azuma examined the issue in an incisive and sophisticated way. Closely reading Japanese-language sources that other researchers had hitherto not used and analyzed, Azuma portrayed a group of people pulled in opposite directions by two growing empires, Japan and the United States, that were locked in competition for hegemony over the Pacific. Beginning in 1927, a number of Issei intellectuals became community historians and took on the task of writing their fellow immigrants' history. They equated themselves with European American pioneers who had conquered and developed the American West and strived to replace the Issei's "crisis of racial subordination with a shared memory of their glorious past." They claimed to be *both* American frontiersmen and Japanese colonists. Their discourse was meant to challenge "the Anglo-American monopoly on frontier expansionism." Leaders in Japan found the Issei's assertions convenient during a period when Japan was engaged in efforts to create "new Japans" overseas in East Asia, islands in the Pacific Ocean, and the Americas. Unlike the Issei historians who spoke of their "racial *compatibility*" with European Americans, Japan's leaders touted the "racial *superiority*" of the Yamato race (emphases added). Accordingly, the Issei historians "prophesized advances for their community with a conviction buoyed by the current ascent of Japan in a world dominated by the West and the white race." They declared, "We are not legally . . . American citizens, but in spirit we have become American citizens. We are loyal to our native land, but in that loyalty we find nothing incompatible with loyalty to our land of adoption."[10] Tragically, that duality was found wanting after Japan bombed Pearl Harbor and Japanese Americans, as well as Japanese Canadians and Japanese Australians, were rounded up and forced to spend the war years in concentration camps.

In the globalized world of the twenty-first century, in which an increasing number of people lead transnational lives and possess multiple identities, the questions of national belonging and political loyalty are once again at the fore. Juxtaposing the sojourning middleman minority theory with the "invasion" narrative throws into bold relief the existential dilemma that Asian Americans have had to confront. Characterized as sojourners, they were/are faulted for failing to assimilate; yet, when they did/do show concrete signs of becoming permanent settlers in their country of adoption, they were/are tarred as "invaders." Today this long-standing contradiction still rears its ugly head from time to time, sometimes overtly but most of the time as a subtext, in both public and scholarly discourse.

The second analytical issue likewise requires researchers to tease out the mentality of certain Asian immigrants—in this instance, those who earned a living as wage laborers. Labor history's master narrative centers on how workers organize unions to pressure their bosses to increase their wages and improve their working conditions. Asian American labor history is relatively underdeveloped because it is dependent on the availability of reliable information about the *consciousness* of Asian American workers. Knowing which rung of the economic ladder individuals or groups may occupy tells us very little about whether they identify themselves as members of a specific class within society. Are they people who act to promote their interests *as members of a distinct class* with common aspirations and strategies for improving their lot *while remaining in the class position they currently occupy,* or do they make every effort to *escape from* the confines of the working class in order to make their way into classes with higher incomes and social status? Historically Asian American workers left few documents that reveal how they thought and felt about their stations in life. Only a few booklength life histories of Asian American labor activists have been published—books by or about Karl Yoneda, Koji Ariyoshi, Pablo Manlapit, and Philip Vera Cruz being the most prominent. Given the thin evidence available, Asian American labor historians must make do with studies that *infer* the workers' consciousness by looking at their visible, recorded actions in the form of strikes, boycotts, or other acts of labor militancy.

In the continental United States, in addition to the strikes by Chinese railroad builders and farm laborers mentioned above, Chinese workers in the post–Civil War South also carried out small-scale strikes as the anthropologist Lucy M. Cohen has documented. During the first decade of the twentieth century there occurred two strikes that involved interethnic cooperation. The sociologist Tomás Almaguer and the historian Yuji Ichioka have told the story of 1,200 Japanese and Mexican sugar-beet field workers in Oxnard (located along California's central coast) who formed the Japanese-Mexican Labor Association in 1903 and jointly struck for higher wages and to break the Western Agricultural Contracting Company's monopoly over who growers would be allowed to hire. The strikers demanded the right to negotiate with the growers directly. As scabs were brought in and several deaths and injuries ensued, the American Federation of Labor, though hostile to nonwhite workers, stepped in to mediate. After some of the strikers' demands were met, they returned to work and applied for a charter to form a local union to be affiliated with the American Federation of Labor (AFL). When the

AFL's longtime president, Samuel Gompers, decided that the local charter would be granted only if no Japanese or Chinese members would be admitted, the Mexican workers declined the offer. They told Gompers, "We would be false to them [Japanese workers] and to ourselves and to the cause of unionism if we now accepted privileges for ourselves which are not accorded to them."[11]

In another rare case of interethnic interaction, Japanese coal miners in southern Wyoming were allowed to join a local affiliated with the United Mine Workers of America in 1907. Ichioka explained that this exceptional event came about because it was in the self-interest of that local union and its white members to invite Japanese workers, who formed the largest component of the mine labor force, to become members. The union would gain because its enlarged membership would give it added strength in negotiations with the company. European American union members would benefit because the company could no longer use nonunionized and lower-paid Japanese workers to displace them. The mining company also saw an advantage because it could keep its operations functioning, given the fact that no alternative labor force was available in the thinly populated area. Therefore, the decision the union made to admit Japanese members was a pragmatic one; it was not a manifestation of class unity.[12]

During the 1930s, Filipino workers became the most active advocates for labor unions. The historian Howard DeWitt researched labor unrest in the Imperial Valley of California where fifty-one large growers, many of whom were absentee landlords, controlled 83 percent of the valley's total arable acreage and where Mexicans, (Asian) Indians, and Filipinos were the main field laborers. Mexican farmworkers formed their own ethnic labor union in 1928, and Filipinos established the Filipino Labor Union (FLU) a few years later. From 1928 to the mid-1930s, labor unrest was rampant among workers in the valley's cantaloupe and lettuce fields. Organizers from several communist labor unions moved in to take advantage of the volatile situation by trying to guide and co-opt these strikes. Their presence enabled law enforcement officers to use red-baiting rhetoric, violent tactics, and mass arrests to shut down the nascent ethnic labor unions and to defeat some two dozen strikes. Thus, ironically, the communist organizers unwittingly made the lives of the strikers more difficult. DeWitt also studied the 1934 lettuce workers' strike in Salinas, California, and the Pajaro Valley, also in California, to this day the nation's prime lettuce-producing areas. The National Industrial Recovery Act, promulgated during the Great Depression, required employers to recognize and negotiate with legitimate unions. An AFL local affiliate, the Vegetable Packers Association (VPA), offered to cooperate with the FLU but tensions soon arose between the two when the former was willing to accept binding arbitration but the latter was not. When members of the VPA returned to work, Filipino farmworkers refused to join them. As the strike continued, growers brought in more Mexican farm laborers and accused the FLU of being a "Communist front group," law enforcement officers arrested hundreds of Filipino strikers, and some canny Filipino labor contractors formed a Filipino Labor Supply Organization to recruit scabs for the growers. The FLU finally called off the strike after it won recognition as a legitimate farmworkers' union, wages were increased from 20 to 40 cents an hour, and better working conditions were specified. After another strike in 1936, the AFL granted a charter to the Field Workers Union, local 30326, that had both Filipino and Mexican members.[13]

In a richly documented and movingly told story, the historian Chris Friday traced the development of the canned-salmon industry in Alaska in which Chinese workers initially dominated the labor supply. As an increasing number of Japanese and Filipinos joined the cannery labor force, the aging Chinese held on to the best jobs for themselves, becoming what Friday dubbed a "labor aristocracy," in the process blocking the later-arriving groups' pathway to upward mobility within the workforce—that is, the chance for workers to become foremen, labor subcontractors, or contractors. Despite the Filipino workers' growing numerical dominance, they were stuck at the bottom of the hierarchy. In time, they realized they had to create an alternate upward path for themselves by forming a union. Their unionizing efforts were vastly complicated by three ongoing struggles for power: (1) the rivalry between the craft-oriented AFL and the industrywide organizing strategy of the Congress of Industrial Organizations (CIO); (2) the fight between the International Brotherhood of Teamsters and the International Longshoremen's and Warehousemen's Union for control of the waterfront along the entire Pacific Coast of North America as well as in Hawai'i; and (3) the deep divisions among Filipinos themselves. In the winter of 1932, several Filipino *Alaskaderos* began planning for a union of their own. The following summer, their Cannery Workers and Farm Laborers Union (CWFLU) became a local affiliate of the AFL. But the fledgling union had a difficult time getting work for its members because canning companies preferred to deal with Chinese and, to a lesser extent, Japanese labor contractors with whom they had done business for many years. Meanwhile, the CWFLU faced competition from the Japanese Cannery Workers Association, led by Clarence Arai, a prominent Nisei lawyer, and the Filipino Cannery Workers Association, headed by Pio de Cano, the most notable Filipino labor contractor.

Then on December 1, 1936, tragedy struck. Virgil Dunyungan, CWFLU's president; Aurelio Simon, another union official; and Placido Patron, the nephew of a contractor, were gunned down in broad daylight. The question of who killed whom and why has never been satisfactorily answered but the killings galvanized Filipino union members to close ranks. To make a long and extremely complicated story short, suffice it to say that in September 1937, the CWFLU left the AFL and accepted a charter as CIO, local 7, proffered by the United Cannery, Agricultural, Packing, and Allied Workers of America. From then until early 1942, when World War II upended all aspects of American life, CIO, local 7, and its AFL-affiliated and Japanese-led rival union managed to diminish the power of labor contractors, ended many of the abuses and financial exploitation that cannery workers had suffered, doubled wages, and improved working conditions.[14]

On the other side of the continent in New York during the 1930s, Chinese seamen, who were employed in increasing numbers during the Great Depression as shipping companies cut costs by hiring lower-paid, nonunion, foreign-born sailors, took action to protest the fact that Chinese sailors were required to sign contracts that allowed shipping companies to hold 50 percent of their wages until they were discharged, to demand that each man post a $500 bond, and to forbid Chinese sailors, unlike seaman of other ethnic origins, from going ashore when ships docked in U.S. ports. Not only that, but the Seamen's International Union, an AFL affiliate, asked immigration officials to search for, arrest, and deport Chinese sailors who were found on shore. In contrast, the National Maritime Union (NMU), established in 1933, prohibited racial discrimination and invited African American and Chinese seamen to join their 1936 strike in New York. As the pro-labor activist and scholar Peter Kwong has brought to light, some 3,000 Chinese seamen participated in that strike when the NMU promised to support their demands for equal wages and shore leave.[15]

The historian Renqiu Yu has told the story of another group of Chinese New Yorkers—approximately 10,000 laundrymen who worked in some 3,500 laundries—who stood up for their rights, not only against a discriminatory city ordinance but also against the elite in their own community—the Chinese Consolidated Benevolent Association (CCBA—the equivalent of the so-called Chinese Six Companies on the West Coast). Combing through a nineteen-year run of the *China Daily News*, a newspaper that laundrymen founded and published, pamphlets and newsletters they produced, as well as conducting in-depth interviews in Chinese with aging laundrymen, Yu recovered the voices of laundrymen that might have remained mute had he not done his research. The Great Depression adversely affected the laundrymen as their European American customer base shrank. Worse, in 1933 New York City's aldermen, at the behest of large white-owned laundries, proposed an ordinance to charge Chinese- operated hand laundries an annual license of $25 and a security bond of $1,000. In addition, the proposed ordinance stipulated that only U.S. citizens would be granted licenses to operate public laundries. Aside from the financial hardship laundrymen would suffer, the proposed ordinance was discriminatory because U.S. laws prohibited Chinese immigrants from becoming naturalized citizens—a fact that would make them ineligible to operate laundries. The laundrymen sought help from the CCBA but the latter demanded $1 from each self-employed laundryman and $2 from laundries with two or more workers before it would consider doing something to help the laundrymen. But after collecting this money, the CCBA did nothing.

Angered by the CCBA's high-handedness, the laundrymen established the Chinese Hand Laundry Alliance (CHLA) to defend their interests. Within a month of its founding, some 2,000 members had joined the organization. Their opposition to the aldermen's legislative action eventually led the aldermen to reduce the license to $10 and the bond to $100. An amendment also exempted "Orientals" from the U.S. citizenship requirement. Buoyed by this victory and learning new ideas from immigrant Chinese leftists, leaders among the laundrymen developed an increasingly sophisticated political consciousness that they disseminated among their fellow laundrymen. As Japan's armies conquered more and more Chinese territory in the 1930s, the laundrymen in New York became actively involved in anti-Japanese efforts in the United States and made contributions to the movement for "national salvation" in China. Their slogan, "to save China, to save ourselves," epitomized their transnational perspective. Chinatown's merchant elite tried to destroy the CHLA through blackmail and physical intimidation, secretly sending reports to U.S. immigration officials to finger various laundrymen as illegal aliens or as communists who should be deported.[16]

The history of Asian American labor activism in the 1930s, especially among immigrant Filipinos and Chinese, when juxtaposed against the nineteenth-century crusade against cheap Chinese labor and the twentieth-century use of scare tactics to undermine immigrant Japanese farmers, reveals yet another facet of the dialectical predicament fettering the lives of Asian Americans. When they performed difficult jobs diligently and quietly, they were impugned as disguised slaves; yet when they stood up for their rights as workers, they were maligned as un-American—indeed, anti-American—communist radicals who should be expelled from the body politic.

The strikes undertaken by Hawai'i's plantation workers are better known than the unionization efforts on the mainland because the strikes in Hawai'i lasted longer, involved more people, and have been more thoroughly analyzed by the historians Ronald Takaki, Edward D. Beechert, John E. Reinecke, Masayo Umezawa Duus, and Melinda Tria Kerkvliet, and by the ethnic studies scholar Ruben R. Alcantara.[17] Japanese plantation workers—1,200 fieldworkers, mill hands, stable boys, and carpenters—undertook the first organized strike in 1904 at Waialua on Oahu; 900 workers revolted in 1905 in Lahaina on Maui; and a third strike occurred in Waipahu on Oahu in 1906. Newspaper reporters called the strikers "outside agitators" and "conspirators." The three largest strikes occurred in 1909, 1920, and 1924, lasting four, six, and eight months, respectively, with an estimated 7,000, 8,000, and 2,000 participants, respectively.

One thread that runs through all three large and long-lasting strikes is that individuals who themselves were not working in plantations played key roles in organizing and sustaining the strikes. In 1909, the Higher Wages Association (HWA) established by Japanese Hawaiian journalists and merchants, among whom Frederick Kinzaburo Makino, a drugstore owner fluent in both Japanese and English, was the most active, helped plantation workers to formulate their demands based on the fact that plantation workers' wages had not risen even as the cost of living in Hawai'i kept going up. The HWA sent a report documenting the economic squeeze on plantation workers to the Hawaiian Sugar Planters Association (HSPA) but no response came. After waiting almost five months for a reply, 7,000 workers went on strike, which ended only when workers were evicted from plantation housing and all the resources offered by their supporters (including food on credit from Chinese shopkeepers) ran out. Strike leaders, including Makino, were arrested, charged with conspiracy, and sent to jail. Three months after the strike, however, the planters ended the practice of paying workers of various ethnic origins different wages when they did the same kind of work. After the 1909 strike, plantation owners also stepped up their efforts to recruit more laborers from the Philippines.

In 1919, Japanese workers in the Waialua plantation on Oahu formed a union with some eight hundred members. Workers on other plantations followed suit. These plantation-level unions amalgamated into the Associated Japanese Labor Union of Hawaii. The nonplantation leadership came mainly from members of the Young Men's Buddhist Association. The number of Filipino plantation workers had been increasing rapidly since 1907 but they had not yet formed their own union. However, they had an emergent leader in Pablo Manlapit, who had come to Hawai'i in 1909 at age nineteen and had worked for three years on a sugar plantation. At the end of that three-year stint, he led a strike to protest the plantation management's unilateral move to reduce the agreed-on price for cutting each hectare of cane. The plantation reported the strike to the HSPA, which then blacklisted him while the plantation fired him. After leaving the plantation, Manlapit managed to find work as a stevedore, janitor, court interpreter, manager of a pool hall, and editor of a weekly newsletter. When he became an assistant to a Honolulu lawyer, he began studying law on his own and in time obtained a license to practice law. But his heart was in labor organizing. During 1919, he followed Fred Makino around as the latter traveled to all the Hawaiian Islands to talk to plantation workers. He also became friends with George Wright, a committed union organizer who was president of the AFL Labor Council in Hawai'i. Even though the AFL was hostile to nonwhite workers, Wright himself was a strong advocate of multiethnic and multiracial labor unity. Out of these interpersonal relationships grew the idea that Japanese and Filipino plantation workers could rise up jointly to carry out the first dual-ethnic strike in Hawai'i in 1920. On August 31, 1919, Manlapit helped establish the Filipino Labor Union (that became the model for the FLU formed in the early 1930s in California at Manlapit's urging) to unify Filipino workers. Listening to his open-air speeches to plantation workers, a major newspaper in Hawai'i denounced him as a dangerous and un-American agitator who was preaching class hatred.

As Melinda Kerkvliet has stressed (but Edward Beechert and Ron Takaki did not), tensions roiled the efforts at coordination and cooperation. Tensions existed between Japanese and Filipino workers and between their respective leaders. Distrust also marred the relationship between these leaders and their co-ethnic followers. Due to the underlying strains and the difficulty of communicating with workers in several plantations simultaneously, Filipinos went on strike before the Japanese strike organizers thought it was prudent to do so. The latter asked Manlapit to call off the premature strike but the Filipino workers would not listen to him. In this climate of uncertainty, Honolulu newspapers began to characterize the strike as a "Japanese conspiracy" to take over Hawai'i's sugar business. As Masayo Duus has analyzed insightfully, what began as a *labor* dispute was reinscribed as a "*race* war." Manlapit, sad to say, believed the invidious allegations against the Japanese and distanced himself from them. The owners and managers of the plantations that were struck resorted to the same tactics as those used in 1909 to defeat the strikers: evicting them from plantation housing, arresting them, and getting the courts to convict the strike leaders for "conspiracy in the first degree" and imprisoning them.

The 1924 strike, the first multi-island strike, involved mainly Filipino workers. Reinecke called it a "piecemeal strike" because workers on the different islands followed their own schedule regarding when to launch their strikes. Instead of dubbing the 1924 series of strikes as a race war and as a manifestation of Japan's efforts to colonize Hawai'i, a new dynamic appeared on the scene. For years, Filipino workers had yearned for a resident commissioner to be sent from the Philippines with the hope that such an official could represent them and speak on behalf of their interests. Unfortunately, the first resident commissioner, Cayetano Ligot, who arrived in 1923, did exactly the opposite: he became the HSPA's best ally. Filipino Protestant ministers, and evangelical missionaries likewise sided with plantation management. What emerged, then, was an *inter*ethnic class alliance between the local Filipino elite and plantation owners who worked jointly to defeat the strikers. Instead of showing ethnic solidarity, the Filipino elite waged an *intra*-ethnic class war against their co-ethnic workers. Manlapit, who was deemed less important than his Japanese labor-leader peers during the 1920 strike, now became the HSPA's main target. He was arrested and convicted of several charges and spent the next three years in jail.

Comparing the U.S. mainland and Hawai'i, workers' class consciousness was more apparent in the islands because the situation in which they found themselves gave them fewer options. In the nineteenth century, plantation contract laborers could not walk away from their jobs without severe penalties while the free laborers knew of few opportunities in the world outside the plantations. They led isolated lives because many of the plantations were located quite a distance from the nearest towns. Unlike the mainland where ethnic communities sprang up in many localities, plantation workers had no nearby co-ethnic communities that might have served as sanctuaries into which they could disappear if they escaped from the plantations. Even after the contract-labor regime ended, their lives did not improve much. They continued to be oppressed by plantation owners, managers, and *luna* who treated them as nothing more than beasts of burden. Accordingly, class divisions within the plantations, which coincided with racial divisions (at least until the 1924 strikes), were clearly demarcated. Those who wished to improve their lives had few options other than to go on strike. As the journalist Sanford Zalburg, the historians Edward D. Beechert and Gerald Horne, and the sociologist Moon-Kie Jung have recounted, in the years following World War II multiethnic unions were finally successfully established in Hawai'i largely under the dynamic leadership of the International Longshoremen's and Warehousemen's Union.[18] Hawai'i remains today as the state with the highest percentage of unionized workers. Those same postwar decades also witnessed the spectacular ascent of the Democratic Party, which would dominate Hawaiian politics for decades to come. Unions and Democrats together have transformed the lives of Asian Hawaiians and other working people in fundamental ways.

In contrast, Asian immigrant workers in the continental United States had relatively more opportunities to leave their jobs to look for new ones. They were not confined within "total institutions" (a concept propounded by the sociologist Erving Goffman that is applicable to sugar plantations) that encumbered every aspect of their lives in the same way that plantation workers in Hawai'i were tethered. Asian workers in the continental United States were less often compelled to remain in cruel and exploitative situations so long as they were willing to take risks and face uncertainties after they left unbearable jobs. They knew that some of their compatriots managed to improve their lot economically and socially by starting small businesses or leasing and even buying land to farm. Given such hopeful, albeit limited, possibilities, fewer individuals felt permanently trapped at the very bottom of society. So, going on strike was only *one of several* possible options that might conceivably lead to better days. In many economic sectors, Asian labor contractors—two-faced creatures who simultaneously helped and exploited their co-ethnic workers—often acted as buffers between discontented workers and their employers to dampen or forestall labor militancy. In businesses that hired co-ethnic workers, reactive ethnic solidarity in the face of hostility from mainstream society helped mute potential class conflicts between employers and employees. Furthermore, for almost a century a very large number of the Asians on the mainland were migrant workers and it was very difficult for them to remain together long enough in any one place to discuss, plan, and carry out possible strikes even if they wanted to. Finally, few Asian immigrant workers joined mainstream unions because with rare exceptions white union leaders and members helped spearhead the anti-Asian movements as racism trumped class unity. All these factors contributed to the somewhat porous boundaries between different classes within Asian American communities in the continental United States that in certain circumstances rendered class differences ambiguous and indeterminate.

Since Congress reformed U.S. immigration laws in 1965 and amended them several times thereafter, the world of Asian America has expanded in multiple ways. The Asian American population has burgeoned, and immigrants from many Asian countries—Thailand, Malaysia, Singapore, Indonesia, Pakistan, Bangladesh, Sri Lanka, and Iran (that had not hitherto sent emigrants to America)—set foot on U.S. soil, greatly increasing the diversity within Asian America. The very large influx of refugees from Vietnam, Laos, and Cambodia from 1975 through the early 1990s, followed by the entry of smaller numbers of refugees from Afghanistan, Iraq, Myanmar (formerly known as Burma), Tibet, and people of Nepalese origin in Bhutan from the early 1990s to the present, further enhanced the multiplicity of Asian America.

There is an ironic paradox in post-1965 Asian American history, however. As the proportion of foreign-born Asian Americans increased vis-à-vis the U.S.-born, the pan-Asian coalitional identity, "Asian Americans," formulated in the late 1960s began to fray. Foreign-born immigrants now form a large majority among every Asian ethnic group except Japanese Americans, and they are much less likely to call themselves Asian Americans. Most of them do not share the multiethnic Asian American worldview of the 1960s generation who first coined the term; rather, they think of themselves in terms of a single national/ethnic origin. Furthermore, many of the immigrants from countries that are still ruled by communist governments strongly disapprove of—indeed, condemn—the left-leaning tendencies of the individuals who had participated in various aspects of the Asian American movement. More are inclined to be Republicans than Democrats if they participate in electoral politics at all. Middle-class and well-to-do Asian immigrants and their progeny usually do not mingle with poorer Asian Americans except when the latter happen to provide childcare, housecleaning, and lawn care for them. Cleavages based on national/ethnic origins, generation within the United States, class, gender, sexual orientation, political ideology, and attitudes toward and connections with ancestral homelands now divide communities that outside observers and government agencies continue to assume are homogeneous entities. Funding agencies, law enforcement officers, health providers, and government officials all find it convenient to deal with a single amalgamated group, and it is this public usage that is helping scholars in Asian American studies to perpetuate the notions of "Asian Americans" and "Asian America." Pacific Islanders were included in the demographic mix for several decades until they lobbied to be removed from the Asian/Pacific American rubric. The U.S. Census Bureau acceded to their request, but many community organizations continue to use the terms "Asian and Pacific Americans" or "Asian/Pacific Americans" even when they show little real interest in and concern for the well-being of Pacific Islander Americans.

Social scientists (a vast majority of them sociologists), rather than historians, are the scholars who have been and are most actively studying these new social formations. For this reason, a consideration of theoretical constructs is inescapable in discussing the research on post-1965 developments. Laissez-faire market economics, human capital, segmented (or dual) labor market, social capital, and ethnic enclave economies are the main concepts guiding the research that has been done. Two sets of questions emerge from the existing literature. First, what "modes of incorporation" have post-1965 Asian immigrants followed or are following as they entered/enter American society and its economy, and how has each mode impacted their socioeconomic status? Second, how has globalization affected the lives of Asian Americans and how, in turn, have Asian Americans contributed to the globalizing process by virtue of the choices they make and the actions they take?

Classical economic theory postulates that in a laissez-faire market system that is unencumbered by government regulations or other noneconomic forces the price of a commodity is arrived at when supply and demand are in equilibrium. Similarly, the wage that an individual worker earns results from the interaction between the demand for and supply of the particular kind of work he or she can perform. International migration occurs when wages in different countries are so obviously different that workers from low-wage (unusually "underdeveloped") countries migrate to higher-wage (usually "developed" but also "developing") countries in pursuit of better lives. Early studies of Asian international labor migrations either explicitly or implicitly relied on the assumptions of classical economic theory—that is, poor economic conditions in Asian (or other Old World) countries "push" emigrants out while the lure of higher wages, available farmland, or opportunities to go into business "pull" immigrants into more prosperous economies or societies. This push-pull framework continues to be used in some studies of Asian immigration to this day.

Human capital theory refined laissez-faire economic theory by making the latter less mechanistic. Human capital refers to an agglomeration of education, job experience, and other personal attributes that enable people to perform work that produces economic value. Unlike material capital (machines, factories, and technology), human capital resides within individuals. However, it is fungible: individual workers possessing a certain kind or amount of human capital can be interchanged with other workers with the same endowment of desirable traits. When sociologists began looking at the socioeconomic status of Asian Americans through the lens of human capital theory, they assumed that if Asian Americans earn less than European Americans, it must be because the amount of human capital Asian Americans possess is less than that possessed by the canonical "white male." Or the source of the disparity might be due to the fact that the education and work skills that immigrant Asians had acquired abroad are not transferable to the U.S. context.

The data that social scientists use to study socioeconomic status are drawn largely from the computerized Public Use Microdata Sample (PUMS) files prepared by the U.S. Census Bureau, beginning with the 1960 census. Similar computer-accessible files for a 1 percent stratified sample are also available for the 1940 and 1950 censuses, which were assembled in a collaborative effort between the Census Bureau and the Center for Demography and Ecology at the University of Wisconsin. The Census Bureau, in cooperation with Archives.com, released digital images of all 3.8 million pages of the 1940 manuscript census on April 2, 2012. These digital images are useful to genealogists and others searching for information about specific individuals, families, or households, but they are not usable in the same way as PUMS files. Other databases produced by the Census Bureau that scholars who research Asian Americans' socioeconomic status have used include the Survey of Income and Program Participation (SIPP), Survey of Minority-Owned Business Enterprises (SMOBE), and Survey of Business Owners (SBO). The SBO information is broken down by individual Asian ethnic groups instead of being lumped together as "Asian." The individual groups include (Asian) Indians, Chinese, Filipino, Japanese, Koreans, Vietnamese, and "other Asians." Social scientists themselves also create databases of their own, including survey questionnaires tailored to whatever topics they are studying, ethnographic work in the form of in-depth interviews and participant observations, and reviews of available written sources. The main methods used to make sense of such data are statistical analysis and discursive interpretations.

The first two Asian American sociologists to study the changing socioeconomic status of Asian Americans were Robert M. Jiobu and Morrison G. Wong (alone and with his coauthor Charles Hirschman) who analyzed the PUMS files from the 1960 and 1970 censuses. They, as well as the economist Barry R. Chiswick, found that by 1970 the educational level of both immigrant and U.S.-born Asian Americans equaled or exceeded that of European Americans. Proportionately more Asian Americans were professionals than whites but a significantly larger percentage of immigrant Chinese and Filipinos worked in low-paid service occupations and in retail trade. U.S.-born Japanese Americans had reached parity with white males in terms of income while U.S.-born Chinese Americans were not quite there yet in 1970. U.S.-born Filipinos, who had fewer years of both schooling and work experience, had a lower socioeconomic status than Chinese and Japanese Americans. Overall, the "cost" of being Asian Americans, as measured by the income gap between a particular Asian-origin group and European American males, had decreased between 1960 and 1970. However, given the higher educational attainment levels of Asian Americans, their returns from schooling did not produce the higher earnings that should have been commensurate with their educational investment. Thus, whatever income parity certain groups of Asian Americans had attained came from their overachievement in higher education and not from wage equality.[19]

By the time that the 1980 PUMS files became available, more sociologists had developed an interest in the socioeconomic status of Asian Americans. The sociologists Victor Nee, Jimy Sanders, Herbert R. Barringer, David P. Takeuchi, Peter C. Xenos, Min Zhou, and the physicist-turned-sociologist Amado Cabezas and his coauthor Gary Kawaguchi, all did research using the 1980 census data. Nee and Sanders found that the four groups with the highest earnings were U.S.-born whites, U.S.-born Chinese Americans, and both immigrant and U.S.-born Japanese Americans. The "cost" of being immigrants was least for those with college degrees. U.S.-born Filipino Americans continued to lag behind and their returns to education were "unusually modest." Based on these findings, Nee and Sanders argued that the "cost" of ethnicity should be distinguished from the "cost" of being foreign-born. Barringer, Takeuchi, and Xenos examined Korean and Indian Americans in addition to Chinese, Japanese, and Filipino Americans. Due to the large number of immigrants among Chinese, Filipinos, Koreans, and Indians by the time the 1980 census was taken, these groups still suffered income losses when educational attainment is taken into account. Zhou compared persons of black, Mexican, Puerto Rican, Cuban, Chinese, and Japanese ancestries and concluded that the different ways in which members of these groups are utilized in the labor force result in differential economic outcomes. Cabezas and Kawaguchi found that race has a greater dampening effect on earnings than does place of birth.[20] The general picture that emerges from the 1980 census is a contradictory one: some Asian Americans had reached parity with white males in terms of earnings but the socioeconomic status of others was becoming less positive than it had been in earlier years partly due to the large influx of immigrants struggling to find their economic footing in the labor market. In other words, the Asian American population was becoming a bimodal one, with a large cluster of low-income earners and another large grouping of highly educated professionals and successful businesspeople.

Such a socioeconomic bunching reflects post-1965 U.S. immigration policy that admits individuals on the basis of two principles: family reunification and skills needed in the U.S. economy. Potentially low-income earners enter largely via family reunification while well-educated individuals come under the needed-skills principle. As over a million refugees from Vietnam, Laos, and Cambodia entered the country, the bimodal distribution became even more pronounced and national/ethnic origins became a key variable requiring analysis. Meanwhile, the positive aspects of the socioeconomic status of Asian Americans were seen as proof that Asian Americans were indeed a model minority—an idea first disseminated in the late 1960s. This image, based on treating Asian Americans as an aggregate, camouflages the internal disparities within the population. So the aggregate data must be disaggregated into separate Asian ethnic groups to provide a more accurate picture.

In the early 1970s, the segmented or dual labor-market theory was developed to explain why such a bifurcation exists. It posits that there are actually two labor markets in existence—a primary market where jobs are well paid, prestigious, and stable with high returns to human capital and opportunities for career advancement as well as good fringe benefits, and a secondary market where jobs are low paid, insecure, dangerous, dirty, and difficult with no fringe benefits and few, if any, chances for upward mobility regardless of what human capital workers in that sector may possess. Segmented labor-market theorists argue that immigrants, including foreign-born Asians, and women are slotted into the secondary market because of racism, nativism, and sexism; it helps to account for how discrimination based on race, ethnicity, nativity, and gender impacts the socioeconomic status of Asian Americans.

To overcome the secondary labor-market trap, many immigrants turn to self-employment in small business. Observing this phenomenon, sociologists developed the twin concepts of social capital and the ethnic-enclave economy that, taken together, illuminate the existence of an alternative path to upward mobility other than insertion into the primary labor market. Social capital theory highlights the significance of shared group resources available under certain conditions to enable particular activities to take place. Groups can range from families to various institutions to entire communities, and such group-based capital can facilitate the acquisition of individual human capital. This phenomenon is called "bounded solidarity." Conversely, social capital can also be used to enforce group norms and to police errant behavior and lack of accountability, a phenomenon called "enforceable trust." These are cultural components of ethnic-enclave economies that are based on norms of reciprocity. Segmented labor-market theory and social capital theory both reject the individualistic premises of classical laissez-faire and human capital conceptualizations. In addition to being used in studies of immigrant entrepreneurship, the concept of social capital has also been deployed in two books, by the psychologist Nathan Caplan and his coauthors John K. Whitmore and Marcella H. Choy and by the sociologists Min Zhou and Carl L. Bankston III, that dissect the factors behind the academic achievements of the children of Vietnamese refugees.[21]

An ethnic-enclave economy has a spatial dimension—the existence of a clustering of ethnic firms as well as co-ethnic owners and workers in a particular location. The sociologist Alejandro Portes and his various coauthors formulated the ethnic-enclave economy theory based on their empirical studies of Cuban Americans in Miami, Florida. An ethnic-enclave economy differs from a traditional ghetto in that the former makes positive outcomes possible whereas the latter traps most of its residents in permanent poverty. In an ethnic-enclave economy, ethnically owned and managed businesses provide jobs for a large number of co-ethnic workers, as well as other ethnic minority workers in certain industries, most of whom speak little English. Many ethnic entrepreneurs were *not* merchants in their countries of origin. However, given the difficulty of transferring the human capital they had acquired in their countries of origin to the U.S. labor market, especially its primary sector, former professionals or individuals who had been in noncommercial occupations decided to open businesses so that they could be their own bosses and avoid the discrimination they faced due to their limited English proficiency and foreign credentials. As Min Zhou put it, an ethnic-enclave economy is "more than just a shelter for the disadvantaged . . . [it] possesses the potential to develop a distinct structure of economic opportunities as an effective alternative path to social mobility." Methodologically, because of the heavy reliance on PUMS files, researchers have to decide *how* an ethnic-enclave economy is operationalized: should the enclave be defined according to place of residence or place of work and business? Choosing one or the other can lead to different findings.

Victor Nee and Min Zhou and their respective coauthors have published the most thought-provoking writings on Asian American ethnic-enclave economies within a large body of studies about not only immigrant Asian entrepreneurs but also similarly situated businesses owned and operated by other ethnic groups. Nee and Sanders questioned the conclusion of Portes and his coauthors that immigrants in an ethnic-enclave economy receive returns to their human capital equal to the earning returns of immigrants in the primary labor market. Comparing Chinese immigrants to Cuban immigrants, Nee and Sanders found that the ethnic-enclave economy theory is only partially correct. Whereas immigrant entrepreneurs do indeed obtain returns commensurate with their human capital, their co-ethnic workers do not. In fact, enclave workers often earn less than their counterparts in the outside labor market (even in its secondary sector), which means an enclave economy can actually be a mobility trap. There *are* limits to ethnic solidarity: class matters. In a 1992 book about New York City's Chinatown, Zhou depicted a more positive picture of the rewards that exist within an ethnic-enclave economy. She pointed to the opportunities that workers have to learn how a business is run and the possibility of employers helping loyal employees to start their own business by offering both advice and financial resources. However, Nee, Sanders, and Scott Sernau in a 1994 study based on over a hundred in-depth interviews found that many immigrants actually prefer jobs outside the ethnic economy because they can get higher wages and encounter fairer work rules in the larger economy. As studies proliferated, sociologists became increasingly cognizant of the fact that there are multiple modes of economic incorporation that occur simultaneously. Zhou and three coauthors, in a 2000 article, documented this fact while Nee and Sanders discussed in a 2001 article how the mix of human, social, and financial capital that immigrants possess sorts them into different sectors of the labor market and economy. In an effort to clarify the conceptual foundations of ethnic entrepreneurship, Zhou in 2004 reviewed the various approaches that had been used to date.[22]

Economists, in contrast to sociologists, have found less to celebrate with regard to the advantages of owning businesses and working within ethnic-enclave economies. The economist Timothy Bates, for example, in multiple articles has argued that the success and survival of Asian immigrant firms derive more from their large financial investments and the business owners' high educational attainment than from social capital. Among Korean immigrant entrepreneurs in particular, their current occupation is actually a form of *under*employment.[23] Robust debates over ethnic economy theory and its various offshoots—ethnic-enclave economies, middleman minorities, ethnic occupational niches, and ethnically owned businesses that operate within the larger economy—have been going on since the 1980s and they continue to engage social scientists in the twenty-first century.[24]

As the 1990 and 2000 censuses and other databases released by the Census Bureau became available and as researchers began to analyze them, the issue of how the various modes of incorporation affect the socioeconomic status of Asian Americans has broadened with more factors being taken into consideration. The sociologists Zhen Zeng and Yu Xie analyzed 1990 PUMS files and discovered that while U.S.-born and U.S.-educated Asian Americans had reached parity with U.S.-born and U.S.-educated white males, foreign-born Asians had not. Immigrant Asians educated in non-U.S. universities earned 16 percent less than their U.S.-born and U.S.-educated peers. *Where* an immigrant Asian was educated is a variable that researchers had hitherto not considered. Based on an analysis of data in the 2000 and 2004 SIPP and PUMS files in the 2006 Community Survey released by the Census Bureau, the economist Paul M. Ong and the urban planners R. Varisa Patraporn and Douglas Houston found that the wealth (measured by a combination of income, homeownership, ownership of other resources, and investments) gap between Asian Americans and non-Hispanic white Americans was beginning to close largely as a result of the high Asian American homeownership rate and their other realty investments. The sociologists Arthur Sakamoto, Kimberly A. Goyette, and ChangHwan Kim credited an increase in Asian American class resources in closing the gap. After more than a century and a half of Asian American history, class is finally able to trump race. In another article, Kim and Sakamoto found that immigrant Asians who come at a relatively young age and are educated in the United States (the so-called 1.5 generation) are also catching up to non-Hispanic whites, but immigrants who arrive at older ages still lag behind.[25]

Meanwhile, the higher-than-average poverty and unemployment rates of substantial numbers of Indochinese refugees and other low-paid Asian immigrant workers cannot be forgotten. Only two books about Chinese Americans in the New York metropolitan area by the sociologist Jan Lin and the historian Xiaojian Zhao devote one chapter each to the class divisions within the Chinese American community. Even that old scholar-activist, Peter Kwong, allocated only nine pages to the contemporary disenfranchised working class in a book he coauthored with Dusanka Miscevic.[26] More research needs to be done on the Asian American working poor and the welfare-dependent population so that the dark underside of the Asian American success story can be exposed and a more rounded and balanced picture of the changing socioeconomic status of Asian Americans can emerge.

The group of Asian immigrant small-business owners that has received the greatest scholarly attention are immigrant Korean merchants who locate their small businesses in neighborhoods with a large number of African Americans and, less often, Latino immigrants. The intense scrutiny came as a result of interracial conflicts in both New York City and Los Angeles in the early 1990s. More than a dozen books, numerous journal articles, and hundreds, if not thousands, of newspaper articles have explored these businesses and their owners, in particular their fraught relationship with African American customers. Fewer scholars have examined their conflicts with white suppliers and their more sanguine relationship with their Latino employees. These works investigate earnings, work conditions, the impact of small business on the families that run them (particularly the changes in gender roles), and race relations with non-Asian minorities. The sociologists Pyong Gap Min, Ivan Light, Edna Bonacich, John Lie, In-Jin Yoon, Kwang Chung Kim, and Jennifer Lee; the political scientists George O. Totten III, E. Eric Schockman, Claire Jean Kim, and Patrick D. Joyce; and the anthropologists Nancy Abelmann and Kyeyoung Park have all produced works of significant scholarship on a difficult and controversial topic, examining multiple facets of the racial tensions that marked the conflicts that occurred in the early 1990s in New York City and especially in Los Angeles. Pyong Gap Min's academic output that spans three decades, based on multisited research in Atlanta, New York City, and Los Angeles, has been particularly insightful. He has demonstrated conclusively that it is situational, structural factors in the form of conflicts with other racial/ethnic groups that help build and strengthen the collective and politicized ethnic *solidarity* among Korean immigrant entrepreneurs—solidarity being a phenomenon that Min distinguishes from ethnic *attachment*, a matter of personal identity.[27]

During the same decades of steady socioeconomic improvement for Asian Americans, the forces of globalization have changed the face of Asian America in multiple ways. Globalization has created a worldwide labor market in which disparities between the rich and the poor have become wider. Low-paid Asian American workers are now part of a global working class whose privations are even worse than those of disadvantaged minorities in the United States. They serve an emerging global middle class and a global capitalist class. What is new about twenty-first-century Asian migrants is that they become members of both a global elite stratum (highly skilled information technology engineers, medical professionals, and entrepreneurs being the most visible examples) and an oppressed global working class. This is a more geographically extensive form of the demographic and socioeconomic bifurcation that has been apparent since the late 1970s. Asian members of these classes migrate repeatedly from one country to another. Asian women now outnumber men among Asian global migrants, and the literature on their socioeconomic situations is growing.[28]

A critical characteristic of globalization is that even though capital, certain kinds of jobs, as well as workers, can now all migrate (that is, be outsourced), there still remains work that needs to be done in situ. Houses and offices cannot be shipped abroad to be cleaned. Workers and engineers who build, maintain, and repair highways, bridges, and other infrastructure must do their work where such structures exist. Freshly cooked food needs to be prepared where people eat it. It is in these nonmovable sectors of the labor market that low-paid workers, regardless of their ethnic origins, increasingly now earn a living. They serve the local needs of professionals, entrepreneurs, and families in which both spouses work, as well as wealthy people.

Contemporary Asian American labor history focuses on women who sew clothing in dingy, overcrowded shops owned by Asian subcontractors. Their situation has been analyzed by the historian Xiaolan Bao, the sociologist Margaret Chin, and the labor activist Miriam Ching Yoon Louie, while the business professor Biju Mathew and the sociologist Diditi Mitra have studied taxi drivers who come from India, Pakistan, the Middle East, and Africa to work in large metropolitan areas like New York City.

The historians Glenna Matthews and Stephen J. Pitti have studied low-paid computer assembly workers, a vast majority of whom are immigrant women from Asia and Latin America, in California's so-called Silicon Valley. Aside from this handful of studies on the Asian American working class, scholars have paid far more attention to an emerging Asian American professional-cum-capitalist class. The sociologist Bernard P. Wong, the professor of landscape architecture Shenglin Chang, the information-technology theorist AnnaLee Saxenian, the public administration scholar Roli Varma, the anthropologist Xiang Bao, and the business consultant Angelika Blendstrup have focused on computer and information-technology companies and the well-educated and well-paid professionals of Asian ancestry (mostly Chinese and Indians) who establish and run them. The geographer William S. Harvey has compared Indian and British scientists working in Boston's pharmaceutical and biotechnology companies. Among Asian immigrant health professionals, Filipina nurses were the pioneers; the historian Catherine Ceniza Choy has portrayed their lives and careers sensitively in a book that follows the historical trajectory of nurse migrations from the American colonial period in the Philippines to the present day. The struggles of foreign-trained medical doctors, many of them Asians, to obtain credentials and licenses in the United States and Canada are documented by the professor of medicine and health policy Linda G. Lesley and the economists James T. McDonald, Casey Warman, and Christopher Worswick.[29] These writings illuminate what the analysis of census statistics has already made apparent: the class divide within Asian American communities is getting ever wider as conspicuous displays of wealth exist alongside working-class misery—not a comforting picture in the eyes of scholars and students in Asian American studies who care about social justice; legal, economic, and political equality; and human rights and dignity.

NOTES

1. Patricia Cloud and David W. Galenson, "Chinese Immigration and Contract Labor in the Late Nineteenth Century," *Explorations in Economic History* 24, no. 1 (1987): 22–42; Charles J. McClain, Jr., "Chinese Immigration: A Comment on Cloud and Galenson," *Explorations in Economic History* 27, no. 3 (1990): 363–378; Patricia Cloud and David W. Galenson, "Chinese Immigration: Reply to Charles McClain," *Explorations in Economic History* 28, no. 2 (1991): 239–247.

2. Ping Chiu, *Chinese Labor in California, 1850–1880: An Economic Study* (Madison: State Historical Society of Wisconsin, 1967); Sucheng Chan, *This Bittersweet Soil: The Chinese in California Agriculture, 1860–1910* (Berkeley: University of California Press, 1986), 32–78; Sucheng Chan, "Chinese Livelihood in Rural California, 1860–1880," *Pacific Historical Review* 53, no. 3 (1984): 273–308; Moon-Ho Jung, *Coolies and Cane: Race, Labor, and Sugar in the Age of Emancipation* (Baltimore, MD: Johns Hopkins University Press, 2006).

3. Robert J. Steinfeld, *Coercion, Contract, and Free Labor in the Nineteenth Century* (New York: Cambridge University Press, 2001).

4. Chiu, *Chinese Labor*, 40–51; Paul M. Ong, "The Central Pacific Railroad and Exploitation of Chinese Labor," *Journal of Ethnic Studies* 13, no. 2 (1985): 119–124; William F. Chew,

Nameless Builders of the Transcontinental Railroad: The Chinese Workers of the Central Pacific Railroad (Victoria: Trafford, 2004).

5. Chiu, *Chinese Labor*, 67–88; Richard Steven Street, *Beasts of the Field: A Narrative History of California Farmworkers, 1769–1913* (Stanford, CA: Stanford University Press, 2004); Chan, *This Bittersweet Soil*, 272–340.

6. Masakazu Iwata, *Planted in Good Soil: The History of Issei in United States Agriculture*, 2 vols. (New York: Peter Lang, 1992); Marn J. Cha, *Koreans in Central California (1903–1957): A Study of Settlement and Transnational Politics* (Lanham, MD: University Press of America, 2010); Karen I. Leonard, *Making Ethnic Choices: California's Punjabi Mexican Americans* (Philadelphia: Temple University Press, 1992).

7. The statistics are in Katharine Coman, *The History of Contract Labor in the Hawaiian Islands* (1903; repr., New York: Cambridge University Press, 2010), Table B, 548.

8. John E. Reinecke, *Feigned Necessity: Hawaii's Attempt to Obtain Chinese Contract Labor, 1921–1923* (San Francisco: Chinese Materials Center, 1979).

9. Edna Bonacich, "A Theory of Middleman Minorities," *American Sociological Review* 38, no. 5 (1973): 583–594; Edna Bonacich and John Modell, *The Economic Basis of Ethnic Solidarity: Small Business in the Japanese American Community* (Berkeley: University of California Press, 1980).

10. Eiichiro Azuma, *Between Two Empires: Race, History, and Transnationalism in Japanese America* (New York: Oxford University Press, 2005).

11. Lucy M. Cohen, *Chinese in the Post–Civil War South: A People without a History* (Baton Rouge: Louisiana State University Press, 1984); Tomás Almaguer, "Racial Domination and Class Conflict in Capitalist Agriculture: The Oxnard Sugar Beet Workers' Strike of 1903," *Labor History* 25, no. 3 (1984): 325–349; Yuji Ichioka, *The Issei: The World of the First Generation Japanese Immigrants, 1885–1924* (New York: Free Press, 1998), 96–102.

12. Yuji Ichioka, "Asian Immigrant Coal Miners and the United Mine Workers of America: Race and Class at Rock Springs, Wyoming, 1907," *Amerasia Journal* 6, no. 2 (1979): 1–23.

13. Howard DeWitt, *Violence in the Fields: California Filipino Farm Labor Unionization during the Great Depression* (Saratoga, NY: Century Twenty One, 1980); Howard DeWitt, "The Filipino Labor Union: The Salinas Lettuce Strike of 1934," *Amerasia Journal* 5, no. 2 (1978): 1–21.

14. Chris Friday, *Organizing Asian American Labor: The Pacific Coast Canned Salmon Industry, 1870–1942* (Philadelphia: Temple University Press, 1994).

15. Peter Kwong, *Chinatown, N.Y.: Labor and Politics, 1930–1950* (New York: Monthly Review, 1979), 116–130.

16. Renqiu Yu, *To Save China, to Save Ourselves: The Chinese Hand Laundry Alliance of New York* (Philadelphia: Temple University Press, 1992).

17. Ronald Takaki, *Pau Hana: Plantation Life and Labor in Hawaii* (Honolulu: University of Hawai'i Press, 1983); Edward D. Beechert, *Working in Hawaii: A Labor History* (Honolulu: University of Hawai'i Press, 1985); John E. Reinecke, *The Filipino Piecemeal Sugar Strike of 1924–1925* (Honolulu: Social Science Research Institute, University of Hawai'i, 1996); Masayo Umezawa Duus, *The Japanese Conspiracy: The Oahu Sugar Strike of 1920* (Berkeley: University of California Press, 1999); Melinda Tria Kerkvliet, *Unbending Cane: Pablo Manlapit, a Filipino Labor Leader in Hawaii* (Honolulu: Office of Multicultural Student Services, University of Hawai'i at Manoa, 2002); Ruben

R. Alcantara, *Sakada: Filipino Adaptation in Hawaii* (Washington, DC: University Press of America, 1981).

18. Sanford Zalburg, *A Spark Is Struck: Jack Hall and the ILWU in Hawaii* (Honolulu: University of Hawai'i Press, 1979); Beechert, *Working in Hawaii*; Gerald Horne, *Fighting in Paradise: Labor Unions, Racism, and Communists in the Making of Modern Hawaii* (Honolulu: University of Hawai'i Press, 2011); Moon-Kie Jung, *Reworking Race: The Making of Hawaii's Interracial Labor Movement* (New York: Columbia University Press, 2006).

19. Robert M. Jiobu, "Earnings Differentials between Whites and Ethnic Minorities: The Case of Asian Americans, Blacks, and Chicanos," *Sociology and Social Research* 61, no. 1 (1976): 24–38; Charles Hirschman and Morrison G. Wong, "Trends in Socioeconomic Achievement among Immigrant and Native-Born Asian Americans, 1960–1970," *Sociological Quarterly* 22, no. 4 (1981): 495–513; Morrison G. Wong, "The Cost of Being Chinese, Japanese, and Filipino in the United States, 1960, 1970, 1976," *Pacific Sociological Review* 5, no. 1 (1982): 59–78; Barry R. Chiswick, "An Analysis of the Earnings and Employment of Asian-American Men," *Journal of Labor Economics* 1, no. 2 (1983): 197–214.

20. Victor Nee and Jimy Sanders, "The Road to Parity: Determinants of the Socioeconomic Achievements of Asian Americans," *Ethnic and Racial Studies* 8, no. 1 (1985): 75–93; Herbert R. Barringer, David T. Takeuchi, and Peter C. Xenos, "Education, Occupational Prestige, and Income of Asian Americans," *Sociology of Education* 63, no. 1 (1990): 27–43; Min Zhou, "Underemployment and Economic Disparities among Minority Groups," *Population Research and Policy Review* 12, no. 2 (1993): 139–157; Amado Cabezas and Gary Kawaguchi, "Empirical Evidence for Continuing Asian American Income Equality: The Human Capital Model and Labor Market Segmentation," in *Reflections on Shattered Windows: Promises and Prospects for Asian American Studies*, ed. Gary Y. Okihiro, Shirley Hune, Arthur A. Hansen, and John M. Liu (Pullman: University of Washington Press, 1988), 144–164.

21. Nathan Caplan, John K. Whitmore, and Marcella H. Choy, *The Boat People and Achievement in America: A Study of Family Life, Hard Work, and Cultural Values* (Ann Arbor: University of Michigan Press, 1989); Min Zhou and Carl L. Bankston III, *Growing Up American: How Vietnamese Children Adapt to Life in the United States* (New York: Russell Sage Foundation, 1998).

22. Jimy M. Sanders and Victor Nee, "Limits of Ethnic Solidarity in the Enclave Economy," *American Sociological Review* 52, no. 6 (1987): 745–773; Min Zhou, *Chinatown: The Socioeconomic Potential of an Urban Enclave* (Philadelphia: Temple University Press, 1992); Victor Nee, Jimy M. Sanders, and Scott Sernau, "Job Transitions in an Immigrant Metropolis: Ethnic Boundaries and the Mixed Economy," *American Sociological Review* 59, no. 6 (1994): 849–872; John R. Logan, Richard D. Alba, Michael Dill, and Min Zhou, "Ethnic Segmentation in the American Metropolis: Increasing Diversity in Economic Incorporation, 1980–1990," *International Migration Review* 34, no. 1 (2000): 98–132; Victor Nee and Jimy Sanders, "Understanding the Diversity of Immigrant Incorporation: A Fo rms-of-Capital Model," *Ethnic and Racial Studies* 24, no. 3 (2001): 386–411; Min Zhou, "Revisiting Ethnic Entrepreneurship: Convergence, Controversies, and Conceptual Advancements," *International Migration Review* 38, no. 3 (2004): 1040–1074.

23. Timothy Bates, "Social Resources Generated by Group Support Networks May Not Be Beneficial to Asian Immigrant-Owned Small Businesses," *Social Forces* 72, no. 3 (1994): 671–689, Timothy Bates, "An Analysis of Korean-Immigrant-Owned

Small-Business Start-Ups with Comparisons to African-American and Nonminority-Owned Firms," *Urban Affairs Quarterly* 30, no. 2 (1994): 227–248.

24. The journal literature is large and it continues to grow, but delving further into these debates is beyond the scope of this essay.

25. Zhen Zeng and Yu Xie, "Asian-Americans' Earnings Disadvantage Reexamined: The Role of Place of Education," *American Journal of Sociology* 109, no. 5 (2004): 1075–1108; R. Varisa Patraporn, Paul M. Ong, and Douglas Houston, "Closing the Asian-White Wealth Gap?" *Asian American Policy Review* 18 (2009): 35–48; Arthur Sakamoto, Kimberly A. Goyette, and ChangHwan Kim, "Socioeconomic Attainments of Asian Americans," *Annual Review of Sociology* (2009): 255–276; ChangHwan Kim and Arthur Sakamoto, "Have Asian American Men Achieved Labor Market Parity with White Men?" *American Sociological Review* 75, no. 6 (2010): 934–957.

26. Jan Lin, *Reconstructing Chinatown: Ethnic Enclave, Global Change* (Minneapolis: University of Minnesota Press, 1998); Xiaojian Zhao, *The New Chinese America: Class, Economy, and Social Hierarchy* (New Brunswick, NJ: Rutgers University Press, 2010); Peter Kwong and Dusanka Miscevic, *Chinese America: The Untold Story of America's Oldest New Community* (New York: New Press, 2005), 388–397.

27. Pyong Gap Min, *Ethnic Business Enterprise: Korean Small Business in Atlanta* (New York: Center for Migration Studies, 1988); Ivan Light and Edna Bonacich, *Immigrant Entrepreneurs: Koreans in Los Angeles, 1965–1982* (Berkeley: University of California Press, 1988); Nancy Abelmann and John Lie, *Blue Dreams: Korean Americans and the Los Angeles Riots* (Cambridge, MA: Harvard University Press, 1995); Pyong Gap Min, *Caught in the Middle: Korean Communities in New York and Los Angeles* (Berkeley: University of California Press, 1996); In-Jin Yoon, *On My Own: Korean Businesses and Race Relations in America* (Chicago: University of Chicago Press, 1997); Kyeyoung Park, *The Korean American Dream: Immigrants and Small Business in New York City* (Ithaca, NY: Cornell University Press, 1997); Kwang Chung Kim, ed., *Koreans in the Hood: Conflict with African Americans* (Baltimore, MD: Johns Hopkins University Press, 1999); Claire Jean Kim, *Bitter Fruit: The Politics of Black-Korean Conflict in New York City* (New Haven, CT: Yale University Press, 2000); Jennifer Lee, *Civility in the City: Blacks, Jews, and Koreans in Urban America* (Cambridge, MA: Harvard University Press, 2002); Patrick D. Joyce, *No Fire Next Time: Black-Korean Conflicts and the Future of America's Cities* (Ithaca, NY: Cornell University Press, 2003); Pyong Gap Min, *Ethnic Solidarity for Economic Survival: Korean Greengrocers in New York City* (New York: Russell Sage Foundation, 2008).

28. Kathleen M. Adams and Sara Dickey, eds., *Home and Hegemony: Domestic Service and Identity Politics in South and Southeast Asia* (Ann Arbor: University of Michigan Press, 2000); Rhacel Salazar Parreñas, *Servants of Globalization: Women, Migration, and Domestic Work* (Stanford, CA: Stanford University Press, 2001); Mary Beth Mills, *Thai Women in the Global Labor Force* (New Brunswick, NJ: Rutgers University Press, 2003); Nicola Piper and Mina Roces, eds., *Wife or Worker: Asian Women and Migration* (Lanham, MD: Rowman and Littlefield, 2003); Barbara Ehrenreich and Arlie Russell Hochschild, eds., *Global Women: Nannies, Maids, and Sex Workers in the New Economy* (New York: Metropolitan, 2003); Nan Oishi, *Women in Motion: Globalization, State Policies, and Labor Migration in Asia* (Stanford, CA: Stanford University Press, 2005); Dewi Anggraeni, *Dreamseekers: Indonesian Women as Domestic Workers in Asia* (Jakarta: PT Equinox, 2006); Pei-Chia Lan, *Global Cinderellas: Migrant Domestics and Newly Rich Employers in Taiwan* (Durham, NC: Duke University Press, 2006); Rhacel Salazar Parreñas, *The Force of Domesticity: Filipina Migrants and Globalization* (New York: New York University

Press, 2008); Anna Romina Guevarra, *Marketing Dreams, Manufacturing Heroes: The Transnational Labor Brokering of Filipino Workers* (New Brunswick, NJ: Rutgers University Press, 2010); Robyn Magalit Rodriguez, *Migrants for Export: How the Philippine State Brokers Labor to the World* (Minneapolis: University of Minnesota Press, 2010).

29. Xiaolan Bao, *Holding Up More Than Half the Sky: Chinese Women Garment Workers in New York City, 1948–1992* (Champaign: University of Illinois Press, 2001); Margaret M. Chin, *Sewing Women: Immigrants and the New York City Garment Industry* (New York: Columbia University Press, 2005); Miriam Ching Yoon Louie, *Sweatshop Warriors: Immigrant Women Workers Take on the Global Factory* (Cambridge, MA: South End, 2001); Biju Mathews, *Taxi! Cabs and Capitalism in New York City* (New York: New Press, 2005); Diditi Mitra, "Punjabi American Taxi Drivers: The New White Working Class?" *Journal of Asian American Studies* 11, no. 3 (2008): 303–336; Glenna Matthews, *Silicon Valley, Women, and the California Dream: Gender, Class, and Opportunity in the Twentieth Century* (Stanford, CA: Stanford University Press, 2003); Stephen J. Pitti, *The Devil in Silicon Valley: Northern California, Race, and Mexican Americans* (Princeton, NJ: Princeton University Press, 2003); Bernard P. Wong, *The Chinese in Silicon Valley: Globalization, Social Networks, and Ethnic Identity* (Lanham, MD: Rowman and Littlefield, 2006); Shenglin Chang, *The Global Silicon Valley Home: Lives and Landscapes within Taiwanese American Trans-Pacific Culture* (Stanford, CA: Stanford University Press, 2006); AnnaLee Saxenian, *Silicon Valley's New Immigrant Entrepreneurs* (San Francisco: Public Policy Institute of California, 1990); AnnaLee Saxenian, *The New Argonauts: Regional Advantage in a Global Economy* (Cambridge, MA: Harvard University Press, 2007); Roli Varma, *Harbingers of Global Change: India's Techno-Immigrants in the United States* (Lanham, MD: Lexington, 2006); Xiang Bao, *Global "Body Shopping": An Indian Labor System in the Information Technology Industry* (Princeton, NJ: Princeton University Press, 2007); Angelika Blendstrup, *They Made It! How Chinese, French, German, Indian, Iranian, Israeli, and Other Foreign-Born Entrepreneurs Contributed to High-Tech Innovation in Silicon Valley, the United States, and Overseas* (Cupertino, CA: HappyAbout.com, 2007); William S. Harvey, "Brain Circulation? British and Indian Scientists in Boston, Massachusetts, USA," *Asian Population Studies* 4, no. 3 (2008): 294–309; William S. Harvey, "Strong or Weak Ties? British and Indian Expatriate Scientists Finding Jobs in Boston," *Global Networks* 8, no. 4 (2008): 453–473; Catherine Ceniza Choy, *Empire of Care: Nursing and Migration in Filipino American History* (Durham, NC: Duke University Press, 2003); Linda G. Lesley, "Physician Migration to the United States and Canada: Criteria for Admission," in *High-Skilled Immigration in a Global Labor Market*, ed. Barry R. Chiswick (Washington, DC: American Enterprise Institute for Public Policy Research, 2011), 155–164; James Ted McDonald, Casey Warman, and Christopher Worswick, "Earnings, Occupations, and Schooling Decisions of Immigrants with Medical Degrees: Evidence for Canada and the United States," in *High-Skilled Immigration in a Global Labor Market*, ed. Barry R. Chiswick (Washington, DC: American Enterprise Institute for Public Policy Research, 2011), 165–198.

FURTHER READING

Bao, Xiaolan. *Holding Up More Than Half the Sky: Chinese Women Garment Workers in New York City, 1948–1992.* Champaign: University of Illinois Press, 2001.

Beechert, Edward D. *Working in Hawaii: A Labor History.* Honolulu: University of Hawaiʻi Press, 1985.

Chan, Sucheng. *This Bittersweet Soil: The Chinese in California Agriculture, 1860–1910*. Berkeley: University of California Press, 1986.

Chiu, Ping. *Chinese Labor in California, 1850–1880: An Economic Study*. Madison: Wisconsin Historical Society, 1967.

Choy, Catherine Ceniza. *Empire of Care: Nursing and Migration in Filipino American History*. Durham, NC: Duke University Press, 2003.

Friday, Chris. *Organizing Asian American Labor: The Pacific Coast Canned Salmon Industry, 1870–1942*. Philadelphia: Temple University Press, 1994.

Iwata, Mazakazu. *Planted in Good Soil: The History of Issei in United States Agriculture*. 2 vols. New York: Peter Lang, 1992.

Jung, Moon-Ho. *Coolies and Cane: Race, Labor, and Sugar in the Age of Emancipation*. Baltimore, MD: Johns Hopkins University Press, 2006.

Jung, Moon-Kie. *Reworking Race: The Making of Hawaii's Interracial Labor Movement*. New York: Columbia University Press, 2006.

Leonard, Karen Isaksen. *Making Ethnic Choices: California's Punjabi Mexican Americans*. Philadelphia: Temple University Press, 1994.

Mathew, Biju. *Taxi! Cabs and Capitalism in New York City*. New York: New Press, 2005.

Min, Pyong Gap. *Ethnic Solidarity for Economic Survival: Korean Greengrocers in New York City*. New York: Russell Sage Foundation, 2008.

Park, Kyeyoung. *The Korean American Dream: Immigrants and Small Business in New York City*. Ithaca, NY: Cornell University Press, 1997.

Parreñas, Rhacel Salazar. *The Force of Domesticity: Filipina Migration and Globalization*. New York: New York University Press, 2008.

Street, Richard Steven. *Beasts of the Field: A Narrative History of California Farmworkers, 1869–1913*. Stanford, CA: Stanford University Press, 2004.

Varma, Roli. *Harbingers of Change: India's Techno-Immigrants in the United States*. Lanham, MD: Lexington, 2006.

Yoon, In-Jin. *On My Own: Korean Businesses and Race Relations in America*. Chicago: University of Chicago Press, 1997.

Yu, Renqiu. *To Save China, to Save Ourselves: The Chinese Hand Laundry Alliance of New York*. Philadelphia: Temple University Press, 1992.

CHAPTER 19

ASIAN AMERICANS, POLITICS, AND HISTORY

GORDON H. CHANG

Do Asian Americans have a political history? The answer is "no" or "virtually no," if one accepts the traditional definition of "political history."

Conventional historiography takes American political history as the study of the people, institutions, and processes in the various levels and realms of government as well as of organized efforts to influence the functioning of the state. It is, in other words, the history of electoral politics and civic functioning. With this understanding, a hundred years of scholars wrote about presidents and other officials, the making of policy, the activity of parties, the judiciary, elections, and the expression of opinions about politics. This was largely a history of the Euro-American elite self. By the 1960s, such an approach came to be seen not only as inadequate but also as intellectually conservative and racially prejudiced—emphasizing as it does a conception of American history whose sole actors were privileged white males. It was also intellectually constipated in the constricted and restricted ways that power and political thought were defined and understood. Over time, however, historians came to recognize and appreciate new actors (women, bureaucracies), new social forces (African Americans, radicals), and new approaches and contexts (the power of social movements, the salience of belief systems such as religion or racism in political discourse, gender, and international contexts). The result has been that today there is an expanded notion of what constitutes political history.

The authoritative *Concise Princeton Encyclopedia of American Political History* seeks to exemplify this enhanced vision. The editor, Michael Kazin, claims that the volume "assumes an expansive definition of politics: the meaning and uses of power in the public sphere and the competition to gain that power."[1] The volume studies the presidency but also, for example, the influences of region, race, and gender on the uses of political power. Kazin, whose first book examined anti-Chinese sentiment in the San Francisco labor movement during the Progressive Era, is himself a highly respected historian of radicalism in American history and a leading public intellectual.

The *Encyclopedia*'s expanded definition of political history, however, still did not lead its various authors to devote significant attention to the politics of racial minorities such as Asian Americans who were limited, or excluded altogether, from the functioning of the state and from electoral politics generally. The construction and functioning of the formal nation-state and electoral politics remain the *Encyclopedia*'s center of attention: the locus of politics is the *activity of the voting citizenry*. But what of those who were unable to become citizens and part of the electorate or whose citizenship was so restricted as to preclude full participation? Asian Americans do appear in a few lines in the more than six-hundred-plus pages of the *Encyclopedia* but largely as objects acted upon by immigration laws or World War II internment. One thinks of what Roger Daniels wrote forty years ago, characterizing Asian Americans as having been treated by scholars largely as the "objects" and not subjects of history.[2] This meant political as well as social history.

Responding to this portrayal, scholars identifying themselves as Asian Americanists in the late 1960s began to locate and study the voices and energy of Asian American actors to fill the void in the literature. As with other ethnic studies, the new field of Asian American studies focused on minority power and lived humanity. Other concurrent intellectual currents also encouraged greatly expanded considerations of the forms of power beyond old approaches that considered only elite political institutions and established social structures as worthy of study. With the new social and ethnic history, voice, agency, and power came to be seen as ubiquitous as well as defused, inhabiting every social and cultural space and expressed and practiced in myriad ways. Everything, in a sense, became an expression of power and everything became political. Traditional political history became inverted: all history became "political." All, or virtually all, history produced by Asian Americanists could then be seen as a sort of political history. Though imbuing historical study with a certain creative energy and purpose, this approach came to be so expansive it obliterated any specific meaning for analytical categories such as politics, law, economics, or even culture itself.

Taking a middle path between that which emphasizes traditionally defined activities related to the state and that which maintains that everything is politics, this essay sees Asian American political history as history that studies the past efforts of persons of Asian ancestry, with some level of self-awareness and purpose, to affect group social position and alter the relationship with state power. This altered definition of political history arises out of the actual lived experience of Asian Americans and challenges the conventionally understood category that a very different historicity produced.

In this light, Asian American political history can be understood conceptually in perhaps fresh ways. Four dimensions of Asian American politics arise out of the unique circumstances of Asian American life and history. These categories are as follows:

Politics of the excluded
Politics of the transnational
Politics of the radicalized
Processes of politicization

POLITICS OF THE EXCLUDED

Before Asians were excluded from scholarly attention, they were historically excluded from the United States and from the rights and privileges of full citizenship. They were not politically absent, however, because many contemporaneous writers in the nineteenth and early twentieth centuries actually feared that Asians threatened American political institutions and wrote about the Oriental danger. Chinese and Japanese immigrants, it was widely alleged, aspired not just to enter American politics but to take them over. They were not docile tools present on American soil only to labor. This extremist yellow peril literature of the late nineteenth and early twentieth centuries maintained that Asians were far from being disinterested in American politics or marginal to the country's political health. Indeed, the Chinese, according to the polemicist Pierton W. Dooner, threatened the very survival of the republic, as the title of his sensationalist book, *Last Days of the Republic* (1880), announced. Chinese ambition was nothing less than the conquest of America, through the ballot box and gun.

The Chinese immigration restriction acts of the 1880s aimed in part to prevent that possible nightmare. Even after their passage, however, white commentators continued to express anxiety about Chinese political influence in America. In 1898, the respected journal *North American Review* published "The Chinaman in American Politics," which described the Chinese as especially capable political animals who had an extraordinary and undesirable influence over American politics. "It is the prevailing opinion that politics as a profession is unknown to the Chinese, but nothing could be farther from the truth," the article began. "As a race they are astute politicians, and singularly, one of the most active fields for the demonstration of their skill is found, not in China, but on the American continent and among the American people." Although they were virtually without the power of the vote, the essay accused the Chinese of wielding political power far beyond what their numbers should allow. They allegedly were even more influential and capable politically than the much more numerous African American population. The Chinese supposedly had a political machine that successfully frustrated congressional efforts to further control and limit them. Despite the importance of the exclusion movement, mainstream American political history, continues to inadequately consider the implications of the Asian exclusion movement in the construction of modern definitions of citizenship and civic functioning.[3]

Yellow peril ranting has often been dismissed as displays of racial and turn-of-the-century cultural anxiety, as expressions of exaggerated, unfounded fear about other matters, such as masculinity. But what if we took an alternative point of view and considered the ways that Chinese in America actually took creative, effective, and untraditional means to affect American politics? Indeed, federal efforts to pass anti-Chinese legislation actually failed to satisfy ardent exclusionists. The anti-Chinese measures, as draconian as they were, and the mistreatment of the Chinese, as cruel and inhumane as it was, still left many Americans unsatisfied, and they expressed frustration about their inability to do *more* against the recalcitrant Chinese. An important reason the Chinese succeeded in challenging further efforts was their ability to win defenders among whites, to use the courts to challenge restrictions, and to enter the arena of international politics to influence American opinion and policy.[4]

Work arising from the study of American legal history actually offers wonderful insight into a particular form of the "politics of the excluded." Unable to use the power of the ballot box, Chinese turned to the courts to advance individual as well as group rights and address grievances. The success of the Chinese and their attorneys in the courts, all the way up to the United States Supreme Court, is impressive evidence of the Chinese engagement with American institutions. Historians, however, have only scratched the surface of this Chinese strategy and should consider the ways that legal history should be seen as a form of politics. Chinese, and other Asians, challenged discriminatory city ordinances, state antimiscegenation statues, and federal immigration and citizenship legislation and enforcement, thereby influencing politics and helping shape the functioning of the judiciary, one of the principal forms of state power in America.

The international arena also provides a venue to understand the "politics of the excluded." Take, for example, the career of Wu Tingfang, the Chinese minister to the United States in the years 1897 to 1909. He was by all accounts one of the most effective and highly respected spokespersons on behalf of Chinese in the United States. Mary Coolidge, one of the early sympathetic writers about Chinese in America, described the ability of Wu to remonstrate forcefully against outrages and employ ways to moderate or even overturn extreme aspects of immigration restriction enforcement. The historian Shih-shan Tsai properly describes Wu as doing "more than any other single individual to present China's case [on immigration exclusion] to the American public." Wu had extensive contact with Chinese in America and received many reports from them about their lives and the abuses they suffered. They urged him to speak out on their behalf. He himself had been a target of hooligan violence in New York City and drew from the voices of his abused countrymen in his eloquent writing and his effective speeches (many examples of which were in English) that he delivered across the United States. He helped articulate a "politics of the excluded," though his name rarely appears in books on Chinese American history, and his extensive writing remains a rich, understudied, historical trove on the Chinese in nineteenth-century America.[5]

In ways somewhat similar with the Chinese, Japanese immigrants in the early twentieth century articulated their own "politics of the excluded" through a number of journalists, writers, and diplomats who aimed to influence American public and official opinion. The journalists Kiyoshi Kawakami and Kiyutao Abiko; Stanford University professor, Yamato Ichihashi; returned missionary, Sidney L. Gulick; businessman, Wallace M. Alexander (president of the Hawaii firm Alexander & Baldwin and a director of the Matson Navigation Company); and a succession of capable Japanese diplomats worked energetically to influence American public opinion in favor of the Issei. They were so effective that they provoked anti-Japanese agitator Montaville Flowers to declare that the Japanese had even "conquered" American public opinion. He did not think he exaggerated and cried out that the presumptuous Japanese immigrants wanted all the rights and privileges of the American-born white man—the right of free entrance for [Japanese] nationals into the United States; the right to vote; the right to own American land anywhere, in any quantity, for any purpose; the right to be legislators and governors of states; the right to go to Congress and make the laws; the right to sit upon our supreme Courts of State and Nation, and there to determine the very genius of our future civilization.[6]

The Japanese were not intimidated by Flowers or by the passage of the 1924 Immigration Act but continued to work to overturn the restrictions on them, making the cause for equal citizenship one of the most important international issues in the interwar years. Despite the significance of these efforts, scholarship in understanding the actors, their strategies, the connections between the immigrants and these leaders, the relationships with American political leaders, and the role of the Japanese government in responding to the American anti-Japanese movement is still in its beginning stages. The importance of the subject and richness of the materials make the study of Japanese American politics in the interwar years especially valuable and provide insight into the features of the "politics of the excluded" and strategies to affect the American mainstream.[7]

POLITICS OF THE TRANSNATIONAL

Life circumstances required Asian immigrant populations up through at least World War II to be transnational, that is, to lead lives that did not singularly focus on amalgamation into the American nation-state under which they lived but from whose political processes they were largely excluded. State policies precluded that possibility. International law, personal sentiment, and social custom also continued to link them tightly to their lands of ancestry. They lived their lives between states. They were squeezed between states, and their lives transcended state boundaries and their politics followed suit. It was a politics that traditional accounts in America have not recognized or appreciated, though it is one of the most important contributions of Asian American historiography.[8]

Some of the most exciting work out of Asian American history investigates this politics of the transnational. It is an approach not bounded by the U.S. nation-state in order to capture the great vitality of Asian American lives and political activism. These accounts dispute traditional interpretations that Asians were indifferent to politics or simply acquiesced to their marginalization by the American state. They also reveal the inner complexity of Asian immigrant politics and the creative efforts that activists adopted to simultaneously involve themselves in the politics of the homeland and in the policies of the American state toward their homelands. "Issues of state power and its uses," observes Richard Kim, "were central to all Korean immigrant political concerns" and, in turn, their political activism became central to their lived lives in America. The state is returned to a central place in Asian American historical study. What Kim writes about Korean immigrants could be asked about other Asian immigrant groups: how did these marginalized and "in between" populations, virtually powerless in regards to the American state (and without a Korean state for Korea immigrants), pursue their political agendas? What were the consequences of such politics for their own identities?

As Kim shows, Korean immigrants often turned to what he calls the model of "clientelist" politics. Korean activists looked for powerful patrons to represent their interests and present their points of view to others in America. Koreans wanted to appeal to the American state on behalf of the people in their land of ancestry. Clientelist politics, however, was unstable and unpredictable, as patrons could be unreliable partners and Korean activists often competed among themselves for attention as much as they cooperated to be heard. Along the way, however, as they campaigned for the independence of their homeland, Koreans forged a unique "ethnic identity" for themselves in America. Politics on behalf of their homeland became, for Korean immigrants, the politics of their new land and was their path to an American identity.[9]

In some similar ways, Filipino migrants to America also found that their lives were deeply embedded in the inextricable tangle of international and national politics and racial identities. But in their case, Filipinos, with their land of ancestry under American imperial rule, experienced the dubious privilege of being the only Asian migrants who were simultaneously American nationals as well as foreign aliens. Their unique legal position fundamentally shaped their historical experiences as well as their political struggles. It was as difficult for them to figure out what they were in terms of national identity, and what they wanted, as it was for American political figures to determine their status within the American empire. Were they American nationals who could be excluded from America? Did the promise of independence for their homeland make them into aliens as with other Asians or into an immigrant population with the possibility of naturalized citizenship? With war in the Pacific, were the undesirable Filipinos now expected to serve America loyally and patriotically despite their anomalous status? The political history of Filipinos in America provides especially useful insight into the functioning of the American state and about ideas of nationality and citizenship. Filipinos were themselves actively involved in confronting these questions and contributing to the discourse on citizenship and nationality.[10]

The study of the history of Chinese transnational politics is particularly rich. Many Chinese went overseas in the nineteenth and twentieth centuries, and their difficult, often tragic experiences led them to be especially active and influential in the politics of their homeland as they searched for a way to address their grievances and improve their conditions of life. The close relationship of the Chinese in America to reform and revolutionary movements in China, including surrounding the 1911 Revolution, and the story of Sun Yatsen, who spent many years in Hawai'i and in the mainland United States, are well known, for example, but study of the full extent of the involvement of the Chinese in America with Sun's movement is still in its early stages. Work on other areas of Chinese transnational politics (sometimes referred to as diasporic politics) is revealing a wonderful complexity of experiences, organizations, and thinking. Far from being an apolitical people, the Chinese in America are emerging as an especially resourceful community in its efforts to forge a politics from within its highly constricted confines.[11]

Why hasn't work produced by Asian Americanists had a greater impact on the writing of the wider field of American political history? In large part, it is because of the way that the field has been defined, as discussed at the start of this essay. But there is another reason. In recent years, observers have noted the high degree of specialization in all fields of scholarship; in the area of ethnic history, this has sometimes been dismissed as "balkanization." This charge suggests a "self-segregation" in academia, with the blame placed on scholars of color. But the charge should be reversed, with the responsibility placed on those who have not taken the work of Asian Americanists and others as seriously as they should. "Balkanization" is very much imposed. At the same time, Asian Americanists themselves might assume a level of responsibility in the underappreciation of their work. Asian Americanists can be more aggressive in interjecting their work into the mainstream of historical scholarship.

Take the fate of the extraordinary research of the undeniable dean of Chinese American studies, Him Mark Lai. Not trained as a "professional" historian, he produced the singular accounts of Chinese life, community, and politics in America. Over a long and productive career, Lai wrote studies of depth and texture. He was able to do so in part because he began his study long before many others; identified and collected unrivaled research material, especially Chinese-language material; and drew from his personal involvement in Chinese American community life to identify deeply relevant questions, issues, and interpretations that will remain foundational for years to come. Yet his work has not had the impact it should on established historical scholarship, especially in American political history. Lai was not especially interested in speaking to scholars in that realm, it is true, but the challenge to Asian Americans who are in the academe is to speak to the mainstream and use our study of the particular experiences of Asian Americans to address more general historiographic, narrative, and interpretive issues. That is a task that is too important to be left to others.[12]

The work of Lai and others who work in Asian American history should make an impact on American historical writing as large as, say perhaps, Robin D. G Kelley's *Race Rebels* has. This is a work that emerges from African American history but is justly seen as speaking to other historical investigations, raising as it does new methodological and interpretive approaches to understanding the politics of those with "hidden transcripts" and in the African diaspora.

In contemporary historical study, Asian Americanists were among the earliest to explore diaspora and transnational political history, beginning long before the ground-breaking round table, "The Nation and Beyond: Transnational Perspectives on United States History," in the December 1999 issue of the *Journal of American History* that signaled the start of the mainstream's interest in transnationalism. (In more than 350 pages of journal text, by the way, the issue does not include any discussion of Asia or Asian Americans, even though there are essays considering new views on empire, race, labor, borders, migration, and immigration in American history.) Work from Asian American studies has been especially innovative and yet few references appear in the essays that serve as the now-standard reference on the internationalization of American history.[13]

What might Asian Americanists do? They should engage in historiographic discussions, draw implications from their work for other fields, and challenge those who are preoccupied with narrowly conceived nation-state history. Asian Americanists might investigate the actual efforts of Asian Americans to influence state power in America. Asian Americans should reject being placed in a "particularist" niche" and help shape an expanded notion of what constitutes American political history that includes those who were excluded from formal politics.[14]

Politics of the Radicalized

From the moment of birth of Asian American studies, Asian Americanists, with a passion befitting the search for self, have been interested in recovering the history of social activism and radical politics in Asian American history. Excavating this genealogy has been one of the animating curiosities of the field. Among the first scholarly articles in Asian American history were studies about early leftists, socialists, and labor organizers among Asians in America.[15] More recently, as Asian American studies and the concurrent Asian American movement that helped generate it became the stuff of historical study, writing about that generative moment in the late 1960s and 1970s has proliferated. Of particular note is the effort devoted to understanding the early years of the movement, especially its most radical elements. Asian Americans have a growing number of memoirs, biographies, reflections, and interpretations that variously seek to record, reclaim, or reinspire the politics of those early years. Some nicely capture the personalities, mood, and ideas of the early movement; others border on hero worship and are enamored of image and rhetoric.[16]

The radical political history of Asians in America, however, remains a field rich in potential and importance. Important topics include the participation of the Chinese in America in Sun Yatsen's revolutionary movement; the Asian American response to the revolutionary and anticolonial movements in Asia (one can think of the activist Koji Ariyoshi from Hawai'i or Tang Mingzhao, who left New York for China after 1949, among many others); Asian Americans and the American communist and socialist movements (Karl Yoneda and his Issei communist comrades in the 1920s and 1930s); and the influential leftwing Japanese and Chinese artists in New York and Los Angeles in the interwar years. As for the Asian American movement, there is still no study that goes much beyond the use of published materials and oral histories to study federal records, organization archives, and personal manuscripts. Obtaining those materials, including from the federal government, will require creativity and initiative but is not impossible. There has been very little consideration of Asian American activism from the late 1970s to the present.[17]

PROCESSES OF POLITICIZATION

Until quite recently, Asian Americanists have displayed little interest in the history of the actual involvement of Asian Americans in electoral politics. Though not as exhilarating or as inspiring as uncovering a left lineage, the history of Asian Americans in electoral politics offers rich insight into the formation of Asian American communities and their growing influence on American politics. Among the questions that can be asked are how and in what ways do social groups, and individuals, who were previously largely unfamiliar with American electoral politics come to understand and participate in mainstream political processes? How do other communities respond when Asian Americans become politically active? In what ways does their activity change the structure, language, and institutions of American politics? In what ways have Asian Americans been transformed by the experience of their own political engagement? These are questions about the "processes of politicization," a historical phrase nicely employed by the anthropologist Tricia Toyota in her study of these issues related to Chinese Americans in Southern California.[18]

An emerging literature, which has largely been from disciplines other than history, has begun to consider these questions in recent years,[19] and has begun addressing new topics. Still virtually unexplored, however are the lives and careers of the Asian Americans who have held important state and national elected offices. A quickly compiled list would include Hiram Fong, Patsy Mink, Daniel Akaka, Spark Matsunaga, S. I. Hayakawa, Dalip Singh Saund, David Wu, Mike Honda, Gary Locke, March Fong Eu, Jay Kim, and others. The list is growing quickly, yet no scholarly study has considered the processes of politicization and experience of these important Asian American elected officials. This is not an unimportant issue by any means: in 2011, Don Nakanishi and James Lai tabulated more than 3,000 elected and appointed officials of Asian ancestry in the United States and its territories.[20] They are from every Asian ethnic group, with a significant number from those who arrived post-1965. In areas of population concentration, such as the San Francisco Bay Area, the greater Los Angeles area, New York, Minnesota, and now even Nevada, Asian Americans are important political constituencies, and their rapidly growing influence and sophistication in electoral politics beg consideration. How did Asian Americans, once dismissed as apolitical and disinterested in politics, emerge as an energized political force? What is the historical background for this development? What have been the particular issues, interests, and approaches that have marked this political force? The work of historians interested in the politics of Asian Americans would do well to take the lead of our colleagues in political science and sociology and seek to offer a historically grounded perspective on what is clearly emerging as one of the most important dimensions of Asian American life.

Brief mention must also be made of one other arena of Asian American political life whose absence in the literature is conspicuous: the history of conservatives of Asian ancestry in America. Far more attention has been devoted to the left and protest movements, but almost none has been given to the groups, individuals, and thinkers on the right, despite the fact that rightist politics have historically played a prominent, even dominant role, at times and places within Asian American communities. They have also been far more important in broader American life than those of the left. One can point to the strong anticommunist sentiment and organizations among Chinese, Koreans, and Southeast Asians. There is no study of the Soong Family and the many other Guomintang post-1949 exiles in the country; none on the anticommunist forces among the Vietnamese, Cambodians, and Laotians; none on S. I. Hayakawa, Frances Fukuyama, Sun Myung Moon's Reunification Church, Dinesh D'Souza, or Michelle (Maglalang) Malkin.[21]

The history of the right may be less appealing to activist-inclined students and academics, but its story remains one of the largest and most significant lacuna in the study of Asian American political history.

Even if one takes the state and its functioning as the principal unit of scholarly analysis, which is political history's conventional approach, the political history of Asian Americans could still enrich the narrative and analysis. American politics, as has often been argued, has been shaped by the political mainstream's confrontation with the challenges from without. Certainly, the history of Asian Americans, who were largely excluded from mainstream politics before World War II and who since then have been increasingly visible in various dimensions of American political life, has much to offer to those interested in the politics of the excluded, marginalized, radicalized, or transnational. The interpretation of American political history should be recast to embrace those who had been formally denied access to the political processes but who pursued politics by other means. The processes of politicization for Asian Americans have been historical and ongoing. The significance of Asian Americans as a political force in national and international politics is growing quickly and suggests that Asian American political history is more than a historical curiosity. It is one that has important connections to the present and future. It is time for the construction of a self-conscious Asian American political history.[22]

NOTES

1. Michael Kazin, ed., *The Concise Princeton Encyclopedia of American Political History* (Princeton, NJ: Princeton University Press, 2011), vii–ix.

2. Roger Daniels, "American Historians and East Asian Immigrants," *Pacific Historical Review* 43, no. 4 (1974): 449–472.

3. Studies that could be understood as contributions to American political history, for example, are Moon-Ho Jung, *Coolies and Cane: Race, Labor, and Sugar in the Age of Emancipation* (Baltimore, MD: Johns Hopkins University Press, 2006); Najia Aarim-Heriot, *Chinese Immigrants, African Americans, and Racial Anxiety in the United States, 1848–1882* (Champaign: University of Illinois Press, 2003); and Ellen Wu, *The Color of Success: Asian Americans and the Origins of the Model Minority* (Princeton,

NJ: Princeton University Press, 2013). The *Princeton Encyclopedia*, for example, does not even mention the yellow peril movement.

4. Gordon H. Chang, "China and the Pursuit of America's Destiny: Nineteenth-Century Imaging and Why Immigration Restriction Took So Long," *Journal of Asian American Studies* 15, no. 2 (2012): 145–169; Charles J. McClain, *In Search of Equality: The Chinese Struggle against Discrimination in Nineteenth-Century* America (Berkeley: University of California Press, 1994); Lucy E. Salyer, *Laws Harsh as Tigers: Chinese Immigrants and the Shaping of Modern Immigration Law* (Chapel Hill: University of North Carolina Press, 1995); Bill Ong Hing, *Making and Remaking Asian America through Immigration Policy, 1850–1990* (Stanford, CA: Stanford University Press, 1993); and Mary Roberts Coolidge, *Chinese Immigration* (New York: Henry Holt, 1909), 459–485. For the immigration politics of the "excluded" in the twentieth century and the Chinese, see Erika Lee and Judy Yung, *Immigrant Gateway to America* (New York: Oxford University Press, 2010), 90–109; and Mae Ngai, *Impossible Subjects: Illegal Aliens and the Making of America* (Princeton, NJ: Princeton University Press, 2004), 202–224.

5. Shih-shan Henry Tsai, *China and the Overseas Chinese in the United States, 1868–1911* (Fayetteville: University of Arkansas Press, 1983), 100. The most complete study of Wu in English is Linda Pomerantz-Zhang, *Wu Tingfang: Reform and Modernization in Modern Chinese History* (Hong Kong: Hong Kong University Press, 1992). Also see Wu Tingfang, *America through the Spectacles of an Oriental Diplomat* (New York: Frederick A. Stokes, 1914).

6. Montaville Flowers, *The Japanese Conquest of American Opinion*(New York: George H. Doran, 1917), 52–53.

7. See Yuji Ichioka, *The Issei: The World of the First Generation Japanese Immigrants, 1885–1924* (New York: Free Press, 1988), 176–243; Gordon H. Chang and Eiichiro Azuma, eds., *Before Internment: Essays in Prewar Japanese American History* (Stanford, CA: Stanford University Press, 2006); the biographical essay in Gordon H. Chang, *Morning Glory, Evening Shadow: Yamato Ichihashi and His Internment Writings, 1942–1945* (Stanford, CA: Stanford University Press, 1995); Izumi Hirobe, *Japanese Pride, American Prejudice: Modifying the Exclusion Clause of the 1924 Immigration Act* (Stanford, CA: Stanford University Press, 2001); and Eiichiro Azuma, *Between Two Empires: Race, History, and Transnationalism in Japanese America* (New York: Oxford University Press, 2005).

8. On transnationalism, see Azuma, *Between Two Empires*, and Erika Lee and Naoko Shibusawa, "What Is Transnational Asian American History? Recent Trends and Challenges," *Journal of Asian American Studies* 8, no. 3 (2005), vii–xvii.

9. Richard S. Kim, *The Quest for Statehood: Korean Immigrant Nationalism and U.S. Sovereignty, 1905–1945* (New York: Oxford University Press, 2011); David K. Yoo, *Contentious Spirits: Religion in Korean American History, 1903–1945* (Stanford, CA: Stanford University Press, 2010). A parallel argument is advanced in Renqiu Yu, *To Save China, to Save Ourselves: The Chinese Hand Laundry Alliance of New York* (Philadelphia: Temple University Press, 1992).

10. Rick Baldoz, *The Third Asiatic Invasion: Empire and Migration in Filipino America, 1898–1946* (New York: New York University Press, 2011), 156–236. Also see Dorothy Fujita-Rony, *American Workers, Colonial Power: Philippine Seattle and the Transpacific West, 1919–1941* (Berkeley: University of California Press, 2003).

11. See, for example, the work by Eve Armentrout-Ma, *Revolutionaries, Monarchists, and Chinatowns: Chinese Politics in the Americas and the 1922 Revolution* (Honolulu: University of Hawai'i Press, 1990); Yu, *To Save China*; K. Scott Wong and Sucheng Chan, eds., *Claiming America: Constructing Chinese American Identities during the Exclusion Era* (Philadelphia: Temple University Press, 1998); Sucheng Chan, ed., *Chinese American Transnationalism: The Flow of People, Resources, and Ideas between China and America during the Exclusion Era* (Philadelphia: Temple University Press, 2006); Shehong Chen, *Being Chinese, Becoming Chinese American* (Champaign: University of Illinois Press, 2002); and Madeline Y. Hsu, *The Good Immigrants: How the Yellow Peril Became the Model Minority* (Princeton, NJ: Princeton University Press, 2015). From Chinese studies, see Adam McKeown, *Chinese Migrant Networks and Cultural Change: Peru, Chicago, Hawaii, 1900–1936* (Chicago: University of Chicago Press, 2001); Guanhua Wang, *In Search of Justice: The 1905–1906 Chinese Anti-American Boycott* (Cambridge, MA: Harvard University Asia Center, 2001); and, of course, the extensive work by Wang Gungwu.

12. From 1967 until his passing in 2009, Him Mark Lai published scores of articles, essays in books, and several books in Chinese and English. These include *Becoming Chinese American: A History of Communities and Institutions* (Walnut Creek, CA: AltaMira, 2004), Madeline Y. Hsu, ed., *Chinese American Transnational Politics* (Champaign: University of Illinois Press, 2010); and Judy Yung, ed., *Him Mark Lai: Autobiography of a Chinese American Historian* (Los Angeles: UCLA Asian American Studies Center, 2011).

13. See Thomas Bender, ed., *Rethinking American History in A Global Age* (Berkeley: University of California Press, 2002). In addition to the authors cited above, many other Asian Americanists have creatively explored the possibilities of transnational history and its political implications. They are too numerous to list here.

14. Fine examples of the effort to have the particular speak to broad scholarly issues is Ngai, *Impossible Subjects* and Greg Robinson, *By Order of the President: FDR and the Internment of Japanese Americans* (Cambridge, MA: Harvard University Press, 2003).

15. See Him Mark Lai, "A Historical Survey of Organizations of the Left among the Chinese in America," *Bulletin of Concerned Asian Scholars* (1972); Yuji Ichioka, "A Buried Past: Early Issei Socialists and the Japanese Community," *Amerasia Journal* 1, no. 2 (1971): 1–25; and Editorial Board, "Interview with Philip Vera Cruz," in *Roots: An Asian American Reader*, ed. Amy Tachiki, Eddie Wong, Franklin Odo, and Buck Wong (Los Angeles: UCLA Asian American Studies Center, 1971), 305–310. For more recent perspectives, see Josephine Fowler, *Japanese and Chinese Immigrant Activists: Organizing in American and International Communist Movements, 1919–1933* (New Brunswick, NJ: Rutgers University Press, 2007). On what might be called early civil rights activism, see Wong and Chan, *Claiming America*.

16. I will just offer here some personal reflections as a historian who participated in the activities of those formative years. This curious dual position offers advantage as well as limitations. It is a blessing and a curse, to some extent, to be an "artifact" of history, as one of my students once said of me. She was trying to be complimentary, I think. Indeed, it is unusual for a historian to have been an active participant in a moment of historical study. Personal experience provides a special vantage point but also makes it difficult to be dispassionate as scholarship requires. I now understand better why historical actors often complain that "historians just don't get it right." With this caveat, I offer these thoughts.

My first reaction to much of the literature on Asian American activism is one of ambivalence. Much of what I have read is inaccurate, according to my memory and record, and certainly less substantial and nuanced than the subject warrants. William Wei's study, *The Asian American Movement*, for example, is full of errors and misidentifications. He did not understand the layers of activities and complexity of views of many of those whom he discusses. The book commits the basic error in a historical study of not critically understanding source material and drawing conclusions from very limited evidence. The book takes oral histories and published material at face value, for example, and the author had little or no access to documentation, archives, or even personal manuscripts from the time. The result is that the interpretation reflects the author's own political naivete. This is a serious shortcoming in trying to understand a complex, diverse, and oft-vexed process as was the early Asian American movement. Other literature, though well intentioned, often emphasizes appearance over substance, the performance of radicalism rather than content, and media individuals rather than substantive organization and working activists. See William Wei, *The Asian American Movement* (Philadelphia: Temple University Press, 1993). Some useful corrections are Steve Louie and Glenn Omatsu, *Asian Americans: The Movement and the Moment* (Los Angeles: UCLA Asian American Studies Center Press, 2001); Estella Habal, *San Francisco's International Hotel: Mobilizing the Filipino American Community in the Anti-Eviction Movement* (Philadelphia: Temple University Press, 2007); Daryl J. Maeda, *Chains of Babylon: The Rise of Asian America* (Minneapolis: University of Minnesota Press, 2009); Daryl J. Maeda, *Rethinking the Asian American Movement* (New York: Routledge, 2012); and Michael Liu, Kim Geron, and Tracy Lai, *The Snake Dance of Asian American Activism: Community, Vision, and Power* (Lanham, MD: Lexington, 2008). Also see, Diane Carol Fujino, *Heartbeat of Struggle: The Revolutionary Life of Yuri Kochiyama* (Minneapolis: University of Minnesota Press, 2005), and *Samurai among Panthers: Richard Aoki on Race, Resistance, and a Paradoxical Life* (Minneapolis: University of Minnesota Press, 2012).

17. Work that relies on archives includes the highly original work by Fowler, *Japanese and Chinese Immigrant Activists*; also see, Judy Tzu-Chun Wu, *Radicals on the Road: Internationalism, Orientalism, and Feminism during the Vietnam Era* (Ithaca, NY: Cornell University Press, 2013). For work that uses U.S. government documents released through the Freedom of Information and Privacy Act, see Gordon H. Chang, "The Many Sides of Happy Lim: aka Hom Ah Wing, Lin Jian Fu . . . ," essay and translated poems, *Amerasia Journal* 34, no. 2 (2010): 70–98. Federal agencies, such as the Department of Justice, hold a large amount of material on Asian American activists that would be essential for historians. See the controversy around Richard Aoki provoked by Seth Rosenfeld, *Subversives: The FBI's War on Student Radicals and Ronald Reagan's Rise to Power* (New York: Farrar, Straus and Giroux, 2012).

18. Tritia Toyota, *Envisioning America: New Chinese Americans and the Politics of Belonging* (Stanford, CA: Stanford University Press, 2010), 6. Along similar lines is John Horton, *The Politics of Diversity: Immigration, Resistance, and Change in Monterey Park, California* (Philadelphia: Temple University Press, 1995); Leland T. Saito, *Race and Politics: Asian Americans, Latinos, and Whites in a Los Angeles Suburb* (Champaign: University of Illinois Press, 1998); and Linda Trinh Vo, *Mobilizing an Asian American Community* (Philadelphia: Temple University Press, 2004). Historical views are presented by Scott Kurashige, *The Shifting Grounds of Race: Blacks and Japanese Americans in the Making of Multiethnic Los Angeles* (Princeton, NJ: Princeton University Press, 2010), and Angie Chung, *Legacies of Struggle: Conflict and Cooperation in Korean American Politics* (Stanford, CA: Stanford University Press, 2007).

19. See, for example, Leslie T. Hatamiya, *Righting a Wrong: Japanese Americans and the Passage of the Civil Liberties Act of 1988* (Stanford, CA: Stanford University Press, 1993); Pei-te Lien, *The Making of Asian America through Political Participation* (Philadelphia: Temple University Press, 2001); various essays in Gordon H. Chang, ed., *Asian Americans and Politics: Perspectives, Experiences, Prospects* (Washington, DC: Woodrow Wilson Center Press, 2001); and Christian Collet and Pei-Te Lien, eds., *The Transnational Politics of Asian Americans* (Philadelphia: Temple University Press, 2009). Don Nakanishi has long called for a more expansive approach to thinking about Asian Americans and politics. See his many essays, including "Beyond Electoral Politics: Renewing a Search for a Paradigm of Asian Pacific American Politics," in the Chang volume cited above. .

20. Don Nakanishi and James Lai, *2011–2012 National Asian Pacific American Political Almanac*, 14th ed. (Los Angeles: UCLA Asian American Studies Center, 2011).

21. Biographies of two important Asian American conservatives come from diplomatic history. See Stephen G. Craft, *Wellington Koo and the Emergence of Modern China* (Lexington: University Press of Kentucky, 2003); and Catherine Forslund, *Anna Chennault: Informal Diplomacy and Asian Relations* (Wilmington, DE: Scholar Resources, 2002).

22. The importance of an international dimension is suggested in Peter H. Koehn and Xiao-huang Yin, eds., *The Expanding Roles of Chinese Americans in U.S.-China Relations: Transnational Networks and Trans-Pacific Interactions* (Armonk, NY: M. E. Sharpe, 2002), which has a foreword by Him Mark Lai. Also see Warren I. Cohen, *The Asian American Century* (Cambridge, MA: Harvard University Press, 2002). Charlotte Brooks has published a pioneering study in *Between Mao and McCarthy: Chinese American Politics in the Cold War Years* (Chicago: University of Chicago Press, 2015); also see Joyce Mao, *Asia First: China and the Making of Modern American Conservativism* (Chicago: University of Chicago Press, 2015).

CHAPTER 20

··

ASIAN AMERICAN
INTELLECTUAL HISTORY

··

AUGUSTO ESPIRITU

UNLIKE established subfields in Asian American history, such as social, women's, or labor history, no appraisal has ever been done on Asian American intellectual history. Neither has such a subfield of Asian American studies ever been recognized. Asian American intellectual history, drawing from the U.S. intellectual historian David Hollinger's insightful definition, might be described as the historical study of the ways in which intellectuals of Asian descent in the United States have sought to grapple with the governing *questions* of their time. Such a definition is necessarily arbitrary, but perhaps indispensable if one is to constitute a field of inquiry that is neither too narrow nor too broad. Still, if we are to understand Asian American intellectuals and their history, we will need to define the term "intellectual," a concept that few historians of Asian America have used or acknowledge. Antonio Gramsci, the Italian social theorist of the 1920s, and his illuminating discussion of the subject, provides guidance on this point.[1]

Every person, Gramsci argues, is an "intellectual" to the extent that he or she is capable of rational thought, religious worldviews, and philosophical concepts. Gramsci writes, however, that what distinguishes intellectuals from the masses is their *social function* as intellectuals. Indeed, not every thinking, rational person plays such a societal *role*. Gramsci distinguishes between age-old "traditional" intellectuals, as for instance those who make up the multilayered, hierarchical Catholic clergy so powerful in Latin countries, in contrast to "organic" intellectuals who provide the "intellectual and moral leadership" for Northern Italy's modern, capitalist, industrial society. For Gramsci, what matters in the theorizing of intellectuals is that they as a *social group* emerge and remain central to the construction of hegemonic values, habits, self-consciousness, and social practices. Hence, Gramsci's intellectual contrasts with common stereotypes of the intellectual as disengaged, unrealistic, out of touch with common people, and divorced from relations of power. Indeed, intellectuals *are* engaged, enmeshed in relations of power, and involved in relationship with institutions and other collective groupings.

The assumption of a social function, of leadership in a wide variety of senses, transforms the character of intellectual life from individual speculation, to something of broader significance, which is perhaps more aligned with Asian American studies' original, socially oriented, activist goals. The virtue of this definition is that it matters less what *kind* of occupation or social *class* a particular individual might come from, as those concerned about the elitism of intellectual history are apt to object. Rather, the emphasis is on the social *role* that that individual plays in a given place and time. To say this is not to deny that intellectuals do for the most part come from middle and upper classes. At the same time, such a definition acknowledges that working people, from indentured servants to slaves to clerical and auto workers—indeed, any kind of subalterns—can be and have been intellectuals.

In terms of Asian American historiography, such a view of intellectuals helpfully expands, though not in too elastic a manner, to a wide range of social actors beyond the usual pale of writers and academics. Indeed, given the great social pressures that have played an inordinate role in the lives of Asian Americans, Asian American history is rich with interesting intellectual figures, including brokers, translators, journalists, labor unionists, social movement leaders, and political figures among them, in addition to writers (poets, fiction writers, and essayists) and academics (in various fields of study).

Moreover, such a view of intellectuals and their social function transcends the question of intentionality, viz. whether historians are conscious or not of writing intellectual history. Indeed, many historical works were not consciously written as intellectual history. However, if one looks at the singular figures they examine and their articulation of ideas, or their characterization of the social roles of Asian American intellectuals, it is evident, to me at least, that they are writing some form of Asian American intellectual history.

One final point: Of great importance is singularity as a criterion—that is, of works that focus on individual Asian Americans—precisely because Asian American history, being closely related to the social movement for Asian American empowerment, has shied away from such examinations. The 1960s American social histories, of which Asian American history was a part, arose in reaction to a conservative tendency in historical writing known as the "consensus" school, which argued that the course of American history "had been shaped by a broadly accepted set of values that overrode ethnic and class distinctions," a school that was perhaps not surprisingly dominated by intellectual history.[2]

An insistence on "singularity," however, need not necessarily be exclusivist but can be a way of highlighting collective Asian American experiences while recuperating unique, exceptional, or marginal voices. The term "singularity" is consciously used as opposed to "individuality." Individuality connotes discrete bodies, wills, and experiences, and it emphasizes difference. Singularity, on the other hand, is inextricable from the general. In the Saussurean sense, it highlights the contextual nature of signification and, as Jacques Derrida argues, deconstructs the binary between the individual and the general, highlighting difference without making an essentialism out of it.[3] That is to say, one of its virtues is to highlight how that difference emerges out of the general, or how it might

point to the general in a dialectical way. Indeed, examination of the seemingly exceptional, the queer, the strange, the marginal, or the repressed singular figure often provides a sharper understanding of general social norms, collective experiences, and mass
movements. At the same time, it also highlights the importance of the irreducibility of
the "individual" (here, I'm consciously using the word) to the general, the unique voices,
experiences, and sense of alterity of the individual as Other.

In this renewed conception of Asian American intellectuals, one discovers then that
intellectual history is no stranger to Asian American history but has been there from its
earliest stages, as the following survey suggests.

Several examples from the first few decades of Asian and Asian American research
are arguably intellectual histories, as much as they are biographies. For instance, Emily
Brown's study of Har Dayal (1884–1939) provides an example of this tendency. Dayal was
a leading intellectual in the Indian diaspora committed to India's freedom from British
rule and equally one who was not wedded to Gandhi's nonviolent, cultural nationalist
ideology emerging in the Indian subcontinent, similar to other expatriate Indians like
Taraknath Das, Ram Chandra, M. N. Roy, and Lala Lajpat Rai.[4] Brown spends considerable space tracing Dayal's political education and his development of an uncompromising approach to British colonialism. As revealed in the records of his court trial in San
Francisco, Dayal eschewed anarchism and the use of terror, though he did not renounce
those who chose these methods in the struggle against the injustices of colonialism. He
did believe in the importance of both oral and literary propaganda, both of which came
together in the Ghadar ("Rebellion") Party, which he founded. The success of this effort
among Indians in the diaspora, he believed, led to his arrest and prosecution. Of this,
Dayal remarked that the United States should not allow itself to be pushed around by the
British, whose empire at once oppressed India, Egypt, and Ireland. Rather, he thought
America should be a haven, or asylum, for those resisting colonialism.[5]

Meanwhile, Leonard Gordon's study of Kumar Goshal (1899–1971) echoes Brown's
earlier work. Though Goshal came well after Dayal, he shared Dayal's sense of political
conviction and his itinerant movements across the globe. The son of an Indian nationalist from Bengal, he began as an actor in India. He left for Europe, spending four weeks
in France and three months in England before arriving in the United States. There, he
started a fourteen-year career as an actor, playing especially ethnic roles, including
that of a Chinese, a Latin Valentino, and an American Indian. He did political theater
and weekly radio broadcasts for the League for Industrial Democracy, though he was
denied a job for the federal theater program because, as an Indian, he could not become
a U.S. citizen. He married Julia Fox, a singer he met in Greenwich Village. During
and immediately after World War II, he started writing analyses of political conflicts
in British India and postcolonial India and Pakistan, eventually contributing to the
National Guardian in Britain for the next three decades. Gordon traces the evolution
of the ideas of this Indian intellectual, who shared the fate of being blacklisted during
the McCarthy years with his friend Paul Robeson. Goshal's recurring political concerns involved Third World nationalism and anti-imperialism. Indeed, South Asia and
its postcolonial struggles preoccupied him, but just as important, he studied what he

perceived as the troubling rise of American power and cultural arrogance during the Cold War era.[6]

Meanwhile, Hyman Kublin's portrait of Sen Katayama (1859–1933) explores not only his itinerant life but also his intellectual emergence as a socialist and the evolution of his revolutionary ideas. Drawing from Kublin, Yuji Ichioka has already sufficiently explored the broad outlines of Katayama's life in his *Issei* (a term for the first generation of Japanese immigrants), regarding him as one of the few significant student-laborers to lay the groundwork for Japanese immigrant society. What remains of interest in the book from an Asian American intellectual history standpoint are the chapters in which Kublin explores Katayama's struggles to survive and become educated in the United States, which in a sense provide the incubation period for his development as a socialist.

In these, Kublin tells the story of Katayama's ironic Americanization, how he dropped out of Hopkins Academy in Oakland, because of, among other things, the insufficient time he had to learn the English language and the racist taunts he received from other students. Seeking a better place for an education, and upon the advice of one of his patrons, he matriculated at Maryville College in Tennessee where he just managed to fulfill the courses required and had difficulty finding a job (probably from racial discrimination, as he would attack the city for its racially discriminatory policies at a later time). Finally, he landed at Grinnell College in Iowa where he obtained a great education in the classics and where he found help from his friend Iwasaki. Still, his education, moving from classics to literature to political writings about Japan, as well as Sunday school, which helped him to understand Christianity at a deeper level, was too erratic, and at the end of it all, he was unhappy that he had not concentrated on any particular skill. So much for the training of an Asian American "intellectual" and such a contrast to the future "marginal men" and "model minority" figures of a later age!

Following Kublin's pioneering work, Ichioka's writings on the Issei, from his pathbreaking monograph to his posthumously published collection of essays, display a marked concern for the singular figures, cases, and controversies that encapsulate the Japanese American community's evolving struggles for identity. Ichioka understood well the Horatio Alger myth and the myth of Asian American success, both of which have structured the immigrant story in American life. Instead, he presents a countermythic, counterhegemonic narrative of a people's hopes and struggle for survival and the tragic irony of their barren future. Especially through the seminal figure of Abiko Kyutaro, at once a colonial and settler immigrant figure, Ichioka argues for the ideological transformation of the prevailing Japanese immigrant ethos, from the *dekaseginin*, or "sojourner," ethos to the desideratum of "settlement" (acculturation to assimilation).[7]

As Eiichiro Azuma writes in an introduction to his essays, Ichioka's *Issei* as well as the essays collected in *Before Internment*, a continuation of *Issei*, broke new ground not only in turning the attention of scholars in Japanese American studies to the period of immigration and the interwar period but also in methodically raising questions, including controversial questions of loyalty and disloyalty in the years leading up to World War II as well as the strong transnational and sentimental ties to Japan, to challenge the field at key junctures in its development. Of particular significance, in this respect, is Ichioka's concept of Asian American intellectual figures as a "bridge of understanding." This he develops in the article on the influential editor of Seattle's *Japanese American Courier*, James Sakamoto. For as long as he could, Sakamoto sought to play the role of interpreter between "East" and "West." He sought as well to direct the Japanese American community toward the maintenance of cultural ties to Japan, until the 1937 Japanese invasion of China and, subsequently, the Pearl Harbor attack, made it difficult and then impossible to do so.[8]

This hybrid biographical-intellectual history genre from the early stages of Asian American studies, as much as the bridge of understanding figures, continues into the 1990s and the twenty-first century. It assumes new heights in Gordon Chang's work on Yamato Ichihashi, the first tenured Japanese American scholar out of Stanford, ardently pro-Japan as much as a believer in bringing America and Asia together. Chang builds upon Ichioka's initial research and critique of this pioneering Issei historian. In his introduction to Ichihashi's wartime correspondence, Chang's biographical gloss on Ichihashi (at seventy-six pages, along with brief essays introducing various stages of Ichihashi's correspondence, it is a mini-treatise in itself) explores the contexts of race and ethnicity, gender relations, academic culture, and imperial state encounters that shaped and were reshaped by Ichihashi's rich intellectual life and widespread encounters in social, academic, and political life.[9] The overall effect is to magnify the dramatic irony of his incarceration, similar to many Nikkei incarceration narratives. However, what distinguishes Ichihashi from many Japanese American lives are the complexities of his local, national, and international connections—which were constructed by his important research work, diplomacy, and activism and which mark him as an *institution* in his own right.

Similar to works on South Asian and Japanese immigrant intellectuals discussed above, and building from earlier explorations of Sucheng Chan and Eve Armentrout Ma,[10] K. Scott Wong's seminal essays explore the diasporic Chinese intellectual figures of Wu Ting Fang, Yan Phou Lee, Yung Wing, and Liang Qichao, among others. Wong not only provides a study of the nationalist visions of elite expatriates and Chinese Americans but also contributes to the emerging field of Asian American transnationalism. In his three essays, Wong explores Chinese intellectual perspectives on the United States in China as a "contact zone" and a space of "transculturation" and explores the ways in which Liang Qichao, a prominent elite reformer in exile, recognized his political perspectives in his brief but meaningful encounter with Chinese immigrants in the United States. Wong discovers as well how Chinese intellectuals in the United States aligned themselves as "cultural defenders" of the Chinese community and as "brokers" (a concept of recurring significance in Chinese American intellectual history), that is, those who, like the pioneer Yale graduate and transnational figure, Yung Wing, saw no contradiction between America and China and who sought to mediate the cultural differences between the two societies. Wong is especially adept at highlighting the dualities facing both Chinese elites and Chinese immigrants in the United States—between Asia and America, between Sinocentrism and Americanization, between maintenance of one's Confucian beliefs and embrace of American Protestantism—especially during a period of great transformation in China and an era of extreme racial discrimination and violence directed against the Chinese in the United States.[11]

K. Scott Wong's concerns about the dual pressures facing Chinese American intellectuals find renewed articulation in three subsequent studies: Yong Chen's reading of the life of the businessman Ah Quin; Madeline Hsu's account of Chen Yuxiu, the Chinese American industrialist; and Mae Ngai's study of the Tape family. By mining Ah Quin's diary as a cultural resource, Chen provides a window into the attempts of San Francisco Chinatown's immigrants to cling to Chineseness even as they aspired to succeed economically in the United States. Ah Quin wrote in English, though ostensibly for doing business with the white world, reserving his deeply personal events for Chinese. Quin also acted as court interpreter for his fellow countrymen. Interestingly, Chen finds that while go-betweens, interpreters, and translators like Ah Quin had access to the white world, their prestige as intellectuals could not match those of the "scholars," who represented "tradition" and homeland ties for the Chinese immigrant community. Meanwhile, Hsu explores the struggles of Chen Yuxiu, the American industrialist and repatriate. Like the earlier figure of Yung Wing, who returned to China and worked with the Chinese government, Chen sought to build a profitable railroad in Taishan just as he had done in his successful career as an industrialist in the Western United States. Chen, however, faced enormous challenges in transplanting U.S. industrial techniques and U.S.-style entrepreneurialism from the American West to the Asian rural landscape in the early twentieth century. Finally, Ngai's study of three generations of the Tape family echoes the role of the cultural broker. For Ngai, the cultural broker describes the resourceful, in-between, and entrepreneurial Chinese during Exclusion-era America. Indeed, members of the Tape family played such roles as court interpreter, translator, bond agent, immigration officer, and import-export trader, finding a niche in the racialized American economy that excluded Chinese from a wide variety of occupations. Driven by relentless ambition, these mediating Chinese economic intellectuals played by the rules and, as Ngai writes, also broke the rules, relying upon smuggling, graft, and vice in order to get ahead.[12]

These explorations of Japanese and Chinese American intellectuals find their counterparts among Filipino and Indian Americans. For instance, the late Steffi San Buenaventura's dissertation and essay on the mutual aid organization the Filipino Federation of America is inevitably intertwined with the leading figures of Hilario Moncado and Lorenzo de los Reyes, whose "nativism" exemplifies the performance of ethnicity in the U.S. racial context, the founding and expansion of an esoteric folk Christian religion, and Filipino Americans' attempt to exercise political leadership in the U.S. colonial Philippines. Meanwhile, Jonathan Okamura explores another seminal figure of Hawai'i, the sociologist Roman Cariaga, whose master's thesis, *Filipinos in Hawaii*, Okamura reinterprets. While Cariaga believed in assimilationism, hence toward a hegemonic view of race relations, Okamura argues that Cariaga's works need to be placed in the context of the incredibly racist environment toward Filipinos in territorial Hawai'i during the 1920s and 1930s. From this vantage point, *Filipinos in Hawaii* can be reread as an antiracist document, an assertion of Filipinos' humanity and emerging nationalism, especially in the context of U.S. colonialism and the rise of the Philippine Commonwealth. The book's exploration of remittances and other aspects of Filipino migrants' continuation of ties to the Philippines likewise makes Cariaga an early contributor to the later study of diaspora and transnationalism. Contemporaneous with San Buenaventura and Okamura, Melinda Tria Kerkvliet's account of Pablo Manlapit's activism, which transgresses the imperial spaces of the U.S. colonial Philippines, territorial Hawai'i, and the emergent American West, might be read as an exploration of the lasting impact of American ideas of interracial unionism, antiracism, and labor republicanism, combined with anticolonialism, Filipino nationalism, and pro-independence thought, upon this prominent labor activist.[13]

In the meantime, Gordon Chang's introduction to Dhan Gopal Mukerji's *Caste and Outcast* shows this elite Indian intellectual's connections to prominent Indian and American thinkers alike, including Jawaharlal Nehru, M. N. Roy, Van Wyck Brooks, Roger Baldwin, and Will Durant. Beyond this, the essay highlights not only the specific social structures in British India and America that South Asians had to navigate, but also Mukerji's struggles as a student activist in American anarchist and socialist circles, his pro-independence activity in support of the Ghadar Party, and the class differences between this budding writer from the Brahmin class and the mass of lower-class, predominantly Sikh and Muslim Indians in America.[14]

Mukerji's and other Indian elite intellectuals' experiences in America had been prefigured by the pioneering Indian feminist and nationalist reformer Pandita Ramabai, whom historians Meera Kosambi and Kumari Jayawardena have rescued from long neglect, especially in the American context. In Kosambi's introduction to the translation and republication of *The Peoples of the United States*, Ramabai's penetrating series of readings of Gilded Age America, Kosambi situates Ramabai "in the interstices between British imperialism and American Orientalism." Kosambi argues that Ramabai weaves together narratives of "the USA, England and India," criticizing British colonialism in India through her largely positive, though not uncritical, appraisal on American attitudes, practices, and institutions, especially of their racial and gendered dimensions. Meanwhile, Kumari Jayawardena explores Ramabai's tangled relationship with her Protestant and American middle-class women patrons during her long sojourns in the American heartland, as well as her uncompromising feminist criticism of the masculinist foundations of Indian nationalism.[15]

Even in the twenty-first century, explorations of Asian American intellectuals remain under the purview of social and cultural history rather than intellectual history. Judy Wu's focus on the avant-garde figure "Mom Chung" from San Francisco exemplifies the illumination that singular figures can cast on the history of social groups. Mom Chung's claim to fame was hosting weekly gatherings in San Francisco during World War II that brought together the famous (actors, celebrities like John Wayne and Admiral Nimitz) and the not so famous (soldiers on furlough). It was the maternal image she projected, at once exotic and assuring, Judy Wu says, that made her such a popular figure. Yet "Mom Chung" was a persona, the staid mother image belying her subversive romantic affairs with other women and her presence in a budding queer community.

Wu calls her work a "biography," but one wonders why it would not also be an intellectual history. She is interested in doing both a reconstruction of this medical professional and celebrity's life that is meaningful along with a treatment that connects Chung's life to larger themes of race, gender, and sexuality about which intellectual historians are similarly concerned. Her question of "how Mom Chung accomplished what she did"—what Wu calls her "self-Orientalism," which is at once racial as it is gendered (maternal) and a strategy that is itself limited—is an intellectual history question as much as a social historical one. Indeed, the question of how Mom Chung constructed a community (at first of 75 and then over 1,500 "fair haired bastards") involves questions of "strategy," popularization, power, and performance that involve intellectual history.

Wu's narrative of Mom Chung's interstitial role connects her experiences to K. Scott Wong's, Mae Ngai's, and Yong Chen's concept of the cultural "broker." Mom Chung—American-born, proficient in English, and an American citizen—parlayed her skills between her parents condemned by exclusion laws and the white world. However, recalling Yong Chen's observation about the social status of brokers among Chinese immigrants, Mom Chung's sense of independence, reform, and queer sexuality, while making her more acceptable to whites and other non-Chinese, made her simultaneously less acceptable among Chinese Americans.[16]

Similarly, Karen Leong makes an interesting decision to study the transformation of American Orientalism through the prism of biographical studies of the fascinating, multilayered lives of Pearl Buck, Anna May Wong, and Soong May Ling (Madame Chiang Kai-shek). What concerns Leong is a large cultural problematic, that of American Orientalism, that congeries of Occidental (specifically American) racial and gendered attitudes toward the Chinese, which contributed both to the nativist violence and the Chinese Exclusion Act of the late nineteenth century and the shift toward a more tolerant attitude of the 1930s. That transformation takes place as a result of many historical factors, including the influence of the Protestant missionary efforts in China, Japanese aggression in China, and the shift in American foreign policy inaugurated by President Franklin D. Roosevelt's more egalitarian view of international relations. That shift, Leong argues, occurred as well through the agency of important intellectual figures who transformed social attitudes in various arenas of Asian-American life: Buck in the world of letters and politics, Wong on the movie screen, and Soong as China's First Lady and as Generalissimo Chiang Kai-shek's representative to the United States during China's struggle against Japanese invasion.

Much is revealed of race and gender relations in the 1930s and 1940s by studying the thinking and activism of these figures. Since much is already known about Anna May Wong, it is appropriate to focus on Leong's discussion of Pearl Buck and Mayling Soong. Both Buck, who was raised in China, and Soong, who was educated in the United States, especially gained the attention of a broad American audience. Buck, the Nobel Prize winner, transformed attitudes toward China not only through her novel, *The Good Earth*, which humanizes a Chinese family's struggle for survival, but also by publicly attacking the racist foundations of the American missionary effort and her activism on behalf of improving general race relations in the United States, principally for African

Americans, but also for Chinese Americans. Meanwhile, through Soong May Ling's extended official visit in the United States during World War II, Leong shows the complex reasons that belie Soong's seemingly erratic actions, which were explained away as due to the fickleness or deceitfulness of her race and sex, but which, in truth, reflected Soong's roundabout anti-imperialism and her forthright demands for racial dignity for the Chinese. These include her obsession with demanding that the White House declare her visit an official state visit; her stubborn demand to have Winston Churchill visit her, rather than the other way around (in response to White House efforts to broker a meeting between the two world leaders); and her lecturing of Hollywood producers on their racial stereotyping of the Chinese.[17]

Mention here should also be made of the works of scholars of Asian American activism, coming not from a historical approach but from an ethnic studies focus, whose works on intriguing political leaders of the Asian American movement involve exploration of their ideas. For example, Diane Fujino's books on Yuri Kochiyama and Richard Aoki combine extensive oral history with political biography to tell the story and draw out the social significance of these activists. Kochiyama's and Aoki's contributions to Asian-African solidarities as well as the radical wing of the African American freedom movement and international struggles, including membership in Malcolm X's Organization for African-American Unity and the Black Panthers, were just as extensive as or exceeded their contributions to the Asian American movement. To this group should be added Jennifer Jung Hee Choi's reconstruction of Grace Lee Boggs's political development as a Marxist and her associations with C. L. R. James, Runa Dunaevskaya, and Carl Boggs. While appreciative of Grace Boggs's potential significance for Asian Americans, including her contributions to the Asian American struggles in Detroit in the 1970s and 1980s, Choi is nonetheless critical of Boggs's subordination of Asian American struggles to the black liberation movement as a foundation for true interethnic organizing.[18]

From the opposite political vantage point, Daryl Maeda's " 'Down with Hayakawa': Assimilation vs. Third World Solidarity at San Francisco State College" explores Asian American activism from the unique viewpoint of the controversial San Francisco State College president, political conservative, and renowned linguistics scholar of the 1960s. Hayakawa, as Maeda writes in this exploration of the politics of his work, concerned himself with the problem of racism in American society. Unlike Kochiyama, Aoki, and Boggs, however, Hayakawa believed in "liberal assimilationism," in the essential goodness of American institutions and the need for immigrants to assimilate American values, cultural norms, and institutions. He viewed race essentially as a matter of semantics and ending racism as a matter of changing the key words we used. Maeda points out that Hayakawa maintained this view from its emergence in the 1930s and 1940s all the way through the 1970s, even as the civil rights and antiwar movements, not to mention the student movements on college campuses such as San Francisco State College, were exposing the model minority as a myth and the structural foundations of American racism in capitalism, the military-industrial complex, and U.S. imperialism.[19] Such a sclerotic position set him in confrontation with Asian

American youth in particular, for whom assimilationism had proved bankrupt, given the pervasiveness of racism in American society, and for whom cultural pluralism combined with newfound political assertiveness provided a more attractive model for ethnic participation in American life.

Ironically, historians of Asian American intellectuals self-consciously identified as intellectual historians, have proven, in the long run, to be the exceptions. Of the historians examined here, only two, Henry Yu and Augusto Espiritu, make such a conscious methodological choice. In the history departments of both Princeton University and the University of California, Los Angeles, from which Yu and Espiritu received their doctorates, respectively, there have been strong intellectual history influences. Yu, for instance, was a former student of Daniel Rodgers, a historian of ideas and of American social policy across the Atlantic, while Espiritu was influenced by a strong American and European intellectual history program. Still, this cannot serve as an explanation for why these two historians chose to embrace intellectual history. Nor does it explain why other historians, coming from departments with strong intellectual history backgrounds, did not make such a choice. Perhaps, the anti-elitist politics and the vogue of social history might provide better starting points. Indeed, even the works of Yu and Espiritu exhibit the strong influences of social history, if not methodologically, then in terms of their pressing concerns.

Yu's *Thinking Orientals* is a case in point of intellectual history written with great awareness of social history. His work on Chinese and Japanese American doctoral students in the University of Chicago's sociology department is a penetrating examination of the social dynamics of race, class, ethnicity, and gender. Yu may not have been the first to identify the "Oriental problem" in American life, but his work has been the most compelling argument about its significance for Chinese and Japanese American academics during the first half of the twentieth century. Yu's exploration of the marginal man theory, the role of interpreter between dominant and subordinate cultures (recalling a kind of *domestic* "bridge of understanding" or "cultural broker") and his original phrase, "the commodification of authentic identity," the ways in which Asian American sociologists consciously sought to refashion the marginal man concept in order to set themselves up as experts, authorities, on matters involving Asian Americans, helped to revivify interest in this particular period and sector of Asian American history and to establish interest in Asian American intellectual history in general.

One cannot miss here as well the ways in which these early sociologists' concerns about issues of race, immigration, assimilation, and social distance established the basis for the rise of the Asian American social movement in the 1960s. One can see precursors of Asian American movement criticisms of American life within Paul Siu's painstaking though flawed examination of the "sojourner attitude" among Chinese immigrants and in Kazuo Kawai's searing portrayal of racism in Charlie Company in the segregated Japanese regiment's experience in World War II. On the other hand, the effect of these early Asian American sociologists might have been just as great in serving as a foil for the 1960s generation of Asian Americans. For instance, Rose Hum Lee, who became the first Asian American, man or woman, to head a department of sociology, eschewed the powerful impact of structural forces of racism and social discrimination and had seen that race relations primarily in terms of personal, individual intercultural relations would become controversial.[20] Yu's insights on the racially conservative tendency among these early Asian Americans finds support in Daryl Maeda's " 'Down with Hayakawa.' "

The fundamental drawback in Yu's book, according to other historical works on Chinese Americans, is the fact that its gaze is trained exclusively on the American racial landscape. Adam McKeown makes this observation in his own reading and examination of Paul Siu's significance, from a global, transnational context. Because he uses the word "sojourner," McKeown argues that contemporary Asian American scholars have too easily dismissed his work as reinforcing the stereotype of the Asian as racial outsider. However, McKeown argues for a rereading of Siu from a global, transnational perspective. Unlike Yu, who argues that the marginal man was salutary for early Asian American intellectuals, McKeown argues that Siu's account of the sojourner in his essay on the subject reveals Siu's rejection of the term as accurately describing the in-between reality of the sojourner, who neither gives up his/her homeland nor becomes a "settler." From this view, Siu's insight and rich ethnographic work on Chinese hand laundrymen shows their challenge to a teleological immigrant narrative of assimilation and, instead, demonstrates their continuing engagement with friends, family, home, and national developments in China.[21] By a different path, through the critique of the historiography, McKeown thus arrives at a similar conclusion as Yong Chen and Madeline Hsu.

Similarly, Espiritu's *Five Faces of Exile* draws in part from American social history's concerns. His work on the elite Filipino writers and intellectuals draws on literatures of race, masculinity, and patronage relations in Asian American studies and U.S. history. One immediately notices the differences in the subject matter of Yu's and Espiritu's works. Yu's work has the benefit of being centered around a prominent institution, the Chicago School of Sociology, during a determinate time, the 1920s and 1930s, with a core of prominent mainstream, hegemonic intellectuals that have been much written about and a group of Chinese and Japanese American students that were generationally quite similar. Hence, its sharp analytic focus, especially on race and ethnic relations. Espiritu's subjects, however, involve pioneering Filipino American writer-intellectuals, including known quantities, such as Carlos Bulosan, Ben Santos, and Jose Garcia Villa, and less recognized figures like Carlos P. Romulo and N. V. M. Gonzalez, who were among the precursors of contemporary Asian American intellectuals. There is no one school that unifies them. In fact, they have different regional, class, and educational backgrounds. In contrast with Yu's focus on the United States, what Espiritu's work shows is these intellectuals' common longing for acceptance in the emerging Filipino nation, the transnational reality of their lives as well as their difficult attempts at "adjusting" to American life, and the cultures of travel, exile, and alienation that such a reality produced.[22] Still, the idea of transnationalism extends rather than contradicts the concepts of the "bridge of understanding," the navigation of "Orientalism" and "self-Orientalism," and "cultural brokers," all of recurring significance in Asian American intellectual history.

CONCLUSION

In line with a view of intellectuals as social agents in structured relations of power, drawing from Gramsci's writing on intellectuals, the focus on historical studies highlights and critically examines singular figures in Asian American history, especially individuals who attempt to carry out a particular idea, play a mediating function between social groups, play a vanguard role artistically or politically, or resist hegemonic structures.

A synoptic reading of the texts shows that Asian American intellectual histories exist, even if epiphenomenally, and despite the qualms Asian American historians might feel about embracing the analytical category of "Asian American intellectual" or the subfield of "Asian American intellectual history." Asian American intellectual history need not be an essentially elitist or socially disengaged form of historical writing, but as these classic texts show, it can instantiate concerns about gender, race, class, nation, empire, and power as much as any other methodological approach. And inasmuch as there is a wide range of historical Asian American actors, there is also a correspondingly wide range of models for doing intellectual history, including a critical reading of intellectuals' writings, extensive use of oral history and interviews, exploration of intellectuals' social and cultural milieu, the way intellectuals might embody or depart from a school of thought, the ways intellectual strategies are expressed in political life, and the ways they rearticulate larger discourses of social identification like race, class, or gender. Asian American intellectual history is a richly varied subfield of Asian American history, though its potential for combining engaging historical narratives with explorations of ideas and the agency of singular figures has yet to be fully tapped.

NOTES

1. David A. Hollinger, *In the American Province: Studies in the History and Historiography of Ideas* (Baltimore, MD: Johns Hopkins University Press, 1985), 132; David Forgacs, ed., *The Antonio Gramsci Reader: Selected Writings 1916–1935* (New York: New York University Press, 2000), 300–311, 320–322. See also the International Gramsci Society's "Gramsci Bibliography," http://www.internationalgramscisociety.org/resources/recent_publications/index.html.

2. Eric Foner, ed., *The New American History: Revised and Expanded Edition* (Philadelphia: Temple University Press, 1997), 233.

3. Jacques Derrida, "Structure, Sign, and Play in the Discourse of the Human Sciences," in *Writing and Difference*, trans. Alan Bass (Chicago: University of Chicago Press, 1978), 351–370.

4. Sucheng Chan, "European and Asian Immigration Reconsidered," in *Immigration Reconsidered*, ed. Virginia Yans-McLaughlin (New York: Oxford University Press, 1990), 56–55; Erez Manela, *The Wilsonian Moment: Self-Determination and the International Origins of Anticolonial Nationalism* (New York: Oxford University Press, 2007), 85–95.

5. Emily C. Brown, *Har Dayal: Hindu Revolutionary and Rationalist* (Tucson: University of Arizona Press, 1975), 21–30, 158–163.

6. Leonard A. Gordon, "Bridging India and America: The Art and Politics of Kumar Goshal," *Amerasia Journal* 15, no. 2 (1989): 68–84.

7. Yuji Ichioka, *The Issei: The World of the First Generation Japanese Immigrants, 1885–1924* (New York: Free Press, 1988), 1–5, 28. See also chapters 5 and 6 of Hyman Kublin, *Asian Revolutionary: The Life of Sen Katayama* (Princeton, NJ: Princeton University Press, 1964), 47–74.

8. Eiichiro Azuma, "Introduction," in *Before Internment: Essays in Prewar Japanese American History* (Stanford, CA: Stanford University Press, 2006), xx, xxiii, xxiv; Yuji Ichioka, "A Study in Dualism: James Yoshinori Sakamoto and the *Japanese American Courier*," in Azuma, *Before Internment*, 100–117.

9. Gordon Chang, "Introduction," in *Morning Glory, Evening Shadow: Yamato Ichihashi and His Internment Writings, 1942–1945* (Stanford, CA: Stanford University Press, 1999), 11–87.

10. Sucheng Chan, "European and Asian Immigration Reconsidered," in *Immigration Reconsidered: History, Sociology, and Politics* (New York: Oxford University Press, 1991); L. Eve Armentrout Ma, *Revolutionaries, Monarchists, and Chinatowns: Chinese Politics in the Americas and the 1911 Revolution* (Honolulu: University of Hawai'i Press, 1990).

11. K. Scott Wong, "The Transformation of Culture: Three Chinese Views of America," *American Quarterly* 48, no. 2 (1996): 207–208; K. Scott Wong, "Liang Qichao and the Chinese of American: A Re-evaluation of His Selected Memoir of Travels in the New World," *Journal of American Ethnic History* 11, no. 4 (1992): 17, 20; and K. Scott Wong, "Cultural Defenders and Brokers: Responses to the Anti-Chinese Movement," in *Claiming America: Constructing Chinese American Identities during the Exclusion Era*, ed. K. Scott Wong and Sucheng Chang (Philadelphia: Temple University Press, 1998), 28, 32. Religious differences are also explored in an insightful manner in Qingsong Zhang's essay on the early civil rights leader Wong Chin Foo, "The Origins of the Chinese Americanization Movement: Wong Chin Foo and the Chinese Equal Rights League," in *Claiming America: Constructing Chinese American Identities during the Exclusion Era*, ed. K. Scott Wong and Sucheng Chan (Philadelphia: Temple University Press, 1998), 44–47.

12. Yong Chen, *Chinese San Francisco: A Trans-Pacific Community* (Stanford, CA: Stanford University Press, 2000), 106, 108–110; Madeline Y. Hsu, *Dreaming of Gold, Dreaming of Home: Transnationalism and Migration between the United States and South China, 1882–1943* (Stanford, CA: Stanford University Press, 2000), 158; Mae Ngai, *The Lucky Ones: One Family and the Extraordinary Intervention of Chinese America* (New York: Houghton Mifflin Harcourt, 2010), 225.

13. Steffi San Buenaventura, "The Master and the Federation: A Filipino American Social Movement in California and Hawaii," *Social Process in Hawai'i* 33 (1991): 174–178; Steffi San Buenaventura, "Nativism and Ethnicity in a Filipino-American Experience" (Ph.D. dissertation, University of Hawai'i, 1990); Jonathan Okamura, "Writing the Filipino Diaspora," *Social Processes in Hawai'i* 37 (1996): 41, 49; Melinda Kerkvliet, *Unbending Cane: Pablo Manlapit, a Filipino Labor Leader in Hawai'i* (Manoa: Office of Multicultural Student Services, University of Hawai'i at Manoa, 2002), 21, 67, 121.

14. Gordon Chang and Dhan Gopal Mukerji, eds., *Caste and Outcast* (Stanford, CA: Stanford University Press, 2002), 1–44.

15. Meera Kosambi, "Introduction: Returning the American Gaze: Situating Pandita Ramabai's American Encounter," in *Pandita Ramabai's American Encounter* (Bloomington: University

of Indiana Press, 2003), 4, 6; Kumari Jayawardena, "Going for the Jugular of Hindu Patriarchy: American Women Fundraisers for Ramabai," in *Unequal Sisters: A Multicultural Reader in U.S. Women's History*, ed. Vicki Ruiz and Ellen Du Bois (New York: Routledge, 2000).

16. Judy Wu, *Doctor Mom Chung of the Fair-Haired Bastards: The Life of a Wartime Celebrity* (Berkeley: University of California Press, 2005), 3–5, 97, 165.

17. Karen Leong, *The China Mystique: Pearl S. Buck, Anna May Wong, Mayling Soong, and the Transformation of American Orientalism* (Berkeley: University of California Press, 2005), 1–3, 31–32, 46–48, 146–149.

18. Diane Fujino, *Heartbeat of Struggle: The Revolutionary Life of Yuri Kochiyama* (Minneapolis: University of Minnesota Press, 2005), xxiv; Diane Fujino, *Samurai among Panthers: Richard Aoki on Race, Resistance, and a Paradoxical Life* (Minneapolis: University of Minnesota Press, 2012), 22; Jennifer Jung Hee Choi, "At the Margins of the Asian American Political Experience: The Life of Grace Lee Boggs," *Amerasia Journal* 25, no. 2 (1999): 30–33, 37.

19. Daryl Maeda, *Chains of Babylon: The Rise of Asian America* (Minneapolis: University of Minnesota Press, 2009), 40–72.

20. Henry Yu, *Thinking Orientals: Migration, Contact, and Exoticism in Modern America* (New York: Oxford University Press, 2002), 108–110, 159–160, 134, 142, 147, 125–128.

21. Adam McKeown, "The Sojourner as Astronaut: Paul Siu in Global Perspective," in *Re/collecting Early Asian America: Essays in Cultural History*, ed. Josephine Lee, Imogene L. Lim, and Yuko Matsukawa (Philadelphia: Temple University Press, 2002), 128, 131.

22. Augusto Espiritu, *Five Faces of Exile: The Nation and Filipino American Intellectuals* (Stanford, CA: Stanford University Press, 2005), xiii, 192.

FURTHER READING

Brown, Emily C. *Har Dayal: Hindu Revolutionary and Rationalist*. Tucson: University of Arizona Press, 1975.

Chang, Gordon H., ed. *Morning Glory, Evening Shadow: Yamato Ichihashi and His Internment Writings, 1942–1945*. Stanford, CA: Stanford University Press, 1997.

Chang, Gordon H., and Dhan Gopal Mukerji, eds. *Caste and Outcast*. Stanford, CA: Stanford University Press, 2002.

Chen, Yong. *Chinese San Francisco: A Trans-Pacific Community*. Stanford, CA: Stanford University Press, 2000.

Choi, Jennifer Jung Hee. "At the Margins of the Asian American Political Experience: The Life of Grace Lee Boggs." *Amerasia Journal* 25, no. 2 (1999): 18–40.

Espiritu, Augusto. *Five Faces of Exile: The Nation and Filipino American Intellectuals*. Stanford, CA: Stanford University Press, 2005.

Fujino, Diane. *Heartbeat of Struggle: The Revolutionary Life of Yuri Kochiyama*. Minneapolis: University of Minnesota Press, 2005.

———. *Samurai among Panthers: Richard Aoki on Race, Resistance, and a Paradoxical Life*. Minneapolis: University of Minnesota Press, 2012.

Gordon, Leonard A. "Bridging India and America: The Art and Politics of Kumar Goshal." *Amerasia Journal* 15, no. 2 (1989): 68–88.

Hollinger, David. *In the American Province: Studies in the History and Historiography of Ideas*. Baltimore, MD: Johns Hopkins University Press, 1989.

Hsu, Madeline Y. *Dreaming of Gold, Dreaming of Home: Transnationalism and Migration between the United States and South China, 1882–1943*. Stanford, CA: Stanford University Press, 2000.

Ichioka, Yuji. *Before Internment: Essays in Prewar Japanese American History*. Stanford, CA: Stanford University Press, 2006.

———. "A Study in Dualism: James Yoshinori Sakamoto and the *Japanese American Courier, 1928–1942*." In *Before Internment: Essays in Prewar Japanese American History*, edited by Yuji Ichioka. Stanford, CA: Stanford University Press, 2006.

Jayawardena, Kumari. "Going for the Jugular of Hindu Patriarchy: American Women Fund-Raisers for Ramabai." In *Unequal Sisters: A Multicultural Reader in U.S. Women's History*, edited by Vicki Ruiz and Ellen Du Bois. New York: Routledge, 2000.

Kerkvliet, Melinda Tria. *Unbending Cane: Pablo Manlapit, a Filipino Labor Leader in Hawaii*. Manoa: Office of Multicultural Student Services, University of Hawai'i at Manoa, 2002.

Kosambi, Meera. *Pandita Ramabai's American Encounter: The Peoples of the United States*. Bloomington: Indiana University Press, 2003 [1889].

Kublin, Hyman. *Asian Revolutionary: The Life of Sen Katayama*. Princeton, NJ: Princeton University Press, 1964.

Leong, Karen. *The China Mystique: Pearl S. Buck, Anna May Wong, Mayling Soong, and the Transformation of American Orientalism*. Berkeley: University of California Press, 2005.

McKeown, Adam. "The Sojourner as Astronaut: Paul Siu in Global Perspective." In *Re/collecting Early Asian America: Essays in Cultural History*, edited by Josephine Lee, Imogene L. Lim, and Yuko Matsukawa, 127–142. Philadelphia: Temple University Press, 2002.

Maeda, Daryl. *Chains of Babylon: The Rise of Asian America*. Minneapolis: University of Minnesota Press, 2009.

Ngai, Mae. *The Lucky Ones: One Family and the Extraordinary Invention of Chinese America*. New York: Houghton Mifflin Harcourt, 2010.

Okamura, Jonathan. "Writing the Filipino Diaspora." *Social Process in Hawai'i* 37 (1996): 36–56.

San Buenaventura, Steffi. "The Master and the Federation: A Filipino American Social Movement in California and Hawaii." *Social Process in Hawai'i* 33 (1991): 169–193.

Wong, K. Scott. "Cultural Defenders and Brokers: Chinese Responses to the Anti-Chinese Movement." In *Claiming America: Constructing Chinese American Identities during the Exclusion Era*, edited by K. Scott Wong and Sucheng Chan, 3–40. Philadelphia: Temple University Press, 1998.

———. "Liang Qichao and the Chinese of America: A Re-evaluation of His Selected Memoir of Travels in the New World." *Journal of American Ethnic History* 11, no. 4 (1992): 3–24.

———. "The Transformation of Culture: Three Chinese Views of America." *American Quarterly* 48, no. 2 (1996): 201–232.

Wu, Judy Tzu-Chun. *Doctor Mom Chung of the Fair-Haired Bastards: The Life of a Wartime Celebrity*. Berkeley: University of California Press, 2005.

Yu, Henry. *Thinking Orientals: Migration, Contact, and Exoticism in Modern America*. New York: Oxford University Press, 2002.

CHAPTER 21

....

ASIAN AMERICAN
RELIGIOUS HISTORY

....

HELEN JIN KIM, TIMOTHY TSENG,
AND DAVID K. YOO

THE subfield of Asian American religions, and in particular, Asian American religious history, is located at the intersection of Asian American history and American religious history. (We understand the nomenclature "Asian American religions" to include "North America" and "Asian Pacific America.") The sheer lack of attention that historians have paid to Asian American religions risks essentializing and rendering invisible Asian American religious subjects as historical actors, resulting in reductive and binary conceptualizations: religious Asian Americans are cast either as the perpetually foreign religious "other" or the racially assimilated model minority.[1] Such flat and stereotypical characterizations limit the complexity, nuance, and agency available to religious Asian Americans as subjects of history.

The ethnic and religious composition of Asian Americans and Native Hawaiian and Pacific Islanders has been historically diverse, though the contemporary growth of Asian Americans religions is primarily a result of the 1965 Immigration Act, which ended a long period of Asian exclusion. As of 2012, Asian Americans religiously affiliate as 42 percent Christian, 26 percent unaffiliated, 14 percent Buddhist, 10 percent Hindu, 4 percent Muslim, 2 percent Other Religion, 1 percent Sikh, and 1 percent Don't Know/Refused to Answer.[2] A deeper dive into these numbers shows high concentrations of religious affinity by ethnic group: approximately half of Indian Americans identify as Hindu; a majority of Filipinos (89 percent) and Koreans (71 percent) identify as Christian; and, over half of all Chinese Americans identify as non-religious (52 percent), the largest ethnic group in the United States to affiliate as "religious nones."[3]

Much literature has been devoted to studying this heterogeneous Asian American religious landscape. Yet these contemporary statistics can be traced back to a longer religious history within Asian homelands, new immigrant contexts and transnational connections. Thus, the contemporary focus in extant Asian American religious scholarship reveals an opportunity to take the long view for more historical excavation—specifically, to write Asian American religious histories. This essay, therefore, argues that to address the essentialization and invisibility of Asian American religious subjects, not only are theoretical interventions and social scientific analyses needed, but also stories and historical narratives.

The 1960s and 1970s: The Asian American Movement and Theologies of Liberation

The subfield of Asian American religions has its roots in the Asian American movement of the 1960s and 1970s, a watershed historical moment when the term "Asian American" was first coined. A growing generation of college-age Asian Americans mobilized politically by identifying with Third World struggles for decolonization and resistance to the Vietnam War. Ideologically, they allied with Marxist and Maoist struggles for justice and liberation, forming reading groups that studied a combination of Marxist-Leninist-Maoist thought. Students formed revolutionary groups, including the Red Guard Party, Wei Min She, I Wor Kuen, and the Asian Study Group. They allied with the Third World Liberation Front to fight for ethnic studies programs, including Asian American Studies, at universities. As much as the movement was born out of an identification with the masses, it was also an intellectual movement that protested the Eurocentrism of university curriculum, resulting in one of its hallmark achievements: the nation's first School of Ethnic Studies at San Francisco State University in 1968.

The secular roots of the Asian American intellectual tradition were sown during this time, and it had largely omitted religion as a category of analysis. Ironically, however, this movement was also the context in which theologies of Asian American liberation were sown, providing some of the initial seeds for the development of a subfield of Asian American religions. Though mainstream Asian American studies had overlooked religion because of its secular movement roots, it was also the case that the movement provided an important context out of which a tradition of Asian American religious thought emerged. The Asian American intellectual tradition has, then, from the beginning blurred the meaning of the sacred and secular even if it has purported to be, and primarily has been, considered in secular terms.[4]

Within a movement that drew on the class analysis of Marx and Mao, a small number of ministers and theologians were influenced by the movement, blurring the sacred and secular through religious activism and theological imagination. They produced theologies of liberation and writings specific to the Asian American experience, akin to black theologies of liberation. They not only wrote about "ethnic theology of liberation," "yellow theology," and "Asian American theology," but also lived them out in their everyday activities. Though they were small in number, they became forerunners to a larger critical mass of scholars and activists of Asian American studies and theological/religious studies.[5]

Indeed, in charting the intellectual roots of the subfield of Asian American religions, at least one significant stream can be traced to the development of Asian American theologies of liberation, which spawned a series of networks developed for Asian American ministers and scholars. Lloyd Wake and Roy Sano created in 1972 the Pacific Asian American Center for Theology and Strategies (PACTS), which became an affiliate of the Graduate Theological Union in Berkeley, California. Thereafter, in 1984, the feminist theologians Kwok-Pui Lan and Letty Russell created the Pacific Asian North American Asian Women in Theology and Ministry (PANAAWTM), focused on postcolonial and feminist Asian and Asian American theologies and ministries. In 2000, the Pacific School of Religion created the Institute for Leadership Development and Study of Pacific and Asian North American religion (PANA Institute). Led by the theologian Fumitaka Matsuoka, PANA's mission resonated with the goals of PACTS in fostering a community for those interested in Asian American religious traditions.

These networks and organizations laid a foundation for future intellectual communities. Early on, the PANA Institute became an institutional home for the Asian Pacific American Religions and Research Initiative (APARRI), which began in 1998; those who created the Asian North American Religions, Culture, and Society (ANARCS) in 1997 as a formal section of the American Academy of Religion also had connections to these forerunners. Thus, the roots of Asian American religions date back to a multifaceted historical moment when theologies of liberation germinated alongside movements of social protest, even when such protest was largely undergirded by ideas that neglected, rejected, or contested those theological or religious ideas as resources.[6]

THE 1990S AND 2000S: ASIAN AMERICAN RELIGIONS

If theologians of the movement era were forerunners, then the critical mass of scholars who came of age in the 1980s and 1990s more formally founded the interdisciplinary subfield of Asian American religions. In 1996, *Amerasia Journal* published a special issue titled "Racial Spirits," which first documented the scholarly debate among graduate students and early career scholars who became leading voices of the emerging subfield of Asian American religions. Eventually, "Racial Spirits" culminated in the publication of the first edited volume, *New Spiritual Homes: Religion and Asian Americans* (1999), which argued for the "reconceptualization of Asian American Studies" so that a "serious and critical treatment of religion becomes an interpretive rule rather than an exception."[7] Since the late 1990s, scholars affiliated with APARRI and ANARCS have produced multiple single-authored journal articles, monographs, and team-authored edited volumes, including Jung Ha Kim and Pyong Gap Min's *Asian American Religions: Building Faith Communities* (2002) and Jane Naomi Iwamura and Paul Spickard's *Revealing the Sacred in Asian and Pacific America* (2004).[8]

In addition to these, scholars studying the theological and religious experiences of Asian and Asian American women published a number of resources. Scholars affiliated with PANAAWTM published the edited volume *Off the Menu: Asian and Asian North American Women's Religion and Theology* (2007). Around the same time, a group of Asian American women, primarily affiliated with evangelical Christian communities, published for a lay audience *More Than Serving Tea: Asian American Women on Expectations, Relationships, Leadership, and Faith* (2006).[9] Many of the contributors were affiliated with Asian American Women on Leadership (AAWOL), which in 2004 grew out of informal gatherings among Asian American evangelical women in ministry and academia. AAWOL, moreover, was an outgrowth of the Institute for the Study of Asian American Christianity (ISAAC), a think tank founded in 2006 to bridge church and academia as well as evangelical and mainline Protestant Asian American leaders.[10]

More Than Serving Tea was one out of a series of publications on Asian American Christians published by Intervarsity Press—the largest evangelical press for Asian American publications—and it was written for a popular audience. Lay campus ministers and clergy also published practical ministerial books, including *Following Jesus without Dishonoring Your Parents* (1998) and *Growing Healthy Asian American Churches* (2006).[11] Because these works are not academic texts, they are not part of the scholarly conversation on Asian American religions; they are mentioned here, however, to note the growing interest in Asian American Christian traditions within a popular audience at a time when scholars were publishing academic literature.

THE INTELLECTUAL FOUNDATIONS OF ASIAN AMERICAN RELIGIONS

Since its movement roots, scholarship in Asian American religions has burgeoned into a wide-ranging field of study. Given this heterogeneity, what intellectual and communal goals brought these scholars together? What are the scholarly foundations of their work? At least three significant intellectual concerns, discussed below, undergird the subfield of Asian American religions, including but not exclusive to the critique of disciplinary traditions, rigorous analysis of Orientalism and race, and nuanced treatment of an otherwise reductive approach to religion.

First, there was the critique of disciplinary traditions. In Rudy Busto's essay "DisOrienting Subjects" (2004), he called for the development of an intellectual path at the intersections and interstices of Asian American studies and American religions, acknowledging that these fields had operated as two nonintersecting parallel narratives. Busto identifies a need for Asian American religionists to not only bridge disciplinary divides but also play an "indicting function" of disciplinary traditions themselves. Analogous to the field of Asian American literature, which also critiques from an interstitial space, Busto identifies in Asian American religions a scholarly position from which to critique "a liberal 'multiculturalism' that flattens out the differences among groups, ignores history and hides inequality."[12] Busto's analysis highlights a critical issue at stake in Asian American religions, which is a matter of not only including Asian American subjects, but, more urgently, a critique of privilege and power in disciplinary traditions.

Along with a critique of disciplinary traditions, Asian American religionists have rigorously analyzed Orientalism and race. As Edward Said has written, at stake in the critique of Orientalism is the agency of the "Orient": "In brief, because of Orientalism the Orient was not (and is not) a free subject of thought or action."[13] The Saidian critique of Orientalism has become a theoretical foundation for the development of various fields of study, including Asian American religions. The subfield is concerned with a Saidian notion of agency, including the freedom of "Oriental" subjects in modern Western scholarship. It shares this intellectual labor with mainstream scholars of Asian American studies, but distinctly, at the busy intersection of the category of religion and the study of religious subjects, where rich but incomplete knowledge, discussion, and critique remain.

Third, those who study Asian American religions are interested in treating religion as an independent category of analysis. One does not have to go far to observe "religion" at work either in the lives of Asian Americans or in Asian American scholarship, for it is a latent but operative category even if it not theorized or treated thoroughly. A brief look at Said's critique of Orientalism suggests it is born out of the tensions between the Occident's Christian and the Orient's Islamic world. Similarly, scholars have narrated Asian American history by beginning with the European and American imagination of the "Orient," which is concomitantly a religious narrative—the Christian imagination of the "Orient." The historian Shelley Lee provides that it was the lure of Confucian philosophy, which structured the American elite's gaze of the Orient as simultaneously mysterious, irrational, and sensuous.[14] Yet it is curious that even as Said and Asian American historians speak of religion—in Christian, Islamic, and Confucian terms—as central in constructing the pernicious categories they contest, it remains largely undertheorized. Asian American history has been much more structured by an ambivalent tension between secular and sacred than has been acknowledged and studied.

These aforementioned intellectual foundations of Asian American religions have laid the groundwork to address the invisibility and essentialization of Asian American religious subjects. As such, narrating the religious history of Asian Americans is not a straightforward proposition, but one that calls for the reworking of fundamental categories in both Asian American studies and American religions. To write Asian American religious history, then, historians need to take into account the challenges named above in terms of the critique of disciplinary traditions, the genealogy of Orientalism and race, and the reduction of religion. Scholars have addressed these frameworks in studies of Asian religions in the United States and of Christian traditions in Asian America.

ASIAN RELIGIONS IN THE UNITED STATES: ORIENTALISM AND REIMAGINING ASIAN RELIGIOUS TRADITIONS

Asian Americans have historically been the majority practitioners of Asian religions including Buddhism and Hinduism, yet the subfields of neither American religious history nor Asian American history have claimed them as subjects. American religious historians have called for a geographic reorientation toward the Pacific in narrating religious history, and they have studied the presence of Asian religious traditions in the United States, yet this has largely been to the neglect of studying Asian American practitioners, and the histories of inequality between practitioners of Asian and European descent.[15] Indeed, the intellectual challenge in studying Asian religions in the United States is not merely the acknowledgment of Asian and Asian American bodies, or even a geographic turn toward the Pacific, but even more fundamentally, an understanding of the conditions of power that have rendered these subjects invisible in the historiography.

"The when and where of the Asian American experience," writes the historian Gary Okihiro, "can be found within the European imagination and construction of Asians and Asia."[16] Even Columbus, Okihiro notes, was searching for the exotic lands of the "Orient," which he believed he found, when he arrived on American soil. Similarly, Lee suggests that not only bodies but also ideas of Asia, or the "Orient," provide a productive starting point for narrating Asian American history.[17] This "Orientalism before Asian America" paradigm has helped historians take the long view of the formation of Asian America in U.S. history, and it has provided a productive corrective for American religious history in its study of Asian religions in the United States.

At the same time, as discussed above, it is also important to note that scholars of Asian America have been relatively blind to a robust analysis of religion. It was not just scholars of American religion, but also historians of Asian America, who did not claim practitioners of Asian religions as their subjects of study. They did not theorize religion as an independent category of analysis to make these subjects visible. Even though there were ambivalent strains in the 1960s and 1970s within the intellectual heritage of Asian American studies, the Marxian framework did predominate, creating a long "secular bias" in Asian American studies, which has prompted intellectual interventions among scholars of Asian American religions.

The task, then, for Asian American religionists has been to rectify these multiple historiographical oversights. Carolyn Chen, Khyati Joshi, Jane Iwamura, and Sharon Suh, to name a few, began to address this in their work on contemporary Asian religions in the United States.[18] Suh, Chen, and Joshi have provided ethnographic and sociological studies of Korean American and Taiwanese American Buddhists as well as Indian American Hindus, providing crucial data on understudied communities. In *Virtual Orientalism: Asian Religions in American Popular Culture* (2011), Iwamura uniquely bridges theoretical gaps, simultaneously taking to task the Orientalist gaze of American religions and the reduction of religion among Asian Americanists.

In *Virtual Orientalism,* Iwamura reveals the importance of studying Orientalism in a religious key and the religious gaze in an Orientalist key. She traces a genealogy of the "oriental monk" in American popular culture to uncover the Orientalist gaze upon Asian religions in the United States, lodged into American consciousness through the virtual realm. American media had portrayed Japanese American Buddhists as less "authentic" than white American Buddhists who took up elite and sophisticated Eastern religions. In her ominous last lines, she highlights how the logic of the "oriental monk" in popular culture has ultimately limited the "Oriental" subject's agency: "At our immediate disposal and making no demands of his own, [the Oriental monk] has indeed become virtually ours."[19] Iwamura exposes the process of commodification and commercialization of Asian religions in the United States, suggesting that Asian practitioners themselves have been relegated to the status of nonsubjects, more closely paired with objects available for consumption.

Indeed, the Orientalist gaze continues to be discussed in the study of Asian American religions. Most recently in their study of the 2012 Pew Research report, scholars have critiqued the categories that have been used to evaluate the practice of "Asian religions" in the United States as Christian normative assumptions have gone unnoticed in the surveying and analysis.[20]

ASIAN AMERICAN CHRISTIAN TRADITIONS: ASSIMILATION, HYBRIDITY, AND TRANSNATIONALISM

The scholarship on Asian American Christian traditions has wrestled with interpreting what it means for Asian people to subscribe to the dominant religious tradition of the United States, especially as it has been integral in propagating Orientalism, including projects of empire and colonialism. Among the heterogeneous strands of Asian American Christian traditions, the literature on evangelicalism is a significant one, as it debates assimilation of Western culture versus retention of Asian heritage: Is Asian American Christianity in general and Asian American evangelicalism in particular a form of colonial mimicry or indigenous expression? The categories of assimilation, hybridity, and transnationalism emerge as central concepts in debating this question.

The initial literature on Asian American evangelicalism argues for assimilation. Busto suggests that evangelicalism reinforces the stereotype of the "model minority" for Asian American evangelical college students, pressuring them to conform to ideals of piety and performance. While they have made it into the elite halls of American higher education, their upward mobility paradoxically burdens them as the exoticized "model *moral* minority." Yet another "trap," evangelicalism "reinforces" the pressure of academic per-formance with moral performance.[21] The sociologist Antony Alumkal provides a simi-lar critique of the evangelical ethos to which contemporary Asian Americans subscribe, diagnosing them as suffering from the "scandal of the 'model minority' mind." In spite of their racially marginalized status, they uncritically suffer from the same scandal of anti-intellectualism as the evangelical mainstream.[22] Asian American evangelicals, as analyzed by Busto and Alumkal here, adopt their beliefs by passively adopting and col-laborating with the mythic status of the "model minority," rendering them essentially duped by mainstream evangelical thought.

Both scholars' works have had considerable traction in intellectual debate, even as others have departed from their theorizations. In the sociologist Sharon Kim's work, she concludes that Korean American evangelicals neither assimilate into mainstream churches nor remain in the ethnic churches of their immigrant parents, but establish their own "independent religious institutions," revealing that there are "hybrid third spaces to inhabit."[23] Instead of reading Korean American evangelicalism as white mim-icry, she suggests that practitioners have innovated a hybrid religious expression. The scholarly debate over assimilation and hybridity reflects an underlying concern about the agency that Asian American Christians, specifically evangelicals, are able to exercise as a minority population within a brand of Christianity that prioritizes a theology of universalism that can obscure and ignore difference.

The discussion concerning assimilation and hybridity, however, can be pushed one step further. The literature in African American religious studies provides a helpful point of comparison. In Jonathan Walton's work, for example, he argues that the black liberation theology paradigm has cast a long intellectual shadow that has rendered others, including black Pentecostals and televangelists, as invalid subjects of study.[24] His work highlights the complex and heterogeneous landscapes of reli-gious black America, which includes not just the prophetic social movement figures, but also televangelists and accommodating Christians—and much more. A simi-lar assessment can be made about the intellectual trajectory of Asian American religious studies as the lineage of the subfield holds a preference for liberationist critique and subjects. The study of Christian traditions in Asian America reveals a need for more nuanced discussion that not only acknowledges theological and racial binaries, or dichotomous categories such as assimilation versus hybridity, but also moves beyond them to reflect the full range and complexity of Asian American Christian lives.

In part, this complexity and comprehensiveness need to come from acknowledg-ing transnational connections as Asian American Christian traditions are placed within their global contexts. Indeed, the scholarly debate over assimilation and hybridity witnessed among scholars of Asian American Christianity parallels the scholarly discussion in world Christianity. On one hand, historians have argued that Christianity is a world religion that has adapted to non-Western contexts through indigenization and vernacularization.[25] On the other hand, scholars have argued for the primarily Western and American character of world Christianity; still others have viewed Christianity in non-Western contexts as primarily or solely an agent of imperialism and colonization.[26] If Asian American Christianity has roots in Asia, then the indigeneity of Asian Christianity and its transnational dimensions are significant for evaluating the complex agentive possibilities of Asian American Christian traditions.

THE FUTURE OF ASIAN AMERICAN RELIGIONS AND ASIAN AMERICAN RELIGIOUS HISTORY

Almost two decades after the inaugural *Amerasia Journal* issue "Racial Spirits" (1996), the journal published in 2014 a sequel of sorts, entitled "Asian American Religions in a Globalized World."[27] The two journal issues book-end a significant development in the scholarly conversation within the subfield. Indeed, as discussed, in the subfield of Asian American religions, theoretical interventions have been made, and sociological and ethnographic analyses have been conducted to revise the intellectual frameworks used in studying Asian religions in the United States and Christian traditions in Asian America. With this 2014 publication, it could be suggested that there is now a third cohort of scholars and conversations emerging in the 2010s and beyond.

In this third wave, much-needed historical narratives of Asian American religious traditions are emerging as scholars utilize archives and oral histories to excavate the past. A number of graduate students are producing, or have recently produced, dissertations on Japanese American, Chinese American, and Hmong American religious histories.[28] These studies have not yet been published in monograph form but represent a scholarly effort to fill a lacuna in the religious history of Asian Americans, not only as it relates to nonintersecting parallel histories written in Asian American history and American religious history, but also as it concerns the contemporary bias in the subfield of Asian American religions. These works build off of historical projects that have uncovered especially late nineteenth and early twentieth-century Chinese, Japanese, and Korean American religious histories, including David Yoo's *Contentious Spirits: Religion in Korean American History, 1903–1945* (2010) and Derek Chang's *Citizens of a Christian Nation: Evangelical Missions and the Problem of Race in the Nineteenth Century* (2010).[29]

How do we construct a historical imagination of Asian American religious life? This is not a new question but is one that nevertheless needs to be asked perennially for the growth and expansion of Asian American scholarship. The invisibility and essentialization of religious Asian Americans cannot be rectified in the historical record with theory and social scientific data alone, but stories and narratives need to be told and past lives and worlds, reconstructed.

CONCLUSION

The study of Asian American religions as a subfield is situated "betwixt and between" Asian American studies and American religions. A more complex and comprehensive understanding of Asian American agency is at stake in the scholarship as it concerns Asian American religions in general and Asian American religious history in particular.

NOTES

1. Timothy Tseng, "Beyond Orientalism and Assimilation: The Asian American as Historical Subject," in *Realizing the America of Our Hearts: Theological Voices of Asian Americans*, ed. Fumitaka Matsuoka and Eleazar S. Fernandez (St. Louis, MO: Chalice, 2003), 69.
2. Cary Funk, Luis Lugo, and Alan Cooperman, *Asian Americans: A Mosaic of Faiths* (Washington, DC: Pew Research Center, July 19, 2012), http://www.pewforum.org/files/2012/07/Asian-Americans-religion-full-report.pdf, 43 (also, http://www.pewforum.org/2012/07/19/asian-americans-a-mosaic-of-faiths-overview). For more analysis, see Sylvia Chan-Malik and Khyati Joshi, eds., "Asian American Religions in a Globalized World," *Amerasia Journal* 40, no. 1 (2014).
3. For discussion on Chinese Americans' "religious nones," see Russell Jeung, "Second Generation Chinese Americans: The Familism of the Nonreligious," in *Sustaining Faith Traditions: Race, Ethnicity, and Religion among the Latino and Asian American Second Generation*, ed. Carolyn Chen and Russell Jeung (New York: New York University Press, 2012), 197–221.
4. David Kyuman Kim argues that the secular terms of Asian American studies, including key terms such as "diaspora," are actually sacred terms. See David Kyuman Kim, "Enchanting Diasporas, Asian Americans and the Passionate Attachment of Race," in *Revealing the Sacred in Asian and Pacific America*, ed. Jane Iwamura and Paul Spickard (New York: New York University Press, 2004).
5. See the archival holdings at the Graduate Theological Union in Berkeley, California, entitled "Pacific and Asian American Center for Theology and Strategies Collection, 1972–2002." See also Helen Jin Kim, "Niseis of the Faith: Theologizing Liberation in the Asian American Movement" (undergraduate thesis, Stanford University, 2006).
6. Jonathan Y. Tan, *Introducing Asian American Theologies* (Maryknoll, NY: Orbis, 2008).
7. David K. Yoo, ed., *New Spiritual Homes: Religion and Asian Americans* (Honolulu: University of Hawai'i Press, 1999), 10.
8. Pyong Gap Min and Jung Ha Kim, *Asian American Religions: Building Faith Communities* (Walnut Creek, CA: AltaMira, 2002); Iwamura and Spickard, *Revealing the Sacred*, 2004.
9. Rita Nakashima Brock, ed., *Off the Menu: Asian and Asian North American Women's Religion and Theology* (Louisville, KY: Westminster John Knox, 2007); Nikki Toyama et al., eds., *More Than Serving Tea: Asian American Women on Expectations, Relationships, Leadership, and Faith* (Downers Grove, IL: IVP, 2006).
10. ISAAC's publications include *The Journal of Asian American Christianity* and Timothy Tseng and Viji Nakka-Cammauf, eds., *Asian American Christianity: A Reader* (ISAAC, 2009).

11. Jeannette Yep et al., *Following Jesus without Dishonoring Your Parents* (Downers Grove, IL: IVP, 1998); Peter S. Cha, Steve Kang, and Helen Lee, eds., *Growing Healthy Asian American Churches* (Downers Grove, IL: IVP, 2006).

12. Rudy Busto, "DisOrienting Subjects: Reclaiming Pacific Islander/Asian American Religions," in Iwamura and Spickard, *Revealing the Sacred*, 24.

13. Edward Said, *Orientalism* (New York: Vintage, 1978), 3.

14. Shelley Lee, *A New History of Asian America* (New York: Routledge, 2014), 9–13.

15. For a call for a reorientation toward the Pacific, see Laurie Maffly-Kipp, "Eastward Ho! American Religion from the Perspective of the Pacific Rim," in *Retelling U.S. Religious History*, ed. Thomas Tweed (Berkeley: University of California Press, 1997), 127–148. For a treatment of European/white American Buddhism, see Thomas Tweed, *The American Encounter with Buddhism: Victorian Culture and the Limits of Dissent, 1844–1912* (Chapel Hill: University of North Carolina Press, 2000).

16. Gary Okihiro, *Margins and Mainstreams: Asians in American History and Culture* (Seattle: University of Washington Press, 1994), 7.

17. Lee, *New History*, 5–26.

18. Sharon Suh, *Being Buddhist in a Christian World: Gender and Community in a Korean American Temple* (Seattle: University of Washington Press, 2004); Khyati Joshi, *New Roots in America's Sacred Ground: Religion, Race, and Ethnicity in Indian America* (New Brunswick, NJ: Rutgers University Press, 2006); Carolyn Chen, *Getting Saved in America: Taiwanese Immigration and Religious Experience* (Princeton, NJ: Princeton University Press, 2008); Jane Iwamura, *Virtual Orientalism: Asian Religions and American Popular Culture* (New York: Oxford University Press, 2011). For an earlier narration of Buddhism in America from the perspective of Asian Americans, see Tetsuden Kashima, *Buddhism in America: The Social Organization of an Ethnic Religious Institution* (Westport, CT: Greenwood, 1977).

19. Iwamura, *Virtual Orientalism*, 165.

20. See note 3.

21. Rudy Busto, "The Gospel According to the Model Minority? Hazarding an Interpretation of Asian American Evangelical College Students," in Yoo, *New Spiritual Homes*, 178–179. See also Rebecca Kim, *God's New Whiz Kids? Korean American Evangelicals on Campus* (New York: New York University Press, 2006).

22. Antony Alumkal, "Scandal of the 'Model Minority' Mind? The Bible and Second-Generation Asian American Evangelicals," *Semeia* 90 (91) (2002): 237–250.

23. Sharon Kim, *A Faith of Our Own: Second-Generation Spirituality in Korean American Churches* (New Brunswick, NJ: Rutgers University Press, 2010), 3.

24. Jonathan Walton, *Watch This! The Ethics and Aesthetics of Black Televangelism* (New York: New York University Press, 2009).

25. Dana Robert and Lamin Sanneh respectively argue for Christianity as a world religion and indigenization through vernacularization. See Dana Robert, *Christian Mission: How Christianity Became a World Religion* (Malden, MA: Wiley-Blackwell, 2009); and Lamin Sanneh, *Disciples of All Nations: Pillars of World Christianity* (New York: Oxford University Press, 2008).

26. Mark Noll emphasizes the American character of world Christianity in *The New Shape of World Christianity: How American Experience Reflects Global Faith* (Downers Grove, IL: IVP Academic, 2009). A close reading of Said's work, for instance, shows the role of missionaries as primarily forces of imperialism and colonization.

27. See note 3.

28. See the work of Dean Adachi (Claremont, U.S. history, Ph.D. candidate), Melissa Borja (Columbia University, U.S. history, Ph.D.), Chris Chua (UC Berkeley, ethnic studies, Ph.D. candidate), and Chrissy Lau (UC Santa Barbara, history, Ph.D.).

29. Derek Chang, *Citizens of a Christian Nation: Evangelical Missions and the Problem of Race in the Nineteenth Century* (Philadelphia: University of Pennsylvania Press, 2010); David K. Yoo, *Contentious Spirits: Religion in Korean American History 1903–1945* (Stanford, CA: Stanford University Press, 2010). See also the work of Timothy Tseng in the following works: "Chinese Protestant Nationalism in the United States, 1880–1927" in Yoo, *New Spiritual Homes*, 19–51; "Trans-Pacific Transpositions: Continuities and Discontinuities in Chinese North American Protestantism," in Iwamura and Spickard, *Revealing the Sacred*, 241–271; and "Unbinding Their Souls: Chinese Protestant Women in Twentieth-Century America," in *Women and Twentieth-Century Protestantism*, ed. Margaret Lambert Bendroth and Virginia Lieson Brereton (Urbana: University of Illinois Press, 2002), 136–163.

FURTHER READING

Brock, Rita Nakashima, ed. *Off the Menu: Asian and Asian North American Women's Religion and Theology*. Louisville, KY: Westminster John Knox, 2007.

Carnes, Tony, and Fenggang Yang. *Asian American Religions: The Making and Remaking of Borders and Boundaries*. New York: New York University Press, 2004.

Chan-Malik, Sylvia, and Khyati Joshi, eds. "Asian American Religions in a Globalized World." *Amerasia Journal* 40, no. 1 (2014).

Chang, Derek. *Citizens of a Christian Nation: Evangelical Missions and the Problem of Race in the Nineteenth Century*. Philadelphia: University of Pennsylvania Press, 2010.

Chen, Carolyn. *Getting Saved in America: Taiwanese Immigration and Religious Experience*. Princeton, NJ: Princeton University Press, 2008.

Chen, Carolyn, and Russell Jeung. *Sustaining Faith Traditions: Race, Ethnicity, and Religion among the Latino and Asian American Second Generation*. New York: New York University Press, 2012.

Iwamura, Jane. *Virtual Orientalism: Asian Religions and American Popular Culture*. New York: Oxford University Press, 2011.

Iwamura, Jane Naomi, and Paul Spickard, eds. *Revealing the Sacred in Asian and Pacific America*. New York: New York University Press. 2004.

Jeung, Russell. *Faithful Generations: Race and New Asian American Churches*. New Brunswick, NJ: Rutgers University Press, 2005.

Joh, Anne. *Heart of the Cross: A Postcolonial Christology*. Louisville, KY: Westminster John Knox, 2006.

Kim, Jung Ha. *Bridge-makers and Cross-bearers: Korean-American Women and the Church*. Atlanta: Scholars Press, 1997.

Kim, Rebecca. *God's New Whiz Kids? Korean American Evangelicals on Campus*. New York: New York University Press, 2006.

Kim, Sharon. *A Faith of Our Own: Second-Generation Spirituality in Korean American Churches*. New Brunswick, NJ: Rutgers University Press, 2010.

Kwok Pui-Lan. *Postcolonial Imagination and Feminist Theology*. Louisville, KY: Westminster John Knox, 2005.

Kwon, Ho-Youn, Kwang Chung Kim, and Stephen Warner, eds. *Korean Americans and Their Religions: Pilgrims and Missionaries from a Different Shore*. University Park: Pennsylvania State University Press, 1991.

Matsuoka, Fumitaka. *Out of Silence: Emerging Themes in Asian American Churches*. Cleveland, OH: United Church Press, 1995.

Matsuoka, Fumitaka, and Eleazar S. Fernandez, eds. *Realizing the America of Our Hearts: Theological Voices of Asian Americans*. St. Louis, MO: Chalice, 2003.

Min, Pyong Gap, and Jung Ha Kim. *Asian American Religions: Building Faith Communities*. Walnut Creek, CA: AltaMira, 2002.

Pak, Su Yon, Unzu Lee, Jung Ha Kim, and Myung Ji Cho, eds. *Singing the Lord's Song in a New Land: Korean American Practices of Faith*. Louisville, KY: Westminster John Knox, 2005.

Rah, Soong-Chan. *The Next Evangelicalism: Freeing the Church from Western Cultural Captivity*. Downers Grove, IL: IVP, 2009.

Suh, Sharon. *Being Buddhist in a Christian World: Gender and Community in a Korean American Temple*. Seattle: University of Washington Press, 2004.

Tseng, Timothy. "Asian American Religions." In *The Columbia Guide to Religion in American History*, edited by Paul Harvey and Edward J. Blum, 253–264. New York: Columbia University Press, 2012.

———. "Beyond Orientalism and Assimilation: The Asian American as Historical Subject." In *Realizing the America of our Hearts: Theological Voices of Asian Americans*, edited by Fumitaka Matsuoka and Eleazar S. Fernandez, 55–72. St. Louis, MO: Chalice, 2003.

———. "Trans-Pacific Transpositions: Continuities and Discontinuities in Chinese North American Protestantism." In *Revealing the Sacred in Asian and Pacific America*, edited by Jane Naomi Iwamura and Paul Spickard, 241–271. New York: Routledge, 2003.

———. "Unbinding Their Souls: Chinese Protestant Women in Twentieth-Century America." In *Women and Twentieth-Century Protestantism*, edited by Margaret Lamberts Bendroth and Virginia Lieson Brereton, 136–163. Urbana: University of Illinois Press, 2002.

Yoo, David K., ed. *New Spiritual Homes: Religion and Asian Americans*. Honolulu: University of Hawai'i Press, 1999.

———. "Racial Spirits: Religion and Race in Asian American Communities." *Amerasia Journal* 22, no. 1 (1996).

Yoo, David K., and Ruth H. Chung, eds. *Religion and Spirituality in Korean America*. Urbana: University of Illinois Press, 2008.

Yoo, David K., and Albert Park, eds. *Encountering Modernity: Christianity in East Asia and Asian America*. Honolulu and Los Angeles: University of Hawai'i Press in association with UCLA Asian American Studies Center, 2014.

....

CHAPTER 22

RACE, SPACE, AND PLACE IN ASIAN AMERICAN URBAN HISTORY

....

SCOTT KURASHIGE

NOTWITHSTANDING the rural origins of community formation in Asian American history, it is clear that the development of Asian American communities has been a predominantly urban phenomenon in the twentieth century. For instance, the history of Japanese Americans in the twentieth century represents a dramatic case of urbanization (and later suburbanization) that was accompanied by notable social and economic consequences. Japanese immigrants established literal and figurative roots by toiling as agricultural workers and small farmers during the late nineteenth and early twentieth centuries. By the 1980s, 88.9 percent of Japanese Americans lived in urban areas with residential spatial patterns so diffused that Bill Ong Hing was moved to argue that "the predominantly American-born Japanese prefer suburban living."[1]

While some important studies have been situated within urban contexts, Asian American urban history as a subfield is still largely in the process of formation. Interestingly, urban history has been far more pivotal to the development of immigration and African American history—fields for which Asian American historians have felt considerable affinity. A comparative analysis of Asian American and urban historiography allows us to explain some of the theoretical and methodological factors accounting for the gulf between the two fields. Subsequently, it is possible to trace developments of the past two decades that have begun to bring the fields more into line with each other as historians have looked to bring concerns about spatiality into dialogue with analyses of race, class, and gender/sexuality. In particular, scholars have deployed the city as a critical site to study the construction of Orientalism within the United States, interethnic and multiracial interactions, and the production of transnational communities and subjectivities. To be certain, popular discourse on Asian Americans in urban areas—especially that which revolved around ethnic communities as segregated ghettoes, such as the ubiquitous Chinatown—dates back to the nineteenth century.

The scholarship on Asian American urban history that has been produced from the origins of Asian American studies in the late 1960s and early 1970s to the present is worthy of special attention.

URBANISM AND THE ORIGINS
OF ASIAN AMERICAN STUDIES

When student and community activists gave birth to Asian American studies during the Asian American movement of the 1960s and 1970s, the field was largely born within urban settings. One obvious reason was that campuses like San Francisco State and the University of California at Berkeley, home of the foundational Third World Liberation Front student strikes, were both located in urban centers and had significant Asian American student populations. Urbanism, however, was a constitutive rather than coincidental or residual factor in the rise of Asian American studies. Asian American urban communities provided much of the purpose and content for the field during its formative stages of growth.

For instance, the issue of urban redevelopment loomed central in the minds of Asian American scholars and activists. Movements of resistance to redevelopment and gentrification—be they in Philadelphia's or Boston's Chinatowns, San Francisco's Manilatown and Nihonmachi, Little Tokyo's Los Angeles, or Seattle's International District—emphasized place attachment to ethnic neighborhoods and defense of historic communities. Such a language, which radical organizers funneled through Malcolm X's notion of self-determination and the Black Power movement's call for community control, contrasted sharply with the integrationist and assimilationist tendencies of the upwardly mobile postwar generation that viewed suburbanization as a form of progress.

Battles over redevelopment forced activists to confront policy makers from the local level (e.g., zoning laws, land usage, community redevelopment agencies) to the federal level (e.g., interstate highway construction, urban renewal programs, federally subsidized housing). Yet in many instances the whole struggle over space crystallized into one defining struggle over a distinct place. This occurred most notably in the 1970s battle over San Francisco's International Hotel (a.k.a. the I-Hotel), the historic residential hotel where elderly Chinese and Filipino Americans teamed with community activists to fight eviction by speculative landlords backed by the power of the state. The struggle over the I-Hotel demonstrated the power of place to represent many things simultaneously—a place of residence for retired *manongs*, a place of refuge from a racist society, a place of affordable housing in a market of skyrocketing rents, and a place of community organizing and cultural production.

Capturing this protracted struggle, Curtis Choy's landmark documentary *The Fall of the I-Hotel* (1983) could be viewed as one of the most important early "texts" to give rise to the study of Asian American urban history. Without question, the elderly I-Hotel residents are the central actors in the film, with a supporting cast made up of Asian American movement generation organizers, epitomized by Al Robles. Tense scenes of conflict and confrontation between I-Hotel supporters and the police provide a sense of immediacy to the struggle unfolding before the eyes of the viewers. However, the film should also be properly seen as a historical statement; indeed, history itself might be viewed as a protagonist within the film. The film provides a series of interviews with Filipinos who immigrated to the continental United States before World War II, recounting their dreams as well as the hardships and discrimination they endured individually and collectively. At the same time, *The Fall of the I-Hotel* seeks to forge a consciousness of the contemporary struggle against displacement and gentrification as part of a long and unbroken struggle for justice, dignity, and a decent material living by pioneering, working-class Asian immigrants. The proliferation of the community struggle provides the opportunity to learn and teach about (and even create) Asian American history, while the teaching of history and the participation of (formal and informal) students of the emerging field of Asian American history become indispensable to developing the struggle and fostering an appreciation for its significance.[2]

Similar efforts by movement activists seeking to implement "serve the people" programs were also connected to historic places of survival and resistance. Delano's Agbayani Village, established by the United Farm Workers and supported by Filipino and Asian American student and community activists, became a marker of the lifelong struggle of the manong generation against labor exploitation and racism, then signified by a quest for affordable and dignified housing for retirees. Likewise, Little Tokyo Towers, built in Los Angeles in the 1970s, represented more than a concession by the purveyors of corporate redevelopment. It signified a refuge for working-class Issei whose lives had been marked by displacement, from the exclusion drives of the 1910s and 1920s to World War II internment and the gentrification of the 1960s and 1970s. In San Francisco's Chinatown, organizers established Freedom Schools and fought for bilingual education to serve a community that had once been relegated to second-class segregated schools.

I hope that my highly abbreviated review of this history serves to make clear how much both the topic of Asian American history and the practice of Asian American history making at this foundational stage were highly urban enterprises. It might seem peculiar, therefore, that Asian American studies as it emerged as a scholarly field would remain largely disconnected from urban history. To explain this development, we must shift focus to the lineage of U.S. urban history as a scholarly field.

AMERICAN HISTORY BECOMES URBAN

The early development of urban history left little space for consideration of Asian Americans. As Eric Monkkonen noted, grand works of "urban biography" that "treated an individual city as an anthropomorphic identity with a unique personality, working out its individual destiny," generally focused on the so-called great men that made a city great.[3] Even as scholars in this genre began to focus on the more mundane aspects of what made cities function and grow and turned greater attention toward nonelites, Asian ethnic groups were still seen as too small and marginal to factor crucially into the narrative.

But the prospects for convergence between urban history and Asian American history brightened with the advance of the new social history in the 1960s and 1970s. First of all, the new social history sought to tell history from the bottom up. Second, in contrast to the consensus view that defined American historiography in the chilling Cold War climate of the 1950s, the new social history stressed conflict and change as the driving force in U.S. history. Third, new social historians marshaled new theories and quantitative methods to conduct their analyses.

All of these elements came together in the new urban history, which Monkkonen argues "probably flew the highest . . . of all the 'new' histories that were launched."[4] While immigration and ethnicity were at the forefront of the new urban historians' consciousness, their emphasis on "mobility" studies led to a privileging of working-class European immigrants of the industrial Northeast and Midwest, for these were the historical subjects who could best be used to settle debates about American exceptionalism. However, several factors militated against the inclusion of Asian Americans in mobility studies of the industrial era. Asian immigrants were concentrated on the West Coast, and they were largely excluded from blue-collar industrial work and labor unions. Moreover, from a quantitative historian's perspective, studying Asian Americans created special quandaries. Little published census data existed for Asian ethnic groups beyond the aggregate level, what data did exist were not always reliable, and shifting definitions of who fit the categories applied to people of Asian descent made working with relatively good data a challenge.

In the end, the mobility studies decided little. No study could successfully answer whether America transcended the class orders and conflicts of the Old World, and it would ultimately fall upon the historians of whiteness to provide the next qualitative leap in our understanding of class formation in U.S. history. Instead, the urban rebellions of the mid- to late 1960s convinced social scientists that the black ghetto provided the best example of halted mobility in America. Urban historians thus looked to understand the origins of the black ghetto as a key to the mystery of persistent inequality. Studies of urban centers like Harlem and Chicago revealed the discriminatory factors that produced segregated living patterns, creating what Joe Trotter has characterized as the "ghetto synthesis" in African American urban historiography.[5]

Just as they were missing from mobility studies, Asian Americans were largely absent from the ghettoization studies not because they were immune to segregation and discrimination but primarily because such studies, focused on urban centers of the Northeast and Midwest where Asian populations were relatively small, generally viewed race as a bipolar black/white construction. In a slight twist, Robert Fogelson's *The Fragmented Metropolis*, arguably the most foundational treatise on Los Angeles history produced in this era, identified processes of white hegemonic ascendancy but downplayed the agency of Asian Americans alongside Mexican and African Americans.[6]

During the 1980s, a second wave of "new urban history" served to expand the study of segregation across time and space while offering a more detailed perspective of the social actors who engaged in "race relations." For instance, Trotter's corrective argument in *Black Milwaukee* was to insist that segregation be situated within the context of political economy. His emphasis on "proletarianization" transcended the institutionalized perspective of ghettoization studies to offer a more nuanced analysis of black urban community formation.[7] Whereas Trotter's work added the important component of African American agency, Arnold Hirsch's *Making the Second Ghetto* provided new insight into the grassroots character of white resistance, often violent, to postwar racial integration.[8] Moreover, Kenneth Jackson's *Crabgrass Frontier* demonstrated the important link between public policy—specifically federal housing, urban renewal, and transportation policies—and the polarization between predominantly white suburbs and increasingly impoverished nonwhite ghettos.[9]

Meanwhile, as neoconservatives deployed Asians as central actors in narratives designed to preserve the central elements of the assimilation paradigm, scholars of Asian American studies pushed to inject their perspectives into debates on multiculturalism during the 1980s. Nevertheless, Asian Americans remained for the most part off the radar screen of American urban history with the black-white binary remaining at the center of "race-relations" discourse. Perhaps, for some, there remained a tacit assumption that Asian Americans were a "model minority" that escaped the stigma of ghettoization. Conscious of the need to dispel the model minority myth, Asian American movement activists had portrayed ethnic enclaves as dynamic sites of both interracial and intraracial class struggle. In a complementary manner, Peter Kwong's pioneering scholarship helped to trace the roots of class formation in New York's Chinatown beginning with his 1979 monograph, *Chinatown, N.Y.: Labor and Politics, 1930–1950*, published by the book division of the left-wing journal *Monthly Review*.[10] Highlighting the intersection of race and class helps us to appreciate how Asians have historically been at most a plurality and usually a minority of neighborhood residents in enclaves like New York's Chinatown or Los Angeles's Koreatown today. This has generally been the case because the same traits that made such places desirable for Asian immigrants—being low-rent, supportive of bachelor laborers, and sites of open occupancy passed over by middle-class whites—rendered them as sites of transience that attracted other immigrants and new arrivals.

Another notable outlier in this era was John Modell's *The Economics and Politics of Racial Accommodation* (1977) examining Japanese Americans in Los Angeles. Viewing Japanese Americans as a middleman minority, Modell consciously positioned Japanese American history between mobility and ghetto formation studies. He argued that the city's "uncertainty about how to draw a line that could exclude Japanese from some endeavors but not from those which were important to the smooth functioning of business in the area" provided a basis for Japanese Americans to experience economic mobility in spite of social segregation.[11] This degree of "success" was a tradeoff for their accommodation to racism, defined not only by an acceptance of white antipathy toward them but also by an aura of superiority over other nonwhites. Though his thesis about the subjective dynamics of political accommodation is susceptible to challenge, Modell's work is seminal for its connection of the Asian American experience to urban processes, especially for pushing beyond the focus on ethnic enclaves.

THE DIALECTICS OF TOWN AND GOWN

Notwithstanding these examples, the development of Asian American studies as a field involved wrestling with social and intellectual tensions that complicated the relationship of scholarship to urban communities. While those working to build Asian American studies on university campuses recognized the importance of urban community struggles and worked to build a curriculum that situated them at the center, the campus was itself a different place that could not be portrayed as an undivided whole with Chinatown, Little Tokyo, and Manilatown. The rapid incorporation of people of color, especially African Americans, in the aftermath of the urban rebellions of the 1960s was a contradictory development. Following its study of the rebellions and analysis of its causes, the blue-ribbon Kerner Commission recommended that policies consciously promote the creation of a black middle class to help stabilize the American capitalist social order. The rapid admission of people of color to schools like Berkeley, UCLA, and the University of Michigan represented simultaneously the breaking down of discriminatory barriers to upward mobility and the effort to separate an educated professional-managerial class of minorities from the rebellious urban masses.

The Kerner Commission report was a defining moment in American capitalism's creation of a new system of hierarchical rule, which Adolph Reed, Jr., has termed "race relations management." The advance of the civil rights movement from the 1950s to the mid-1960s pushed the U.S. state to abandon support for Jim Crow and to grant civil and political rights to African Americans. Instead of total exclusion, the state began promoting the incorporation of elite "minorities" into the system to act as "brokers" or "custodians" of their race. By co-opting leading elements of minority groups into the system, the state could more easily channel opposition to racism into forms that were manageable within the system.[12]

It is in this context that we should properly situate the original call for ethnic studies to "give back to the community" or break down the divide between the campus and community. There was a real sense that students of color were being plucked from minority communities and co-opted into the power structure. Universities in the eyes of activists existed not only to reproduce social inequality but also to conduct military and corporate-sponsored research. The mandate to "serve the community" or "go back to the community" sought to prevent this occurrence—to remind university students that their newfound human capital should be used for the movement for social change, not the reproduction of the status quo.

For instance, advocates of Asian American studies (initially identified as contemporary Asian studies) at Berkeley wrote, "In a sort of 'brain-drain' process, the University has educated many young and talented Asians, prepared them to work in the professions, and drawn them away from their communities." They called instead for placing a "community orientation" at the "core" of the curriculum, stemming from their recognition "that the knowledge upon which its courses are based is derived from the community, and developed in unity with the people in the community."[13] By promoting student involvement in the community through field studies and what today falls under the rubric of "service learning" and encouraging community participation in governance, their goal was to advance a counterhegemonic agenda for research and pedagogy.

The focus on community heightened the emphasis on social justice as the mission of ethnic studies and led the creation of wonderfully imaginative campus-community collaborations that challenged the traditional role of the elite university. Community meant more than place; it served a politicizing function, linking upwardly mobile university students to working-class populations. In this sense, "community" became a key word connoting class consciousness within the academy. Yet defining community ideologically created new pitfalls. While the concept of serving the "community" acted as a kind of transmission belt physically transporting students from one place (the campus) to a socially if not geographically distant place (working-class neighborhoods) it did so at a price. As the idea of "community" needed to be expansive and omnipresent to perform its political service, it became a slippery concept lacking a scientific definition. In practice, community often became synonymous with race or ethnicity; belonging to a community thus became a question of identity politics. As Lane Hirabayashi has pointed out, "One of the key issues that was often taken for granted, and thus essentialized, was the existence of a community that could be characterized in terms of its internal unity and solidarity, in contrast to the generally accepted understanding today that communities are necessarily internally diverse."[14]

In some measure then, the equation of community with race/ethnicity blunted the power of community as place, foregrounding racial/ethnic solidarity at the risk of slighting the multiple histories that informed shared territories. This problem, however, was blunted by the political commitment to panethnicity and Third World solidarity during the early stages of Asian American studies. Thus, even if a Chinese American student activist identified Chinatown as "my community" through a sense of ethnic solidarity, she was just as likely to believe in a sense of (borrowing Huey Newton's term) "intercommunalism" that linked the struggles of oppressed communities across racial, ethnic, and national lines. Moreover, since the philosophy behind ethnic studies stressed practice, community activist campaigns regularly promoted the type of coalition building and interaction that helped to stem the rise of narrow ethnic chauvinism.

To be certain, Asian American historians generally maintained some kind of political commitment to antiracism and solidarity among communities of color. In practice, however, Asian American historical research did not intersect with urban studies to the degree that black history did. Although driven by the new social historians' concern with nonelite subjects, Asian American historians of the 1970s generally did not have the same desire as urban historians did to detail social scientific structures and processes. Rather, their overriding concern—consistent with the Asian American movement's drive to hegemonize a new political identity that transcended passive concepts of assimilation and the model minority—was with showing how Asian immigrants and their ancestors were agents of history. They sought to document acts of injustice and patterns of oppression but were just as determined to record a history of resistance, survival, and perseverance in America.

The project of Asian American social historians in the 1970s and 1980s was best articulated by Yuji Ichioka. Writing about Japanese Americans but speaking in ways analogous to the marginalized history of other Asian American groups, Ichioka spoke of recovering the "buried past" through research specifically of primary-language sources and more generally through recovery of the voices that provided a distinctive and usable past.[15] Indeed there was so much work to be done to recover the "buried past" that scholars tended to focus on specific ethnic histories while documenting experience in ways that gave presence to previously invisible subjects. Moreover, searching for the roots of Asian American history often entailed digging into the soil that pioneering Asian immigrants had toiled within while using agriculture and rural community formation to establish economic and social foundations in America.

While some research was place based, the primary concern of early work in Asian American history was to show how race and ethnicity functioned in the construction of imagined communities or communities without propinquity. Perhaps the most exemplary example of ethnic-specific social history to be rooted in an urban place is Judy Yung's *Unbound Feet*, which charts the development of collectivity, consciousness, and empowerment among Chinese women in San Francisco. In addition, Yung opened her treasure trove of primary research findings to others through the publication of her book of documents, *Unbound Voices*.[16]

During the 1990s, a new interest in Asian American urban history began to develop in large measure as the study of urban communities became a vehicle for the cultural/linguistic turn in Asian American historiography. Without completely overturning the Marxist foundations of Asian American social history, a new wave of scholars swayed by postmodernist and postcolonialist currents began to make its mark as Asian American scholars and graduate students expanded their footprint within American research universities and elite Ph.D. programs during the decade. Conventional ideas of power as a material force wielded by the ruling class and also something that historical actors could possess and harness as an oppositional force began to yield to the notion of power situated instead within the discourses that structure subjectivity. But if the real challenge of historians is unpacking the genealogy of these nebulous underlying forces, experience was then something to be viewed with increasing suspicion.

Two influential works by John Kuo Wei Tchen and Nayan Shah, both of which rework Edward Said's notions of Orientalism for an American historical context, especially signaled the cultural turn in Asian American urban history. With his extensive research on New York City, Tchen has probably been more closely connected to urban history over the past two decades than anyone else in Asian American studies. Tchen's work was widely hailed in the 1980s as a model of community-based history based upon his central involvement in the New York Chinatown History Project, which grew into the Museum of Chinese in the Americas. Groundbreaking exhibits such as "The Eight Pound Livelihood: A History of the Chinese Laundry Workers in America" exemplified history from the bottom up in the truest sense of the word. Critical of the academy's tendency to separate expert scholars from an ignorant public, Tchen argued in 1992 that public history institutions should work from a "dialogic-driven approach" in which our understanding of history is constantly being reshaped by the recovery of experience. Indeed, exhibits would not have been possible without the involvement of community members (whose participation was solicited through ingenious methods such as class reunions). Tchen remarked, "Without a base of scholarship and with no archival collections to draw upon, we had to rely upon those who had lived the experience to collaborate with us in reconstructing the community's history." Thus, even the exhibits themselves had built-in mechanisms to draw out historical remembrances from patrons.[17]

Though first developed through his work with the Chinatown museum, Tchen's monograph *New York before Chinatown* combines his earlier emphasis on the recovery of community history with an analysis of dominant cultural representations as generated by prominent whites like George Washington and P. T. Barnum. Studying the nineteenth-century history of Chinatown precluded a reliance on oral history and other methods of recovery that shaped previous community-based projects. The impressive archival research he conducted definitely shows in the book's footnotes, which by themselves will be a tremendous contribution to future research in the field. The narrative of Quimbo Appo, in particular, serves to explain the chronological manifestation of what Tchen terms patrician, commercial, and exclusionary Orientalisms. While the book also recovers the more plebian culture that emerged in the multiethnic neighborhoods surrounding the port in lower Manhattan and documents the relatively prevalent instances of Chinese-Irish intermarriage, what ultimately stands out is the role of the dominant culture in setting the terms under which the formation of a Chinese American community would occur. Tchen writes, "The history of Chinatown and how it emerged and developed, therefore, was shaped not so much by the actual presence of Chinese in the metropolis as by their systematic erasure and omnipresent 'otherness' in New York before Chinatown."[18]

Nayan Shah's *Contagious Divides* has had a profound impact within Asian American studies and more generally on scholars of race, culture, public health, and urbanism in U.S. history. While Shah documents various forms of racism and material discrimination endured by Chinese American residents of San Francisco, his primary concern and innovation is to track the evolving discourse of Chinatown as expressed through the languages of science, medicine, and health, particularly as such discourse shifted "from menace to model minority." Drawing on queer theory to make sense of Chinese Americans as deviant subjects, he helps us to understand the role of the state in enacting technologies of power through processes of regulation, classification, and administration. In turn, he analyzes the changing responses of the Chinese American community, which initially relied on white surrogates to represent its interests during the nineteenth century but later developed its own immigrant and American-born leadership.[19]

Complicating prior notions of oppression and resistance, Shah helps us to understand how the modern art of government deploys "ruling at a distance" to foster governable citizen-subjects. Thus, his work cautions us to scrutinize the operation of power—even within reform discourses and movements—in the quest to achieve liberal citizenship. In this manner, *Contagious Divides* (though released in 2001) was a timely product of the Clinton era, when Asian Americans became more incorporated into both the liberal academy and the neoliberal state's multicultural logic. Furthermore, several subsequent monographs of this period complemented Shah's attempt to make new sense of power and hegemony through a cultural analysis of urban-based subjects, including Mary Ting Li Lui's *The Chinatown Trunk Mystery* on turn-of-the-century New York, as well as Linda España-Maram's *Creating Masculinity in Los Angeles's Little Manila* and Lon Kurashige's *Japanese American Celebration and Conflict* on twentieth-century Los Angeles. Though not explicitly a work of urban history, Henry Yu's *Thinking Orientals* also added to an understanding of how Orientalist discourses shaped ideas about race and urbanism through a study of Asian American students emanating from the Chicago School of sociology.[20]

The Origins of the Urban Crisis and the Return of Urban History

Over the past two decades, urbanism has reasserted itself as a central topic within the study of U.S. history. Urban history, particularly as connected to the study of race relations, had taken off during the 1960s at a time when urban social movements and urban rebellions were regularly headline news and urban social policy had been at the forefront of American political debate. But as the urban agenda nearly disappeared from the political radar screen during the Reagan era, urban history began to languish as a field. Where faculty positions dedicated to urban history existed within academic departments and programs, they were likely to be filled by those hired during the upsurge of demand in the 1960s and 1970s. Nonetheless a new interest in urbanism began to develop in response to several developments during the 1990s. First, a whole generation raised in the suburbs began to question the "vanilla" character of suburban culture. Second, owing partly to this return of youth to the cities, the cyclical nature of investment, and the economic restructuring caused by the rise of the information sector, a new wave of urban renewal emerged during the Clinton years. Third, scholars and citizens have become increasingly critical of the social costs of urban sprawl for our fragile ecology and for human relations.

Crystallizing the concerns that problematized suburbanization, Thomas Sugrue's award-winning 1996 case study of Detroit, *The Origins of the Urban Crisis*, has done more to revitalize the field of urban history than any monograph of the past two decades. Sugrue demonstrates that post–World War II deindustrialization, combined with discriminatory policies and white homeowner resistance to integration, foreclosed upon the options for black social and geographical mobility. The result was the crushing of hopes for tens of thousands of African Americans, whose expectations had been raised by the social advances of World War II and whose frustrations were unleashed in the 1967 Detroit rebellion. *The Origins of the Urban Crisis* is particularly groundbreaking in its seamless linkage of race, space, class, and politics. Among his many contributions, Sugrue points out that one of the reasons why the American racial divide seems so intractable is that we as a society have failed to come to terms with the corresponding polarization between the city and suburb.[21]

Given how much the postindustrial urban crisis has shaped the post-1965 experience of Asian Americans—and particularly how Detroit's crisis provides the context for the Vincent Chin murder and civil rights case in ways that are largely underappreciated—these findings are of vital relevance to the field of Asian American studies. On the one hand, the "black/Korean conflicts" of the early 1990s made imperative the study of urban interethnic relations in the inner city. On the other hand, the tremendous growth of middle-class and professional Asians viewing suburban homeownership—with its troubled relationship to the historical construction of whiteness—as a marker of comfort and success has added new motivation to analyze the urban/suburban dialectic. In this same era, a new wave of African American urban histories made particularly constructive use of analyses of place and space in ways that should prove instructive for Asian American historians. As Earl Lewis has argued, the history of communities cannot be understood without coming to terms with "the power of place." As residents gain a sense of "self" through identification with places, personal and community memory remains bound to consciousness of place.[22]

Meanwhile, coming from the study of architecture and public history, Dolores Hayden extended analyses of place to address the multiracial history of Los Angeles. During her time at UCLA, before departing for Yale, Hayden undertook an imaginative project called "The Power of Place: Urban Landscapes as Public History," while serving as the founder and president of a nonprofit arts and humanities organization. In Hayden's words, the power of place signaled "the power of ordinary urban landscapes to nurture citizens' public memory, to encompass shared time in the form of shared territory."[23] The project became a cogent vehicle to recover and highlight the multiethnic heritage of Los Angeles, challenging a legacy of official municipal discourse that often prioritized Euro-American settlement and achievement. Two of the wonderful displays of public history projects linked to public art installations included the Biddy Mason Wall, dedicated to one of the city's pioneering African American migrants (an ex-slave who courageously manumitted herself through a legal battle), and the Little Tokyo Sidewalk, which engraves a timeline of Japanese American community history alongside images testifying to ethnic cultural resilience.

Hayden, who did most of the work on the project with collaborators between 1984 and 1991, also exhibited impeccable timing. Her installations, demonstrating how, in their struggles to make Los Angeles their home, diverse residents had left an indelible mark on the city, were the perfect anecdote to the portrayals of Los Angeles as a multiethnic dystopia, which appeared for the first time as farce in the film *Blade Runner* and for the second time as tragedy in the urban rebellion following the Rodney King trial in April 1992.

I have drawn great inspiration from "The Power of Place" project, which in many ways serves as a model of public history in the way it connects microhistories of specific places to larger structures and processes occurring at the level of the city and the nation. At the same time, the project missed some golden opportunities to use the concept of "shared territory" to draw out the cooperative and competing histories that define place attachment within multiethnic populations. Little Tokyo, for instance, has been a Japanese American business district since the early twentieth century. But for most of the century, it was also a residential district housing not only Japanese American workers and families but also a multiethnic and largely working-class population of blacks, Mexicans, whites, and other Asians. The idea of Little Tokyo as a distinctly "Japanese" space emerged primarily from the redevelopment and rebranding of Los Angeles as a "world city" during the 1960s and 1970s. During this period, blocks of historic structures, often claimed through eminent domain, were demolished. As city planners and boosters remade Little Tokyo into a tourist destination, low-rent apartments and boarding houses, along with the small businesses catering to their occupants, were displaced by luxury hotels and shopping malls.

The Little Tokyo Sidewalk installation could also have been enhanced by highlighting the crucial intersections between black and Japanese American history in Los Angeles that I have sought to identify through my own research. As I detailed in *The Shifting Grounds of Race*, Little Tokyo, following the internment of Japanese Americans during World War II, was remade into Bronzeville, an African American business, entertainment, and residential district.[24] Through recounting such narratives, I have deployed the big city as a key site for examining the evolution of multiracial and interethnic relations and for promoting the study of intersecting historical trajectories. My efforts have been aided by a generation of ethnic studies scholars situating the histories of Asian Americans within the multiethnic and polycultural social fabric of the city. A seminal study demonstrating links between Chinese, Japanese, and Mexican American in history in late nineteenth and early twentieth-century Los Angeles, Natalia Molina's *Fit to Be Citizens?* focuses on public health discourses to demonstrate how comparative Asian American and Latino studies reveal race to be a relational construct.[25]

As I have worked to forge connections between Asian American and urban history, I have been excited to be a part of what is an unprecedented new current of scholarship in Asian American urban history. This work, including Cindy I-Fen Cheng's recent book, *Citizens of Asian America*, builds on the prior studies of both urban racial discourse and the urban crisis while also pushing in new directions to help us make better sense of Asian American history within multiracial and transnational contexts. To be certain, the urban dimensions of the post-1965 rise of Asian migration and the corresponding heightening of diversity and globalization have primarily been studied by social scientists within Asian American studies. For instance, urban sociologists and geographers, such as Timothy Fong, John Horton, Leland Saito, Wei Li, and Wendy Cheng have dissected the immigrant transformation of multiethnic Monterey Park in suburban Los Angeles, the expansion of new Chinatown and Southeast Asian settlement into the greater San Gabriel Valley, and the post-Fordist production of the ethnoburb in Southern California.[26]

In time we will see the up-and-coming generation of Asian American historians produce studies of the post-1965 urban landscape. What has recently been published and is coming into print right now, however, are studies that trace the pre-1965 roots of multiethnic diversity, transnational discourse, and Asian American urban community formation. By offering a critical historicization of such developments, this work also helps us to problematize essentialist Asian American urban success stories that reinforce the model minority stereotype and to avoid viewing them through a teleological or celebrationist lens. For instance, Dawn Mabalon and Clement Lai have both drawn from the urban crisis paradigm to critique the marginalization of Asian Americans and the destruction of ethnic communities through processes of urban redevelopment and gentrification while adding new dimensions of analysis. Mabalon's book, *Little Manila Is in the Heart: The Making of the Filipina/o American Community in Stockton, California*, both recounts the early twentieth-century dreams and hardships of the pioneer generation of Filipino immigrants and reveals how the recovery of these histories has inspired projects of historic preservation in more recent times. Through his articles on twentieth-century San Francisco, Lai helps us to situate the aforementioned dramatic and paradigmatic struggle over the I-Hotel within a broader geographical and historical context that runs through both the bureaucratic offices of city planners and the dynamic streets of communities like the Fillmore District. Both Mabalon and Lai are highly conscious of the reality that their research necessitates an understanding of panethnic and multiracial relations.[27]

Seattle has also served as a critical location for new insights into Asian American urban history. Doug Chin and Bob Santos provide insights into community history and urban activism in their respective books, *Seattle's International District* and *Hum Bows, Not Hot Dogs*. One of the first works of African American urban history to pursue comparisons and intersections with Asian American history was Quintard Taylor's study of Seattle's Central District, *The Forging of a Black Community*. Focusing on Filipino Americans in the age of U.S. imperial rule over the Philippines, Dorothy Fujita-Rony's *American Workers, Colonial Power* helps us to see the role urbanism played in the lives of Filipino immigrant workers who constantly migrated up and down the Pacific Coast in search of agricultural harvesting work but also looked to Seattle as a place to find off-season work and to establish ethnic community institutions. Furthermore, Shelley Lee's *Claiming the Oriental Gateway* examines Japanese Americans in pre–World War II Seattle to provide a model for tracing the relationship between race, culture, and internationalism in Asian American urban history.[28]

Unquestionably, one of the glaring shortcomings of work in Asian American urban history is the lack of attention to South Asian and Southeast Asian communities.

In turn, therefore, we might expect the most interesting new work in the field to emerge from scholarship on South Asian and Southeast Asian Americans. Pathbreaking writings on the historical construction of South Asian identity, politics, and culture in the United States are now being published. Exemplified by the pre–World War II research of scholars such as Vivek Bald and Seema Sohi, this work, while often engaging with urban historical subjects, has understandably—much like the earliest scholarship on East Asian immigrants—sought to trace the origins of the Indian and South Asian American community as an imagined entity across space and time. Working in the realm of postcolonial cultural studies and addressing the post–World War II era, Sandhya Shukla's study of race, migration, and representation provides a foundation for analyses of diasporic Indian communities in cities like New York and London, where migrancy is defined by "the persistent motion between community life in the city of settlement and an idea of homeland."[29] At the same time, Southeast Asian communities have become a prominent fixture across much of urban and suburban America, particularly as the processes of refugee resettlement and secondary migration have led to concentrations developing in places like San Jose, Orange County, and St. Paul. To this point, the struggles of working-class Southeast Asian refugees in inner-city environments have largely been examined by social scientists, such as Nazli Kibria, and interdisciplinary American studies scholars, such as Eric Tang and Karin Aguilar-San Juan.[30]

CONCLUSION

Given the rapid changes that are remaking commerce, culture, and community among Asian Americans in the United States and throughout the global order, urban studies will remain a critical site for examining social reality and social transformation. Undoubtedly, interest in Asian American urban studies will continue to expand in multiple directions, given the increasing role that Asian Americans are playing in the reshaping of urban foodways, the built environment, arts, social movements, and now, in some striking ways, electoral politics. In 2010 and 2011, for instance, Asian American politicians and their supporters made headlines by winning elections to become the mayors of Oakland and San Francisco.

Asian American historians can and should play a central role in making sense of these new urban realities. Our research has already demonstrated the role Asian Americans have played in the construction of vibrant and diverse urban cultures and communities. It has further shown how cities as increasingly multiracial and transnational entities cannot be comprehended without the critical perspective that Asian American historians have to offer. However, it also cautions us to refrain from one-sided, overly optimistic ideas of urban futures. Asian American urban struggles reveal important insights into the logic and sometimes dominance of capital and market forces in shaping community and remaking the built environment. Moreover, we can expect Asian Americans to be increasingly found on varying sides of urban social conflicts, particularly as diasporic Asian subjects become more and more central to the globalized working class and propertied class. All in all, it's an important and exciting time in which to study Asian American urban history.

NOTES

1. Bill Ong Hing, *Making and Remaking Asian America through Immigration Policy, 1850–1990* (Stanford, CA: Stanford University Press, 1993), 109.

2. For a written account of the I-Hotel struggles, which is part scholarly research and part memoir, see Estella Habal, *San Francisco's International Hotel: Mobilizing the Filipino American Community in the Anti-Eviction Movement* (Philadelphia: Temple University Press, 2007).

3. Eric H. Monkkonen, *America Becomes Urban: The Development of U.S. Cities and Towns, 1780–1980* (Berkeley: University of California Press, 1988), 25.

4. Ibid., 26.

5. See Joe W. Trotter, "African Americans in the City: The Industrial Era, 1900–1950," *Journal of Urban History* 21, no. 4 (1995): 438–457.

6. Robert M. Fogelson, *The Fragmented Metropolis: Los Angeles, 1850–1930* (Cambridge, MA: Harvard University Press, 1967).

7. Joe William Trotter, Jr., *Black Milwaukee: The Making of an Industrial Proletariat, 1915–1945* (Champaign: University of Illinois Press, 1985).

8. Arnold Hirsch, *Making the Second Ghetto: Race and Housing in Chicago, 1940–1960* (Cambridge: Cambridge University Press, 1983).

9. Kenneth Jackson, *Crabgrass Frontier: The Suburbanization of the United States* (Oxford: Oxford University Press, 1985).

10. Peter Kwong, *Chinatown, N.Y.: Labor and Politics, 1930–1950* (New York: Monthly Review, 1979). See also Renqiu Yu, *To Save China, to Save Ourselves: The Chinese Hand Laundry Alliance of New York* (Philadelphia: Temple University Press, 1992).

11. John Modell, *The Economics and Politics of Racial Accommodation: The Japanese of Los Angeles, 1900–1942* (Champaign: University of Illinois Press, 1977), 32.

12. Adolph Reed, Jr., *Stirrings in the Jug: Black Politics in the Post-Segregation Era* (Minneapolis: University of Minnesota Press, 1999).

13. Contemporary Asian Studies Division, University of California, Berkeley, "Curriculum Philosophy for Asian American Studies," *Amerasia Journal* 2, no. 1 (1973): 37–39.

14. Lane Ryo Hirabayashi, "Back to the Future: Re-Framing Community-Based Research," *Amerasia Journal* 21, nos. 1 and 2 (1995): 103.

15. Yuji Ichioka, Yasuo Sakata, Nobuya Tsuchida, and Eri Yasuhara, "Introduction," in *A Buried Past: An Annotated Bibliography of the Japanese American Research Project Collection*, ed. Yuji Ichioka et al. (Berkeley: University of California Press, 1974).

16. Judy Yung, *Unbound Feet: A Social History of Chinese Women in San Francisco* (Berkeley: University of California Press, 1995); Judy Yung, *Unbound Voices: A Documentary History of Chinese Women in San Francisco* (Berkeley: University of California Press, 1999).

17. John Kuo Wei Tchen, "Creating a Dialogic Museum: The Chinatown History Museum Experiment," in *Museums and Communities: The Politics of Public Culture*, ed. Ivan Karp et al. (Washington, DC: Smithsonian Institution Press, 1992), 285–326; see also Renqiu

Yu, *To Save China, To Save Ourselves: The Chinese Hand Laundry Alliance of New York* (Philadelphia: Temple University Press, 1992).

18. John Kuo Wei Tchen, *New York before Chinatown: Orientalism and the Shaping of American Culture, 1776–1882* (Baltimore, MD: Johns Hopkins University Press, 1999), 295.

19. Nayan Shah, *Contagious Divides: Epidemics and Race in San Francisco's Chinatown* (Berkeley: University of California Press, 2001).

20. Mary Ting Li Lui, *The Chinatown Trunk Mystery: Murder, Miscegenation, and Other Dangerous Encounters in Turn-of-the-Century New York City* (Princeton, NJ: Princeton University Press, 2004); Linda España-Maram, *Creating Masculinity in Los Angeles's Little Manila: Working-Class Filipinos and Popular Culture, 1920s–1950s* (New York: Columbia University Press, 2006); Lon Kurashige, *Japanese American Celebration and Conflict: A History of Ethnic Identity and Festival, 1934–1990* (Berkeley: University of California Press, 2002).

21. Thomas J. Sugrue, *The Origins of the Urban Crisis: Race and Inequality in Postwar Detroit* (Princeton, NJ: Princeton University Press, 1996).

22. Earl Lewis, "Connecting Memory, Self, and the Power of Place in African American Urban History," *Journal of Urban History* 21, no. 3 (1995): 347–371.

23. Dolores Hayden, *The Power of Place: Urban Landscapes as Public History* (Cambridge, MA: MIT Press, 1995), 9.

24. Scott Kurashige, *The Shifting Grounds of Race: Black and Japanese Americans in the Making of Multiethnic Los Angeles* (Princeton, NJ: Princeton University Press, 2008).

25. Natalia Molina, *Fit to Be Citizens? Public Health and Race in Los Angeles, 1879–1939* (Berkeley: University of California Press, 2006).

26. Cindy I-Fen Cheng, *Citizens of Asian America* (New York: New York University Press, 2013); Timothy P. Fong, *The First Suburban Chinatown: The Remaking of Monterey Park, California* (Philadelphia: Temple University Press, 1994); John Horton, *The Politics of Diversity: Immigration, Resistance, and Change in Monterey Park, California* (Philadelphia: Temple University Press, 1995); Leland T. Saito, *Race and Politics: Asian Americans, Latinos, and Whites in a Los Angeles Suburb* (Champaign: University of Illinois Press, 1998); Wei Li, *Ethnoburb: The New Ethnic Community in Urban America* (Honolulu: University of Hawai'i Press, 2009); and Wendy Cheng, *The Changs Next Door to the Díazes: Remapping Race in Suburban California* (Minneapolis: University of Minnesota Press, 2013).

27. Dawn Bohulano Mabalon, *Little Manila Is in the Heart: The Making of the Filipina/o American Community in Stockton, California* (Durham, NC: Duke University Press, 2013); Clement Lai, "The Racial Triangulation of Space: The Case of Urban Renewal in San Francisco's Fillmore District," *Annals of the Association of American Geographers* 102, no. 1 (2012): 151–170; and Clement Lai, "Saving Japantown, Serving the People: The Scalar Politics of the Asian American Movement," *Society and Space* 31, no. 3 (2013): 467–484. See also Lynne Horiuchi, "Coming and Going in the Western Addition: Japanese, Japanese Americans, and African Americans," *Annals of Scholarship* 17, no. 3 (2008): 33–67.

28. Doug Chin, *Seattle's International District: The Making of a Pan-Asian American Community* (Seattle: University of Washington Press, 2001); Bob Santos, *Hum Bows, Not Hot Dogs: Memoirs of a Savvy Asian American Activist* (Seattle: International Examiner Press, 2002); Quintard Taylor, *The Forging of a Black Community: Seattle's Central District from 1870 through the Civil Rights Era* (Seattle: University of Washington Press, 1994); Dorothy Fujita-Rony, *American Workers, Colonial Power: Philippine Seattle and the Transpacific West, 1919–1941* (Berkeley: University of California Press, 2003); Shelley

Sang-Hee Lee, *Claiming the Oriental Gateway: Prewar Seattle and Japanese America* (Philadelphia: Temple University Press, 2010).

29. Vivek Bald, *Bengali Harlem and the Lost Histories of South Asian America* (Cambridge, MA: Harvard University Press, 2013); Seema Sohi, *Echoes of Mutiny: Race, Surveillance, and Indian Anticolonialism in North America* (New York: Oxford University Press, 2014); Sandhya Shukla, *India Abroad: Diasporic Cultures of Postwar America and England* (Princeton, NJ: Princeton University Press, 2003), 20.

30. Nazli Kibria, *Family Tightrope: The Changing Lives of Vietnamese Americans* (Princeton, NJ: Princeton University Press, 1993); Eric Tang, *Unsettled: Cambodian Refugees in the New York City Hyperghetto* (Philadelphia: Temple University Press, 2015). On Vietnamese Americans in Boston and Orange County, see Karin Aguilar-San Juan, *Little Saigons: Staying Vietnamese in America* (Minneapolis: University of Minnesota Press, 2009).

FURTHER READING

Bald, Vivek. *Bengali Harlem and the Lost Histories of South Asian America*. Cambridge, MA: Harvard University Press, 2013.

Cheng, Cindy I-Fen. *Citizens of Asian America*. New York: New York University Press, 2013.

Kwong, Peter. *Chinatown, N.Y.: Labor and Politics, 1930–1950*. New York: Monthly Review, 1979.

Lee, Shelley Sang-Hee. *Claiming the Oriental Gateway: Prewar Seattle and Japanese America*. Philadelphia: Temple University Press, 2010.

Lui, Mary Ting Li. *The Chinatown Trunk Mystery: Murder, Miscegenation, and Other Dangerous Encounters in Turn-of-the-Century New York City*. Princeton, NJ: Princeton University Press, 2004.

Mabalon, Dawn Bohulano. *Little Manila Is in the Heart: The Making of the Filipina/o American Community in Stockton, California*. Durham, NC: Duke University Press, 2013.

Modell, John. *The Economics and Politics of Racial Accommodation: The Japanese of Los Angeles, 1900–1942*. Champaign: University of Illinois Press, 1977.

Molina, Natalia. *Fit to Be Citizens? Public Health and Race in Los Angeles, 1879–1939*. Berkeley: University of California Press, 2006.

Shah, Nayan. *Contagious Divides: Epidemics and Race in San Francisco's Chinatown*. Berkeley: University of California Press, 2001.

Tang, Eric. *Unsettled: Cambodian Refugees in the New York City Hyperghetto*. Philadelphia: Temple University Press, 2015.

Taylor, Quintard. *The Forging of a Black Community: Seattle's Central District from 1870 through the Civil Rights Era*. Seattle: University of Washington Press, 1994.

Tchen, John Kuo Wei. *New York before Chinatown: Orientalism and the Shaping of American Culture, 1776–1882*. Baltimore, MD: Johns Hopkins University Press, 1999.

Yung, Judy. *Unbound Feet: A Social History of Chinese Women in San Francisco*. Berkeley: University of California Press, 1995.

CHAPTER 23

FROM ASIA TO THE UNITED STATES, AROUND THE WORLD, AND BACK AGAIN

New Directions in Asian American Immigration History

ERIKA LEE

IN 1996, the historian Sucheng Chan proudly proclaimed that Asian American history was "finally coming of age." Asian Americans had been the subject of articles, books, and studies since the mid-nineteenth century, but these works, mostly written by white missionaries, labor leaders, journalists, and politicians, expressed partisan views in the debate over Asian immigration. In the early twentieth century, Asian Americans became the focus of study by social scientists, but they were viewed as social problems to be solved. It would take the Asian American movement and the "new" social historians of the 1960s and 1970s to fully give voice to Asian Americans, "unearth" their "buried pasts," and document their everyday lives, struggles, and triumphs and their contributions to the making of America.[1]

Today's Asian American historians have built on these pioneering studies to complicate, broaden, and deepen the history of Asian immigration to the United States and elsewhere. New archival sources, theoretical frameworks, and methodologies have changed the questions that historians are asking, where they are doing their research, and the focus of their inquiries. Interdisciplinary influences from sociology, critical race and ethnic studies, gender and sexuality studies, Asian studies, and world history have brought new insights. New definitions of migration and migrants and broader chronological and geographical frameworks have helped expand the study of Asian American immigration history across time and space. Closer attention to race, ethnicity, class, and gender and sexuality has complicated our understandings of Asian immigrant families, communities, and interethnic and interracial relations. And new scholarship has focused on recent immigrant and refugee communities, the use of Asian-language sources, and the centrality of transnational, diasporic, and global perspectives.

The first part of this essay examines recent theoretical and methodological trends in Asian American immigration history. It then analyzes how recent scholarship has shaped our understandings of specific eras of Asian immigration to the United States.

Rethinking Migration

Immigration has traditionally been defined as a push-and-pull process. Conditions in one country, like war, natural disaster, civil unrest, economic instability, and so on "push" desperate peoples out as another country "pulls" them to its shores with better-paying jobs, land, and freedom from persecution. This approach portrays individual immigrants as making free, rational decisions about leaving their homelands. Immigration is a one-way journey to a better life. Immigrants are "uprooted" and then successfully "transplanted" into their new countries of residence, where they readily assimilate into the mainstream.[2]

Since the mid-1980s Asian American and immigration historians have challenged these paradigms to instead focus on the complex factors shaping international migration. Lucie Cheng and Edna Bonacich charted the connections among capitalism, imperialism, uneven economic development, population displacement, and migration abroad in Asia. Yong Chen used Chinese sources to reconsider how Western imperialism and its economic and ideological impact on the Pearl River Delta in China established important preconditions for migration in the nineteenth century. Similarly, scholars studying Filipino migration have clearly placed it within the context of U.S. imperialism and colonialism in the Philippines. Dorothy Fujita-Rony focuses on the "powerful reach of colonialism in Philippine-American relations" and how networks of transpacific trade and militarism as well as American colonial education encouraged Filipino migration to Seattle, Washington. Catherine Ceniza Choy uses a "two-shores" approach of archival and ethnographic research in both the United States and the Philippines to locate Filipino nurse migration to the United States within the long history of U.S. colonialism and colonial education in the Philippines.[3]

Asian American immigration historians are also adopting more flexible definitions and frameworks of migration and mobility to refer to the multiple ways in which people move. As Christiane Harzig and Dirk Hoerder explain, migration can be many-directional and multiple, temporary or long-term, voluntary or forced. Migration studies emphasize that men and women on the move have agency. They negotiate their options and constraints and sometimes change directions to keep on the move or return to where they began. This broader framework allows scholars to look at "both ends of mobility," to examine how migration affects both the sending and receiving societies. Donna Gabaccia has also called on immigration historians to pay more attention to the "continuous, multidirectional, and circular character of migrations" rather than relying upon the older "immigrant paradigm and its well-worn paths of immigration and adaptation to the United States." Included under the rubric of immigration are peoples who have not followed a unidirectional pattern of movement, whose stay in the United States has been temporary, or whose migration is via nontraditional routes: slaves, indentured laborers, sailors, sojourners, students, visitors, refugees, adoptees, and individuals engaged in serial migrations. Like these migration scholars, the Asian American immigration historian Madeline Hsu has argued for a transnational, "ambulatory" approach that recognizes migrants' "complicated sets of negotiations, multilayered realities, and multidirectional orientations." She describes how early twentieth-century Taishanese moved back and forth across the Pacific and often changed their migration strategies and plans along the way. An intention to stay in the United States only temporarily sometimes turned into a lifetime abroad. Triumphant retirements to childhood homes in Taishan were cut short when Chinese Americans returned to the United States out of economic necessity or by choice.[4]

DIASPORIC/GLOBAL/TRANSNATIONAL FRAMEWORKS

Global, transnational, and diasporic frameworks are also becoming increasingly central for the explanation of Asian migration patterns as well as the ongoing social relations and networks that immigrants maintain across geographic, cultural, and political borders. It is no longer possible to think of Asian immigration to the United States as being solely defined by the U.S. nation-state. Instead, scholars seek to explain how Asian immigration to the United States fits within larger global patterns of mobility around the world.[5]

For example, the Chinese and world historian Adam McKeown has illustrated how the "practices and ideologies of migration are embedded in larger global trends and transnational activities." Instead of tracking distinct streams of people moving from one nation to another, he advocates for an approach that centers "mobility and dispersion as a basis from which to begin analysis." His work highlights how both global and local processes shaped Chinese migration, Chinese migrant networks, and international regulation in the late nineteenth and early twentieth centuries. Similarly, Eiichiro Azuma has called for a "remapping" of global Japanese migration history that connects Japanese labor migration to the Americas with the history of Japanese colonial expansionism within Asia. Examining the dual influences of both U.S. and Japanese national expansionisms, Azuma's "two-empire" approach emphasizes the role of the Japanese homeland in shaping migrants and their journeys, and it connects the Japanese to the Americas and the Japanese to East and Southeast Asia together into a more complex portrait of the Japanese diaspora prior to World War II.[6]

A key aspect of diasporic and transnational approaches to Asian American immigration is the use of non-English-language sources. Shih-shan Henry Tsai was among the first to use Chinese-language sources to examine the roles of Chinese diplomats and government officials in protecting Chinese citizens abroad and the ways in which Chinese immigrants challenged discriminatory immigration laws in the name of human rights. Alan Moriyama and Yuji Ichioka used Japanese-language sources both to explain how the Japanese government and private emigration companies organized Japanese migration and to demonstrate the complex lives of Japanese immigrants. Madeline Hsu drew from Chinese-language gazetteers to illustrate how Taishanese in the United States maintained transnational ties with their families and villages in Guangdong province and vice versa.[7]

Using Chinese-, English-, and Spanish-language sources, scholars have offered new interpretations of how Asian migrants have lived their lives across national borders in the Americas. McKeown's study of Chinese in Peru, Chicago, and Hawai'i during the early twentieth century documented transnational Chinese migrant social, economic, and cultural connections. Focusing on the U.S.-Mexico borderlands, Robert Chao Romero, Julia Camacho Schiavone, and Grace Peña Delgado have documented how Chinese migrant families and businesses were connected together across national borders, oceans, and continents. They show how the Chinese in Mexico maintained economic and familial ties with their southern Chinese villages, while simultaneously developing transnational ties with other Chinese communities in the Americas, notably the United States and Cuba. These took the form of merchant networks, transnational commercial orbits, wholesale trade, contract-labor recruitment, human trafficking, and transnational, interracial families.[8]

Diasporic frameworks have also illustrated how Asian migrants form identities that were often simultaneously tied to their local ethnic communities, their homelands, and communities within diasporas. Collaborative research coming out of the International Nikkei Research Project, for example, documents the long and rich histories of *nikkei,* peoples of Japanese descent, in the Americas as well as the changing patterns and processes of Japanese emigration from the late nineteenth century to the end of the twentieth. Eiichiro Azuma's portrait of Japanese in America also suggests that Japanese migrants were caught between the two empires of the United States and Japan, and, as a result, had conflicted and complex identities, loyalties, and behaviors.[9]

Early twentieth-century Korean and South Asian migrants in the United States practiced diasporic nationalisms that maintained their political connections to their colonized homelands and contributed to larger anticolonial movements. Lili M. Kim has argued that transnational approaches to studying the Korean American experience are "not only useful but necessary," especially during the years of Japanese colonialism in Korea. Because Korean immigrants remained passionately involved in Korean homeland politics, she warns that any failure "to connect the concerns and experiences of Koreans in the United States back to the conditions and realities of Korea would result in inadequate, partial interpretations of Korean immigrant experiences." Richard Kim's study of Korean diasporic nationalism in the early twentieth century illustrates this point even further. Korean immigrants in the United States "saw themselves inextricably linked to their compatriots geographically dispersed across national boundaries and borders," he writes. When Korean immigrants convened the "Korean Congress" in Philadelphia in April 1919 to mobilize support for the Korean independence movement and the new Korean Provisional Government of the Republic of Korea, they saw themselves as part of a larger diasporic movement that represented all Koreans in and outside of Korea.[10]

Under the leadership of charismatic Indian nationalist leaders, South Asians in Canada and the United States became politically active in the cause of Indian independence. The discriminatory treatment they faced in Canada and the United States fed growing anti-British sentiment and mobilized them into nationalist politics. At the same time, they developed a unique ethnic identity as South Asians in North America. Their encounters with white prejudice, anti-Asian riots, disfranchisement, and exclusion bounded them together. Joan Jensen and Seema Sohi have demonstrated that the interconnected movements in Canada and the United States explicitly linked the unequal status of South Asians in North America to the colonized state of their homeland. Nationalists and their activities routinely crossed the U.S.-Canadian border and together were part of a global anticolonial movement in which South Asians challenged laws all over the British empire.[11]

At the same time that scholars are expanding their perspectives far beyond the borders of the United States, they are also asking new questions about Asian immigration within the broader context of American history, including the making of the modern American state, American national identity, and international relations. Legal historians like Charles McClain, Jr. and Lucy Salyer have analyzed how the Chinese immigrant community's efforts to combat immigration restrictions and housing, employment, and educational discrimination were instrumental in establishing several legal landmarks as well as the national development of immigration laws and procedures. Erika Lee's study of Chinese immigration during the exclusion era showed how the Chinese exclusion laws not only transformed Chinese American lives, immigration patterns, identities, and families but also recast the United States into a "gatekeeping nation." Immigrant identification, border enforcement, surveillance, and deportation policies were extended far beyond any controls that had existed in the United States before. Similarly, Mae Ngai's history of immigration policy traced the origins of the "illegal alien" in American law and society. These included Filipino colonial subjects caught up in the Filipino repatriation program of the 1930s, incarcerated Japanese Americans during World War II, and Chinese American "paper sons" forced to enter the United States with fraudulent documents. Cast as "problems" in U.S. immigration policy, these groups helped shape ideas and practices about race, national identity, citizenship, and state power.[12]

While reconsidering the role of Asian immigration in the broader context of U.S. history, Asian American immigration historians have also examined how Asian American women and gender relations shaped immigration patterns, family and community formations, and work and labor.[13] In addition, controlling the admission of Asian immigrant women and measuring their fitness to enter the country based on gender and sexuality were key components of immigration policies and border control.[14]

New research has continued to document the central roles women have played in changing immigration patterns and community formation. Lili Kim and Ji-yeon Yuh, for example, have written about the central roles that Korean immigrant women and Korean military brides played in sustaining the early Korean immigrant community in the United States and in laying the groundwork for future family-sponsored Korean immigration after 1965. Scholars have also used intersectional analyses of race, gender, and class to explain the dynamics of immigration in the past and present. Catherine Ceniza Choy's study of Filipino nurse migration to the United States illustrates how U.S. colonialism in the Philippines, the racialization of Filipinos, and gendered assumptions about the nursing profession helped to institutionalize the migration of Filipino women for nursing positions in the United States beginning in the early twentieth century.[15]

Utilizing new archival sources and historical methodologies; intersectional analyses of race, class, and gender; and transnational and diasporic frameworks, Asian American immigration historians are asking new questions of Asian immigration to the United States and helping to revise our understandings of U.S. history in general.

The rest of this article examines the major periods of Asian immigration to the United States and highlights recent scholarship using these new perspectives and sources.

ASIANS IN THE AMERICAS

From 1830 to 1930, more than one million Asians entered the United States. Until recently, most studies of Asian immigration largely focused on the period of mass migration and community formation beginning in the late nineteenth century. A common starting point has been the arrival of thousands of Chinese gold seekers in California during the midcentury Gold Rush. Increasingly, however, historians have begun to explore how the roots of Asian American history extend far beyond and before this time period. Gary Okihiro's *Margins and Mainstreams: Asians in American History and Culture* (1994) sought to expand the "canvas of Asian American history" by asking "when and where does the history of Asians in the United States begin?" In tracing how Asians entered into the European historical consciousness through Greek representations of Asia in the fifth century B.C.E., Okihiro makes the point that "Asians did not first come to America; Europeans went to Asia." The resulting European American understandings of Asia as exotic, foreign, and other influenced the European colonization of Asia as well as Europe's search for Asia that ended up in America. "The when and where of Asian American history," Okihiro thus proclaims, "are of an ancient vintage and of a global scale."[16]

A number of scholars inside and outside of the field of Asian American history have contributed to Okihiro's vision to revise the "when and where" starting points of Asian immigration to the United States.[17] One first step in this endeavor has been to connect the history of Asian immigration to the United States to the histories of Asians in the

Americas and to world history more generally. Evelyn Hu-DeHart's pioneering scholarship on the Chinese in Mexico and Cuba and her efforts to transnationalize the field of Asian American studies helped to establish a field that can be called "Asians in the Americas."[18] Placing the history of Asian immigration to the United States within the broader history of Asians in the Americas has inspired major reconceptualizations of the Asian American past.

For example, historians have looked back to the history of the Manila galleon trade from 1565 to 1815, during which massive trading ships sailed from Manila and connected Europe, Asia, and the Americas together in a global, transpacific trading network for the first time. The galleons brought an estimated 40,000 to 100,000 Filipinos, Chinese, Japanese, and others from Southeast Asia and India across the Pacific to New Spain (colonial Mexico). As late as 1860, there were more Chinese in Latin America and the Caribbean than there were in North America.[19]

Scholars like Evelyn Hu-DeHart, Denise Helly, Lisa Yun, and Kathleen Lopez have also turned their attention to the so-called coolie trade, which brought 250,000 Chinese indentured laborers to Cuba and Peru from 1847 to 1874 and another 430,000 South Asians to the British West Indies from 1834 to 1918. Tied to the Black Atlantic world of slavery, the coolie trade helped initiate the transition from slavery to free labor and set the stage for the mass migrations of Asians to the Americas during the late nineteenth and early twentieth centuries. As Moon-ho Jung, Matthew Guterl, and Christine Skwiot have demonstrated, the coolie trade also prompted a global discussion about race and labor across the Atlantic and Pacific oceans and throughout the Caribbean and Latin America. Chinese coolies were both a desirable source of cheap labor and a disruptive social force in the communities in which they lived. These debates over Asian coolies left an indelible mark on the debates over Chinese immigration in the United States and in other white settler societies around the world. In the study of Asian immigration to the United States, historians like John Kuo Wei Tchen have also expanded their inquiries to the East Coast in the early nineteenth century. Together, these works and perspectives help set the stage for a broader understanding of the origins and global roots of Asian immigration to the United States and to the Americas.[20]

ASIAN IMMIGRATION DURING
THE EXCLUSION ERA: 1882 TO WORLD WAR II

With the help of newly discovered sources and different methodological choices, historians have also greatly expanded our understandings of Asian mass migration during the late nineteenth century and early twentieth century and the related exclusion laws that eventually curtailed that migration: the 1875 Page Law and the 1882 Chinese Exclusion Act, which curtailed the immigration of Chinese laborers and women suspected of being prostitutes, but allowed certain "exempt" classes, including merchants, students, teachers, diplomats, and travelers to enter. Later court challenges by Chinese immigrants resulted in allowing the wives and children of merchants and U.S. citizens to enter. Other exclusion laws were the 1907 Gentlemen's Agreement, which barred the immigration of Japanese laborers but allowed family members to apply for admission; the Immigration Act of 1917, which barred all within the newly constructed "Asiatic Barred Zone"; the 1924 Immigration Act, which prohibited the entry of all "aliens ineligible for citizenship," meaning Asians; and the 1935 Tydings-McDuffie Act, which granted the Philippines nominal independence and thereby revoked Filipinos' status as "U.S. nationals" and reclassified them as foreigners subject to the country's immigration and exclusion laws.

Sucheng Chan's edited and coedited volumes on Chinese exclusion laid the foundation for a new generation of scholarship on the history of the Chinese exclusion era. The books that resulted include: George Anthony Peffer's study of Chinese immigrant women and the 1875 Page Law; Lucy Salyer's legal history of the judicial and administrative enforcement of the Chinese exclusion laws; Adam McKeown's examination of Chinese migrant networks in Hawai'i, Peru, and the United States; Madeline Hsu's study of Chinese immigrant transnationalism during the era of exclusion; Erika Lee's book on Chinese immigration during the exclusion era; and Estelle Lau's exploration of Chinese immigrant "paper families."[21]

Comparative works like Mae Ngai's legal history of "illegal immigration," Anna Pegler-Gordon's examination of photography and immigrant documentation, Martha Gardiner's analysis of how immigration and naturalization laws were applied to immigrant women, and Erika Lee and Judy Yung's history of Asian, European, and Mexican immigration through the Angel Island Immigration Station in San Francisco have begun to place Asian immigration and exclusion within the broader context of immigration regulation and comparative racial formation in the United States. Together, these works have demonstrated how immigrants have been both excluded and admitted on the basis of their race, ethnicity, class, gender, sexuality, moral standing, health, and political affiliation, among other factors. These justifications for exclusion and admission often intersected and overlapped with each other to regulate not only foreign immigration, but also domestic race, class, and gender relations within the United States. Moreover, a complex state bureaucracy was established to enforce the immigration laws and to exercise the state's control over its geographical borders as well as its internal borders of citizenship and national membership.

Immigrants were profoundly affected by the new laws. But one of the crucial aspects of this new scholarship focuses on how Asian immigration continued in spite of the exclusion laws: Chinese immigrants with fraudulent documents as U.S. citizens, who were paper sons, wives, and daughters; Japanese "picture brides"; Korean laborers, students, and families; South Asian laborers, students, and revolutionaries; and Filipinos who entered as "U.S. nationals." Asian immigrants actively challenged the laws and their discriminatory treatment wherever they could and by any means possible—in the streets, in court, in the barracks of the Angel Island Immigration Station; by writing letters of protest, crossing the border without proper documentation, and telling their stories to future generations to remember.[22]

WORLD WAR II TO 1965

America's emergence as a superpower following World War II forced the country to reconsider its discriminatory immigration policies, and significant transformations in U.S. immigration policy resulted. The first step came in 1943 when Congress repealed the Chinese exclusion acts. By 1946, Congress passed bills to grant quotas of one hundred to India and the Philippines and allowed for the naturalization of immigrants from those countries as well. In 1945 and in 1947, Congress continued to relax the country's immigration laws by passing the so-called War Brides Acts, which allowed the spouses of American servicemen to enter the country.

The repeal of Asian exclusion laws did not open America's doors wide open to Asian immigration, and until recently, the decades between World War II and 1965 have received little scholarly attention. It has been a "historical blind spot," forgotten between the two periods of immigration exclusion and immigration liberalization. Recent scholarship, however, has illustrated how new migrations of military brides, students, refugees, professionals, adoptees, and others during these years laid the foundations for contemporary Asian American communities. Xiaojian Zhao, for example, has demonstrated how these newly arrived Chinese immigrant women and newly reunited Chinese American families played crucial roles in the transformation of Chinese American communities across the nation. Some Filipinos who served in the U.S. military during and after World War II were able to enter the United States under the Selective Service Act as military brides of U.S. servicemen and as professional migrants sponsored by the U.S. government. Between 1946 and 1965, more than 39,000 Filipinos entered the United States.[23]

Historians examining the Cold War period have also noted how Asian immigration directly followed the growing U.S. hegemony in Asia. The Cold War struggle with the Soviet Union placed a premium on foreign students and professionals within the United States, and new professional and elite Chinese immigrants began to arrive from Taiwan and Hong Kong in the 1950s as part of government-sponsored programs to recruit scientific workers and engineers in the field of military technology. They joined a small group of Chinese students who chose to remain in America after the 1949 revolution. The Cold War–inspired U.S. Exchange Visitor Program also brought small numbers of elite Filipina nurses to the United States to gain skills as well as firsthand knowledge about the United States and its values. These migrants opened the door for the later mass migration of Filipino nurses in the post-1965 period.[24]

Since 1945, the U.S. military presence and dominance in Korea has resulted in ongoing U.S. military troop deployments in South Korea. Relationships between Korean women and U.S. military personnel—sometimes begun in the "camptowns" established near U.S. military bases where prostitution and other illicit businesses were "supported and regulated by the U.S. military for the benefit of its soldiers"—ended in marriage and migration to the United States. Ji-yeon Yuh's research on Korean military brides places their migration to the United States within the context of the neoimperialist and gendered relationship between South Korea and the United States after 1950. Nearly 100,000 Korean military brides immigrated to the United States between 1950 and 1989.[25]

The migration of transracial, transnational Asian American adoptees also has its roots in the U.S. Cold War relationship with South Korea. Since 1953, the United States has received over 110,000 adopted children from South Korea. New scholarship has demonstrated how transnational Korean adoption became institutionalized as a "national custom" in Korea and as a humanitarian project and an evangelical Christian mission in the United States. An estimated 200,000 Korean children have been transnationally adopted worldwide. Beginning in the 1990s, the United States became a major receiving nation for children adopted from China. Echoing the history of Korean adoption in the United States, the Chinese adoption program provided healthy young infants free of ties to birth families with a "desirable" ethnic background and "flexible" racial status. They soon became known as "model adoptees." Adoption became understood as a humanitarian act that "rescued" "unwanted" children, as well as a symbol of progress for multicultural America. By 2000, China became the top sending country for international adoption, with more than 5,000 Chinese adoptees arriving that year.[26]

1965 to the Present

Contemporary Asian America has been largely formed by changes in U.S. immigration policy after 1965 as well as several global factors, including global economic restructuring in both the United States and Asia and increased U.S. political, economic, and military roles in Asia. Scholarship from a wide range of disciplines is filling important historiographical gaps as well as introducing new theoretical frameworks and methodologies for studying Asian American immigration in general.

Motivated by Cold War politics and civil rights activism, the 1965 Immigration and Nationality Act abolished the national origins quotas and created a new set of preference categories based on family reunification and professional skills. Although the 1965 Immigration Act was intended to facilitate emigration from Europe, Asians and Latin Americans have made up the bulk of new arrivals. Since the 1980s, 88 percent of all immigrants came from either of these two geographic regions. Asian immigrants make up around 35 percent of all immigrant admissions. Among the top ten sending countries since 1980 are the Philippines, China/Taiwan, Korea, India, and Vietnam. The majority are family-sponsored migrants or employer-sponsored skilled workers.

Min Zhou and James Gatewood have explained how U.S. investments in developing countries like Asia also resulted in rapid economic growth and high emigration from those countries to the United States. U.S. capital in Asian economies targeted production for export and led to uneven economic development, increased rural-urban migration, underemployment, displaced workers, and the creation of a large pool of potential emigrants. At the same time, the global integration of higher education in many developing countries like India, Korea, the Philippines, and Taiwan resulted in a sizable professional class frustrated with the widening gap between expectations of a higher standard of living and the uneven economic development and lack of mobility opportunities. One result has been "tremendous pressure for emigration." In the United States, a severe shortage of skilled workers equipped for high-tech industries and services encouraged employer-sponsored skilled migration to the United States. Since the 1980s, Asian immigrant engineers and medical personnel have made up about one-third of the professionals in their industries.[27]

While historical analyses of post-1965 Asian immigration patterns are just emerging, scholars from a broad range of disciplines are offering rich data on these immigrant communities and how they are adjusting in the United States. Like the new histories focusing on earlier Asian migrations, researchers emphasize the importance of global, transnational, and international frameworks in shaping contemporary Asian immigration and the ways in which diasporic Asian identities have been formed.

CONTEMPORARY CHINESE IMMIGRATION

Most of the new scholarship on contemporary Asian immigration emphasizes how different the new arrivals are from early twentieth-century Asian immigrants. For example, unlike the first generations of mostly working-class male Chinese immigrants who came from China's Pearl River Delta, the new Chinese immigrants, or *san yi man,* come from mainland China, Hong Kong, and Taiwan and include both men and women, members of the working and professional classes, and Cantonese and Mandarin speakers. The difference in numbers is striking as well. In 1960, there were just under 100,000 Chinese-born immigrants in the United States. In 2010, the U.S. Census reported over 3.3 million adult Chinese Americans in the United States. Making up the largest group of Asian Americans and the largest ethnic Chinese population (including Taiwanese) outside Asia, they represent 24 percent of the United States' adult Asian population and in 2015 they became the single largest immigrant group entering the United States.[28]

Some are elite migrants who are part of the "uptown, high-tech Chinese" and are English-speaking scientists, real estate moguls, capitalist entrepreneurs, and professional elites. There are also "downtown, low-tech" Chinese who are low-skilled, blue-collar workers, waiters, domestic workers, cooks, and laundrymen. Some members of the "downtown," "low-tech" Chinese work under exploitative working conditions in crowded garment factories in American cities. Others include those who have entered the country without proper documentation, sometimes with the help of smugglers, or "snakeheads." With neither professional skills nor relatives already in the United States who could sponsor them, an estimated 150,000 Chinese chose to enter without documentation during the 1990s. Their experiences echo many exclusion-era paper sons who also lived in the shadows of society because of their immigration status.

New Chinese immigrants in the United States have helped to revive older Chinatowns in big urban centers like New York City. At the same time, they have also formed new ethnic enclaves in the suburbs, complete with Chinese-owned banks, restaurants, and malls, and Chinese-language newspapers. Monterey Park in Southern California, where Chinese make up more than one-third of the city's population, has been nicknamed "the first suburban Chinatown." Just as with earlier Chinese ethnic enclaves established throughout the Americas beginning in the late nineteenth century, the high concentration of Chinese immigrant-serving businesses and services ease the transition into the United States while fostering close community and homeland ties. Chinese Americans have also successfully integrated into local and national communities. In the United States, the number of elected officials of Asian Pacific American descent almost tripled from 1978 to 2000. In 2012, both the mayors of Oakland, California, and San Francisco were Chinese Americans.

Just as new Chinese immigrants are adapting to and integrating into their new homes, many also remain transnational migrants simultaneously connected to both their old and new homelands. Some Hong Kong and Taiwanese families are literally spread across the Pacific Ocean between North America and Asia. Choosing to split up the family unit in order to make the most of business opportunities in Asia and educational opportunities for the children in the United States and Canada, "astronaut" Chinese fathers shuttle across the Pacific for business while their wives and children live and attend school in North America. Similarly, Taiwanese "parachute" kids have been left in the United States alone or with caretakers and relatives to go to school and better their chances of gaining admission to a prestigious U.S. university. These transnational "split-family households" are similar to the working-class Chinese immigrants who were also divided from their families during the exclusion era. But unlike these earlier sojourners, who often never saw their families again, today's elite transnationals are able to travel back and forth much more frequently. New technologies such as email, international phone lines, and the Internet make transnational connections much more frequent, intense, and direct. A number of Chinese immigrants simultaneously express their ethnicity in their adopted homelands and their transnational relationships to their ancestral homelands through flexible and selective citizenship. Globe-trotting Chinese elites with multiple homes and passports exemplify what the anthropologist Aihwa Ong describes as "flexible citizens," who enjoy privileged access to multiple nations.[29]

CONTEMPORARY FILIPINO IMMIGRATION

Scholars of contemporary Filipino migration to the United States emphasize its place within the larger global mass migration of Filipinos around the world. Over eight million Filipinos, around 10 percent of the entire Philippine population, currently work overseas in 140 countries. Made up of nurses, schoolteachers, entertainers, domestic workers, and seafarers working as deck hands, cleaners, mechanics, and cooks aboard container ships and luxury cruise liners, the Filipino diaspora is perhaps the largest in the world.

Filipino immigration to the United States has been shaped by the long-standing colonial and military relationships between the two countries. Many post–World War II migrants were sent to the United States by the U.S. military or through military-based networks. After the 1965 Immigration Act opened up more avenues to immigration, Filipino migration has increased dramatically. Between 1965 and 1985, almost 665,000 Filipinos entered the United States. Between 1990 and 2000, the Filipino population grew by 66 percent. Political conditions in the Philippines, especially the repressive government of Ferdinand Marcos (1965–1985) and the civil unrest caused by communist rebels and Islamic separatists, also spurred migration abroad. Continuing massive unemployment and underemployment as well as income inequality have sustained a culture of migration abroad. In 2010, there were 2.55 million Filipinos in the country, making up 18 percent of the adult Asian population in the United States.[30]

The Filipinos who came to the United States in the early twentieth century were largely working-class immigrant laborers. In contrast, since the 1960s, the Philippines has sent the largest number of professional immigrants to the United States. Filipino nurses, doctors, and other medical practitioners have been heavily recruited to the United States to help alleviate a shortage of medical personnel in the country, especially in inner cities and rural areas. Almost 25,000 nurses entered the United States between 1966 and 1985. Another 10,000 arrived between 1989 and 1991. More recently, family-based immigration has brought a greater diversity of Filipino immigrants to the United States as well. Like earlier generations of Filipinos in the United States, contemporary Filipino immigrants continue to maintain strong transnational identities and ties with the Philippines. For example, the Filipino *balikbayan,* permanent residents of the United States, have long been championed as national Filipino heroes for the billions of dollars in remittances that they send to the Philippines each year. More recently, Filipinos' transnational philanthropy has become more organized and direct. As Joyce Mariano has found, there are now thousands of transnational hometown, regional, and national associations, as well as professional and alumni organizations that link Filipino Americans to direct transnational investment and partnership with communities in the Philippines.[31]

CONTEMPORARY KOREAN IMMIGRATION

Since 1965, Korean immigration to the United States has skyrocketed. In 1970, the U.S. Census reported 70,598 persons of Korean ancestry in the United States. Twenty years later, the Census counted almost 800,000. This rapid migration occurred within the context of political instability and economic dislocations in South Korea beginning in the 1970s and 1980s. Rapid industrialization and a population explosion resulted in diminished socioeconomic mobility among the middle class, overall income inequality, intense rural-to-urban migration, and increased population density. Koreans—encouraged by the South Korean government—actively engaged in emigration.

Like the earlier wave of Korean immigrants to the United States, the newcomers come intending to stay and migrate as families. A majority have quickly become naturalized citizens. Professionals and students made up the majority of the initial wave of Korean migrants, including physicians, nurses, pharmacists, and dentists. The peak years of Korean immigration were in the late 1970s and 1980s, when many family members of immigrants already in the country began to arrive. Since the 1990s, when South Korea's living standards and democratization have increased, immigration to the United States has declined, but the Korean American population remains vibrant. In 1997, there were almost 136,000 Korean-owned businesses, and in 2010, the Korean population in the United States was estimated to be 1.26 million.

As in the case of other contemporary Asian migrations, scholars frame Korean immigration to the United States within a larger global framework. The Korean diaspora encompasses Koreans in China, Japan, the former Soviet Union, South America, and the United States formed out of necessity during and after Japanese colonialism and the Korean War. An estimated 5.7 million Koreans live in 160 different countries. Ji-yeon Yuh has focused on this Korean "refuge migration" of military brides, adoptees, labor migrants, political exiles, and international students turned immigrants seeking peace of mind. She finds that Koreans abroad are increasingly developing a diasporic consciousness that "takes the diaspora, not the homeland, as the point of reference." They seek to create international communities of Koreans outside of Korea that are connected to the Korean diaspora, host countries, and the Korean homeland.[32]

CONTEMPORARY EMIGRATION
FROM SOUTH ASIA

In the years directly following the passage of the 1965 Immigration Act, emigration from both India and Pakistan—two independent nations created in 1947—increased. The U.S. Census recorded 371,630 South Asians in the country in 1980, including those from India, Pakistan, Bangladesh, and Sri Lanka. In 1990, the number had almost tripled to 919,626. By 2010, there were over 1.73 million Indian Americans in the United States along with 409,000 Pakistanis and over 147,000 Bangladeshis.[33]

Unlike the small numbers of emigrants who arrived mostly from the Punjab region of what is now India and Pakistan in the early twentieth century, today's newcomers come from throughout India. While the early twentieth-century migration was almost exclusively male laborers, both men and women are contemporary Indian immigrants. The majority are fluent in English and are highly educated professionals, including physicians, engineers, and computer scientists. During the 1960s and 1970s, India's economy could not keep pace with the number of college graduates it produced. Educated professionals sought opportunities abroad just as the Immigration Act offered visas to those with technical skills. Since the 1990s, the rate of Indian immigration has increased as professionals arrive through employment-based immigration programs, and as a growing number of Indian immigrants already in the country sponsor their families to join them. The 2000 Census counted 1.7 million Indian Americans. They were the fastest-growing Asian American group in the 1990s and are highly diverse in terms of language, religion, and, increasingly, class, as more working-class family members arrive to join those already here.

Indian Americans also maintain strong transnational homeland ties, often with the assistance of the Indian government. Beginning in the 1970s, Indians in the United States began to form ethnic organizations and newspapers as part of new community-building efforts. Like their early twentieth-century predecessors, they actively claim an "Indian" identity that is formed at the intersection of India and the United States. In 1999, India began to issue special immigration documents, known as "Persons of Indian Origin Card" that allow "non-resident Indians [NRIs]" to visit India without a visa, own property, buy government bonds, and apply to universities in India. By granting nonnationals the rights of nationals, the Indian government has sought to encourage financial investments and long-term transnational ties between Indians in the diaspora and India. In 2005 alone, India received $27 billion in remittances. As Verne A. Dusenberry and Darshan S. Tatla observe, "NRIs are the new VIPs."[34]

SOUTHEAST ASIAN REFUGEE MIGRATIONS

Although there was hardly any emigration from Southeast Asia prior to 1975, Southeast Asians now make up a significant proportion of contemporary Asian immigration. The United States' long involvement in Southeast Asia ended in 1975 following the victory of the North Vietnamese communist forces in Vietnam. After the fall of Saigon in April 1975, the United States engaged in emergency evacuations of American military personnel and a small number of South Vietnamese allies. Over the next several months, the total number of evacuees totaled over 130,000. By 1978, the annual admission of Southeast Asian refugees had increased exponentially, most of them admitted under the Indochinese Parole Programs that granted the attorney general ad hoc authority to "parole" into the United States any alien on an emergency basis with no real numerical limit or oversight from Congress. From 1978 to 1980, 267,800 refugees were admitted into the United States. The latter arrivals included second-wave Vietnamese "boat people" who were primarily former political prisoners and ethnic Chinese expelled from Vietnam, as well as a third and fourth wave of

Cambodian refugees fleeing the "killing fields" of Cambodia, and Laotian, Mien, and Hmong from Laos who had fought the United States' "secret war" in Laos. Since 1975, around 1.5 million Vietnamese, Lao, and Cambodian refugees have resettled in the United States.

Oral history collections, first-person narratives, and ethnographic studies dominate the field of Southeast Asian American history, and they richly document the refugees' experiences of war, revolution, flight, and resettlement. Booklength historical studies are just beginning to emerge and include Sucheng Chan's study of Cambodian refugees. Based on interviews with community leaders, government officials, resettlement agency workers, and others, *Survivors: Cambodian Refugees in the United States* is the definitive study of how and why Cambodians sought refuge in the United States and how they have fared. Aihwa Ong uses the case of Cambodian refugees to understand "everyday strategies and techniques of citizen-making" in their attempts to cope, navigate, and survive life in the United States. The first generation of Hmong American scholars have been publishing and entering the academy in recent years. Chia Vang's two books on Hmong Americans examine the formation of the Hmong American community in Minnesota, in the United States, and in the diaspora.[35] And Yen Le Espiritu's "critical refugee studies" approach has introduced new frameworks for understanding the importance of U.S. imperialism in creating the refugee subject and the role of memory in preserving Southeast Asian American histories.[36]

CONCLUSION

Asian American immigration historians have helped pave the way toward a dramatic rethinking of the Asian American past. We now have a much more diverse and complicated portrait of Asian immigration that follows Asians across the Pacific and back again, as well as throughout the Americas and around the world. Recent scholarship asks how Asian immigration was formative in the making of the United States and American race, class, and gender relations; how it intersected with U.S.-Asian relations; and how it connects to trends in world history and global migration more generally.

In looking toward the future, we need more interdisciplinary exchange to connect historical and contemporary perspectives. This will allow us to examine how earlier patterns set the foundation for the newest migrations; how migration patterns, communities, and identities are similar and different; and how historical methodologies, sources, and frameworks can inform scholarship on the newest Asian immigrants. Similarly, historians should consider how insights from anthropology, sociology, political science, cultural studies, and other fields shed new light on the past. By continuing to draw on the latest interdisciplinary scholarship, historians and others can continue to push the boundaries of Asian American immigration history while also highlighting the historical contexts that frame contemporary phenomena.

NOTES

1. Sucheng Chan, "The Writing of Asian American History," *OAH Magazine of History* 10, no. 4 (1996): 15; Yuji Ichioka et al., *A Buried Past: An Annotated Bibliography of the Japanese American Research Project Collection* (Berkeley: University of California Press, 1974), 3–15; Yuji Ichioka and Eiichiro Azuma, *A Buried Past: A Sequel to the Annotated Bibliography of the Japanese American Research Project Collection* (Los Angeles: UCLA Asian American Studies Center, 1999).

2. Donna Gabaccia, "Do We Still Need Immigration History?" *Polish American Studies* 55 (1998): 54–55.

3. Lucie Cheng and Edna Bonacich, *Labor Immigration under Capitalism: Asian Workers in the United States* (Berkeley: University of California Press, 1984); Gary Okihiro, *The Columbia Guide to Asian American History and Culture* (New York: Columbia University Press, 2001), 71–74; Yong Chen, *Chinese San Francisco, 1850–1943: A Trans-Pacific Community* (Stanford, CA: Stanford University Press, 2000); Dorothy Fujita-Rony, *American Workers, Colonial Power: Philippine Seattle and the Transpacific West, 1919–1941* (Berkeley: University of California Press, 2002), 19; Catherine Ceniza Choy, *Empire of Care: Nursing and Migration in Filipino American History* (Durham, NC: Duke University Press, 2003). See also Augusto Espiritu, *Five Faces of Exile: The Nation and Filipino American Intellectuals* (Stanford, CA: Stanford University Press, 2005); and Augusto Espiritu, "Transnationalism and Filipino American Historiography," *Journal of Asian American Studies* 11, no. 2 (2008): 171–184.

4. Christiane Harzig, Dirk Hoerder, with Donna Gabaccia, *What Is Migration History?* (Cambridge: Polity, 2009), 3; Donna Gabaccia, "Is Everywhere Nowhere? Nomads, Nations, and the Immigrant Paradigm of United States History," *Journal of American History* 86, no. 3 (1999): 1116; Madeline Y. Hsu, "Transnationalism and Asian American Studies as a Migration-Centered Project," *Journal of Asian American Studies* 11, no. 2 (2008): 185; Madeline Y. Hsu, *Dreaming of Gold, Dreaming of Home: Transnationalism and Migration between the United States and South China, 1882–1943* (Stanford, CA: Stanford University Press, 2000): 11.

5. Linda G. Basch, Nina Glick Schiller, and Cristina Blanc-Szanton, *Nations Unbound: Transnational Projects, Postcolonial Predicaments, and Deterritorialized Nation-States* (London: Routledge, 1994); David Thelen, "Nation and Beyond: Transnational Perspectives on U.S. History," *Journal of American History* 86, no. 3 (1999): 968–969; Shelley Fisher Fishkin, "Crossroads of Cultures: The Transnational Turn in American Studies—Presidential Address to the American Studies Association, November 12, 2004," *American Quarterly* 57, no. 1 (2005): 17–57; Erika Lee and Naoko Shibusawa, "What Is Transnational Asian American History? Recent Trends and Challenges," *Journal of Asian American Studies* 8, no. 3 (2005): vii–xvii; Hsu, "Transnationalism and Asian American Studies."

6. Adam McKeown, "Conceptualizing Chinese Diasporas, 1842 to 1949," *Journal of Asian Studies* 58, no. 2 (1999): 307–308; Adam McKeown, *Melancholy Order: Asian Migration and the Globalization of Borders* (New York: Columbia University Press, 2008); Adam McKeown, *Chinese Migrant Networks and Cultural Change: Peru, Chicago, and Hawaii, 1900–1936* (Chicago: University of Chicago Press, 2001); Eiichiro Azuma, "Remapping a Pre–World War Two Japanese Diaspora: Transpacific Migration as an Articulation of Japan's Colonial Expansionism," in *Connecting Seas and Connected Ocean Rims*, ed. Donna R. Gabaccia and Dirk Hoerder (Leiden: Brill, 2011), 415–439.

7. Shih-shan Henry Tsai, *China and the Overseas Chinese in the United States, 1868–1911* (Bloomington: Indiana University Press, 1986); Yui Ichioka, *Issei: The World of the First Generation Japanese Immigrants, 1885–1924* (New York: Free Press, 1990); Yuji Ichioka, with Eiichiro Azuma and Gordon Chang, eds., *Before Internment: Essays in Prewar Japanese American History* (Stanford, CA: Stanford University Press, 2006); Alan Takeo Moriyama, *Iminigaisha: Japanese Emigration Companies and Hawaii, 1894–1908* (Honolulu: University of Hawai'i Press, 1985); Hsu, *Dreaming of Gold*.

8. McKeown, *Chinese Migrant Networks*; Robert Chao Romero, *The Chinese in Mexico, 1882–1940* (Tucson: University of Arizona Press, 2010); Grace Delgado, *Making the Chinese Mexican: Global Migration, Localism, and Exclusion in the U.S.-Mexico Borderlands* (Stanford, CA: Stanford University Press, 2012); Julia Maria Schiavone Camacho, *Chinese Mexicans: Transpacific Migration and the Search for a Homeland, 1910–1960* (Chapel Hill: University of North Carolina Press, 2012).

9. Akemi Kikumura-Yano, *Encyclopedia of Japanese Descendants in the Americas: An Illustrated History of the Nikkei* (Walnut Creek, CA: AltaMira, 2002); Lane Ryo Hirabayashi, Akemi Kikumura-Yano, and James A. Hirabayashi, *New Worlds, New Lives: Globalization and People of Japanese Descent in the Americas and from Latin America in Japan* (Stanford, CA: Stanford University Press, 2002); Eiichiro Azuma, *Between Two Empires: Race, History, and Transnationalism in Japanese America* (New York: Oxford University Press, 2005).

10. Lili M. Kim, "Doing Korean American History in the Twenty-first Century," *Journal of Asian American Studies* 11, no. 2 (2008): 204; Richard S. Kim, "Inaugurating the American Century: The 1919 Philadelphia Korean Congress, Korean Diasporic Nationalism, and American Protestant Missionaries," *Journal of American Ethnic History* 26, no. 1 (2006): 51–53, 70–71; Richard S. Kim, *The Quest for Statehood: Korean Immigrant Nationalism and U.S. Sovereignty, 1905–1945* (New York: Oxford University Press, 2011).

11. Joan Jensen, *Passage from India: Asian Indian Immigrants in North America* (New Haven, CT: Yale University Press, 1988), 121; Seema Sohi, "Race, Surveillance, and Indian Anticolonialism in the Transnational Western U.S.-Canadian Borderlands," *Journal of American History* 98, no. 2 (2011): 420–436; and *Echoes of Mutiny: Race, Surveillance, and Indian Anticolonialism in North America* (New York: Oxford University Press, 2014).

12. Charles J. McClain, *In Search of Equality: The Chinese Struggle against Discrimination in Nineteenth-Century America* (Berkeley: University of California Press, 1996); Lucy Salyer, *Laws Harsh as Tigers: Chinese Immigrants and the Shaping of Modern Immigration Law* (Chapel Hill: University of North Carolina Press, 1995); Erika Lee, *At America's Gates: Chinese Immigration during the Exclusion Era, 1882–1943* (Chapel Hill: University of North Carolina Press, 2003); Mae Ngai, *Impossible Subjects: Illegal Aliens and the Making of Modern America* (Princeton, NJ: Princeton University Press, 2005).

13. Shirley Hune and Gail M. Nomura, eds., *Asian/Pacific Islander American Women: A Historical Anthology* (New York: New York University Press, 2003); Evelyn Nakano Glenn, *Issei, Nisei, War Bride: Three Generations of Japanese American Women in Domestic Service* (Philadelphia: Temple University Press, 1986); Valerie Matsumoto, *Farming the Home Place: A Japanese American Community in California, 1919–1982* (Ithaca, NY: Cornell University Press, 1993); Judy Yung, *Unbound Feet: A Social History of Chinese Women in San Francisco* (Berkeley: University of California Press, 1995); Judy Yung, *Unbound Voices: A Documentary History of Chinese Women in San Francisco* (Berkeley: University of California Press, 1999); Choy, *Empire of Care*; Xiaojian Zhao, *Remaking Chinese*

America: Immigration, Family, and Community, 1940–1965 (New Brunswick, NJ: Rutgers University Press, 2002); Yen Le Espiritu, *Asian American Women and Men: Labor, Laws, and Love* (Lanham, MD: Rowman and Littlefield, 2007).

14. George Anthony Peffer, *If They Don't Bring Their Women Here: Chinese Female Immigration before Exclusion* (Champaign: University of Illinois Press, 1999); Martha M. Gardner, *The Qualities of a Citizen: Women, Immigration, and Citizenship, 1870–1965* (Princeton, NJ: Princeton University Press, 2005); Erika Lee and Judy Yung, *Angel Island: Immigrant Gateway to America* (New York: Oxford University Press, 2010); Eithne Luibhéid, *Entry Denied: Controlling Sexuality at the Border* (Minneapolis: University of Minnesota Press, 2002).

15. Lili M. Kim, "Redefining the Boundaries of Traditional Gender Roles: Korean Picture Brides, Pioneer Korean Immigrant Women, and Their Benevolent Nationalism in Hawai'i," in Hune and Nomura, *Asian/Pacific Islander American Women*, 106–119; Ji-yeon Yuh, *Beyond the Shadow of Camptown: Korean Military Brides in America* (New York: New York University Press, 2002); Choy, *Empire of Care*.

16. Gary Okihiro, *Margins and Mainstreams: Asians in American History and Culture* (Seattle: University of Washington Press, 1994), ix–xi, 7.

17. See Erika Lee, *The Making of Asian America: A History* (New York: Simon and Schuster, 2015) and Gary Okihiro, *American History Unbound: Asians and Pacific Islanders* (Berkeley: University of California Press, 2015).

18. Evelyn Hu-DeHart, "Racism and Anti-Chinese Persecution in Sonora, Mexico, 1876–1932," *Amerasia* 9, no. 2 (1982): 1–27; "Race Construction and Race Relations: Chinese and Blacks in Nineteenth-Century Cuba," in *Encounters: People of Asian Descent in the Americas*, ed. R. Rustomji-Kerns (Lanham: Rowman and Littlefield, 1999), 105–112; "Huagong and Huashang: The Chinese as Laborers and Merchants in Latin America and the Caribbean," *Amerasia* 28, no. 2 (2002): 64–92.

19. Erika Lee, *The Making of Asian America*, 15–33; Edward R. Slack, "The *Chinos* in New Spain: A Corrective Lens for a Distorted Image," *Journal of World History* 20, no. 1 (2009): 35–67; Edward R. Slack, "Sinifying New Spain: Cathay's Influence on Colonial Mexico via the *Nao de China*," in *The Chinese in Latin America and the Caribbean*, ed. Walton Look Lai and Tan Chee-Beng (Leiden: Brill, 2010), 7–34; Melba E. Falck Reyes and Héctor Palacios, *El japonés que conquistó Guadalajara: La historia de Juan de Páez en la Guadalajara del siglo XVII* (Guadalajara: Biblioteca Pública del Estado de Jalisco Juan José Arreola, 2009); Roshni Rustomji-Kerns, "Mirrha-Catarina de San Juan: From India to New Spain," *Amerasia* 28, no. 2 (2002): 29–36; Walton Look Lai, "Introduction," in *The Chinese in the West Indies, 1806–1995: A Documentary History* (Mona: University Press of the West Indies, 2000), 6–7.

20. Erika Lee, *The Making of Asian America*, 34–58; Denise Helly, *The Cuba Commission Report: A Hidden History of the Chinese in Cuba. The Original English-Language Text of 1876* (Baltimore, MD: Johns Hopkins University Press, 1993); Evelyn Hu-DeHart, "Coolies, Shopkeepers, Pioneers: The Chinese of Mexico and Peru, 1849–1930," *Amerasia* 15, no. 1 (1989): 91–116; China Cuba Commission, *The Cuba Commission Report: A Hidden History of the Chinese in Cuba* (Baltimore, MD: Johns Hopkins University Press, 1993); Lisa Yun, *The Coolie Speaks: Chinese Indentured Laborers and African Slaves in Cuba* (Philadelphia: Temple University Press, 2009); Kathleen Lopez, "Migrants between Empires and Nations: The Chinese in Cuba, 1874–1959" (Ph.D. dissertation, University of Michigan, 2005); Matthew Guterl and Christine Skwiot, "Atlantic and Pacific

Crossings: Race, Empire, and the 'Labor Problem' in the Late Nineteenth Century," *Radical History Review* 91 (2005): 40–61; Moon-Ho Jung, *Coolies and Cane: Race, Labor, and Sugar in the Age of Emancipation* (Baltimore, MD: Johns Hopkins University Press, 2006); John Kuo Wei Tchen, *New York before Chinatown: Orientalism and the Shaping of American Culture, 1776–1882* (Baltimore, MD: Johns Hopkins University Press, 2001).

21. Sucheng Chan, ed., *Entry Denied: Exclusion and the Chinese Community in America, 1882–1943* (Philadelphia: Temple University Press, 1991); Sucheng Chan and K. Scott Wong, *Claiming America: Constructing Chinese American Identities during the Exclusion Era* (Philadelphia: Temple University Press, 1998); Sucheng Chan, ed., *Chinese American Transnationalism: The Flow of People, Resources, and Ideas between China and America during the Exclusion Era* (Philadelphia: Temple University Press, 2006); Sucheng Chan and Madeline Hsu, eds., *Chinese Americans and the Politics of Race and Culture* (Philadelphia: Temple University Press, 2008); Peffer, *If They Don't Bring Their Women Here*; Salyer, *Laws Harsh as Tigers*; McKeown, *Chinese Migrant Networks*; McKeown, *Melancholy Order*; Hsu, *Dreaming of Gold*; Lee, *At America's Gates*; Estelle Lau, *Paper Families: Identity, Immigration Administration, and Chinese Exclusion* (Durham, NC: Duke University Press, 2007).

22. Ngai, *Impossible Subjects*; Anna Pegler-Gordon, *In Sight of America: Photography and the Development of U.S. Immigration Policy* (Berkeley: University of California Press, 2009); Gardner, *Qualities of a Citizen*; Lee and Yung, *Angel Island*.

23. Catherine Ceniza Choy, "Asian America History: Reflections on Imperialism, Immigration, and 'the Body,'" *Amerasia* 26, no. 1 (2000): 119–140; Mae M. Ngai, "The Strange Career of the Illegal Alien: Immigration Restriction and Deportation Policy in the United States, 1921–1965," *Law and History Review* 21, no. 1 (2003), 69–108; Zhao, *Remaking Chinese America*; Philip Q. Yang, *Asian Immigration to the United States* (Cambridge: Polity, 2011), 102–103.

24. Peter Kwong and Dusanka Miscevic, *Chinese America: The Untold Story of America's Oldest New Community* (New York: New Press, 2005), 231–233; Madeline Hsu, *The Good Immigrants: How the Yellow Peril Became the Model Minority* (Princeton, NJ: Princeton University Press, 2015); Choy, *Empire of Care*, 59–118.

25. Ramsey Liem, "History, Trauma, and Identity: The Legacy of the Korean War for Korean Americans," *Amerasia* 29, no. 3 (2003): 114; Ji-yeon Yuh, *Beyond the Shadow of Camptown: Korean Military Brides in America* (New York: New York University Press, 2002).

26. Kim Park Nelson, "Mapping Multiple Histories of Korean American Transnational Adoption," U.S.-Korea Institute Working Paper Series (2009); Richard Lee and Matthew Miller, "History and Psychology of Adoptees in Asian America" in *Asian American Psychology*, ed. A. Alvarez and N. Tewari (Mahwah, NJ: Lawrence Erlbaum, 2008), 337–363; Eleana J. Kim, *Adopted Territory: Transnational Korean Adoptees and the Politics of Belonging* (Durham, NC: Duke University Press, 2010); Catherine Ceniza Choy, *Global Families: A History of Asian International Adoption in America* (New York: New York University Press, 2013); Arissa Oh, *To Save the Children of Korea: The Cold War Origins of International Adoption* (Stanford, CA: Stanford University Press, 2015); Sara Dorow, *Transnational Adoption: A Cultural Economy of Race, Gender, and Kinship* (New York: New York University Press, 2006); "International Adoption Facts," Evan B. Donaldson Adoption Institute, http://www.adoptioninstitute.org/FactOverview/international.html (accessed October 17, 2011).

27. Min Zhou and James V. Gatewood, "Transforming Asian America: Globalization and Contemporary Immigration to the United States," in *Contemporary Asian America: A Multidisciplinary Reader* (New York: New York University Press, 2000), 115–138.

28. Kristen McCabe and Migration Policy Institute, *Chinese Immigrants in the United States*, January 18, 2012, http://www.migrationinformation.org/USfocus/print.cfm?ID=841 (accessed November 12, 2012); Elizabeth M. Hoeffel et al., *The Asian Population: 2010* (Washington, DC: U.S. Department of Commerce, Economics and Statistics Administration, U.S. Census Bureau, 2012), 14; Pew Research Center, *The Rise of Asian Americans* (Washington, DC, 2013), 38; Min Zhou, *Contemporary Chinese America: Immigration, Ethnicity, and Community Transformation*, 2nd ed. (Philadelphia: Temple University Press, 2009), 43; Erika Lee, "Chinese Immigrants Now Largest Group of New Arrivals to the U.S.," *USA Today*, July 7, 2015, http://www.usatoday.com/story/opinion/2015/07/07/chinese-immigrants-largest-column/2 9784905/ (accessed September 11, 2015).

29. Ronald Takaki, *Strangers from a Different Shore* (Boston: Little, Brown, 1998), 425; Peter Kwong and Edith Wen-Chu Chen, "Chinese Americans," in Edith Wen-Chu Chen and Grace J. Yoo, eds., *Encyclopedia of Asian American Issues Today*, vol. 1 (Santa Barbara, CA: Greenwood Press, 2010), 19–20; Kwong and Miscevic, *Chinese America*, 233–236, 343–348; Iris Chang, *The Chinese in America: A Narrative History* (New York: Penguin, 2004), 210, 338–346, 349–388; "Immigrant Women Speak Out on Garment Industry Abuse," in *Chinese American Voices from the Gold Rush to the Present*, ed. Judy Yung, Gordon Chang, and Him Mark Lai (Berkeley: University of California Press, 2006), 225–231; Timothy Fong, *The First Suburban Chinatown: The Remaking of Monterey Park, California* (Philadelphia: Temple University Press, 1994); Eric Lai and Dennis Arguelles, "Politics and Civil Rights," in *The New Face of Asian Pacific America: Numbers, Diversity, and Change in the 21st Century* (Los Angeles: UCLA Asian American Studies Center Press, 1998), 210; Min Zhou, *Contemporary Chinese America: Immigration, Ethnicity, and Community Transformation* (Philadelphia: Temple University Press, 2009), 202–220; Aihwa Ong, *Flexible Citizenship: The Cultural Logics of Transnationality* (Durham, NC: Duke University Press, 1999).

30. Hoeffel et al., *The Asian Population*, 14; Pew Research Center, *The Rise of Asian Americans*, 42.

31. Steven C. McKay, "Filipino Sea Men: Identity and Masculinity in a Global Labor Niche," in *Asian Diasporas: New Formations, New Conceptions*, ed. Rhacel Parreñas and Lok Siu (Stanford, CA: Stanford University Press, 2007), 63; Lai and Arguelles, "Filipinos: Swimming with and against the Tide," in *The New Face of Asian Pacific America*, 45, 47; Takaki, *Strangers from a Different Shore*, 432, 383; Carl L. Bankston III and Danielle Antoinette Hidalgo, "The Waves of War: Immigrants, Refugees, and New Americans from Southeast Asia," in Zhou and Gatewood, *Contemporary Asian America*, 140–143; L. Joyce Zapanta Mariano, "Homeland Developments: Filipino America and the Politics of Diaspora Giving" (Ph.D. dissertation, University of Minnesota, 2011), 3–4, 48–53, 102–126.

32. Yang, *Asian Immigration*, 114; Eui-Young Yu and Peter Choe, "Korean Population in the United States as Reflected in the Year 2000 Census," *Amerasia* 29, no. 3 (2003): 5, 2; Edward Taehan Chang, "What Does It Mean to Be Korean Today? One Hundred Years of Koreans in America and More," *Amerasia* 29, no. 3 (2003): xxiii; Ji-yeon Yuh, "Moved by War: Migration, Diaspora, and the Korean War," *Journal of Asian American Studies* 8, no. 3 (2005): 287.

33. Hoeffel et al., *The Asian Population*, 14.

34. Raymond Brady Williams, "South Asians in the United States," in *The South Asian Religious Diaspora in Britain, Canada, and the United States*, ed. Harold Coward, John R. Hinnels, and Raymond Brady Williams (Albany: State University of New York Press, 2000), 215; Takaki, *Strangers from a Different Shore*, 446; Yang, *Asian Immigration*, 114; Sandhya Shukla, "New Immigrants, New Forms of Transnational Community: Post-1965 Indian Migrations," *Amerasia* 25, no. 3 (1999): 19, 23–25, 27, 30–33; Verne A. Dusenberry and Darshan S. Tatla, "Introduction," in *Sikh Diaspora Philanthropy in Punjab: Global Giving for Local Good*, ed. Verne A. Dusenberry and Darshan S. Tatla (New York: Oxford University Press, 2009), 3–4, 7–8.

35. Bankston and Hidalgo, "The Waves of War," 140–143; Bill Ong Hing, *Making and Remaking Asian America through Immigration Policy, 1850–1990* (Stanford, CA: Stanford University Press, 1994), 126; Sucheng Chan, *Hmong Means Free: Life in Laos and America* (Philadelphia: Temple University Press, 1994); James Freeman, *Hearts of Sorrow: Vietnamese-American Lives* (Stanford, CA: Stanford University Press; 1991); Sucheng Chan, *The Vietnamese American 1.5 Generation: Stories of War, Revolution, Flight and New Beginnings* (Philadelphia: Temple University Press, 2006); Sucheng Chan, *Survivors: Cambodian Refugees in the United States* (Champaign: University of Illinois Press, 2004); Aihwa Ong, *Buddha Is Hiding: Refugees, Citizenship, the New America* (Berkeley: University of California Press, 2003); Chia Vang, *Hmong America: Reconstructing Community in Diaspora* (Champaign: University of Illinois Press, 2010); Chia Vang, *Hmong in Minnesota* (St. Paul: Minnesota Historical Society Press, 2008).

36. Yen Le Espiritu, *Body Counts: The Vietnam War and Militarized Refugees* (Berkeley: University of California Press, 2014).

Further Reading

Azuma, Eiichiro. *Between Two Empires: Race, History, and Transnationalism in Japanese America*. New York: Oxford University Press, 2005.

Chan, Sucheng, ed. *Entry Denied: Exclusion and the Chinese Community in America, 1882–1943*. Philadelphia: Temple University Press, 1991.

———. *Hmong Means Free: Life in Laos and America*. Philadelphia: Temple University Press, 1994.

———. *Survivors: Cambodian Refugees in the United States*. Champaign: University of Illinois Press, 2004.

———. *The Vietnamese American 1.5 Generation: Stories of War, Revolution, Flight and New Beginnings*. Philadelphia: Temple University Press, 2006.

Choy, Catherine Ceniza. *Empire of Care: Nursing and Migration in Filipino American History*. Durham, NC: Duke University Press, 2003.

———. *Global Families: A History of Asian International Adoption in America*. New York: New York University Press, 2013.

Espiritu, Yen Le. *Body Counts: The Vietnam War and Militarized Refugees*. Berkeley: University of California Press, 2014.

Hsu, Madeline Y. *Dreaming of Gold, Dreaming of Home: Transnationalism and Migration between the United States and South China, 1882–1943*. Stanford, CA: Stanford University Press, 2000.

———. *The Good Immigrants: How the Yellow Peril Became the Model Minority*. Princeton, NJ: Princeton University Press, 2015.

Hune, Shirley, and Gail M. Nomura, eds. *Asian/Pacific Islander American Women: A Historical Anthology*. New York: New York University Press, 2003.

Jensen, Joan. *Passage from India: Asian Indian Immigrants in North America*. New Haven, CT: Yale University Press, 1988.

Jung, Moon-Ho. *Coolies and Cane: Race, Labor, and Sugar in the Age of Emancipation*. Baltimore, MD: Johns Hopkins University Press, 2006.

Kim, Richard S. *The Quest for Statehood: Korean Immigrant Nationalism and U.S. Sovereignty, 1905–1945*. New York: Oxford University Press, 2011.

Lee, Erika. *The Making of Asian America: A History*. New York: Simon and Schuster, 2015.

—— and Judy Yung. *Angel Island: Immigrant Gateway to America*. New York: Oxford University Press, 2010.

McKeown, Adam. *Melancholy Order: Asian Migration and the Globalization of Borders*. New York: Columbia University Press, 2008.

Ngai, Mae. *Impossible Subjects: Illegal Aliens and the Making of Modern America*. Princeton, NJ: Princeton University Press, 2005.

Oh, Arissa. *To Save the Children of Korea: The Cold War Origins of International Adoption*. Stanford, CA: Stanford University Press, 2015.

Okihiro, Gary. *American History Unbound: Asians and Pacific Islanders*. Berkeley: University of California Press, 2015.

——. *Margins and Mainstreams: Asians in American History and Culture*. Seattle: University of Washington Press, 1994.

Ong, Aihwa. *Buddha Is Hiding: Refugees, Citizenship, and the New America*. Berkeley: University of California Press, 2003.

Sohi, Seema. *Echoes of Mutiny: Race, Surveillance, and Indian Anticolonialism in North America*. New York: Oxford University Press, 2014.

Vang, Chia. *Hmong America: Reconstructing Community in Diaspora*. Champaign: University of Illinois Press, 2010.

Yuh, Ji-yeon. *Beyond the Shadow of Camptown: Korean Military Brides in America*. New York: New York University Press, 2002.

Yung, Judy. *Unbound Feet: A Social History of Chinese Women in San Francisco*. Berkeley: University of California Press, 1995.

Zhao, Xiajian. *Remaking Chinese America: Immigration, Family, and Community, 1940–1965*. New Brunswick, NJ: Rutgers University Press, 2002.

Zhou, Min. *Contemporary Chinese America: Immigration, Ethnicity, and Community Transformation*. Philadelphia: Temple University Press, 2009.

CHAPTER 24

PUBLIC HISTORY AND ASIAN AMERICANS

FRANKLIN S. ODO

"DEMOCRACY has no monuments. It strikes no medals. It bears the head of no man on a coin," wrote John Quincy Adams, the son of the former president John Adams and himself the sixth president of the United States. The younger Adams is not among our most treasured former heads of state. Many Americans do not realize that, more than a quarter-century after the American Revolution, he had expressed a sense that this new nation should not follow in the footsteps of European monarchies and their veneration of past heroes in the form of monuments and medals.[1] But the young nation soon began to build and preserve numbers of monuments and memorials. And, in the past few decades, this tendency has become much more pronounced. Most of us have memorials/sites of memory, perhaps of loved ones who have died. Pilgrimages to cemeteries and sites of accidents where teddy bears and flowers accumulate become part of the journey. Memory, then, becomes a crucial part of personal and family dynamics. To be remembered is somehow to remain part of the living even in death. At the national level, there are large public memorials, invariably dedicated to great men in American history such as the Lincoln Memorial or the Washington Monument in Washington, D.C., or Mt. Rushmore in the Black Hills of South Dakota, with its gigantic sculptures of the former presidents George Washington, Thomas Jefferson, Abraham Lincoln, and Theodore Roosevelt.[2] More recently, the Vietnam Memorial literally and figuratively broke new ground with a radically new approach to remembering—by listing more than 50,000 names of Americans who had died in the war, on granite walls that appeared to emerge from [or sink into] deep gashes in the earth. Maya Lin, then an architecture student, who designed the memorial, soon became the target of racist criticism; now, however, the memorial is nearly universally heralded as a work of high achievement.[3]

Memory, in the public history form of memorials, museums, and monuments, is important for nearly all peoples and communities, and this is certainly true for Asian Americans, as individuals or ethnic/racial constructs. Certainly, private memory can be highly suspect as dramatized in the Japanese film *Rashomon*.[4] And perhaps "he said, she said," issues are more common than sometimes acknowledged. The particularly disastrous and vicious public recollections of childhood sexual abuse, beginning in the later decades of the twentieth century, were deeply unsettling.[5] In any case, memory, whether private or public, is often complex and conflicted.[6] For Asian Americans, however, there is difficulty dealing with problematic nuances of memorialization because we have only recently achieved the minimal critical mass of demographic, political, and financial power to affect public history—at all—at the national level. While many people memorialize individuals or events or places with markers such as flowers at the site of an accident, not all communities are represented by nationally sanctioned forms of memorials and thus honored collectively as part of public history. And memory involves forgetting as well as remembering. It has been a struggle for the United States, as with all nations, to come to grips with some of its actions and policies—including slavery, genocide, xenophobia, wars of aggression, and racism. Sometimes famous images have become complicit in national amnesia, such as the formal photograph celebrating the completion of the transcontinental railroad that connected America's Atlantic and Pacific coasts at Promontory Summit, Utah, in 1869.[7]

On May 10 of that year, the symbolic golden spike was gently tapped into a highly polished laurel tie [the tie was made of laurel wood], symbolically connecting the Central Pacific and Union Pacific railroads. The East and West Coasts were thus joined, and both tie and spike were immediately removed for safekeeping. Most students of Asian American history are aware of the enormous sacrifices made by thousands of Chinese immigrant laborers in the process of building the Central Pacific Railroad. It is jarring, therefore, to learn that they were deliberately barred from formal photographs and paintings. These representations took pains to include other participants, including the Irish workers who created the Union Pacific as well as incidental Native Americans and, of course, the owners and financiers.[8] Memory making, whether for individuals or nation-states, includes what is remembered and highlighted as well as what is forgotten or obscured. The process of public memory making, of memorializing, of creating monuments, or of building archives or exhibitions, is ongoing, fraught with contestation, and subject to enormous change.

An examination of the major memory-keeping and memory-making institutions at the national level, such as the Library of Congress, the Smithsonian Institution, and the National Historic Landmarks Project of the National Park Service, leads to two important discussions on memory and memorials in the making of two major events in American history. First, World War II forced the removal and incarceration of 120,000 Japanese Americans and a redress movement culminating in the signing of the Civil Liberties Act of 1988 by President Ronald Reagan. Second, we must look at the 1882 Chinese Exclusion Act (and subsequent acts that excluded Asians and Pacific Islanders) as well as the successful efforts to have Congress express "regret" for these racist laws in 2011 and 2012.[9]

Asian American studies share a particular kinship with public history. Both began as parts of the more general social and political movements in the United States in the 1960s and 1970s. Both Asian American studies and public history emerged to challenge the orthodox scholarship embodied in academic research across the nation, confronting the top-down nature of academic interpretation, of "truths" revealed by scholars upon whom credentials had been conferred by colleagues similarly situated on equivalent campuses. Most important, both public history practitioners and Asian American specialists argued that one critical way to engage important ideas was through a "shared authority" with individuals and groups—the communities—that had experienced the events being described or analyzed and who understood the consequential impact of otherwise theoretical treatises.[10] Asian American history, from its inception as a field in the 1970s, like allied enterprises in ethnic, social, and women's studies, often anchored research projects in, with, or for perceived needs within their communities, often to address or redress issues of deprivation or oppression.[11] Public history and its many and varied venues became valuable mechanisms to accomplish these aims.

Public history is often defined by what it is not: it is not scholarly activity conducted for peer review by professional historians largely on the faculties of colleges and universities. Most public history is conducted in museums, galleries, historical societies, foundations, national parks, historic houses, libraries, film and television programs, oral/video projects, and increasingly websites. Simply listing these media and institutions convinces us that the vast majority of people learn "history" and "heritage" through public venues rather than from scholarly texts or lectures. Ideally, of course, the revelations made possible by scholarly research eventually reach these public arenas. In contrast, some history is "private" rather than public—here, we might consider classified government projects as uncirculated corporate reports outlining the histories of drug tests or market research. The conclusions or interpretations contained in this type of research are intended to remain hidden from the public and revealed only occasionally; further, those who make this information public may be criminalized, as the Pentagon Papers or Wikileaks scandals have demonstrated.

In the past, academic historians have generally dismissed public history as less rigorous and less significant. There are ambiguous areas, however, when scholars write for the general public but with a firm control of traditional academic protocols. Recently, more university-based research, publication, and instruction has included public history. Indeed, mainstream academic history departments are becoming increasingly supportive of public history efforts. In the 1990s, there were no more than a few recognized public history programs in academia but by 2012 there were more than one hundred campuses boasting these units. In the process, academic disdain for public historians has diminished. Part of the reason for this evolution is the decreasing numbers of positions for academic historians, forcing more newly minted Ph.D.s and their advisors to turn to public history institutions for employment opportunities.[12] Every state and region and many localities have some form of public site or forum in which historians work to transmit the legacies of specific people, events, or issues, from generation to generation.

These institutions remind generations of people about values crucial to the individuals and groups that create and maintain them. Many of our most memorable national sites are monuments to heroes and battles from the Revolutionary War: Concord and Lexington in Massachusetts; Trenton and Princeton in New Jersey; the Washington Monument or Mt. Vernon in the District of Columbia and Virginia. All proclaim the righteous nature of the struggle by the thirteen colonies for liberation from the oppression of the British empire. And the arc of those monuments and memorials bends far toward inculcating pride and patriotism in the American public. At the same time, there are hundreds of memorials commemorating the valor of Confederate troops who lost the Civil War. These monuments and memorials, like Stone Mountain in Georgia, praise the courage and commitment of southern military leaders like Robert E. Lee, who, in other circumstances, might simply be dismissed as traitors, and, like Benedict Arnold from the Revolutionary War, be consigned to the dustbin of history. But there are other, very different and extremely complex examples; these memorials seek to highlight issues that can appear to negate the generally positive image of America by noting specific values such as pride in Native American heritage or celebration of African slave rebellions or the forced removal and incarceration of Japanese Americans, by their own government, during World War II.

The same principle holds true for state or local history. We generally have a sense of which sites qualify and for what reasons in specific instances, and there are many memorials, including those containing Christian iconography, that have been passionately contested. But the most prominent and critical sites of public history are, arguably, national in scope and nature. This is true because their reach extends, at least potentially, to everyone. And, for many, they define the nature of being American—Washington and Jefferson have enormous and enormously popular and powerful monuments in the nation's capital, even though both were slaveowners. The White House and the U.S. Capitol were built by African slaves and maintained by their descendants, but this is not a significant part of their interpretation because these facts are inconvenient to the major message of the governance of a democratic and egalitarian form of government. But if you happen to be part of the community descended from African slaves, then places like the Frederick Douglass House in Washington, D.C., or the W. E. B. Du Bois home in the Berkshires may be as important as the more conventionally acknowledged memorials, to a sense of being or becoming an American—at least a voting American citizen.

If we acknowledge the fact that most Americans absorb their history—the past—from public sources rather than academic publications or college courses, where is Asian American history in this picture? This section examines three important national institutions: the Library of Congress (LoC), the National Park Service (NPS), and the Smithsonian Institution (SI).[13] I have elected to discuss them because they are arguably the most important of our national institutions for acquiring, preserving, interpreting, and presenting Asian American history to the public. They are also institutions in which I have served as a key administrator or as a participant in important committees. As a result, I have had professional interest in them as an academic exercise and have been directly involved in leadership attitudes and behaviors dealing specifically with Asian Americans.

An executive summary would suggest that there has been some progress after a long period of neglect but that Asian American history remains all but ignored on the national level. This is true in spite of the fact that demographic, political, cultural, and economic indicators point to quantum leaps in the significance and impact of Asian Pacific Americans (APAs) in the recent past and that this trend will certainly intensify in the near future.[14] Even mainstream media now note the increasing numbers of APAs in the president's cabinet or among senior federal bureaucrats and within the election campaigns of congressional, state, regional, and local politicians. Dalip Singh Saund, a Sikh American in California, was the first Asian American elected to Congress (1957–1963) but for many years the only representatives in the Senate or House were from Hawai'i, where Asian Americans formed the majority population. Hawai'i is still the only state in the union that has never had a white majority. And being represented in Congress does make a difference in public history—and policy—because without the efforts and influence of Senators Daniel Inouye and, especially, Spark Matsunaga from Hawai'i, or Congressmen Norman Mineta and Robert Matsui from California, redress for the unconstitutional incarceration of Japanese Americans during World War II would never have been achieved in 1988.

Similarly, the 2011 and 2012 passages of resolutions expressing "regret" for the Chinese Exclusion Act of 1882 and for subsequent actions that denied Asians and Pacific Islanders the right to enter the United States or to live there peacefully or to become naturalized citizens and vote, were made possible largely through efforts led by Congresswoman Judy Chu from Los Angeles. Remarkably, she and her allies got both the Senate and the House to deliver bipartisan, unanimous support. This political accomplishment was as momentous as the successful drive for redress, led by the Japanese American community. And Congresswoman Chu and community leaders are absolutely clear that the work ahead in terms of educating the public about the Exclusion Acts must be a major priority. Thus, while there has been considerable scholarly research and publication on this general topic, it is certain that more awareness of these tragic and racist acts will result from public history efforts following these congressional actions. Congress and other political institutions and actions provide a particularly important venue for public history. One result was APA History Month, which began with President Jimmy Carter's designation of an APA History Week and the eventual designation of each May as APA History Month.

The Smithsonian Institution has nineteen museums, including the national museums of American History, Natural History, Air and Space, Portrait Gallery and American Art, as well as dozens of research and educational units, such as the Center for Folklife and Cultural Heritage. The Library of Congress is the world's largest library, with books, prints, photographs, serials, moving images, sound recordings including folk songs, and much more. The National Park Service oversees the natural resources as well as many of the cultural treasures of the United States. There are other institutions and agencies, including the National Archives and Records Administration and the National Endowments for the Arts and for the Humanities, which largely regrant funds from Congress. There are also many ways to deliver public history—various forms of media, including newspapers, popular magazines, radio, television, film, and the Internet all supply vast amounts of public history for mass consumption. Websites, in particular, now include increasing amounts of documents, photos, moving images, oral histories, and genealogies. Some of these collected archives are digitized, allowing for sophisticated searchable databases. Densho, for example, at www.densho.org, is the largest Asian American website. Japanese for "passing on to the next generation," Densho is a digitized collection of more than seven hundred video histories and a massive database of documents from the World War II incarceration of Japanese Americans.[15] But national institutions like the SI, LoC, and NPS remain critically important because they carry the imprimatur of the nation and justify or validate the credibility of claims made by APA communities regarding their value, significance, or, even, very existence.

THE SMITHSONIAN INSTITUTION

The SI was established by Congress in 1846 with a mission to "increase and diffuse knowledge." Like other mainstream institutions, the SI has been vulnerable to criticism for its historical legacy of marginalizing or demeaning people of color. However, in the twenty-first century, there is change in the wind. The National Museum of the American Indian opened to the public in 2004. The National Museum of African American History and Culture will open its doors on the Washington Mall in 2016. There is legislation pending to create a Latino museum; in the meantime a vibrant Latino Center provides guidance to sister units within the Institution and leadership to Latino arts and culture organizations across the country. Established by Congress in 1997, the center has, in addition to operating funds, an annual "pool" of $1,000,000 to support efforts by other SI units in Latino-themed research, collection, public programming, and exhibitions. Finally, while the Asian Pacific American Center was also established in 1997, there is still no indication that any APA museum might be envisioned. The following account is based largely on my direct experiences as director of the APA program in 1997–2010, until I left the Smithsonian.[16]

In those thirteen years, APA communities finally found a congenial home within the Smithsonian. We hosted or created over a dozen exhibitions, partnered with sister units to initiate major programs, acquired significant artifacts, and hosted hundreds of public programs, including book readings, film showings, lectures, professional dance and music performances, and community art festivals. All this was accomplished with two staff positions supported by the Smithsonian. In addition, we had the services, earlier, of a half-time, dedicated development person. Later, we often raised funds for or pleaded with the administration (the "Castle") for modest sums for a part-time development person. Our program raised an average of approximately $500,000 each year for a wide variety of projects. Fundraising became a crucial part of the program, without which few projects could have been implemented and development work immediately and inevitably locked itself into any substantial project we considered. Since this was the only way to increase our presence in the making of public history with and through the Smithsonian, it quickly became part of our DNA.

The APA program was established during 1995–1997, while I was a consultant to SI exploring directions the Institution might consider for this demographic, given the momentum then in motion for the three other major "racial" groups. This initiative depended entirely on the goodwill of James Early, then the assistant secretary for education and public service, who was encouraged by Marshall Wong, the head of the Office of Wider Audience Development, the Smithsonian's version of an affirmative action unit. It was not coincidental that Early was African American and had been a participant in progressive politics decades earlier in the University of California, Berkeley, area where he had personal and political allies who were APA activists. They were involved in what was then known as the Third World movement, composed of left-leaning organizations from communities of color. For the SI, the major accomplishment in that early period was the creation of an advisory group carefully selected to provide maximum impact on the Institution. This group was absolutely critical to the establishment of the APA program.[17]

On July 1, 1997, I became the founding director of the APA program with critical support from Stacey Suyat, who had been working with Wong in the Office of Wider Audience Development. She and, later, Gina Inocencio were program specialists who became partners in the extraordinary development of the program. To understand the context, it is important to note that there had been only one major exhibition at SI focusing on Asian Americans in the 150 years prior to 1997—that was the critical and critically acclaimed "A More Perfect Union" show—which treated the World War II experiences of Japanese Americans, both wholesale forced removal and incarceration as well as the military exploits, in courageous and sensitive fashion. The curator Tom Crouch, not then an authority on the subject, and his assistant, Jennifer Locke (now Jones), crafted a phenomenal exhibition that managed to tell many stories, including that of prisoners resisting government "opportunities" to proclaim their loyalty to the United States, within the main narrative of official actions in violation of the Constitution. The exhibition opened in 1987, receiving many awards. In 2001, principally funded by a Rockefeller Foundation grant which I secured, the American History Museum launched an extensive, also award-winning, website of this exhibit. But the exalted status of this single exhibition ironically highlights the fact of its solitary existence. It is useful to recall, also, that "A More Perfect Union" was not designed to help museumgoers reflect on the experiences of Japanese Americans; rather, it used their World War II history to focus on the fragility of the Constitution. The year 1987 was being commemorated by the American History Museum as the two hundredth anniversary of the Constitution.

The opening of the APA program heralded an unprecedented series of exhibitions when we negotiated the right to space in the Arts and Industries Building, the second oldest on the Mall, after the Smithsonian Castle. The A&I Building would soon be closed for extensive renovations but for a few precious years it provided critical space for us. The first example was a huge success—showcasing a large exhibit from the Japanese American National Museum, "From Bento to Mixed Plate: Americans of

Japanese Ancestry in Multicultural Hawai'i," in 1999.[18] In 2001, we used the same venue to host three separate exhibitions on Chinese Americans: "On Gold Mountain," "Fly to Freedom," and "Gateway to Gold Mountain." "Kahoʻolawe: Ke Aloha Kupaʻa I Kaʻaina" (Steadfast Love of the Land) arrived from the Bishop Museum in Honolulu in 2001.[19] In 2003, the program created an exhibit with eighteen Korean American artists to commemorate the centennial of significant Korean immigration; in that same year, we produced one major public event every month, highlighting Korean American experiences, with large receptions following each.[20] "Through My Father's Eyes," featuring work from a Filipino American photographer, was installed in the American History Museum in 2004. In 2005, we hosted a traveling exhibit of undersea photographs by a Japanese artist. In 2007, we created "Exit Saigon, Enter Little Saigon," a major show on Vietnamese Americans. Then in 2008 we produced "Singgalot: Ties that Bind." Three of the exhibits, two Filipino American and one Vietnamese American shows, became traveling versions, all touring at least fifteen cities in three-year periods. In 2009, I concluded discussions with Indian American leaders in the Washington, D.C., region, to create "Homespun"—an exhibit that opened in 2013. In 2009, I negotiated a grant with the Kellogg Foundation for an introductory "APA 101" exhibition, also in 2013.[21] All of these exhibitions have fascinating stories embedded in their histories, including the many different ways in which significant amounts of funding could be secured. The APA Center was vital in hosting or creating these exhibitions.

It is difficult to overstate the importance of "being at the table" to effect change at large, conservative, mainstream institutions like the Smithsonian. The SI has always found itself subject to political influence, and issues like the *Enola Gay* controversy were dangerous, but sometimes the potential for political influence was extremely useful.[22] The secretary and the Board of Regents were/are ever mindful that two-thirds of SI's operating budget comes from congressional appropriations; hence the presence of influential political figures like Mineta or Inouye made them take notice of the APA program. Our work was both demanding and fulfilling because diversity and balance requirements required that I be present, as the sole senior APA executive, a fact that provided—and required—consistent opportunities to participate in high-level committees, including many with responsibilities for budget and program issues. These working opportunities also secured personal contacts with museum and center directors for direct solicitation of APA interests. This form of intervention was especially critical with the National Museum of American History, where I was soon offered a simultaneous position as a curator—thus providing me authority to collect artifacts with APA significance without having to justify such acquisitions to other curators. Another staff member now continues to add dozens of artifacts every year and participates in creating exhibits emanating from American history initiatives, independent of APA Center support. This also happened with the Smithsonian American Art Museum and the National Portrait Gallery, where Asian American participation has increased dramatically over the last decade.[23] Similar personal connections with the directors of the Sackler Freer Galleries, Air and Space Museum, Natural History, Hirshhorn Gallery, and the National Museum of the American Indian (NMAI) made possible multiple partnerships, enabling the APA program to use their auditoriums and exhibit spaces for displays, lectures, film showings, and community participation. Because the APA Center does not have its own space, we had to broker deals constantly, often years in advance, in order to secure venues for our programs.[24]

Of all federal agencies, SI is best positioned to move forward with vigor and will have a positive impact on a national sensitivity toward Asian American history and culture. We should see, then, increased activity in memory making for APAs. In part, this is because of the Institution's sensitivity to political realities, especially in the national electoral realm, which, as noted, is inexorably moving in the direction of expanding APA influence. Second, the field of Asian American studies, including Asian American history, is stable and growing, extending its reach into all regions of the nation, including the South, which had not previously seen such activity. Third, the APA program itself is firmly embedded in the SI structure.

THE LIBRARY OF CONGRESS

In 2011–2012, I was appointed the acting chief of the Asian Division in the Library of Congress. The Library of Congress (LoC) is the oldest federal cultural agency, having been established in 1800 to serve members of Congress. Its mission was "to support the Congress in fulfilling its constitutional duties and to further the progress of knowledge and creativity for the benefit of the American people."[25] It continues this core mission with more than seven hundred staff whose principal responsibility is to respond to direct inquiries from members of Congress. But the total library staff includes over 3,500 people, including nearly thirty in the Asian Division alone. The library has grown to include vast amounts of published books from across the globe as well as prints, photographs, moving images, and sound recordings in addition to personal papers and manuscripts. The Manuscript Collection includes the papers of the former congresswoman Patsy Takemoto Mink, who authored the famous Title IX legislation, which paved the way for massive changes in women's participation in college athletics and on campus governance and resource allocation in general. The LoC has made no significant attempt to assess or enhance its holdings of American minority groups, including Asian Americans. Perhaps the acquisition process makes such concerns appear trivial to senior leadership—because copyright deposits in 2011 alone included more than 700,000 works. Approximately 22,000 items arrive every working day, and the library selects 10,000 to be added to its permanent collections. In this era of long-term federal budget downsizing, LoC has suffered significant loss of staff while the need for space grows ever more acute. Many volumes spill onto the floors between shelves. Still, the fact remains that Asian American history, in the form of folklife, such as songs and stories, prints and photographs, rare books, moving images, journals, immigrant literature, and newspapers both past and contemporary, continues to suffer benign neglect.

The Library has an active Asian Division, which traditionally acquired works in Asian languages only until, in 2007, Congressman Michael Honda of San Jose, California, requested that it include an Asian American Pacific Islander (AAPI) Collection to acknowledge the growing significance of this demographic group. No other American "ethnic minority" groups are similarly recognized. Fortunately, at the time, the chief of the Asian Division, Hwa-Wei Lee, was both supportive and collaborative and the AAPI Collection was launched in 2008 in spite of LoC resistance. Reme Grefalda was appointed the founding curator of the collection, which continues its impressive growth in substance, volume, and diversity. Among the individuals and institutions now represented in the LoC as a result of this initiative are the playwright Philip Kan Gotanda, the theater photographer Lia Chang, the demographer Juanita Tamayo Lott, Asian American Studies pioneer Betty Lee Sung, the Filipino activist Royal Morales, the author and ceramicist Jade Snow Wong, and the labor organizer and writer Carlos Bulosan. There are also organizational papers from a Vietnamese refugee support group in the United States and from a Japanese American nonprofit that sponsors Vietnamese youngsters into colleges. This latter organization was created by Japanese Americans who had been assisted out of World War II camps and into colleges by the American Friends Service Committee, the Quakers, and who wished to pay the tribute forward to another group requiring financial, cultural, and political support.[26]

Unlike the Smithsonian with its independent Center firmly sited in the institutional structure, LoC's AAPI Collection is fragile, even with its important and growing collection of individual and personal papers. Because it is a "creature of Congress," and was literally established at the behest of one Member the Collection will be hard-put to maintain a vigorous program of acquisition and outreach absent political or public support.[27]

THE NATIONAL PARK SERVICE

In 2010, I was appointed to serve on the Landmarks Committee of the National Park Service Advisory Board. The National Park Service (NPS) is an enormous federal enterprise, formally in existence since 1916 but with earlier antecedents, including Yellowstone, America's first national park, which was established in 1872. The NPS has more than 20,000 staff and an annual budget of over $3,000,000,000. NPS is responsible for much more than its justly famous stewardship of the well-known and intensely visited national parks across the nation. The Service resides in the Department of the Interior and has assigned its imprimatur of "National Historic Place" to over 80,000 sites, notably those associated with the rich and famous. Fewer than 2,500 sites have been designated National Historic Landmarks, however, after a much more rigorous process of application and review. But only a tiny percentage of Historic Places and Historic Landmarks reflects significant Asian American experiences. And it is only recently that NPS has turned its attention to sites that highlight the experiences of

America's diverse peoples of color.[28] I have observed with great interest the Landmarks Committee's focus on ethnic/racial diversity. The NPS has only recently turned serious attention to Asian American sites; progress has been gradual and modest. Much of the credit for any momentum belongs to Dr. Antoinette Lee, who retired in June 2012 after a distinguished career in NPS. She was the Assistant Associate Director of Historical Documentation Programs, overseeing, among others, the National Register of Historic Places and the National Historic Landmarks Program.[29]

The former Secretary of the Interior, Ken Salazar, instructed the NPS to move pro-actively toward identifying historic sites important to Latino/Hispanic experiences. A "theme" study implemented by Latino scholars has been completed and is available for review. A similar study for Asian Americans is currently being implemented through an NPS–Organization of American Historians partnership and is scheduled for completion in 2016.[30] These two studies have the potential of moving the NPS to designate many more Historical Landmarks for significant Latino and Asian American experiences, thus providing the general public with many more opportunities to encounter a broader, more accurate, series of public history sites.

Japanese Americans and World War II

On December 2, 1946, the *Los Angeles Times* noted that "they've knocked down Manzanar and hauled the pieces away." Less than a year after the last of 10,000 Japanese Americans had left the now-notorious War Relocation Authority camp, the barracks had been dismantled and the lumber sold to World War II veterans. The former director of Manzanar, Ralph Merritt, noted that this was "one of the finest ways government money can be spent." Further, Merritt added: "And please say that Manzanar is not being demolished—it's merely being redistributed."[31]

Few Americans know the story of Manzanar or of the forced removal and incarceration of 120,000 Japanese Americans during World War II, after Japan's Imperial Navy attacked Pearl Harbor. President Franklin Roosevelt issued Executive Order 9066 on February 19, 1942, which paved the way for the Army to cleanse the entire West Coast of anyone descended from a Japanese person. No one was charged with any crime and no one was provided a hearing or trial by judge or jury. On August 10, 1988, President Ronald Reagan apologized on behalf of the nation for this travesty, and he helped to establish the mechanism for individual checks of $20,000 for each surviving Japanese American who had been incarcerated.[32] The literature and media sources on this topic are voluminous. Here, I focus on a few salient points regarding the memory and memorialization of this largest forced removal in American history.

In 1948, the U.S. government made token payments to Japanese Americans who had suffered losses due to the incarceration, but these amounted to less than $40,000,000, an amount even at the time estimated to be one-tenth of the value of lost property. Later, economists placed a much larger value on the loss. In 1952 the McCarran-Walter Act for the first time allowed immigrants from Japan the right to become naturalized American citizens and to vote. But it was not until the 1970s, a full quarter-century after the end of the war, that any serious calls were made for the government to apologize and make amends. As the demolition of the Manzanar camp made clear, the nation was then intent upon creating images of "the good war," and the unconstitutional incarceration of its Japanese American population did not fit well with that effort. At the same time, the energies of the Japanese American community were directed toward readjustment into society and securing some of the benefits of an expanding economy. In that process, the Japanese American Citizens League had become the undisputed representative of the group, and it squashed efforts to complicate its message of the wartime unconstitutional incarceration of an innocent, compliant, and heroically patriotic community. Thus, the voices of those who had resisted the incarceration through legal/constitutional venues, by protesting conditions in the camps, by becoming belligerently pro-Japan in their sentiments, and, especially, by insisting that the 1944 imposition of the draft on their numbers while still held in American concentration camps was unconstitutional—those voices were forcibly stilled for two more decades. So what had changed in the years between the 1960s and the 1980s?

Perhaps asking the question in this way leads to some answers. First, the entire political and cultural context of American society had undergone serious transformation as a result of the antiwar and civil rights/antiracism/ethnic power movements. It had become normal to question the validity of state-sponsored and state-driven pronouncements once we learned, publicly and officially, that "the government" could and did lie to its people. It had become far easier, too, to convince Japanese Americans to articulate their collective grievances, especially once younger generations became involved.[33] Second, Asian Americans were actively seeking contemporary and historical bonds with other "Third World" advocates. The World War II incarceration was an ideal example of common oppression. Third, the advent of Asian American studies meant that unprecedented numbers of faculty researchers, graduate and undergraduate students, and individuals in policy settings as well as public history institutions could turn their training and energy into exploration of World War II experiences. Individual memoirs and artistic output, including poetry, novels, and plays, as well as the pioneering efforts of nonprofessional historians like Michi Weglyn fundamentally changed the trajectory of the movements for remembering the incarceration and for redress. Simultaneously, and perhaps ironically, mainstream movements to honor the World War II veterans of the "Greatest Generation" were now induced to include the hitherto unacknowledged combat heroics of the segregated Japanese American military units—the 100th Infantry Battalion and the 442nd Regimental Combat Team, as well as the Military Intelligence Service.[34] The recognition of battlefield heroism underscored the irony of forced removal and incarceration of their families and communities.

All of these projects, individual and collective, coalesced in a movement to secure an official apology and monetary redress from the United States. When this initiative took shape in the mid-1970s, few believed it would ultimately succeed. Most of us felt, nonetheless, that the educational reach of the project, for the general public but primarily for our own communities, would be the best possible outcome. But the timing was perfect and the three different organized efforts eventually used memories of the incarceration and the various media employed to generate ever-widening circles of support.

Two further points: first, Senators Spark Matsunaga and Daniel Inouye led the way by insisting that a Wartime Relocation and Internment Commission be formed to conduct nationwide public hearings before submitting a report and recommendation to Congress. They reasoned that any legislative attempt at redress prior to an overwhelming recommendation from a prestigious commission was doomed to failure. A total of 789 witnesses testified before the commission in 1981. A few non–Japanese Americans were involved in the process but the overwhelming majority of witnesses were persons incarcerated for no reason other than their ethnic heritage. The outpouring of memory was overwhelming; indeed, the opportunity to gather their memories of such a traumatic experience was itself galvanizing. Reopening the venues to memories they had considered, for three decades, to be obsolete, much too damaging, and simply too dangerous, became not only possible but also potentially therapeutic. The result was a report in 1983, which recommended that Congress approve legislation for a formal apology and reparations of $20,000 to each person incarcerated.[35] Second, there was concern that Reagan would veto the legislation and undo all the work to date. But someone recalled that, during World War II, Ronald Reagan had participated in an official presentation of a gold star service banner to the mother of a Japanese American in the 442nd who was killed in combat in Europe. When reminded of this event, Reagan remembered the circumstances and was moved to sign the bill. Memories, then, individual and collective, private and official, cohered to influence public policy decisively even when the memorialization contradicted the official narrative of the nation.[36]

One indication of the energy released by earlier efforts to remember Japanese American World War II experiences was the sheer number of institutions and memorials formally dedicated after 1980. In 1981, the National Japanese American Historical Society was formed in San Francisco; in 1987, the Japanese Cultural Center of Hawai'i was established in Honolulu and, in 1992, the large and impressive Japanese American National Museum was dedicated in Los Angeles. There followed, in succession, the Japanese American Historical Plaza in Portland, Oregon (1990), the Japanese American Internment Memorial in San Jose, California (March 5, 1994), the Go for Broke Monument in Los Angeles (1999), the Gordon Hirabayashi Recreation Site in the Coronado National Forest (1999), the National Japanese American Memorial to Patriotism during World War II (2000), the Oregon Nikkei Legacy Center (2004), and the Japanese-American Detainment Camp Memorial in the Merced, California, fairgrounds (2010). Among the former War Relocation Authority camps, Manzanar and Tule Lake (California), Poston (Arizona), Topaz (Utah), Amache (Colorado), Minidoka (Idaho), Jerome and Rohwer (Arkansas), and Heart Mountain (Wyoming) have varying degrees of historic site designation and memorials, monuments, or recreated facilities as well as interpretive centers.[37]

I was on the original board that created the National Japanese American Memorial Foundation (NJAMF), which lies in the shadow of the U.S. Capitol, close to Union

Station in Washington, D.C. I recently rejoined its board, which oversees educational programming for the NJAMF. The full title of the memorial is the National Japanese American Memorial to Patriotism during World War II. This title reflects a compromise with a D.C. policy prohibiting memorials to specific ethnic groups. "Patriotism during World War II" placed the memorial in a different category. It has been cited as one of the ten most beautiful memorials in D.C. and devotes equal space both to the exploits of the World War II veterans as well as the mass removal and incarceration of 120,000 Japanese Americans. It also emphasizes the redress movement and Reagan's signing of HR 442. Its history and vicissitudes are stark reminders of the challenges of memory and memorialization; the memorial itself was funded ($16,000,000) largely by Japanese Americans themselves), but issues of whose voices should be carved in granite troubled the board.[38] The wounds were severe, deep, and enduring.[39] The NJAMF will need to work through issues of representation carefully to determine whose memories are publicly honored and in what ways.

The 1882 Chinese Exclusion Act

In 1882 Congress enacted legislation singling out the Chinese as the only national/racial group unfit to immigrate to the United States or to become naturalized citizens. It was the first incidence of ethnic/racial targeting for purposes of denying entry to American shores. Subsequent acts led to the exclusion of all immigrants from Asia and, eventually, Pacific Islanders as well. These acts ruptured numerous families, causing enormous hardship. This cruel circumstance led to extra-legal efforts to reunite families and led to the practice of "paper sons" and "paper daughters," who entered the United States formally as fictitious children of Chinese Americans who had fathered them while on return trips to China. Immigration officials soon learned of this practice and attempted to exclude these paper sons and daughters through intense questioning of lineage, household, and village details to "expose" the fraudulent applicants. In response, the Chinese resorted to extraordinary "coaching books," which required applicants to memorize details to thwart the officials. These included questions like requiring prospective immigrants to list the names of all second cousins on the mother's side, provide the number of stone steps from front door to village square, describe the view from a bedroom window on the south side, or count the number of apple and pear trees in the back garden. In the process, men, women and children were kept in detention for weeks or months at the Angel Island Immigration Station in San Francisco Bay, which functioned to deter newcomers, as opposed to Ellis Island, which served largely as a welcoming entry point for most Europeans.[40] But unlike the decades-long efforts to secure redress for Japanese Americans, an apology for the Chinese Exclusion Act was achieved with unanimous resolutions from the House in 2011 and the Senate in 2012, after only two years of lobbying and educational outreach.

The public history and memorializing stories of the 1882 Chinese Exclusion Act Project have just begun. Coincidentally, the exhibition "Attachments: Faces and Stories from America's Gates" opened in the National Archives Building in Washington, D.C., in 2012 with an impressive number of Asian/Chinese examples. Martin Gold, an attorney, provided expert professional assistance and managed to complete a book on the project as well, *Forbidden Citizens: Chinese Exclusion and the U.S. Congress.*[41] I joined this effort early and, as with Japanese American redress, seriously miscalculated its chances for success, believing that securing the resolutions would be impossible in the current political climate. The ultimate success of these efforts amounts to a textbook account of successful lobbying at its finest in the halls of Congress, tied to impressive grassroots organizing across the country. It is more than likely that the ensuing educational program, in the form of television and film documentaries, museum exhibitions, oral histories, and websites emanating from this legislative achievement will, as in the Japanese American redress movement, do much to increase general awareness of the history and heartache imposed by these exclusion acts.

The leaders of the project were Michael Lin, the former head of the Organization of Chinese Americans, and Ted Gong, who did much of the groundwork. Gong suggests that the effort connects him to the early mission of Asian American studies: "The 1882 Project became more and more an effort to demand that our history would not be invisible and that we would not let someone else tell our stories for us. It became about forcing America to recognize that we were here building the United States alongside with everyone else despite that photo at Promontory Point [Utah]. And, with that recognition, the struggles of our parents and forebears could be properly honored, which gives me a great sense of fulfillment."[42]

Scholars and public historians of Asian America have made considerable progress in attempts to insert their previous "margins" into the American "mainstream" narrative, as the historian Gary Okihiro has suggested.[43] Academic research and publication, the serious and gritty work of digging into archives and solitary hours thinking and writing, created the foundational bedrock of intellectual firepower for the arsenal used by public history warriors. But the sheer amount of public education and political persuasion to date owes much to public history. There are enormous gaps in both academic and public histories, and filling them in can both broaden our understanding of the experiences of Asian Americans and Pacific Islander Americans as well as expand the ways in which these stories enhance and deepen our comprehension of American history writ large.

NOTES

1. Michael Kammen, *Mystic Chords of Memory: The Transformation of Tradition in American Culture* (New York: Vintage, 1993), 19.
2. Gutzon Borglum, the sculptor who designed Rushmore, was also involved in the massive frieze of Confederate heroes on Stone Mountain in Georgia. Borglum was a member of the

Ku Klux Klan. The official website of the city of Stone Mountain, which was the site of the Klan's rebirth in the 1920s, makes no mention of Borglum.

3. See, for example, G. Kurt Piehler, *Remembering War the American Way* (Washington, DC: Smithsonian Institution, 1995).

4. Donald Richie, *The Films of Akira Kurosawa* (Berkeley: University of California Press, 1984).

5. See Maryanne Garry and Harlene Hayne, eds., *Do Justice and Let the Sky Fall: Elizabeth Loftus and Her Contributions to Science, Law, and Academic Freedom* (Mahwah: Lawrence Erlbaum, 2006).

6. Some issues of public memory are far more consequential and complex. See, for example, Erika Doss, *Memorial Mania: Public Feeling in America* (Chicago: University of Chicago Press, 2010); Edward Linenthal, *Preserving Memory: The Struggle to Create America's Holocaust Museum* (New York: Columbia University Press, 2001 [1995]); Roy Rosenzweig and David Thelen, *The Presence of the Past: Popular Uses of the Past in American Life* (New York: Columbia University Press, 1998); Greg Dickinson, Carole Blair, and Brian Ott, eds., *Places of Public Memory: The Rhetoric of Museums and Memorials* (Tuscaloosa: University of Alabama Press, 2010); and James Gardner and Peter LaPaglia, eds., *Public History: Essays from the Field* (Malabar, FL: Krieger, 2004).

7. See, especially, Michel-Rolph Trouillot, *Silencing the Past: Power and Production of History* (Boston: Beacon, 1995).

8. Gordon Chang, a professor in Stanford's History Department, reports that his university, created by Leland Stanford, one of the original owners of the Central Pacific, has now agreed to support the creation of a new archive for the history of these Chinese workers. Courtesy Dongfang Shao, Chief of the Asian Division, Library of Congress, personal communication, September 10, 2012.

9. There is extensive literature on this subject; for a quick and reliable summary, see the online "encyclopedia" of terms, events, and people involved in incarceration at www.densho.org. Efforts to parlay the unexpectedly rapid passage of resolutions by both the Senate (unanimous consent of Senate Resolution 201, on October 6, 2011) and House (unanimous voice vote of House Resolution 683 on June 18, 2012) of the 1882 apologies into large-scale educational projects are ongoing. See, for example, "1882 Project: A Voice for Protecting American Civil Rights" (Washington, DC: 1882 Project, 2012).

10. Shared authority is a concept made popular by Michael Frisch in his work on the importance of oral history as a vital part of public history. See *A Shared Authority: Essays on the Craft and Meaning of Oral and Public History* (Albany: State University of New York Press, 1990).

11. See, for example, the first anthology widely used as a text in the field: *Roots: An Asian American Reader*, ed. Amy Tachiki, Eddie Wong, Franklin Odo, with Buck Wong. It was published in 1971 by UCLA's Asian American Studies Center.

12. The National Council on Public History was established in 1979. It publishes, with the University of California, Santa Barbara, the major journal in the field, *The Public Historian.* Its stated mission is "making the past useful in the present and to encouraging collaboration between historians and their public. Our work begins in the belief that historical understanding is of essential value in society."

13. There are others, including the National Trust for Historic Preservation, which was formed as a federal agency but now operates as a very large and influential private institution.

14. Asian Pacific Americans (APAs) or Asian Americans and Pacific Islanders (AAPIs) include Pacific Islander Americans who require their own considered treatment. For evidence that APAs are quickly becoming critically important in many areas, including regional and national electoral politics, see the pamphlet "Up for Grabs: America's Swing Vote, Asian Americans and Pacific Islanders" (Washington, DC: Asian American Justice Center, 2012); and *2012 Policy Platform: Framing Issues and Recommendations to Improve the Lives of Asian American, Native Hawaiian and Pacific Islander Communities* (Takoma Park, MD: National Council of Asian Pacific Americans, 2012).

15. See www.densho.org. Since the summer of 2012, I have been a senior scholar at Densho. A more recent site is the South Asian American Digital Archive: www.saadigitalarchive.org.

16. This section on SI is the most detailed because I was directly involved for an extended period of thirteen years. There is, of course, more to the story than my personal involvement but much of what happened then was directly or indirectly influenced by being "at the table." The Smithsonian is now irrevocably committed to some form of distributive justice for the four major "racial" groupings in America; see the proceedings of the symposium "(Re)Presenting America: The Evolution of Culturally Specific Museums" (Washington, DC: National Museum of the American Indian, April 25, 2004).

17. Norman Mineta became the chairperson of the group; he was the senior APA member of the House of Representatives (San Jose, CA) but also a sitting member of the Smithsonian's Board of Regents. The Regents oversee policy at the Smithsonian; they hire and fire the secretary, the head of the institution. Senator Daniel Inouye was already a very senior senator from Hawai'i. Dr. Amy Agbayani, an administrator at the University of Hawai'i at Manoa and a major player in Democratic Party circles in the islands, was a member as was David Kim, then responsible for outreach to APAs for Anheuser-Busch. David had his corporation write the first check to support the APA program. Professor Yen Espiritu, a professor of ethnic studies at the University of California, San Diego, was also then president of the Association for Asian American Studies. Irene Hirano was the executive director of the Japanese American National Museum in Los Angeles.

18. This was an exhibit that could not be accommodated at the time by the American History Museum so the presence of the APA program was critical.

19. Fortunately, the conflict between Native Hawaiians and the U.S. Navy over control of Kahoolawe had ended with the former reclaiming the island, thus foreclosing any protest from the public or some member of Congress. Otherwise, loud protests were hardly unlikely, since controversial exhibits, especially those with content deemed "un-American," routinely drew the ire of vociferous guardians of national "pride." The most notorious example was over the proposed exhibition featuring the *Enola Gay*, the aircraft that delivered the atomic bomb that devastated Hiroshima. The exhibit was basically derailed in the 1990s and the director of the Air and Space Museum was forced to resign. At the time, in 2001, I reported to Dennis O'Connor, assistant secretary and second in command at the Institution; he asked pointedly if the Smithsonian would become a target because the United States was then regularly bombarding Vieques in Puerto Rico in the face of growing popular anger. I told him I did not think so but was braced for trouble.

20. This took considerable negotiating because we wanted to engage a local Korean restaurant in the community. The Smithsonian had its own circle of caterers and, not surprisingly, none was a "minority" firm. Insurance, regulations, and codes were part of the barrier. We did eventually prevail, much to the delight of our audiences who enjoyed fine Korean

cuisine. But some of the museum staff objected to the pungent aromas, including some delightful kim chee.

21. Support for the introductory exhibit came after extended conversation with Dr. Al Yee of the Kellogg Foundation, who felt that many institutions and audiences would appreciate such an exhibit.

22. For a detailed analysis, see Edward T. Linenthal and Tom Englehardt, eds., *History Wars: The Enola Gay and Other Battles for the American Past* (New York: Holt, 1996).

23. The American Art Museum's director, Elizabeth "Betsy" Broun, has been most support- ive, collecting works from APA artists, supporting APA art historians, and providing a venue for a major traveling show of Japanese American World War II camp art: "The Art of Gaman: Arts and Crafts from the Japanese American Internment Camps, 1942–1946" was a major success. The Portrait Gallery's "Portraiture Now: Asian American Portraits of Encounter" was a major show featuring seven outstanding artists. The National Portrait Gallery's director, Martin Sullivan, said that it "is a provocative and path breaking show that affirms the complex realities of Asian identity in today's culture." Konrad Ng, the cur- rent director of the APA program, says, "These exceptional works are portals into the souls of the American experience, world cultures and their intersections." See the website of the APA program: www.apanews.si.edu.

24. NMAI has been especially helpful for our Native Hawaiian and Pacific Islander American communities because its mandate includes issues concerning indigenous peoples in the entire hemisphere, which includes the islands of Hawai'i.

25. *Library of Congress Magazine* 1, no. 1, September/October 2012.

26. See www.loc.gov/rr/asian/aapi.

27. Reme Grefalda, the current curator of the collection, is nearing retirement and there is widespread fear that she may not be replaced by the library.

28. For example, Hawai'i has thirty-three National Historic Landmark sites but in spite of extensive Asian American presence and participation, extending back to the 1850s, not a single one deals with this demographic, which has been the majority "racial" grouping since the early 1900s. Of the thirty-three sites, eighteen deal with Native Hawaiian sites, primarily archaeological, such as *heiau*, or sacred/burial grounds. Eleven are military dealing with World War II; two record encounters with Western powers, including an old Russian fort; one is an old sailing vessel; and one commemorates the oldest commercial sugar mill in Koloa, Kauai. See S. Allen Chambers, Jr., *National Landmarks, America's Treasures: The National Park Foundation's Complete Guide to National Historic Landmarks* (New York: John Wiley and Sons, 2000).

29. Lee inserted me into two important NPS projects: first, the planning and creation of *Asian Reflections on the American Landscape: Identifying and Interpreting Asian Heritage* (2005), for which I served as scholar/advisor; second, as a member of the National Historic Landmarks Advisory Committee. Toni's father is Chinese American. Absent her initia- tives, independent Asian American scholarly input might not have been secured at execu- tive levels of the NPS.

30. I have been asked to lead that effort; when the scholars group is organized, this will mark the first time that the NPS has engaged a formal unit of Asian American historians/ scholars.

31. Ingrid Gessner, "Erasure and Visual Recovery: Displaying Japanese American Internment Experiences," in *Visual Culture Revisited: German and American Perspectives on Visual Culture(s)*, ed. Adelmann Ralf, Andreas Fahr, Ines Katenhusen, Nic Leonhardt, Dimitri Liebsch, and Stefanie Schneider (Koln, Germany: Halem, 2007). Note that the author is

a German scholar of American studies. Gessner has done valuable work on incarceration and memory.

32. Aleuts from Alaska had also been removed from homes and communities; and several thousand Japanese Latin Americans, mostly from Peru, had been kidnapped and brought to American internment camps. Some of them received redress payments, albeit less than provided to Americans. See, for one of many resources, Yasuko Takezawa, *Breaking the Silence: Redress and Japanese American Ethnicity* (Ithaca, NY: Cornell University Press, 1995).

33. It should not be forgotten that second-generation Nisei like Edison Uno pioneered efforts to advocate for redress. We might recall also that many people were more receptive to historical examples of government wrongdoing.

34. Michi Weglyn, *Years of Infamy: The Untold Story of America's Concentration Camps* (New York: Morrow Quill, 1976). Perhaps it need be mentioned that, in 2000, President Bill Clinton conferred twenty Medals of Honor on Japanese Americans for heroism in World War II combat. This was a belated but extraordinary acknowledgment of Japanese American achievement in American mobility.

35. *Personal Justice Denied: Report of the Commission on Wartime Relocation and Internment of Civilians*, 2nd ed. (Washington, DC: Civil Liberties Public Education Fund, 1997).

36. Of course, there had to be a way to reconcile this move with the narrative; for many this became evidence that the United States was "indeed a great nation capable of admitting its errors."

37. In Canada, where treatment of Canadians of Japanese heritage was even more barbaric, there is the Japanese Canadian National Museum, which began life as the Nikkei National Museum in 2000 in British Columbia. In Japan, several impressive museums have emerged to mark the experiences of their diaspora; see the website, www.Japanese-American and Nikkei Museums in Japan.

38. This was a classic example of writing or rewriting history in the form of a national memorial. There is not yet a synthesis of the dispute and its resolution; among the major players are Mike Masaoka, Grant Ujifusa, Frank Sogi, Mel Chiogyoji, Kelly Kuwayama, Bill Hosokawa, Gerald Yamada, Deborah Lim, Daniel Inouye, and the D.C. Commission on Fine Arts.

39. They resurfaced in a musical named *Allegiance*, which premiered in San Diego in September 2012. It featured George Takei and Lea Salonga. See www.allegiancemusical.com for reviews and background information about Mike Masaoka.

40. Erika Lee and Judy Yung, *Angel Island: Immigrant Gateway to America* (New York: Oxford University Press, 2010), is the latest and most detailed of many treatments of this subject.

41. See www.TheCapitol.Net.

42. Personal communication, email, September 25, 2012.

43. Gary Okihiro, *Margins and Mainstreams: Asians in American History and Culture* (Seattle: University of Washington Press, 1994).

FURTHER READING

Chambers, S. Allen, Jr. *National Landmarks, America's Treasures: The National Park Foundation's Complete Guide to National Historic Landmarks.* New York: John Wiley and Sons, 2000.

Lee, Erika, and Judy Yung. *Angel Island: Immigrant Gateway to America.* New York: Oxford University Press, 2010.

Linenthal, Edward. *Preserving Memory: The Struggle to Create America's Holocaust Museum*. New York: Columbia University Press, 2001 [1995].

Piehler, G. Kurt. *Remembering War the American Way*. Washington, DC: Smithsonian Institution, 1995.

Rosenzweig, Roy, and David Thelen. *The Presence of the Past: Popular Uses of the Past in American Life*. New York: Columbia University Press, 1998.

Trouillot, Michel-Rolph. *Silencing the Past: Power and Production of History*. Boston: Beacon, 1995.

CHAPTER 25

ASIAN AMERICAN LEGAL HISTORY

GREG ROBINSON

THE legal history of Asian Americans is a complex tapestry that joins together many different strands: federal and state laws, military decrees, administrative regulations, and diverse forms of executive intervention. Nevertheless, federal and state court rulings constitute the core of this history. The reason is evident: throughout most of the two centuries spanned by their presence in the United States, people of Asian ancestry faced legalized racial inequality on the national level in the shape of restrictions on immigration and bars to naturalization (and thereby suffrage), which were then aggravated by discriminatory laws in many states. As with other racialized groups denied full access to voting rights, the main avenue of recourse for Asian Americans was through the courts.

From the time of their first arrival in the early nineteenth century, Asian immigrants and their children continually brought legal action in defense of their civil rights. Although they won some landmark victories over the following century, their record was at best mixed, and even such success as they had in the courts was generally limited in larger terms. Beginning in the 1940s, however, the arc of Asian American legal history underwent a major swing. On the one hand, the national government undertook a sweeping race-based denial of constitutional freedoms in the shape of the official wartime removal of West Coast Japanese Americans, a policy upheld by the judiciary. On the other hand, the wartime period signaled an epochal reversal in federal policy, from hostility toward Asian Americans to support for their civil rights, one gradually followed by the states. An additional seismic shift took place in the generation after 1965, when changes in immigration law—including the entry of large numbers of Southeast Asian refugees—reshaped the demography and legal status of Asian America, bringing new legal questions to the fore. Meanwhile, the Japanese American redress movement, working through interconnected legislative and legal campaigns, helped usher in both official recognition of past injustices and a new birth of freedom for American society.

Even as the legal status of Asian Americans has advanced over time, the scholarly literature covering it has mushroomed in dramatic fashion.[1] The field scarcely existed before 1970, yet by the 1980s research in legal history came to play a decisive role in the redress movement, notably in the *coram nobis* (writ of error) lawsuits of the former defendants in the "Japanese internment" cases. The last generation has seen a shift in both the methodological and intellectual foundations of writing on the subject. Many newer works reflect the influence of overall trends in historiography, such as multigroup approaches or the inclusion of issues of gender and sexuality. Like Asian American history generally, legal histories have reframed their subject within larger discussions of transnationalism and U.S. empire: in the process, Hawai'i, home of the nation's most concentrated and influential Asian population, has assumed a more central place in historical discussions of Asian Americans and the law. At the same time, advances in legal scholarship, most notably the rise of the school of critical legal studies (an offshoot of critical race theory), have left their traces on these discussions.

THE EARLY PERIOD

While some accounts contend that the first Asians to immigrate to the United States were the "Manilamen," successive groups of Filipino sailors who jumped ship and settled in Louisiana before statehood in 1812, and a few individuals entered the United States in succeeding decades, the legal history of Asian Americans can properly be said to start with 1849. The California Gold Rush catalyzed the arrival of 10,000 Chinese, the first large group of East Asian people to migrate to the United States. With their settlement emerged a unique legal regime to classify and cover them—and this is a development of capital importance because the same regime would later be extended to fit all other groups. According to the 1790 naturalization act, only "free white" immigrants were allowed to become naturalized American citizens. It is not clear whether this provision reflected the will of the nation's founders to limit citizenship to Caucasians, or simply to exclude the involuntary African immigrants brought as slaves—"white" thus meaning not black. In either case, officials in California and Washington, DC alike understood these new immigrants as falling on the black side of the color line and as unfit for citizenship on racial grounds. Ironically, even after Congress approved the 14th Amendment, assuring citizenship to black Americans, in the midst of the politically tinged humanitarianism of the early Reconstruction era, and opened naturalization to free African immigrants—an all-but-nonexistent category—it declined to lift the corollary bar on Asian citizenship that had sprung from it.

The upshot was that the Chinese were harassed by a series of discriminatory laws, a pattern that persisted for nearly a century. (The tide of hostility lessened only during the 1860s, when the urgent needs of business interests for Chinese labor to build a transcontinental railroad and for a commercial treaty with China to expand trade temporarily diluted anti-immigrant efforts.) Chinese residents in California and other states were successively barred from testifying against whites in court, removed from jury service, subjected to unequal taxation, and limited in their right to work and own businesses.

In a number of states, ethnic Chinese were barred from intermarrying with whites. In addition, as Jean Pfaelzer reminds us, Chinese were singled out for persecution in dozens of Western towns, where they were robbed of their possessions and forcibly expelled by mobs, often with the collusion of police and judicial authorities.[2]

On the federal level, although in the Burlingame Treaty of 1868 the United States and China formally granted permission to each other's nationals to reside legally in their countries, beginning in 1882 Congress enacted a series of measures forbidding entry to the United States to all but a select few categories of Chinese immigrants. (Even before formal exclusion, Chinese women had been discouraged from entry due to the Page Law of 1875, under which they were subject to humiliating examination as suspected prostitutes.) Those men already in the country, like black Americans in the era of the Fugitive Slave Act, were required to carry passes. They were also banned from bringing in wives from China, which meant that Chinatowns remained largely bachelor enclaves and few ethnic Chinese children were born in America.

In response, Chinese immigrants established the pattern by which Asian Americans deprived of their rights used the courts to obtain redress. The Chinese brought successful actions to force prosecution of rioters, reimburse property losses, and overturn laws preventing them from being hired for trades. In 1885, the Tape family secured a ruling assuring all their children admission (albeit segregated) to public schools in California. Chinese Americans won a pair of historic victories in the U.S. Supreme Court. In the case of *Yick Wo v. Hopkins* (1886), the Court ruled that laws that were race-neutral on their face but were enforced in discriminatory fashion, or had a "disparate impact" on some groups, were unconstitutional under the 14th Amendment. The very next year, however, the Court vitiated much of that ruling by its decision in *In re Thomas Baldwin* (1887) that the 14th Amendment did not apply to Chinese aliens. A more influential precedent was set in *United States v. Wong Kim Ark* (1898), in which the Court decreed that all children born in the United States, irrespective of race or citizenship of parents, were birthright citizens. Nevertheless, the balance of power weighed against Chinese Americans. In cases at the turn of the century, the Court upheld the Chinese Exclusion Act, with its unequal access to entry, and approved the requirement that resident Chinese carry identity cards. Even more importantly, the Chinese Exclusion cases laid the first basis for the courts to decree the "plenary power" doctrine, still considered as controlling in immigration and national security. According to this doctrine, Congress is presumed to have full authority over those seeking entry, and the courts have no power to protect the rights of such individuals.

OTHER GROUPS

Once the Chinese were excluded, the legal history of Asian Americans over the next sixty years was dominated by the efforts of white racists, both on the West Coast and in Congress, to ensure that Asian immigrants remained stuck with African Americans and

Native Americans on the underside of the color line. The main group to face this pressure was the Japanese. In the generation after the Chinese were excluded, some 100,000 Japanese were recruited or encouraged to come to the United States, or migrated to Hawai'i and were absorbed once the islands were annexed in 1898. These Japanese immigrants, known as Issei, were folded upon arrival into the same legal regime as the Chinese, though with some notable differences. Like their Chinese counterparts (as well as the several thousand Korean "Ilse" who immigrated at the turn of the century, primarily to Hawai'i, and likewise a few thousand East Indians who settled in the states of Washington and California), the Issei were forbidden from becoming citizens and thus from voting or entering certain professions such as law. Ethnic Japanese were equally barred in many states from intermarrying with whites (though this did not stop a large number of Issei men outside the West Coast from taking white brides). The difference was that because of the economic and military power of the Japanese empire, whose networks of consular officials abroad intervened in support of Japanese nationals, the Issei were not as easy to exclude and harass as the other groups.

In 1906 San Francisco's school board officials, channeling nativist sentiment, attempted to relegate ethnic Japanese pupils to the segregated schools already occupied by Chinese pupils, in order to target them as undesirables. President Theodore Roosevelt persuaded the board to reverse its decision on national security grounds. In exchange, he pledged to restrict Japanese immigration. The result was the so-called Gentlemen's Agreement of 1907–1908 (in fact, an exchange of diplomatic notes) under which Americans promised not to legally bar Japanese immgration or discriminate against existing residents as long as Tokyo made sure that no more Japanese laborers came. Instead, only select categories were allowed entry, mostly wives and children of existing residents. By executive order, Roosevelt also barred Japanese aliens in Hawai'i from migrating to the mainland. California legislators soon violated the spirit of the Gentlemen's Agreement by the ruse of enacting laws barring "aliens ineligible to citizenship"—a category composed exclusively of Asians—from owning agricultural land. The Issei (and other Asian immigrants) were thus forced to place title to land with white friends or in the names of their American-born children (the so-called Nisei). In the years that followed, alien land statutes were adopted by states across the nation.

The Issei challenged this discrimination in court. Although in the 1894 case of Shebalto Saito, a federal judge ruled that Japanese were not eligible for naturalization (a ruling confirmed by the 1902 cases of Takuji Yamashita in Washington and Lee Guy Dean in Chicago), a handful of early Japanese immigrants did acquire citizenship. In the 1922 case of *Ozawa v. United States*, however, the U.S. Supreme Court definitively declared that Japanese were ineligible for citizenship as members of an Asian race, and on that basis the justices proceeded to uphold the alien land laws in *Terrace v. Thompson* (1923). The Court reached the same exclusionary conclusion in the 1923 case of Bhagat Singh Thind, an East Indian of "Caucasian racial stock," though on grounds that completely contradicted its reasoning in *Ozawa*.

By this time, national political leaders had undertaken a campaign to restrict Asian immigration entirely. In 1917 Congress barred entry to nationals from an "Asiatic barred zone" that included India and Southeast Asia. In 1924 West Coast congressmen pushed through an absolute ban on Chinese and Japanese immigration. Korean immigration, which had been halted by Tokyo in 1905 after the Japanese established their rule over Korea, was likewise formally banned. The one Asian group not barred was Filipinos, who held an anomolous status under American law. Although the United States annexed the Phiippines following the Spanish-American War of 1898, in a series of so-called Insular Cases over the following years the Supreme Court decreed that residents of annexed territories, while they might be considered U.S. nationals, did not thereby become citizens. Thus, while Filipinos could migrate to the United States without restriction, they might still be targeted for discrimination as "aliens ineligible to citizenship." Ultimately, under the 1934 Tydings-McDuffie Act, which established a roadmap to independence for the Philippines, migration of Filipinos was severely restricted and put on the path to extinction.

In addition to discrimination against "aliens ineligible to citizenship," various states enacted racial laws against American-born citizens of Asian ancestry (who also faced a great deal of unofficial discrimination, especially on the West Coast). Several states enacted statutes barring intermarriage. California continued to relegate Chinese Americans to "Oriental" schools and its 1921 public school law empowered local districts to segregate Nisei (although in practice only a handful ever did). Six years later, in turn, the Supreme Court upheld in *Gong Lum v. Mississippi* a southern state's right to classify a Chinese American as colored and to require her to attend a segregated school. Hawai'i segregated most of its ethnic Asian students by the legal device of restricting admission to elite "English standard" schools to whites and to the few others who could "talk white" (i.e., not in pidgin), and relegating others to separate schools. Meanwhile, territorial authorities in Hawai'i enacted special restrictions on Japanese schools, hoping to shut them down. However, in *Farrington v. Tokushige* (1927) the Supreme Court struck down the restrictions.

THE WAR YEARS

The wartime removal and confinement of Japanese Americans (often, if imprecisely, called the "Japanese internment") dominates Asian American history. Its main outlines are well known. In the wake of the Japanese attack on Pearl Harbor in December 1941, all Issei became "enemy aliens" subjected to a curfew and restrictions on travel and banking. (Korean immigrants, initially included in the restricted group as Japanese nationals, won their removal from the enemy list in early 1942.) In the days that followed the outbreak of the Pacific War, several hundred Issei community leaders and businessmen were arrested and held incommunicado. Gradually the government instituted a series of loyalty hearings for enemy aliens (German and Italian as well as Japanese), in which those accused could attempt to prove their loyalty, but from whch legal counsel was forbidden. In the end, over a thousand Japanese aliens were ordered interned indefinitely.

They would be joined by some 2,200 ethnic Japanese from Peru and other Latin American countries, who were abducted by their home governments and shipped to Panama and then the United States for internment. (After a protracted struggle against deportation to Japan, the remaining Latin American Japanese who had been interned in the United States were granted permanent residency in 1952.)

Meanwhile, in the weeks that followed, Western Defense Commander General John DeWitt began to insist on the total removal of the local Japanese population, on the grounds that Issei and Nisei might prove disloyal in case of a potential invasion by Tokyo. Despite a lack of good evidence of any disloyal activity, the pressure from DeWitt, seconded by West Coast whites inspired by racism and economic self-interest and further amplified by a solid bloc of opportunistic West Coast congressmen, set off debate within the White House. The War Department, whose chiefs felt obliged to back their local commanders, recommended mass removal, while Attorney General Francis Biddle saw no necessity for such action and refused to undertake it. President Franklin Roosevelt sided with the military and signed Executive Order 9066. Under authority of this order, with enforcement power provided by Congress via P.L. 502 and 503, the Army declared the entire West Coast a military area, imposed a special curfew, then decreed the wholesale removal of the entire ethnic Japanese population. With the approval of Roosevelt and the War Department, this removal (officially termed an evacuation) in turn led to the mass confinement of those removed, first in Army-run holding centers, then in government camps inland operated by the newly created War Relocation Authority (WRA). While WRA officials later designed a cumbersome and confessedly unconstitutional system of "leave permits," which enabled some inmates with outside sponsors to be released from camp to places outside the West Coast, the majority remained in confinement throughout the war.[3]

While the mass of Japanese Americans complied with government orders, a handful of Nisei, with support from different sets of non-Japanese sympathizers and attorneys, brought suits challenging Executive Order 9066. Mary Asaba Ventura of Seattle, a Nisei married to a Filipino American, brought a *habeas corpus* petition challenging Executive Order 9066 in March 1942. Judge Lloyd D. Black rejected the petition on the grounds that Asaba was not imprisoned, and he also gratuitously claimed that the order was constitutional and Asaba ought to be glad to cooperate. Lincoln Seiichi Kanai, a Hawai'i-born YMCA official in San Francisco, challenged the order "with his feet" by leaving the West Coast area without official permission in order to attend a conference and to investigate possibilities for resettlement. Arrested in Wisconsin and brought back to the West Coast for trial, he was convicted of violating military orders. Ernest and Toki Wakayama, a Nisei couple from Los Angeles, filed habeas corpus petitions with assistance from ACLU attorneys Edgar Camp and A. L. Wirin, plus an African American attorney, Hugh Macbeth. They asserted that there was no military necessity for removal and that General DeWitt's exclusion order was an arbitrary race-based violation of rights. In October 1942, a three-judge panel heard the petitions, and on February 4, 1943, they granted a writ of habeas corpus. However, by that time the Wakayamas, worn down by their treatment at the Manzanar camp, had withdrawn their suit and requested "repatriation" to Japan. In 1944, Wirin undertook the defense of a third Nisei, Dr. George Ochikubo, who challenged his "individual exclusion" from the West Coast, but the case remained unresolved at the end of the war.

Four cases reached the Supreme Court: those of Gordon Hirabayashi, Minoru Yasui, Fred Korematsu, and Mitsuye Endo. While all arose and were argued independently, the first three centered on a common set of legal questions: can a president, acting under his "war powers," constitutionally single out a group of citizens for special restrictions? In the cases of Hirabayashi and Yasui, decided in 1943, the government won a unanimous decision from the Court. The justices, denying the manifest result of the policy, ruled only on the curfew and registration requirements imposed on American citizens of Japanese ancestry rather than their mass removal. Even though there was no firm evidence of any disloyal conduct by Japanese Americans, they rushed to accord deference to military authority and agreed that military commanders could take cognizance of the influence of "racial strains" or ancestral identity by taking group-based action.[4]

It was in the case of *Korematsu v. United States* (1944) that the Court examined the question of mass removal itself. There, by a 6–3 vote, the justices upheld the mass "evacuation" of West Coast Japanese Americans. As in the previous cases, the majority opinion artificially (and disingenuously) separated out removal from the confinement that followed. Accepting the official argument that the Army had no time to determine individual loyalty, the justices held that removal was a rare case where separate treatment of a single racial group was constitutionally permissible. Conversely, in the case of *Ex Parte Endo*, decided on the same day as *Korematsu*, the Court unanimously ordered the release of the inmate Mitsuye Endo. To avoid ruling directly on whether the goverment could ever engage in arbitrary imprisonment of its own citizens as a matter of law, the Court decreed (with ludicrous logic) that the confinement of concededly loyal citizens had never been explicitly contemplated under Executive Order 9066—in essence holding that the agency operating the camps had throughout its existence been responsible for acting in an unauthorized and illegal fashion. In a consuming irony, the *Korematsu* decision, which remains a landmark in American constitutional law, had virtually no immediate impact on the position of Japanese Americans—it approved official actions already long since completed. By contrast, the *Endo* ruling, while largely forgotten today, forced the White House to open the camps and gave constitutional sanction to the Army's reopening of the West Coast in January 1945.

In addition to the "Japanese internment" cases, there was an important wartime court battle over citizenship rights. In 1942 the nativist group Native Sons of the Golden West, with support from the American Legion, brought suit in federal court to strip Nisei of voting rights, with the avowed final goal of overturning birthright citizenship for all Asian Americans. The case, entitled *Regan v. King*, was heard by Federal District Court judge Adolphus St. Sure, who refused to overturn the *Wong Kim Ark* precedent. The Native Sons then appealed. In response, the Japanese American Citizens League (JACL), whose decision not to oppose mass wartime removal had aroused outrage among many Japanese Americans, submitted an *amicus curiae* brief in defense of the Nisei's permanent citizenship rights, a brief cosigned by the African American attorneys Hugh Macbeth and Thomas Griffith. In February 1943 the Ninth Circuit Court of Appeals proceeded to throw out the case even before the defense could present its arguments. Not only did the victory reaffirm the constitutional doctrine of birthright citizenship, but it also laid the groundwork for postwar alliances for civil rights between blacks and Japanese Americans.[5]

The wartime confinement also led to other legal battles. When the War Department, which had excluded Nisei from enlistment in early 1942 and then approved formation of a volunteer all-Nisei combat battalion in 1943, reversed policy and undertook conscription of Japanese Americans in early 1944, individual Nisei men in the various camps protested, while at the Heart Mountain camp a group of confined Nisei organized a Fair Play Committee (FPC) to express their opposition. The FPC members carefully explained that they were prepared to fight for their country, but only once their civil liberties had been restored—how could they fight for freedom when their own families were stuck behind barbed wire? In a series of mass criminal trials, sixty-three resisters from Heart Mountain were convicted of draft evasion and sentenced to prison sentences. Soon after, thirty-three individuals from Minidoka were convicted in hurried trials (a handful pleaded guilty) and were sent to prison. The only draft resisters to escape prison were those from Tule Lake. Following their trial, a federal judge, Louis Goodman, ruled that it was "shocking to the conscience" to convict those already deprived of their civil rights for refusing to exercise the obligations of citizenship. An additional contest erupted over the portion of the inmate population whom the government had deemed "disloyal" and segregated in a cheerless high-security prison camp at Tule Lake. In 1944, after a disturbance there, the Justice Department pushed through Congress a denationalization law that permitted U.S. citizens to more easily renounce their citizenship. The government's goal was to ease arbitrary confinement of recalcitrant inmates under the Constitution. Some 5,000 inmates renounced their citizenship in the months that followed, but once the war ended approximately 80 percent sought to avert deportation to Japan and regain their lost citizenship, citing evidence of duress, including from pro-Axis inmates. Following a series of federal court rulings, most notably the Ninth Circuit Court of Appeals decision *Acheson v. Murakami* (1949), these "renunciants" were able to avert involuntary deportation, but regaining their lost citizenship was far more difficult, and in some cases restoration took over a decade.

THE POSTWAR PERIOD

World War II changed the legal landscape for people of Asian ancestry. The contributions of Asian Americans as soldiers and defense workers, especially in Hawai'i, plus the essential need to win support from Asian nations for the war against imperial Japan by demonstrating that the United States was a true multiracial democracy, led the federal government to adopt a policy of encouraging equal citizenship for Asians. The Fair Employment Practices Committee, a wartime civil rights watchdog agency created in 1941 under pressure from African Americans, investigated cases of job discrimination against Asians as well. In 1943, as a gesture to America's wartime ally, Congress repealed the Chinese Exclusion Act, instituting a token immigration quota for China and for the first time offering naturalization to Chinese immigrants. In 1946, Congress voted similar legislation for immigrants from South Asia and the Philippines Commonwealth, which became an independent country in July of that year. In addition, American residents of all nationalities who served in the Army were granted citizenship. The end of the war, however, brought about an injustice to Filipino soldiers, who had been recruited by the Army on the promise that they would enjoy veterans' benefits. In 1946, President Harry S. Truman signed the Rescission Bill, which stripped Filipino veterans of benefits under the GI Bill. Only in 2009 did Congress offer surviving veterans a cash settlement as damages for their losses. The end of the war also led to the entry of selected new Asian immigrants. Under the Soldier Brides Act of 1946, which permitted entry to wives of GIs, numerous Americans, both Asian and non-Asian, brought their new brides from Asia to live in the United States. A series of private bills enacted by Congress opened the doors to other individuals deemed worthy. Conversely, in 1947, during the Indonesian War of Independence, the Justice Department deported some 300 Indonesian sailors who had jumped ship in the United States and sought asylum, a move upheld by the courts.

The war with Japan and its aftermath also left its traces on the legal status of Japanese Americans. There was a flurry of court cases involving loss of citizenship by Nisei who assumed Japanese nationality or voted in Japanese elections. In 1949, Iva Toguri d'Aquino, a Nisei who had been stranded in Japan at the outbreak of war and who had returned to the United States afterward, was accused of broadcasting propaganda for the Japanese enemy as "Tokyo Rose" and was charged with treason. After a trial featuring testimony that was later revealed to be tainted and perjured, she was convicted and sentenced to ten years in prison. Another Nisei, Tomoya Kawakita, was also convicted of treason for abusing American POWs as a prison camp guard in Japan. At the same time, the Truman administration made halting efforts to repair the damage of wartime confinement. In December 1947, Truman officially pardoned the Nisei draft resisters (all but one of whom had already completed their prison terms) and restored their civil rights. He also campaigned in favor of evacuation claims legislation. The Japanese Evacuation Claims Act, enacted in mid-1948, provided token restitution of up to $2,500 to each Japanese American for losses of property during the initial removal, but in practical terms the legislation failed in its purpose. The government demanded receipts for sales, and the administrative process was contentious and wearisome. The Truman administration also supported the lifting of bars on Japanese immigration. Ironically, it was the 1952 McCarran-Walter Act, vetoed by Truman on other grounds and overridden by Congress, that finally lifted the ban on entry by Japanese, Koreans, and other excluded Asian groups and opened naturalization to the Issei (some of whom had already lived a half-century in the United States).

In tandem with these legislative and executive actions, Asian Americans fought state-level discrimination in the courts. The JACL spearheaded an intergroup legal struggle for civil rights, most notably in partnership with African Americans. The campaign came to fruition with a trio of landmark Supreme Court victories in 1948. In *Oyama v. California*, the Court struck down California's Alien Land Act as applied to citizens. The ruling not only halted the iniquitous use of escheat suits by California officials to strip Japanese Americans of their land, but also established the Court's constitutional doctrine imposing "strict scrutiny" on race-based laws, which it presumed unconstitutional absent exceptional circumstances. In *Takahashi v. California Fish and Game Commission*, the Court overturned California's 1945 law barring "aliens ineligible to citizenship" from obtaining fishing licenses. Meanwhile, the JACL joined a circle of civil rights groups backing the NAACP's successful legal challenge to racially restrictive covenants in the cases of *Shelley v. Kraemer* and *Hurd v. Hodge*. JACL lawyers produced an *amicus* brief in support of the NAACP's cases and also brought a pair of appeals, *Kim v. California* and *Amer v. California*, on its own. These cases, which involved Korean American and Chinese American veterans evicted from their respective homes under restrictive covenants, were designed to dramatize to the justices the discrimination against Asian Americans. Although the Court deferred consideration of the cases, they were decided in accordance with *Shelley*. The JACL subsequently submitted amicus briefs in support of the NAACP campaign against school segregation, which climaxed in the epochal 1954 Supreme Court ruling *Brown v. Board of Education*.

The JACL associated with other groups as well. JACL lawyers produced an *amicus curiae* brief in the 1947 Ninth Circuit Court of Appeals case *Mendez v. Westminister*, in which Mexican Americans in California successfully challenged school segregation. (In the wake of the decision, the state legislature repealed its segregation laws for Chinese and Japanese students.) In 1949, the JACL supported Chinese Americans who challenged a Hawai'i law that limited the operation of schools teaching Chinese and other foreign languages. After the case of *Stainback v. Mo Hock Ke Lock Po* came before the Supreme Court in 1949, it was remanded to the Hawai'i courts, where it broke no further legal ground. The JACL meanwhile continued to lobby for repeal of state laws barring white-Asian intermarriage, and intervened in legal challenges. In 1955 the JACL provided backing for the Supreme Court appeal of Han Say Naim, a Chinese American whose marriage to a white woman had been annulled under Virginia's antimiscegenation law. However, the justices ultimately decided not to hear the case. JACL counsel were granted permission to argue in the 1967 Supreme Court case *Loving v. Virginia*, in which the Court struck down all state laws against interracial marriage. The JACL and other groups also lobbied Congress to grant statehood to Hawai'i and give its majority Asian American population equal voting privileges. When Hawai'i became the fiftieth state in 1959, Hiram Fong became the first U.S. senator of Asian ancestry, while Representative Daniel Inouye started his decades-long congressional career.

THE CONTEMPORARY ERA

Asian American life changed durably as a result of the 1965 Hart-Celler Immigration Act, which ended race-based national quotas and opened immigration from Asia on a formally equal basis. While small numbers of Asian immigrants, notably students, adoptees, and wives of American citizens, plus refugees from communist China, had settled in the United States during the postwar decades, the 1965 law led to a dramatic expansion of the Asian population. Under the law's family reunification and immigrant investor provisions, Asian families and kin groups engaged in chain migration. Korean, Filipino, and South Asian American populations, which had previously been a relatively small demographic fraction, soon outpaced the long-dominant Japanese population. Another law, the Indochinese Migration and Refugee Assistance Act of 1975, enacted after the end of the Vietnam War in response to the fall of the American-backed regime in Saigon, authorized the entry of 130,000 Vietnamese and Cambodian nationals who had worked with American forces, and provided limited government assistance alongside aid from private sponsors. As a result of this law, along with the Refugee Act of 1980, which provided asylum and aid for a share of Vietnamese "boat people" (many of them ethnic Chinese) and Hmong (ethnic minority peoples from Laos) fleeing brutal communist regimes, plus the 1988 American Homecoming Act, which admitted some 25,000 Amerasian children of American soldiers as permanent residents, the Southeast Asian American population expanded exponentially by the end of the century.

The achievement of equal legal status did not automatically terminate the legal struggles of Asian Americans. Rather, there were notable court cases in the decades that followed that illuminated diverse issues. One facet was educational opportunity. In 1974, the Supreme Court case of *Lau v. Nichols*, brought by Chinese American students in San Francisco with limited English proficiency, expanded rights to bilingual education. Asian American groups, most notably the Asian American Legal Defense and Education Fund, campaigned for affirmative action and minority assistance programs in education and other areas, including furnishing *amicus* briefs in Supreme Court cases. Conversely, in a few high-profile cases, Asian Americans opposed affirmative action. For instance, in 1994 Chinese American parents in San Francisco, ignoring opposition by Asian American civil rights groups, sued to overturn a 1983 consent decree that had established race-based quotas to boost admission of African Americans to the city's elite Lowell High School. The suit, *Ho v. San Francisco Unified School District*, led to a settlement in 1999 that replaced racial identity by a broader "diversity index" of various factors for the purpose of determining student admission.

Asian American communities were forced during these decades to react to numerous episodes of interracial violence. The most notorious was the case of Vincent Chin, a young Chinese American from Detroit. In 1982, following a scuffle in a strip club, Chin was beaten to death by two white men, Ronald Ebens and Michael Nitz, who mistook him for Japanese and blamed him for the nation's economic crisis. After county court judge Michael Kaufman sentenced the men to probation with no jail time, Asian American activists pressured federal authorities to prosecute the murderers on civil rights charges. The widespread coalition for justice is often considered a founding event of Asian American activism. While Ebens was convicted on federal civil rights charges, the conviction was later overturned on retrial.[6] Two other racially-inflected murder cases also had a large impact on Asian Americans. In 1992, a sixteen-year-old Japanese exchange student, Yoshihiro Hattori, was shot dead in Louisiana by a meat market manager named Rodney Peairs after he and a white friend knocked mistakenly on Peairs's door in search of a Halloween party. Peairs claimed the right of self-defense and was acquitted of manslaughter. JACL observers protested the sentence, noting that Peairs had shot only the Japanese boy and not his white companion. Meanwhile, in 1991, Soon Ja Du, a Korean-born shopowner in Los Angeles, fatally shot a fifteen-year-old African American girl, Latasha Harlins, following an altercation over a bottle of juice. Judge Joyce Karlin praised Du and sentenced her to probation with no jail time. Many commentators later noted that the outrage in the black community over the light sentence was a prime causal factor in the 1992 Los Angeles riot, in which rioters targeted Korean-owned businesses.

A final area was racial profiling and discrimination, often under the heading of national security. In 1968, under pressure from Asian American activists, the JACL announced as its new major legislative goal the repeal of Title II, the section of the Internal Security Act of 1950 that had authorized the executive branch to confine suspected subversives within concentration camps. The movement to repeal Title II soon brought together major civil rights and political organizations, churches, and labor unions, plus a wide spectrum of nonwhite groups, and repeal was enacted by a large majority in Congress in 1971. In the following decades, there remained various allegations of abuses under cover of national security, even before the terrorist attacks of September 11, 2001. Bruce Yamashita, subjected to racial harrassment following his enlistment in the Marine Corps in 1989 and "disenrolled" from Officer Candidate School (OCS) on racial grounds, was forced to sue the government. After his legal team uncovered a pattern of persistent discrimination against racial minorities in OCS, the case was settled in 1996. Yamashita received an official apology and was reinstated. Another emblematic case was that of Wen Ho Lee, a Taiwanese American scientist working at Los Alamos National Laboratory in New Mexico. In 1999, a federal grand jury indicted Lee on charges of giving classified information to the People's Republic of China. Federal prosecutors publicly accused him of having stolen the "crown jewels" of America's nuclear arsenal. Lee was denied bail and placed in solitary confinement. Ultimately, federal prosecutors admitted that they had no proof of transmission of any "top secret" materials, and Lee was released after pleading guilty to a minor charge. In 2006, Lee settled a civil suit against the federal government for $1.6 million, and the trial judge formally apologized to him for official abuses of power.

Finally, at the center of contemporary Asian American legal history was the movement to gain reparations for Japanese Americans confined during World War II. A grassroots campaign, the Japanese American redress movement, coalesced in the

1970s. Its first success came in 1976, when President Gerald Ford formally revoked Executive Order 9066 and stated his regret over the policy. It culminated twelve years later in the Civil Liberties Act of 1988, enacted by Congress and signed by President Ronald Reagan. The law provided an official apology and a $20,000 payment to each surviving former inmate.

In addition to these legislative and executive victories, there was an essential judicial component to the movement. In 1981, as part of the process of writing a book on the Supreme Court "Japanese internment" cases of Gordon Hirabayashi, Minoru Yasui, and Fred Korematsu, the author/lawyer Peter Irons hit on the idea of bringing a new court challenge to their convictions, by using the historical material that he and a researcher, Aiko Herzig-Yoshinaga, had uncovered regarding official fraud and manipulation in the original cases. After obtaining the consent of the three former defendants, Irons recruited a volunteer legal team, directed by the Sansei attorneys Dale Minami, Peggy Nagae, and Kathryn Bannai, to handle the three cases. The lawyers filed petitions under the ancient, seldom-used writ of *coram nobis*, through which courts could reexamine past cases in order to correct fundamental errors of justice.

On November 10, 1983, following a hearing, a U.S. judge, Marilyn Hall Patel, summarily granted Fred Korematsu's *coram nobis* petition, reversing his conviction. In her opinion, Patel found that there was substantial support in the evidentiary record that the government had deliberately omitted relevant information and provided misleading information in its papers before the Supreme Court. The cases of Yasui and Hirabayashi proved more complicated and protracted in their progress through the courts. In 1984, district judge Robert C. Belloni issued an order vacating Yasui's conviction but declined to either grant Yasui's *coram nobis* petition or to make findings of fact regarding the record of official misconduct. Yasui died before any appeal could be decided, mooting the case. Conversely, Hirabayashi's *coram nobis* petition drew an inconclusive Federal District Court ruling, which both sides appealed. In September 1987, a three-judge panel of the U.S. Court of Appeals for the Ninth Circuit ordered Hirabayashi's petition granted in its entirety, proclaiming that the record demonstrated that racial bias was "the cornerstone of the internment orders" and that government misconduct had materially affected the argument of the case. Because the *coram nobis* cases involved specific charges of official misconduct and not just protest over the government's larger actions, and because they were tried before judicial tribunals widely perceived as more objective and less political than Congress, the final court rulings had a validity that was hard to ignore, and they were fundamental in persuading lawmakers to enact the redress legislation.

Even as the *coram nobis* petitions and the triumphs of the legal redress team were made possible by historical research, they signaled in turn the coming of age of Asian American legal scholarship. Before the advent of the larger field of Asian American history, there had been scattered law review pieces and books on law with a historical dimension, such as those by Dudley McGovney and Thomas A. Bailey, as well as biographies of non-Asian lawyers, judges, and political leaders that featured discussion of cases involving the rights of people of Asian ancestry.[7] Nevertheless, there was little in the way of historical reflection on the structure of law in defining Asian American subjects and shaping their development over time. Perhaps in this sense, the first major work in the field was Milton R. Konvitz's *The Alien and Asiatic in American Law* (1946), though it was primarily descriptive rather than analytical. The 1954 study *Prejudice, War, and the Constitution*, penned by a team of social scientists and a legal specialist, broke new ground in exploring the wartime confinement of Japanese Americans from both a historical and constitutional angle. Fred Warren Riggs's *Pressures on Congress*, on the repeal of Chinese exclusion, though fundamentally a political science study of lesislative lobbying, included a historical section. S. W. Kung's *Chinese in American Life* (1962) was probably the first full-length study by an Asian American author to include a history of law approach.[8] Still, Asian American issues remained absent from overall casebooks and monographs on immigration and constitutional law.[9]

It was in the late 1970s and 1980s that the field of Asian American legal history began to coalesce. This development was the product of several related factors. First, following the pattern set by the civil rights movement, advocates of racial equality and social reform turned increasingly to the courts (most notably the U.S. Supreme Court) to achieve progressive goals. Meanwhile, in concert with the growth of the Asian American movement, a network of Asian American legal defense groups and law student caucuses sprang up. As activist lawyers sought historical support for their arguments, historical analysis of past legal change became of greater interest to outside readers. Ironically, even partisans of the developing school of critical legal studies, who challenged the notion of an objective law, turned to history to investigate how social power influenced jurispridence. Yet legal academics still paid hardly any attention to the subject. Instead, in the heyday of the redress movement, various independent or semi-independent scholars launched notable studies of the legal background to confinement. *The Bamboo People* (1976), by the attorney/JACL activist Frank Chuman, was a synthesis of legal history that ably went over the different categories of cases in which the rights of Japanese Americans were concerned. Moritoshi Fukuda's *Legal Problems of Japanese Americans* (1980) focused on immigration and land rights. Peter Irons's *Justice at War* (1983) centered on the wartime Japanese internment cases and revealed the official fraud and manipulation in the government presentation. Radical author Richard Drinnon's powerful attack on WRA director Dillon Myer, *Keeper of Concentration Camps*, focused on the unconstitutional segregation and detention policies that Myer implemented.[10]

In contrast, it was not until the 1990s that academic specialists in Asian American history began contributing in a serious way to legal history. Apart from intellectual interest, some material factors favored such an opening. First, there was an identifiable and growing student and popular audience—especially with the multiplication of ethnic studies programs in universities during these years. Moreover, legislation and court records offered historical researchers a clear and readily accessible corpus of material for study. Finally, although legal academics continued to produce substantial works on their own,[11] there was an explosion of collaborative projects between the two groups. The four-volume set *Asian Americans and the Law: Historical and Contemporary Perspectives*, directed by the law professor Charles McClain, brought together outstanding articles culled from law reviews and academic journals on (respectively) Chinese immigrants, Japanese immigrants, Japanese internment and redress, and "Asian Indians, Filipinos, Other Asian Communities and the Law." Meanwhile, Hyung-Chan Kim, a professor of education, contributed a pair of volumes (the first one in partnership with a set of lawyers and legal scholars that included Dale Minami, Lorraine Bannai, and Neil Gotanda) that provided the first synthetic overviews of Asian American legal history. Kim's own writings, though marred by various factual errors and by a somewhat simplistic approach that presented American society as unfailingly exclusionist, were impressively thorough, considering the significant gaps in the secondary literature then available, and also covered multiple Asian groups.[12]

Once engaged with legal history, historians began to mine legal sources and materials, which they used to advantage in illuminating larger issues. For example, Lucy Salyer's groundbreaking *Laws as Harsh as Tigers* (1995) remade popular understandings of Chinese exclusion by using immigrant case files and judicial decisions to reveal the sophisticated legal strategies that Chinese immigrants used to win admission to the United States during the period and also to demonstrate how such immigration jurisprudence catalyzed the development of the "plenary power" doctrine that limits judicial review of congressional power over immigration.[13] Salyer's work would soon be extended by a set of kindred works. Xiaojin Zhao's *Remaking Chinese America* (2002) explored the post-exclusion period by using Immigration and Naturalization Service case files. Erica Lee's *At America's Gates* (2003) documented how the policy of excluding Chinese transformed the United States into a "gatekeeper" nation with modern coercive immigration apparatus. Mae Ngai's *Impossible Subjects* (2004) discussed the historic construction of the immigrant, including Asians, as "illegal."[14] In counterpoint, George Peffer's slim volume *If They Don't Bring Their Women Here* (1999) examined the prehistory of exclusion by focusing on the legal bars imposed on Chinese women, while Jeanne Pfaelzer's study *Driven Out* (2007) recounted how Chinese immigrants turned to the courts to counter mob violence and pogroms designed to chase them from the country.[15] Lisa Rose Mar's *Brokering Belonging* (2010), though it focused on Canada rather than the United States, turned popular understandings of Chinese exclusion in the two countries on their head by revealing the agency of ethnic Chinese interpreters and middlemen within the policing of exclusion.[16]

The legal history of Japanese American confinement, a subject on which little new had been written since redress and which many observers believed exhausted, was itself transformed in 2001 by three distinctive new works. The multiauthored volume *Race, Rights, and Reparation* presented the wartime internment cases in connection with larger issues of racism and individual liberty. A rare legal casebook with substantial historical treatment, it was widely adopted for schoolroom use as a historical text. Eric Muller's *Free to Die for Their Country*, which offered an unprecedented full-length study of the Nisei draft resisters and the legal cases triggered by their long-hidden campaign, in the process posed the larger question of whether patriotism was best served by military service or by legal challenge in defense of constitutional principle. Greg Robinson's *By Order of the President*, the first work to focus on Franklin Roosevelt's role in Executive

Order 9066 and the wartime events, not only provided an executive history of the camp policy, but also equally dramatized how long-standing racial bias informed presidential decision- making.[17] Muller and Robinson would each go on to produce further works that used legal cases as tools for analysis of larger questions surrounding confinement. Muller's *American Inquisition* (2007), which delved into the "loyalty program" and questionnaires inposed on inmates, showed how the indefinable quality of "loyalty" was substituted for "security" as a basis for judging arbitrarily confined inmates. Robinson's *A Tragedy of Democracy* (2009), a transnational study of confinement in the United States, Canada, and Mexico, explored the legal history of martial law in wartime Hawai'i alongside mass confinement as twin episodes of military overreaching and rejection of civilian authority.[18]

In the first decade of the twenty-first century, Asian American legal history came more visibly into its own, with breakthroughs in different areas. While it is not possible to cover the gamut of themes, three especially fruitful sectors are worthy of note: transnational and multiracial studies; gender and sexuality; and examinations of administrative regulations and policies. The theme of border-crossing, whether national or racial, informed a series of works about the largely uncovered postwar era that centered on multigroup alliances in legal struggles for civil rights. Mark Brilliant's *The Color of America Has Changed* (2010) analyzed how California's racial diversity shaped the legal campaigns for civil rights in the state. Charlotte Brooks's *Alien Neighbors, Foreign Friends* (2009) traced multigroup legal struggles over open housing as a window into Asian American life.[19] A pair of interrelated articles by Toni Robinson and Greg Robinson, which were later compiled into a book, on postwar alliances among Japanese Americans, Mexican Americans, and African Americans, revealed the uneasy and even contradictory nature of such coalitions.[20]

On questions of gender and sexuality, a major focus of attention was interracial sex. Susan Koshy's *Sexual Naturalization* (2005) was a historical study of Asian-white "miscegenation" and the shaping of the laws that regulated it. Building on Koshy's work, Peggy Pascoe's *What Comes Naturally* (2010) provides a transracial study of laws against intermarriage and the ways in which they structured American society over time.[21] Leti Volpp's much-cited article "Divesting Citizenship" (2005) traced the history of the Cable Act, which stripped Asian American women of citizenship for marrying "ineligible" aliens.[22] Nayan Shah's *Stranger Intimacy* (2012), which traced the official exclusion of nonwhite immigrants in the United States and Canada, explored the intersection between sexuality and citizenship. Also, while not strictly speaking a historical work, the law professor Kenji Yoshino's widely-publicized essay on "covering" drew a fascinating, historically informed parallel between the stigmatization of Asian Americans who did not conform to white mainsteam culture and that of gays and lesbians who openly expressed their sexuality.[23]

Finally, a number of new works examined how recourse to administrative procedures and practices shaped the legal status of Asian Americans over time. Nayan Shah's *Contagious Divides* (2001) examined in novel fashion how city authorities used public health concerns as a pretext for residential segregation and exclusion of Chinese

Americans. Tetsuden Kashima's *Judgment Without Trial* (2003) detailed the prewar administrative momentum created for mass Japanese confinement by the development of ever-greater plans for control of suspicious groups. John Howard's scintillating *Concentration Camps on the Home Front* (2008) recounts how WRA officials attempted to influence confined Issei and Nisei by policies to ensure monoracial and heterosexual couplings, and through systemic pro-Christian bias. In addition to Lisa Mar's previously- mentioned work on the administrative operation of Chinese exclusion, Estelle Lau (herself a practicing attorney) contributed the historical study *Paper Families* (2007), which underlined the extent to which the Chinese Exclusion Act reconfigured administrative practice, even as it reshaped Chinese American family structure.[24] These works demonstrate not only the richness of the existing literature in Asian American legal history, but also the potential utility and adaptability of such source materials and approaches for works in other fields of study.

NOTES

1. In keeping with this volume's larger focus on Asian American historical studies, my essay deals primarily with how monographs and essays written from the historian's viewpoint have treated legal questions. This definition certainly embraces essentially historical writing done by legal scholars (which already comprises a good deal of the best work in the field). However, it excludes the mass of casebooks and law journal articles, both because they are too numerous to list and because they generally include a technical or theoretical dimension that goes beyond the bounds of strict historiography.

2. Jeanne Pfaelzer, *Driven Out: The Forgotten War against Chinese Americans* (New York: Random House, 2007).

3. The legal and other literature on Executive Order 9066 is enormous. See, for example, United States Commission on Wartime Relocation and Internment of Civilians, *Personal Justice Denied* (Seattle: University of Washington Press, 1996 [1983]). It is important to underline that Executive Order 9066 followed a snowballing evolution of misplaced official concern for security during the prewar period. It is also important to note that lawyers from the Army Provost Marshal General's office, led by Captain (later Colonel) Karl Bendetson (later Bendetsen), played a central role in pushing DeWitt's demands for arbitrary power. These officials were motivated not only by mistrust of Japanese Americans but also by the desire to exert military authority in war zones, free of civilian interference. Bendetsen's actions were mirrored by those of the Chief of the Provost Marshal General's office in Hawai'i, Colonel Thomas Green. Before Pearl Harbor, Green drafted a secret martial law proclamation, abolishing all civilian government. Once Japanese airplanes attacked the Hawaiian bases, Green and his commanding officer, General Walter Short, sprang the proclamation on the territorial governor, John Poindexter, and browbeat him into signing it. The Army then suspended the U.S Constitution, closed civilian courts, and established dictatorial rule in Hawai'i. Due to Army resistance, full civilian rule was not restored in Hawai'i until late 1944. That same year, a defense worker, Lloyd Duncan, brought a *habeas corpus* suit challenging his assault conviction by a military tribunal. During the trial before Judge Delbert Metzger, government lawyers justified the use of military courts to try civilians as a necessary response to the "menace" represented by the

territory's racial diversity and the presence of ethnic Japanese. Metzger nonetheless struck down the military tribunals as unconstitutional, a ruling later affirmed by the Supreme Court in *Duncan v. Kahanamoku* (1946).

4. Peter Irons, *Jusice at War: The Japanese Internment Cases* (New York: Oxford University Press, 1983). The cases were also linked by the shocking official manipulation that marked their presentation before the courts—Assistant Secretary of War John McCloy ordered General DeWitt's Final Report on Evacuation, which had affirmed that no Japanese American could be trusted, destroyed and altered to reflect the fallacious official line that the Army lacked the time to determine individual loyalty. In *Korematsu*, Justice Department lawyers presented DeWitt's report, with its allegations of Japanese American signaling of enemy ships, for judicial notice as uncontroverted fact, even though the government's own agencies had debunked his evidence and refuted his central conclusions.

5. On *Regan*, see Greg Robinson, August 9, 2010, "The Last Time That Birthright Citizenship Was 'Reconsidered,'" *The Faculty Lounge*, http://www.thefacultylounge.org/2010/08/when-birthright-citizenship-was-last-reconsidered-regan-v-king-and-asian-americans-1.html.

6. On Vincent Chin, see Christine Choy and Renée Tajima-Pena, "Who Killed Vincent Chin?" (New York: Filmmakers Library, 2009 [1988]); Curtis Chin, "Vincent Who?" Curtis Chin, 2008.

7. Some examples include Dudley O. McGovney, "Anti-Japanese Land Laws of California and Ten Other States," *California Law Review* 35 (1947): 7–60; and Thomas A. Bailey, *Theodore Roosevelt and the Japanese-American Crisis: An Account of the International Complications Arising from the Race Problems on the Pacific Coast* (Stanford, CA: Stanford University Press, 1934). Other examples include Henry F. Pringle, *The Life and Times of William Howard Taft: A Biography*, 2 vols. (New York: Farrar and Rinehart, 1939); and (somewhat later) J. Woodford Howard, *Mr. Justice Murphy: A Political Biography* (Princeton, NJ: Princeton University Press, 1968).

8. Milton R. Konvitz, *The Alien and Asiatic in American Law* (Ithaca, NY: Cornell University Press, 1946); Jacobus tenBroek, Edward Norton Barnhart, and Floyd W. Matson, *Prejudice, War, and the Constitution* (Berkeley: University of California Press, 1954); Fred Warren Riggs, *Pressures on Congress: A Study of the Repeal of Chinese Exclusion* (New York: King's Crown, 1950); S. W. (Shien-Woo) Kung, *Chinese in American Life: Some Aspects of Their History, Status, Problems, and Contributions* (Seattle: University of Washington Press, 1962). An even earlier study than this first generation, but a rather obscure one, was Macaomi Yoshitomi, *Les confits Nippo-Américains et le problème du Pacifique* (Paris: A. Pedone, 1926), a revision of the author's thesis in international law that convincingly demonstrated the impact of anti-Japanese prejudice on the making and intepreting of law.

9. Curiously enough, even works on African Americans did not cover the Asian American component of civil rights. Discussion of Asian Americans appears nowhere in classic legal studies of the period: see Clement E. Vose, *Caucasians Only: The Supreme Court, the NAACP, and the Restrictive Covenant Cases* (Berkeley: University of California Press, 1959); Loren E. Miller, *The Petitioners: The Story of the Supreme Court of the United States and the Negro* (New York: Pantheon, 1966); and Richard Kluger, *Simple Justice: The History of Brown v. Board of Education and Black America's Struggle for Equality* (New York: Vintage, 1977).

10. Frank F. Chuman, *The Bamboo People: The Law and Japanese Americans* (Del Mar, CA: Publisher's Inc., 1976); Moritoshi Fukuda, *Legal Problems of Japanese Americans: Their History and Development in the United States* (Tokyo: Keio Tsushin, 1980); Irons, *Justice at War*; Richard Drinnon, *Keeper of Concentration Camps: Dillon S. Myer and American Racism* (Berkeley: University of California Press, 1987).

11. See, for example, Bill Ong Hing, *Making and Remaking Asian America through Immigration Policy, 1850–1990* (Stanford, CA: Stanford University Press, 1993); Angelo Ancheta, *Race, Rights, and the Asian American Experience* (New Brunswick, NJ: Rutgers University Press, 1997). The multitalented Mari Matsuda, in addition to developing the field of critical race theory and coauthoring a manifesto in favor of affirmative action, directed a historical study of women lawyers in Hawai'i, including Asian Americans. Mari J. Matsuda, ed., *Called from Within: Early Women Lawyers of Hawaii* (Honolulu: University of Hawai'i Press, 1992).

12. Charles McClain, ed., *Asian Americans and the Law: Historical and Contemporary Perspectives*, 4 vols. (New York: Routledge, 1994); Charles McClain, *In Search of Equality: The Chinese Struggle against Discrimination in Nineteenth Century America* (Berkeley: University of California Press, 1996); Hyung-Chan Kim, ed., *Asian Americans and the Supreme Court: A Documentary History* (Westport, CT: Greenwood, 1992); Hyung-Chan Kim, *A Legal History of Asian Americans, 1790–1990* (Westport, CT: Greenwood, 1994). The question of "borders" and "international law" infused an important anthology of legal and historical scholarship that dealt with the "War on Terror" and the prison at Guantanamo. Leti Volpp and Mary Dudziak, eds., *Legal Borderlands: Law and the Construction of American Borders* (Baltimore, MD: Johns Hopkins University Press, 2006).

13. Lucy E. Salyer, *Laws as Harsh as Tigers: Chinese Immigrants and the Making of Modern Immigration Law* (Chapel Hill: University of North Carolina Press, 1995). Salyer had earlier presented an aspect of her research in a volume on the legal history of exclusion. Sucheng Chan, ed., *Entry Denied: Exclusion and the Chinese Community in America, 1882–1943* (Philadelphia: Temple University Press, 1994).

14. Xiaojin Zhao, *Remaking Chinese America: Immigration, Family, and Community, 1940–1965* (New Brunswick, NJ: Rutgers University Press, 2002); Erika Lee, *At America's Gates: Chinese Immigration during the Exclusion Period, 1882–1943* (Chapel Hill: University of North Carolina Press, 2003); Mae Ngai, *Impossible Subjects: Illegal Aliens and the Making of Modern America* (Princeton, NJ: Princeton University Press, 2004). Lee's and Ngai's works would in turn inform Natsu Taylor Saito's historically informed study, *From Chinese Exclusion to Guantanamo Bay: Plenary Power and the Prerogative State* (Boulder: University Press of Colorado, 2007).

15. George Anthony Peffer, *If They Don't Bring Their Women Here: Chinese Female Immigration before Exclusion* (Urbana: University of Illinois Press, 1999); Pfaelzer, *Driven Out*.

16. Lisa Rose Mar, *Brokering Belonging: Chinese in Canada's Exclusion Era, 1885–1945* (New York: Oxford University Press, 2010).

17. Eric K. Yamamoto, Margaret Chin, Carol L. Izumi, Jerry Kang, and Frank H. Wu, *Race, Rights, and Reparation: Law and the Japanese American Internment* (New York: Aspen, 2001); Greg Robinson, *By Order of the President: FDR and the Internment of Japanese Americans* (Cambridge, MA: Harvard University Press, 2001). There were some further notable studies of the different "internment cases" by legal scholars. See Patrick Gudridge, "Remember Endo?" *Harvard Law Review* 116 (2003): 1933–1970; Neil Gotanda,

"The Story of *Korematsu*: The Japanese-American Cases," in *Constitutional Law Stories*, ed. Michael C. Dorf (New York: Foundation, 2004), 249–296; and Jerry Kang, "Dodging Responsibility: The Story of *Hirabayashi* v. United States," in *Race Law Stories*, ed. Devon Carbado and Racel Moran (New York: Foundation, 2008), 311–342.

18. Eric L. Muller, *American Inquisition: The Hunt for Japanese American Disloyalty in World War II* (Chapel Hill: University of North Carolina Press, 2007); Greg Robinson, *A Tragedy of Democracy: Japanese Confinement in North America* (New York: Columbia University Press, 2009).

19. Mark Brilliant, *The Color of America Has Changed: How Racial Diversity Shaped Civil Rights Reform in California, 1941–1978* (New York: Oxford University Press, 2010); Charlotte Brooks, *Alien Neighbors, Foreign Friends: Asian Americans, Housing, and the Transformation of Urban California* (Chicago: University of Chicago Press, 2009). Two leading works in consolidating the multiethnic trend, though they did not feature legal analysis, were Kevin Leonard, *The Battle for Los Angeles: Racial Ideology and World War II* (Albuquerque: University of New Mexico Press, 2006); and Scott Kurashige, *The Shifting Grounds of Race: Blacks and Japanese Americans in the Making of Modern Los Angeles* (Princeton, NJ: Princeton University Press, 2007).

20. Greg Robinson and Toni Robinson, "*Korematsu* and Beyond: Japanese Americans and the Origins of Strict Scrutiny," *Law and Contemporary Problems* 68, no. 2 (2005): 29–55; Toni Robinson and Greg Robinson, "The Limits of Interracial Coalition: *Méndez v. Westminster* Reconsidered," in *Racial (Trans)formations: Latinos and Asians Remaking the United States*, ed. Nicholas de Genova (Durham, NC: Duke University Press, 2006), 93–119. Both essays appeared in revised form in Greg Robinson, *After Camp: Portraits in Midcentury Japanese American Life and Politics* (Berkeley: University of California Press, 2012). Robinson and Robinson were also apparently responsible for a modest methodological shift in focusing primarily on *amicus* briefs to trace the evolution of legal discourse and arguments.

21. Susan Koshy, *Sexual Naturalization: Asian Americans and Miscegenation* (Stanford, CA: Stanford University Press, 2005); Peggy Pascoe, *What Comes Naturally: Miscegenation Law and the Making of Race in America* (New York: Oxford University Press, 2010).

22. Leti Volpp, "Divesting Citizenship: An Asian American History and the Loss of Citizenship through Marriage," *UCLA Law Review* 53 (2005): 405–483. Though she was the most thorough in detailing cases of women who lost their citizenship, Volpp was not the first scholar to deal with the Cable Act. Esther Ngan-Ling Chow had previously treated the Cable Act in "The Development of Feminist Consciousness among Asian American Women," *Gender and Society* 1, no. 3 (1987): 284–299.

23. Nayan Shah, *Stranger Intimacy: Contesting Race, Sexuality and the Law in the North American West* (Berkeley: University of California Press, 2012); Kenji Yoshino, *Covering: The Hidden Assault on Our Civil Rights* (New York: Random House, 2006).

24. Nayan Shah, *Contagious Divides: Epidemics and Race in San Francisco's Chinatown* (Berkeley: University of California Press, 2001); Tetsuden Kashima, *Judgment without Trial: Japanese American Imprisonment during World War II* (Seattle: University of Washington Press, 2004); John Howard, *Concentration Camps on the Home Front: Japanese Americans in the House of Jim Crow* (Chicago: University of Chicago Press, 2008); Estelle T. Lau, *Paper Families: Identity, Immigration Administration, and Chinese Exclusion* (Durham, NC: Duke University Press, 2007).

Further Reading

Aarim-Heriot, Najia. *Chinese Immigrants, African Americans, and Racial Anxiety in the United States, 1848–1882.* Urbana: University of Illinois Press, 2002.

Asato, Noriko. *Teaching Mikadoism: The Attack on Japanese Language Schools in Hawaii, California, and Washington, 1919–1927.* Honolulu: University of Hawai'i Press, 2006.

Barth, Paul Gunther. *Bitter Strength: A History of the Chinese in the United States, 1850–1870.* Cambridge, MA: Harvard University Press, 1964.

Daniels, Roger. *The Politics of Prejudice: The Anti-Japanese Movement in California, and the Struggle for Japanese Exclusion.* Berkeley: University of California Press, 1962.

Duus, Masayo. *Tokyo Rose: Orphan of the Pacific.* Tokyo: Kodansha, 1979.

Elinson, Elaine, and Stan Yogi. *Wherever There's a Fight: How Runaway Slaves, Suffragists, Immigrants, Strikers, and Poets Shaped Civil Liberties in California.* Berkeley, CA: Heyday, 2010.

Gardiner, C. Harvey. *Pawns in a Triangle of Hate: The Peruvian Japanese and the United States.* Seattle: University of Washington Press, 1981.

Geiger-Adams, Andrea. "Writing Racial Barriers into Law: Upholding B.C.'s Denial of the Vote to Its Japanese Canadian Citizens, *Homma v. Cunningham,* 1902." In *Nikkei in the Pacific Northwest,* edited by Lois Fiset and Gail Nomura, 20–43. Seattle: University of Washington Press, 2005.

Gotanda, Neil. "Multiculturalism and Racial Stratification." In *Asian American Studies: A Reader,* edited by Jean Yu-wen Shen Wu and Min Song, 379–390. New Brunswick, NJ: Rutgers University Press, 2004.

Gyory, Andrew. *Closing the Gates: Race, Politics and the Chinese Exclusion Act.* Chapel Hill: University of North Carolina Press, 1998.

Irons, Peter. *Justice Delayed: The Record of the Japanese American Internment Cases.* Middletown, CT: Wesleyan University Press, 1989.

Izumi, Masumi. "Prohibiting 'American Concentration Camps': Repeal of the Emergency Detention Act and the Public Historical Memory of the Japanese American Internment." *Pacific Historical Review* 74, no. 2 (2005): 165–193.

Maki, Mitchell T., Harry H. L. Kitano, and S. Megan Berthold. *Achieving the Impossible Dream: How Japanese Americans Obtained Redress.* Urbana: University of Illinois Press, 1999.

Newbeck, Phyl. *Virginia Hasn't Always Been for Lovers: Interracial Marriage Bans and the Case of Richard and Mildred Loving.* Carbondale: Southern Illinois University Press, 2004.

Ngai, Mae. *The Lucky Ones: One Family and the Extraordinary Invention of Chinese America.* Boston: Houghton Mifflin, 2010.

Pfaelzer, Jeanne. *Driven Out: The Forgotten War against Chinese Americans.* New York: Random House, 2007.

Saxton, Alexander. *The Indispensable Enemy: Labor and the Anti-Chinese Movement in California.* Berkeley: University of California Press, 1995 [1971].

Stevens, Todd. "Tender Ties: Husbands' Rights and Racial Exclusion in Chinese Marriage Cases, 1882–1924." *Law and Social Inquiry* 27, no. 4 (2002): 271–305.

CHAPTER 26

··

ASIAN AMERICAN
EDUCATION HISTORY

··

EILEEN H. TAMURA

WHEN compared with European American, African American, and Latino education histories, Asian American education history, a potentially fruitful arena of inquiry, has been largely unexplored. While there have been publications and conference papers that scholar-authors have explicitly identified as Asian American education history, they have been relatively few and far between. While this may seem puzzling, since education is such a huge field of study, several reasons account for this situation: the fairly small field of educational history; the comparatively small population of Asian American youths who grew up before 1970; and the nature of education being part of a larger sociocultural phenomenon. Taken together, these three factors have resulted in its relative invisibility. Moreover, many of those who have had articles published on Asian American education history do not self-identify as historians of education, and thus they have published their studies in non-history-of-education and non-education journals. This essay expands on the three factors mentioned above, discusses the extant literature on Asian American education history, and suggests areas for further investigation.

Despite its importance, educational history has been a rather small field of inquiry within the huge arena of educational research, so it is not surprising that Asian American education history is an even smaller area of scholarly endeavor. Nevertheless, when compared to African American and Latino education histories, the scarcity of works on Asian American education history is noteworthy. The smaller proportion of Asian Americans in the population contributes to this lack, a situation that should change as the Asian American population increases.

The second contributing factor is the post-1965 arrival of most immigrants from Asia. Although Asians have been migrating to the Americas since the late eighteenth century, the vast majority have arrived since the U.S. Congress passed the 1965 Immigration and Nationality Act. As a result, significant numbers of Asian American children attended schools beginning in the 1980s. While a plethora of social science studies have appeared on these Asian American youths, historical studies on post-1965 Asian

American educational history have had to wait for the passage of time. My comments are not meant to ignore the youths who grew up before the 1965 law, but to highlight the greater numbers in the United States in the later decades of the twentieth century. And while historians have examined the education of Asian American youths in the first half of the twentieth century, most of these studies have focused on Chinese and Japanese Americans, the two largest Asian American groups of this period.

In a historiographical essay published in 2001, I discussed the lack of scholarly focus on Asian American education history. To help remedy the situation, I proposed to the editor of the *History of Education Quarterly* that the journal offer a special issue on Asian American educational history. The editorial team accepted my proposal and invited me to serve as guest editor. Most of the papers submitted were on Japanese and Chinese, as were the final three accepted for publication by the review panel. Insufficient time had passed for solid historical works to be developed on the education of the large numbers of Asian American youths growing up in the United States in the 1980s and beyond.[1]

Yet another reason for the apparent dearth of publications explicitly on Asian American education history is the sociocultural nature of education. Because of this, historians have embedded their discussion of education within larger studies. Schooling thus becomes part of the studies' political, economic, cultural, and social analyses. As a result, the inclusion of education history is not readily apparent by reading titles of monographs. In *Americanization, Acculturation, and Ethnic Identity*, for example, Eileen Tamura embeds her analysis of schooling within the post–World War I Americanization hysteria that swept Hawai'i. Americanizers who feared the potential political and economic power of the Nisei—second-generation Japanese Americans—wanted to control their schooling in order to have cheap, manageable labor for the sugar plantations. At the same time, the Nisei had their own ideas about their lives and futures, actively shaping and using the environment—including both English-language and Japanese-language schools—for their own purposes. In *Growing Up Nisei*, David Yoo examines the ways in which Nisei negotiated their lives in California, developing and affirming their American identity through community institutions, among them schools, churches, and the immigrant press. In *Children of Chinatown* Wendy Jorae breaks through the dominant image of Chinese men living and working in urban America during the nineteenth and early twentieth centuries by making visible the role that children—albeit a small proportion of the Chinese population—played in the development of what was then the largest community of Chinese in the United States. She discusses the youths' segregated schooling within the context of their lives amidst anti-Chinese hostility, crime, and violence. And in "History as Law and Life," Mae Ngai analyzes Chinese American access to schooling in San Francisco within a larger analysis of assimilation and the emergence of a Chinese middle class.[2]

While most studies on the Chinese, like Jorae's and Ngai's, are situated on the West Coast and particularly in California because of the predominance of the Chinese population there, other places in the United States offer fruitful areas for research. In her article "Crafting a Delta Chinese Community," Sieglinde Lim de Sánchez demonstrates the importance of the Deep South in Asian American education history. She complicates the black-white dichotomy by examining how the Chinese, considered neither black nor white, sought schooling for their children at a Baptist mission school, to the unfortunate marginalization of those of mixed African and Chinese descent. Articles in noneducation journals have illuminated other little-known aspects of Asian American education. Yuki Yamazaki's "St. Francis Xavier School" and Lillian Pereyra's "The Catholic Church and Portland's Japanese" examine Catholic schools that taught its Japanese American students in both English and Japanese during the decades before World War II. In offering bilingual education, these schools were like the ethnic parochial schools that served millions of European immigrant children during the nineteenth and early twentieth centuries. As these examples indicate, Catholic and Protestant mission schools played an important role in educating Asian American children.[3]

Since the 1980s there have been a plethora of nonhistorical studies on the education of a wide diversity of Asian American groups, including East, Southeast, and South Asian groups, such as Koreans, Filipinos, Vietnamese, Hmong, and Asian Indians. Because historical studies emerge decades after the events in question, educational histories of these groups have emerged more slowly. Such studies will grapple with issues of identity, and language, which have been central to post-1965 children of Asian immigrants as they were with youths of the earlier period. Gender issues, largely missing in historical studies of pre–World War II youths, will become fruitful areas of investigation for studies of both pre- and post-1965 youths. Available to historians will be statistical studies on post-1965 youths, like the one by Valerie Ooka Pang, Peggy Han, and Jennifer Pang, which disaggregates data on the performance of Asian American students, thereby demonstrating the fallacy of the Asian American model minority stereotype, which lumps together diverse youths who are heterogeneous in ancestral lands, cultural values, socioeconomic levels, and parental levels of schooling. Fewer social science studies have been available about Asian American teachers, principals, and school staff members—to be sure, a small proportion of all school personnel and yet an important segment of Asian America. Historians will want to examine, for example, the experiences of Asian American school personnel across the country; their feelings of acceptance and rejection; their interactions with students, parents, and school personnel; and their ability or inability to move up the bureaucratic hierarchy.

Furthermore, post-1965 Asian Americans, and increasingly so in the twenty-first century, have had a different human environment from those of the pre–World War II period. That is, the growing proportion of the nonwhite population since 1965 and the increasing acceptance of LGBT persons bring up the question of what we mean by "mainstream society." Then, too, differences between the working class and professional class within Asian America have added to the changed demographic milieu. Additionally, technological advances, permitting easier communication with people in other countries and more frequent travel to and from their ancestral lands, have resulted in increasing instances of transnationalism. What has this meant in terms of integration into American society? Investigating the ways in which Asian immigrants and their descendants have become part of the various segments of American society is a potentially rich area of study. Also important would be comparative studies between pre- and post-1965 immigrant youths. Then, too, awaiting historians of education are much-needed studies on Asian American interethnic collaboration and conflict in schooling—such as Jeff Chang's essays, which examine tensions in the 1970s among Filipino immigrant professionals and Japanese Americans. Yet another promising area of historical research is that of bi-ethnic or multiethnic youths who can trace part of their ethnic ancestry to Asia. In Hawai'i the proportion of such people has grown substantially, constituting 50 percent of the population in the 2010s. California's multiethnic population has also grown, and other states are following suit. Historians might well investigate the ways in which bi-ethnic and multiethnic youths confronted issues of ethnic identity and the ways in which these issues affected the youths' schooling experiences and their interactions with others.[4]

In addition to K–12 schooling, institutions of higher education have been an area of historical inquiry. Before the 1970s, it was rare to have an Asian American at the helm of a university. But that was not the only reason why Gerald and Janice Haslam's biography and Daryl Maeda's chapter about S. I. Hayakawa are important to Asian American education history. A respected academic who in 1968 was appointed acting president of San Francisco State (SFS), Hayakawa found himself at the center of a bitter student strike. During the struggle between administrators on one side, and students and faculty on the other, SFS became the first institution of higher education to establish a college of ethnic studies. Asian American students, as Karen Umemoto reveals, were active participants in this effort. In *Chains of Babylon*, Maeda places the strike within the larger context of the rise of Asian America. William Wei, in *The Asian American Movement*, recounts the drive to establish Asian American studies programs on university campuses. As a result of the success of this student-led movement, the next three decades witnessed the appearance of Asian American courses and programs on college campuses nationwide. While the aforementioned studies focus on Asian Americans, emerging scholars have examined student activism that involved interracial collaboration on college campuses during the 1960s and 1970s. Such studies promise to provide new avenues for understanding Asian American college-student life.[5]

An area rich for scholarly study has been Asian American college/university students—in the many facets that this topic entails. One historical period that I discuss later in this essay is World War II, when imprisoned Japanese American youths were allowed to leave the U.S. War Relocation Authority camps in order to attend institutions of higher education away from the West Coast. Another is the Asian American student movement mentioned previously. But the increasing number of Asian American college students since the late 1970s has given historians much more to study. An issue that became the subject of controversy in the 1980s was the debate over affirmative action. Activists declared that administrators of elite universities were limiting the admission of Asian American students. Dana Takagi has argued that neoconservatives were able to turn this discussion in their favor by portraying Asian Americans as victims of affirmative action, whereby—according to neoconservatives—less qualified blacks and Latinos were being admitted. As Sharon Lee argues, in "Over-Represented and De-Minoritized," the perceptions of Asian Americans as a model minority on the one hand and foreign on the other have intersected in debates over Asian American overrepresentation in elite institutions of higher education. In "The De-Minoritization of Asian Americans," which focuses on admissions to University of California campuses, Lee provides one of the few historical studies on Asian Americans in higher education during the post-1965 period. Another aspect of Asian American higher education, student campus life—the encouragement or discouragement they received, services they received or were denied, instances of discrimination and racism, comfort zones or social alienation, gender issues, and other aspects of campus climate—is a subject that has been examined by nonhistory scholars but has as yet been largely untouched by historians. Moreover, there is a need for historians to examine student life at nonelite as well as elite institutions of higher education, including community colleges. Still another area for historians is the experiences of Asian American faculty and administrators in higher education, among them access to employment, work life, barriers encountered, and gender issues.[6]

Since the 1990s, there have been increasing discussion and critique of the epistemol-ogy of Asian American studies. Scholars have problematized once-accepted notions that decades later will become fodder for historians interested in analyzing the ways in which scholars in Asian American studies have understood the field. What have been the prevailing assumptions, theories, frames of reference, and methodologies over time? How have the debates over the nature of Asian American studies been played out in scholarly works and in college and university classrooms? What have been the institu-tional and academic places and positions of Asian American studies in higher education across different regions of the country? In 1999, Mitchell Chang offered an early critique of the field, and a few years later *Amerasia Journal*'s guest editor Aril Dirlik brought together essays on the direction and possibilities of the field. Still later, Mark Chang pro-duced a thought-provoking monograph, Erika Lee situated Asian American studies in the Midwest, and the *Journal of Asian American Studies*, with the coeditors Susie J. Pak and Elda E. Tsou, devoted an entire issue on the subject. These works and others should provide rich sources for historical analysis.[7]

While some historians might argue against engaging in historical studies on col-lege campus life of the more recent past, such studies can be used effectively to inform the present. This is especially so in regards to Asian American education history, since the bulk of immigration since 1965 has resulted in a wider diversity of Asian American college students, such as Filipino, Vietnamese, Korean, and Asian Indian Americans. Historians, with their emphasis on context, continuity, change, and causation, can pro-vide a much-needed perspective. The same argument can be made about post-1965 K–12 schooling. As is always the case with history, later generations of historians will interpret the same events anew, with an eye to their own contemporary concerns.

While schooling accounts for just a fraction of people's lives, the field of educational history has been dominated with studies on formal education: both K–12 and post-secondary schooling. The same can be said about Asian American education history. However, there have been some exceptions. Hannah Tavares's work, which I discuss fur-ther in this essay, examines the dark side of educational efforts at the turn of the twenti-eth century, when the U.S. government justified its military aggression in the Philippines by sponsoring reports and studies and by producing large-scale Filipino exhibits at world's fairs, all with the purpose of representing the colonized people as childlike, ignorant, and needing the guidance of Americans. Tamura examines another nonformal educational effort by the U.S. government, this time during World War I, when it took concerted action to instill patriotism in its citizens through the millions of posters it distributed nationwide. In addition, in its boot camps, the military worked with progressive reformers to Americanize enlisted men who were immigrants and children of immigrants. Tamura also reveals the ways in which adult Nikkei at the War Relocation Authority camp at Manzanar made meaning of their incarceration through discussions and often rancorous debates. These exchanges, while unstructured and informal, proved their power, as demonstrated by the inmates' ensuing revolt against injustice. As the foregoing indicates, much education occurs outside the formal school curriculum. The influential philosopher John Dewey, with his ideas on thinking, reflection, and experience in learning, is closely associated with nonformal and informal education. By nonformal education, I refer to the organized and purposeful transmission of ideas and values outside the schoolhouse walls. The educational historian Lawrence Cremin has been influential in articulating this aspect of education. By informal education, I refer to learning that occurs spontaneously and unsystematically. In the nineteenth century, Frederick Packard noted that education happens not always by "direct intentional methods, but by the numberless incidental influences which act upon the minds and hearts [of people] as silently and mysteriously as light and air upon vegetable life." Donald Warren picked up on these ideas. In "The Wonderful Worlds of the Education of History," he wrote that this meant looking for "certain qualities of experience," staying "alert for phenomena that seem to reveal places [of learning]," and "[probing] for consequences, even buried ones" to "expose . . . varied instances of processes legitimately classified as educational." Both nonformal and informal education are rich areas of inquiry awaiting historians of Asian American education.[8]

Possibilities for historians of Asian American education also lie in the use of theory to inform their work. While educational research scholars generally embrace theory, most U.S. educational historians tend to eschew it. This tendency was the subject of a history of education panel at a 2009 conference of the American Educational Research Association. Defining theory as "an interpretive framework that emerges from primary sources and serves as a lens to analyze evidence and experience in order to explain identities, actions, events, realities, rationalities, and other human phenomena," the panel challenged the lack of theoretical works among U.S. educational historians. While one could argue that narrative is a theoretical approach, panelists distinguished its definition by specifically referring to "the engagement and mobilization of Marxist, feminist, critical race, queer, and social-constructivist theories as well as 'post' approaches to historical interpretation, including postmodern, poststructuralist, and postcolonial theories." The panel presentation created lively discussion among education historians during the conference and led to a special issue of *History of Education Quarterly* (*HEQ*), in which seven prominent historians of education, some who had earlier used theory and others who had not, were asked to respond to three essays that derived from the panel presentations. Their responses ranged from enthusiastic support to heated criticism, which reflected their acceptance and nonacceptance of theory, and its use and nonuse in their own works.[9]

Like other educational historians, few of those working on Asian America engage in theory extensively. The reason may come from the nature of doing history, which takes an inductive, interpretive approach and gives primacy to the particular and to a multiplicity of sources, which often means turning away from what can be an imposition of theoretical constructs. Yet theory does not necessarily need to work at cross-purposes with an evidence-centered approach. As Nancy Beadie wrote in her response to the three essays in the *HEQ* issue discussed in the previous paragraph, theory can be used "as a kind of intellectual tool or probe . . . to explore and investigate relationships in a particular case" . . . [making] "visible stories that otherwise [may] not be seen." Roland Coloma, in "'Destiny Has Thrown the Negro and the Filipino under the Tutelage of America,'" demonstrates this use of theory as a tool. He engages Michel Foucault's concept of archaeology to unearth issues of race and empire in public education in the Philippines at the turn of the twentieth century. Coloma uses Foucault to explore ways in which the schooling of colonized Filipinos, who were deemed racially black by American imperialists, was patterned after the nonacademic, manual-industrial curriculum for African Americans of the U.S. South. Tavares likewise uses theory to help her analyze the racial subordination of Filipinos during the turn of the twentieth century. Drawing on Judith Butler's concept of subjection, Tavares examines so-called expert accounts that depicted Filipinos as subaltern and rationalized their colonization to the American public. Perhaps because both Coloma and Tavares were both imbued with theory in their doctoral programs and did not have educational historians as advisors, they have felt unconstrained by the canons of educational history and comfortable in using theory as other educational researchers do.[10]

While one can argue that Asian American education history should be clearly distinguished from Asian education history—as one can argue that Asian American studies should be distinguished from Asian studies—the two fields intersect in at least two important ways. One intersection is evident in instances of transnationalism. In *Seeking Modernity in China's Name*, Weili Ye examines the experiences of a small group of pioneering young Chinese men and women who studied in U.S. colleges and universities during the early decades of the twentieth century, a time of strong anti-Asian hostilities in the United States. While many had thought to initiate political reform in their homeland, political upheaval there disheartened them. Yet they returned to become leaders in government, industry, and education, introducing ideas that contributed to China's emerging modernity. Their experiences, like the experiences of Chinese cadets at West Point, illustrate instances of early twentieth-century transnationalism, when Asian youths studying in the United States negotiated their way between the contrasting mores of Chinese and American societies.[11]

The reverse transnational experience occurred when Japanese American youths left their birth country to study in Japan. Using both Japanese- and English-language sources, Eiichiro Azuma, in "'The Pacific Era Has Arrived,'" examines the educational experiences in Japan of Americans of Japanese ancestry. During the 1930s, thousands of such youths sojourned in Japan to attend high school or college, in order to learn the language and culture of their ancestral land. Such transnational education in a time of increasing tensions between Japan and the United States was viewed with suspicion by the U.S. government and the public. Caught up in the opposing ideologies and interests of the two countries, these youths found themselves as targets of suspicion in both countries. Scholars in Japan have also been interested in Japanese American education history. For example, like Azuma, Yuko Konno has examined Japanese American youths studying in Japan during the decade before World War II.[12]

On the borderline between Asian education history and Asian American education history are works that examine the lives of Asians who attended schools in the United States and then remained there in succeeding decades. Gordon Chang and Yuji Ichioka have each examined the experiences of Yamato Ichihashi, one of the earliest Asian scholars in the United States, a Japanese national who was schooled in American educational institutions and subsequently taught at Stanford University, a person who had a foot in each country while never feeling fully comfortable in either. Barbara Posadas and Roland Guyotte provide the case of Filipino students in Chicago who, in the 1920s, attended U.S. colleges at the behest of the Philippine government. While the students were expected to return to their homeland, many instead remained in the United States.[13]

The other point of intersection between Asian American education history and Asian education history is the element of Americanness in their respective histories. While Asian American education history is first and foremost an American historical phenomenon, and Asian education history is not, U.S. power and hegemonic relations with Asian countries dictate the necessity for historians to interrogate American influences in the development of Asian educational ideas and institutions. In *The History of Modern Japanese Education*, for example, Benjamin Duke demonstrates how Japan during the Meiji period borrowed American and other Western ideas and incorporated them within a Japanese educational framework. More frequently, scholars have examined the ways in which the U.S. government used education to control and regulate its colonized people, and the political and cultural implications of its imperial educational policies. In *Empire and Education*, Coloma analyzes U.S. efforts at formal and nonformal education in the Philippines. Using primary sources in English, Spanish, and Tagalog, he discusses educational policy, curricula, teacher preparation, sports, and sanitation programs. In "Colonial Lessons," Funie Hsu demonstrates how colonial educational policy in the Philippines was modeled after late nineteenth-century policies concerning American Indians and African Americans, at the same time that it was both influenced by and contributed to educational policies in Hawai'i, Puerto Rico, and Cuba. Another example of imperialism can be seen in the efforts of American missionaries, who proselytized across Asia during the late nineteenth and early twentieth centuries. Among the many publications on this subject is one by Gael Graham, who recounts the work of American Protestants. Establishing schools in China in order to spread Christianity and the ideas of Western civilization, their vision was to bring a superior way of life to a backward people. Revolutionary changes in China, the rise of Chinese nationalism, and secular American consumerism back home, however, led these missionaries to reconsider Confucianism as a positive force and to question their efforts to change Chinese society. The challenge for these and other scholars of U.S. imperialism is to uncover the worldviews, social relationships, and agency of those subjugated.[14]

Much has been argued—by both Chinese and American scholars—about the American philosopher John Dewey's 1919–1921 stay in China, where he was enthusiastically received as he traversed the country, lecturing on education and democracy, participating in conferences, and meeting with educational and political leaders. While much has been written, the significance of his visit remains an open question. Also in question has been the educational impact of the U.S. occupation in Japan, a subject of keen interest among both American and Japanese scholars. For one, Hans Martin Kramer, in "Reforms of Their Own," disputes assumptions that Americans took a dominant role in shaping Japan's educational reforms. Focusing on higher education, Kramer argues that U.S. efforts were counterbalanced by Japanese resistance. Nevertheless, Kramer agrees that American influence was strong, a view argued in Ruriko Kumano's "Anticommunism and Academic Freedom." Kumano, like Kramer, uses both Japanese- and English-language sources to examine the role of the civilian educationist Walter Eells in the U.S. effort to pressure Japan's national universities to fire communist professors. She demonstrates how the United States—through Eells—was able to voice its views without issuing direct orders. Other Japanese scholars have also published works on American educational influences in this pivotal period of Japanese-U.S. history, and dissertations continue to be written on this subject.[15]

These examples of America in Asia occurred within the context of international relations between the United States and particular Asian nations. Likewise, instances of educational controversy in Asian America often occur during times of tension between nations. In an early study, *All Deliberate Speed*, Charles Wollenberg examines the international situation in his analysis of the Japanese immigrant challenge to efforts to block their children from attending San Francisco public schools with whites. Wollenberg discusses the issue within the framework of Japan's victory in the Russo-Japanese War of 1904–1905 and its growing military strength, which escalated U.S. anti-Japanese sentiment at the same time that it caused a diplomatic crisis. President Theodore Roosevelt was forced to intervene, resulting in the Gentlemen's Agreement of 1907–1908, a compromise in which the San Francisco school board agreed to rescind its segregation policy, Japan agreed to end labor migration to the United States, and Roosevelt agreed to issue an executive order that prevented Japanese laborers from entering the U.S. mainland through Hawai'i, Mexico, and Canada. In yet another way, international tensions affected the schooling of Japanese American youths in the attempt to eliminate Japanese-language schools in Hawai'i, California, and Washington. Using both English- and Japanese-language sources, Noriko Asato's *Teaching Mikadoism* connects the controversies in the three locales, building on earlier works on the subject at the same time that it critiques their shortcomings.[16]

A more direct effect on the education of Japanese American youths occurred during World War II, when they and their parents were exiled into U.S. concentration camps. The first important study on the youths' schooling is Thomas James's *Exile Within*. James illuminates the irony of the attempt to infuse ideas of democracy in the curriculum for students impounded during the war because of their race. James succeeds in interweaving a complicated story of schooling with the backdrop of unrest and turmoil of life within barbed wire. Patricia Roy discusses the war situation of Japanese Canadian youths, who had been removed with their parents to the interior of British Columbia. Roy examines their schooling in poorly staffed, substandard facilities that were barely funded by the federal government. As Roger Daniels notes, what is lacking in education histories of the concentration camps is a serious study of the teachers who taught in the schools there. In contrast, there is no lack of publications on the more than 4,000 youths who were allowed to leave their confinement in order to attend Midwest and East Coast colleges and universities. Allan Austin's *From Concentration Camp to Campus* examines the efforts of European and Japanese Americans to counter racism through the National Japanese American Student Relocation Council (NJASRC), a nongovernmental group established to assist the Nisei in their relocation, and Gary Okihiro's *Storied Lives* recounts the experiences of Nisei who benefited from the efforts of the NJASRC. A little-explored educational aspect of this period is the schooling of children of enemy aliens who were allegedly suspected of engaging in subversive activities. They were incarcerated in a set of camps administered by the Justice Department's Immigration and Naturalization Service (INS). In *Schools behind Barbed Wire*, Karen Riley tackles this subject by examining schooling in the Crystal City camp in Texas. Had the author included some context for the INS camps—for example, the number of such camps, their location, and the uniqueness or similarity of the Crystal City camp with other INS camps—the reader would have a useful framework with which to better understand the Crystal City camp. Nevertheless, her study on an INS camp, like other studies on the War Relocation Authority camps, informs contemporary concerns in a time of global tensions and the rhetoric of war.[17]

There is much yet to be examined in the educational history of Asian Americans, in both the pre- and post-1965 periods. In selecting issues for examination, the historian should not shy away from considering present-day concerns. While most historians can agree that understanding the past helps to understand the present, and while present-day issues influence noneducation historians in their choices of research topics, it is particularly in the field of education that scholars are confronted with the pressing need to understand contemporary problems. This is understandable, given the hotly debated subject of schooling. In this light, historians who write on Asian America might well consider grappling with educational issues that have obvious relevance to current questions. Their studies would have a wide audience among the public as well as educational researchers, and they have the potential to make a profound contribution to our understanding of the present.

NOTES

1. Eileen H. Tamura, "Asian Americans in the History of Education: An Historiographical Essay," *History of Education Quarterly* 41, no. 1 (2001): 58–71; *History of Education Quarterly*, special issue, 43, no. 1 (2003).

2. Eileen H. Tamura, *Americanization, Acculturation, and Ethnic Identity: The Nisei Generation in Hawaii* (Champaign: University of Illinois Press, 1994); David K. Yoo, *Growing Up Nisei: Race, Generation, and Culture among Japanese Americans of California, 1924–49* (Champaign: University of Illinois Press, 2000); Wendy Rouse Jorae, *The Children of Chinatown: Growing Up Chinese American in San Francisco, 1850–1920* (Chapel Hill: University of North Carolina Press, 2009); Mae Ngai, "History as Law and Life: *Tape v. Hurley* and the Origins of the Chinese Middle Class," in *Chinese Americans and the Politics of Race and Culture*, ed. Sucheng Chan and Madeline Y. Hsu (Philadelphia: Temple University Press, 2008), 62–90.

3. Sieglinde Lim de Sánchez, "Crafting a Delta Chinese Community: Education and Acculturation in Twentieth-Century Southern Baptist Mission Schools," *History of Education Quarterly* 43, no. 1 (2003): 74–90; Yuki Yamazaki, "St. Francis Xavier School: Acculturation and Enculturation of Japanese Americans in Los Angeles, 1921–1945," *U.S. Catholic Historian* 18, no. 1 (2000): 54–73; Lillian A. Pereyra, "The Catholic Church and Portland's Japanese: The Untimely St. Paul Miki School Project," *Oregon Historical Quarterly* 94 (1993): 399–434.

4. Valerie Ooka Pang, Peggy P. Han, and Jennifer M. Pang, "Asian American and Pacific Islander Students: Equity and the Achievement Gap," *Educational Researcher* 40, no. 8 (2011): 378–389; Jeff Chang, "Local Knowledge(s): Notes on Race Relations, Panethnicity and History in Hawai'i," *Amerasia Journal* 22, no. 2 (1996): 1–29; Jeff Chang, "Lessons of Tolerance: Americanism and the Filipino Affirmative Action Movement in Hawai'i," *Social Process in Hawai'i* 37 (1996): 112–145; *State of Hawai'i Databook 2010* (Honolulu: DBEDT, 2011), Table 1.38.

5. Gerald W. Haslam and Janice E. Haslam, *In Thought and Action: The Enigmatic Life of S. I. Hayakawa* (Lincoln: University of Nebraska Press, 2011); Daryl Maeda, *Chains of Babylon: The Rise of Asian America* (Minneapolis: University of Minneapolis Press, 2009); Karen Umemoto, "'On Strike!' San Francisco State College Strike, 1968–69: The Role of Asian American Students," *Amerasia Journal* 15, no. 1 (1989): 3–41; William Wei, *The Asian American Movement* (Philadelphia: Temple University Press, 1993).

6. Dana Y. Takagi, *The Retreat from Race: Asian-American Admissions and Racial Politics* (New Brunswick, NJ: Rutgers University Press, 1992); Sharon S. Lee, "Over-Represented and De-Minoritized: The Racialization of Asian Americans in Higher Education," *InterActions: UCLA Journal of Education and Information Studies* 2, no. 2 (2006), http://escholarship.org/uc/item/4r7161b2#page-1; Sharon S. Lee, "The De-Minoritization of Asian Americans: A Historical Examination of the Representations of Asian Americans in Affirmative Action Admissions Policies at the University of California," *Asian American Law Journal* 15 (2008): 129–152; Jennifer C. Ng, Sharon S. Lee, and Yoon K. Pak, "Contesting the Model Minority and Perpetual Foreigner Stereotypes: A Critical Review of Literature on Asian Americans in Education," *Review of Research in Education* 31 (2007): 113–119; Robert T. Teranishi, Laurie B. Behringer, Emily A. Grey, and Tara L. Parker, "Critical Race Theory and Research on Asian Americans and Pacific Islanders in Higher Education," *New Directions for Institutional Research*, no. 142 (2009): 57–68.

7. Mitchell J. Chang, "Expansion and Its Discontents: The Formation of Asian American Studies Programs in the 1990s," *Journal of Asian American Studies* 2, no. 2 (1999): 181–206; Mark Chiang, *The Cultural Capital of Asian American Studies: Autonomy and Representation in the University* (New York: New York University Press, 2009); Erika Lee, "Asian American Studies in the Midwest: New Questions, Approaches, and Communities," *Journal of Asian American Studies* 12, no. 3 (2009): 247–273; *Journal of Asian American Studies* 14, no. 2 (2011).

8. Hannah M. Tavares, "The Racial Subjection of Filipinos in the Early Twentieth Century," in *The History of Discrimination in U.S. Education: Marginality, Agency, and Power*, ed. Eileen H. Tamura (New York: Palgrave Macmillan, 2008), 17–40; Eileen H. Tamura, "Value Messages Collide with Reality: Joseph Kurihara and the Power of Informal Education," *History of Education Quarterly* 50, no. 1 (2010): 1–33; John Dewey, *How We Think: A Restatement of the Relation of Reflective Thinking to the Educative Process* (Boston: D. C. Heath, 1933); John Dewey, *Experience and Education* (New York: Macmillan, 1959 [1938]); Lawrence A. Cremin, *Public Education* (New York: Basic Books, 1976), 21, 22, 27; Frederick A. Packard, *The Daily Public School in the United States* (Philadelphia: Lippincott, 1866), 15–16, quoted in Richard Storr, "The Education of History: Some Impressions," *Harvard Educational Review* 31, no. 2 (1961): 130; Donald Warren, "The Wonderful Worlds of the Education of History," *American Educational History Journal* 32, no. 1 (2005): 109.

9. Eileen H. Tamura, Caroline Eick, and Roland Sintos Coloma, "Theory in Educational History," *History of Education Quarterly* 51, no. 2 (2011): 148; *History of Education Quarterly* 51, no. 2 (2011).

10. Nancy Beadie, "Probing the Deep: Theory and History," *History of Education Quarterly* 51, no. 2 (2011): 212; Roland Sintos Coloma, " 'Destiny Has Thrown the Negro and the Filipino under the Tutelage of America': Race and Curriculum in the Age of Empire," *Curriculum Inquiry* 39, no. 4 (2009): 295–319; Tavares, "Racial Subjection of Filipinos," 1–40.

11. Sau-ling C. Wong, "Denationalization Reconsidered: Asian American Cultural Criticism at a Theoretical Crossroads," *Amerasia Journal* 21, nos. 1 and 2 (1995): 1–28; Shirley Hune, "Asian American Studies and Asian Studies: Boundaries and Borderlands of Ethnic Studies and Area Studies," in *Color-Line to Borderlands: The Matrix of American Ethnic Studies*, ed. Johnnella E. Butler (Seattle: University of Washington Press, 2001), 227–239; Jonathan Y. Okamura, "Asian American Studies in the Age of Transnationalism: Diaspora, Race, Community," *Amerasia Journal* 29, no. 2 (2003): 171–193; Weili Ye, *Seeking Modernity in China's Name: Chinese Students in the United States, 1900–1927* (Stanford, CA: Stanford University Press, 2001); Charles D. Krumwiede, "Chinese Cadets at West Point," in *West Point: Two Centuries and Beyond*, ed. Lance Betros (Abilene, TX: McWhiney Foundation, 2004), 299–320.

12. Eiichiro Azuma, " 'The Pacific Era Has Arrived': Transnational Education among Japanese Americans, 1932–1941," *History of Education Quarterly* 43, no. 2 (2003): 39–73; Yuko Konno, "Kyoiku niokeru Toransu-nashonarizumu: Senzen ni Rainichishita Nikkei Amerikajin 2sei Gakuto no Kyogu, Doki, oyobi Taiken no Bunseki" [Transnationalism in education: The backgrounds, motives, and experiences of Nisei students in Japan before World War II]. *Amerika-Kanada Kenkyu* (Tokyo) 27 (2009): 81–113.

13. Gordon H. Chang, ed., *Morning Glory, Evening Shadow: Yamato Ichihashi and His Internment Writings, 1942–1945* (Stanford, CA: Stanford University Press, 1997); Yuji Ichioka, *Before Internment: Essays in Prewar Japanese American History* (Stanford,

CA: Stanford University Press, 2006), 227–257; Barbara M. Posadas and Roland L. Guyotte, "Unintentional Immigrants: Chicago's Filipino Foreign Students Become Settlers, 1900–1941," *Journal of American Ethnic History* 9, no. 2 (1990): 26–48.

14. Benjamin C. Duke, *The History of Modern Japanese Education: Constructing the National School System, 1872–1890* (New Brunswick, NJ: Rutgers University Press, 2009); Roland Sintos Coloma, *Empire and Education: Filipino Subjects under United States Rule*, forthcoming; Funie Hsu, "Colonial Lessons: Racial Politics of Comparison and the Development of American Educational Policy in the Philippines," in *The "Other" Students: Filipino Americans, Education and Power*, ed. Dina C. Maramba and Rick Bonus, 39–64 (Charlotte, NC: Information Age, 2013); Gael Graham, *Gender, Culture, and Christianity: American Protestant Mission Schools in China, 1880–1930* (New York: Peter Lang, 1995).

15. Zhixin Su, "A Critical Evaluation of John Dewey's Influence on Chinese Education," *American Journal of Education* 103, no. 3 (1995): 302–325; Hans Martin Kramer, "Reforms of Their Own: The Japanese Resistance to Changes in Higher Education Administration under the U.S. American Occupation, 1945–1952," *Paedagogica Historica* 43, no. 3 (2007): 327–345; Ruriko Kumano, "Anticommunism and Academic Freedom: Walter C. Eells and the 'Red Purge' in Occupied Japan," *History of Education Quarterly* 50, no. 4 (2010): 513–537.

16. Charles Wollenberg, *All Deliberate Speed: Segregation and Exclusion in California Schools, 1855–1975* (Berkeley: University of California Press, 1978); Noriko Asato, *Teaching Mikadoism: The Attack on Japanese Language Schools in Hawaii, California, and Washington, 1919–1927* (Honolulu: University of Hawai'i Press, 2006); Hironori Watari, "Senzen Hawai Nihongo Gakko Mondai: Amerika 'Shimin' Ronso to Nihongo Kyoiku Hoshin no Henkan" [The Japanese language school controversy in Hawaii before World War II: The debate over the American 'citizen' and the change in Japanese-language education policy]. *Shakai Shisutemu Kenkyu* (Kyoto) 13 (2010): 221–233.

17. Thomas James, *Exile Within: The Schooling of Japanese Americans, 1942–1945* (Cambridge, MA: Harvard University Press, 1987); Patricia E. Roy, "The Education of Japanese Children in the British Columbia Interior Housing Settlements during World War Two," *Historical Studies in Education/Revue d'histoire de l'éducation* 4, no. 2 (1992): 211–231; Roger Daniels, "Educating Youth in America's Wartime Detention Camps," *History of Education Quarterly* 43, no. 1 (2003): 91–102; Allan W. Austin, *From Concentration Camp to Campus: Japanese American Students and World War II* (Champaign: University of Illinois Press, 2004); Gary Y. Okihiro, *Storied Lives: Japanese American Students and World War II* (Seattle: University of Washington Press, 1999); Karen L. Riley, *Schools behind Barbed Wire: The Untold Story of Wartime Internment and the Children of Arrested Enemy Aliens* (Lanham, MD: Rowman and Littlefield, 2002). See also Yoon K. Pak, *Wherever I Go, I Will Always Be a Loyal American: Schooling Seattle's Japanese Americans during World War II* (New York: RoutledgeFalmer, 2002).

FURTHER READING

Austin, Allan W. *From Concentration Camp to Campus: Japanese American Students and World War II*. Champaign: University of Illinois Press, 2004.

Azuma, Eiichiro. "'The Pacific Era Has Arrived': Transnational Education among Japanese Americans, 1932–1941." *History of Education Quarterly* 43, no. 2 (2003): 39–73.

Chang, Jeff. "Local Knowledge(s): Notes on Race Relations, Panethnicity and History in Hawai'i." *Amerasia Journal* 22, no. 2 (1996): 1–29.

Coloma, Roland Sintos. "'Destiny Has Thrown the Negro and the Filipino under the Tutelage of America': Race and Curriculum in the Age of Empire." *Curriculum Inquiry* 39, no. 4 (2009): 295–319.

Daniels, Roger. "Educating Youth in America's Wartime Detention Camps." *History of Education Quarterly* 43, no. 1 (2003): 91–102.

James, Thomas. *Exile Within: The Schooling of Japanese Americans, 1942–1945*. Cambridge, MA: Harvard University Press, 1987.

Lee, Sharon S. "The De-Minoritization of Asian Americans: A Historical Examination of the Representations of Asian Americans in Affirmative Action Admissions Policies at the University of California." *Asian American Law Journal* 15 (2008): 129–152.

Ngai, Mae. "History as Law and Life: *Tape v. Hurley* and the Origins of the Chinese Middle Class." In *Chinese Americans and the Politics of Race and Culture*, edited by Sucheng Chan and Madeline Y. Hsu, 62–90. Philadelphia: Temple University Press, 2008.

Tamura, Eileen H. *Americanization, Acculturation, and Ethnic Identity: The Nisei Generation in Hawaii*. Champaign: University of Illinois Press, 1994.

———. "Value Messages Collide with Reality: Joseph Kurihara and the Power of Informal Education." *History of Education Quarterly* 50, no. 1 (2010): 1–33.

Wollenberg, Charles. *All Deliberate Speed: Segregation and Exclusion in California Schools, 1855–1975*. Berkeley: University of California Press, 1978.

CHAPTER 27

....

NOT ADDING AND STIRRING

Women's, Gender, and Sexuality History and the Transformation of Asian America

....

ADRIENNE ANN WINANS
AND JUDY TZU-CHUN WU

TRANSFORMATIVE possibilities emerge from placing Asian American women, gender, and sexuality at the center of Asian American history. The anthropologist Sylvia Junko Yanagisako noted over twenty years ago that the existing scholarship and courses on Asian American history tended to privilege "a masculine working-class past" that "molds a uniform ethnic, gender, and social-class consciousness out of more divergent material realities."[1] Calling for attention to Asian American women's experiences, Yanagisako argued that these "women disrupt these seemingly exclusive, natural boundaries of class, nation, and ethnic identity by signaling the boundary crossings that have occurred."[2] In other words, a focus on women would not just expand the subject matter worthy of historical attention. The lives, perspectives, and representations of Asian American women alter fundamental paradigms in Asian American history.

The rich scholarship published since the late 1980s in Asian American women's, gender, and sexuality history validates Yanagisako's claims. While women's history focuses on women as historical subjects, gender history examines the social construction of masculinity and femininity and how these constructions vary across time and context. The interpretation of gender as a form of performativity further argues that there are no essential categories of sex differences. Instead, gender is enacted through repeated and oftentimes unconscious patterns of behaviors or gender scripts that create a fiction of a cohesive and preexisting identity of manhood or womanhood. In addition, gender scholars examine how gender hierarchies serve as a constitutive basis for power that are used to justify forms of social inequality. In fact, Asian American historians tend to adopt an intersectional analysis of gender; they explore how gender inequalities are intertwined with other power differences based on race, class, nationality, dis/ability, religion, sexuality, and so on.

Although less explored than Asian American women's and gender history, sexuality history examines the social norms, actual practices, fantasies, and identities associated with bodily pleasure and desire. Queer theoretical approaches to analyzing sexuality challenge essentialist understandings of normative sexuality. Instead, queer theorists posit a range of practices, fantasies, and identifications that transcend either heterosexuality or homosexuality. In addition, sexuality historians and queer theorists deconstruct heteronormativity, the assumption that heterosexuality should be the underlying basis of social and cultural reproduction. Analyzing heteronormativity allows scholars to understand how social, political, economic, and cultural institutions shape sexual norms and practices as well as how sexual hierarchies intersect with and underlie other social inequalities.

THE DEVELOPMENT OF THE FIELD OF ASIAN AMERICAN WOMEN'S, GENDER, AND SEXUALITY HISTORY

Asian American women's history became a significant intellectual field in the late 1980s and 1990s. Nancy I. Kim, in her study on the teaching of Asian American women's history courses, notes that this period was one of transition.[3] After an era of experimentation in course content and pedagogy from 1970 to 1975, Kim argues that Asian American women's history classes became increasingly institutionalized within the mainstream academy from 1976 to 1989 before becoming professionalized in the 1990s. During the experimentation phase of the early 1970s, instructors utilized Asian American activist writings. These writers conducted pioneering research on Asian American women. Influenced by the politics of Third World liberation and the idea of pan-ethnic sisterhood, syllabi during this period included studies about women in Asia. The *Asian Women's Journal*, written and published by a student collective at the University of California, Berkeley, is a canonical text of this era. Originally issued in 1971, the journal was eventually reprinted three times by 1975.[4] During the era of institutionalization from the mid-1970s through the end of the 1980s, courses commonly assigned novels, biographies, and autobiographies by and/or about Asian American women. In addition, the groundbreaking scholarship of the historian Yuji Ichioka, the sociologist Lucy Cheng Hirata, as well as others illuminated a significant group of Asian American "foremothers," namely Japanese and Chinese immigrant prostitutes.[5] The "professionalization" of Asian American women's history courses since the 1990s coincided with the publication of monographs and anthologies on the histories of Asian American women. We believe that this scholarship, which is the primary focus of this essay, could be conceptualized into two cohorts.

The first cohort of Asian American women's historians was part of a larger community of academics invested in foregrounding the lives, perspectives, and significance of women of color. They sought to transform the study of race (gendered as masculine) and womanhood (racialized as white) by examining intersectional and comparative under-standings of social hierarchy and identity.[6] These scholars, who published their works from the mid-1980s through the mid-1990s, included individuals trained in historical analysis, such as Valerie Matsumoto, Peggy Pascoe, and Judy Yung, as well as academics in other fields but invested in historical analysis, such as the political scientist Sucheng Chan and the sociologist Evelyn Nakano Glenn.[7] Inspired by new social histories, they worked with community historians, adopted oral history methodologies, and searched for and helped to archive overlooked Asian American material and textual sources.

A second and larger cohort of professional Asian American women's historians emerged in the late 1990s and the first decade of the twenty-first century. They benefited from the mentorship of the first cohort of scholars and also were influenced by the turn toward cultural, gender, sexuality, and transnational/diasporic forms of history.[8] Rather than accept the subject of "Asian American womanhood" as a given, these works tended to analyze the historical construction of racialized gender roles and identities in rela-tion to evolving normative understandings of nation, citizen, family, and community. Utilizing feminist, queer, and postcolonial theory, this cohort of scholars included his-torians as well as other academics, particularly social science and cultural studies schol-ars. As a result, interdisciplinary works became a key site for new historical analysis and knowledge. Simultaneously, scholars reached beyond the bounds of the American nation-state, they engaged in multishore and multilingual research and analysis in order to understand the gendered dynamics of diaspora, globalization, and empire. Critical attention to the histories of indigenous Pacific Islander women also developed analysis of Asian settler colonialism, of Asian people not as pawns but as perpetrators of empire.

This schematic overview of Asian American women's, gender, and sexuality histori-cal scholarship is by nature selective rather than comprehensive. However, the transi-tion from experimentation to institutionalization and then to professionalization that Nancy Kim identifies in terms of pedagogical practices does shed light on the evolution of research as well. The next four sections will elaborate on the intellectual contribu-tions of the first and second cohorts of historical and interdisciplinary scholarship from the past twenty-plus years. By focusing on Asian American and to a lesser degree on Pacific Islander scholarship on women, gender, and sexuality, this collective literature has helped to transform the analysis of (1) migration, citizenship, and empire; (2) labor and class; (3) family, community, and sexuality; and finally (4) Orientalism, activism, and feminism.

IMMIGRATION, CITIZENSHIP, AND EMPIRE

Immigration and exclusion have been central themes in Asian American history, because the two topics explain the presence and the racialization of Asians in the United States. The most common narrative for understanding the experiences and pat-terns of Asian migration focuses on two primary waves. The first wave, lasting roughly from the mid-nineteenth century through the early decades of the twentieth century, has drawn more historical attention. This rich literature documents and analyzes the legal, economic, social, and cultural exclusions that the disproportionately male Asian migrants faced during this time period. Even as they provided essential labor for the development of the U.S. West, they were designated perpetually foreign as "aliens ineligible to citizenship." Less historical attention has been paid to the second large wave of immigration, which was unleashed by the 1965 Immigration Act that modified discriminatory national-origin quotas. Perhaps due to the more contemporary nature of this period, nonhistorians, particularly sociologists and anthropologists, have studied this era in greater detail. In contrast to the first wave, the second wave had more gender-balanced and even female-dominated forms of migration due to the privileging of family reunification and professional migration. The historical scholarship on Asian American and Pacific Islander women during the past twenty years has enriched and complicated the understanding of migration, citizenship, and empire. These works collectively raise new questions and offer new conceptions about the periodization of immigration, the transnational and sexualized process of crossing borders, and the gendered nature of citizenship.

The scholarship on Asian American women's immigration patterns and experiences identifies new turning points and periods worthy of historical attention. First, in contrast to many synthetic and monograph works that tend to date the first federal act of immigration exclusion to the Chinese Exclusion Act of 1882, scholars interested in the surveillance and exclusion of Chinese women foreground the historical significance of the Page Law of 1875, which targeted both Asian (male) contract laborers as well as Asian (female) prostitutes. Since Chinese women were presumed to be sexually immoral unless they could prove otherwise, the Page Law severely curtailed their migration and established a federal legal precedent for immigration exclusion based on race, class, and sexuality.[9] In addition, historians interested in female migration have increasingly examined the period between the two waves. The era of World War II and the Cold War have received greater recognition as periods of transformative migration, particularly for women who gained entry as military brides, adoptees, refugees, as well as professionals.[10] Their presence significantly changed the nature of family and community formation for Asian as well as non–Asian Americans as these female migrants formed monoracial as well as multiracial kinship units.

A focus on Asian American women not only shifts how we think about key historical events as well as periods of time but also about the transnational process of border crossing. By utilizing government records, immigration files, court cases, oral histories, newspaper accounts, and material culture, scholars have provided new insight into the gendered process of migration. Due to exclusion laws, the legal principle of coverture, as well as racialized cultural assumptions regarding Asian womanhood and sexuality, Asian women faced a plethora of barriers for gaining entry into the United States. Their success in surmounting these barriers during the first wave of migration varied based on nationality, class, access to legal and community resources, and, very importantly, marital status as well as kinship ties, particularly to male migrants.[11] In the post-9/11 era, Islamophobic racialization has impacted the ability of Asian immigrant women, particularly those of West and South Asian ancestry, to enter the United States.[12] And, in the current neoliberal climate, Asian immigrant women also must pass suspicion of being welfare cheats. Their reproductive capability places them under intense government and public scrutiny. As actual or potential mothers, these women are perceived as limited in their ability to economically contribute to the U.S. economy. Simultaneously, reproductive women are suspected of draining American resources through social service utilization.[13]

In addition to this analysis of the gendered enforcement of the border, scholars of Asian American women have emphasized the necessity of understanding immigration transnationally. Sucheta Mazumdar, for example, calls for a comparative analysis to explain why so few Chinese and Indian women migrated not only to the United States but also to other parts of the Asian diaspora during the late nineteenth and early twentieth centuries.[14] She argues that it was due not only to U.S. immigration exclusion laws but also to the increased significance of Asian female productive and reproductive labor in their respective homelands. In addition to the need to understand historical conditions and changes in "sending" countries, other scholars point to the extra-national reach of the U.S. state. In some cases, the American border extended outward through the prescreening of potential migrants on their native lands. In other cases, the expansion of the U.S. empire facilitated migration through economic dislocation, militarized/sexualized encounters with Asian women, and the globalization of American culture. As Catherine Ceniza Choy has argued, Filipina professional migration to the United States in the post–World War II era originated from the gendered impact of the U.S. empire in the Philippines during the first half of the twentieth century.[15] Ji-Yeon Yuh's study also points out that the presence of Korean military brides on American soil stemmed from a broader and longer history of U.S. militarization of Asia during the Cold War.[16] And, Adria L. Imada's work on hula considers how U.S. colonization of Hawaii created transportation and cultural circuits that allowed Native Hawaiians to travel and perform throughout the American empire.[17]

In addition to the gendered analysis of the border and the call for transnational as well as comparative works on migration, scholars of Asian American women's history also contribute to the scholarship on the racialized, gendered, and classed nature of citizenship. In the legal realm of citizenship, Martha Gardner, Laura Kang, and Judy Yung point to the contradictory impact of severing coverture for Asian immigrant and Asian American women.[18] Beginning with the 1907 Expatriation Act, all American women who married immigrant men lost their U.S. citizenship. Due to racial restrictions for naturalization, American-born women of Asian ancestry could not regain their U.S. citizenship. Following the passage of female suffrage, the 1922 Cable Act allowed U.S. women to retain their citizenship status independent of their husbands. Women who married "aliens ineligible to citizenship" remained the sole exception to this principle of female legal independence until 1931. Given the extensive legal restrictions and social sanctions against miscegenation or interracial marriage, these women were most likely to be of Asian ancestry. Coverture or being covered by the legal identity of their husbands and fathers both punished Asian American women and also benefited them. Asian women were more likely to gain entry as wives and daughters of Asian men compared to when they immigrated based on an independent status.[19]

In the face of raced and gendered restrictions, Asian American women worked to build community and made claims to legitimacy and inclusion. The works of Gloria Heyung Chun, Shirley Jennifer Lim, and Valerie Matsumoto illuminate the efforts by American-born women of Asian ancestry to assert their cultural citizenship.[20] As flappers, beauty queens, and sorority members, Asian American women reinvented their assigned outsider identities to make claims for national, ethnic, and at times diasporic belonging. In addition, the works by Brenda Moore, Judy Tzu-Chun Wu, and Judy Yung illuminate the efforts by American-born Asian women to claim national legitimacy by entering the military, the bastion of white male citizenship.[21] Given the prevalence of Orientalist assumptions regarding Asian women, however, their attempts to gain acceptance in the United States at times depended on their ability to perform otherized racial and gender roles.[22] In other words, Asian American women at time engaged in acts of self-Orientalization in order to establish national belonging.[23]

Much of the scholarship in Asian American women's history has focused on attempts to enter into the United States and gain membership in an exclusionary nation-state. In contrast, the emerging studies on Pacific Islanders question the goal of full citizenship and call instead for an alternative vision of obtaining national sovereignty.[24] Indigenous feminist approaches critique U.S. empire as a form of racialized patriarchy and also name Asian American complicity in dislocating indigenous people and their cultures and communities. In some instances, there are efforts to reclaim alternative gender systems that provide opportunities for female political, economic, and spiritual leadership.[25]

Cumulatively, these works on Asian American and Pacific Islander women shed new light on the periodization of immigration and the transnational and sexualized nature of border crossing. This body of scholarship also examines the gendered and racialized constructions of U.S. legal and cultural citizenship. These historical studies both call for full national inclusion and critique U.S. imperialism. These works not only illuminate the experiences, perspectives, and symbolic significance of Asian American and Pacific Islander women. They also offered gendered and sexualized understandings of migration, border enforcement, national belonging, and colonial resistance.

LABORING WOMEN

Asian American women's history also prompts a rethinking of the central categories of labor and class in Asian American history. Deeply influenced by Marxist paradigms as well as social history, the pioneering works in Asian American history focused on the first wave of Asian laborers, who contributed to the economic development of the United States during a crucial era of national expansion and industrialization.

Social scientists also have examined the economic endeavors of the second wave of Asian migrants through three primary sectors: as service and manufacturing laborers; as family-based business owners as well as transnational corporate entrepreneurs; and as highly educated professionals, particularly in the medical and engineering fields.[26] Scholars who focus on Asian American women's work experiences add to this rich scholarship on class and labor. They do so by analyzing the gendered as well as racialized stratification of an increasingly globalized labor market; highlighting the paid as well as unpaid, productive as well as reproductive, labor that women perform; and examining the diversity of occupational and class status that Asian American women occupy.

Studies that focus on Asian American women's work experiences highlight the stratified nature of the labor market. Whether as prostitutes, waitresses, domestics, health care providers, seamstresses, factory operatives, plantation workers, waitresses, flight attendants, or nail-salon beauticians, Asian American women have performed economic roles deemed uniquely suitable for women, particularly women of color.[27] In certain historical periods and social contexts, Asian American men and non–Asian American women have occupied similar roles. Their presence in these positions, however, does not suggest a color-blind or gender-blind economic labor market; in fact, Chinese male laundry workers and Japanese houseboys or Irish, African American, and Latina female domestics confirm that gender and racial stratification are social constructions that change over time and place. Those designated as outsiders (due to racial or legal status or perceived deficiencies of masculinity) and/or as secondary workers (based on patriarchal assumptions of female economic dependence) tend to be slotted into lower-paying occupations that offer little security and provide few to nonexistent benefits. Consequently, Asian American women's economic roles reinforce their marginal citizenship status and provide rich opportunities for comparative racial and gender analysis.[28]

The scholarship on labor stratification has increasingly embraced transnational frameworks of analysis, particularly in this contemporary moment of globalization. Xiaolan Bao, for example, examines how Chinese garment workers in post–World War II New York drew upon a longer history of immigrant female labor organizing within the International Ladies' Garment Workers' Union as well as their own work and activist experiences in Taiwan and the People's Republic of China. Sociologist Rhacel Parreñas also has explored the impact of Filipina domestic worker migration on the national economy of the Philippines as well as on their family members, particularly their children who remain at home.[29] These studies emphasize that the gendered immigrant labor force in the United States is intricately connected to a stratified global economy.

The studies that focus on Asian American women's labor point to the important contributions that they make—in paid as well as unpaid work, through productive as well as reproductive labor. Yanagisako argues that Japanese American women's labor enabled class mobility among Japanese American farmers and family-based businesses over the first half of the twentieth century.[30] Not only were Nikkei women charged with domestic reproductive responsibilities, but they also undertook significant economic roles, most of which were not paid. These women could benefit from the upward mobility of their families, although it is not clear how much direct control they had over collective finances. In other instances, the labor of Asian American women yielded limited rewards for their personal livelihoods. For example, the pioneering sociologist Hirata examined how Chinese immigrant prostitutes, through their sex work as well as their forced participation in manufacturing during "slow" work days, enabled the wealth accumulation of Chinese immigrant male merchants during the late nineteenth century.[31] In more contemporary times, the relatively "cheap" labor of Asian women (either abroad or in the United States) allows American and transnational businesses, including those owned and operated by Asian Americans, to economically compete by lowering production costs in garment and electronics factories. Also, the care work performed by Asian and Asian American women, whether as employees or as family members, frees both men and women, including those of Asian ancestry, to pursue paid work outside of the home with reduced childcare and elder-care responsibilities.

The straddling of un/paid and re/productive labor by Asian American women occurs not only within the United States but also across national borders. During the first wave of mostly Asian male emigration, Asian women performed reproductive as well as productive labor in Asian homelands. Since World War II, when women increasingly become the lead migrants within family kinship networks, they might serve as the primary breadwinners, even if they only find work in secondary or informal job markets. In these scenarios, some families are again "split" transnationally. However, as Parreñas points out, working overseas mothers tend to face greater cultural and emotional pressures compared to working overseas fathers. While both parents might economically contribute to their families, women also are expected to perform the necessary work to reproduce and nurture their kin. When male partners refuse these responsibilities, working mothers more commonly turn to female kin or female employees to fulfill this function. As more women enter the paid labor force, both as producers and reproducers, the previously "unpaid" work of social reproduction within their families becomes subject to gender renegotiation and/or a site for commodification.[32]

The studies of Asian American women's labor have tended to focus on the working class and the economically exploited. This emphasis reflects the social justice mission of the field of Asian American studies. However, more recent works also have examined those who broke gender and racial barriers or occupied positions of influence, such as physicians, midwives, nurses, lawyers, actresses, fashion designers, and business owners. These studies have been careful not to reaffirm the model minority myth, which positions Asian Americans as success stories that confirm the fairness of meritocracy. Rather, these studies point to the persistent racial, gendered, and sexualized barriers that Asian American women negotiate even as they cross these borders. For example, Margaret Chung, the first American-born female physician, adopted an Orientalized maternal persona to cater to client expectations, even as she entered the male profession of Western medicine.[33]

"Success" for these Asian American women does not result merely from a work ethic or a strong family, attributes perceived as inherent to Asian "culture." Instead, the scholarship analyzes shifting structural and historical conditions as well as individual and collective strategies. For example, Stephanie Smith's study on Japanese American midwives notes how changing educational opportunities in Meiji Japan as well as the nature of the health care system in the U.S. West enabled Nikkei women to establish a professional niche prior to World War II.[34] Rather than a story of continual progress, these studies on Asian American women and work illuminate the historical contingencies, the interplay between structure and agency that facilitate particular forms of economic mobility.

While historians have contributed to the study of Asian American women's labor experiences, sociologists and anthropologists have consistently and increasingly provided intellectual leadership in this field. Together, their works have introduced and elaborated on the global stratification of labor, the concepts of un/paid and re/productive work, as well as the efforts and conditions that create economic and professional opportunities.

FAMILY, COMMUNITY, AND SEXUALITY

While Asian American men have been the primary historical focus for narratives about immigration and labor, Asian American women have been central to discussions of family and community. Furthermore, conceptions of kinship and sexuality have been integral to the overall racialization of Asian Americans. During the late nineteenth and early twentieth centuries, the presumed "deviancy" of Asian American sexuality, gender roles, and communities reinforced their status as perpetual foreigners to U.S. society.[35] Given the gender imbalance among Asian immigrants, Asian Americans were perceived as "lacking" in heteronormative nuclear families. Instead, these predominantly "bachelor" communities were characterized as sexually deviant due to the prevalence of prostitution, households of residents not related through nuclear family structures, and other religious and social practices outside the norms of white, Protestant, middle-class America. The presence of Asian American women did not necessarily rectify this presumption. Asian American women were alternately portrayed as hypersexual or as overly passive and oppressed by "Asian" culture and society.[36] The Cold War re-construction of Asian Americans as a "model minority" ironically reversed these gender and sexual stereotypes. In the context of the 1965 Moynihan Report (which critiqued the lack of nuclear families among African Americans as a cause for social dysfunction and social unrest) and the emerging women's movement in the post–World War II era, Asian Americans became perceived as members of model heteronormative nuclear families. These strong kinship units presumably allowed Asian Americans to excel beyond racial barriers, thereby confirming U.S. meritocracy.[37] Historians of Asian American women, gender roles, and sexuality counter and complicate both these tropes of "lack" and "excess." The first cohort of scholars highlighted female agency in Asian American family and community formation both in the United States and transnationally. They also worked to rebut raced and gendered essentializations of Asian American deviant femininity and masculinity, at times reinforcing the normative narrative of the Cold War nuclear family structure. More recent works critique a focus on monoracial heteronormativity. Instead, the scholarship highlights Asian American participation in multiracial, multicultural, queer, and fictive notions of family and community.

Initially, historians challenged the long-standing trope of the deviant nature of "bachelor" societies with a narrative of Asian American family formation in the face of structural barriers of racist immigration laws. First-wave Asian immigrants faced obstacles in forming heteronormative family units due to immigration exclusion as well as antimiscegenation laws.[38] The combination of societal and legal pressures fueled the Orientalist depictions of Asian immigrant communities as "bachelor" societies of sojourners, deviant due to their lack of family formation. In one example of a refutation of this trope, a two-shore approach by the historian Madeline Hsu reframed the bachelor sojourners as family breadwinners within a transnational community.[39]

Women's historians also examined the importance of gendered work in building Asian American communities in the United States through relational networks and cultural institutions, all within the trope of normative nuclear families.[40] Scholarship by historians such as Judy Yung and Valerie Matsumoto placed women's roles within the Asian American community at the forefront of constructing a new vision of the Asian American family.[41] In particular, these works emphasized women's agency in the creation of solidarities through work, activism, and local organizations.[42] Women's relational ties functioned as connections within the community and as bridges to the dominant white society.[43] For example, Yung's pioneering social history of Chinese American women showcases middle-class women's organizations that worked for the betterment of their ethnic community. Yung tells a story of generational change over time as Chinese American women acculturated and as dominant societal restrictions loosened over the first half of the twentieth century.[44]

As studies of Asian American families and communities refuted Orientalist notions of deviancy, the creation of normative nuclear families became part of a master narrative. As the scholars Jennifer Ting and Nayan Shah have pointed out, a long history of exclusionary attempts to prevent Asian American family formations in the United States led historians to focus on a counternarrative that emphasized the normalcy of "bachelor societies."[45] This has led to silences and gaps in the literature of examinations of intimate relations and community ties outside of the nuclear family. Post-1965 changes in immigration law also reinforced a structural privileging of heteronormativity through the principle of family reunification.[46] As Rita Brock suggests, historians could use women's roles as a fulcrum of negotiation and networks of relational kinship to reexamine the histories of Asian America beyond the constraints of the heteronormative nuclear family.[47]

Works on multiracial Asian Americans help displace normative understandings of family and also illuminate structural attempts to control marriage and reproduction.[48] As the historian Peggy Pascoe has shown, mixed-race relationships became a site in the contestation over the "natural" and the deviant. Antimiscegenation laws were passed by various states to create and reinforce gender and racial boundaries of inclusion and exclusion.[49] In challenging these legal restrictions and social sensibilities that prescribe intraracial marriage, the very presence of mixed-race individuals complicates notions of belonging and legitimacy. Anthropologist Karen Leonard's examination of Punjabi-Mexican families suggests that a multiracial identity can form a new ethnic identity, even as monoracial immigrant populations challenge the legitimacy of these hybrid formations.[50] Meanwhile, Historian Ji-Yeon Yuh's study of migration and multiracial marriages for military brides foregrounds individual efforts to negotiate racialized/cultural obstacles in mainstream American society and among Korean American communities.[51]

In addition to complicating the reification of monoraciality, historical examinations of fictive and queer formations of kinship offer nonnormative understandings of family and community. Nayan Shah points out how Asian Americans created "alternative domesticities and homosocial domesticity."[52] They also engaged in homoerotic and homosexual acts of "stranger intimacy." "These queer formations of cohabitation and sexuality challenge heteronormative accounts of Asian American family formation and sexuality. Historian Linda España-Maram also shows that contestations of masculinity took place in public spaces of heterosocial leisure. She examines how Filipino American popular culture served as a site for defining community understandings of masculinity.[53] These social and cultural histories analyze the connections among raced, gendered, and sexual identities and performativity. They open the historical narrative to alternative, heterogeneous, and queer possibilities as sites for resistance to societal and state exclusions.

Two other possibilities for intersection between these new questions and women's history lie in examinations of public performances and women's cultural production. As Rebecca King examines multiraciality in beauty pageants, she does so within a historiography of Asian American community performances as political acts of identity formation. Her work also speaks to a broader trend in women's history in examining the body, presentation, and consumption of femininity.[54] Another way to access fictive kinship is to analyze cultural productions as historical sources. Creative works such as art, poetry, novels, and personal narratives reflect on queer and multiracial negotiation and belonging.[55] The inclusion of these writings about mixed-race and queer identities in anthologies and shared histories on Asian American women acknowledges the diversity within this collective identity.

The scholarship on Asian American women, sexuality, gender, and community has moved the field of Asian American history from claiming to critiquing normativity. Communities are not just questions of connections between mono-ethnic, heteronormative nuclear families, but also of kinship ties that can be heterogeneous, fictive, transnational, queer, and/or multiracial. New investigations into the historical compositions of families and communities will continue to develop understandings of heterogeneity in Asian American history.[56]

ORIENTALISM, ACTIVISM, AND FEMINISM

Historical work on women's experiences, gender, and sexuality has helped to compli-cate an essentialized notion of Asian America. To add to the ways in which historians have examined women's roles as migrants, laborers, family members, and community builders, we now turn to women's activism. Scholars who focus on Asian American women's forms of resistance, conceived as everyday acts as well as organized forms of mass action, apply the lens of intersectionality. In this theoretical framework, oppres-sion because of race, class, ethnicity, nationality, gender, or sexuality forms dynamic lay-ers to be negotiated by historical actors. This approach contrasts with claiming a solitary functionalist or primary cause for oppression and resistance. We examine how recent historical studies portrayed women as they advocated for political change and orga-nized for local, national, and global causes. In many instances, these histories of Asian American women's activism show their efforts to challenge the gendered and sexualized dynamics of Orientalism that resulted in stereotypes of "dragon ladies," "china dolls," or "tiger moms."

The literature on women's activism covers various political goals and strategies. As previously discussued, scholars have examined how Asian American women engaged in claiming American, Asian, and Asian American belonging through public cultural performances in pageants and parades.[57] Asian American women also agitated for workers' rights through strikes, union activism, and the formation of community and gender-based groups that foster class alliances across ethnic and racial boundaries.[58] The fruitful period of activism known as the Asian American movement mobilized women through calls for pan-ethnicity, transnational solidarity with the Third World, domestic social justice, and women's liberation.[59]

The scholarship on women's activism during the Asian American movement is still emerging. Despite the lack of monographic research specifically on Asian American women's activism, scholarship on the social movement does incorporate topics related to women and gender. As historian Daryl Maeda has explored, members of the Asian American movement, as part of its effort to achieve liberation, sought to redefine Asian American masculinity and femininity.[60] Female activists of the Asian American movement, which extended from the late 1960s through the 1970s and beyond, intro-duced an early variant of intersectionality by naming "triple oppression," the oppres-sion that women of color or Third World women experience due to race/nationality, class, and gender.[61] As Laura Pulido and others have examined, the demand to address "triple oppression" met with resistance at times within ethnically/racially based radical organizations that tended to prioritize issues related to racial injustice or class oppres-sion.[62] Asian American women, however, focused attention on and developed analyses of the manifestations of triple oppression. These included gender inequalities within Asian American activist organizations that relied on female labor but privileged male leadership; the exploitation of Asian immigrant female workers; and the expectations that women perform a double shift of productive as well as reproductive labor. Asian American women also developed critiques of racialized heterosexuality, particularly the emasculation of Asian American men, the hypersexualization of Asian American women, and the romantic/sexual value placed on whiteness. Some Asian American women also critiqued heteronormativity and proclaimed lesbian and queer identities. In developing critiques of triple oppression, Asian American women drew inspiration from both women of color in the United States and from Third World women. As Judy Tzu-Chun Wu has analyzed, Asian American women tended to look to female Asian revolutionaries, fighting the U.S. military in Southeast Asia and building socialist societies, for political role models.

These studies of Asian American women's activism encourage critical reflection as to what constitutes Asian American feminism. Activists of the 1960s, 1970s, and even the 1980s and 1990s commonly claimed pan-ethnic Asian American sisterhood and identified strongly with women of color both domestically and worldwide.[63] Life stories of radical women, such as Yuri Kochiyama and Grace Lee Boggs provide insight into ongoing social justice activism beyond the 1960s and 1970s and into the twenty-first century.[64] However, these women did not always identify as Asian American or feminist. In addition, other Asian American women who challenge inequality may do so while also accepting gender and kinship inequalities. Nazli Kibria analyzed how Vietnamese women, as they transitioned from wartorn Viet Nam to the United States as refugees, negotiated for greater agency but did so within patriarchal family structures.[65] And, Bindi Shah documented how young Laotian women embrace their family and community roles as daughters to engage in anti-racist environmental justice movements.[66] Given the sparse historical studies on and the elusiveness of Asian American feminism, interdisciplinary anthologies as well as cultural studies works are often used to teach this topic.[67]

Asian American women's, gender, and sexuality historians of both the first and second cohort were deeply influenced by feminist analysis of history. Their collective works are extending gendered insights about migration, labor, family, and activism. There, however, is a need for further studies of women's activism from the local to the transnational. Doing so will develop our understandings of the historical convergences and cleavages of feminism and Asian American activism.

CONCLUSION

The histories of Asian American and Pacific Islander women—as integral agents in transnational migration flows; as working-class, entrepreneurial, and professional women; as members of diverse forms of family and communities; and as labor, community, radical, and feminist activists—all serve to enhance, complicate, and enrich Asian American history as well as women's history. In doing so, the scholarship of the past twenty years has challenged fundamental conceptions about gender, sexuality, nation, class, kinship, and resistance. Yet much more work remains to be done.

While Asian American women's history has benefited from interdisciplinary collaboration, are historians fully engaging as equal partners in these conversations, particularly in the fields of gender and sexuality studies? For early Asian American histories, one of the challenges remains the paucity of pre-twentieth-century sources. However, creative uses of materials in English-language as well as Asian-language sources could help historians to question and decenter masculinist as well as heteronormative narratives of history. More broadly, while the gender division between men and women is recognized as salient in Asian American history, scholars have not fully interrogated the construction of such gendered categories. Even the designation of "woman" could be deconstructed to consider cis and trans formulations of gender. In addition, the study of sexuality within Asian American history tends to receive relatively less attention.

The further we get from 1965, the greater the as-yet unanswered potential becomes for historical studies of women of these new migrations. For example, the so-called second wave of Asian American migration could be further subdivided to consider the post-1975 refugee migration from Southeast Asia as well as the impact of 9/11 and neoliberalism on national borders and conceptions of belonging. Although historians have increasingly been influenced by gender and cultural approaches, perhaps a renewed interest in social and labor history could position them as significant interpreters of the contemporary political economy.

Women's, gender, and sexuality history also could benefit from more comparative histories on the diversity of Asian America as well as comparative work beyond the United States. Studies of Asian Americans have tended to focus on ethnic-specific groups and increasingly include a more diverse range of Asian ethnicities. However, studies on Chinese and Japanese Americans still dominate the historical scholarship, and few studies on Pacific Islanders exist. Comparative and interactive histories between Asian ethnicities and across racial groups could illuminate more complex social interactions. Also, while "radical" women have attracted the attention of Asian American studies scholars, what about "reformist" or even "conservative" activists and their involvement with U.S. mainstream as well as homeland politics?

In addition to these suggestions to expand the methodology and focus of Asian American women's, gender, and sexuality history, there also are issues related to the position of these studies within the broader academy. There is increasing acknowledgment of the need to study women and sexuality as well as to include a gender analysis in Asian American as well as overall history courses. At the same time, there is reluctance to do so in scholarship and courses not specifically about these topics. Simultaneously, there are increasing numbers of women who are Asian American historians but not necessarily women's or gender or sexuality historians. And, more broadly, there is still a tendency to overlook the historical significance of Asian American and Pacific Islander women within the broader academy. The categories of "women" and "race" still too often default to a binary of whiteness and blackness. And Asian American history still commonly centers on masculine and heteronormative subjects.

Despite these ongoing challenges, scholars in Asian American women's, gender, and sexuality history have been producing groundbreaking work and there is the potential for generating even more conceptually relevant studies. Most members of the first and second cohorts of Asian American women's, gender, and sexuality historians since the 1990s continue to be active in the academy and are assuming positions of intellectual leadership. In addition, there is a new cohort beginning research and on the verge of publishing their works. Their collective insights will be increasingly necessary as Asian Americans maintain their status as the fastest-growing group in the United States and as Asian American and Pacific Islander "women" play central roles as migrants, workers, and family and community members, as well as activists seeking to create a better world.

NOTES

1. Sylvia Junko Yanagisako, "Transforming Orientalism: Gender, Nationality, and Class in Asian American Studies," in *Naturalizing Power: Essays in Feminist Cultural Analysis*, ed. Sylvia Junko Yanagisako and Carol Lowery Delaney (New York: Routledge, 1995), 282.

2. Ibid., 289.

3. Nancy I. Kim, "The General Survey Course on Asian American Women: Transformative Education and Asian American Feminist Pedagogy," *Journal of Asian American Studies* 3, no. 1 (2000): 37–65.

4. *Asian Women's Journal* (University of California, Berkeley, 1971; Asian American Studies Center, University of California, Los Angeles, 1975, 3rd printing).

5. Yuji Ichioka, "Ameyuki-san: Japanese Prostitutes in Nineteenth-Century America," *Amerasia* 4, no. 1 (1977): 1–22; Lucie Cheng Hirata, "Free, Indentured, Enslaved: Chinese Prostitutes in Nineteenth-Century California," *Signs: A Journal of Women in Culture and Society* 5, no. 1 (1979): 3–29.

6. Kimberlé Crenshaw is credited with introducing the term "intersectionality" in her article "Mapping the Margins: Intersectionality, Identity Politics, and Violence against Women of Color," *Stanford Law Review* 43, no. 6 (1991): 1241–1299. Ellen DuBois and Vicki Ruiz's important anthology, *Unequal Sisters: A Multicultural Reader in U.S. Women's History*, was first published in 1990. DuBois and Ruiz would include important work in Asian American women's history in this edition and in future editions of *Unequal Sisters*.

7. Examples include Asian Women United of California, *Making Waves: An Anthology of Writings by and about Asian American Women* (Boston: Beacon, 1989); Sucheng Chan, *Entry Denied: Exclusion and the Chinese Community in America, 1882–1943* (Philadelphia: Temple University Press, 1991); Shamita Das Dasgupta, *A Patchwork Shawl: Chronicles of South Asian Women in America* (New Brunswick, NJ: Rutgers University Press, 1998); Nancy Donnelly, *Changing Lives of Refugee Hmong Women* (Seattle: University of Washington Press, 1994); Yen Le Espiritu, *Asian American Women and Men: Labor, Laws, and Love* (Thousand Oaks, CA: Sage, 1997); Evelyn Nakano Glenn, *Issei, Nisei, War Bride: Three Generations of Japanese American Women in Domestic Service* (Philadelphia: Temple University Press, 1986); Barbara Kawakami, *Japanese Immigrant Clothing in Hawaii, 1885–1941* (Honolulu: University of Hawai'i Press, 1993); Nazli Kibria, *Family Tightrope: The Changing Lives of Vietnamese Americans* (Princeton, NJ: Princeton University Press, 1993); Mary Paik Lee, *Quiet Odyssey: A Pioneer Korean Woman in America* (Seattle: University of Washington Press, 1990); Valerie J. Matsumoto, *Farming the Home Place: A Japanese American Community in California, 1919–1982* (Ithaca,

NY: Cornell University Press, 1993); Mei Nakano, *Japanese American Women: Three Generations, 1890–1990* (San Francisco: Mina and National Japanese American Historical Society, 1990); Peggy Pascoe, *Relations of Rescue: The Search for Female Moral Authority in the American West, 1874–1939* (New York: Oxford University Press, 1990); George Peffer, *If They Don't Bring Their Women Here: Chinese Female Immigration before Exclusion* (Urbana: University of Illinois Press, 1999); Benson Tong, *Unsubmissive Women: Chinese Prostitutes in Nineteenth-Century San Francisco* (Norman: University of Oklahoma Press, 1994); Haunani-Kay Trask, *From a Native Daughter: Colonialism and Sovereignty in Hawaii* (Honolulu: University of Hawai'i Press, 1999); Judy Yung, *Unbound Feet: A Social History of Chinese Women in San Francisco* (Berkeley: University of California Press, 1995).

8. Examples include Xiaolan Bao, *Holding Up More Than Half the Sky: Chinese Women Garment Workers in New York City, 1948–92* (Urbana: University of Illinois Press, 2001); Catherine Ceniza Choy, *Empire of Care: Nursing and Migration in Filipino American History* (Durham, NC: Duke University Press, 2003); Gloria Heyung Chun, *Of Orphans and Warriors: Inventing Chinese American Culture and Identity* (New Brunswick, NJ: Rutgers University Press, 1999); Diane Carol Fujino, *Heartbeat of Struggle: The Revolutionary Life of Yuri Kochiyama* (Minneapolis: University of Minnesota Press, 2005); Martha Gardner, *The Qualities of a Citizen: Women, Immigration, and Citizenship, 1870–1965* (Princeton, NJ: Princeton University Press, 2005); Shirley Hune and Gail Nomura, eds., *Asian Pacific Islander American Women: A Historical Anthology* (New York: New York University Press, 2003); Susan Koshy, *Sexual Naturalization: Asian Americans and Miscegenation* (Stanford, CA: Stanford University Press, 2004); Laura Hyun Yi Kang, *Compositional Subjects: Enfiguring Asian/American Women* (Durham, NC: Duke University Press, 2002); Karen J. Leong, *The China Mystique: Pearl S. Buck, Anna May Wong, Mayling Soong, and the Transformation of American Orientalism* (Berkeley: University of California Press, 2005); Shirley Geok-Lin Lim, Larry E. Smith, and Wimal Dissanayake, eds., *Transnational Asia Pacific: Gender, Culture, and the Public Sphere* (Urbana: University of Illinois Press, 1999); Shirley Jennifer Lim, *A Feeling of Belonging: Asian American Women's Public Culture, 1930–1960* (New York: New York University Press, 2005); Brenda Moore, *Serving Our Country: Japanese American Women in the Military during World War II* (New Brunswick, NJ: Rutgers University Press, 2003); Rhacel Parreñas, *Servants of Globalization: Women, Migration, and Domestic Work* (Stanford, CA: Stanford University Press, 2001); Rhacel Parreñas, *Children of Global Migration: Transnational Families and Gendered Woes* (Stanford, CA: Stanford University Press, 2005); Nayan Shah, *Contagious Divides: Epidemics and Race in San Francisco's Chinatown* (Berkeley: University of California Press, 2001); Susan Lynn Smith, *Japanese American Midwives: Culture, Community, and Health Politics, 1880–1950* (Urbana: University of Illinois Press, 2005); Linda Võ, *Asian American Women: The Frontiers Reader* (Lincoln: University of Nebraska Press, 2004); Judy Tzu-Chun Wu, *Doctor Mom Chung of the Fair-Haired Bastards: The Life of a Wartime Celebrity* (Berkeley: University of California Press, 2005); Christine Yano, *Crowning the Nice Girl: Gender, Ethnicity, and Culture in Hawaii's Cherry Blossom Festival* (Honolulu: University of Hawai'i Press, 2006); Christine Yano, *Airborne Dreams: "Nisei" Stewardesses and Pan American World Airways* (Durham, NC: Duke University Press, 2011); Mari Yoshihara, *Embracing the East: White Women and American Orientalism* (New York: Oxford University Press, 2002); Ji-Yeon Yuh, *Beyond the Shadow of Camptown: Korean Military Brides in America* (New York: New York University

Press, 2002); and Xiaojian Zhao, *Remaking Chinese America: Immigration, Family, and Community, 1940–1965* (New Brunswick, NJ: Rutgers University Press, 2002).

9. Chan, *Entry Denied*; Erika Lee, "Exclusion Acts: Chinese Women during the Chinese Exclusion Era, 1882–1943," and Jennifer Gee, "Housewives, Men's Villages, and Sexual Respectability: Gender and the Interrogation of Asian Women at the Angel Island Immigration Station," in *Asian/Pacific Islander American Women: A Historical Anthology*, ed. Shirley Hune and Gail M. Nomura, 77–105; Erika Lee and Judy Yung, *Angel Island: Immigrant Gateway to* (New York: Oxford University Press, 2012); Peffer, *If They Don't Bring Their Women Here*.

10. Choy, *Empire of Care*; Glenn, *Issei, Nisei, War Bride*; Yuh, *Beyond the Shadow of Camptown*; Zhao, *Remaking Chinese America*.

11. Gardner, *Qualities of a Citizen*.

12. Lalaie Ameeriar, "The Gendered Suspect: Women at the Canada-U.S. Border after September 11," *Journal of Asian American Studies* 15, no. 2 (2012): 171–195.

13. Lisa Sun-Hee Park, *Entitled to Nothing: The Struggle for Immigrant Health Care in the Age of Welfare Reform* (New York: New York University Press, 2011).

14. Sucheta Mazumdar, "What Happened to the Women? Chinese and Indian Male Migration to the United States in Global Perspective," in *Asian/Pacific Islander American Women: A Historical Anthology*, ed. Hune and Nomura, 58–76.

15. Choy, *Empire of Care*.

16. Yuh, *Beyond the Shadow of Camptown*.

17. Adria L. Imada, *Aloha America: Hula Circuits through the U.S. Empire* (Durham, NC: Duke University Press, 2012).

18. Kang, *Compositional Subjects*

19. Gardner, *Qualities of a Citizen*.

20. Chun, *Of Orphans and Warriors*; Lim, *Feeling of Belonging*; Valerie J. Matsumoto, "Japanese American Girls' Clubs in Los Angeles during the 1920s and 1930s," in *Asian/Pacific Islander American Women: A Historical Anthology*, ed. Hune and Nomura, 172–187.

21. Moore, *Serving Our Country*; Wu, *Doctor Mom Chung of the Fair-Haired Bastards*; Yung, *Unbound Feet*.

22. Karen J. Leong and Judy Tzu-Chun Wu, "Filling the Rice Bowls of China: Staging Humanitarian Relief during the Sino-Japanese War," in *Chinese Americans and the Politics of Race and Culture*, ed. Sucheng Chan and Madeline Yuan-yin Hsu (Philadelphia: Temple University Press, 2008), 132–152; Yoshihara, *Embracing the East*.

23. Henry Yu, *Thinking Orientals: Migration, Contact, and Exoticism in Modern America* (New York: Oxford University Press, 2002); Leong, *China Mystique*.

24. Trask, *From a Native Daughter*. Also see Davianna Pomaika'i McGregor, "Constructed Images of Native Hawaiian Women," in *Asian/Pacific Islander American Women: A Historical Anthology*, ed. Hune and Nomura, 25–41.

25. Melinda L. De Jesus, ed., *Pinay Power: Peminist Critical Theory: Theorizing the Filipina/American Experience* (New York: Routledge, 2005).

26. Espiritu, *Asian American Women and Men*.

27. Some examples of this scholarship not cited previously include Bao, *Holding Up More Than Half the Sky*; Miliann Kang, *The Managed Hand: Race, Gender, and the Body in Beauty Service Work* (Berkeley: University of California Press, 2010); Thuy Linh Nguyen Tu, *The Beautiful Generation: Asian Americans and the Cultural Economy of Fashion* (Durham, NC: Duke University Press, 2010); Charlene Tung, "Caring across Borders: Motherhood,

Marriage, and Filipina Domestic Workers in California," in *Asian/Pacific Islander American Women: A Historical Anthology*, ed. Hune and Nomura, 301–318; Yano, *Airborne Dreams*.

28. Evelyn Nakano Glenn, *Unequal Freedom: How Race and Gender Shaped American Citizenship and Labor* (Cambridge, MA: Harvard University Press, 2002).

29. Parreñas, *Servants of Globalization*; Parreñas, *Children of Global Migration*.

30. Yanagisako, "Transforming Orientalism."

31. Hirata, "Free, Indentured, Enslaved."

32. For a discussion of how South Asian immigrant working women negotiate home responsibilities, see Vibha Bhalla, "'Couch Potatoes and Super-Women': Gender, Migration, and the Emerging Discourse on Housework among Asian Indian Immigrants," *Journal of American Ethnic History* 27, no. 4 (2008): 71–99.

33. Wu, *Doctor Mom Chung of the Fair-Haired Bastards*.

34. Smith, *Japanese American Midwives*.

35. Mary Ting Yi Lui, *The Chinatown Trunk Mystery: Murder, Miscegenation, and Other Dangerous Encounters in Turn-of-the-Century New York City* (Princeton, NJ: Princeton University Press, 2005); Shah, *Contagious Divides*; Paul C. P Siu, *The Chinese Laundryman: Study of Social Isolation* (New York: New York University Press, 1987).

36. Peffer, *If They Don't Bring Their Women Here*.

37. Christina Klein, *Cold War Orientalism: Asia in the Middlebrow Imagination, 1945–1961* (Berkeley: University of California Press, 2003).

38. Lui, *Chinatown Trunk Mystery*; Peffer, *If They Don't Bring Their Women Here*; Shah, *Contagious Divides*.

39. Madeline Y. Hsu, *Dreaming of Gold, Dreaming of Home: Transnationalism and Migration between the United States and South China, 1882–1943* (Stanford, CA: Stanford University Press, 2000).

40. Matsumoto, *Farming the Home Place*; Smith, *Japanese American Midwives*; Yung, *Unbound Feet*.

41. Yung, *Unbound Feet*; Matsumoto, *Farming the Home Place*.

42. Rita Nakashima Brock, "Private, Public, and Somewhere in Between: Lessons from the History of Asian-Pacific American Women," *Journal of Feminist Studies in Religion* 12, no. 1 (1996): 127–132.

43. Yung, *Unbound Feet*.

44. Choy, *Empire of Care*; Donnelly, *Changing Lives of Refugee Hmong Women*; Leong, *China Mystique*; Matsumoto, *Farming the Home Place*; Yuh, *Beyond the Shadow of Camptown*.

45. Jennifer Ting, "Bachelor Society: Deviant Heterosexuality and Asian American Historiography," in *Privileging Positions: The Sites of Asian American Studies*, ed. Gary Okihiro et al. (Pullman: Washington State University Press, 1995), 271–280; Shah, *Contagious Divides*.

46. Eithne Luibheid, *Entry Denied: Controlling Sexuality at the Border* (Minneapolis: University of Minnesota Press, 2002); Susan C. Pearce, Elizabeth J. Clifford, and Reena Tandon, *Immigration and Women: Understanding the American Experience* (New York: New York University Press, 2011).

47. Brock, "Private, Public, and Somewhere in Between."

48. Shah, *Contagious Divides*; Nayan Shah, *Stranger Intimacy: Contesting Race, Sexuality and the Law in the North American West* (Berkeley: University of California Press, 2012); Wu, *Mom Chung of the Fair-Haired Bastards*.

49. Peggy Pascoe, *What Comes Naturally: Miscegenation Law and the Making of Race in America* (New York: Oxford University Press, 2009).

50. Karen Isaksen Leonard, *Making Ethnic Choices: California's Punjabi Mexican Americans* (Philadelphia: Temple University Press, 1992).

51. Yuh, *Beyond the Shadow of Camptown*.

52. Shah, *Contagious Divides*, 15.

53. Linda España-Maram, *Creating Masculinity in Los Angeles's Little Manila: Working Class Filipinos and Popular Culture, 1920s–1950s* (New York: Columbia University Press, 2006).

54. Rebecca Chiyoko King, "Multiraciality Reigns Supreme? Mixed-Race Japanese Americans and the Cherry Blossom Queen Pageant," *Amerasia Journal* 23, no. 1 (1997): 113–128; Leong, *China Mystique*; Leong and Wu, "Filling the Rice Bowls of China."

55. Asian Women United of California, *Making Waves*; Dasgupta, *Patchwork Shawl*; Sangita Gupta, *Emerging Voices: South Asian American Women Redefine Self, Family, and Community* (Thousand Oaks, CA: Sage, 1999); *Chinese Women Traversing Diaspora: Memoirs, Essays, and Poetry* (New York: Garland, 1999); *The Politics of Life: Four Plays* (Philadelphia: Temple University Press, 1993); Sonia Shah, ed., *Dragon Ladies: Asian American Feminists Breathe Fire* (Boston: South End, 1997); Võ, *Asian American Women*; Yung, *Unbound Feet*.

56. Ji-Yeon Yuh, "Moved by War: Migration, Diaspora, and the Korean War," *Journal of Asian American Studies* 8, no. 3 (2005): 277–291.

57. Leong, *China Mystique*; Leong and Wu, "Filling the Rice Bowls of China"; Lon Kurashige, *Japanese American Celebration and Conflict: A History of Ethnic Identity and Festival, 1934–1990* (Berkeley: University of California Press, 2002); Lim, *Feeling of Belonging*; Valerie J. Matsumoto, "Japanese American Women and the Creation of Urban Nisei Culture in the 1930s," in *Over the Edge: Remapping the American West*, ed. Valerie J. Matsumoto and Blake Allmendinger (Berkeley: University of California Press, 1999), 291–306; Yung, *Unbound Feet*; Chiou-lin Yeh, *Making an American Festival: Chinese New Year in San Francisco's Chinatown* (Berkeley: University of California Press, 2008).

58. Bao, *Holding Up More Than Half the Sky*; Miriam Ching Yoon Louie, *Sweatshop Warriors: Immigrant Women Workers Take on the Global Factory* (Cambridge, MA: South End, 2001); Yung, *Unbound Feet*.

59. Laura Pulido, *Black, Brown, Yellow, and Left: Radical Activism in Los Angeles* (Berkeley: University of California Press, 2006). See Pulido's section on gender, East Wind, and Gidra.

60. Daryl J. Maeda, *Chains of Babylon: The Rise of Asian America* (Minneapolis: University of Minnesota Press, 2009).

61. Jeanie Dere, "A Wei Min Sister Remembers," *Chinese America: History and Perspectives* (2009): 64–94; Mary Kao, "Three-Step Boogie in 1970s Los Angeles: Sansei Women in Asian American Movement," *Amerasia Journal* 35, no. 1 (2009): 112–138.

62. Pulido, *Black, Brown, Yellow, and Left*.

63. Kao, "Three-Step Boogie."

64. Grace Lee Boggs, *The Next American Revolution: Sustainable Activism for the Twenty-First Century* (Berkeley: University of California Press, 2011); Jennifer J. H. Choi, "At the Margins of the Asian American Political Experience: The Life of Grace Lee Boggs," *Amerasia Journal* 25, no. 2 (1999): 18–40; Diane Carol Fujino, *Heartbeat of Struggle: The Revolutionary Life of Yuri Kochiyama* (Minneapolis: University of Minnesota Press, 2005); Yuri Kochiyama, *Passing It On: A Memoir* (Los Angeles: UCLA Asian American Studies Center, 2004).

65. Nazli Kibria, *Family Tightrope: The Changing Lives of Vietnamese Americans* (Princeton, NJ: Princeton University Press, 1995).

66. Bindi V. Shah, *Laotian Daughters: Working toward Community, Belonging, and Environmental Justice* (Philadelphia: Temple University Press, 2011).

67. Kim, "General Survey Course on Asian American Women"; Dasgupta, *Patchwork Shawl*; De Jesus, *Pinay Power*; Shah, *Dragon Ladies*.

FURTHER READING

Asian Women United of California. *Making Waves: An Anthology of Writings by and about Asian American Women*. Boston: Beacon, 1989.

Bao, Xiaolan. *Holding Up More Than Half the Sky: Chinese Women Garment Workers in New York City, 1948–92*. Urbana: University of Illinois Press, 2001.

Choy, Catherine Ceniza. *Empire of Care: Nursing and Migration in Filipino American History*. Durham, NC: Duke University Press, 2003.

Dasgupta, Shamita Das. *A Patchwork Shawl: Chronicles of South Asian Women in America*. New Brunswick, NJ: Rutgers University Press, 1998.

Donnelly, Nancy D. *Changing Lives of Refugee Hmong Women*. Seattle: University of Washington Press, 1994.

España-Maram, Linda. *Creating Masculinity in Los Angeles's Little Manila: Working Class Filipinos and Popular Culture, 1920s–1950s*. New York: Columbia University Press, 2006.

Espiritu, Yen Le. *Asian American Women and Men: Labor, Laws, and Love*. Lanham, MD: Rowman and Littlefield, 2008.

Fujino, Diane Carol. *Heartbeat of Struggle: The Revolutionary Life of Yuri Kochiyama*. Minneapolis: University of Minnesota Press, 2005.

Hirata, Lucie Cheng. "Free, Indentured, Enslaved: Chinese Prostitutes in Nineteenth-Century California." *Signs: A Journal of Women in Culture and Society* 5, no. 1 (1979): 3–29.

Hune, Shirley. *Asian Pacific Islander American Women: A Historical Anthology*. New York: New York University Press, 2003.

Kibria, Nazli. *Family Tightrope: The Changing Lives of Vietnamese Americans*. Princeton, NJ: Princeton University Press, 1993.

Leong, Karen J. *The China Mystique: Pearl S. Buck, Anna May Wong, Mayling Soong, and the Transformation of American Orientalism*. Berkeley: University of California Press, 2005.

Lim, Shirley Jennifer. *A Feeling of Belonging: Asian American Women's Public Culture, 1930–1960*. New York: New York University Press, 2006.

Matsumoto, Valerie J. *Farming the Home Place: A Japanese American Community in California, 1919–1982*. Ithaca, NY: Cornell University Press, 1993.

Peffer, George Anthony. *If They Don't Bring Their Women Here: Chinese Female Immigration before Exclusion*. Urbana: University of Illinois Press, 1999.

Shah, Nayan. *Stranger Intimacy: Contesting Race, Sexuality, and the Law in the North American West*. Berkeley: University of California Press, 2012.

Shah, Sonia, ed. *Dragon Ladies: Asian American Feminists Breathe Fire*. Boston: South End, 1997.

Smith, Susan Lynn. *Japanese American Midwives: Culture, Community, and Health Politics, 1880–1950*. Urbana: University of Illinois Press, 2005.

Ting, Jennifer. "Bachelor Society: Deviant Heterosexuality and Asian American Historiography." In *Privileging Positions: The Sites of Asian American Studies*, edited by Gary Okihiro et al., 271–280. Pullman: Washington State University Press, 1995.

Võ, Linda Trinh. *Asian American Women: The Frontiers Reader*. Lincoln: University of Nebraska Press, 2004.

Wu, Judy Tzu-Chun. *Doctor Mom Chung of the Fair-Haired Bastards: The Life of a Wartime Celebrity*. Berkeley: University of California Press, 2005.

———. *Radicals on the Road: Internationalism, Orientalism, and Feminism during the Vietnam Era*. Ithaca, NY: Cornell University Press, 2013.

Yanagisako, Sylvia Junko. "Transforming Orientalism: Gender, Nationality, and Class in Asian American Studies." In *Naturalizing Power: Essays in Feminist Cultural Analysis*, edited by Sylvia Junko Yanagisako and Carol Lowery Delaney, 275–298. New York: Routledge, 1995.

Yuh, Ji-Yeon. *Beyond the Shadow of Camptown: Korean Military Brides in America*. New York: New York University Press, 2002.

Yung, Judy. *Unbound Feet: A Social History of Chinese Women in San Francisco*. Berkeley: University of California Press, 1995.

INDEX

Printed in the USA
CPSIA information can be obtained
at www.ICGtesting.com
LVHW081448211123
764194LV00002B/7

9 780197 547915